@ online resource centre

www.oxfordtextbooks.co.uk/orc/gillespie_els3e/

The book is accompanied by an innovative Online Resource Centre offering a range of resources to support teaching and learning:

- Lecturers can track student progress using a **test bank of 300 multiple choice questions**, offering immediate answers and feedback, which can be loaded on to the university's VLE and customized

- **Regular updates** are an indispensable resource providing easy access to changes and developments in the law that have occurred since publication of the book

- A selection of **annotated web links** facilitate further research in areas of particular interest

- A **glossary** provides a useful one-stop reference point for key words and terms used within the text

- **Suggestions for practical activities** are provided to help take learning further

- **Audio podcasts** by the author outline opposing viewpoints on controversial topics in this area, encouraging critical thinking and debate

The English Legal System

Third edition

ALISDAIR A. GILLESPIE

LL.B.(HONS), M.A.(ED), M.JUR.
OF THE MIDDLE TEMPLE, BARRISTER

PROFESSOR OF CRIMINAL LAW AND JUSTICE
DE MONTFORT UNIVERSITY

OXFORD
UNIVERSITY PRESS

OXFORD
UNIVERSITY PRESS

Great Clarendon Street, Oxford OX2 6DP

Oxford University Press is a department of the University of Oxford.
It furthers the University's objective of excellence in research, scholarship,
and education by publishing worldwide in

Oxford New York

Auckland Cape Town Dar es Salaam Hong Kong Karachi
Kuala Lumpur Madrid Melbourne Mexico City Nairobi
New Delhi Shanghai Taipei Toronto

With offices in

Argentina Austria Brazil Chile Czech Republic France Greece
Guatemala Hungary Italy Japan Poland Portugal Singapore
South Korea Switzerland Thailand Turkey Ukraine Vietnam

Oxford is a registered trade mark of Oxford University Press
in the UK and in certain other countries

Published in the United States
by Oxford University Press Inc., New York

First edition 2007
Second edition 2009

British Library Cataloguing in Publication Data

Data available

Library of Congress Cataloging in Publication Data
Library of Congress Control Number: 2011921198

Typeset by Newgen Imaging Systems (P) Ltd., Chennai, India
Printed in Italy
on acid-free paper by
L.E.G.O S.p.A

ISBN 978–0–19–959916–5

1 3 5 7 9 10 8 6 4 2

Preface

This book has been written for you, the student. It is likely that you are just starting to learn about law and this text is designed to provide an introduction to the English Legal System in a way that you can engage with. The subjects in this book are presented in a way that allows you to understand the key aspects of the English Legal System and help you to question why the law has evolved in this way. Each chapter includes suggestions for you to reflect upon what you are reading and learning. It also provides suggested further reading so that you can increase the depth of your student learning by engaging with other sources.

This textbook is only one part of the learning experience and there is an Online Resource Centre that accompanies this book. Many online resource centres simply act as an 'updating service' whereby anything that happens to arise between editions will feature on a website. That is not the case here. Whilst new developments will, of course, be featured on the Online Resource Centre, the site includes many more resources. There are extra reading resources that it was not practicable to include in the text of this book. There are links to many of the specific documents that are discussed in the book so that rather than rely on my interpretation of what a document says you can read it yourself and come to your own understanding of its importance. There are also exercises that will allow you to test and develop your knowledge. Sometimes these will be application tests, such as allowing you to complete forms for litigation so that you can understand how a case progresses. Others are knowledge tests which involve multiple choice tests, short answer questions, etc. It is designed to be fully interactive.

The third edition continues with the use of 'viewpoints'. When reading this book you will see a number of questions for reflection: these are here to highlight particular issues of controversy and help you put them into context. Some of these questions for reflection are accompanied by a symbol (see page xviii) which indicates that a related podcast is to be found on the ORC. The podcast will discuss some of the key themes surrounding that question for reflection, providing you with ideas on both sides of the argument.

As usual, thanks are due to a number of people in respect of this book. I would like to thank my colleagues at De Montfort University who have answered questions and read sections of the book. I also wish to continue to thank my former colleagues at the University of Teesside who assisted me with the first edition. I continue to acknowledge the assistance of the Crown Prosecution Service, HM Court Service, the Tribunal Service, and the Ministry of Justice who answered a number of questions in a prompt and efficient manner.

In the first edition of this book I thanked a number of academics who reviewed each chapter of the book. For subsequent editions they were joined by a number of academics who provided detailed anonymous reviews of the later editions. These reviews were invaluable, not only because they helped check the content and style of the book, but also because they provided assistance in ensuring that the book is matched with many *English Legal System* courses. There are now too many academics to name personally but I am extremely grateful to them and can assure them that I read each review carefully.

Special thanks needs to be given to some within Oxford University Press. Readers of the previous editions of this book will note that I seem to be very careless with editors, and this new edition is accompanied with another change of editor. Rachael Willis left OUP but Helen Davis took over and I am very grateful for her assistance in preparing this third edition and, like all my previous editors, for not telling me what she really thinks when I say, "You know I said I would get you the copy by [date] but actually it may be another couple of weeks…". And finally thank you to my family to whom the book continues to be dedicated, and a very special 'hello' to Murron, my newly-arrived niece.

AAG
Leicester
October 2010

New to this edition

This third edition has been substantially updated to take into account key developments in the English Legal System.

- The new edition has been updated to reflect the replacement of the House of Lords with the Supreme Court
- In the opening chapter new material has been included on common law vs equity
- The chapter on *International Law* now discusses the impact that the ratification of the Lisbon Treaty has had on EU law
- Additional material on the Coroner's Court has been included within the chapter on *The Courts*
- The chapter on *Funding Legal Services* has been substantially revised to present in detail the various competing arguments in this controversial area
- The chapter on *Trials on Indictment* has been updated to include coverage of trial by judge alone

Outline contents

Detailed contents

Guide to the book

The English Legal System is enriched with a range of features designed to help support and reinforce your learning. This guided tour shows you how to fully utilize your textbook and get the most out of your study.

Learning outcomes

Each chapter begins with a bulleted outline of the main concepts and ideas you will encounter. These serve as helpful signposts to what you can expect to learn by reading the chapter.

> **By the end of this chapter you will be able to:**
>
> * Define the United Kingdom.
> * Identify how many legal systems exist in the United Ki
> * Begin to understand the concept of law and how laws
>   mere rules.
> * Begin to think about 'systems' and understand the key
>   English Legal System.

> **◉ Example** Private and public law
>
> **Private law**
>
> Rhiannon agrees with Alison to purchase twenty-four bottles of red w
> When Rhiannon comes to collect them, there are only twenty bottles
> full £150. If not resolved amicably it is quite possible that this dispu
> courts, with Rhiannon suing Alison for breach of contract.
>   This is a classic example of private law as it is a dispute between
> involve the state in its sovereign capacity.[5]
>
> **Public law**

Examples

Everyday scenarios explain and illustrate how a particular law or legal practice would apply in a real life situation.

Questions for reflection

Why was a particular decision reached in a certain case? Is the law on this point rational and coherent? Is the English legal system fit for purpose? Questions for reflection encourage you to think about contentious issues and critique the law.

> **❓ QUESTION FOR REFLECTION**
>
> Lord Cooke suggests that the *Parliament Act 1949* cannot be
> *Parliament Act 1911* in such a way as to remove the safeguards
> or the extension of Parliament. Consider the case of *Jackson* (ab
> speech of Lord Bingham. Do you think Lord Cooke is right? If so,
> are no safeguards to prevent a rogue government indefinitely ext
> Parliament?

> **🎧 LISTEN TO THE PODCAST**
> For guidance on how to answer this question and a discussion of
> to the author's podcast on the Online Resource Centre:
> www.oxfordtextbooks.co.uk/orc/gillespie_els3e/

Listen to the podcast

Selected questions for reflection are supported by audio podcasts by the author which appear on the accompanying website (see the Guide to the Online Resource Centre for details). These outline the contrasting viewpoints you may wish to consider and offer advice on how to answer the questions.

Case boxes

Real life cases demonstrate the way in which legal concepts are used in practice. The facts and decisions are presented to assist you in understanding why the court reached its decision and what the wider implications are.

Case box *R v Dooley*

In *R v Dooley* [2005] EWCA Crim 3093 the Court of Appeal needed to the words 'with a view to' which appeared in s 1(1)(c) *Protection of C* did not define these words but it is a not uncommon phrase to be fou the court examined how it had been construed in other legislation, 21 *Theft Act 1968* and the *Obscene Publications Act 1964*. The Court the same interpretation to the 1978 Act would be logical and it can be other legislation acted as an extrinsic aid.

THEFT

Theft is defined under s 1 *Theft Act* 1968 thus: '[a] person is guilty of appropriates property belonging to another with the intention of per other of it'. The *actus reus* of this crime is appropriating property bel *mens rea* of the crime is doing so dishonestly and with the intention of the other of the property.

Terminology

Some key concepts and important legal terms are highlighted, illustrated, and explained.

Chapter summaries

The central points and concepts from each chapter are distilled into succinct summaries. These help you to reinforce your understanding and can also be used as a revision tool.

 Summary

In this chapter we have examined the basic concept of domestic so identified that there are two sources of law (primary sources and s particular we have noted that:

- *Primary sources* are considered to be those 'authoritative' sour by the legal process itself. *Secondary sources* are sources that a and are, in essence, a commentary on the law.
- Primary sources of law include statutory material and this its types of material: *primary legislation* (Acts of Parliament) and (Statutory Instruments, Orders in Council, etc).

End-of-chapter questions

1. Should the Parliament Acts be used in politically controversial pie House of Lords is the second chamber of the legislature and thus right to block controversial legislation? By allowing the House o this block does this not mean there is no protection against, for ex to diminish human rights?

2. The Supreme Court of the United States of America is allowed to tion that is incompatible with their Constitution. Should the Supre allowed to 'strike down' legislation that is incompatible with the E

3. If the intention of Parliament is important in the construction of leg

End-of-chapter questions

Problem questions and essay-type questions at the end of each chapter will help to develop your analytical and problem-solving skills.

Further reading

Suggestions for further reading are included at the end of each chapter as a springboard for reliable further study. Each source is accompanied by an explanation of its relevance to your study, guiding you to the key academic literature in the field.

Further reading

Kavanagh A (2005) 'Unlocking the Human Rights Act: The radical appr revisited' 3 *European Human Rights Law Review* 259–275.

This is another authoritative article from this commentator where i courts have been reluctant to make the full use of their powers of i

Kavanagh A (2005) '*Pepper v Hart* and matters of constitutional princip *Review* 98–122.

This is an interesting article that examines the modern application Hart.

Marshall G (2003) 'The lynchpin of parliamentary intention: Lost, stole *Law* 236–248.

Guide to the
Online Resource Centre

The Online Resource Centre that accompanies this book provides students and lecturers with ready-to-use teaching and learning resources. They are free of charge and are designed to maximize the learning experience.

www.oxfordtextbooks.co.uk/orc/gillespie_els3e/

FOR STUDENTS

Accessible to all, with no registration or password required, enabling you to get the most from your textbook.

Regular updates

Any changes and developments in the legal system since publication of the textbook are highlighted here. They include page references to the relevant section of the book to enable you to keep up to date and to continue benefitting from the textbook throughout your course.

> **Departing from Strasbourg:**
> **R v Horncastle et al [2009] UKSC 14**
>
> The second case of relevance is *R v Horncastle*
> a different opinion from the European Court o
> meaning of Article 6 of the European Convention
>
> It will be remembered from chapters 2 and 5 of t
> *Act 1998* compels courts to "take account of"
> Ordinarily this will mean that they will follow the E
> of a situation when they did not.

Podcasts: viewpoints on questions for reflection

These audio podcasts support some of the questions for reflection which appear in the textbook (see Guide to the book). The author outlines opposing viewpoints on controversial topics and offers advice on points to consider when answering the questions.

Glossary

A useful one-stop reference point for definitions of key terms used within the text. This glossary is useful for learning and revision.

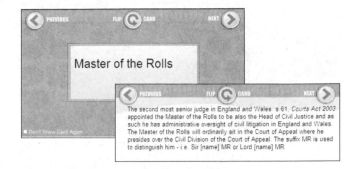

Activities

Suggestions for practical activities are provided to help you take your learning further. These include dealing with source material to ensure you understand how it is created, visiting a court, and approaching lawyers for work experience.

Web links

This selection of annotated web links chosen by the author enables you to research topics of particular interest. These links are checked regularly to ensure they remain up to date.

FOR LECTURERS

Password-protected to ensure only lecturers can access this resource. Adopting lecturers should complete the simple registration form and, subject to verification, access will be granted within three working days. Each registration is personally checked to ensure the security of the site.

Chapter 06 - Question 06
Who is the head of the judiciary?
○ Attorney-General
○ Lord Chancellor
◉ Lord Chief Justice
○ Senior Law Lord

1 out of 1
Correct! The Constitutional Reform Act accordingly the head of the judiciary.
Page reference: 184

Test bank

A fully customizable resource containing ready-made assessments with which to test your students. Offers versatile testing tailored to the contents of the textbook, including questions in several different formats.

Table of Cases

European Court of Human Rights

Courts of Justice of the EU

Table of Statutes

Table of Statutory Instruments

Table of International Instruments

General Treaties

1

The English Legal System

By the end of this chapter you will be able to:

- Define the United Kingdom.
- Identify how many legal systems exist in the United Kingdom.
- Begin to understand the concept of law and how laws differentiate from mere rules.
- Begin to think about 'systems' and understand the key issues within the English Legal System.

Introduction

In this introductory chapter the words 'English', 'Legal', and 'System' will be discussed. These words are often used but it is not always clear why they are used in this phrase and why so many modules now refer to the English Legal System. This chapter will also prepare you for the later chapters as it will help put them into context.

1.1 England

The first word to examine is that of 'England'. The question of identity is something that appears to be raised perpetually in the media and countries are given numerous different wordings. In this country, it is common to refer to living in 'Britain', 'the UK', or the 'United Kingdom'. The country does have a formal legal title, that of the *United Kingdom of Great Britain and Northern Ireland*. The Queen, as sovereign, has many other titles representing many of the dependent territories that exist but the title is as above. The latest version of the title became relevant in 1920 when Ireland was partitioned and twenty-six counties were given independence, forming the Republic of Ireland.[1] The title also demonstrates that 'Britain' or, more correctly, 'Great Britain'[2] is actually the main island grouping of which England is one part.

1.1.1 The constituent parts

The United Kingdom of Great Britain and Northern Ireland consists of four countries (although one was originally a principality). The countries are England, Wales, Scotland, and Northern Ireland. The status of Wales differs from England, Scotland, and Northern Ireland. Traditionally Wales was a principality (a province ruled by a prince) and this is a term that continues to be used by some, not least because the Crown Prince of the United Kingdom is known as the *Prince of Wales* and thus the logic, to some, is that it follows that Wales is a principality. Others disagree and argue that Wales is a country and should be accorded that title. In reality the distinction between principality and country is moot and either title could be used although it would seem that many in Wales itself dislike the term principality. Wales does differ from the other constituent countries in that it has not had its own legal system since the sixteenth century.

---

1. It is often erroneously said that the twenty-six counties constitute 'Southern Ireland', presumably as the opposite of 'Northern Ireland'. However this is both legally incorrect (the formal name of the state is The Republic of Ireland (in English) or Eire (in Gaelic)) and geographically incorrect since the County of Donegal is as northerly as the six counties that constitute Northern Ireland.

2. Since the term is derived from Brittany, a French region, what we understand to be Britain is 'Great' (meaning large) Britain.

1.1.1.1 England and Wales

Wales does not, as yet, have its own legal system (see, however, the *Government of Wales Act 2006* and 17.1 below) and following the *Laws of Wales Act 1535*, Wales in effect became legally 'annexed' by England and ensured that the laws of England would apply in Wales. This Act was passed by an English-only Parliament but part of its purpose was to ensure that there could be Welsh representation in the (then) English Parliament. A further *Laws of Wales Act* was passed in 1543 and gave further effect to the governance of Wales and the long title of the Act makes express reference to its status as a principality.

The effect of this is that this book, along with every other book on this topic, and most modules are technically wrong. It is not the *English* Legal System; it is technically the Legal System of *England and Wales*. That this is correct can be seen when one examines the main legal institutions. The senior courts are technically known as the *Superior Courts of England and Wales* (see *Constitutional Reform Act 2005*, Sch 15). The body for solicitors, known as the Law Society, is actually the *Law Society of England and Wales* and the body for barristers, known as the Bar Council, is actually the *General Council of the Bar for England and Wales*. This extends to judicial offices with the Lord Chief Justice technically being the *Lord Chief Justice for England and Wales*.

1.1.1.2 Scotland

Scotland is a country and joined the United Kingdom as a result of an Act of Union. The history of England and Scotland is probably well known to most readers and involved numerous battles between the two countries, sometimes with England winning, sometimes with Scotland winning. Indeed some of the battles occurred after the union with perhaps the most notable being the uprising led by 'Bonnie Prince Charlie'[3] who believed that he was the rightful heir to the throne.

Prior to the countries uniting, England and Scotland had shared a sovereign, when King James VI of Scotland assumed the throne of England as King James I. This continued even through the 'Glorious Revolution' of 1688 when King William III and Queen Mary II jointly ruled both thrones. The countries were joined by the *Act of Union 1707*. In fact two statutes were passed as both the English and Scottish Parliaments had to pass the Act. The effect of the Act was to extinguish the Parliaments of *both* England and Scotland and create a Parliament of the United Kingdom. This can be contrasted with the position with Wales where Welsh members simply joined the English Parliament. The seat of Parliament was Westminster and this continues to be the case regardless of devolution (see below).

Perhaps one of the most important aspects of the Act was the preservation of Scots law. Title 19 of the Act expressly preserved the Scottish Legal System and governed how appointments to the senior judiciary would be made. The principle of a separate legal system has continued throughout and devolution has merely altered the mechanics of this. That is not to say that Westminster does not have power to create Scottish laws since it clearly does—it is the Parliament of the United Kingdom—but there is no *automatic* assumption that laws passed will extend to Scotland (below).

---

3. More properly known as Charles Edward Stuart.

1.1.1.3 Northern Ireland

Northern Ireland is the most recent addition to the United Kingdom, it being created by 1920. However prior to that Ireland was a whole country and it was a member of the United Kingdom as a result of the *Act of Union 1801*. There were many similarities between the Acts of Union 1707 and 1801 and it was intended that it would be a merger: Ireland did not become part of the United Kingdom of Great Britain but transformed it into a new body, the United Kingdom of Great Britain and Ireland. The merger was political expediency: the two countries had shared the same King since the sixteenth century and there was close cooperation between the Parliaments but it was believed more appropriate to create a single country. Like Scotland, Ireland retained its own legal status and although there were United Kingdom laws (ie laws that applied across the entire United Kingdom) there were also individual Irish laws.

Throughout the nineteenth and twentieth centuries pressure grew for Ireland to have more responsibility for its own actions; a series of 'Home Rule' Bills (in effect devolution) failed but pressure grew for full independence. Eventually the United Kingdom Parliament passed the *Government of Ireland Act 1920* which partitioned Ireland. Twenty-six counties became 'Southern Ireland' and six counties became 'Northern Ireland'. The division was broadly upon religious grounds with Ulster (which included the six counties)[4] being mainly Protestant and the twenty-six counties being mainly Roman Catholic. Of course this is a very crude approximation and there was a significant Protestant population in 'Southern Ireland' and vice versa. However 'Southern Ireland' never came into existence as a result of the independence movement and Ireland became an independent Republic, meaning the United Kingdom became the United Kingdom of Great Britain and Northern Ireland. The 1920 Act was repealed by the *Northern Ireland Act 1998* which was part of the devolution process (below) but also in pursuance of the *Good Friday Agreement*, an agreement between the Irish and UK governments to deal with the question of Irish unification.

1.1.2 The United Kingdom

Whilst this book is about the *English Legal System* (but really the Legal System of England and Wales) it is necessary to pause briefly to consider the United Kingdom. The election of a Labour government to the Westminster Parliament in 1997 led to the process of devolution. Theoretically devolution does not affect purely English matters; the law continues to be passed by the Parliament at Westminster. Devolution principally affects Northern Ireland and Scotland and this is outside the scope of this book although it is likely you will discuss them in *Constitutional Law* or similar modules.

Westminster remains the Parliament of the United Kingdom and the devolution instruments expressly preserve the right of Westminster to pass legislation that affects both Scotland and Northern Ireland. This is known as 'extent'. Both prior to and following devolution, the convention is that if an Act of Parliament is silent as to its extent (ie there is not a section within the Act of Parliament that discusses its extent) then it applies only to England and Wales. If the Act is to apply to either Scotland or Northern Ireland then a section within the Act will expressly state this and also the provisions that apply.

---

4. Although 'Ulster' is commonly now thought of as being Northern Ireland, it technically includes the counties of Cavan, Donegal, and Monaghan.

⮑ SEXUAL OFFENCES ACT 2003

The Sexual Offences Act 2003 was a major piece of legislation that reformed the criminal law relating to sexual offending. Section 142 states:

142 Extent, saving etc.
   (1) Subject to section 137 and to subsections (2) to (4), this Act extends to England and Wales only.
   (2) The following provisions also extend to Northern Ireland–
      (a) sections 15 to 25, 46 to 54, 57 to 60, 66 to 72, 78 and 79,
      (b) Schedule 2,
      (c) Part 2, and
      (d) sections 138, 141, 143 and this section.
   (3) The following provisions also extend to Scotland–
      (a) Part 2 except sections 93 and 123 to 129 and Schedule 4, and
      (b) sections 138, 141, 143 and this section.

By reading this section (don't worry about the language used within it, this is explained in the next chapter) it can be seen that the whole of the Act applies to England and Wales. Only certain parts of the Act apply to Northern Ireland (those mentioned in subsection (2) so, for example, ss 1–5 which are not mentioned would not apply in Northern Ireland) and even less of it applies to Scotland (principally only Part 2 of the Act and even then ss 93 and 123–129 do not apply either).

1.2 Legal

The second word to examine is 'legal' which is the adjective for 'law' but what is 'law'? One of the first things to note is that we talk about a 'body of law' meaning that there is more than one law. Indeed those of you who are studying for a law degree can find that out from your degree title. Most of you will be reading for the degree of LLB (Hons) but do you know what that stands for? It is the abbreviation for *Legum Baccalaureus*, which means Bachelor of Laws. Why is it that there are two 'L's? It is because in Latin the abbreviation for a plural is to repeat the first letter (whereas we use 's', ie Law becomes Laws).

1.2.1 Classifying law

Before considering what law is (which will require a brief examination of the philosophy of law) it is worth reflecting on the types of law that exist. Law can be classified in various ways and the approach that is taken to the law will be governed by its classification.

1.2.1.1 Substantive or procedural

The first division that perhaps has to be discussed is that which exists between substantive and procedural law. It will be seen below that some theorists, most notably Hart, argue that law can be classified into primary and secondary rules. Primary rules are considered to be laws that set out rights, duties, and obligations. Secondary rules determine how the primary rules are to be recognized, interpreted, and applied. Whilst this can be considered relatively simplistic it does assist in our understanding of the distinction between substantive and procedural laws.

What is the first thing you think about when you think of law? There is a reasonably high chance that it will be a crime (see 1.2.1.3 below). This is not uncommon because it is one of the few areas of law that most people know something about but also because it is an interesting area of law and one that the media deal with on a daily basis. The actual crime is *substantive* law, in other words substantive law is that which sets out the rule which must be followed. Where someone is suspected of breaching this substantive law, there has to be an investigation, prosecution, and trial. All of these areas are also governed by laws so that an individual is protected against arbitrary interference by the state. These laws differ from the rule that says a person cannot commit a crime but they are, nonetheless laws, and must be followed. These rules are *procedural* law and they set out the framework by which the substantive law will be determined.

⮑ SUBSTANTIVE AND PROCEDURAL LAW

Section 1 *Theft Act 1968* states:

(1) A person is guilty of theft if he dishonestly appropriates property belonging to another with the intention of permanently depriving the other of it; and 'thief' and 'steal' shall be construed accordingly.

This is a substantive law. It, in combination with section 7 (which prescribes the punishment for theft) states that a person must not steal.

Section 24 of the Police and Criminal Evidence Act 1984 states:

(1) A constable may arrest without a warrant–

   (a) anyone who is about to commit an offence;

   (b) anyone who is in the act of committing an offence;

   (c) anyone whom he has reasonable grounds for suspecting is about to commit an offence;

   (d) anyone whom he has reasonable grounds for suspecting to be committing an offence.

(2) If a constable has reasonable grounds for suspecting that an offence has been committed, he may arrest without a warrant anyone whom he has reasonable grounds to suspect of being guilty of it.

This is procedural law. It sets out the circumstances when a police officer may arrest someone, those being (approximately) that a person has committed, or is about to commit, a breach of the substantive law.

1.2.1.2 Private or public law

The next distinction that needs to be drawn is between private and public law. This is a more subtle distinction as it straddles both substantive and procedural law; ie both substantive and procedural law could be either private or public law. A crude but effective separation is to suggest that private law concerns disputes that exist between citizens and public law is disputes that exist between the state and the individual. It is perhaps the definition of 'public' that is more relevant since certain disputes between public bodies may actually give rise to private law matters.

👁 Example Private and public law

Private law

Rhiannon agrees with Alison to purchase twenty-four bottles of red wine for the price of £150. When Rhiannon comes to collect them, there are only twenty bottles and yet Alison wants the full £150. If not resolved amicably it is quite possible that this dispute will end up before the courts, with Rhiannon suing Alison for breach of contract.

This is a classic example of private law as it is a dispute between two parties and does not involve the state in its sovereign capacity.[5]

Public law

Jack, a (fictitious) media commentator made derogatory statements about accountants in a newspaper. Sarah runs a campaign group that attempts to raise the profile of accountants. Sarah wishes to lead a march through the home town of Jack but the local police force refuses permission.

This is a good example of public law. Sarah may think that the police force is acting unreasonably and may wish to apply to the courts to challenge this decision. This would be done through the process known as judicial review (considered at 14.3) and is a public law matter because it involves the relationship between a private citizen (Sarah) and the state (the police).

AV Dicey, a nineteenth-century jurist, and someone who is considered to be one of the pre-eminent authorities on constitutional law, stated that there was, in England and Wales, no such thing as 'administrative' law. By this he meant to contrast the position with the continental-based systems (see 1.3 below) which have always believed that there is a distinction between public- and private-law matters. Indeed the continental system created separate courts and legal processes to resolve administrative disputes. Dicey argued that this was not the position within England and Wales because everyone was equal under the law, ie the state was bound by the same law as the citizen.

Whilst, during the nineteenth century, this may have been true it is extremely difficult to continue this approach today. The legal system has now created a specific court to deal with administrative law (called the Administrative Court) although it is, theoretically, within the ordinary court system since it merely constitutes a Divisional Court of the Queen's Bench Division of the High Court of Justice. However there is no doubt that the system has now become a body of law in its own right and there is now an express and specific procedure that governs administrative disputes (Part 54 of the *Civil Procedure Rules*).

1.2.1.3 Civil or criminal

It may seem that one of the more obvious distinctions to make is between civil and criminal but, as we will see, this is not always a simple distinction. The distinction does not, as is sometimes believed, necessarily follow the private and public split.

---

5. If the dispute existed between two councils this would remain a private law matter even though it now involves two public (state) bodies. This is because the dispute is not with the state acting in its capacity as the state, ie the sovereign.

Civil law is effectively anything that is not criminal. This may appear a trite statement but to an extent it is easier to say this than to suggest that a crime is anything that is not civil. This is because it is generally easier to identify what is criminal rather than civil. The civil law encompasses many different bodies of law mixing both private and public law. Ordinarily criminal matters can be categorized as public law in that the state is becoming involved in its sovereign capacity in relation to a citizen. In criminal matters the state will ordinarily be the prosecutor (for offences that take place in the Crown Court this will normally be through the sovereign (known as Regina when the sovereign is female and Rex when the sovereign is male) and in magistrates' courts ordinarily through the *Director of Public Prosecutions* or *Crown Prosecution Service* (10.1.1)). Whilst many crimes will have a victim, who will almost certainly be a citizen, it is not necessarily a private dispute between the citizens. Indeed the state can, if it so wishes, bring a prosecution regardless of the views of the victim (10.4.2). This would make it a public law matter.

However, criminal law can, under certain circumstances, be a private-law matter too. Although the state sets out the legal framework and will ordinarily prosecute, there remains in England and Wales the right to undertake a 'private prosecution'. This will be discussed elsewhere (10.1.3) but in essence means that a private citizen acts as the prosecutor and brings court proceedings. Whilst the state can intervene it need not do so, and accordingly in that guise it would appear to be private law (because the state is not present); but the laws are made on the assumption that the state will be the prosecutor so is this not still public laws merely instigated privately? This is confusing but does demonstrate an important point: there are no clear answers in law and thus the divisions noted in this chapter will always be somewhat imprecise in practice.

What then is a crime? An example was noted earlier (1.2.1.1 above) and s 1 *Theft Act 1968* appears quite a simple example of a crime. It is a law that prohibits something and carries with it a sanction for breaching the law. The courts have traditionally linked punishment with the idea of a crime (Adams and Brownsword (2006) 153) but this can in itself cause difficulty. There are many examples of situations where a person may appear to receive a punishment but it would not amount to a crime. A good example would be tax. If you need to complete a self-assessment tax form (to let the government know how much tax you must pay) there is a deadline by which you must submit it. If you miss this deadline then a surcharge (which is sometimes even called a 'fine') is payable. Is this a punishment? The person who receives it probably thinks so but a person surcharged in these circumstances is not considered to have a criminal record or to have committed a crime.

The European Court of Human Rights (ECtHR) has always adopted its own approach of what amounts to a 'crime' when adjudicating upon the *European Convention on Human Rights* (see, most notably, *Welch v United Kingdom* (1995) 20 EHRR 247). In considering whether a matter is a crime the ECtHR said that domestic labelling (ie whether the state considered it to be a crime) was important but not conclusive. Other factors would include the purpose of any sanction and, in particular, its severity. As a general rule, the stricter the 'punishment' the more likely it is that it will be considered a crime.

1.2.2 What is law?

Trying to define what law is, is a question that has taxed jurists and philosophers for centuries and will undoubtedly continue do so. Some jurists, most notably Hart, never answered the question, appearing to suggest that it was the wrong question (Bix (2003) 6) and that the more appropriate question would be to consider what distinguishes law from other regulations or what the purpose of law is.

It is beyond the scope of this introductory text to consider this question in detail and you should (eventually) refer to texts on legal theory, philosophy, or jurisprudence to consider (note I am not suggesting you will ever be able to answer) this question. Some of you will have the opportunity to study modules on jurisprudence or legal theory and this will be at the heart of the module.

Law has to be more than just a simple set of rules and regulations. Every society has rules and regulations; most families will have a series of informal rules that must be obeyed. Would anyone categorize these as laws? Every university has a set of rules and some will even refer to the documents holding these rules as statutes. There may be a punishment for breaching some of these rules, but again can it be suggested that a university rule is a law? It is sometimes said that a law must be of general application but this need not be the case. In the next chapter the concept of *Private Acts of Parliament* will be discussed and these are of limited application. The simplistic answer is to say that a law is something that is handed down from the state, and that in the United Kingdom it is a rule set out by the Crown to which we, the subjects of the Crown, are bound. Are there limits to law, or where do laws come from, however? It is necessary, at least briefly, to introduce some of the philosophical debates.

1.2.2.1 Positivism

One of the more important theories of legal governance is known as positivism. There are a number of positivist theorists but the most important are Bentham and Austin, both nineteenth-century philosophers, and Hart, a twentieth-century jurist. Positivism focuses on what the law *is* rather than what it *should* be. It is often criticized as suggesting that even evil laws are valid and should be followed but this is a misunderstanding of positivism (Bix (2003) 34) not least because positivism is not concerned with whether a law should be followed but simply what law is.

Austin believed in the premise of commands. He believed that an action would either be mandated, prohibited, not mandated or not prohibited (Harris (1997) 29). In other words, he believed that there was an imbalance in the state and that the Sovereign Head of State had the power to issue commands that detailed how a citizen could act, and that any other principles (eg commands from God, individual commands of employers, etc) were not laws but merely moralistic or private requirements (Harris (1997) 31).

Hart disagreed with this contention. He preferred the notion of rules rather than commands as he believed the notion of 'command' was problematic (Bix (2003) 36). A significant problem with the idea of commands is that it relies on an unfettered sovereign, ie nobody can command the sovereign. Yet this is not the case in many states where there are limits on what the state can do—sometimes referred to as the 'Rule of Law'. Another key difficulty Hart had with the command theory is that a command requires a sanction, but does every law have a sanction? If one thinks of procedural law especially it is not easy to think of what a sanction would be. Hart argued that the basis of law was rules and that there were two types of rules: primary rules and secondary rules.

⊙ PRIMARY AND SECONDARY RULES

Primary rules are those that apply directly to citizens. They are the rules that provide what our rights, duties, and obligations are.
Secondary rules are those that govern the operation of the primary rules. They put them into effect.

This, to an extent, mirrors the 'substantive' and 'procedural' rules that were discussed above. Hart also believed that these rules had to be set within a context of societal norms, ie that it was not just a fear of sanction that led people to follow the rules but the fact that they believed that it was 'normal' to do so.

1.2.2.2 Natural law

It has been noted already that a particular criticism of positivism is the belief that moral judgements have little to do with law. Natural-law theorists believe that law is not simply that which our rulers create but that there is a 'higher law' that constrains laws. The concept of natural law dates back millennia, probably first appearing in ancient Greek philosophies (Bix (2003) 66) and was certainly strong in the early years of the Christian Church with Aquinas, who later was made a saint, being one of the principal proponents of natural law. The influence of the Church in natural law is perhaps not surprising since to someone of faith, the 'higher' law will be their God.

Aquinas believed that there were four types of law: eternal law, natural law, divine law, and human law (Bix (2003) 67). He believed that human law derived from natural law, so that natural law requires a law of murder and accordingly society must create such a law. Aquinas also believed that human law had to be compatible with natural law. For a human law to be valid and enforceable it must be consistent with natural law, that being the requirements of the common good (Bix (2003) 68). Where a law is incompatible then Aquinas believed that it was unenforceable and unjust.

A criticism of natural law is that it is not necessarily practicable. Austin, a positivist, suggested that if a crime was punishable by death it meant very little whether it was an unjust law or not since it would, in all probability, be followed leaving the 'criminal' dead but apparently secure in the knowledge that he has become a martyr. The argument of natural lawyers however is that it empowers judges not to follow the law. In a common-law-based system (see 1.3 below) it is accepted that judges are the guarantors of law and indeed they can create law. The suggestion is that where a law is incompatible with natural law it should not be followed by judges.

Modern natural-law theorists, most notably Finnis, argue that natural law can be equated with ethical conduct and that it is about the creation of laws that are necessary for man to live ethically (Bix (2003) 72). This is an interesting approach and demonstrates one advantage of natural law, that it acts as a valid justification for the creation of many of the most fundamental laws (on murder, theft, marriage, and property) since without these basic laws society could not operate.

Natural law is, to an extent, considered to be the main opponent of positivism and yet there are a number of similarities between them. Both assume the concepts of rules and both accept that a state can produce the rules that surround us. Where the two appear to deviate is that natural law goes beyond positivism and seeks to discuss what the law *should* say. There is constantly a benchmark against which human laws will be measured, that of the 'higher' law.

1.2.2.3 Interpretative/rights theory

One of the more recent philosophical theories on law is referred to as the 'rights thesis' and is propagated by Dworkin, a twentieth-century jurist. Dworkin rejected the principles of positivism because he believed that law was not simply based on a series of rules but on principles, policies, and more general standards (McCoubrey and White (1999) 158). Some of these standards will include morality and it has been suggested that this can be equated, to an extent, with parts of natural law (McCoubrey and White (1999) 176) but it is different in that Dworkin did not believe that there is a 'higher' law; merely that the community has institutional morality, ie a common base of principles to which its members adhere.

The centre of Dworkin's criticism is that law is based on the difference between rights (principles) and policy (goals) (McCoubrey and White (1999) 161). The importance of policy was that it was a decision for the public good, a decision that influenced the community. This interplays with principles that give rise to individual rights and these may be contrary to the policy goal albeit for appropriate reasons. More than this, however, he argues that judges are obligated to decide matters on the basis of principles (rights) and not policy. This distinction is based on a similar premise to the distinction between politics and the law.

He later sought an interpretative approach to law. This is not interpretation as we understand it (ie reviewing a statute and deciding what it means) but has a more philosophical abstract sense. Dworkin believes that the law is a series of constructive interpretations, that in order for a judge to adjudicate on a problem he must look for a pattern that is discernible in the rights and policies relevant to the issue (Bix (2003) 89).

This theory of law fits the common-law system (1.3.1 below) because precedent is an important part of the interpretative approach. The previous decisions of judges help identify a pattern that could lead one to determine what the legal solution to a problem is. Alongside these principles, however, are the moral policies and Dworkin believed that a judge should attempt to make the law as 'good' as it can be, meaning that, where there are different alternatives, the one closest to the moral norm may be best (Bix (2003) 90). This is also a response to the argument that positivism neglects amoral laws whereas in the rights-based approach the amoral law is unlikely to ever be the 'best' solution to a given problem and thus the judge will reinterpret the matter.

1.3 System

The final word to examine is that of 'System'. Identifying precisely what a system is can be open to debate but it is probably more than the individual rules or laws and is instead the concept of how law is administered. In the same way that law can be divided into civil and criminal law (1.2.1.3 above) there are two systems, the criminal justice system and the civil justice system. Thus the system is how the law is to be applied and envelops some procedural law together with the courts etc.

1.3.1 Common law

The English Legal System is an example of a common-law-based system. This can be contrasted with the other principal system which is sometimes known as the civil system (which can be confusing as it does not mean civil as in the distinction between civil and criminal law) and more readily understood as the continental system. These two legal systems can be found throughout the world and their use reflects the geopolitical influence of Britain, Spain, and France. Accordingly, those areas of the world that were parts of the British Empire (eg the United States of America, Canada, Australia, New Zealand, and certain African states) have all tended to follow the common-law-based system of law whereas those that formed part of the French and Spanish Empires (eg Continental Europe, Latin America, and certain parts of Africa) have adopted the continental approach.

1.3.1.1 Common-law system

The principal hallmark of the common-law system is, as its name suggests, the recognition of something called 'common law'. In England and Wales law is not only passed by Parliament (known as statutory law) but also can develop from the previous decisions of courts. It is for this reason that precedent (which is explained in further details during Chapter 3 but may be summarized here as the basis upon which certain courts set out rulings which they and other courts must follow) is so important to the common-law system.

The term 'common law' was used to distinguish between law that was decided by the Royal Courts in London and which was applied throughout the kingdom (thus a 'common' approach to the law) and ecclesiastical (Church) law (which remained an important source and application of law until the nineteenth century) and local customary law. Eventually the common law took over the other sources of law, especially as the reporting of decisions became more ordered and it was thus easier to see how judges were applying the law.

The common law remains strong today and, whilst it is comparatively rare for the courts to create a new legal principle, there continues to be a significant amount of law that exists without statutory definition.

⮕ COMMON-LAW CRIME

Perhaps the best example of a common law is that of murder. The crime of murder is not defined in statute (although its punishment now is: see *Murder (Abolition of Death Penalty) Act 1965*). The definition has evolved through the common law with its basis in the definition given by Coke, an eighteenth-century judge. The definition has been amended by statute (see *Law Reform (Year and a Day Rule) Act 1996*) but its definition continues to be a matter of the common law.

Where there is a 'gap' in the law the superior courts will sometimes continue to rely on their common-law powers. A good example of this is in respect of the protection of the vulnerable (particularly children) where the Family Division of the High Court of Justice claims an 'inherent jurisdiction' which means that it has the power to draw upon the common law to act in the best interests of the vulnerable person.

Common law v equity

Whilst we now refer to the system in England and Wales being a common-law system it is also necessary to refer to the place of equity. Prior to the *Judicature Acts* of 1873 and 1875 equity was considered a parallel system to the common-law courts. It is not true to think of it as being separate to the common law as its jurisdiction was inextricably linked to the common law but the common-law courts were restricted to granting damages and so if somebody could not petition the court, or wished for something other than damages, the common-law courts could not assist. There was also a belief that the common-law courts were too mechanistic and that the strict rules of law sometimes created unfairness. People began to petition the King (as Sovereign) for justice and he began to delegate these matters to the Lord Chancellor and eventually created a separate series of courts, the courts of Chancery, to resolve such matters. The courts of Chancery proceeded not on the basis of the strictures of common law but on the principles of justice and they could dispense equitable rather than legal resolutions, something based on fairness, and which incorporated other remedies, including injunctions and the ability to recognize beneficial, and not just legal, interests.

Equity introduced a series of new and innovative resolutions but it became quickly apparent that in many instances a dispute could be resolved either under the common law or equity and the two parallel systems often conflicted. In the *Earl of Oxford's case* (1615) 1 Rep Ch 1 the courts were called upon to decide whether common law or equity took priority. It is not necessary to consider the facts of this case in depth and you will probably read about it in *Equity & Trusts* but, in essence, there was an allegation that a judgment of the common-law courts had been obtained by bribery. The Chancery court issued an injunction preventing the common-law order being enforced and this led directly to a conflict between the two jurisdictions. It was ultimately resolved by it being ruled that in a dispute between the common law and equity, equity would prevail.

The *Judicature Acts* of 1873 and 1875 resolved this tension by unifying the jurisdictions and creating one supreme court of judicature (now embodied by the Senior Courts of England and Wales). All courts—not just the courts of Chancery—were able to exercise the equitable remedies and hence now the part of the High Court that is seen as the successor to the common-law courts (the Queen's Bench Division) readily issues equitable remedies such as injunctions or mandatory orders. It is important to note the jurisdictions did not merge and it is possible today to distinguish equity from the common law (and indeed you will do so when you study the module *Equity and Trusts*). Equity is based on a series of principles—known as equitable maxims—which continue to be used and which were considered to encapsulate the inherent fairness of equity.

1.3.1.2 Continental system

The continental system differs from a common-law system in that it is based on the primacy of written laws. Continental systems tend to be codified, meaning that the laws are all set out in a document. This is not only the hallmark of the continental system since in many common-law countries (most notably America) they have a codified criminal law whereby all of the crimes and procedural rules relating to the criminal justice system are set out in one document, commonly referred to as a Penal Code.

The codification system means that judges are not 'creating' new laws or rights but simply interpreting the laws set out by the legislature. Accordingly if there is a 'gap' in the law then it cannot be filled by the judges. However, of course, in practice the concept of 'interpretation' is almost as fluid as the idea of judicial creations and the fact that many courts will 'follow' the decisions of other judges (even though they arguably do not have a formal system of precedent per se) means that the law will develop in the way that the judges desire.

1.3.2 **An adversarial system**

The second hallmark of the English Legal System (and indeed all common-law systems) is that it is an adversarial system. This refers to how cases are adjudicated upon and can be distinguished from the inquisitorial system that is frequently found within the continental system.

1.3.2.1 Adversarial approach

The adversarial approach to law is where the adjudication is seen as a contest between two or more sides and that it is fought out before a neutral umpire (the judge and/or jury). The judge, whilst able to ask questions, should not seek to become an investigator and should rather concentrate on ensuring that both sides are obeying the procedural rules governing the presentation of their case (*Jones v National Coal Board* [1957] 2 QB 55).

A central plank of the adversarial process is the fact that the parties, not the court, call witnesses. Both parties will gather their evidence, including asking witnesses to give statements. The parties will then decide which witnesses they are going to call to give evidence in court. The opposing party is able to challenge this evidence in two ways. The first is through calling their own witnesses who may provide an alternative viewpoint on the issues. The second, and more combative method, is to allow witnesses to be cross-examined. Cross-examination is where a party directly challenges the witnesses' evidence and puts the contrary case to them.

The other key principle of the adversarial system is that of the importance of orality. In both the criminal and civil systems of justice there is still the assumption that providing live oral evidence is the best way of arriving at the facts. Indeed in a criminal trial where there is no dispute between the parties as to what the witness will say (ie there will be no cross-examination) then the statement given by that person will be tendered as evidence. The way it is tendered is that it is read out aloud. It is quite possible, or indeed likely, that giving it to the jury to read would be at the very least as effective but the tradition of oral evidence continues.

It will be seen later in this book that changes are being made to the adversarial system in order to take the edge off some of its harshness (see in particular Chapters 14 and 16). However these are only minor modifications and it is not a shift towards a purely inquisitorial system.

1.3.2.2 Inquisitorial approach

The continental system tends to adopt an inquisitorial approach. In this sense the court becomes the investigator itself. Rather than the judge being a neutral umpire, he is given the authority to seek out the truth by asking questions of the witnesses. The respective lawyers seek to control this questioning by reference to the procedural rules and to this extent it can be argued the roles of counsel and the judiciary are almost mirrored. It has been suggested that one advantage of this model is that it ensures that all relevant witnesses are heard (Zander (2007) 395) whereas in the adversarial system, if a witness's evidence is not helpful to a side, he or she may not be called.

Consideration was given to whether the English Legal System should move towards an inquisitorial approach but the *Royal Commission on Criminal Justice* argued that this would be a significant cultural shift (Zander (2003) 377). Arguably this is correct and it cannot be accidental that common-law systems tend to be adversarial with continental systems being inquisitorial, suggesting that any shift to either model may involve a rethink of the legal system as a whole.

 ## Summary

In this chapter we have noted that:

- There is a United Kingdom of Great Britain and Northern Ireland. Whilst this is our formal state, it is constituted from four parts; England, Scotland, Wales, and Northern Ireland.

- Historically England annexed the law of Wales and so when we refer to the English Legal System we are actually including Wales too.

- Scotland and Northern Ireland have separate legal systems, these being retained as part of the Acts of Union that created the United Kingdom.

- It is difficult to identify what precisely law is and it is probably a philosophical rather than a practical problem. Law is probably a collection of rules governing rights, duties, and obligations but the extent of these rules and where the authority comes from to use them is more open to debate.

- Law can be divided into different classifications including substantive and procedural, public and private, and civil and criminal. These classifications affect how we think about law and what the law does.

- The English Legal System is based on the common law, meaning that judges are able to progress the law themselves. Decisions from previous court hearings still form part of our law.

- The English Legal System is an adversarial system meaning that a case is adjudicated by two competing sides presenting their evidence with a neutral judge or jury deciding which case they prefer.

PART I

Sources of Law

2

Domestic Sources of Law: parliamentary material

By the end of this chapter you will be able to:

- Understand the primary sources of domestic law.
- Differentiate between primary and secondary sources of law.
- Differentiate between primary and secondary legislation.
- Identify, and use, the different approaches to statutory interpretation.

Introduction

You are studying the law but how do you know what the law is? Where do you find law? The skill of being able to find law and the knowledge of knowing how to interpret law are two of the most important abilities of any lawyer. Indeed it is possible to go so far as to say that these are the two most important abilities of a lawyer and of a law student. If you are able to find and interpret law then you can apply those skills to any law—it does not matter whether you have studied the subject or not because all law has the same basic components in it.

Sources of law are an important (and arguably *the* most important) part of legal study since a proper grounding in the subject will allow you to access any substantive legal issue. The next two chapters will introduce you to this knowledge but reference should also be made to Legal Skills texts that will help you put this knowledge into practice. This chapter examines parliamentary material, that is to say laws passed by the Houses of Parliament, and Chapter 3 examines material produced by the courts through cases.

2.1 Domestic law

This chapter discusses the sources of domestic law and we need to be clear at the very beginning of this chapter what that means.

2.1.1 International relations

As has already been noted the United Kingdom consists of four countries (England, Scotland, Northern Ireland, and Wales) and there are three legal systems (England and Wales, Scotland, and Northern Ireland) each of which approaches its sources of law in similar (although not exactly the same) ways. However, the United Kingdom is also a signatory to a number of treaties, most notably the *European Convention on Human Rights* (ECHR) and the *Treaty of Rome* which led to the UK joining what was the European Economic Community (EEC) and is now the European Union (EU).

The ECHR is directly relevant because the *Human Rights Act 1998* created a situation where it was deemed that all public bodies would abide by the Convention and provided authorities to the domestic courts to hear challenges to any breach. This chapter will look at how the *Human Rights Act 1998* has altered the way courts approach domestic legislation but will not discuss the sources of the jurisprudence surrounding the ECHR as this will be discussed in Chapter 4 (International Sources of Law). The individual rights established within the ECHR will be examined in Chapter 5 as will some of the effects of the *Human Rights Act 1998*.

The relationship that the United Kingdom has with the EU is more complicated and this too will be examined in Chapter 4. Some EU law becomes directly part of UK domestic law without any domestic proceedings occurring but this is because

Parliament has provided for this (see the *European Communities Act 1972*) and if it wished to do so it could legislate to prevent this from happening. Accordingly, in this chapter the interface with EU law will not be considered because apart from those situations where a measure is directly applicable into domestic law, any changes are brought about in the same way. Chapter 4 will examine how EU law is created, how decisions are reached as to whether it is directly applicable to individual states and how that law is implemented.

2.1.2 Constitution

This text is not a textbook on the constitution of the United Kingdom and those of you who are studying law as an undergraduate programme will almost certainly study the constitution of the United Kingdom in a specific module, sometimes called *Constitutional Law* and sometimes known as *Public Law*. However, it is necessary to summarize some aspects of the constitutional law so as to understand the sources of domestic law.

Every country must have a constitution which can be defined as a series of legal and non-legal rules that define how a country is governed (Barendt (1998) 2). However, the term 'constitution' in many countries means a document that enshrines the fundamental rules of governance. Perhaps the most obvious example of this is the Constitution of the United States of America which quite clearly sets out the machinery of governance, expressly creating three instruments of state: the executive (President of the United States of America), the legislature (Congress), and the judiciary (Supreme Court of the United States of America). The American Constitution is not static in that it can be changed (and indeed there are currently twenty-seven amendments, the last having been passed in 1992).[1]

Most constitutions will enshrine the laws in their constitution, ie they will require a special resolution to amend the instrument. Most democracies will normally operate on a simple majority system to pass legislation but constitutions will require a higher standard to ensure that the constitution, which will normally also prescribe the rights and freedoms of citizens, cannot be abused by rogue governments. In the United States of America any amendment to the Constitution requires Congress to pass an amendment by a two-thirds majority *and* for three-quarters of the individual state legislatures to pass the amendment.

2.1.2.1 Does the United Kingdom have a constitution?

The United Kingdom does not have a written constitution:

> There is no document in the United Kingdom equivalent, say, to the United States Constitution...Nor, for that matter, is there a set of statutes clearly indicated by their titles as 'Constitutional' or 'Basic' laws. (Barendt (1998) 26)

However, this is no longer strictly true as the *Constitutional Reform Act 2005* obviously contains the word 'constitutional' in it, but the basic point remains intact; within the United Kingdom the legislature rarely expressly refers to pieces of legislation as constituting part of a formal constitution. That is not to say that measures do not exist because quite apart from the 2005 Act, the *Acts of Union 1707* and *1801* which created

---

1. Which protects the 'compensation' (salary) of senators and congressmen.

the United Kingdom (see 1.1.1 above) must be considered constitutional as must the *European Communities Act 1972* and the *Human Rights Act 1998*. However, the presumption is that so-called 'constitutional' pieces of legislation are no different from any other piece of legislation and could be amended or repealed by a simple majority.

2.1.3 Primary and secondary sources

When locating law it is important to draw a distinction between primary and secondary sources of law. Primary sources of law are authoritative sources of law, ie they are statements of what the law is. Secondary sources of law are not authoritative and are interpretations of the law. Whilst you will use secondary sources quite frequently through your law studies you should not misunderstand their place and should cite primary sources where possible (see Diagram 2.1).

Diagram 2.1 demonstrates that within each division of sources there are different subcategories and this chapter will discuss which sources should be cited when.

2.1.3.1 Primary sources

It was discussed above that there is no enshrined specific constitutional law and thus primary sources of law can be separated into two general parts. The first is legislation, ie measures that come from the legislature (Parliament) and this is known as 'statutory law', and the second is from the decisions of courts and this is known as the 'common law'. The interaction between these forms of law will be discussed in this chapter but theoretically statutory law is supreme. The United Kingdom is a monarchy. The formal Head of State is the Queen (which can be contrasted with the President of the United States of America or the President of France) but at the same time we are a democracy and the head of the executive is the prime minister.[2] Sovereign power in the United

Primary	**Secondary**
Acts of Parliament	Books of authority
Statutory Instruments	Peer-refereed articles in law journals
Orders in Council	Leading textbooks in the field
Decisions of superior courts	Non-refereed articles in key law journals

Diagram 2.1 Primary and secondary sources

2. Although interestingly there is no *legal* rule that states that the prime minister is the head of the executive and until comparatively recently, the office did not even necessarily legally exist as it was not mentioned in statutes. It is a *convention* that the prime minister is the head of the executive and this demonstrates the importance of conventions (unwritten rules of custom and practice).

Kingdom resides in the Queen in Parliament. This means that all legislation requires the approval of the monarch (see below) but that subject to this Parliament may pass such laws as it wishes. There are different types of democracies but the UK version of parliamentary democracy means that rather than citizens taking votes on issues (known as referendums) the convention is that we elect Members of Parliament who have the right to pass laws subject to their being voted out of office at the next election.

As the Queen in Parliament is supreme then this means that where a statute conflicts with a decision of the court, the statute (legislation) should prevail but whether this happens in practice will be discussed below. However, there are examples of situations where Parliament has passed legislation with the specific intention of overturning a decision of the courts[3] and the courts have had to accept that version of the law.

2.1.3.2 Secondary sources

It can be seen from the diagram above that secondary sources are, in essence, academic material, although other material (for example, government policy papers etc) may also come within this band. The use of the material will be discussed below but it should be noted at the outset that whilst you may use secondary sources frequently in your studies (either to find primary sources or to complete an essay) they will very rarely be mentioned in court. That said, the courts do appear to be citing academic material more than they ever did and at one point authors would only be cited when they were dead and could not change their mind! Perhaps the growth in academic writings over recent years has led judges to consider that it can be useful to see how others have interpreted the law. However, caution should always be used when citing contemporary academic sources.

2.2 Statutory law

The first source to discuss is statutory law, that being law passed by Parliament. It was noted above that statutory law is a primary source of law but to confuse matters statutory law itself is divided, into primary legislation and secondary legislation, with primary legislation itself being divided into two! Diagram 2.2 may assist.

Diagram 2.2 shows that primary legislation is that which is known as an Act of Parliament and that these may exist as either a Public or Private Act. Whilst all forms of parliamentary legislation are statutory, an Act of Parliament is often referred to as a 'statute'. The statutes that you will encounter most of the time are known as Public Acts and these are measures that apply to all of society. Private Acts are those that are limited to a particular company or organization that requires powers beyond those prescribed by the normal law. They tended to be used for the creation of docks, transport links, or other major building programmes.

➲ PRIVATE ACT

The University of Wales, Cardiff Act 2004 is a private (sometimes referred to as 'local') Act. Its purpose was to merge the University of Wales Medical School with the University of Wales,

3. For example the *Sexual Offences Act 2003* states that the test for whether an offender believed a rape complainant was consenting is an objective test whereas the courts had traditionally said that it was a subjective test.

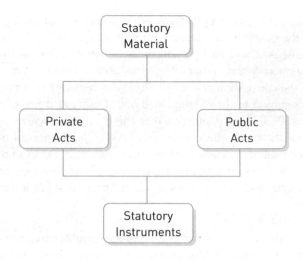

Diagram 2.2 Legislation

Cardiff. Universities can be divided into two groups: those that existed before 1992 and those that gained university status after 1992. The former were generally established by Royal Charter whereas the latter acquired their authority from the *Further and Higher Education Act 1992* and articles of governance approved by the Privy Council. Universities are independent bodies but are limited to the powers set out in either the Royal Charter or the 1992 legislation. In 2004 it was decided that the University of Wales Medical School would be incorporated into the larger University of Wales, Cardiff but neither institution had the power to do this as their status was regulated as described above. They petitioned Parliament and the *University of Wales, Cardiff Act 2004* gave the institutions the power to merge and become a single unit.

The Act thus provided one institution a power that it did not previously have and doing so did not involve it granting any wider power to either that institution or any other institution, the essence of a private Act.

⮕ PUBLIC ACT

The *Education Act 2005* is a public Act. Its purpose is to reform the way in which failing schools are identified and required to reform. The Act is of general importance as it applies not to a specific school or authority but to all schools in England.[4] It creates an Inspectorate for Schools in England and provides specific powers and duties for that body.

As the Act provides a general power that applies beyond a single company or authority it is a Public Act and applies as a general law of the land subject to the limitations contained within its drafting.

Secondary legislation is slightly easier to define although it is normally referred to as *statutory instruments*. An Act of Parliament will generally provide the general scope of a law and its powers but it will commonly leave some consequential matters out. Such

---

4. The *Education Act 2005* is also unusual in that it provides a general application for just England rather than England and Wales because education is a devolved matter for Wales (see 1.1.2 above).

matters could include when a piece of legislation comes into effect (a majority of Acts of Parliament do not come into effect immediately so that preparations can be made for any requisite training or public awareness campaigns) or the precise application of a law (eg what grade a person must be to exercise a power).

The balance between what goes in primary and secondary legislation is a delicate one. Parliament only has a finite amount of time to debate legislation and so if every detail of a law was placed in primary legislation then any changes (eg an organization changes its name) would require another piece of primary legislation to permit this. This would quickly lead to a situation where Parliament would have no time to discuss any other legislation. However, if too much is placed into secondary legislation then Parliament as a whole could lose control of how the law is being implemented because it is far easier for secondary legislation to be passed (see below). To put this all into context if we look at the figures for 2009, Parliament passed twenty-seven Public Acts of Parliament while 3,468 pieces of secondary legislation were passed. It is inconceivable that each piece of secondary legislation could have been passed in the same way as primary legislation.

⊕ SECONDARY LEGISLATION

Part II of the *Regulation of Investigatory Powers Act 2000* permits certain public bodies the right to undertake covert surveillance. The Act does not say who these public authorities are or who within the organization may authorize surveillance to be carried out. These details are provided for in the *Regulation of Investigatory Powers (Directed Surveillance and Covert Human Intelligence Sources) Order 2010, SI 2010/521*. The order lists each organization that may undertake surveillance (eg the police, local authorities, etc) and who within each organization may authorize its use (eg police inspector, director of housing, etc). The advantage of this is that where a new public agency requires the right to conduct surveillance Parliament need only pass a new statutory instrument rather than amend the 2000 Act.

The manner in which legislation is passed, reviewed, and treated depends on whether it is primary or secondary legislation, as will be seen.

2.2.1 Primary legislation

The most important type of legislation is primary legislation. Although noting the existence of Private Acts of Parliament above, the remainder of this chapter will focus on Public Acts of Parliament as these are the more important and also the pieces of legislation that you are more likely to encounter.

It was noted that the Queen in Parliament is the sovereign body in this country and in practice this means Parliament through its Acts of Parliament. There are (theoretically) no limits to the power of Parliament and it could legislate to do anything it wishes.

👁 Example Smoking in Paris

A common example that is used when discussing the supreme nature of Parliament is that of smoking on the streets of Paris. If Parliament wished to do so it could pass a law that states it is illegal to smoke on the streets of Paris. Could this be enforced? Possibly not but it does not matter because whether a law can be enforced is not relevant to its validity. A statute banning smoking in Paris would be valid and assuming that evidence existed to show that D had smoked in Paris then if D ever set foot in the United Kingdom he could be arrested, tried, and convicted.

The fact that Parliament can legislate for anything has not been compromised by the constitutional changes that have taken place in recent years. It was noted in Chapter 1 that Scotland, Northern Ireland, and (to a much more limited extent) Wales have devolved authority whereby they can create their own law. However, Parliament could as easily choose to withdraw this power and centralize all legislation again. It was noted at the beginning of this chapter that no legislation is enshrined into law (2.1.2 above) and, accordingly, an Act of Parliament could repeal the devolution legislation. Even without doing this, however, we can see that the UK Parliament remains supreme because the legislation expressly states that the devolution legislation does not preclude the UK Parliament from legislating over devolved areas (see, for example, s 28(7) *Scotland Act 1998*).

The *Human Rights Act 1998* (HRA 1998) is also compatible with this convention that Parliament can legislate to do anything. Whilst there is a presumption that all legislation will be compatible with the ECHR the statute expressly preserves the power of Parliament to legislate in a way that is *not* compliant with the ECHR (see s 19(2) HRA 1998). This also serves as an example of the second principal convention that exists on the sovereignty of Parliament which is that Parliament cannot bind its successors. In other words, the current Parliament in any current session may not pass a law that is not subject to repeal. This convention is also likely to ensure that Parliament cannot enshrine legislation as although this would not prevent Parliament from repealing it (enshrining legislation merely raises the threshold for repeal) the setting of a threshold would restrict the competency of Parliament and accordingly all statutes have (theoretically) the same status as each other.

2.2.1.1 Process of creating an Act

We now know what an Act of Parliament is but how is it established? Reference should be made to your constitutional-law/public-law texts which will describe this process in more detail, but it is necessary at least to summarize the parliamentary process in order to understand the impact of statutes.

The general process can be represented in diagrammatic form as shown in Diagram 2.3.

For the purposes of Diagram 2.3 a Bill has been introduced into the House of Commons but a Bill can begin its parliamentary life in either House. Whilst a Bill is progressing through Parliament it is easy to identify where it originated as the letters '[HL]' are appended to those Bills that start in the House of Lords. Where this happens the boxes in Diagram 2.3 listed 'House of Commons' and 'House of Lords' would simply be switched. Each substantive stage will be detailed in brief.

House of Commons

Regardless of whether the House receives the Bill first or second the same format is always adopted.

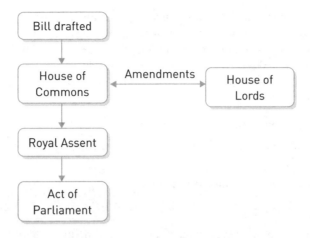

Diagram 2.3 The parliamentary process

Table 2.1 The legislative stages

First Reading	Title of the Bill is read out and the Bill is printed.
Second Reading	Debate on the *general* principles of the Bill. Vote taken on whether to proceed.
Committee Stage	Passes to a Committee of the House.[5]
Report Stage	Amended Bill is reprinted and voted on.
Third Reading	Final amendments and vote. Passed to House of Lords if relevant.

The matter will only not return to the House of Lords if either the Parliament Act is used (see below) or the two Houses have agreed the content of the Bill following the process described.

House of Lords

The process adopted in the House of Lords is virtually identical but the committee is normally a committee of the whole House and the rules relating to the choice and content of the amendments is not as regulated as it is in the House of Commons. The other significant difference is that by convention a Finance Bill is never defeated in the House and a government Bill that was included in an election manifesto is never defeated at second reading (although it may be later on).

Consideration of amendments

In many cases it is likely that the second House to consider the Bill will produce a slightly different Bill than that which was handed to them not least because members of

---

5. Where this is a constitutional Bill or part of the Finance Bill ('the budget') then it would normally be a committee of the whole House, otherwise it is more likely that an ad hoc committee of up to 50 MPs is established according to party strength.

the second House have had the opportunity to table amendments. Assuming that this happens then the matter returns to the originating House (so in our example the House of Commons) where that House must consider the amendments. If they do not agree them (and therefore make further amendments themselves) then the matter returns to the other House and the process is repeated in a 'ping-pong' fashion until one of three things happens:

- the two Houses agree the content of the Bill
- the Houses cannot agree and parliamentary time runs out in which case the Bill is normally lost[6]
- the Parliament Act is invoked (see below).

Royal Assent

Assuming that the two Houses manage to agree the content of the Bill then the Bill is sent to the Queen for Royal Assent. The date on which the Royal Assent is given is also marked on the Act and it becomes itself part of the Act (see below). The constitutional position of Royal Assent is often debated but it is usually accepted that the sovereign no longer has power to decline assent (see, for example, Barendt (1998) 41).

2.2.1.2 Parliament Act

The normal process by which an Act will be established is as discussed below but an important exception to this is when the Parliament Act is invoked. In fact there are two Parliament Acts, the first is the *Parliament Act 1911* and the second is the *Parliament Act 1949* which amended the 1911 Act. The 1911 Act was created to solve an impasse between the House of Commons and House of Lords whereby government business was being rejected by the upper House. The prime minister of the day, Herbert Asquith, sought to introduce legislation that would limit the right of the House of Lords to reject the wishes of the (democratically elected) House of Commons. If the legislation was not passed then Asquith had gained the support of the king to create sufficient new peers to ensure that the government would have a majority in the upper House, which would have been disastrous in terms of the authority and efficiency of the upper House. With that threat the House of Lords passed the 1911 Act.

The main provisions of the 1911 Act are to be found in ss 1 and 2 of the Act. Section 1 states that the House of Lords may only delay a money Bill for one month and that after this has elapsed the Bill may receive Royal Assent without the authority of the House of Lords. Whether a Bill is a 'money Bill' will depend on whether the Speaker of the House of Commons certifies it as such under s 1(2). The certificate of the Speaker cannot be subject to review by any court of law (s 4). This severely restricts the powers of the upper House and was imposed because one of the Bills that was rejected in Asquith's Parliament was the Finance Bill (the government budget).

The second, and more important, part of the 1911 Act is provided for in s 2. This also limits the time in which the upper House can delay a Bill. When it was originally enacted the Bill had to be rejected on the third occasion before s 2 could be used (ie the Bill had failed to gain parliamentary support in at least two successive parliamentary sessions (years)) and the rejection had to be for virtually identical Bills (subject to

---

6. However, since 1998 the House of Commons can, in certain circumstances, agree that a government Bill can be held over to the next session (see House of Commons Factsheet L1: *Parliamentary Stages of a Government Bill*, 6–7).

amendments to reflect the passage of time). If the criterion was met—and the Speaker certified the criterion as being met (s 2(4) with s 4 applying to deny the opportunity to review this certificate)—then after its rejection for the third time the Bill could receive Royal Assent without the House of Lords approving it. The only exceptions to this were money bills (covered by s 1) and any provision that purported to lengthen the duration of Parliament.[7]

The *Parliament Act 1911* has only been used seven times, twice in 1914[8] and four times in the last twenty years,[9] but its most controversial use was when it was used to pass the *Parliament Act 1949* which amended the 1911 Act itself. The principal purpose of the 1949 Act was to reduce the threshold in s 2 to one year, meaning that a Bill must merely fail after it has been entered in two consecutive Parliaments and would be passed after the second, rather than third, defeat.

One important point to note about the *Parliament Act 1911* is that it applies only to legislation introduced to the House of Commons. If a Bill introduced into the House of Lords is amended by the House of Commons and the Lords refuse to accede to these amendments over two consecutive years then the Act cannot be invoked (see Barnett (2011) 444).

Validity of the Parliament Act 1949

There has for a number of years been a debate over the validity of the *Parliament Act 1949*. The sole purpose of this Act was to amend the 1911 Act and two criticisms have been made of the 1949 Act. The first, as Loveland (2009) notes, is that some consider it unconstitutional because the 1911 Act was not designed to limit further the power of the upper House (Loveland (2009) 165) but from a legal standpoint this argument carries little weight due to the competency of Parliament to legislate in any manner. The second argument is that legislation under the 1911 Act is not primary legislation per se but delegated legislation (the delegation being the 1911 Act permitting law to be made in a way contrary to the usual parliamentary process) and that delegated legislation cannot be used to alter primary legislation without express permission to do so.

The debate about the validity of the Act had been played out in the pages of academic books and journals but in 2005 it became a real proposition when it formed the basis of a case before the courts. The *Hunting Act 2004* was arguably one of the most controversial statutes in recent years and it banned certain types of hunting with live animals. The debate in Parliament was acrimonious and the House of Lords refused to pass the legislation. The government used the Parliament Act to force the provision through but the *Countryside Alliance*, an organization created to lobby against the Act, sought to challenge the ruling.

The challenge was rejected by the High Court and the matter proceeded to the Court of Appeal (*R (Jackson and others) v Attorney-General* [2005] QB 579) who needed to consider the status of the 1949 Act. The court agreed that legislation under the 1911 Act was delegated legislation rather than true primary legislation. The court argued that this conclusion was inevitable because delegated means the authority arises

---

7. Ensuring that a rogue government could not legislate to continue in power where it had a majority but knew it was unlikely to be re-elected.

8. To legislate for the disestablishment of the Church of Wales (*Welsh Church Act 1914*) and once to legislate for home rule in Ireland (*Home Rule Act 1914*) although this Act was never implemented.

9. To legislate for war crimes (*War Crimes Act 1991*), European parliamentary elections (*European Parliamentary Elections Act 1999*), to legalize certain homosexual acts and to reduce the age of consent for sexual activity (*Sexual Offences (Amendment) Act 2000*), and to ban hunting (*Hunting Act 2004*).

from another piece of legislation and this is what happens when the Parliament Act is invoked. The Bill which is to become an Act can only do so because of the authority vested in the 1911 Act. If the 1911 Act was repealed then a Bill rejected by the House of Lords could not become an Act of Parliament (pp 589–593). However, the court also rejected the suggestion that because it was delegated legislation it was somehow not as effective as an Act of Parliament and held that the legitimacy of an Act passed under the Parliament Act was present. In terms of the 1949 Act the court held that although the 1911 Act could not be used to bring further significant constitutional change (as it did not expressly so provide) the 1949 Act could not be so categorized. The court also made the important point that the amended Act had been used three times already without challenge and that the sovereign, Parliament, and the courts had acted on that Act implicitly acquiescing to the validity of the Act (pp 606–607). This perhaps marks the ultimate conclusion of the courts: if the 1949 Act had been deemed invalid it would have caused numerous difficulties in its exercise in the past twenty years and that alone was cause for the courts to be slow to question its validity.

The matter inevitably proceeded to the House of Lords ([2005] 3 WLR 733) where their Lordships upheld the decision of the Court of Appeal by dismissing the appeal but reversed the Court of Appeal on several aspects of its judgment, most notably over whether legislation passed under the Parliament Acts is delegated legislation. Lord Bingham, who gave the leading speech in the case, stated that the 1911 Act makes clear that the legislation should be an 'Act of Parliament' and Parliament did not at that time envisage any different status (p 744). This, it was submitted, is a crucial point. Constitutionally there has never been any distinction drawn between the status of Acts of Parliament as distinct from legislation in general. Acts of Parliament have always been considered to be not only primary sources of law but also primary legislation— and accordingly although the courts can interpret the provisions (see below) they cannot rule them illegal. The submissions of the appellants would have created a situation where a distinction was drawn between Acts of Parliament, which could have undermined the supremacy of Parliament.

Lord Bingham went further and argued that the case being litigated came extremely close to disrupting the separation of powers, with his Lordship noting that the courts have consistently stated that they do not have the power to look at the validity of an Act of Parliament but must merely interpret and implement its provisions (p 746). This was not a view shared by all the Law Lords sitting on the case and Lord Nicholls, for example, argued that it is not a case of looking at the validity of a properly passed Act but questioning whether the Act was properly passed (p 754). This is probably an important distinction to be drawn as who else could decide this point? The balance of powers in the state does not provide Parliament with any power to adjudicate on individual cases but instead leaves that to the judiciary. Whilst Parliament can overrule a decision of the courts by legislating to overrule the principle this will ordinarily have no impact on the specific case being litigated. The only way that the validity of the Parliament Act process could be raised is through the courts and for this reason a relaxation of the traditional rules would appear appropriate.

Importantly, the decision in *Jackson* leaves open some questions on the limits of parliamentary accountability to the judiciary, with Cooke (a former Lord of Appeal in Ordinary) suggesting that some judges were prepared to hold that there are certain measures (eg the abolition of judicial review or a similar restriction of judicial access) that could not be passed under the Act (see Cooke (2006) 226). However, it is quite clear from the unanimous decision of the House that legislation passed under the Parliament Acts is not delegated but has exactly the same status as legislation that is passed in the usual way. It is, of course, open to Parliament to repeal the Parliament Acts but unless the repealing Act expressly stated that it was to operate retrospectively the decision of the House of Lords in this case demonstrates that all Acts passed under those instruments are as valid as any other statute.

❓ QUESTION FOR REFLECTION

Lord Cooke suggests that the *Parliament Act 1949* cannot be used to amend the *Parliament Act 1911* in such a way as to remove the safeguards against a money bill or the extension of Parliament. Consider the case of *Jackson* (above), in particular the speech of Lord Bingham. Do you think Lord Cooke is right? If so, does that mean there are no safeguards to prevent a rogue government indefinitely extending the lifetime of Parliament?

🎧 LISTEN TO THE PODCAST

For guidance on how to answer this question and a discussion of the main issues, listen to the author's podcast on the Online Resource Centre:
www.oxfordtextbooks.co.uk/orc/gillespie_els3e/

2.2.2 Content of a statute

Having now discussed what legislation is, what does one look like and what are its contents. If we take, as an example, the *Constitutional Reform Act 2005* (CRA 2005) which we have already used it can be seen that the beginning of the Statute will look similar to Diagram 2.4.

The relevant aspects to discuss are:

1. Short title
2. Royal Coat of Arms
3. Chapter number
4. Long title
5. Date of Royal Assent
6. Enacting formula
7. Part number and heading
8. Marginal note
9. Section

Short title

Most statutes will be referred to by their short title, ie in the example above the statute will normally be called the *Constitutional Reform Act 2005*. This short title is always displayed at the beginning of the Act but the authority to use a short title must be expressly provided within the statute itself and it will normally come towards the end of the statute. For this statute, s 149 CRA 2005 says: 'This Act may be cited as the Constitutional Reform Act 2005.'

Ordinarily the short title of an Act is uncontroversial but occasionally its use can be misunderstood. Perhaps a classic example of this was in 2008 during the midst

> **1**   Constitutional Reform Act 2005
>
> **2**   [Royal Coat of Arms]
>
> **3**   2005 CHAPTER 4
>
> **4**   An Act to make provision for modifying the office of Lord Chancellor, and to make provision relating to the functions of that office; to establish a Supreme Court of the United Kingdom, and to abolish the appellate jurisdiction of the House of Lords; to make provision about the jurisdiction of the Judicial Committee of the Privy Council and the judicial functions of the President of the Council; to make other provision about the judiciary, their appointment and discipline; and for connected purposes.
>
> **5**   [24th March 2005]
>
> **6**   BE IT ENACTED by the Queen's most Excellent Majesty, by and with the advice and consent of the Lords Spiritual and Temporal, and Commons, in this present Parliament assembled, and by the authority of the same as follows:—
>
> **7**   **Part 1**
> The Rule of Law
>
> **8** The rule **1.** This Act does not adversely affect—
> of law. **9**   (a) the existing constitutional principles of the rule of law; or
>   (b) the Lord Chancellor's existing constitutional role in relation to that principle.

Diagram 2.4 An example of a statute

of the global financial crisis. An Icelandic bank called *Landsbanki Islands hf* was in financial difficulties and after it went into liquidation the Chancellor of the Exchequer used powers given to him under the *Anti-Terrorism, Crime and Security Act 2001* to seize control of the bank's British assets. This led to the Icelandic government and many global media outlets stating that the British government had used its anti-terrorist legislation against Iceland, the inference being that Iceland was being compared to terrorists. However, the relevant provisions used by the Chancellor were not in the Anti-Terrorism parts of the Act, they were in later sections of the Act. It is easy to see how this could be misrepresented, however, given the short title of the Act. It is perhaps a warning of the political difficulties in putting too much disparate legislation in an Act of Parliament, and also of the requirement to choose short titles with care!

Royal Coat of Arms

An Act of Parliament is made under the authority of the Queen in Parliament because the United Kingdom is a constitutional monarchy. Accordingly when any legislation is passed the Royal Coat of Arms is affixed to the statute to act as a seal for the legislation.

Chapter number

The second official way in which a statute should be cited is in respect of its chapter number. Each Act that is passed by both Houses of Parliament and which receives

Royal Assent is assigned a sequential number to identify what order the legislation was passed in any parliamentary session. Modern statutes are governed by the *Parliament Numbering and Citation Act 1962* which provides that the chapter number is assigned by reference to the calendar year. The first statute to be given Royal Assent after 31 December is given the chapter number 1, and each successive piece of legislation is given a sequential number (s 1). Accordingly in the example above, the *Constitutional Reform Act 2005* was the fourth Act to be given Royal Assent in the calendar year 2005.

Prior to the 1962 Act the position was significantly more complicated. Statutes were assigned a chapter number according to the regnal year in which the parliamentary session was begun. The regnal year was the year of the reign of the current monarch. The regnal year starts on the accession to the throne (eg Queen Elizabeth II acceded to the throne on 6 February 1952)[10] and continues until the day before the anniversary of accession (eg the first regnal year of Queen Elizabeth II was 6 February 1952 to 5 February 1953; on 6 February 1953 Her Majesty's second regnal year began). This inevitably meant that there may be an overlap between the regnal years and the parliamentary sessions which typically begin in October or November of each year with the Queen's Speech. The system was extremely confusing because of this overlap and, for example, the twenty-third Act that was passed in the parliamentary session which began in 1961 and lasted to 1962 would be referred to as *10&11 Eliz.2 c.23* which is translated to mean the 23rd Act in the 10th and 11th years of the reign of the Monarch Elizabeth II. This meant that one would need to know the year of accession for all the monarchs in order to identify what year the Act was! Even today in law libraries you will normally find a list of monarchs and their regnal years in order to facilitate paper-based searching of these Acts.[11] Thankfully the 1962 Act simplified this process and most electronic legislative search engines (eg *Westlaw*, *LexisNexis*, etc) use the calendar rather than regnal year for ease of reference.

It has been argued that the only significance of the chapter number is that it allows the courts to identify in which order Parliament is deemed to have acted (Bennion (1990) 128). If, for example, in the extremely unlikely event that two pieces of legislation are given Royal Assent on the same day but appear to contradict each other, the chapter number identifies which is the later Act and would, therefore, be deemed to have implicitly repealed the earlier legislation.[12]

Long title

Although each Act is given a short title by which it will ordinarily be known, there is also a 'long title' to the Act which serves a description of the purposes of the Act. Bennion also notes that procedurally it is important because when a Bill is being debated in the House of Commons (see 2.2.1.1 above) an amendment can only be tabled to the Act if it is within the scope of the legislation and the long title broadly governs the scope of legislation (Bennion (1990) 42). Bennion also notes that it should be an aid to construction and this will be considered below (see 2.3.5.1 below).

---

10. Note it is the date of the *accession* (ie assumption) of the throne and not the date of the *coronation*. A monarchy is never without a sovereign and thus as soon as a monarch dies the heir presumptive becomes monarch with this assumption being *confirmed* by coronation but the rule starts at the time of accession. The coronation of Queen Elizabeth II was not until 1953 but she was Queen from 1952.

11. A list can also be found on the Online Resource Centre that accompanies this book.

12. For more on implicit repeal see Loveland (2009) 33–34. The issue is not necessarily academic discussion. In *R v Richards* [2007] 1 WLR 847 the President of the Queen's Bench Division held the fact that two pieces of legislation were enacted on the same day was evidence that they did not contradict (and thus implicitly repeal) each other (at 853).

Date of Royal Assent

It was discussed above that Royal Assent is the final part of the process required to enact legislation (see 2.2.1.1 above) and the date on which assent is given is placed on the Act and on all copies of the Act. The sovereign no longer signs each Act and the process is now regulated, in part, by the *Royal Assent Act 1967*, s 1(1)(b) of which permits the Speaker of the House of Commons and the Lord Speaker of the House of Lords to notify their House that Royal Assent has been granted.

Enacting formula

The enacting formula is just a formal wording that demonstrates that the legislation passed the relevant legislative processes. The formula identified in the example above is the usual one but where the Parliament Act has been invoked (see 2.2.1.2 above) the formula changes to:

> Be it enacted by the Queen's most Excellent Majesty, by and with the advice and consent of the Commons, in this present Parliament assembled, in accordance with the provisions of the Parliament Acts 1911 and 1949, and by the authority of the same, as follows–

Obviously it is necessary for this formula to be used as the usual one refers to the advice and consent of the Lords which, of course, did not occur if the Parliament Acts needed to be invoked.

Part number and heading

The organization of statutory material is important since, especially with long pieces of legislation, it ensures that there is a consistency of approach and permits provisions to be grouped together for interpretation. Where an Act is long it is not uncommon for the Act to be split into Parts. The *Constitutional Reform Act 2005* is divided into seven Parts each dealing with a discrete set of provisions in a broad area. Each Part is usually accompanied by a heading, or more properly referred to as a 'note' and these have the same status as marginal notes (see below).

Where an Act is particularly long or complicated it is possible to further divide the Parts into chapters. For example the *Constitutional Reform Act 2005* divides Part 4 (judicial appointments and discipline) into four chapters. In this context is important to note that 'chapter' merely means a subdivision of a Part and is not the same as a chapter number.

Marginal note

Each section within a statute (see below) is accompanied by a marginal note, which is sometimes also referred to as a side note. In effect it has the appearance of a heading and on electronic versions of statutes it appears alongside the section number with the appearance of a heading; eg s 1, as noted above, is presented in electronic versions as:

1. The Rule of Law

This Act does not adversely affect–

    (a) the existing constitutional principle of the rule of law, or

    (b) the Lord Chancellor's constitutional role in relation to that principle.

However it is referred to as a marginal note because, as was seen in Diagram 2.4, in printed form the notes appear in the margins alongside text. A debate appears to exist as to whether marginal notes are part of the Act or whether they are annotations. This will be discussed in more detail below as it is relevant only to the interpretation of a statute (see 2.3.5.1 below).

Section

Each provision within a statute is known as a section. Each section will ordinarily deal with only one topic but it may not be possible to deal with a single topic with only one level of heading within the provision. Accordingly, it is possible to subdivide a section. Four levels are recognized.

Table 2.2 Dividing sections

Level	Name	Appearance
1	Section	1
2	Subsection	(1)
3	Paragraph	(a)
4	Subparagraph	(i)

 Example Section 9 *Constitutional Reform Act 2005*

Section 9 states:

(1) The President of the Family Division is Head of Family Justice.

(2) The Lord Chief Justice may appoint a person to be Deputy Head of Family Justice.

(3) The Lord Chief Justice must not appoint a person under subsection (2) unless these conditions are met–
  (a) the Lord Chief Justice has consulted the Lord Chancellor;
  (b) the person to be appointed is an ordinary judge of the Court of Appeal.

(4) A person appointed as Deputy Head of Family Justice holds that office in accordance with the terms of his appointment.

It can be seen that s 9 is broken into four subsections each of which deals with a discrete aspect of the section's provision. Subsection (3) has to be subdivided itself in order to provide for discrete conditions and this division consists of two paragraphs. If either paragraph needed to be divided then this division would be known as subparagraphs and would be represented as (i), (ii), etc.

It is important to note that each level has a distinct appearance. If I wanted to refer to the second paragraph of subsection 3 I would do so by writing s 9(3)(b). Not using the brackets could cause confusion as s 9 3 b might be taken to mean either section 93 or a new section that follows s 93.[13]

The provisions themselves are at the heart of the statute and it is these that the courts need to interpret when adjudicating on cases brought before them.

---

13. A further explanation of the appearance of provisions is given on the Online Resource Centre accompanying this book.

2.3 **Statutory interpretation**

Having now seen a statutory provision it can be seen that the language used is somewhat formal. Section 25 CRA 2005 was relatively easy to understand but some statutory provisions are less than clear and consist of highly technical language. Sometimes because of the complexity of a statute it is not immediately clear what the section provides; in other situations it may not be immediately clear who is within the provisions. One of the principal jobs for courts is to interpret statutory material (both primary and secondary legislation)[14] and apply their interpretation to the facts at hand.

It has been suggested that since 2001 there have been two principal means of interpreting a statute: the purposive approach and the interpretative approach (Marshall (2003) 236). Marshall argues that the former is the traditional manner in which legislation is construed and the latter arises from s 3 *Human Rights Act 1998* which provides that a court must, so far as possible, interpret a statute to comply with the ECHR. Whether the distinction is as profound as Marshall argues is perhaps more debatable and Bennion, writing a decade earlier, argued that there is no distinction between construction and interpretation (Bennion (1990) 84) but s 3 undoubtedly introduces a new aspect of statutory interpretation and its importance cannot be denied.

Statutory interpretation is unique to common-law-based jurisdictions (Bennion (1990) 83). The principal comparator to the common-law-based system is continental Europe where civil law is primary and where the courts feel they have no need to construe a statute because the texts are more often considered to be more flexible and more akin to 'living instruments' with the judges having final say over what the law should mean in a particular case (ibid). Common-law countries, however, now prefer to state that the legislature creates the law and the courts merely apply the law which, of course, means that the will of Parliament must be identified. This requires a system of rules known as statutory interpretation to assist the judiciary.

Given that the common-law countries seek to separate the powers between the instruments of law (with Parliament creating the law, the executive implementing the law and the judiciary applying the law) it is perhaps not unsurprising that tension exists between the instruments. Whilst each would appear to have a distinct role, there is undoubtedly overlap and tension. For example, much of the law that is passed by Parliament comes from the executive but neither branch can by itself apply the law. The judiciary considers itself to be the custodian of rights in the country and does not act in a way that is necessarily popular but in a way that it sees as just. In recent years the tension between the executive and the judiciary has becoming increasingly fraught, especially in the fields of criminal justice and asylum issues. It is perhaps not surprising that these are the areas of increased tension as they are also the most politically active areas of law with the impression that the electorate is most concerned with these matters. In the early 1990s when John Major was the prime minister and Michael Howard was the Home Secretary this tension began to become somewhat noticeable but in the early 2000s the battle recommenced when David Blunkett was appointed Home Secretary (see Stevens

---

14. The remainder of this section will discuss how to interpret statutes as this will be the most usual practice. However, the same rules and procedures govern interpreting statutory instruments too.

(2002) 129–136). The tension arises from the way that judges interpret statutes but is this a deliberate attempt by the judiciary to thwart the will of the elected body or is it something else?

⊘ **PARLIAMENTARY SOVEREIGNTY: 'GINGER HAIR' TEST**

Earlier in this chapter the concept of parliamentary sovereignty was discussed and the ambit of Parliament was discussed in connection with the 'smoking on the streets of Paris' example (p 25 above). If Parliament can do what it wishes then does this mean there are no balances and that a corrupt Parliament could use its powers to act in an improper way? Those who argue that the courts are either supreme or, at the very least, a safeguard to an overzealous legislature and executive sometimes point to the 'ginger hair' example.

The essence of this example is that Parliament passes a law that states anyone with ginger hair is to be arrested and sent to gaol. Theoretically Parliament could enact such a law but it is an unjust law and one that is a direct affront to human rights and the right to liberty. Given that the courts will be the ultimate arbitrators of this law it is argued that they could interpret the law so as to make it impossible to implement. For example, if a judge was called upon to rule whether someone had ginger hair, she could adjudicate that the person in fact had red hair or a dark copper colour hair. In this way the courts could act as a 'brake' to Parliament's desire to infringe human rights by ensuring that the law was interpreted in such a way that no injustice is done.

Before the 'interpretative' rule arose the courts stated that they would interpret legislation in accordance with one of three rules:

- literal rule
- golden rule
- mischief rule.

By examining these rules we can begin to understand how the courts interpret statutes and where tensions between the executive and legislature begin to be introduced. However, the notion of these rules is controversial with Bennion, arguably one of the leading authorities on parliamentary drafting and interpretation, suggesting that it is erroneous to argue that there are only three rules governing interpretation (Bennion (1990) 104–105). This is an important point and is undoubtedly true. There is also the difficulty of using the term 'rules' since the courts themselves do not consider themselves bound by them, they are conventions rather than strict rules, and some refer to them as 'canons of interpretation'. However the three principles discussed below are the most commonly referred to.

2.3.1 Literal rule

The literal rule is considered to be the 'normal' rule and it complies with the traditional view of the courts that their role is not to make or subvert the law but rather to apply the law created by Parliament. The essence of the literal rule is that the courts simply look at the words and apply them as they are written with the suggestion that Parliament must have known what they meant.

> ### 👁 Example   Literal rule
>
> Parliament (hypothetically) creates a law that states:
>
> (1) A person aged 18 must pay the sum of £150 to the government.
>
> (2) On receipt of the £150 the government shall grant to the person a certificate.
>
> (3) No person shall be entitled to drink an alcoholic beverage in a public house without a certificate.
>
> There are a number of parts of this law that may need to be interpreted, including 'aged 18', 'on receipt', 'alcoholic beverage', and 'public house'. The literal approach would simply look towards the ordinary meaning of these words. Accordingly in subsection (1) it is likely that the courts would hold that a person could not pay £150 until the eighteenth anniversary of their birth, but that they had until the day before their nineteenth anniversary of their birth to pay the £150. A literal interpretation would not suggest that the sum must be paid on the person's eighteenth birthday because it does not literally say that. A literal interpretation of subsection (2) would mean that as soon as the money has been received by the government they should give a certificate and so, for example, an executive decision taken by the Home Secretary not to issue any certificates until two months after receipt in order to enable people to attend alcohol education programmes would be ruled illegal as it contravened a literal interpretation of the Act. A literal interpretation of subsection (3) would mean that a person could not drink any alcoholic drink in a public house regardless of whether they bought it or indeed knew whether it was alcoholic.

Where the literal interpretation can begin to come unstuck, however, is when grammar is introduced, not least because grammatical rules and styles change over the years (see Bennion (1990) 130). Some have argued that grammar should be ignored but that would be a false premise as punctuation must have been used for a reason. One commentator has suggested that where there are conflicting grammatical meanings the courts must decide between them by looking at the possibilities and the section as a whole (Bennion (1990) 96–97) but to remember above all that the purpose of statutory interpretation is to adopt a legal meaning and not necessarily a grammatical meaning (p 88).

In deciding the literal meaning of the word the judge will sometimes refer to their own interpretation of the meaning, usually arguing that it is so well known that people know what it means. Alternatively the judge will make reference to a dictionary, usually the *Oxford English Dictionary*, and suggest that this amounts to the literal meaning. The literal rule can sometimes appear harsh with one leading commentator citing the example of *Diane Blood* who was denied the right to conceive by artificial insemination using her late husband's sperm which had been harvested whilst he was in a coma (Darbyshire (2001) 27).[15] The relevant Act (*Human Fertilisation and Embryology Act 1990*) required the consent of the donor before artificial insemination could be undertaken and this was not, of course, possible in these circumstances. Although the courts were deeply sympathetic to the predicament faced by Mrs Blood they were forced to rule that the literal language employed by statute was obvious and they were bound to follow the wording of the Act.

---

15. *R v Human Fertilisation and Embryology Authority, ex p Blood* [1997] 2 WLR 807.

2.3.2 Golden rule

Whilst the literal rule will normally be applied there are occasions when its use could actually defeat the intention of Parliament rather than apply it. On those occasions the courts will not feel constrained to obey the literal rule but will follow what is known as the 'golden rule'.

It has been suggested that this rule should be used when Parliament intended its provision to have a wider definition and not one restricted to the literal meaning of its words (Bennion (1990) 105) and this is corroborated by other commentators who note that the rule is traditionally employed when it is decided that a literal interpretation would not give rise to the will of Parliament (Manchester et al (2000) 41) although they then argue that it is commonly applied when it is thought that the literal rule would lead to an absurdity (p 42). An absurdity may arise of course not just because of the intentions of Parliament but because of poor drafting but this need not contradict Bennion's belief because the key to the ruling is that Parliament's intention is to be discovered and applied notwithstanding the drafting of the words.

It is important to note that the courts cannot just cast off the literal rule for the golden rule when it so wishes. The clear presumption is that it must follow the literal rule unless not to do so would contravene the intentions of Parliament (with it being implicit that Parliament will not normally wish to legislate in such a way to create an absurd situation). In the preceding section it was noted that the courts had sympathy with Mrs Blood who wished to conceive using her dead husband's harvested sperm. Given that the courts and indeed the parties directly related to the litigation morally supported her[16] it may be thought that the courts would reject the literal rule but there were no grounds to do so: there was no uncertainty in the legislation nor was there any absurdity created. It was undoubtedly Parliament's intention that the consent of both parties was required and they probably just did not contemplate this situation. The failure of Parliament to contemplate a situation is not a reason to depart from the literal rule and all a court can do in these circumstances is bring the matter to the attention of Parliament and suggest that it passes new legislation.

👁 **Example** Golden Rule

Section 57 *Offences Against the Person Act 1861* defines bigamy as:

> Whosoever, being married, shall marry another person during the life of the former husband or wife, whether the second marriage shall have taken place in England or Ireland or elsewhere, shall be guilty [of an offence].

It is not possible to use the literal rule here since the application of that rule would defeat the intention of Parliament. Section 57 says it is illegal to marry another person but as a matter of civil law a second marriage under such circumstances would not be legally valid so the person has not, by law, married anyone. Also, the statute says during the life of the 'former' husband or wife. The purpose of bigamy is to deal with situations where they are still

---

16. The hospital that in effect refused to undertake the procedure did not do so because it objected in principle to the idea but rather because it believed it had no statutory right to do it and was obliged to reject the approach. This is a common feature in medical cases where there is no 'dispute' as such but doubt exists about the legality of a situation.

married so 'former' would not apply. If they were the former husband or wife then it would not be bigamy.

The courts, to overcome this obstacle, have used the golden rule so as to construe bigamy as when somebody purports to marry someone else (ie go through a marriage ceremony) whilst already legally married.

❓ QUESTION FOR REFLECTION

The Online Resource Centre accompanying this book has a summary of the Diane Blood litigation. Read this. Do you think that the courts were unduly harsh here? Nobody doubts that the golden rule could have been used to create an exemption where a partner is dead but the question is whether the rule could be used. Instead of looking at absurdity in *the law* (ie on the face of the legislation) could the absurdity not be *in fact* (ie in this case, the fact that it was impossible to gain consent from a dead person)?

🎧 LISTEN TO THE PODCAST

For guidance on how to answer this question and a discussion of the main issues, listen to the author's podcast on the Online Resource Centre:
www.oxfordtextbooks.co.uk/orc/gillespie_els3e/

2.3.3 Mischief rule

The third rule that is most commonly employed by the courts is the mischief rule. This rule differs from the previous two rules in that the importance of the words is less important than the underlying reason why Parliament legislated (Manchester et al (2000) 42). Bennion argues that the rule is historic as it dates back to the time when statutory law did not have a pre-eminent position—ie common law was the more usual and statutory law was only passed when the common law did not cover an issue (Bennion (1990) 161) or, presumably, Parliament wished to remedy what it saw as a 'defect' in the law.

Bennion also argues that allied to the mischief rule is the purposive rule which is when Parliament has legislated to remedy a defect in a previous statute that has been identified (Bennion (1990) 163). The purposive approach takes as its starting point that Parliament intended to remedy the previous defect and accordingly the courts should construe the amending legislation in such a way as to ensure that it recognizes the intention of Parliament was to correct the error.

The mischief rule is sometimes used when a statute is in force for many years. Some statutes will remain current law for many years, and will be in continuous use. A good example of this is the *Offences Against the Person Act 1861* which is probably one of the most commonly used statutes in the criminal law. However, a statute will invariably use words that were appropriate at the time and may no longer necessarily be correct in contemporary society. The mischief rule permits a court to depart from the literal meaning of a word used at that time and apply the intention of Parliament—to legislate for a particular mischief—in such a way that it can be applied to modern society.

> **Example** Obscenity
>
> An example of the use of the mischief rule can be seen from the case of *R v Stamford* [1972] 2 QB 391 where the appellant had been convicted of sending postal packets containing indecent or obscene material. The relevant statute creating the offence, the *Post Office Act 1953*, did not provide any definition of 'indecent' or 'obscene' and this could be contrasted with the *Obscene Publications Act 1959*, which did. The Court of Appeal was called upon to consider whether it was possible to call expert evidence on what amounted to 'indecent' or 'obscene' material if someone was charged under the 1953 Act. Counsel submitted that they should be able to because expert evidence was permitted under the 1959 Act. In rejecting the submission the court looked to the mischief behind the 1953 and 1959 Acts and decided that the statutes were intended to deal with different mischiefs (see pp 396–397 per Ashworth J) with the 1953 Act being intended to prevent the misuse of the postal service and the 1959 Act being intended to regulate, inter alia, the publication of obscene material. The court argued that this meant that the test of obscenity under the 1953 Act would be purely objective as it matters not what the addressee thinks of the material as the postal service has been misused irrespective of the intentions of both parties. This could be contrasted with the 1959 Act where it was thought that the views of the likely audience at the publication would be relevant.
>
> It can be seen that the court believed that in order to understand Parliament's intention it was not enough to look literally at the wording of the Act but rather to focus on the mischief and conclude as to Parliament's intention.

2.3.4 The Human Rights Act 1998

Whatever the status of the traditional 'rules' of statutory interpretation, the process of statutory interpretation was altered by the *Human Rights Act 1998*. The Act was one of the first major pieces of constitutional legislation enacted by the Labour administration elected in 1997. The Act itself will be the subject of discussion in Chapter 5 but at least part of its provisions need to be discussed in this chapter as they unquestionably impact upon the construction of legislation.

Labour, in 1997, was elected with a manifesto promise to incorporate the *European Convention on Human Rights* into domestic law, that is to say to ensure that citizens of the United Kingdom could exercise the rights and freedoms contained within the Convention by bringing actions for breach in UK courts rather than before the European Court of Human Rights as had to happen prior to the implementation of the 1998 Act. The government also wished to enact a presumption that Parliament would always intend to act in accordance with the ECHR. Its instrument to do so was s 3 of the 1998 Act which states:

(1) So far as it is possible to do so, primary legislation and subordinate legislation must be read and given effect in a way which is compatible with Convention rights.

(2) This section–

    (a) applies to primary legislation and subordinate legislation whenever enacted;

    (b) does not affect the validity, continuing operation or enforcement of any incompatible legislation; and

    (c) does not affect the validity, continuing operation or enforcement of any incompatible secondary legislation if (disregarding any possibility of revocation) primary legislation prevents removal of the incompatibility.

The new rule of statutory construction is contained within s 3(1) which states that, where it is possible to do so, both primary and secondary legislation should be read in such a way to make the statutes compatible with the ECHR. This is quite clearly an exception to the literal rule of statutory interpretation as it is quite possible that a literal interpretation of a provision will conflict with a right or freedom contained within the ECHR and yet s 3(1) states that in those circumstances the literal rule should not be followed. Neither can it be said that s 3 is the application of either the golden or mischief rule as it may be that the intention of Parliament, at the time the legislation was passed, was incompatible with the ECHR and yet s 3(1) and (2)(a) make clear that where conflicting intentions arise then the *presumption* should be that Parliament intended to enact in a compatible way. Tension can exist between two competing intentions of Parliament (Kavanagh (2005a) 269) but Kavanagh argues that the wording of s 3 makes clear that Parliament clearly wishes its intention that statutes comply with the ECHR to take priority over any original intention (ibid).

This priority is subject to two important exceptions, however. The first is that the 1998 Act expressly reserves the right of Parliament to act in a way incompatible with the Convention (see s 19(1)(b)) and the second is that the wording of s 3(1) expressly signals that Parliament contemplated situations when it would not be possible to reconcile a compatible interpretation—'so far as it is possible to do so'. The courts were not to be given the ability to act in a way contrary to the clear intentions of Parliament, with the legislature retaining the decision as to how (or even whether) to make the law compatible (see ss 4 and 10). The expectation of the government was, however, that these exceptions would be rarely required with the belief that the court would in the vast majority of cases be able to interpret legislation in such a way as to comply with the Convention (Klug (1999) 252–253). Interestingly, the main debate that has arisen over s 3(1) does not concern legislation passed *before* the 1998 Act came into force but later legislation. This should be more straightforward since if Parliament states that it wishes to act in a way compatible with the Convention (see s 19) then interpretation should be possible but Kavanagh notes that some have argued that s 3 should not be used to circumvent the mischief of the Act notwithstanding the ministerial statement of compliance.

Case box *R v A*

Kavanagh (2005a) argues that one of the most contentious cases where s 3(1) has been used is *R v A (No 2)* [2002] 1 AC 45 and this is undoubtedly correct. The case of A concerned the construction of s 41 *Youth Justice and Criminal Evidence Act 1999* which purported to prevent the victim of a sexual offence being questioned about previous sexual history. This provision was widely welcomed at that time and was introduced in the context of a number of cases where rape complainants had been cross-examined as to their complete sexual history, including number of partners and methods used to have sex, in great detail and in public. Parliament believed that such questioning should stop and enacted s 41 to do so.

The appellant A had been charged with the rape of a woman. He sought to question the complainant about consensual sexual intercourse that had taken place between her and the appellant in the weeks preceding the alleged rape. This was quite clearly 'sexual history' and would be excluded by virtue of s 41. However, the House of Lords argued that this evidence was vital in establishing a defence of consent and that excluding the use of what could be probative evidence would breach Article 6 of the ECHR. Their Lordships therefore unanimously invoked s 3(1) and stated that the exclusion should be subject to an overriding power of the judge to permit such questioning when a failure to do so would amount to a breach of Article 6, the right to a fair trial.

The decision of the House of Lords was unquestionably contrary to the intentions of Parliament and Kavanagh (2005a) notes that it has been vociferously attacked on that basis (pp 268–269). However, Parliament had also made clear that it wished legislation to be interpreted in a way that made it compatible with the Convention and the decision of the House and *R v A* certainly made the provision compatible even though it was contrary to what Parliament had itself intended. Some argue that the House should have made a declaration of incompatibility instead (see Kavanagh (2005a) 273) but this would arguably have been contrary to the intention of Parliament expressed in the 1998 Act. It was possible to interpret the legislation and the House did so.

How does a court approach constructing a statute under s 3? Clearly the first stage is to identify what the incompatibility with the ECHR is. In the case study above it was thought that the application of the provision unchallenged would breach Article 6 but in other cases the breach has related to other articles of the convention. It is important that the breach is real and not theoretical—given that some articles in the Convention are qualified (see Chapter 5) this means assessing whether the statute is within the qualification before deciding that incompatibility arises. Discovering a breach is not merely a technical issue; it is the foundation for s 3. Lord Woolf CJ has ruled that, in the absence of a prima facie breach of the Convention, s 3 can be ignored (see *Poplar Housing and Regeneration Community Association Ltd v Donoghue* [2002] QB 48 at 71–72) and this must be correct. The 1998 Act does not provide the judiciary with an opportunity to turn its back on statutory interpretation but rather it provides it with the ability to follow the legislature's desire that the law should comply with the ECHR.

Assuming that an incompatibility is detected then the courts must decide whether it is possible to interpret the statute in such a way as to remove that incompatibility. Laws LJ argued, albeit in an extrajudicial capacity, that s 3 'will abolish the old lynch pin of the search for parliamentary intention' (Marshall (2003) 237) although that comment cannot be taken literally. In deciding whether the provision can be interpreted it must surely be relevant to decide what Parliament's intention was (probably through examining the mischief of the legislation). Only then will it be possible to discuss the court's two options (interpretation or a declaration of incompatibility).

How far can the courts take their interpretation? The courts should not adopt a 'strained' interpretation (Marshall (2003) 238), that being a 'far-fetched' interpretation or, in other words, one that is too far removed from the mischief the Act sought to tackle. If this is applied to the case study above it can be seen that this provides further assurance that *R v A* did not overstep the boundaries as the mischief of that provision—that previous sexual history should not be permitted—is still being tackled and the decision itself stated there was a strong presumption in not permitting the evidence but that it was subject to an overriding principle that where exclusion of the evidence undermines the fairness of the trial the evidence should be heard. Where it is not possible to interpret the statute then the court must consider whether to declare the legislation to be incompatible with the Convention (see s 4 of the 1998 Act) but it should be noted that this does not affect the validity of the statute and the courts must, therefore, rule on the matter following the traditional rules of interpretation.

❓ QUESTION FOR REFLECTION

If a statute cannot be interpreted without significantly altering the provision against the intentions of Parliament should they not use their power to issue a declaration of incompatibility? In the context of *R v A*, what would have happened to Mr A had the courts made such a declaration?

2.3.5 **Aids to interpretation**

Although it has been noted that subject to the qualification put forward by Bennion it can be said that there are rules governing statutory interpretation, it should also be noted that the courts have a number of tools at their disposal to assist them in their interpretation of statutory material. These aids can normally be classified into one of two categories.

2.3.5.1 Intrinsic aids

Intrinsic aids are those contained within the statutory instrument itself. Quite what can be considered to be 'part of a statute' is open to debate. The contents of a statute were discussed above and the individual components of legislation may become relevant in deciding how to construe a statute.

A number of issues arise as to what is within the statute however. The two principal issues are the wording of the provisions and the explanatory features of the Act.

Wording of the statute

The first issue to examine is the wording of the Act. An important canon of interpretation is that the Act should be read as a whole (Bennion (1990) 187) which gives rise to three examples, all of which are known by a Latin term notwithstanding the fact that we are trying to remove Latin from the legal language! The common rules are:

- *noscitur a sociis*
- *ejusdem generis*
- *expressio unius exclusio alterius*.

Noscitur a sociis

The first rule is that a statutory provision should be read in conjunction with its neighbouring provisions. Certainly this canon has been employed by the courts on a number of occasions and is a logical step. Given that even the most disparate of Acts will

Intrinsic aids	**Extrinsic aids**
Looking at the content of the statutory material to assist in the interpretation of a provision	Looking at material outside the Act but within the contemplation of the legislature

Diagram 2.5 Intrinsic and extrinsic aids

normally be divided into Parts, the neighbouring provisions should assist in ascertaining either the meaning of a word or the mischief behind the Act.

This rule can, in effect, be divided into two aspects. The first of these looks at similar words. A word should have the same meaning throughout an Act (Bennion (1990) 188) although it should be noted that this is only a presumption and accordingly if Parliament expressly wishes to act differently it may do so. A good example of this can be found in the *Sexual Offences Act 2003* where 'sexual' is defined within s 78 but the Act expressly states that a different meaning of the word shall be employed for s 71.

The second aspect to this rule is its logical conclusion: that different words in a statute should normally bear different meanings (Bennion (1990) 189). Whilst this would appear to be obvious it is not necessarily so and indeed this construction has caused difficulties before.

COMPLICITY

The *Accessories and Abettors Act 1861* is a good illustration of how different words should have different meanings. The provision makes it clear that a person can become an accomplice to the principal offender by acting in one of four ways:

- aiding
- abetting
- counselling
- procuring.

At first sight it is unclear what the difference is between 'aiding' and 'abetting' or 'abetting' and 'counselling' or even 'counselling' and 'procuring'. Certainly common usage will frequently refer to someone as 'aiding and abetting' and the thesaurus provides 'aid' as the first alternative to 'abet'. In *Attorney-General's Reference (No 1 of 1975)* [1975] 2 All ER 684 the Court of Appeal held, however, that each had a different meaning because if it were otherwise then Parliament would not have listed these four separate ways of acting.

This canon can still be controversial however and there is sometimes a debate in the courts as to whether different words must necessarily mean anything. A good example of this is the words 'cause' and 'inflict' within the *Offences Against the Person Act 1861*. At first sight they appear to be two different words but they appear in two related sections of the Act (ss 18 and 20 which relate to grievous bodily harm). The difference between the words exercised the courts for many years and in *R v Ireland; R v Burstow* [1998] AC 147 the House of Lords held that for practical purposes there is no longer a distinction between 'cause' and 'inflict' (see p 160 per Lord Steyn and in particular p 164 per Lord Hope of Craighead).

Ejusdem generis

This second rule is similar to the first but relates to similar words rather than identical or contrasting words. The expression can be translated into English as 'of the same kind or nature' and it demonstrates the purpose of this rule. The basic principle of the rule is that where words of general meaning are to be found in a provision following words with a specific meaning then the general words are to be read narrowly as though they were linked to the specific words (see Bennion (1990) 196). In other words the general words are considered to be a continuation of any list of words preceding them.

The rule is subject to some restrictions. The first is that all the words must constitute a genus (or 'set' of words) and this genus should be narrower than the literal interpretation of the provision (Bennion (1990) 197). Bennion provides the following example:

> The *Customs Consolidation Act 1876*, s 43 reads: 'The importation of arms, ammunition, gunpowder or any other goods may be prohibited.' (p 197)

There is no doubt that the words 'or any other goods' are general words and their literal interpretation would encompass virtually any form of trade. However, the *ejusdem generis* rule would seek to limit the meaning of those general words to a context related to the preceding words, ie the 'any other goods' must be comparable to ammunition, eg gelignite (a high explosive) may come within this provision. Bennion continues by arguing that the 'genus' must also be restricted narrowly:

> The string specified as 'boots, shoes, stockings and other articles' would import the genus 'footwear' rather than the wider category of 'wearing apparel'.

Clearly this is a useful and sensible approach to adopt and does ensure that a provision is no wider than it needs to be.

Expressio unius exclusio alterius

This final rule is related to the *ejusdem generis* rule in that it concerns lists of words but where the rules differs is that the *expressio* rule operates on the premise that in the absence of any general words a list will be exhaustive and accordingly any term not listed within the list will be deemed not to be included within the provision. This principle can be identified from its English translation, 'to list one thing is to exclude another'.

The rule arguably goes further by limiting general words. Bennion's argument is that if a specific word is used to limit a general word (cf the *ejusdem generis* rule where a general word was used to *extend* or *complement* the specific words) then the specific word is taken to mean that it excludes other words that come within that general class (Bennion (1990) 202). He provides the following example:

> The *Immigration Act 1973*, s 2(3) states that for the purposes of s 2(1) of the Act the word 'parent' includes the *mother* of an illegitimate child. The class to which this extension relates is the *parents* of an illegitimate child. (p 202)

The logical conclusion of this rule is that the father of an illegitimate child would not be within s 2(1) because the use of the word 'mother' as an express inclusion must be to limit the meaning of the general word 'parent' and accordingly 'father' which is obviously within the general term has been implicitly excluded.

Explanatory issues

Although it will be noted below that some explanatory material is outside of the Act, the statute itself will contain some provisions that explain the significance of the detailed provisions. The two most important features are marginal notes and the long title.

Marginal notes

It was noted that sections will normally be accompanied by something called a 'marginal note' or 'side note'. These are, in effect, descriptions of the section but are they part of the statute and capable of being used as an intrinsic aid? Some commentators argue that the answer is 'no' and they do not form part of the Act and accordingly cannot be used as an intrinsic aid (Manchester et al (2000) 46). However, others disagree and argue that they *are* part of the statute albeit they usually provide only an indication of the provision rather than a necessarily accurate description of the provision (Bennion (1990) 128). It is submitted that there is no reason why a court could not take account of the marginal note of a provision although caution should be shown because the notes are not debated within Parliament but are placed on the Act by the draftsman (p 127). Accordingly, not only is it not necessarily an accurate description of the provision it is the draftsman's deduction of the meaning of the provision.

Case box *R v Tivnan*

In *R v Tivnan* [1999] 1 Cr App R(S) 92 the Court of Appeal demonstrated that it does occasionally use marginal notes in order to assist in understanding the intentions of Parliament. The appellant had been convicted of drug dealing and a confiscation order had been made against his assets. He claimed that as it could not be proven his assets had been obtained through the proceeds of drug dealing the confiscation order should be quashed. The Court of Appeal considered Parliament's intention was to deprive drug dealers of assets equal to the proceeds obtained by drug dealing not necessarily just those assets that were purchased directly from the proceedings. The Court made reference to the marginal note in seeking the intent (see p 97).

Long title

The long title of the Act may provide assistance in the construction of a provision. It will be remembered that the long title is part of the preamble to the Act which sets out the purpose of the Act. As the long title is part of, if not the official title, for the Act it would appear appropriate that it should be considered.

Example Animal cruelty

The *Protection of Animals (Amendment) Act 2000* permits a court to make an order, upon the application of a prosecutor, for an order for the care, disposal, or slaughter of animals that have been kept cruelly. In *Cornwall County Council v Baker* [2003] 1 WLR 1813 the Divisional Court was asked to rule on the meaning of 'animals in question'. The Council had prosecuted the respondent for cruelty to seven farm animals. It also sought an order under the 2000 Act relating to other animals at the farm which were not subject to the prosecution. The magistrates' court refused to make an order in respect of the other animals contending that the 2000 Act applied only to animals subject to proceedings under the 1911 Act. The Divisional Court upheld this ruling on appeal and referred to the long title to demonstrate its purpose (see pp 1819–1820 per Toulson J).

2.3.5.2 Extrinsic aids

In certain circumstances it may be possible to look outside of the Act for assistance in construing a statutory provision and this is known as using extrinsic aids. There are a number of extrinsic aids that the courts will consider but rules do sometimes exist as to when courts may look outside of the Act for assistance. Broadly speaking, the following aids will be examined:

- explanatory notes accompanying an Act
- parliamentary material
- other statutory provisions
- academic writing
- pre-parliamentary material.

Explanatory notes

Since 1999 all government Bills introduced into Parliament are accompanied by explanatory notes and upon Royal Assent these notes are amended to reflect the agreed wording of the Act (see Munday (2005) 340–341). The notes do not form part of the Act and are indeed created by the government department sponsoring the Bill (see *Westminster City Council v National Asylum Support Service* [2002] 1 WLR 2956 at pp 2958–2960 per Lord Steyn) so they have not been approved within Parliament because whilst they may be the subject of discussion during the progress of the Bill there is no mechanism for the notes to be amended by Parliament. Further, parliamentary draftsmen have argued that 'explanatory notes are informal in style, are there to improve clarity for the reader, and to this end may be highly discursive' (Munday (2005) 341). Clearly, it is contemplated that the reader of a piece of legislation will refer to the notes but does a 'reader' include members of the judiciary? Also, given that the notes are written by draftsmen and not members of the legislature, they arguably suffer from the same problem as marginal notes (discussed above).

The courts readily refer to explanatory notes (Munday (2005) 341–342) but some question whether they go too far and accord them a 'quasi-legislative' status that it was never intended for them to have. To support this argument reference is made to the comments of Lord Bingham in *Attorney-General's Reference (No 5 of 2002)* [2005] 1 AC 167 where his Lordship argued that the explanatory notes 'strongly supported' his conclusion as to the meaning of the provisions. Given that they are a creature of the executive rather than the legislature it is somewhat surprising that the notes are so readily referred to, especially in light of the rule governing the use of parliamentary material (see below). However, Lord Steyn in *Westminster City Council v National Asylum Support Service* argued that they were akin to pre-parliamentary material but arguably of more assistance than, for example, White or Green Papers since they reflect the initial wording of the provisions (p 2960). One concern is that ready use of these notes by the courts could encourage sloppy draftsmanship (on the basis that so long as the notes explain the provision it need not matter whether the provision is tightly defined) (Munday (2005) 347). The fact that the notes are created by the executive rather than the legislature also creates the possibility that recourse to the notes could give rise to a confusion as to whether a provision reflects the intentions of Parliament or the government with the two not necessarily coinciding. Notwithstanding these points, however, the use of the notes has become an accepted part of statutory construction although recent decisions of the House of Lords would appear to suggest that a fundamental review of their use (akin to that undertaken in *Pepper v Hart* [1993] AC 593; see 2.3.5.3 below) may soon occur (see Munday (2005) 346–349 and 352–354 for a discussion of these issues).

Parliamentary material

Parliament is a formal body and is a body of record, ie a number of documents exist governing its proceedings and one possible extrinsic aid may be to use these documents. However, this is one of the more controversial uses of an extrinsic aid and for this reason, and to demonstrate the importance of the general rule, the use of such material is considered in its own section below (see 2.3.5.3 above).

Other statutory provisions

Whilst some statutes will act as amending or consolidating instruments for existing legislation, a significant amount of legislation is 'new' in that it creates stand-alone laws and procedures. It may be thought therefore that there is little use in examining other pieces of legislation but it is not unusual for similar words to be found in other statutes. Where the mischief is similar between the Acts then comparing or contrasting statutory words could prove useful in helping construct the meaning of the provision under scrutiny.

> ### 📖 Case box *R v Dooley*
>
> In *R v Dooley* [2005] EWCA Crim 3093 the Court of Appeal needed to consider the meaning of the words 'with a view to' which appeared in s 1(1)(c) *Protection of Children Act 1978*. The Act did not define these words but it is a not uncommon phrase to be found within legislation and the court examined how it had been construed in other legislation, including ss 1(2), 20, and 21 *Theft Act 1968* and the *Obscene Publications Act 1964*. The Court then argued that applying the same interpretation to the 1978 Act would be logical and it can be seen, therefore, that the other legislation acted as an extrinsic aid.

Perhaps the most common alternative statute to examine is that of the *Interpretation Act 1978* which, as its short title suggests, was designed to provide assistance in the interpretation of statutes. The 1978 Act is merely the latest reincarnation of the Interpretation Act and it is unlikely to be the last. The Act itself provides a series of common words and the presumption is that if one of these words is used in a statutory provision then it is deemed to have that meaning unless Parliament intended differently, this intention normally being evidenced expressly. Perhaps the most important interpretative presumptions in the Act are contained within s 6:

> In any Act, unless the contrary intention appears–
>
> (a) words importing the masculine gender include the feminine;
>
> (b) words importing the feminine gender include the masculine;
>
> (c) words in the singular include the plural and words in the plural include the singular.

The use of such presumptions is important because otherwise an Act of Parliament could become cluttered and unreadable when a simple provision refers constantly to 'he or she', 'him or her', 'that or those', etc. Where the context clearly means the masculine or feminine gender then obviously the interpretation is so construed as the 1978 Act creates presumptions rather than mandatory rules.

Academic writing

It is often said that the English courts have been somewhat sceptical about the use of academic writings but this is not necessarily the case. Perhaps the most basic example of the use of books as an extrinsic aid is that of the dictionary; it was noted above that the usual rule in statutory interpretation is to use the literal meaning of the word and a dictionary is not infrequently consulted to achieve that aim. A dictionary cannot be anything other than an external aid.

The use of academic writing through texts and journals has been slowly developing but was used in even the nineteenth century. However its use has arguably been growing not least because there is a greater respect between 'academic' and 'practising' lawyers.[17]

The appellate courts are now increasingly turning to the use of academic sources of writing and indeed a failure to do so has led to criticism about the courts taking an unduly lenient approach to construction (see, for example, the commentary by Professor Andrew Ashworth on the Privy Council decision of *Attorney-General for Jersey v Holley* [2005] 2 AC 580 at [2005] Crim LR 966 at 970). That is not to say that academic sources will be automatically consulted and certainly where textbooks are concerned it is not unusual for only the most authoritative to be cited, but where a narrow point of law arises where there has been little case law or what case law there is has been debated amongst eminent academics then the citation of academic writings can be of assistance to the judges although, of course, they are not bound by them.

⮕ ACADEMIC WRITING

BOOKS

In *R v Dooley* discussed in the previous case study the Court of Appeal did not just use alternative statutes as an aid but also made reference to Smith and Hogan's Criminal Law, undoubtedly the leading criminal law textbook. The arguments made in the text by its (new) editor and author, Professor David Ormerod, were cited by the Court as being of assistance (para 14).

ARTICLES

In *R v Lang et al* [2005] EWCA Crim 2864 the Court of Appeal expressly stated that it had examined an article by Dr David Thomas QC, arguably the leading authority on sentencing, and thanked him in the judgment as they found the article of assistance (see para 2).

Pre-parliamentary sources

Legislation does not 'just happen' especially when a Bill is introduced by the government. There will normally be a significant number of documents that were produced and published prior to the Bill being introduced. When the Bill arises out of government policy it is quite likely that a series of official 'papers' may have been published, with a *White Paper* being a statement of the policy with a broad indication as to how the government intends to legislate to tackle the mischief, and a *Green Paper* being

---

17. Indeed this 'glasnost' has led to a debate as to whether academics could be appointed direct to the bench (see Chapter 7). Arguably the most famous 'academic' lawyer was Professor Brenda Hoggett QC who moved from academia to the Law Commission. She was then appointed to the High Court bench as Hale J before being promoted to the Court of Appeal and then appointed the first female Law Lord in 2004. However, this cannot be said to be a 'pure' academic appointment as she was appointed from the Law Commission rather than from the academe.

a discussion paper issued by the government for assistance in structuring the way in which the mischief should be tackled. The government may also have asked the Law Commission to examine a particular issue and if so the Law Commission will almost certainly have produced a consultation paper and a report to Parliament.[18] In exceptional circumstances where issues of importance need to be examined it is possible that a Royal Commission will be established which will issue a report to Parliament.

Outside of the executive-controlled bodies Parliament itself may have created documents that are relevant to the provision. Both Houses of Parliament create *select committees* that investigate areas of interest to Parliament. Some of these committees are standing committees in that they remain in existence at all times (eg Home Affairs Select Committee, Defence Select Committee) and others will be created for a specific purpose. Committees will produce reports that are publicly available and sometimes these reports will call for legislation to be introduced which the executive may heed.

The use of such material is accepted by the courts but the degree to which it will be useful is perhaps more open to question since it may not reflect the proceedings in Parliament. That said the material will allow the provision to be placed into context and this could assist in its interpretation.

⮕ MODEL CODES

Pre-parliamentary material need not necessarily be accepted, or even debated, by Parliament for it to be used in the construction of a statute. Perhaps the best example of this is *R v G and R* [2004] 1 AC 1034 which is an important criminal law case where the House of Lords used its right to depart from its own decisions (see 3.4.3 below) to overrule *R v Caldwell* [1982] AC 341 which it stated was a 'mistake' even though it had been used for over ten years. Lord Bingham, who gave the leading speech in the House, used the model penal code to construe the meaning of the word 'reckless'. The model penal code was created by the Law Commission and was designed as an exercise to demonstrate how the criminal law could be codified. Parliament has not yet decided that the criminal law should be codified so the proposals have not been debated by Parliament but this does not stop Lord Bingham from using it as a source of identifying the meaning of 'reckless' (pp 1046 and 1054).

2.3.5.3 The rule in *Pepper v Hart*

It has been seen that a basic distinction can be drawn between the legislature and judiciary in that Parliament enacts the law but the courts interpret it. How a court interprets legislation has been discussed and the ability to use extrinsic aids to assist in interpretation has also been identified as a source of help for the judiciary. A logical supposition that could be drawn is that an easy way of interpreting the law would be to examine what was said in Parliament when passing the provision. Debates and written answers in both Houses of Parliament are reported in a series known as *Hansard* and it is published daily both on the Internet and in hard copy.

Where the courts wish to analyse what Parliament's intention is then it may appear sensible to examine *Hansard* to provide clues as to the meaning of the legislation. However, the traditional rule was that it was not permissible to look at parliamentary proceedings to assist in interpretation; in part this was because it was thought that it

---

18. Although the executive will refer a matter to the Law Commission the report will always be to Parliament.

would lead to unnecessary expense and delays (see *Beswick v Beswick* [1968] AC 58) but it was also because it was thought that it might be a challenge to parliamentary supremacy in that it was thought that the law was that which was passed by Parliament not that which was discussed, ie the wording of Bills change and only the final Act is relevant and looking at the proceedings may lead to the suggestion that the courts were questioning or impeaching the process of Parliament contrary to Article 9 of the *Bill of Rights 1689*.

However, in the landmark case of *Pepper v Hart* [1993] AC 593 the House of Lords, exercising its power to reverse previous decisions of the House (see *Practice Statement (Judicial Precedent)* [1966] 1 WLR 1234 and see 3.4.3 below), decided to relax this rule and introduced rules governing when recourse to *Hansard* would be permitted for statutory interpretation. The rule permitted courts to make reference to ministerial statements or the promoter of a Bill so long as three rules were met:

1. The legislation in question was ambiguous, obscure, or led to absurdity.
2. The material relied on consisted of statements by a minister (or the promoter of a Bill).
3. The statements relied on were clear.

It was never thought that this would lead to *Hansard* being referred to frequently, in part because it could be considered an abrogation of the duty of a court to invoke the rule. The clear presumption is that the courts will interpret the law according to the words used (see below) and accordingly only where this is not possible will it be possible to consider using the rule. Lord Browne-Wilkinson, who gave the leading speech in the case, stated: 'In many...cases reference to Parliamentary material will not throw any light on the matter' (p 634). This is partly because many provisions of a Bill are not subject to detailed comment or consideration and in part because where the language is obtuse it is unlikely that any ministerial statement will be particularly clear either. Kavanagh (2005b) argues that restricting an analysis of *Hansard* to the comments of ministers inevitably misrepresents the position and confuses the distinction between the legislature (Parliament) and the executive (government) (p 106). She argues that Parliament passes legislation even if the majority of legislation is sponsored by the executive as the largest parliamentary party. It does not follow automatically that the language of the legislation will necessarily reflect the executive's desire and most Bills will be full of amendments, and it is always open to Parliament to enforce its powers and pass a Bill different to that required by the executive.

👁 Example   Parliament *v* Executive

A good example of where Parliament and the executive may depart is over terrorism legislation. The executive has an interest in obtaining wider powers to deal with terrorists because of the threat that they pose to society at large. Terrorism differs from traditional crimes in the way that it is carried out and most developed countries will have special rules for dealing with terrorism. However, powers can be abused as easily as used and the legislature is therefore careful to ensure that there is a check on any increase in the power of the executive, and indeed this is its very purpose.

In 2005 the Terrorism Bill was being discussed and the government wished to extend the time a terrorist suspect could be held by the police without charge from fourteen days to ninety days. Parliament did not agree and it eventually defeated the government clause proposing this measure, accepting a reduced increase to twenty-eight days. The case for the government was put forward by the Home Secretary and he outlined the reasons why the powers were necessary. If there was any legislative uncertainty as to the meaning of cl 23 of the Bill would recourse to *Pepper v Hart* help? Probably not because the rule permits only statements by ministers to be cited and yet in this case the House of Commons rejected these arguments and put forward its own viewpoint.

The debate on powers may help clarify any uncertainty and the comments of the backbenchers as to why they would not support ninety days would certainly help a court understand the intention of Parliament in this provision but the rule, as drafted, would be of no assistance—the courts would have to ignore parliamentary debates and reach their own conclusions.

Kavanagh, citing Corry, argues that a further difficulty with the rule is that Parliament is not a bipartisan place. A minister making a statement to either House will not be giving a fully independent rationale comment but will be making the point to support his, and the government's position (Kavanagh (2005b) 108). Whilst it is true to state that the rules of Parliament make clear that a minister may not mislead either House[19] this is a far step from an independent comment and Kavanagh argues this can be contrasted with a witness who gives testimony in court under oath (ibid). Of course others will be sceptical as to whether a witness necessarily gives independent and unbalanced evidence in court but the political nature of Parliament inevitably means that the ministers' statements will be geared towards their desire.

However the threat to *Pepper v Hart* appears to have retreated for some time as the House of Lords shows no desire to widen the scope of its enquiry into parliamentary legislation. Kavanagh notes that when the Court of Appeal sought to widen the scope of the rule in *Wilson v Secretary of State for Trade and Industry* [2003] 3 WLR 568 the Speaker of the House of Commons and Clerk to the Houses of Parliament sought the right to make representations to the House as to the application of the rule (Kavanagh (2005b) 112). Their fear was that a wider treatment of parliamentary legislation could lead to the courts scrutinizing the proceedings of Parliament, something that they are expressly not permitted to do (see Article 9 of the *Bill of Rights 1689*).[20] In *Wilson* the House did not simply prevent the rule in *Pepper v Hart* from being widened but it actually constrained its use by noting that the statement of a minister will not necessarily reflect the intention of Parliament as a whole. The House also stated that it was important to emphasize that any statement was not *law* but an aid to deciding *what* the law was. Accordingly, any statement permitted under the rule of *Pepper v Hart* was simply a tool to help the court decide what the law should be and not a definitive statement of the law. This latter point is to be welcomed and whilst Kavanagh argues that it is a restriction (p 115) some doubt must exist as to this because it is difficult to believe that Lord Browne-Wilkinson, when formulating the rule, ever intended that a ministerial statement should ever bind a court when deciding the meaning of the law.

---

19. See McKay (2004) 439 ('Erskine May').

20. For more on this see Lord McKay's speech in *Pepper v Hart* [1993] AC 593 at 614–616 and Lord Browne-Wilkinson at 621–629, 638–640.

So what is the status of *Pepper v Hart*? Kavanagh argues that it has been significantly reduced but in *Jackson v Attorney-General* [2005] UKHL 56 Lord Nicholls of Birkenhead appeared to disagree:

> In some quarters the *Pepper v Hart* principle is currently under something of a judicial cloud. In part this is due to judicial experience that references to *Hansard* seldom assist…It would be unfortunate if *Pepper v Hart* were now to be sidelined. The *Pepper v Hart* ruling is sound in principle, removing as it did a self-created judicial anomaly. (para 65)

His Lordship argues that the rule continues to be important even if his enthusiasm is tempered by the reminder that the rule is perhaps not as useful as some suggest. Yet Lord Steyn, in the same case, suggests that it may not be as important:

> If it were necessary to do so, I would be inclined to hold that the time has come to rule…that *Pepper v Hart* should be confined to the situation which was before the House in *Pepper v Hart*. That would leave unaffected the use of Hansard material to identify the mischief at which the legislation was directed and its objective setting. But trying to discover the intentions of the Government from Ministerial statements in Parliament is unacceptable. (para 97)

Although the ruling in *Pepper v Hart* was about ascertaining the intentions of Parliament and not the government, the difference between what Parliament intends and what the government intends arguably goes to the heart of some of the difficulties that have been raised about this rule. Lord Walker of Gestingthorpe appears to summarize the crux of this area when his Lordship noted that there was a disagreement as to the application of the *Pepper v Hart* principle in the House although his Lordship argued that this need not be resolved in that case (para 141) and this is probably true with the statements of the other Lords concerning its application being *obiter dicta*. *Jackson* is the latest decision of the House to examine this rule and it would appear to demonstrate that the rule remains controversial and one that is not simply understood or applied.

2.3.6 Presumptions

Alongside the rules governing interpretation and the aids used by the courts to identify the correct meaning of words are presumptions that operate in respect of the construction of statutory material. The key presumptions that will be discussed here are:

- against altering the common law
- Crown not bound by Act
- *mens rea* required for criminal offences
- against retrospective approach
- presumption in favour of the defendant.

2.3.6.1 Common law

It has already been noted that until comparatively recently the vast majority of law was judge-made rather than statutory, with Parliament initially simply amending or correcting defects within the common law (see 2.3.3 above). However, as one would expect, Parliament began to take control of the law and now it is often contended that judges no longer have any right to make law (although as will be seen in the next chapter this is contentious). Notwithstanding this however, there remains a presumption that a statute will not alter the common law unless it was the intention of Parliament to do so. The rationale behind the presumption is that Parliament must know the law before it enacts legislation and accordingly unless it identifies a defect in that law then it is presumed not to be interfering with its course. In *Deeble v Robinson* [1954] 1 QB 77 the Court of Appeal held that only plain words would suffice to interfere with common-law rights (p 81) which is taken to mean that the intention of Parliament to interfere with the common-law power should be obvious.

⊙ DOLI INCAPAX

Whilst the intention to interfere with the common law need not be express it is not uncommon for Parliament, when wishing to end a common-law rule, to use express blunt terms to do so. A good example of this can be found in the *Crime and Disorder Act 1998* where s 34 ended the common-law rule of *doli incapax* (where a child between the ages of ten and fourteen was presumed not to be capable of committing a criminal offence unless evidence was adduced to demonstrate they knew it was legally or morally wrong). Section 34 states:

> The rebuttable presumption of criminal law that a child aged 10 or over is incapable of committing an offence is hereby abolished

which would seem to leave little room for doubt but see *R v JTB* [2009] 1 AC 1310 where the House of Lords had to rule on whether the *presumption* or the substantive doctrine had been abolished. The House ruled that despite the literal phrasing, the substantive defence and not just its presumption, was removed by the CDA 1998.

It has been argued that the presumption is extremely controversial (Bailey et al (2002) 459) and given that Parliament is supreme and can legislate against any matter it does appear strange that there should continue to be a presumption that judge-made law will not normally be affected.

2.3.6.2 Crown not bound by the statute

As the United Kingdom is a constitutional monarchy its Head of State is actually the sovereign, currently Her Majesty The Queen Elizabeth II.[21] The term 'the Crown' however is normally used to denote the machinery of the state through the executive (ie government). Since rules are considered to be binding principles handed down from a *ruler* to *subject* the principle has always been that the Crown would not be bound by any law. Note, however, that this does not mean (with the exception of the sovereign) that anyone is personally immune from laws as it is the state rather than an individual who is not subject to laws. The presumption against the Crown not being bound by a statute arises from this doctrine with the principle being that as the Crown is the ruler (the state) it should not be bound unless it expressly says so.

An Act of Parliament will now normally state whether it is bound and it has been considered more appropriate for the Act to state expressly whether it is so bound rather than leave it implied which ensures that the courts must construe the appropriate status.

---

21. Although in Scotland she is technically the first Queen Elizabeth as the Queen Elizabeth who ruled between 1558 and 1603 was Queen of England but not Queen of Scotland.

2.3.6.3 *Mens rea*

Many of the important presumptions relate to the criminal law where certainty is to be expected since transgression of the criminal law could lead to the loss of liberty for the transgressor. One of the most important presumptions is that *mens rea* should be implied into statutes unless it was Parliament's intention for there to be none. It is not possible in this text to provide a precise definition of *mens rea* and you should cross-reference to your set text for *Criminal Law* for a fuller definition but suffice it to say that most crimes require two elements; the *actus reus* (the 'conduct' part of a crime) and the *mens rea* (the 'mental requirement' for a crime). It will often be said that *mens rea* can be approximated to 'guilty mind'.

 THEFT

Theft is defined under s 1 *Theft Act* 1968 thus: '[a] person is guilty of theft if he dishonestly appropriates property belonging to another with the intention of permanently depriving the other of it'. The *actus reus* of this crime is appropriating property belonging to another. The *mens rea* of the crime is doing so dishonestly and with the intention of permanently depriving the other of the property.

Not every statute will, however, necessarily easily identify a mental requirement and it may appear therefore that only the *actus reus* is required for liability to arise.

 Case box *Sweet v Parsley*

The leading case that discusses the absence of *mens rea* is *Sweet v Parsley* [1970] AC 132. The appellant was the tenant of a farm but sublet rooms to other people. At the time of the offence the appellant did not live at the farm. The police found some cannabis resin at the farm and she was charged with the offence of, inter alia, being concerned with the management of premises used for the purpose of smoking cannabis or cannabis resin (s 5(b) *Dangerous Drugs Act 1965*). On the face of the section there was no requirement for *mens rea* and she was convicted by the court as she was concerned with the management of premises—as she was the landlady—at which drugs were found. The House of Lords quashed the conviction and stated that unless Parliament indicated otherwise, *mens rea* should be an essential requirement for any crime. They implied the requirement for knowledge into the criteria.

It is important to note that this is simply a presumption and it can, therefore, be rebutted if it was Parliament's intention to do so. In *B v DPP* [2000] 2 AC 428 and *CPS v K* [2002] 1 AC 462 the House of Lords examined sexual offences against children. Their Lordships argued that indecency with a child and indecent assault (both now repealed) were not crimes of strict liability but they did argue that s 5 *Sexual Offences Act 1956* (now repealed), which created the offence of unlawful sexual intercourse with a girl under thirteen, was intended to be a crime of strict liability. They reached this conclusion by noting that comparable offences within the same legislation did expressly consider mental requirements and accordingly its absence in s 5 must have been deliberate (see [2002] 1 AC 462 at 469–471 per Lord Bingham).

2.3.6.4 Acting retrospectively

The law normally works prospectively—that is to say a law will only change the way we regulate conduct that arises *after* an instrument becomes law. Attempting to regulate conduct that has occurred in the past is known as acting retrospectively and there is a strong presumption that Parliament does not intend to act in this way. Bennion argues that this rule is a matter of fairness since if a person is deemed to know the law (and that well-known saying 'ignorance is no defence to the law' does have a foundation of truth within it) then they should be able to trust the law and act in accordance with their knowledge (Bennion (1990) 151). If a law were retrospective then it would mean that even if a person knew the law and acted in the way that he knew was lawful, he could later be liable under the law as a result of the retrospective law making his actions culpable.

Where the statute relates to the criminal law then the position becomes more complicated because Article 7 of the ECHR prohibits, inter alia, retrospective crimes and punishment. Accordingly, any statute that purports to do this would be subject not only to the common-law presumption but also to s 3(1) *Human Rights Act 1998* as it would prima facie breach Article 7.

That said it should be emphasized that this is a presumption and Parliament, because it is supreme, can act in a way that is retrospective. Perhaps the most obvious example of this is the *War Damage Act 1965* which was enacted specifically to overturn a decision of the House of Lords in *Burmah Oil Co Ltd v Lord Advocate* [1965] AC 75. This Act did not just statutorily overrule the decision but was expressly retrospective and ensured that the appellants did not receive that which the House of Lords had argued was due to them.

Parliament can expressly choose to act retrospectively and certain retrospective acts will not be considered to harm the principle, most notably purely administrative or procedural changes (Bennion (1990) 152). It is not uncommon for procedural rules to change and these can come into effect in respect of conduct that occurs prior to the change becoming effective. Non-punitive regulatory conduct can also come within this rule.

➲ SEXUAL OFFENDING

Section 28 *Criminal Justice and Court Services Act 2000* permits certain courts the power to ban relevant offenders (those convicted of prescribed offences and who have been sentenced beyond a set threshold) from working with children. Whilst this ban is not punitive by itself, breach of the section is a criminal offence (s 35). The Act was silent as to whether a person who was convicted after the date in which the provision came into force but for conduct which occurred prior to that date could be banned. In *R v Field* [2003] 2 Cr App R 3 the appellant contended he could not as this would mean the provision was retrospective in that at the time of his conduct he would not be statutorily banned from working with children. The Court of Appeal rejected this argument and said that it was purely procedural and in any event it was not retrospective by including behaviour that occurred before the provision came into force so long as it did not include cases that were tried before the relevant date.

This can be contrasted with s 106(4) *Sexual Offences Act 2003* which governs Sexual Offence Prevention Orders, a civil order similar to an injunction that can prohibit a convicted sex offender from doing anything listed on the order (see ss 104–108). One of the grounds for making an order is if the chief constable of an area believes that the defendant has acted in a way that makes it necessary for an order to be made to protect the public (s 104(4)–(5)). Section 106(4) expressly states: 'Acts, behaviour, convictions and findings include those occurring before the commencement of this [Act].'

Applying the logic of *Field* this was probably not necessary but Parliament, applying the usual custom, decided to make it clear that there was a degree of retrospectivity in this provision.

2.3.6.5 Presumption in favour of the defence

In the English Legal System—like most developed legal systems—there is, in criminal matters, a presumption of innocence which means that it is not for a defendant to prove that he is innocent but rather for the state to prove that he is guilty. Where the state is not able to demonstrate guilt then the defendant is entitled to an acquittal even if the evidence demonstrates that it is more likely than not that the defendant committed the crime.

The presumption of innocence is taken further and justifies the presumption in favour of the defence. According to this presumption if there are two possible constructions of a statutory provision and one is broadly favourable to the defendant and the other is broadly favourable to the prosecution then this rule states that the construction that favours the defence should be used unless Parliament intends the opposite.

 ## Summary

In this chapter we have examined the basic concept of domestic sources of law. We have identified that there are two sources of law (primary sources and secondary sources). In particular we have noted that:

- *Primary sources* are considered to be those 'authoritative' sources that are produced by the legal process itself. *Secondary sources* are sources that are produced by others and are, in essence, a commentary on the law.

- Primary sources of law include statutory material and this itself is divided into two types of material: *primary legislation* (Acts of Parliament) and *secondary legislation* (Statutory Instruments, Orders in Council, etc).

- Statutes are Acts of Parliament and are either *Public Acts* (Acts that are of general application) or *Private Acts* (which are limited to a certain body).

- An Act will normally have to pass both the House of Commons and House of Lords and then receive Royal Assent before it becomes an Act of Parliament. However, subject to limited exceptions, it is possible to use the Parliament Acts, which will allow the House of Commons to override the House of Lords and enact legislation that has passed only one House.

- A statute will ordinarily be broken down into Parts and Chapters but the most important division is in its clauses known as sections. Sections can also be broken down into sub-sections, paragraphs, and subparagraphs.

- The courts are called upon to interpret legislation and they do this normally by using the *literal rule* where they simply look at the wording of the legislation. Where this leads to an absurdity they can look at either the *golden* or *mischief rules* which allows them to consider what Parliament intended.

- The Human Rights Act 1998 allows greater interpretation and expressly allows courts to decide whether legislation is compatible with the *European Convention on Human Rights*.

End-of-chapter questions

1. Should the Parliament Acts be used in politically controversial pieces of legislation? The House of Lords is the second chamber of the legislature and thus should it not have the right to block controversial legislation? By allowing the House of Commons to bypass this block does this not mean there is no protection against, for example, a state seeking to diminish human rights?

2. The Supreme Court of the United States of America is allowed to 'strike down' legisla-tion that is incompatible with their Constitution. Should the Supreme Court of the UK be allowed to 'strike down' legislation that is incompatible with the ECHR?

3. If the intention of Parliament is important in the construction of legislation why shouldn't the courts be allowed to use parliamentary material whenever they wish and in what-ever form?

4. Reread the section on the use of explanatory notes (p 48) above and also read Munday (2005) 346–349, 352–354 and Kavanagh (2005b) 105–108. Is it right that the courts look to statements produced by the government rather than Parliament as a whole when examining parliamentary material? It is used to gauge Parliament's intent and this need not be the government's intent. Should the rule be relaxed?

Further reading

Kavanagh A (2005) 'Unlocking the Human Rights Act: The radical approach to section 3(1) revisited' 3 *European Human Rights Law Review* 259–275.

This is another authoritative article from this commentator where it is suggested that the courts have been reluctant to make the full use of their powers of interpretation.

Kavanagh A (2005) '*Pepper v Hart* and matters of constitutional principle' 121 *Law Quarterly Review* 98–122.

This is an interesting article that examines the modern application of the rule in *Pepper v Hart*.

Marshall G (2003) 'The lynchpin of parliamentary intention: Lost, stolen or strained' *Public Law* 236–248.

This is an article that examines the place of parliamentary intention in the construction of statutes.

Munday R (2005) 'Bad character rules and riddles: Explanatory notes and the true meanings of s 103(1) Criminal Justice Act 2003' *Criminal Law Review* 337–354.

This is a short but extremely useful and interesting article on the legal status of explanatory notes.

 For multiple choice questions, updates to this chapter and links to useful websites, please visit the Online Resource Centre at

www.oxfordtextbooks.co.uk/orc/gillespie_els3e/

3

Domestic Sources of Law: case law

By the end of this chapter you will be able to:

- Define the principles of *stare decisis*.
- Apply the doctrine of precedent to cases.
- Differentiate between binding, overruling, and distinguishing precedent.

Introduction

The previous chapter introduced the concept of domestic sources of law and it was noted that sources can be divided into primary and secondary sources. Of the primary sources, parliamentary material is supposed to be the most important, with the courts merely implementing the will of Parliament. Often this is expressed as Parliament making the law and the courts applying it but this is not strictly true. It was noted that decisions of the superior courts are a primary source of material in their own right and this is because England and Wales has a common-law-based tradition, ie decisions of the court can amount to law in the same way as statutory law does. It is not just minor matters where the common law becomes involved; quite a significant amount of constitutional law is by convention or through common law, but murder, arguably the most important criminal offence, is a common-law offence. You will not find a statutory definition of murder but it is instead left to the courts to define.

Even where Parliament has passed a law it falls to the courts to decide what this law means and how it will be applied. In the previous chapter it was noted that the courts have created a series of statutory rules to assist them in interpreting the law, but in order to ensure that there is certainty in the law the courts have themselves developed rules on how courts must act when presented with a case. These rules are known as *stare decisis* although the common term of 'precedent' has gained favour. These rules have created a hierarchy of the courts and an understanding of how courts must act when presented with a previous decision.

3.1 Reporting of cases

It has already been noted that the English Legal System is a common-law-based system, which means that historically much of the law was a product of the common law rather than statutes. Even now that statutes are more usual the role of the courts is to interpret the law and many of the common-law rules continue to apply.

At the heart of the common-law system is the system of *stare decisis* or precedent, as it is also known. The term *stare decisis* can be translated as 'let the decision stand' and is designed to bring certainty to the law. The basic proposition of this doctrine is that a case should normally be dealt with in the same way as previous cases were by the courts and that the law can only be changed according to the hierarchy of the courts. How this works in practice will be examined in this chapter but the first issue to consider is how we know what the law is.

One can get the impression that the system of *stare decisis* has a long and distinguished history and to an extent it does. However, until comparatively recently the system was somewhat haphazard because very few cases were ever reported. How could the doctrine be applied therefore? A judge who tried a Chancery case in Preston might not be aware of a similar case that was heard in Plymouth three months earlier. If they were decided differently then it would appear that rather than having a consistent approach to law we would have the exact opposite.

The earliest known reports were known as the 'Year Books' and these date back to the thirteenth century (and can still be seen at the Squire Law Library at the University of Cambridge) but very few cases were reported. Those cases that were mentioned tended to be extremely important cases rather than matters that were considered in typical court cases. Also the reports took a considerable time to be reported which did not contribute to a careful analysis of precedent. In the sixteenth century a series of private reports started to be published. These were reports published by individual reporters and normally cited by reference to their name. A principal difficulty with these reports, however, was that there was no sense of order as to what was reported; it tended to depend on the particular idiosyncrasies of the reporters. There was also considerable doubt as to the accuracy of the reporters as there were no rules and regulations that either required a reporter to check the accuracy of reports or indeed specified what qualification the reporters needed to have, if any. That said private reports continue to be available albeit in a changed format (see below).

Eventually it was decided that if reports were to be produced then it was important that they contributed to, rather than detracted from, the consistency of law. In 1865 the Inns of Court and Law Society, who regulated the legal profession (see Chapter 8), created a new body, the *Council for Law Reporting* and in 1870 it became an incorporated body taking the name, *Incorporated Council of Law Reporting for England and Wales*, the name it continues to be known by today. The patronage of the professions, particularly the Inns of Court where the Masters of the Bench (who are in charge of the Inn) were frequently members of the judiciary (see 8.2.1.2 below), ensured that the Council succeeded and that its reports became authoritative; indeed even today (as will be seen) reports produced by the Council should be cited in preference to any other series.

If the Year Books and private law reports marked the first age of law reporting and the creation of the *Incorporated Council* marked the second age, we are now in the third age. We now live in the era of the Internet and as you will no doubt be aware a significant number of judgments can now be obtained from the Internet. The Law Reports, in all their various guises, never pretend to be able to report every case that occurs in the senior courts but with the Internet this is getting close to being real. For example, let us look at the House of Lords (now replaced by the *Supreme Court*: see chapter 6). The series *Appeal Cases* did not report every case heard by the House, but since 14 November 1996 every judgment of the House appeared on the Internet. To a lesser extent this can also be seen with the Court of Appeal. Whilst not every judgment of the Court of Appeal is reported on the Internet, the vast majority are, and certainly more than would have ever been reported in the traditional law reports.

The courts themselves have mixed emotions about the use of ICT to report cases, as on the one hand electronic reports have facilitated their use through the use of neutral citations (see below) but on the other hand the courts have argued that it is sometimes possible to refer to too many cases. Perhaps the most notable criticism was given by the Lord Chief Justice in *R v Erskine* [2010] 1 WLR 183. The Lord Chief Justice provided a history of law reporting (at p 201) and emphatically restated a principle first enunciated by Viscount Falkland in 1641: 'if it is not necessary to refer to a previous decision of [the] court, it is necessary not to refer to it' (at p 202). Whether *Erskine* will stem the use of repeated authorities (and, quite ironically, it is likely that *Erskine* will become one of the most-cited cases as advocates will cite it as authority as to why a particular case should be allowed to be referred to) has yet to be seen but the Internet certainly continues to provide access to as much of the work of the higher courts as is possible.

3.1.1 Printed series

It has been noted that a number of printed series exist. The *Incorporated Council* is responsible for many of these but a number of private reports, normally produced by recognized legal publishers, are also to be found.

3.1.1.1 Incorporated Council

Judgments reported by the Incorporated Council should normally be cited in preference to any other series (see *Practice Direction (Judgments: Form and Neutral Citation)* [2001] 1 WLR 194). The reports produced by the Council are fully authorized in that the judges check the judgments to see whether they are accurate and can indeed change the wording of the judgment they handed down if it clarifies issues. The reports also contain the submission of counsel which whilst not forming any part of the judgment can be of assistance when identifying the reasoning of the court.

There are three principal series operated by the Incorporated Council which are: the *Law Reports*, the *Weekly Law Reports* and the *Industrial Cases Reports*, the latter of which is a specialist report. Of the three the *Law Reports* are considered to be the definitive reports for the reasons set out above and they are divided into four series, each of which has a different abbreviation and colour.

It is important to note that the titles do not necessarily reflect exactly what their contents are. One of the most common mistakes for law students to make is to think that the *Appeal Cases* series deals with the appellate courts, most notably the Court of Appeal. In fact only matters now heard in either the Supreme Court or Judicial

Table 3.1 The Law Reports

Series	Abbreviation	Colour[a]
Appeal Cases	AC	Brown
Queen's[b] Bench Division	QB	Green
Family Division[c]	Fam	Blue
Chancery Division	Ch	Red

a. The reports will either be bound in this colour or will be bound all in beige with the spine including the Division framed by the relevant colour. This tends to be a less popular method of binding now.

b. When the Sovereign is a King then it is automatically the King's Bench Division and the abbreviation KBD is used.

c. Prior to 1972 this series was known as the Probate Division and carried the abbreviation P. In that year, however, the Family Division of the High Court of Justice was established and the series was retitled.

Committee of the Privy Council are reported in that series.[1] A significant proportion, and perhaps even the majority, of cases reported in the *Queen's Bench Division* series are not heard in the Queen's Bench Division of the High Court of Justice because decisions of the Court of Appeal (Criminal Division), certain decisions of the Court of Appeal (Civil Division), Employment Appeals Tribunal, Consistory Courts,[2] and judgments of the European Court of Justice are reported. Similarly the Family Division and Chancery Division reports encompass decisions of the Court of Appeal (Civil Division) and European Court of Justice that originated in those Divisions.

The *Weekly Law Reports* are so called because they are generally published weekly but this is not for the fifty-two weeks of the year nor are they produced in the same week as the judgment was handed down (see below). There are traditionally three volumes of the *Weekly Law Reports* and it is intended that those reported in volumes 2 and 3 will normally be (eventually) published in the *Law Reports*. That said, it is important to note that this is only an intention and it will not necessarily always occur, in part because by the time a report is produced it may have been considered on appeal.[3] The *Weekly Law Reports* (abbreviated to WLR) are produced much quicker than the *Law Reports*, in part because they are not checked by judges prior to being published. Accordingly, there may be slight differences between the reports. The speed at which they are produced is also reflected by the fact that the arguments of counsel are not contained in the report either.

The *Industrial Cases Law Reports* are the most recent series created by the Council and are comparable to the *Weekly Law Reports* save that they are even more specialist in that they only refer to cases heard by Industrial (now known as Employment) Tribunals and the Employment Appeals Tribunal or appellate decisions where they originated in one of those tribunals. The Tribunals are discussed in Chapter 15 and are quasi-judicial with *stare decisis* being applied to their decisions.

3.1.1.2 Other series

A number of other series exist all of which are private reports. In order to have status within the courts the reports must be prepared by a qualified lawyer (see below). With the exception of the *All England Law Reports* the series tend to be specialist in terms of reporting a narrow range of cases. The primary reason for this is that it is not easy to compete with the Council, especially given the preferential treatment awarded to it by the courts. Where a practitioner wishes to access specialist material, however, it is unlikely that the general law reports will contain many of the cases as they will not be considered 'important' enough. The principal series are referred to in Table 3.2.

Not every report will necessarily be official in that the judges may not necessarily have the opportunity to review them prior to publication although the better reports do allow this. Also very few of these reports will contain the arguments of counsel, the argument for omitting these being that they do not form part of the judgment.

---

1. It previously reported decisions of the House of Lords and the Judicial Committee of the Privy Council.

2. These are ecclesiastical courts and established by the Church of England. Each diocese has a Chancellor who presides over the consistory court. Nowadays the vast majority of cases relate to 'faculties' which are permissions to alter the material content of a church (including its building, windows, or other features that could have a permanent effect on the church).

3. For example, *Davis v Johnson* is reported at [1978] 2 WLR 182 but it has never been reported in *Law Reports* because it was superseded by the House of Lords ruling on that case: see [1979] AC 264.

Table 3.2 Common abbreviations for Law Reports

Series	Abbreviation
All England Law Reports	All ER
Criminal Appeal Reports	Cr App R
Criminal Appeal Reports (Sentencing)	Cr App R(S)
European Human Rights Reports	EHRR
Family Court Reports	FCR
Family Law Reports	FLR
Knight's Industrial Reports	KIR
Local Government Law Reports	LGLR

3.1.1.3 Newspapers and journals

Before leaving the printed series it is worth noting that it is not only specialist publications that report cases but that a limited number of newspaper and journals do so too. *The Times* has long been considered the leading daily newspaper for lawyers in part because it contains law reports usually on an almost daily basis. The reports are highly abridged and would normally only be referred to in court in highly exceptional circumstances (because the case would ordinarily be reported by a series in due course). In contrast to the reporting series above, the words of the judge are not reported verbatim but are simply abridged. The principal advantage of these reports, however, is that the reports are normally produced within days of the judgment being handed down, something that not even the weekly reports can manage. In recent times the *Independent* has also included law reports although on a much less frequent basis.

Legal periodicals also sometimes report cases and perhaps the two most obvious examples of this are the *Solicitors' Journal* and the *New Law Journal*. Both series suffer the same drawbacks as *The Times* in terms of their detail but the speed in which they are reported continues to make them a particularly useful resource.

3.1.1.4 A note on dates

Although all law reports contain a date where the report is carried in print rather than electronically it is likely that there will be a delay between the judgment being handed down and the report being produced. It is a convention that rather than using the date of the judgment the year will normally be taken from the report.

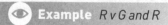 **Example** *R v G and R*

The judgment in the leading case of *R v G and R* was handed down by the House of Lords on 16 October 2003. However, it was reported in the *Appeal Cases* series at [2004] 1 AC 1034 and could, therefore, be abbreviated as *R v G and R* (2004).

Of course nothing is simple and some reports are produced earlier than others, most notably the *Weekly Law Reports*. This may mean that there are different years.

> **◉ Example**   More about *R v G and R*
>
> The case of *G and R*, discussed above, is also reported at [2003] 3 WLR 1060. However, the year can be taken from whichever series you refer to. It could also, therefore, be referred to as *R v G and R* (2003).

Printed reports do not include every case and occasionally there may be a significant delay in reporting a decision. Where a report is particularly late then it would be wiser not to adopt this convention. Perhaps the classic example of this is *Regal (Hastings) Ltd v Gulliver* where the judgment was handed down on 20 February 1942; it was reported by the *All England Law Reports* at [1942] 1 All ER 378 but the official *Law Reports* did not report the case for another twenty-five years ([1967] 2 AC 134)!

3.1.2 Internet sources

The growth in electronic reports led to an increase in the number of unreported cases that were being presented to the courts. Traditionally these were referred to by their case name or the year and 'unreported'. It was difficult for all counsel and the courts to keep track of the cases and clearly as more judgments were becoming available it was preferable for a standardized form to be introduced.

In *Practice Direction (Judgments: Form and Citation)* [2001] 1 WLR 194 Lord Woolf CJ issued a direction that transformed the way that judgments were presented. All judgments would now follow a standard pattern with each paragraph being numbered sequentially through the judgment. Also each case would be assigned a neutral citation number so that even unreported cases could be readily indexed, identified, and retrieved. Initially, the practice was restricted solely to the Court of Appeal and Divisional Court of the Queen's Bench Division but it was later extended to the High Court (see *Practice Direction: Supreme Court: Judgments: Neutral Citations* [2002] 1 WLR 346) but the House of Lords (and now the Supreme Court) followed the system.

The citation has three elements to it: the date, the court code, and the case number. Each number is assigned sequentially by the relevant courts in order of its appearance. The codes are as follows:

Supreme Court	UKSC
House of Lords	UKHL
Privy Council	UKPC
Court of Appeal	
Criminal Division	EWCA Crim
Civil Division	EWCA Civ
High Court of Justice	
Administrative Court[4]	EWHC Admin
Queen's Bench Division	EWHC (QB)
Chancery Division	EWHC (Ch)
Family Division	EWHC (Fam)

---

4. Also known as the Divisional Court of the Queen's Bench Division.

Specialist Courts

Patents Court	EWHC (Pat)
Commercial Court	EWHC (Comm)
Admiralty Court	EWHC (Admlty)

The code EW stands for England and Wales whereas UK is used for those bodies that have jurisdiction throughout the United Kingdom. Confusingly, there is a difference as to where the case number is to be found. Where the court code does not include parentheses then the number occurs immediately after the code whereas where parentheses are used then the case number is written immediately after the code but before the court code which is placed in parentheses.

 Example Neutral citations

The 123rd case in the Court of Appeal (Civil Division) for the year 2003 would be written as:

[2003] EWCA Civ 123

whereas the 45th case to be heard in the Chancery Division of the High Court during the year 2003 would be written as:

[2003] EWHC 45 (Ch).

The neutral citations should be used at least once even in reported cases (see *Practice Direction: Judgments: Form and Citations*) and the reports should not renumber the paragraphs but use the ones assigned in the judgment. Where a paragraph is being referred to the number is placed in square brackets.

 Example Neutral citations—paragraphs

To refer to the 13th paragraph in the (fictional) case of *Smith v Jones*, which has the neutral citation number [2003] EWHC 45 (QB), the following format is used:

[2003] EWHC 45 (QB) at [13].

3.1.3 Reporters

So far it has been recognized that cases are often reported but who reports them? The short answer is qualified lawyers. Traditionally cases were reported by barristers and the vast majority of reporters continue to be barristers. In part this was because of the historical divide between the professions (see 8.2.1 below) with barristers having the exclusive right to litigate in the superior courts. It was thought that as only a barrister could litigate in the superior courts only a barrister would fully understand the procedure and detail of the cases in sufficient detail to report the matter. However, the *Courts and Legal Services Act 1990* ended the Bar's monopoly on accessing the superior courts and s 115 of that Act provides that a law report by a solicitor or other person with a superior court qualification shall have the same authority as one by a barrister. Accordingly, the position is now that either a solicitor or barrister can act as an official law reporter. It is important to note that the reporter, regardless of which profession he belongs to, must be fully qualified, ie have the right (even if they do not avail themselves of it) to conduct litigation in the courts.

3.2 Hierarchy of courts

The system of precedent depends on there being a hierarchy of courts. It is necessary to identify the structure of the courts in order to understand how precedent works. Diagram 3.1 sets out a basic understanding of the English Legal System. It can be seen that the Supreme Court is at the very top of the structure and the magistrates' courts are at the bottom. The position of the European Courts (the European Court of Justice (ECJ) and the European Court of Human Rights (ECtHR)) is somewhat complicated and different texts will place them at different levels of the system. In Diagram 3.1 it can be seen that the ECJ is parallel to the Supreme Court because although the Court, as will be seen, is bound by the ECJ in certain circumstances this is only because the *European Communities Act 1972* says so and if this was repealed then the Supreme Court would continue to be the head of the system. Placing the ECJ above the system would also misrepresent its role in that the vast majority of English law is not impacted by its decisions. The importance of the ECJ will be discussed below. The ECtHR is

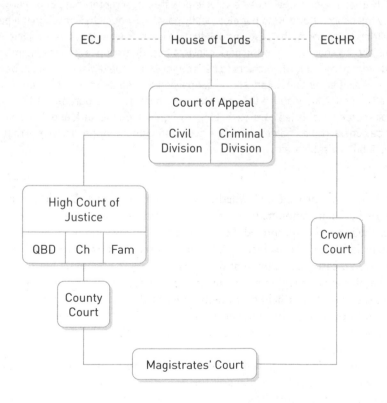

Diagram 3.1 The hierarchy of the courts

linked by a broken line to reflect the fact that technically the ECtHR does not bind any court nor is it reached by an appeal per se (see Chapter 5 for an explanation of this).

The hierarchical principle means that each court will act in accordance with its place in the hierarchy and has responsibilities to those above and below it. When and how the courts can act will be discussed below although it should be noted that the lower courts (ie those below the High Court) do not play any role in *setting* rather than *following* precedent.

3.3 Legal principles

Not every statement of a superior court will necessarily amount to a precedent. Indeed the system of precedent applies only to a narrow part of any case—the legal decision for a case. Harris notes that this is a significant limiting factor as in the vast majority of cases, including appellate cases, there will be no dispute as to the law but rather a dispute as to the facts (Harris (1991) 40). In those situations no precedent will arise as decisions of fact do not bind courts.

> **◉ Example** Facts *v* law
>
> Parliament creates the (fictional) *Motor Vehicle in the Park Act 2006*, which states that a person is guilty of an offence if he drives a vehicle powered by a motor in a public park. Edith is stopped by the police after driving her electrically powered wheelchair through the park.
>
> The District Judge trying the case decides that an electric wheelchair is a vehicle powered by a motor and as she drove it in the park convicts her. Edith appeals to the High Court and they decide that permitting wheelchairs to be brought within the legislation would be 'absurd' and contrary to other parliamentary statutes. Applying the 'golden rule' of statutory interpretation (see Chapter 2) they quash the conviction and hold that the purpose of the legislation was to stop motor vehicles (eg cars, vans, etc) driving through the park and that a wheelchair could not be considered a 'motor vehicle' because although it may be driven by a motor it was not a vehicle but a disability aid.

Whether Edith was driving and whether she was in the park are decisions of fact. Whether a wheelchair amounts to a 'vehicle powered by a motor' is a matter of law as it requires the law to be interpreted. In this situation the decision of the High Court that a wheelchair is not a motor vehicle will become a precedent as it is a decision of law.

However, in a case many apparent decisions of law may be made but some of them may not be binding as they do not form part of the decision of the case. In the example above, the High Court held that the mischief of the Act was to stop cars and vans being driven in the park. This must be a legal rather than factual point but it does not form part of the decision of the case as Edith's case did not involve a car or van; it is an ancillary legal point.

The two types of legal statement identified above are known as the *ratio decidendi* and *obiter dictum*. The *ratio decidendi* is the legal reasoning for the decision and forms the binding precedent, *obiter dicta* are legal opinions that did not go to the decision but are, in essence, side comments on legal issues.

3.3.1 *Ratio decidendi*

The most important principle is the *ratio decidendi* as this is what will form the precedent. The term is often shortened to just *ratio* and notwithstanding the fact that there is a retreat from the use of Latin in law the term remains in use.

Whilst it may seem an easy issue to discuss, in practice the identification and application of the *ratio* can be quite complicated not least because judges do not often signpost exactly why they have reached their decision. The situation becomes even more complicated when more than one judge may be giving judgment, one reason why in some jurisdictions only a single judgment is given (most notably the US Supreme Court).[5]

There is, unfortunately, no clear single rule on how one identifies the *ratio* of a case and with some cases this can be the most difficult part of any case analysis. There are two principal tests that have been considered by theorists to assist in the identification of precedent, those proposed by Wambaugh and by Goodhart.

3.3.1.1 Wambaugh's test

The first possible method of identification is to use the test formulated by Wambaugh. Harris reproduces the earlier text of Cross in considering this work (Harris (1991) 52–57). The test is quite complicated in that it is presented in the negative. It also does not identify the *ratio* but allows a reader to test whether their supposition of what the *ratio* is could be correct. The test, at its most basic level, is that one identifies the supposition of law that the reader believes is a *ratio* and then reverses its meaning (p 52). The reader then considers whether the outcome of the case would have been the same. If the answer is 'yes' then the proposition can only be *obiter* and not the *ratio*.

 Example Edith

Let us return to the example of Edith above. What is the *ratio* of the High Court in that case?

The first possible *ratio* of the case is that only cars and vans are classed as 'motor vehicles'. We reverse the proposition (cars and vans are not classed as motor vehicles) and ask ourselves whether the same decision would have been made in respect of Edith? The answer must be 'yes' because the case did not concern either a car or van and so that proposition will not be the *ratio*.

The second possible *ratio* is that wheelchairs are not motor vehicles. If we reverse our proposition (wheelchairs are motor vehicles) then we need to ask ourselves if the decision would be the same. The answer must be 'no' because the law prohibits the use of motor vehicles so they would have to acquit. Accordingly the proposition that 'wheelchairs are not motor vehicles' may be the *ratio* of that case.

A difficulty with Wambaugh's test is, however, that it does not work particularly well where there is more than one possible *ratio*. For example, it could be decided that the *ratio* of the example above is that a vehicle required for the conveyance of a disabled

---

5. Where the Court is divided then there will tend to be a single majority verdict and a separate single dissenting judgment. As a dissenting judgment will not count towards the *ratio*, this means there is no possibility that the judges contradict each other on the *ratio*.

person is exempt from the legislation. If this proposition was reversed it would not obviously lead to Edith's case being decided differently but is this the *ratio*? Arguably if it does then had Edith not had an electric wheelchair but a quad bike to allow her to move around then are we saying the court would still acquit? It would seem unlikely and yet according to Wambaugh's test is possible. Harris argues that this is a difficulty with the test: it is very good at identifying what *is not* a *ratio* but it is not particularly efficient at identifying what *is* the *ratio* unless there is only a single possible reason (Harris (1991) 56–57).

3.3.1.2 Goodhart's test

The more authoritative test is that which was put forward by the theorist Goodhart. His test is based on the premise that it is possible to identify the *ratio* by examining the material facts of the case that set the precedent. The logic behind this premise is that all decisions are necessarily based on the analysis of facts and is in line with the comments of Lord Halsbury, the then Lord Chancellor, who has stated that 'a case is only author-ity for what it actually decides' (see *Quinn v Leathem* [1901] AC 495 at 506). Harris, reproducing the work of Cross in commenting on this case, notes that his Lordship was not stating that a case has no binding power beyond its decision but rather was indi-cating that precedent only applies where the material facts are similar (Harris (1991) 57–58). We will return to this proposition when examining how to escape precedent (3.4.1 below) but it does validate the premise of Goodhart that an analysis of some facts could reveal the *ratio*.

Not all the facts of a case will be relevant in the search for a *ratio*, indeed a signifi-cant proportion of them are unlikely to be critical. Goodhart, therefore, refers to the need to find 'material' facts which are those that go to the central issues of the case. Goodhart himself, however, noted that one particular difficulty with this theory is that it will be for the judge to decide what the material facts are and this may not neces-sarily be an objective approach to deciding such facts (Goodhart (1931) 11). Whether something is a 'material' fact depends on whether it is essential to the decision of the case.

> 👁 **Example** Material facts
>
> The defendant, a 31-year-old female called Sheila, is accused of stabbing the victim, her hus-band of nine years, in the stomach following an argument. The marriage was a turbulent marriage with frequent allegations of domestic violence including two where the husband was formally cautioned by the police.
>
> There are a series of facts in this example but the age, name of the accused, and duration of the marriage are unlikely to be material facts in that it would not really matter whether they were present or changed. The sex of the defendant may be a material fact but on the other hand it may not.
>
> The material facts in this case would appear to be that the defendant stabbed the victim in the stomach, that the defendant and victim were in a relationship (the fact that it was a mar-riage is probably immaterial), and the allegations (and particularly the proven incidents) of domestic violence.
>
> The material facts are relevant to the decision in the case and therefore go to the *ratio* of the case whereas the immaterial facts are simply irrelevant.

An advantage of Goodhart's theory is that if it were correct then not only would it assist in the identification of a *ratio* but it would also primarily be of assistance in escaping precedent. It will be seen that the most useful tool for a judge or lawyer seeking to escape precedent is the concept of distinguishing (see 3.4.2 below) and if Goodhart is correct then a case can be distinguished if any of the material facts are not present.

The disadvantage of this approach, however, is that not every case necessarily turns on the material facts of the case. The learned editors of a legal encyclopaedia[6] provide the example of *Donoghue v Stevenson* [1932] AC 567, arguably one of the most important cases in English law.[7] The material facts of this case were that a third party purchased a drink (ginger ale but the type of drink cannot be considered material) in a dark glass bottle, and the bottle contained (unbeknown to any party in the case until the material time) a decomposed snail. The judgment of the House of Lords arguably had very little to do with any of these material facts and certainly the use of the *ratio* of this case, which became the very foundations upon which the tort of negligence came to be based, have very little to do with the material facts of this case other than the fact that it was a third party that bought the article (and thus it was not a contract case).

Harris argues that although every case must have a *ratio decidendi* (Harris (1991) 48) it need not be the case that there is only one *ratio* in a case and indeed more than one may exist (p 81). This could be as a result of different reasoning between the judges or because more than one decision is reached. Sadly it is not uncommon for judges to agree as to the decision of a case but disagree as to the reasoning that occurs. Perhaps the most potent example of this is *R (on behalf of R) v Durham Constabulary* [2005] UKHL 21 which concerned the issue of whether a juvenile offender must consent to being given a formal reprimand or final warning rather than being prosecuted. The decision of the House of Lords that no consent was required was unanimous but Lady Hale disagreed radically with Lord Bingham on the reasons for this. What is the *ratio* of this case? Arguably in this particular case it was the reasoning of Lord Bingham because a clear majority of Law Lords backed his arguments but does this necessarily follow? In this case there were two 'primary' judgments that conflict on some aspects: what happens if the other judges all agree with the comments of the other judgments even though they say slightly different things (as arguably happened in *R v Ireland; R v Burstow* [1998] AC 147)?

Bagaric and McConvill (2005) have questioned whether the Australian High Court, which operates on almost identical *stare decisis* principles, has caused itself problems by giving separate judgments rather than a single majority and minority judgment and argued that it made very little difference. Perhaps this demonstrates the fallacy of attempting to identify the *ratio* in every case and that where there could be multiple *rationes* they all have potential force until one is chosen to be followed, with the rest ceasing to be considered as authoritative from that point.

3.3.2 *Obiter dictum*

This second phrase is often shortened to *in obiter* or the *dictum* depending on the preferences of the author although the former is more usual. It is important to note at

---

6. See <www.ivr-enc.info>.
7. Which is somewhat ironic given that it is actually a Scottish case albeit one heard in the House of Lords!

the outset that a judge will often accidentally create *obiter* statements but will, in some cases, wish specifically to raise ancillary issues in this way (see Harris (1991) 42). A difference of opinion appears to exist over whether a judge can ensure that remarks are *only* considered to be *obiter* rather than go to the *ratio* of a case. Lord Devlin in *Behrens v Bertram Mills Ltd* [1957] 2 QB 1 suggested that a judge can, and the principal method of doing so would be to state that the comments are an opinion rather than a cogent statement of the law (p 25) whereas Megarry J has suggested that a judge has no power to prevent a decision from becoming a precedent, ie part of the *ratio* (see *In Re Showerings, Vine Products and Whiteways Ltd* [1968] 1 WLR 1381 and see Harris (1991) 42).

To an extent, Megarry J is correct in that it is for subsequent courts to decide whether they are bound by a decision, but similarly when a court is trying to escape precedent (see below) then the motivation for the statement is undoubtedly going to be a factor. One way that a judge may seek to alter a *ratio* to an *obiter* statement would be to state that the reasoning adopted is restricted to the facts of the case. Such a formula is clearly stating that the judge thinks that he foresees no general application of the principle to other cases and it should, therefore, be considered as persuasive rather than binding. But strictly speaking it remains a decision of the later court as to whether they find themselves so bound.

It is also important to note that just because comments are made *in obiter* does not mean that they are unimportant. *Obiter* comments are *persuasive* authority—ie a court should consider them even if they are not strictly bound by them. Where the statement is made by a particularly authoritative body, eg the Supreme Court or Lord Chief Justice, then it is quite possible that the consideration that should be given to these persuasive comments is significant. Indeed it has been stated:

> *Dicta* of the highest degree of persuasiveness may often, for all practical purposes, be indistinguishable from pronouncements which must be treated as *ratio decidendi*...(Harris (1991) 77)

A good example of this is presented by Harris when he discusses the well-known case of *Donoghue v Stevenson* [1932] AC 562 (Harris (1991) 43–44). The case was an appeal brought under Scottish law to the House of Lords but the House, as it not infrequently does, suggested that English and Scottish law were the same on this point. The case concerned a person who drank a bottle of ginger beer from a brown bottle and found a decomposed snail at the bottom of the glass. No contract exists between the manufacturer and the consumer (as the consumer will purchase the bottle from a shop and not the manufacturer direct) but the House permitted a duty in tort to be established to take reasonable care in the manufacture.

Donoghue v Stevenson is an important case not just for the reasoning in respect of that manufacturer but because of the comments of, in particular Lord Atkin, when he referred to his 'neighbourhood principle', where his Lordship argued that a person owed a duty to a neighbour to take reasonable care. From this statement arguably developed the law of negligence and this comment is still cited today. Yet the comments about neighbours are almost certainly *obiter* because it did not go to the decision of the case. Accordingly it was not part of the *ratio* but these *obiter* comments have undoubtedly become more important than the *ratio* itself.

3.4 The operation of precedent

Harris argues that '[precedent] creates the expectation that, save for the intervention of the legislature, the law will remain as it is stated to be in the precedent' (Harris (2002) 413). However, as will be seen this is not strictly true as the courts do alter precedent through its application. The distinction drawn above between *ratio decidendi* and *obiter dictum* is important because it goes to the heart of how precedent operates. Only the *ratio* is applied to precedent as it is this which encapsulates the law and should, according to Harris, continue to be applied. Whilst the *dictum* of a judge is important it does not set out what the law is but rather illustrates potential ways that the law could be applied or developed.

In order to examine how precedent works in practice it is necessary to identify some more of its key terms. These are all discussed in further detail below but are summarized here for reference.

Table 3.3 The operation of precedent

Term	Meaning
Binding/bound	A court *has* to follow the precedent established in an earlier case
Distinguish	The court believes that the case before it is not factually the same as the precedent and accordingly is not bound by it
Not following	Where two or more conflicting precedents are presented the court chooses to follow one and not follow the remainder
Reverse	When an appeal succeeds the decision of the lower court in that case is reversed
Overrule	A higher court (or the House of Lords) alters a precedent; the original precedent ceases to be good law

These terms, or more properly their actions, are the very operation of precedent as they demonstrate how a court should decide cases before it. It is important that the terms are used appropriately. One of the most common mistakes made by students is to use the term 'overrule' when this is not, in fact, what has happened. It is far more common for a precedent to be escaped by either distinguishing or not following it. In neither situation has there been a change of law—the precedent continues to exist and if another case arises then the courts should be bound by it. Where a precedent is overruled, however, then the law changes—the legal principle that was encapsulated by the precedent no longer applies and where another case arises on these issues the courts cannot follow the original precedent any more but must now follow the principle enunciated by the overruling case which becomes, therefore, the new precedent. It is also important to note that not every court has the power to overrule precedents (see below) and an extremely common mistake is for a student to say that a court has overruled a precedent when it has no power to do so.

3.4.1 **Bound by precedent**

If the notion of *stare decisis* is that decisions continue with courts following the previous decisions then the most important issue is that of binding—ie when is a court bound to follow the *ratio* of a case? This must be considered for each court.

3.4.1.1 Supreme Court

The simplest court to deal with is the Supreme Court. As the highest court in the English Legal System its decisions bind all the courts below it unless they are able to escape the precedent through distinguishing it (see below). The position of the Supreme Court itself will be discussed below (3.4.3.1) but it is likely to follow the position adopted by the House of Lords (its predecessor): see *Practice Direction (House of Lords: Judicial Precedent)* [1966] 1 WLR 1234.

3.4.1.2 Court of Appeal

The Court of Appeal is second in precedence in the English Legal System and is the more usual appellate court (the Supreme Court hearing only a highly limited number of appeals). The simple rule for the Court of Appeal is that it is bound by the Supreme Court and it binds all courts lower than it. Where the complication arises is whether the Court of Appeal is bound by itself.

The leading authority on the matter is *Young v Bristol Aeroplane Co Ltd* [1944] KB 718 where the Court of Appeal stated that it was bound by its own decisions subject to the following exceptions:

1. Where there are two conflicting decisions of the Court of Appeal it may choose which to follow.
2. Where the previous decision of the Court of Appeal, even if not expressly overruled, conflicts with a Supreme Court or House of Lords decision.
3. Where the decision was made *per incuriam*.

Others argue that the second ground of *Young* must have been expanded to include the situation where the previous decision of the Court of Appeal conflicts with the European Court of Justice (Manchester et al (2000) 17) and this is undoubtedly correct. The term *per incuriam* means 'through want of care' and covers those situations where a court neglected to consider an issue that it should have, eg a statutory provision or a binding precedent.

Davis v Johnson

The ruling in *Young v Bristol Aeroplanes* continued for some decades before it came against Lord Denning MR, who was arguably one of the most influential judges of the past century. Lord Denning had been a Lord of Appeal in Ordinary but had accepted the Master of the Rolls position in part because he believed the Court of Appeal was more influential than the House of Lords due to the number of cases it heard. Lord Denning did not like the fact that the Court of Appeal was bound by itself whereas the House of Lords was not. This dislike culminated in the case of *Davis v Johnson* [1978] 2 WLR 182 where Lord Denning empanelled a full Court of Appeal, namely five judges, including Sir George Baker the President of the Family Division. The case concerned a non-molestation order made under the *Domestic Violence and Matrimonial Proceedings Act 1976*. Previous Court of Appeal decisions, most notably *B v B* [1978]

2 WLR 160, had construed this Act in a way that a majority of the court disagreed with[8] but, according to the rule in *Young v Bristol Aeroplanes* the Court of Appeal should have been bound by that decision. However, a majority of the Court of Appeal held that they could choose not to follow the precedent.[9] Lord Denning sought to argue that the Court of Appeal should have the same right to depart from its own decisions as the House of Lords reserved to itself in the *Practice Direction* of 1966. He based his argument on the fact that the House of Lords may never get an opportunity to reverse a bad law because of the cost of litigation and leave requirements (pp 194–195). He also argued that where a ruling was obviously wrong this placed the lower courts in a quandary because an appeal may take a year to be heard by the House but until judgment is handed down by the House the lower courts would be obliged to rule on matters it knows are wrong (p 196).

Lord Denning attempted to argue that the doctrine of precedent was not a legal principle but rather a custom of the courts (pp 197–198). This would be important because if it was mere custom then courts would have the power to alter the principle whereas, of course, if it was a legal rule then *stare decisis* would bind itself, ie only the House of Lords could rule as to whether the Court of Appeal had the authority to depart from its own judgments. He was joined in this by Sir George Baker P who thought that the decisions could be distinguished but argued that this was itself unsatisfactory because it meant a lower court could still consider them valid precedent when his Lordship believed they were wrong. Sir George Baker suggested that the new exception should be slightly narrower by arguing that a new exception should be granted where a decision is wrong and appears contrary to the intentions of Parliament (p 206). The President appeared to be trying to extend the *per incuriam* rule by stating that it goes against Parliament's will but it cannot come within the rule as of right because the provision was (presumably) brought to the court's attention initially.

The matter proceeded to the House of Lords ([1979] AC 264) and their Lordships wasted little time in stating that the Court of Appeal was wrong to believe that it was not bound by itself, with Lord Diplock even suggesting that Lord Denning MR, had 'conducted what may be described…as a one-man crusade with the object of freeing the Court of Appeal from the shackles…of *stare decisis*' (p 325). His Lordship continued by stating that whilst there was a justification in a final appellate court to have a discretion to right obvious wrongs, there is less justification for this in a lesser court where certainty of law should be a primary consideration (p 326) before concluding:

> In my opinion, this House should take this occasion to re-affirm expressly, unequivocably [*sic*] and unanimously that the rule laid down in the *Bristol Aeroplane* case…as to *stare decisis* is still binding on the Court of Appeal. (p 328)

This invitation was taken up by every other member of the House in their speeches. Lord Salmon tackled the argument of Lord Denning that the costs of litigation and leave requirements may lead to an injustice by commenting that the Court of Appeal itself had the power to grant leave to appeal and could order that the costs are paid by the Exchequer (p 344). This is an important point and recognizes the inherent powers of the court. The Court of Appeal did not believe that leave could be granted because

---

8. Only one judge, Cumming-Bruce LJ, dissenting from this part of the case.

9. Goff LJ joined Cumming-Bruce LJ in dissenting from this decision but he expressly stated that he did so reluctantly as he disagreed with the original precedent.

leave had been refused in the earlier cases but this misses the point that where the court believes that its earlier decision was wrong this adds weight to that ground of appeal and introduces a public policy argument in favour of leave.

To an extent, Lord Denning did have a point regarding the custom or law issue. When the Court of Appeal created its rules of precedent in *Young v Bristol Aeroplanes* it must have done so *in obiter*. The actual dispute that led to the litigation in that case had nothing to do with precedent and the comments on precedent did not go to the heart of the reasons for the decision meaning that it could not form part of the *ratio*. Similarly the House of Lords when rebuking the Court of Appeal in *Davis v Johnson* must also have been speaking *in obiter* as it did not go to the heart of the case. Indeed if one looks solely at the judgment of the courts, the law reports record that the House of Lords *affirmed* the decision of the Court of Appeal even though we are discussing it *reversing* the Court of Appeal in terms of precedent. It has already been noted that *obiter* is not strictly binding so to that extent Lord Denning was probably correct.

However, the House of Lords decision in *Davis v Johnson* was inevitable and would probably have arisen through an appeal in any event where the matter could have been dealt with as a *ratio*. It may have been preferable for the House of Lords to clarify this situation by issuing a Practice Direction but the alternative construction is that this is another example of Harris's comment that some *obiter* comments can be as powerful as a *ratio*. Certainly the decision of the House of Lords in *Davis v Johnson* as to the proper function of the Court of Appeal was plain and it did not lead to the Court of Appeal making such a blatant attempt at escaping precedent again.

An emerging exception?

However, some commentators argue that although the Court of Appeal has never expressly challenged the principle in the way that occurred in *Davis v Johnson* they have begun to assert an additional exception to the *Young v Bristol Aeroplane* case, that of declining to follow a case where it was 'manifestly wrong' (Prime and Scanlan (2004) 220). The argument stems from the case of *Cave v Robinson Jarvis & Rolf (A Firm)* [2002] 1 WLR 581 where counsel argued that the Court of Appeal was not bound by a previous decision of a two-judge bench of the Court of Appeal. It had long been since recognized that the Court of Appeal was not bound to follow a decision made on an interlocutory appeal where the full court argued the case was manifestly wrong (*Boys v Chaplin* [1968] 2 QB 1). The Court of Appeal declined, in *Cave*, to rule on this proposition principally because it believed there was no longer any difference between two-, three-, and five-judge benches of the Court and in part because it was not convinced that the decision was 'manifestly wrong'.

Prime and Scanlan argue, however, that the *obiter* comments made in the case demonstrate that the principle of 'manifestly wrong' is a new exception to *Young v Bristol Aeroplanes* and that the court had, albeit *in obiter*, suggested that it had a wider application than merely interlocutory appeals (Prime and Scanlan (2004) 220–221). They also suggested that support for their proposition could be gathered from the case of *Limb v Union Jack Removals Ltd* [1998] 1 WLR 1354 where Brooke LJ stated, inter alia:

> Any departure from a previous decision of the court is in principle undesirable and should only be considered if the previous decision is manifestly wrong. (p 1365)

The difficulty with this is that it is not certain that Brooke LJ was creating a new exception. This line follows a rehearsal of the reasons when the Court of Appeal may depart from its own decisions and was immediately preceded by this passage:

> The doctrine [of precedent] does not extend to a case where, if different arguments had been placed before the court or if different material had been placed before it, it might have reached a different conclusion.

In this context is would appear that Brooke LJ was arguably developing the *per incuriam* ground. Admittedly, the reference to alternative arguments would widen the doctrine further than it has traditionally been but reference to other material does appear to be in line with that exception. More problematic for Prime and Scanlan is that they argue that a majority in *Cave v Robinson* agreed that a new exception exists but the case does not necessarily say that. Whilst Potter LJ does appear to accept that the rule in *Boys v Chaplin* may still exist he is less than convinced that it has any practical modern use (Prime and Scanlan (2004) 594) or that it may be analogous to the current 'leave' hearings; Sedley LJ, who Prime and Scanlan argue also approved of such a distinction (p 221), is less certain. The language used by Sedley LJ is not particularly transparent but his Lordship expressly states: 'the solution which this court felt able to adopt in *Boys v Chaplin* would not be adopted in similar circumstances today' (p 596). Whilst this does not, of course, say that the exception is closed it does suggest that it is unlikely that it will ever be used.

The position does appear therefore to be somewhat transient although Prime and Scanlan (2004) argue that any new exception based on 'manifestly wrong' would be inappropriate (pp 222–4). Given the obtuse statements by the Court of Appeal, upon which their hypothesis is based, it would seem more likely that the Court of Appeal is bound by its own decisions subject to the exceptions identified in *Young v Bristol Aeroplanes*.

The Criminal Division

The decision in *Young v Bristol Aeroplanes* was a decision of the Court of Appeal (Civil Division) and accordingly it could be argued that it only bound that Division. However, the Criminal Division has stated that it too is *normally* bound by its own decisions subject to the exceptions set out in *Young* (see the comments of May LJ in *R v Spencer* [1985] QB 771 at 779) but with an additional exception that arises as a result of the unique cases that the Court of Appeal (Criminal Division) hears. Given that invariably a person who appeals to the Court of Appeal in criminal matters is incarcerated in gaol, the court has, perhaps not unreasonably, taken the approach that where a decision is obviously wrong and would otherwise lead to the appellant remaining in gaol then *stare decisis* should be departed from as even awaiting an expedited Supreme Court ruling would lead to a situation where a person has been deprived of their liberty unnecessarily.

The 'liberty' rule has to be considered exceptional however because if there were any area of law where certainty would be desirable it would be the criminal law (Harris (1991) 117) and the courts appear to have recognized this with Lord Diplock saying:

> although the Criminal Division of the Court of Appeal is not so strictly bound by its own decisions as is the Civil Division, its liberty to depart from a precedent which it

is convinced is erroneous is restricted to cases where the departure is in favour of the accused. (*R v Merriman* [1973] AC 584 p 605)

The latest pronouncement by the Criminal Division was contained in *R v Simpson* [2004] QB 118 where the Court of Appeal (Criminal Division) stated:

> We consider a degree of discretion remains in this court to decide whether a previous decision should be treated as a binding precedent in future or not when there are grounds for saying that the decision is wrong. (p 131 per Woolf LCJ)

Moreover the court suggested that the 'constitution of the court may be relevant' (ibid) and Lord Woolf expressly drew attention to the fact that this was a five-judge bench of the court. This appears to contradict earlier decisions and the custom of the Civil Division where it has been held that the number of judges is irrelevant: the authority flows from the court not the numbers. This is certainly the accepted position and the remarks of Lord Woolf bear a striking similarity to the approach of Lord Denning in *Davis v Johnson*.

Arguably *Simpson* concerns the *per incuriam* rule in that it discusses whether all the relevant authority was before the earlier court. To some degree this mirrors the suggestion of Brooke LJ in *Limb v Union Jack Removals Ltd* which suggests that the Court of Appeal is beginning to push the boundaries of precedent once more. The exception of *per incuriam* has previously been restricted to those situations where the court was not referred to relevant statutory material or a binding precedent but both *Limb* and *Simpson* appear to suggest that where alternative arguments could, or rather should, have been submitted this may justify departure from the precedent. *Simpson* is also important because it appears to contradict the approach in *Merriman* in that in this case the decision to depart from precedent was not favourable to the defendant. There is no question that the ruling in *Simpson* was against the interests of defendants and yet the Court of Appeal still departed from precedent.

That said the limits of *Simpson* should be recognized. In *R v Varma* [2010] EWCA Crim 1575 the Court of Appeal declined to follow *Simpson* when ruling on a matter relating to confiscation orders and their applicability when a defendant has been given a discharge. The facts are not important but the court found itself bound by an earlier decision in *R v Clarke* [2010] 1 WLR 223 but this was the only decision that referred to this point (ie there was no conflict of authorities) and the judges of that court had been referred to all the relevant authority. Whilst the Court of Appeal in *Varma* was prepared to concede that *Clarke* may be wrong, it stated that it was bound by it and that *Simpson* did not apply where there was no conflict of interest and where 'it was considered in meticulous detail, and given the closest possible attention' (at [31]).

It appears therefore that, rather than attempt a full-frontal attack on precedent itself, the Court of Appeal has decided to attempt to broaden the recognized exceptions. The easiest exception to broaden is the *per incuriam* rule and both divisions of the court have sought to tackle this. More importantly the Criminal Division has decided to broaden its approach to errors and widen the meaning of injustice to include a guilty person escaping justice rather than just an innocent person wrongly imprisoned. It will be interesting to see whether the House of Lords feels as strongly now as it did in *Davis v Johnson* and reinforces the narrow interpretation of *stare decisis*.

❓ QUESTION FOR REFLECTION

Read *Davis v Johnson* (1978) and also *R v Simpson* (2004). Do you think that the Court of Appeal should be allowed to depart from its own precedent where it believes it is wrong? Few cases reach the Supreme Court (the number of cases has increased in the last few years but there have never been more than seventy-five) and even fewer cases relate to the criminal law. Is it realistic to suggest that only the Supreme Court can correct mistaken precedent?

🎧 LISTEN TO THE PODCAST

For guidance on how to answer this question and a discussion of the main issues, listen to the author's podcast on the Online Resource Centre: www.oxfordtextbooks.co.uk/orc/gillespie_els3e/

3.4.1.3 The High Court

The High Court of Justice is next in the hierarchy. Whilst there are three principal divisions (Queen's Bench, Family, and Chancery) together with specialist courts (eg Commercial, Admiralty, etc)[10] the other significant court to examine is the Divisional Court, also known as the Administrative Court, which has a supervisory jurisdiction. Of the three divisions the Family Division also requires special attention when it deals with the welfare of children for public-policy reasons akin to the Criminal Division of the High Court.

Non-supervisory jurisdiction

The High Court sits below the Supreme Court and Court of Appeal in the hierarchy and is accordingly bound by their decisions. It binds all lower courts although its principal binding role is in respect of its supervisory jurisdiction (see below).

When the court is not sitting in its supervisory capacity (ie it is not sitting as either an appellate court or hearing a judicial review case but is rather adjudicating on litigation brought between two parties) then its previous decisions are persuasive but are not binding on a judge. That is to say that a judge will normally follow the decision for reasons of consistency but they are able to depart from the decision should they wish to and do not need to find a reason like the Court of Appeal must (see *Police Authority for Huddersfield v Watson* [1947] KB 842).

Where children are concerned it is sometimes suggested that the Family Division adopts a more relaxed attitude to the notion of precedent although Wilson J speaking extrajudicially has suggested this is not strictly true.[11] The latitude is said to arise from the fact that s 1(1) *Children Act 1989* states that where a matter relates to the upbringing of a child then the welfare of the child is to be the paramount consideration. In other words nothing is supposed to be more important than the welfare of the child. That does not mean that courts have the right to disregard *stare decisis* however, something reinforced by Wilson J and evident from cases where matters in the

---

10. Although these are technically part of the other divisions. For example, the Admiralty Court is part of the Chancery Division and the Technology Court is part of the Queen's Bench Division although they are treated for everyday purposes as separate.

11. See '*The Misnomer of Family Law*', The Atkin Lecture 2002 by Hon Mr Justice Wilson.

Family Division have been litigated before the appellate courts.[12] However, the welfare principle does allow some leeway in that every case that involves the upbringing of a child will necessarily have individual facts and accordingly it is perhaps easier for the Family Division to distinguish (see below) precedents than other Divisions may find it. However, where a clear principle of law is enunciated by the appellate courts then the Family Division must follow it.

Divisional Court

Where the High Court is sitting in a supervisory capacity, which will normally involve it sitting as a Divisional court with two or more members[13] then the rules of precedent change and the Divisional Court is treated in much the same way as the Court of Appeal. The Divisional Court is quite clearly below the Court of Appeal in hierarchy so it is bound to follow decisions of that court but it is generally thought that it is bound by *its own* decisions unless the exceptions in *Young v Bristol Aeroplanes* apply (see *Police Authority for Huddersfield v Watson* (above) and *Younghusband v Luftig* [1949] 2 KB 354). However, this has not been conclusively proved and in *R v Greater Manchester Coroner, ex p Tal* [1985] QB 67 the Divisional Court argued that when it was acting in a supervisory role at first instance it was in no different position than the High Court.

Accordingly it would now seem that the general rule for the High Court is that whenever it sits as a court of first instance then no binding precedent is set, but when it sits in an appellate capacity binding precedent does apply, something confirmed, albeit probably *in obiter*, by Laws J in *C (A Minor) v DPP* [1994] 3 WLR 888 (see in particular p 898).

3.4.1.4 Crown Court and inferior courts

It will be seen that the Crown Court is not technically an inferior court (s 45(1) *Senior Courts Act 1981*) but for the purposes of precedent it is de facto an inferior court. No court below the High Court sets a precedent for anyone. Similarly, decisions of each court are not binding on other divisions of that court although it has been said that decisions of a High Court judge sitting in the Crown Court are persuasive although Ashworth argues the status of the judge should be irrelevant (Ashworth (1980) 403).

The position of the Crown Court is interesting because it is unquestionably higher than the magistrates' court and indeed appeals take place from the magistrates' court to the Crown Court. However, any decision reached by that court is restricted to the facts and does not set a precedent. It is for this reason that decisions of law are more frequently taken to the Divisional Court, which does bind all magistrates' courts and Crown Courts sitting in its appellate capacity.

3.4.1.5 The Privy Council

The Privy Council is in an unusual position in terms of precedent. Its current jurisdiction does not include English law (as the *Constitutional Reform Act 2005* transferred

---

12. Perhaps the most notable of these decisions is *Re H (Minors)(Sexual Abuse: Standard of Proof)* [1996] AC 563 where the House of Lords conclusively held that the standard of proof to be used in care proceedings where sexual abuse is alleged was the civil standard but that where a serious allegation was made the more evidence would be required to meet this standard. The Family Division has followed this ruling in accordance with *stare decisis*.

13. Even though judicial reviews are now heard in a court labelled the 'Administrative Court' it continues to be a Divisional Court where more than one judge sits.

the last-remaining UK jurisdiction of the Council to the Supreme Court) and thus it technically has no place in the English Legal System. It is, however, worth noting its place within precedent, albeit briefly.

Precedent within the Council

The Privy Council has always adopted a relatively lax attitude to precedent in respect of its own decisions, considering them only to be persuasive rather than binding (Littlewood (2004) 122). That said, it is also clear that the Council appreciates that certainty is desirable and will therefore seek to follow its earlier decisions where possible (p 123).

Precedent within the English Legal System

Whilst not strictly speaking part of the English Legal System, the Council is in a peculiar position in that those who sit in the judicial committee are usually Justices of the Supreme Court[14] and accordingly their decisions must, at the very least, be considered highly persuasive.

It has been stated:

> It is possible to refer to cases in which a decision of the Privy Council has not been followed by an English judge of first instance, but it is also possible to point to cases in which a decision of the Privy Council has been persistently preferred to a decision of the Court of Appeal, although the decision of that court has never been overruled. (Harris (1991) 102)

In other words, Harris is arguing that the Court of Appeal has, in some cases, used a decision of the Privy Council as a method of invoking the *per incuriam* exception in *Young v Bristol Aeroplanes*. This should be relatively uncontroversial as the Privy Council, whilst not strictly part of the English Legal System, is a senior court and its decisions warrant investigation. The Court of Appeal should be able to consider whether the decision reached in that case alters the understanding of the issues they have previously adjudicated.

Where the position becomes more complicated, however, is what happens when a decision of the Privy Council conflicts with a decision of the Supreme Court or House of Lords? Theoretically since the Supreme Court is the most senior domestic court in the English Legal System the Court of Appeal should follow it as precedent but see *R v Mohammed* [2005] EWCA Crim 1880. The partial defence of provocation[15] entertained the courts for many years prior to its repeal but *R v Smith* [2001] AC 146 appeared to resolve one central part of this partial defence, namely what subjective characteristics could be imputed onto the reasonable man used in the test for provocation. The position seemed clear but in *Attorney-General for Jersey v Holley* [2005] AC 580 the Privy Council stated that it thought *Smith* was wrong. Theoretically this was merely persuasive precedent and the Court of Appeal, together with all courts in the English Legal System, would be required to follow *Smith* but the Court of Appeal in *Mohammed* refused to do so and argued that the position in English law was that put forward by the majority in *Holley* ([2005] EWCA Crim 1880 at [42]). This decision has

---

14. Although it is not restricted to them and certain foreign senior judges and all Lords Justices of Appeal are entitled to sit on the judicial committee.

15. *Homicide Act 1957* s 3. Now repealed by the *Coroners and Justice Act 2009*.

been followed by other decisions of the Court of Appeal (see, for example, *R v Shickle* [2005] EWCA Crim 1881).

It is important to note that this is not a situation where the Court of Appeal has decided that its own decision is *per incuriam* but rather it is making a decision as respects a precedent that it should be bound by, namely the House of Lords decision in *Smith*. It would have been tidier for the court to send the matter to the House of Lords, and it could have done so by granting leave. It is important to note that this was not a case where the liberty of the appellant was at stake (see 3.4.1.2 above) as the appeal in *Mohammed* was dismissed (as it was in *Shickle*) and thus it would have been tidier to do so. If *stare decisis* is supposed to bring certainty then following the decision of a court outside of the English Legal System is contrary to that principle and if a future comparable situation arises it would be tidier to send the matter to the Supreme Court so that the normal rules of precedent apply.

3.4.2 Distinguishing

Whilst a court is bound to follow precedent it is sometimes possible to escape precedent. To an extent this has been discussed above when it was decided that courts were able to fail to follow a precedent (ie not follow) either because it was decided *per incuriam* or because there were two conflicting decisions. The most usual form of escaping precedent, however, is to distinguish a case. It has already been noted that only the *ratio decidendi* binds a court and this only applies therefore where the facts of a case would lead to the same *ratio* being applied. The concept of distinguishing is where a court argues that the *material* facts of a case are different and accordingly the *ratio* will not apply but rather a different reasoning must be adopted.

Where a judge decides to distinguish a case he should normally explain why the precedent is being distinguished and this reasoning will be subject to criticism by later courts and where the decision is itself appealed it could be reversed by the appellate court.

It can be argued that the concept of distinguishing can be taken further and need not be restricted to factual differences but could also include situations where 'societal factual circumstances have changed since [the precedent] was originally decided' (Harris (2002) 411). If this is correct then it would allow courts to develop the law in a way that reacts to society progressing and not require such developments to be constrained by the appellate system.

3.4.3 Overruling

So far the discussion on precedent has concerned situations where a court has either followed precedent or has escaped it. The final issue that needs to be examined is where a precedent ceases to exist because it is overruled. One principal justification for using the power to overrule authority is where the precedent was decided *per incuriam* or its application has left the law unworkable (Harris (2002) 416). In both of these situations the court can safely overrule a case knowing that it will bring certainty to the law, something that is supposedly at the heart of *stare decisis*. Similarly, where a decision has created conflicting precedents then simply following one authority may not lead to certainty arising since the absence of overruling the other could mean that a court is still able to 'resurrect' the other potentially increasing uncertainty. It is for this reason that in *Young v Bristol Aeroplanes* it was said that where the Court of Appeal chooses between two conflicting earlier decisions of the court the one it does not follow is overruled ([1994] KB 718 at 728). Where a difficulty arises, however, is where the court does not consciously attempt to reconcile all the previous decisions as this could lead to an argument that the judgment was made *per incuriam*. It is therefore incumbent on the court to state expressly that it is choosing between conflicting decisions and stating which case is therefore overruled.

Perhaps the more usual method of overruling is when either a more senior court than that which created the precedent or the Supreme Court overturns the precedent. It is important to note the terminology here. The precedent, ie the case that created the *ratio* that was applied in the case which forms the appeal, is *overruled*. The actual case that is being litigated on appeal will be *reversed*.

The simplest situation is where a more senior court overrules a precedent of a lower court (eg Court of Appeal overruling the High Court, Supreme Court overruling the Court of Appeal). In these situations the court has the right to overrule a case and once this has been done then the case that is being litigated forms the *new* precedent with the old one ceasing to be good law although any *dicta* in the court may continue to be relevant (Harris (1991) 128).

 Example Overruling

The (fictional) case of *Smith v Jones* is before the Court of Appeal (Civil Division). The judge at first instance argued that he was bound by the earlier case of *Brown v Bloggs* which was heard by the Divisional Court. The Court of Appeal decides that *Brown v Bloggs* was wrong and that it should no longer be the law. It therefore overrules *Brown v Bloggs* and that case may no longer be cited.

A different judge in the High Court is hearing a case that is very similar to *Brown v Bloggs* and *Smith v Jones*. The judge is bound to follow the Court of Appeal decision in *Smith v Jones*, which is now the only precedent available.

A difficulty arises when the superior court does not state that the case is overruled but merely does not follow the lower precedent (which of course they do not need to) or distinguishes it. The higher court may, in *dicta*, cast doubt on it but without overruling it; then presumably it continues to be a precedent. It will be noted that one of the grounds in *Young v Bristol Aeroplanes* was that it was inconsistent with a House of Lords decision and thus it might be that the court could escape the doubted precedent. But this action itself would not overrule the case and it could mean that the position becomes more confused with an additional precedent being created without any being overruled. This can cause difficulty:

> A High Court judge of first instance when confronted with a decision of the Court of Appeal which has not been expressly overruled by a later House of Lords' case may cease to be bound by it because the House of Lords considered that the Court of Appeal misinterpreted the authorities... The judge is then not obliged to follow the Court of Appeal, but he is not bound to dissent from their conclusion. The previous decision is undermined rather than directly overruled. (Harris (1991) 129–130)

If the purpose of *stare decisis* is to introduce certainty into the law then it is obvious that situations such as that described above would not be helpful and yet this is a not an uncommon outcome. It is submitted that it is incumbent on the superior courts, particularly the Supreme Court, to take care when they discuss authorities and to use their power to overrule a case where they believe it is necessary—merely doubting its application but leaving it open to be used again is a recipe for confusion in law.

3.4.3.1 Supreme Court

The House of Lords (which preceded the Supreme Court) decided in 1966 that it did not consider itself bound by its previous decisions. Interestingly the practice direction did not state that it had the power to overrule its own decisions but rather it claimed the power to 'depart from' previous decisions ([1996] 1 WLR 1234). However, since 1966 the House of Lords had been clear that it did mean the right to overrule its earlier cases (see, for example, *R v G and R* [2004] 1 AC 1034 where the House of Lords expressly overruled the case of *R v Caldwell* [1982] AC 341 ([2004] 1 AC 1034 at 1055 per Lord Bingham)).

The justification for assuming this power was undoubtedly to help bring clarity to the law since previously the House was either not permitted to depart from its own rulings meaning that no matter how sympathetic they were only legislation could remedy the fault or they would do so by distinguishing previous cases and accordingly leave a number of possible precedents 'active'.

The *Practice Statement* did not give the House of Lords complete freedom and they continued to view decisions as *ordinarily* binding on themselves (Harris (1991) 136). The House did, for example, on a number of occasions note that the fact a decision was merely 'wrong' was not enough to justify the use of the statement (see, for example, *Knuller (Publishing, Printing and Promotions) Ltd v DPP* [1973] AC 435). Some commentators suggest that distinguishing should be used wherever possible (Harris (2002) 422). Harris argues that this is needed to make the law more certain and predictable (pp 420–421) but given that he expressly includes precedents that were decided *per incuriam* or are distinguishable because of social movements it is difficult to see why leaving these decisions 'live' would be preferable. It could be argued that simply distinguishing them and labelling them as *per incuriam* etc would be sufficient to inform the lower courts not to follow them. Nevertheless, whilst this may be true, certainty and predictability are not achieved by refusing to tinker with the law unless absolutely necessary, but rather by ending bad decisions. Overruling those types of precedent rather than merely not following them would ensure that no court could resurrect them and would accordingly bring about certainty in the law.

Neither the *Supreme Court Rules* nor its Practice Directions have indicated whether the Supreme Court intends to follow the 1966 *Practice Statement*. Technically as that statement related solely to the House of Lords it is not directly transferred to the Supreme Court. We will no doubt have to wait until the first case where the matter is raised although it is inconceivable the Supreme Court will do anything other than adopt the same approach as the House of Lords.

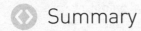 Summary

In this chapter we have examined how the courts use case law. In particular we have noted:

- The courts operate a system of precedent known as *stare decisis* ('let the decision stand').
- The type of precedent set depends on the court sitting, with the most complicated rules arguably occurring in the Court of Appeal. As a general rule of thumb, the court setting the precedent will bind every court below it.
- 'Binding' means setting a precedent that another court must follow.
- Only the *ratio decidendi* of a case forms the precedent. Any other aspects of the case are known as the *obiter dicta*.
- Whilst every case must have a *ratio* there need not necessarily be a single *ratio*. Also, identifying the *ratio* can be quite complicated especially where there is more than one judgment.
- Where a superior court changes the ruling of a lower court this is called 'reversing'. A decision is only 'overruled' when the court is saying that the precedent was wrong and should not be followed.
- Lower courts are able to 'escape' precedent by 'distinguishing' a case. This is where they accept the validity of the precedent but suggest that it does not apply to the case at hand because there are factual differences between the precedent and the case they are adjudicating.

End-of-chapter questions

1. Read Attorney-*General for Jersey v Holley* [2005] UKPC 23 and *R v James; R v Karimi* [2006] EWCA Crim 14. Does this now mean that the Privy Council has become part of the English Legal System for the purposes of *stare decisis*?

2. Consider the following cases and identify their *ratio*:

   (a) *R v G and R* [2003] UKHL 50

   (b) *DPP v Redmond Bates* [2000] HRLR 249

   (c) *Partridge v Crittenden* [1968] 1 WLR 431.

   The Online Resource Centre accompanying this book provides clues and the answers!

3. Read Harris (1991) pp 129–130 and Harris (2002) pp 420–422. Are there circumstances when leaving a precedent 'live' by either distinguishing or disapproving of it would be better than formally overruling it? Does that complicate or ease the burden of the lower courts in applying the principle of *stare decisis*?

Further reading

Ashworth A (1980) 'The binding effect of Crown Court decisions' *Criminal Law Review* 402–403.

This short note discusses whether a judge in the Crown Court sets any precedent for other judges of the Crown Court or magistrates.

Harris B V (2002) 'Final appellate courts overruling their own "wrong" precedents: The ongoing search for principle' 118 *Law Quarterly Review* 408–427.

This is an interesting article that examines whether there is any rationale behind the circumstances governing final appeal courts overruling themselves.

Kavanagh A (2005) '*Pepper v Hart* and matters of constitutional principle' 121 *Law Quarterly Review* 98–122.

This is a wide-ranging but interesting article that examines the role of the courts in precedent and statutory interpretation.

For multiple choice questions, updates to this chapter and links to useful websites, please visit the Online Resource Centre at

www.oxfordtextbooks.co.uk/orc/gillespie_els3e/

International Sources of Law

By the end of this chapter you will be able to:

- Identify the key sources of law in international law.
- Differentiate between the European Union and the Council of Europe.
- Understand how EU law has an impact upon domestic law.
- Identify the ways in which international instruments influence the law.

Introduction

So far we have examined how domestic law is created and found. However, modern-day Britain does not exist in isolation and a significant amount of international law has an impact on domestic law. This can perhaps be best demonstrated from our relationship with Europe where two international agreements creating the European Union (EU) and the Council of Europe (CoE) have significant implications for the way in which our domestic law is interpreted and formed. Outside of Europe there are a significant number of international rules that can influence our laws but how does this relate to domestic law?

It is important at the outset to note that in this chapter we will not be discussing what international law is as such as this is something that is the topic of significant debate, with some even questioning whether it in fact even exists or whether it is a purely political concept. That debate is best left to options that examine the concept of international law. What nobody can deny, however, is that international law is examined in the domestic context and accordingly we should be aware of how to access this law.

4.1 Identifying the institutions

➲ A NOTE ON TERMINOLOGY

When one is referring to an individual country that is party to an international agreement then it is normal to refer to the country as being a 'state'. This, of course, does not mean a 'state' in the same sense as in the United States of America or Australia which operate a federal system whereby the country is broken into regions known as states. In this chapter the term 'state' will be used to signify a sovereign jurisdiction, ie an independent country.

To clarify, the United Kingdom (as noted in Chapter 1) is constituted of four countries but it is one 'state'—the UK. France is another 'state' and Germany, which also operates a federal system, is another—each individual region in Germany is not a sovereign jurisdiction in its own right but is subservient to the 'state' of Germany.

This terminology is commonplace in legal texts and so you are likely to encounter it in other books and articles that relate to international law.

International law differs from domestic law in a fundamental way. Apart from very few exceptions (which are normally confined to international criminal law), international law regulates states and not individuals. The basis of international law is that it is an agreement between two or more countries and this law regulates how these countries will act in accordance with those who have signed this agreement and does not impose obligations on individual citizens. That is not to say that international law is irrelevant to individual citizens since frequently the international agreements will require the state to enact domestic legislation to give effect to the agreement and this may impose rules relating to the international agreement. A good example of this is the *European Convention on Human Rights* which exists as an international agreement binding only on the states but which has now been given domestic effect by the *Human Rights Act 1998.*

Where an international agreement has two planes, the domestic plane (ie that which has an impact upon individuals within the domestic country) and the international plane (ie that which governs the agreements between the signatory states), then in order to understand fully the domestic law it will be necessary to access the international law. Even where the instrument exists solely on the international plane it will be seen that domestic courts are increasingly likely to refer to the international instrument to assist in their understanding of the law as they recognize that the state intends their agreements to be in force. For all of these reasons is necessary to understand where the law is to be found.

That said, however, international law is a complicated subject and not normally one that you will study during the first year of your course and thus the greater part of this chapter will examine the sources of the two international bodies that have most influence on the United Kingdom, ie the EU and the Council of Europe. However, a brief examination of the wider body of international law will be made initially.

At the outset it is vital that you are able to differentiate between the EU and the Council of Europe as they are, contrary to popular belief, completely separate institutions. The EU is the body that many popularly refer to as 'Europe' when they talk about regulation and legal impact. Since 2007 there have been twenty-seven countries within the EU with negotiations ongoing for more to join. The Council of Europe is a much older institution that was set up in the aftermath of the Second World War. Whilst membership of the Council of Europe is a prerequisite for joining the EU, they are separate institutions and some countries belong to the Council of Europe who have no interest in joining the EU (eg Switzerland).

Each of these two European jurisdictions has its own court and you should not, unlike many politicians and journalists, refer to 'the European court' since there are at least two. The *European Court of Justice* (ECJ) is the court for the European Union and has jurisdiction over only community matters. The *European Court of Human Rights* (ECtHR) is the court for the Council of Europe and has jurisdiction only over the European Convention on Human Rights. Confusing the two courts (and indeed institutions) is easily done but it can be a fatal mistake in your studies and is an extremely good way of upsetting your EU lecturer!

4.2 General international sources of law

International law is significantly different from domestic law, not least because there is no machinery of governance. We have already identified in previous chapters that a country will normally have three instruments of state (executive, legislature, and judiciary) and that in common-law systems, such as that operated by England and Wales, the law will normally originate from this machinery. However, in international law there is no hierarchy of states, each nation is sovereign in its own territories, and power is exercised through political and military alliances. Looking at the United Nations it is easy to think that this replicates the machinery of governance but this analogy would be false. The secretary-general does not wield any executive power nor does, for example, the Security Council. The General Assembly (where an ambassador from each signatory nation sits) is not a legislature. The only aspect where there is an element in common is that the United Nations does have its own court, the *International Court of Justice* (ICJ), but it has a limited jurisdiction (see below). Where does the authority come from?

4.2.1 Finding the law

Before deciding whether an apparent rule is a law, it is first necessary to discover where the law can be found.

4.2.1.1 Conventions and treaties

International law normally arises from conventions and treaties. Fitzmaurice notes that a treaty 'provides a precise method of regulating relations between States' (Fitzmaurice (2003) 173) and a simple analogy could be drawn to a contract. Precisely what the difference between a convention and a treaty is, or indeed if such a distinction exists, is not known. One possible way of differentiating between them is a treaty is normally a bilateral document where there are rights and obligations on both sides (see below). This supports the contention of Fitzmaurice above. A convention, on the other hand, is often a lateral contract, ie it is one-sided and not infrequently involves a state accepting responsibilities that could be considered to interfere with its sovereignty. A good example of this is the *Vienna Convention on the Law of Treaties*. This is a document that sets out how treaties are to be defined and enforced. There is no bilateral aspect here in that states agree to sign up to the principles contained in the Convention but there is no 'other side' to this contract. The *European Convention on Human Rights* fits this model in the same way since, as will be seen, there is no 'other party' to the agreement to live up to the expectations of the Convention and to contribute to its machinery.

The *Vienna Convention on the Law of Treaties*, as its name suggests, helps provide a definition for treaties and Article 2(2) defines them as:

> [An] international agreement concluded between States in written form and governed by international law, whether embodied in a single instrument or in two or more related instruments and whatever its particular designation.

Fitzmaurice argues that the latter sentence is important because sometimes documents will be called something else but are intended to be treaties (Fitzmaurice (2003) 174) and indeed she notes that the term 'convention' is arguably covered by this Article even if it can be distinguished in the way suggested above. Malanczuk (1997) argues that the ICJ has drawn a distinction, however, by suggesting that conventions are treaties of 'general application' (p 36) which appears to replicate the distinction drawn above although he is clear that international law does not distinguish between them in terms of legal force. He goes on to identify their importance:

> Treaties are the major instrument of cooperation in international relations, and cooperation often involves a change in the relative positions of the states involved...Treaties, therefore, are often an instrument of change...(p 37)

It would appear that treaties are the closest analogy we can draw to primary legislation within the domestic UK law save that they are drawn up by sovereign states rather than any legislature. The distinction between a treaty and convention is then reintroduced by Malanczuk (1997) who notes that not every treaty is a law-making treaty as some will just act as a contract and are thus subservient to other treaties (ibid). In effect this is demonstrating that some treaties (which could be dubbed conventions) establish the framework of the legal principles, including enforcement action, whilst others seek to use this framework to agree matters between individual states.

4.2.1.2 Custom

In the United Kingdom it has been noted that there is both statutory law and the common law and, to an extent, the same exists for international law. One could easily believe that international law is a relatively modern concept but Neff (2003) notes that arguably the concept dates back to the ancient worlds and cites the discovery of a treaty document between Egypt and the Hittite Emperor in the thirteenth century BC (p 33). In the classical era (seventeenth to nineteenth centuries) when the sea began to be conquered and new lands 'discovered' (colonized) and new geopolitical alliances formed, the use of treaties (and, accordingly, international law) began to increase (pp 37–41) with this acceleration continuing even now.

However in these older times not everything was concluded by treaty, not least because there was frequently no shared language, but shared practice was often followed and this has begun to be recognized as international custom (Malanczuk (1997) 39). However, Malanczuk also warns that it is not sufficient for a custom to have existed, it must also be recognized as law which appears to demonstrate that the division between law-making and contract-like treaties appears to be replicated in international custom; that only where a custom creates a law rather than applies the law will it be considered a source. It may appear that custom is akin to the common law in the United Kingdom and whilst historically it may be so (as the common law arguably arose from custom) it is not a true analogy because custom is the practice between the parties (states) and not the decision of any court. A prime example of when custom can give rise to laws is that of the Law of War, often referred to as the Rules of War. Greenwood (2003) notes that the idea of a law governing war appears somewhat contradictory (pp 790–791) but it is also clear that there are some basic rules within war that have to be obeyed. Some of these are governed by treaty, most notably the *Geneva Convention*, but some are purely based on the custom that has arisen from the conflicts of the past.

4.2.1.3 Court decisions

One of the more problematic sources of law are court decisions. The reason for them being problematic is not that there is any difficulty with the concept of court decisions forming part of the law since this is certainly recognized within common-law jurisdictions, but rather that there is no one single international court. Whilst there is an *International Court of Justice* (ICJ) there is also, amongst others, the *International Criminal Court* (ICC), the *European Court of Human Rights* (ECtHR), and the *European Court of Justice* (ECJ). The jurisdiction of each court is limited to include matters within its competency and indeed to the countries that agreed to abide by the court. A good example of this is the *International Criminal Court*, which the USA refused to abide by; accordingly the court has no jurisdiction over individual Americans.

Malanczuk (1997) notes that the ICJ will normally follow its own decisions (p 51) and in this way it is similar to the domestic courts in common-law systems which recognize that certainty of law is an important issue that helps progress legal development. However, it is also important to note that there is no suggestion that the international courts are bound by their own decisions and thus it would not be appropriate to argue that *stare decisis* exists at international level in its purest form.

Another difficulty that exists in respect of the use of court decisions as a basis of a source of law is that as the number of international courts and tribunals increases there is a risk that they will examine similar issues but resolve matters differently, potentially leading to conflicting decisions. There is no hierarchy of courts within international law and the ICJ, for example, which is operated by the United Nations, does not have any formal relationship with any other tribunal and so cannot act as the ultimate arbitrator in these matters. Similarly, whilst some courts will examine the decisions of other courts (eg the ECtHR has, on occasions, examined the decisions of other international tribunals), it does so purely on an advisory basis and no court considers itself to be subservient to another tribunal and so it is free to decide cases differently.

Malanczuk (1997) makes an interesting point in respect of court decisions when he argues that sometimes decisions of the domestic courts can influence international law (p 51). He suggests that this is perhaps most prominent in the field of diplomatic immunity which is one of the central issues of international law. For diplomacy to work properly countries will normally send diplomatic staff (eg ambassadors, consuls, etc) to another country and they will represent the state in that country. The arrangement is normally reciprocal (ie both countries will send and receive diplomats—eg Canada sends diplomatic staff to the United Kingdom and the United Kingdom sends diplomatic staff to Canada) and the diplomats are given immunity from domestic laws. Wickremasinghe (2003) argues that the reason for this is that senior diplomats require immunity 'for their protection and facilitation' (p 389) which she explains as meaning that if a diplomat were liable to arrest then they could not carry out their function and accordingly arbitrarily arresting diplomats would be an easy method to interfere with the diplomatic efforts of a state.

Although a treaty, the *Vienna Convention on Diplomatic Relations*, primarily governs the area, Malanczuk's point was that this does not set out all the circumstances of diplomatic immunity and that domestic courts will often be called upon to rule on the precise application of diplomatic immunity since the immunity will normally arise from an action that occurs in the diplomatic concept. One of the most recent decisions on this area was the *Pinochet* cases where the House of Lords needed to examine whether General Pinochet, the former dictator and ruler of Chile, had diplomatic immunity. A Spanish magistrate had asked for the general to be extradited from London on the basis that an arrest warrant had been issued alleging that he had undertaken war crimes during his reign (see Millett (2003) 8 for a summary of the facts). One of the issues that needed to be discussed was the limit and proper functioning of diplomatic immunity and some have argued that this analysis is now being used in the international jurisprudence (Shelton (2003) 156–157) which appears to validate Malanczuk's argument.

4.2.1.4 'Soft law'

The last relevant issue that we need to discuss in this brief overview of international sources of law is the concept of 'soft law'. The term 'soft law' has been adopted to describe issues that are covered by treaties but where there is no serious attempt for the agreement to be legally binding, but nonetheless a country is happy to subscribe to a series of 'goals', 'targets', or 'aims' (see Malanczuk (1997) 54). If there is no intention to make the agreement legally binding then it cannot be a true source of law but Malanczuk suggests that 'soft law' sometimes evolves into custom if sufficient countries outside of the agreement begin to follow the treaty (ibid). That said, it would be a slow and controversial process and it would be preferable for law to develop through true law-making treaties and conventions.

4.2.2 Enforceability

Assuming that there is something called international law and that states can bind themselves, how does one enforce international law? In the domestic context the ultimate sanction is imprisonment but this cannot be true in international law, or at least public international law,[1] so how can international disputes be enforced?

The easiest method is where a treaty provides an enforcement action. One particular difficulty in international law is trying to decide what exactly amounts to a breach. Merrills (2003) notes that sometimes disagreements at the international level will amount to a dispute of policy rather than legality (p 530) and accordingly would not be resolved through a legal mechanism.

4.2.2.1 Arbitration

The easiest way in which international disputes are settled is if the treaty that gives rise to the dispute prescribes a particular method of enforceability. Some treaties will do so, eg the ECHR created the ECtHR, but others will leave the matter open. Merrills (2003) argues that the oldest method of dispute resolution is arbitration (p 539). This remains a popular remedy and exists in domestic disputes too (see 16.2.1 below) and involves taking the dispute to an independent third party (agreed by the parties) who will listen to the submissions for both sides before declaring an outcome. Traditionally arbitration was the resolution of choice for land and territory disputes (ibid) and has the attraction that it requires no standing commitment, with an arbitrator being selected when a dispute arises.

Arbitration is based on the concept of consent and although both parties must consent to the matter being taken to an arbitrator there is no sanction if the losing party refuses to cede control of the issues (see Merrills (2003) 541). Where a state does refuse to implement the findings of an arbitrator it is likely that discussions as to the law will give way to diplomacy with both countries, and their geopolitical allies, seeking to implement the decision reached.

4.2.2.2 International courts

It has been noted already that some international courts have been established and accordingly one method of enforcing a law may be to bring an action against a state in the relevant international court. The jurisdiction and powers of each court are set out in the originating treaty. Some courts have the power to impose real sanctions. For example, the ECJ has the power to fine individual states that breach Convention law. The *Treaty of Rome* (see below) gives the Court that power and if the individual state wishes to continue to be a member of the EU, and purport to uphold its laws, then it must abide by the fine.

The ICJ is a permanent court constituted under the auspices of the United Nations although it is independent from the 'executive' of the United Nations in that although it will 'report' to the General Assembly, its Sixth Committee, and the Security Council,

---

1. Different issues arise in respect of international criminal law (see below).

it is not responsible or accountable to any body for its judgments (Higgins (2003) 3). There is, therefore, independence of the judiciary even at the international level. The Court is not an appellate or referral court in that it is not open to citizens of a country to refer a matter to the Court but, rather, it is a means through which individual states can seek to resolve international disputes in a peaceful way after diplomatic means have been exhausted. The Court, unlike most other courts, has no specific jurisdiction but instead has jurisdiction over matters where both parties consent to taking the matter before it.

The Court has fifteen judicial members who are elected by the Security Council and General Assembly and who, at the time of their election, do not represent their country but must act in an independent judicial manner (Thirlway (2003) 362). The judges have diplomatic rank within the United Nations, normally at ambassadorial level, and have the equivalent immunity. However, despite their independent status it is not possible for more than one judge to come from the same country and Thirlway also casts doubt on the independence of their election noting that candidates of the five permanent members of the Security Council tend to be preferred (ibid).[2] The term of office of a judge is nine years although it is possible for them to be re-elected by the United Nations.

In domestic courts it would be extraordinary for a person who had a relationship with one of the parties to sit on a matter (see 7.6.3 below) but in the international context the reverse is true. Where a country brings a matter to the ICJ then they are entitled to appoint an ad hoc judge to the ICJ if one of the judges is not already of that nationality. The argument for this policy at international level is that it is possible for the national judges to explain the legal implications of a particular policy in their own jurisdiction (see Harris et al (1995) 654) but Thirwall (2003) questions the merits of such an approach by noting that whilst permanent judges of the ICJ have not infrequently voted against their own country, no ad hoc judge ever has (p 563). It is perhaps understandable that this is the case given the nature of a temporary appointment (and the desire to be nominated for cases again in the future) but the judges are, theoretically, supposed to take the same oath. This perhaps adds weight to the argument that judicial independence can only be secured when tenure is certain (see 7.5.2 below).

Interestingly Article 38 of the *Permanent Court of International Justice Statute*, which is a statutory instrument issued by the United Nations to give effect to Article 92 of the UN Charter setting up a court, lists the sources of law that are to be considered in disputes and these include international treaties, conventions, custom, general principles of the law, and decisions of tribunals.

Article 60 of the statute states that the judgment of the ICJ is to be final and binding which demonstrates that there is no further judicial appeal from its decision and Article 59 limits the judgment to being binding between the parties and accordingly it can be said that the ICJ does not set precedent per se and that decisions are relevant to future cases but not authoritative. Although the statute refers to matters as being 'binding' this is a relative concept. Article 94(2) of the UN Charter states that where a judgment of the Court is ignored the other party may refer the matter to the Security Council but this is arguably a toothless provision as there is no requirement on the Security Council to act and the actions of the Security Council are political rather than legal. For example, there was widespread debate over whether the decision of the United

2. The five permanent members are China, France, Russia, the United Kingdom, and the United States of America.

States and the United Kingdom to invade Iraq in 2003 was, in terms of international law, legal. A reference to the Security Council under such circumstances would, however, be pointless as both the United States and United Kingdom have a veto on Security Council resolutions meaning one cannot be passed without their acquiescence. Similarly, the conflict between Israel and the Palestinians would appear to be a classic example of when the ICJ should become involved but any judgment would be academic since both parties have traditional allies in the permanent members of the Security Council meaning any attempt at using the Security Council's powers would be defeated.

4.2.2.3 War

The ultimate sanction for the resolution of any dispute between international states is, of course, war. Some international instruments will seek to 'police' war (eg *Geneva Convention relative to the Treatment of Prisoners of War*) but international law will also sometimes permit, or indeed authorize, the use of military force to enforce a legal right. Perhaps the most commonly used justification is that of self-defence, which Article 51 of the UN Charter expressly retains. However, precisely what amounts to self-defence is, of course, open to debate especially in the post-September 11 era when governments, particularly those of the United States, the United Kingdom, and Australia, have considered self-defence from terrorism acts to be legitimate and have used such a justification for the invasion of Afghanistan. The issue of self-defence is extremely controversial (for an introduction to the arguments see Gray (2003) 599–605) and demonstrates the inevitable paradox that arises from the idea that there can be a legal war.

Theoretically, outside of self-defence there should be no right to recourse to war since Article 2(4) of the UN Charter expressly states that parties will not revert to war when disputes arise, the intention being that recourse would be made to diplomatic means or the use of the ICJ. However, it has been seen that the ICJ does not have any enforcement sanctions available to it and thus the UN Charter contemplates that the UN could authorize the use of military force to uphold international law. The UN Charter provides that the Security Council should monitor acts of aggression and 'threats to peace' and provides that they are able to take action to counter such activities (Gray (2003) 607).

Example Iraq

The Attorney-General, Lord Goldsmith QC, had to consider prior to the invasion of Iraq in 2003 whether the United Nations had authorized the use of force. The Attorney-General (controversially) argued that three resolutions of the UN Security Council, taken together, did authorize the use of force (Resolutions 1441, 678, and 687). The argument was controversial because the only resolution that expressly stated that force could be used was Resolution 678, which authorized the use of force to expel Iraq from Kuwait. Resolution 687 suspended Resolution 678 but did not repeal it. The Attorney-General argued that Resolution 1441 lifted the suspension on Resolution 678 but it certainly did not do so expressly. If, however, the Attorney-General was correct then the use of force was legal irrespective of any claim to self-defence.

It had originally been thought that a separate resolution would be required to authorize the use of force and to avoid any uncertainty but the politics of the Security Council became involved again and with the threat of a veto by other permanent members of the Security

Council, the United Kingdom and the United States believed it was better to proceed under the ambiguous authority on the basis that they believed it could authorize the use of force whereas a defeated resolution might be taken as reimposing the suspension on Resolution 678 meaning force would not be authorized. This decision continues to be discussed by international lawyers and it demonstrates how contentious international law can be.

Although the UN Charter does, therefore, allow for the use of force it must be recognized that it is a measure of last resort and Article 41 of the Charter states that the Security Council should normally first consider non-military activities such as the use of economic sanctions. This does normally occur and it is noticeable, for example, that sanctions were imposed on Iraq far earlier than military action was ever contemplated.

Where, however, sanctions are not permissible and where the political will exists, Articles 42–49 of the Charter do authorize the use of force. On occasions the force will operate under the UN banner, with perhaps the best-known example of this being the Korean War in which, at least theoretically, each unit operated under UN command. In modern times, however, it is more usual for UN military actions to be under the banner of peacekeeping, occasionally peacemaking, actions with more offensive actions occurring under national or multinational banners but under authority from the United Nations. A good example of this is the first Gulf War—*Operation Desert Storm*—where the action was not undertaken in the name of the United Nations, nor were any units so badged, but instead it occurred under a coalition led by the United States.

There is no doubt that the most recent Iraq campaign has altered the way that the use of legal force is constrained and it has yet to be seen whether the United Nations will continue to have a role in authorizing the use of force or whether individual states will neglect to seek authorization, relying instead on the premise of 'self-defence' or the 'common good'. Where it is the permanent members of the Security Council that operate such a policy (most notably the United States but the United Kingdom traditionally sides with the United States and with the exception of the case of Iraq, France will normally adopt such a posture) then there is very little the United Nations can do to remedy such actions as these states wield a veto in respect of any action and also are the principal contributors to the work of the United Nations.

4.3 European Union

It was noted at the beginning of this chapter that it is important that you should differentiate between the European Union (formerly the European Economic Community (EEC) and then the European Community (EC)) and the Council of Europe (see 4.1 above). In this section only the EU will be discussed with the Council of Europe being discussed in the next section (4.4 below).

⮑ REFERENCES TO THE TREATY OF ROME

It will be seen below that the Treaty of Rome (now known as the Treaty on the Functioning of the EU) is arguably the most important treaty for EU law. However, it has been renumbered several times, most notably following the Treaties of Amsterdam and Lisbon. All references in this book are to the Treaty as renumbered after Lisbon but you should take care when reading old ECJ cases since they may refer to the old Treaty numbers. The Online Resource Centre accompanying this book provides a table of comparisons between the Treaties in case you get confused.

4.3.1 From EEC to EU

The United Kingdom joined the then European Economic Community on 1 January 1973 but it was not one of the first countries to join the EEC which was established formally in 1957 although its inception would appear to have taken place in the 1950s (Fairhurst (2010) 5). The original grouping of states was: France, West Germany, Italy, Belgium, the Netherlands, and Luxembourg. The original intention was simply to form a community governing European steel and coal and so the *European Coal and Steel Community* (ECSC) was formed in 1952. This was then followed by EURATOM, the *European Atomic Energy Community* and then the *European Economic Community*, these being created by the *Treaties of Rome*.

⮑ TREATIES OF ROME

The status of treaties has already been discussed (4.2.1.1). It became commonplace to talk about the Treaty of Rome, meaning the treaty that established the EEC, but in fact there were two treaties since one created EURATOM. In essence, however, the principal treaty prior to the Lisbon Treaty was the EEC Treaty of Rome and all new members of the EEC had to sign the Treaty of Rome.

In 1967 these communities were, in effect, merged (see *Merger Treaty 1965*) and two institutions were created, the *European Commission* and the *Council of the European Communities*. It is essential that the latter is not confused with *the* Council of Europe since they do remain separate and following the Treaty of Maastricht it became known as the Council of Ministers or, following the Treaty of Lisbon, simply 'the Council'. Although the ministers are in their individual states properly referred to as the executive, within the EU/EEC they are actually, along with the *European Parliament*, the legislature.

The United Kingdom joined the then EEC in 1973 in the second wave of countries to join, the other countries joining at that time being Ireland and Denmark. Joining the Community required, as a result of the legal implications, the passing of domestic legislation (see 4.3.4 below) and this was provided for by the *European Communities Act 1972*. There are, at the time of writing, currently twenty-seven Member States with Turkey, the former Yugoslav Republic of Macedonia, and Croatia seeking to join within the next few years.

As the Community grew so did its mission and it moved from being a purely economic grouping to much more, with greater harmony in respect of laws and more general cooperation. Successive Treaties have then been used to modify the Community and Union and it is certainly clear that the present Union is significantly different from the EEC first created.

4.3.1.1 The road to Lisbon

Whilst the Treaty of Lisbon is undoubtedly the most important of the subsequent Treaties, its predecessors must be placed in context. Perhaps the first Treaty of significance was the *Single European Act* (SEA) which should not be confused with domestic definitions of an Act as it is an international treaty. The SEA was signed in 1986 by ministers of the then Member States and the three new Member States that joined later that year. It came into force in 1987 and its primary purpose was to bring about closer cohesion within the European market. In terms of the policy changes, the SEA defined the internal market as being free from all internal constraints in respect of certain fundamental freedoms, this being enforced by the changes to the Commission etc. The Treaty also sought to harmonize certain laws in respect of health and safety etc. It also, importantly, began the trend away from pure economic considerations with the establishment of the framework for a common foreign policy whereby Member States would work together to assist in the security of the Community.

However, the primary mechanism by which the closer cohesion of the Community was progressed under the SEA was to change the European institutions and by granting them extra powers (the argument being that the institutions would be empowered to act against barriers to a Community market).

Perhaps the first major change that was brought about by the SEA was that certain decisions of the Council of Ministers could be taken by majority rather than unanimity. Prior to the SEA all decisions required unanimity across the countries but by the time the Community had reached twelve Member States it had become more difficult to guarantee unanimity and, in effect, this requirement allowed a country to veto a decision irrespective of whether it would be for the greater good of the Community.

⊙ MAJORITY VOTING

When discussing majority voting it is worth noting that it is not necessarily a simple procedure. It may be thought that when there were twelve Member States a majority would be reached if at least seven states voted for the proposition. However, this was not necessarily true since each state had a 'weighted' vote, in essence replicating its population and so reflecting its importance within the EU. For example, under the current system, the United Kingdom has twenty-nine votes whereas Sweden has ten votes. A majority arises under the total votes although some votes also require a majority of states to be in favour too. Post Lisbon the issue of majority voting will become complicated but this is discussed further below.

The *European Parliament* was also strengthened under the SEA. The Parliament continues to pose an interesting conundrum for Europeans. The Parliament cannot be easily contrasted with the Westminster Parliament since its powers are shared. For example, an important feature of the Westminster Parliament's role is to hold the executive (government) to account. The European Parliament has a similar role but until the *Treaty of Lisbon* this was primarily the responsibility of the Council of Ministers. That said, *Lisbon* has potentially placed the Parliament on an equal footing in respect of most matters. The SEA originally created two principal purposes for Parliament:

- to produce opinions on draft directives and regulations produced by the Commission
- to assent to certain treaties concluded by the Commission, most notably any treaty that leads to the Community becoming enlarged.

In addition to this it would, of course, undertake debates and motions on aspects relevant to the EU. The members of the Parliament (known as MEPs—Members of the European Parliament) are elected in domestic elections and each country sends different numbers of people to the Parliament, again largely according to size. Currently the United Kingdom sends seventy-three MEPs whereas Estonia sends only six and Sweden sends twenty.

Maastricht

Prior to Lisbon the biggest change to the EEC was brought about by the *Treaty on European Union* which was more commonly referred to as the *Maastricht Treaty* (MT) as a result of it being signed in that city in 1992. Its principal change was to create the European Union, it doing so by stating that the Union consisted of three pillars, one of which was the European Communities (the others being the Common Foreign and Security Policy and the Justice and Home Affairs pillar). These pillars have now been abolished and the various functions subsumed within the Union (discussed below when discussing the *Treaty of Lisbon*).

Apart from this change perhaps the most significant other change brought about by the MT was the push towards monetary and economic union. This is certainly the most noticeable change since it led to the establishment of the single European currency, now known as the Euro, although originally known as the Eurodollar. The MT sought to bring in a single currency throughout the Union but this was fiercely rejected by the United Kingdom at the time and was also rejected by Denmark and Sweden (although the latter country is theoretically bound by treaty to join the Euro at some point in the future). Ten of the twelve countries within the European Union at the time of Maastricht did join and it continues to be used within continental Europe. Whilst there were some tensions surrounding the Euro during the global economic crisis, particularly when it was necessary for countries to produce a bail-out package for Greece, there has been no serious suggestion that the single currency will end. All new countries that join the EU must commit to make the Euro their legal tender at some point but, as Sweden has demonstrated, it is perhaps questionable whether breaching this commitment would lead to any sanction.

The MT also made some changes to the democratic accountability of the EU through changes to the European Parliament but these have been further changed by the *Treaty of Lisbon* and will be discussed at that point and when considering the institutions themselves (see 4.3.2.1 below).

Amsterdam

Although the MT was the major legislative instrument prior to *Lisbon*, a further treaty was necessary, this being the *Treaty of Amsterdam* (AT) which was concluded in 1997. Realistically this was not a major treaty and its principal cosmetic change was to renumber the *Treaty of Rome* to take account of the changes brought about since its original drafting. Some commentators have argued that the AT did little other than renumber the Treaty (Foster (2009) 40) and that in essence it was a 'smoke and mirrors' treaty that allowed certain EU countries to work together in a closer way but without the need for all Member States to be involved with ancillary matters.

To an extent, some of the other reforms introduced by the AT were similarly quite cosmetic. The Treaty limited the number of MEPs that could sit in the Parliament (yet Parliament has subsequently increased in numbers) and also defined the powers of the

President of the Commission but it was not a wholesale reform of the EU institutions, something that many commentators believed was necessary (Fairhurst (2010) 17). The AT also made certain changes to the MT but they are not particularly relevant to the discussion here.

One aspect of interest however is the fact that the Treaty made express reference to the *European Convention on Human Rights* which, is of course, run by a separate organization. However, the AT added a provision which allowed the Council to decide to suspend the voting rights of a Member State if it persistently continued to breach the ECHR (Article 7). It will be noted below that there is no direct enforcement action for decisions of the European Court of Human Rights but this provision provided an 'ultimate' sanction for persistent breach of members of the EU.

Treaty of Nice

The last treaty of note before the principal changes brought about by *Lisbon* was the *Treaty of Nice* (TN). This Treaty was concluded in 2000 and its principal purpose was to prepare the Union for expansion. The TN effectively altered the institutions and permitted the Union to increase to twenty-seven Member States.

The interface between the ECHR and the EU returned in the TN, and Article 7 (above)—which permits the suspension of a Member State for persistently breaching the ECHR—ceased to require unanimity and thus suspension could occur if four-fifths of the Council vote (Fairhurst (2011) 22). Again this is undoubtedly a response to the realities of expansion where there are undoubtedly going to be political groupings established within the Community. If a 'rogue' state could persuade one other country to join them it would have ensured that the Union was paralysed and, accordingly, this measure was perhaps necessary, although whether a four-fifths majority would ever be achieved is perhaps open to debate.

The TN began to put in effect the desire of the EU to concentrate on more than just the EC and other parts of the TN dealt with foreign policy, common defence plans, the European arrest warrant, and closer cooperation (Fairhurst (2011) 23). The latter has been particularly controversial in the United Kingdom but it is something that is realistically outside the scope of this chapter, which considers the issue of sources of law.

4.3.1.2 The Treaty of Lisbon

After the conclusion of the TN, considerable effort was spent trying to agree a constitution for Europe. This would have codified all of the treaties but also added to them. As a constitution it required the ratification of all Member States. Voters in both France and the Netherlands rejected the constitution and this led to the suspension of the ratification process.

Following the rejection of the Constitutional Treaty EU leaders attempted to reintroduce certain parts of the Treaty in a new instrument, the *Treaty of Lisbon* (TL). Considerable controversy existed over whether this was, in fact, a distinct treaty or whether it was simply the same treaty but not called a 'constitution'. Countries proceeded to ratify the Treaty and many countries no longer offered their electorate a referendum, arguing that this was no longer necessary. This formed a particular controversy in the United Kingdom since Tony Blair, the then prime minister, stated in the House of Commons that a referendum would be offered in respect of the Constitutional Treaty but Gordon Brown, who later became prime minister, refused to offer a referendum in respect of the TL, arguing the pledge related specifically to the Constitutional Treaty.

Whilst ratification is ordinarily an executive act, s 12 *European Parliamentary Elections Act 2002* states that if a treaty will increase the powers of the European Parliament it requires ratification by the Westminster Parliament and not merely the executive. The government introduced the *European Union (Amendment) Bill* (now Act 2008) providing for ratification. Stuart Wheeler, a prominent eurosceptic, attempted to judicially review the decision of the government to ratify TL without a referendum. In *R (on the application of Wheeler) v Office of the Prime Minister* [2008] EWHC 1409 (Admin) the matter proceeded before the Divisional Court.

The court rejected the application stating that the treaties were, as a matter of fact, different but also, as a matter of domestic law, the pledge could not give rise to an action in law and that the proceedings were an attempt to usurp the sovereign powers of Parliament. The UK has, therefore, now ratified the TL and, after an initial rejection, Ireland ratified the TL, and with the eventual ratification of the Czech Republic it came into force.

The TL has made significant changes to the EU. Some of these will be discussed in further depth below (4.3.1.3) when looking at the institutions and laws of the EU. The limitations of this section should be discussed here. The purpose of this chapter is not to provide a commentary on the EU or identify all the structural changes brought about by the Treaty, its purpose is to consider the *sources* of EU law and accordingly this, and the subsequent sections, of the chapter will concentrate only on those aspects that impact on the sources of law.

It has been stated that the TL renumbers (again) the *Treaty of Rome* but more than this it changes its name. Instead of it being the *Treaty establishing the European Community* it becomes the *Treaty on the Functioning of the European Union* (TFEU) (Article 1(11), TL). This is more than merely a semantic change as it does reflect what the *Treaty of Rome* has become. The subsequent changes have, in essence, changed the Treaty into a 'rulebook' for how the EU operates and referring it to as the founding treaty was becoming less tenable. The TL makes clear that the EU is formed on the basis of two Treaties of equal status, the *Treaty on the European Union* (TEU) and the *Treaty on the Functioning of the European Union* (Article 1(2) TFEU). It has been remarked that in the absence of a formal constitution (which, as noted above, was rejected) the TEU has become the 'repository of the constitutional principles for the European Union' (Craig (2008) 141).

At a constitutional level the Treaty created the post of *President of the European Council*. This will be discussed below (4.3.2.2) but it is worth noting that this is a considerable change from the previous system whereby the presidency of the Council would rotate through the Member States every six months. Other executive positions were created including a *High Representative for Foreign Affairs and Security Policy*. The High Representative is a member of the Commission and is also one of the Vice-Presidents (Article 18(4) TEU). The primary role of the High Representative is to 'conduct the Union's common foreign and security policy' (Article 18(2) TEU) and she also acts as the chair for the Foreign Affairs Council (Article 18(3) TEU). The High Representative is supported by a secretariat drawn from the civil service of the EU.

One of the more important provisions relates to the competence of the EU. It was noted in the previous section that the MT organized the EU into three pillars. Lisbon abolishes these as formal pillars and brings many of the matters into the substantive treaty. Instead of pillars, Lisbon refers to the competences of the EU.

4.3.1.3 The EU post *Lisbon*

The revised treaties state that the EU will be based on the issue of competences. Article 4 TEU states that anything that is not within the competences remains with the Member States and thus the Treaty is making clear the extent to which sovereignty is invested within the EU. Article 5 TEU states 'the limits of Union competences are governed by the principle of conferral' making clear that the EU can only act in situations where the Member States confer sovereignty onto the EU to act in certain areas. This demonstrates the principle of consent: that the EU is established by the Member States joining it and participating in it on the consensual conferral of sovereignty. Allied to this is a new provision contained within the TEU by TL which is Article 50 TEU which states, for the first time, how Member State can withdraw from the EU. Prior to the establishment of Article 50 it was not clear how a Member State would withdraw. It has been suggested that Article 50 reinforces the fact that membership of the EU is voluntary (Love (2010) 14) although it is difficult to see how the EU could have prevented a Member State from leaving prior to the establishment of Article 50.

The competences of the EU are divided into three types:

* areas where the EU has exclusive competence (Article 3, TFEU)
* areas where there are shared competence (Article 4, TFEU)
* areas where the EU can take action to support, coordinate, or supplement action by Member States (Article 6, TFEU).

The differential between these are set out in Article 2 TFEU. Article 2(1) states that where a matter is within the exclusive competence of the EU, 'only the Union may legislate and adopt legally binding acts, the Member States being able to do so themselves only if so empowered by the Union...'. In other words, Member States surrender the power to legislate in these areas save where permitted to do so by the EU. Article 2(2) states that shared competence means that both the EU and Member States may legislate but that 'Member States shall exercise their competence to the extent that the Union has not exercised its competence'. In other words, Member States may legislate in those areas where the EU has not. Article 2(5) states that where the EU takes action to support, coordinate, or supplement action by Member States it does so 'without thereby superseding their competence in these areas'. In other words, the EU will only support the actions of Member States and their laws will not take precedence over domestic laws in these areas.

In addition to these three competences the EU has competence in respect of economic, employment, and social policy (Article 2(3) TFEU) and a common foreign and security policy (Article 2(4)). The latter, in particular, demonstrates the fact that the pillar structure adopted by the MT has been superseded and that the EU now has general competence in these areas, subject to opt-outs negotiated by various countries.

It has been stated that, 'the Treaty of Lisbon distinguishes between the existence of competence...and the use of such competence, which is determined by subsidiarity and proportionality' (Craig (2008) 149). Subsidiarity is explained by Article 5(3) TEU which states that save where a matter is within the exclusive competence of the EU, the EU can only act where it is satisfied that 'the objectives of the proposed action cannot be sufficiently achieved by the Member States....[but can] be better achieved at Union level'. This is limiting the circumstances under which the EU can act outside of situations where it has exclusive jurisdiction and it is notable that the TL has given additional power to national Parliaments in assessing subsidiarity (see Articles 4 and 6 of Protocol 2 to the TFEU on the application of the principles of subsidiarity and proportionality). National Parliaments will be consulted on draft legislation and where, within eight weeks of receiving the draft legislation, it believes that it does not comply with the principle of subsidiarity it may notify the Presidents of the European Parliament, Council, and Commission a reasoned opinion stating why it does not believe that it complies. Such notifications must be taken into account (Article 7, Protocol 2 TFEU) and where at least one-third of all votes allocated to National Parliaments question whether the draft legislation complies with subsidiarity then the relevant institution must formally review the institution.

4.3.2 The institutions

In order to understand how the EU operates it will be necessary to consider its institutions. Article 13 TEU lists the following as institutions of the EU:

- the European Parliament
- the European Council
- the Council
- the European Commission
- the Court of Justice of the European Union
- the European Central Bank
- the Court of Auditors.

It is not necessary to consider all of these institutions since they do not all act as a source of law. For example, the *European Central Bank* will not be considered since although it is, for the first time as a result of TL, an institution it has limited law-making powers of relevance to the English Legal System. It is also notable that the Bank retains its independence and legal personality (Love (2010) 12). The *Lisbon Treaty* also allows for the creation of a *European Prosecutor's Office* (Article 86 TFEU) although this has not yet occurred and accordingly it will not be discussed in this book.

4.3.2.1 The European Parliament

The European Parliament is to an extent a relatively recent addition, with the initial legislative consultancy body simply being drawn from representatives of the individual legislatures of the Member States. The *Single European Act* (discussed above at 4.3.1.1) attempted to make the legislature more democratic and the European Parliament was, for the first time, composed of representatives elected by direct universal suffrage. Its members, known as Members of the European Parliament (MEPs), hold office for a fixed period of five years although they can be re-elected.

Unlike constituencies in the Westminster Parliament which are based on population, the same is not necessarily true of the European Parliament. Each Member State is allocated a number of seats and this differs according not only to the size of the country but also its importance. The TL has attempted to alter this slightly by adjusting the numbers slightly but there continues to be significant differences with, for example, the United Kingdom currently being allocated seventy-three seats (the largest grouping is Germany with ninety-nine seats) and, for example, Sweden being allocated only twenty seats. However, given the variances of population this can mean that the smaller countries do have proportionately better representation than the larger countries (Chalmers et al (2006) 111) but they may have less 'power' than the larger countries. Rather than sitting in national groupings the Parliament divides itself into transnational groupings that reflect the relevant political ethos of the group. Rule 30 of the *European Parliament's Rules for Procedure* dictate when a grouping is recognized. It must currently be a grouping of a minimum of twenty-five MEPs but that these must be representatives from at least one-quarter of the Member States (currently six Member States). Thus if thirty MEPs from five Member States wish to form a grouping this would not be formally recognized and would not, for example, receive staffing or resources beyond that given to individual MEPs.

One of the biggest controversies surrounding the European Parliament arises from where it conducts its business. Its 'official' home is Strasbourg but it also sits in Brussels, which is, in essence, the HQ of the EU. This leads to the rather ridiculous situation where meetings are held in two different cities and the MEPs, officials, and resultant paperwork have to shift between the two 'seats'. The expense and inconvenience this involves is frustrating to many and indeed it is believed that a significant number of MEPs would prefer to be based in Brussels where the other institutions are to be found. However, the location can only be changed with the unanimous agreement of the Council of Ministers and this is unlikely to be forthcoming in the immediate future.

The European Parliament cannot be directly compared to a national Parliament since it forms only one part of the legislature (the other being the European Council). Until the TL the powers of the Parliament were somewhat limited but the TL greatly increased the powers of the Parliament, with it being described as an 'institutional winner' (Craig (2008) 156). Prior to the TL the European Parliament was to an extent inferior to the European Council but they now act primarily on an equal basis. However, the Parliament does not, unlike the Westminster Parliament, have the right to initiate legislation (this being primarily the preserve of the Commission). Article 225 TEU allows the Parliament, by a simple majority, to request the Commission to submit a proposal for legislation but the Commission need not do so, it merely needing to explain to the Parliament why it has failed to do so should it decide not to bring forward any legislation.

Parliament has three principal roles. The first is the participation in the legislative process. The second is its scrutiny of the budget and the third is to supervise the Commission. It also has additional political powers in that it can conduct investigations or hearings into appropriate matters. Its final power is that the Parliament must approve the admission of new Member States (Article 49 TEU).

The Parliament's power to scrutinize legislation is perhaps its most important power. Originally this power was simply to be consulted on legislation and its views could be disregarded. However, the TL has significantly increased the power of the Parliament and it is now involved in the passing of most legislation. The legislative process of the EU is divided into two classes of procedure; the 'ordinary legislative procedure' and the 'special legislative procedure'.

Ordinary legislative procedure

This was, until the TL renamed it, known as the co-decision procedure. Its renaming reflects the fact that the TL has expanded the authority of Parliament into almost all areas of competence and that, in essence, the Parliament and European Council are almost on an equal footing. The ordinary procedure is premised on the basis that Commission legislation only becomes law if it and the Council agree. The stages are as follows (see Article 294):

1. The Commission submits a proposal to the European Parliament and the Council.

First reading

2. The European Parliament adopts its position and communicates this to the Council.

3. If the Council agrees with the position adopted by the Parliament then the relevant act shall be adopted in the wording that corresponds to the position of the European Parliament.

4. If the Council disagrees with the Parliament's position then it adopts its own position, communicates that to Parliament, and states why it adopts the position it does and the Commission indicates what its position is.

Second reading

5. Within three months of receiving a communication from the Council it can:
   (a) approve the position of Council or, if the Parliament fails to adopt a position, it will be deemed to be adopted in the wording of the Council;
   (b) reject the position of the Council by absolute majority (in which case the proposed act is deemed not to have been adopted);
   (c) propose amendments to the Council's position (by absolute majority) in which case the amendment shall be forwarded to the Council and the Commission.

6. Where the Council receives a communication from the Parliament (5(c) above) then acting by a qualified majority (see below) the Council can:
   (a) approve the amendments made by the Parliament, in which case the legislation is adopted;
   (b) disapprove of the amendments, in which case the matter should be referred to a Conciliation Committee.

Conciliation committee

7. A conciliation committee shall be constituted (including equal numbers of members of the Council and the European Parliament) which shall have the task of reaching an agreement on a joint text within six weeks of it being constituted.

8. The Commission shall participate in the committee (although not be a formal party to it) and shall endeavour to bring the parties together on an agreed text.

9. If, within six weeks of being constituted, the parties do not agree a text then the legislative act is deemed not to be adopted.

Third reading

10. If an agreed text is adopted by the conciliation committee then the Parliament, acting by simple majority, and the Council, acting by a qualified majority, shall each have a period of six weeks to accept the text. If they fail to do so then the measure is deemed to be not adopted.

Whilst this is quite a complicated provision it can be seen that it does give the Parliament power to reject most legislation since there are a number of stages where proposed legislation is considered not to be adopted. This marks a significant difference from the previous position whereby for a significant amount of legislation Parliament could, in essence, merely criticize but not block it. It has been remarked that the co-decision procedure (which, in essence, this is) has broadly worked and allows for a proper balance to be given to state (Council) views and citizens (Parliament).

➲ ABSOLUTE MAJORITY

Normally when votes (in any institution) are taken a majority is deemed to be where at least one more vote is cast than the opposing votes. For example, if there are one hundred voters all of whom vote then a majority would be fifty-one. However, if nineteen people abstain (ie decide not to vote) or are not present for the vote then a majority would arise with forty-one as the maximum number of opposing votes would be forty.

An absolute majority, however, is where the number is fixed as at least one more vote than the total number of eligible voters. There are currently 736 MEPs all of whom are entitled to a vote. A majority arises when 369 votes are cast on one side (as only a maximum of 367 votes could be cast in opposition). However, this figure remains regardless of how many people actually vote. Accordingly if 100 MEPs are absent then to carry a resolution, 369 votes still need to be passed even though this equates to 58 per cent of MEPs present voting for the proposition. In essence it is a 'safety net' to ensure that certain powers are exercised only when a true majority of MEPs are in favour of the result.

Special legislative procedure

The second procedure is that known as the 'special legislative procedure'. This procedure is restricted to those areas where the Treaty expressly states that the ordinary procedure is not to be used (see Article 289 TFEU). In these circumstances it is possible that either the Parliament or the Council will have the right to approve the legislation in consultation with the other (although such consultation is more than a mere formality: consideration should be given to its responses (*Roquette Frères v Council* [1980] ECR 3333). Where the Council has the right to approve the legislation then the Parliament has no right of veto and can, in essence, merely make comments as to its own views. Few areas continue to adopt the special legislative procedure although the consultation procedure applies to taxation, competition, and the harmonization of legislation not related to the internal market.[3]

❓ QUESTION FOR REFLECTION

A principal aim of the *Lisbon Treaty* was to increase democratic accountability. Does the Parliament realistically have any teeth in legislative scrutiny? It does not have the right to legislate itself and only has the 'nuclear' option of vetoing legislation rather than demanding that individual amendments be accepted. For example, if in a twenty-section Regulation it objects to one section of it, does it decide to veto the entire Regulation or does it give way on the basis it likes the other nineteen?

---

3. *Fact Sheet: How the European Union Works* (<www.europarl.europa.eu/parliament/expert>).

Could Parliament's powers be increased to allow amendment of individual sections? What would the implications of this be? How do you think the Council of Ministers would react given that national interest is perhaps easier to control in a Committee of twenty-seven rather than a Parliament of 736.

🎧 LISTEN TO THE PODCAST

For guidance on how to answer this question and a discussion of the main issues, listen to the author's podcast on the Online Resource Centre: www.oxfordtextbooks.co.uk/orc/gillespie_els3e/

Supervision of the executive

Perhaps one of the most important functions of the European Parliament is to assist in holding the European Commission, as the EU's executive, to account. The Commission is not part of the Parliament (and in this way can be distinguished from the Westminster Parliament where the executive and legislature consist of the same people) but will frequently be involved in giving evidence to parliamentary committees considering evidence etc. Thus Parliament can question the Commission and consider the reasoning behind appropriate legislation and, in defined circumstances, veto the legislation.

Article 239 TFEU makes clear that the Commission has a legal responsibility to answer questions put to it by MEPs and this includes written questions. Accordingly, this creates another method by which Parliament may hold the Commission to account not least because most questions and answers will be publicly reported. An important extension of the TL was that approval of the budget is based on the ordinary legislative process (Article 314 TFEU) and therefore the Parliament now has considerable power over the proposed budget since it has a number of opportunities to reject it (for a further discussion see Love (2010) 8).

The European Parliament has the right to approve the appointment of the Commission. The President of the Commission is now elected by the European Parliament (Article 14(1) TEU) although this is slightly limited by Article 17(7) TEU, which states that the European Council, acting by a qualified majority (see below), proposes to the Parliament the candidate for President. The Parliament can then approve the appointment by absolute majority and if the candidate fails then the Council must propose a new candidate. Reference to 'new candidate' in Article 17(7) would suggest that it is not open to the European Council to suggest the same person. The Parliament does not have the right to consider individual commissioners (whose appointment is a matter for the Council: see Article 17(7) TEU) but the Commission as a whole is responsible to Parliament via the power of censure.

The European Parliament has the right to censure the Commission. The arithmetic required for such a censure is slightly complicated. The motion must be passed by a two-thirds majority of those MEPs present in the chamber but they must account for a simple majority of the total number of MEPs. If the motion is carried then the entire Commission must resign (Article 234 TFEU).

A simple majority of the total number of MEPs means in essence an absolute majority of MEPs, ie 369. In reality, this means that for a vote to be carried will require a high proportion of the vote to be carried. For example, if there are only 650 MEPs in the chamber then if 370 voted for the motion of censure (an absolute majority) the motion would fail because the 370 votes only equates to 56 per cent of those present.

In order to pass it would require 434 votes to be cast, 64 votes higher than the absolute majority. This is a safeguard to ensure that any vote of censure is only passed in circumstances when it can be ascertained that Parliament as a whole truly wishes to pass the measure.

 Example Edith Cresson

Although the European Parliament has never exercised its powers to dismiss the European Commission it came close to doing so in 1999 and de facto exercised its powers. The European Parliament was angered by the actions of Edith Cresson, a former French prime minister, who was a European commissioner and who had been accused of financial mismanagement and appointing unqualified friends to influential posts.

The European Parliament called on Ms Cresson to resign, something she refused to do. The Parliament had no authority to sack just Ms Cresson and a series of heated discussions and enquiries followed culminating in a vote of censure. Eventually the whole of the EU Commission resigned although the vast majority were automatically reappointed, in part because the Parliament has no power to reject individual commissioners.

Ms Cresson led to further infamy when she became the first commissioner to be stripped of her diplomatic immunity held as a result of being a commissioner. The Commission, on the initiative of Belgium, investigated her for alleged fraud offences although the ECJ ultimately decided not to punish her.

Article 226 TFEU allows the Parliament, where one-quarter of its members so request, an ad hoc Committee of Inquiry to be created that will have the power to examine any alleged contraventions or maladministration of Union law save where the matter is currently being examined by a court (so as to ensure that there is no impact on the fairness of such proceedings). However, the Parliament's powers extend only to the publication of a report as to its findings and not any power to order correction. This system is based on the premise that a negative report would be embarrassing although the effectiveness of this strategy could be questioned when one notes the position that exists in respect of the Court of Auditors (discussed below).

4.3.2.2 The European Council

Confusingly, the TEU lists two institutions that sound similar; the *European Council* and *The Council*. 'The Council' is sometimes referred to as the '*Council of the European Union*' although it is notable that Article 13 TEU does not refer to it in this way. 'The Council' will be discussed below (4.3.2.3) but is a member of the legislature and acts in conjunction with the Parliament (discussed above). The 'European Council' is different, it is a body that comprises the Heads of State or government of each Member State together with the President of the Council and the President of the Commission (Article 15(2) TEU). It only became a formal institution as a result of TL, before that it had an unofficial political existence. The President of the European Council is elected separately by the Council itself using qualified majority voting (see below) and holds office for a term of two and a half years renewable once (Article 15(5) TEU). The move towards a 'permanent' President of the European Council was a major shift from the previous position where the presidency would rotate between the Member States every six months, with the Head of State or government becoming President. It has been suggested that the permanent presidency will allow an individual to develop a wider vision of the EU (Craig (2008) 152).

The European Council must meet twice every six months when convened by its President (Article 15(3) TEU) and its work can be assisted by ministers or commissioners. The European Council is charged with a number of matters but perhaps two of its most important charges are quite generic. The first is, 'The European Council shall provide the Union with the necessary impetus for its development and shall define the general political directions and priorities thereof' (Article 15(1) TEU) and the second is Article 222(4) TFEU which requires the European Council to 'regularly assess the threats facing the Union in order to enable the Union and its Member States to take effective action'. Clearly therefore, the European Council is an important institution not least because it represents the ultimate executive authority for each Member State. It is also clear that the European Council is principally a political body and one that is charged with taking the necessary political steps to facilitate the work. It has no legislative authority (Article 15(1) TEU).

The European Council will have certain policy matters reserved to it, for example, Article 68 TFEU states, 'The European Council shall define the strategic guidelines for legislative and operational planning within the area of freedom, security and justice'. Also numerous other aspects of the Treaties require matters of dispute to be referred to the European Council. Again, this is a pragmatic decision as it means that where there is dispute between Member States it can be resolved by the heads of government. The Council should ordinarily act by consensus (Article 15(4) TEU) which must mean unanimity. However, there are a number of issues within the Treaty that require decisions to be taken by qualified majority (a system discussed below).

4.3.2.3 Council

The second of the two 'Councils' is 'The Council' which is also referred to as either the *Consilium* or the '*Council of the European Union*' and was previously known as the '*Council of Ministers*' although in the TEU and TFEU it is simply referred to as '*The Council*'. Whilst the European Council is a member of the executive and acts on a policy level, the Council is a member of the legislature (it sharing legislative power with the European Parliament (Article 16(1) TEU)).

The Council is established by a representative of each Member State who is of ministerial level (Article 16(2) TEU) and so it is a council of ministers. However, it would be wrong to say that there is a single representative since the actual representation will depend on what is being discussed, this compromise being defined as the Council sitting in different 'configurations'. Accordingly, if, for example, the Council is discussing foreign affairs then the minister will be drawn from the foreign office for each state (which may not be the Foreign Secretary but may be a junior minister depending on the importance of the matter) and if it is discussing the agricultural policy then the minister will be drawn from the department of agriculture. The Presidency of the Council rotates every six months in the way that the European Council did until a permanent President was appointed.

As noted above, the Council operates as the second part of the legislature and ordinarily legislation must be passed by both it and the European Parliament. The method by which legislation is passed was discussed above when considering the European

Parliament (4.3.2.1) and reference should be made to that. The Council's own website states that, in addition to its legislative and budgetary competence, it has the following roles:

- to coordinate the broad economic policies of the Member States
- to define and implement the EU's common foreign and security policy (based on the guidance set by the European Council)
- to conclude, on behalf of the Union, international agreements between the EU and other states or organizations
- to coordinate the actions of the Member States and adopt measures in the area of police and judicial cooperation in criminal matters.[4]

Voting

Perhaps the most controversial aspect of the Council is how it votes. The Council would traditionally act on the basis of consensus but increasingly this became untenable since it meant that the smaller states could, in essence, 'veto' policies or legislation even when the measure was necessary for the good of the EU. As the EU expanded this became increasingly problematic and although some decisions were taken by a simple majority this was considered unfair by the larger states who argued that it could mean that a coalition of the smaller states could block initiatives of the larger states. Accordingly, some measures require decisions to be taken by qualified majority, indeed one of the impacts of the TL is that it has widened the number of instances where decisions can be taken by a qualified majority (see Article 16(3) TEU, which states that all decisions shall be taken by qualified majority save where a Treaty says otherwise). It was noted that identifying precisely how votes would be calculated was one of the most controversial aspects of the Treaty negotiations (Craig (2008) 154).

Perhaps unsurprisingly the actual voting arrangements are somewhat complicated and it is subject to change. The existing arrangement is contained within Protocol 36 of the TFEU. Each Member State is accorded a weighted vote (see Table 4.1 below). A vote is passed if there are at least 255 weighted votes in favour *and* this accounts for at least two-thirds of the Member States. The total number of weighted votes is 345 meaning that 255 accounts for 74 per cent of the votes cast. The weighting of votes and the requirement for a minimum threshold of population acts as a balance to the power of the large countries, who would otherwise be able to push matters through. The actual weighted votes is based on more than just population since, for example, Spain has 27 votes and yet accounts for only 9 per cent of the population whereas Germany has 29 votes and has 16 per cent of the population.

From 2014 (until 2017) Article 16(4) states that a qualified majority requires two elements:

- 55 per cent of the members of the Council; and
- that 55 per cent accounts for at least 15 Member States who account for at least 65 per cent of the population of the Union.

In other words it is not sufficient that 15 Member States take a vote (15 Member States would currently constitute 55 per cent of the members of the Council) since if those 15 Member States were from the smaller countries then they would not be able to pass the

---

4. <www.consilium.europa.eu>.

Table 4.1 Weighted votes of each Member State

Austria	10	Lithuania	7
Belgium	12	Luxembourg	4
Bulgaria	10	Hungary	12
Czech Republic	12	Malta	3
Denmark	7	Netherlands	14
Germany	29	Poland	27
Estonia	4	Portugal	12
Ireland	7	Romania	14
Greece	12	Slovenia	4
Spain	27	Slovakia	7
France	29	Finland	7
Italy	29	Sweden	10
Cyprus	4	United Kingdom	29
Latvia	4		

additional test that the majority must account for at least 65 per cent of the EU. This continues to mean that the larger states will be important as smaller states will need to form alliances with the larger states so as to ensure that the measure is passed. However, an additional complication is that Article 16(4) TEU states that a 'blocking minority' must constitute at least four Council members. This latter takes a little explanation. Let us assume that at least 55 per cent of the Council votes for a particular measure and that this 55 per cent comprised of 24 Member States but that Germany, the United Kingdom, and Spain disagreed with the measure. The combined population of those 24 Member States would only amount to 62 per cent and so the measure should fail. However, Article 16(4) TEU requires the minority to account for at least four Council states and thus the 'block' would not be effective and, according to Article 16(4) the measure should be passed irrespective.

The procedure will change after 2017 and there are also some exceptions to this rule contained within Article 238 TFEU.

4.3.2.4 European Commission

The European Commission is arguably the most powerful of the institutions and prior to the recognition of the European Council as an institution it formed the sole executive of the EU (now it forms the executive alongside the European Council and it is arguably the more powerful of the two). The size of the Commission is controversial (Craig (2008) 155) and currently amounts to one member (commissioners, President, and the High Representative for Foreign Affairs) per country (Article 17(4) TEU). This position will continue until 2014 and afterwards the Commission will number the same as two-thirds of the Member States (currently 27 so it would number 18) unless the European Council decides unanimously to alter this number (Article 17(5) TEU). The members will be adopted on 'a strictly equal rotation between the Member States, reflecting the geographical range of all the Member States' (Article 17(5) TEU). This will mean that the larger countries could, for the first time, lose 'their' commissioner and it will be interesting to see whether this new system comes into effect (Fairhurst states that the European Council is committed to retaining the 'old' system due to commitments given to Ireland (Fairhurst (2010) 93) although the European Council has yet to act on this).

The President of the Commission is now elected by the Council and European Parliament and this was discussed above. The President allocates the 'portfolios' of each commissioner (Article 17(6) TEU) although the President is likely to consult national governments as part of their campaign for election. The creation of a President has also transformed the way in which commissioners can be dismissed. Whilst individual commissioners are able to resign it has traditionally been difficult for them to be removed. However, the TL has altered this position to a certain extent and the President of the Commission is now able to ask an individual commissioner to resign (Article 17(6) TEU). Assuming the President does not do this then the powers of dismissal are limited.

The Court of Justice of the EU has jurisdiction to order the compulsory retirement of a commissioner where he or she 'no longer fulfils the conditions required for the performance of his duties or if he is guilty of serious misconduct' (Article 247 TFEU). This jurisdiction is exercised by the ECJ sitting *en banc* and has never happened. The second method of effective dismissal is where the Commission is required to resign *en masse* if the European Parliament passes a vote of censure passed under Article 234 TFEU (see Article 17(8) TEU). The passing of a motion of censure was discussed above when considering the European Parliament (4.3.2.1).

Whilst Commission members are drawn from the Member States, Article 17(3) TEU makes clear that they are independent of the Member States and must operate on behalf of the EU and not take instructions from the government or other national body. Their term of office is for five years although they can be reappointed. The primary duties of the Commission is summarized in Article 17(1) TEU:

> The Commission shall promote the general interest of the Union and take appropriate initiatives to that end. It shall ensure the application of the Treaties, and of measures adopted by the institutions pursuant to them. It shall oversee the application of Union law under the control of the Court of Justice of the European Union. It shall execute the budget and manage programmes. It shall exercise coordinating, executive and management functions, as laid down in the Treaties...

Article 17(2) TEU expressly notes that the ability to initiate legislation is vested solely with the Commission unless the Treaties say otherwise. This is what provides authority for the Commission to be the key instigator of policy and legislative instruments. Arguably this is one of its more important functions and whilst it shares policy with the European Council, a considerable amount of policy remains with the Council.

An important role of the Commission is to ensure compliance with the Treaties. The Commission is able to take action against Member States where it believes that it is in breach of its applications (Article 258 TFEU). It is also able, in some parts of Union law, to take action against individual private companies that act in a way incompatible with the internal market (Articles 101 and 102 TFEU).

> **Example** Microsoft
>
> One of the biggest examples of the Commission taking action against a private body is its action against Microsoft. The Commission considered that Microsoft had been acting in such a way as to abuse its dominant position in the market, particularly in respect of the way that it 'bundled' software on new computers (for a useful history of this read Vezzoso (2006)).
>
> The Commission required Microsoft to cease its anti-competitive practices and when it believed that it had failed to do so it issued a fine of €280 million.

4.3.2.5 The Court of Justice of the European Union

The TL has altered the judicial branch of the EU. Prior to the TL there were two courts; the *Court of First Instance* (CFI) and the *European Court of Justice* (ECJ). The TL altered this and Article19(1) TEU creates a new institution, the *Court of Justice of the European Union*, which will be comprised of the *Court of Justice* (what was the ECJ), the *General Court* (what was the CFI), and *specialized courts* which is, in essence, a specialist tribunal that deals with matters relating to the Civil Service. All the courts are based in Luxembourg (Protocol 6 TFEU) and are thus separate from the political and legislative offices of Brussels and Strasbourg.

The Court of Justice (CJ) is constituted of one judge from each Member State (Article 19(2) TEU) and it is assisted by eight Advocates-General (see below). It is notable that Article 19(2) TEU states that the General Court (GC) shall be constituted of 'at least' one judge per Member State, meaning that in some instances more than one judge can be sent (although currently the number is capped at 27: see Article 48 of Protocol 3 TFEU). This is in part a reflection on the changing nature of the GC and its increased workload, especially due to the expansion of Member States. Both the judges and Advocates-General (A-G) of the Court of Justice must be qualified for the appointment to 'the highest judicial offices in their respective countries' (Article 253 TFEU) which, in the context of England and Wales, means the same qualification as a puisne judge (discussed in Chapter 7). The judges are appointed for a (renewable) term of six years although their appointment is staggered so that there is a partial replacement every three years (thus ensuring that the CJ does not lose all of its experienced judges at the same time). The judges themselves elect one of their own number as their President. Article 254 TFEU provides comparable requirements for the judges and A-G of the GC. Accordingly, they are appointed for (renewable) terms of six years and must possess the necessary qualification for high judicial office.

> **ADVOCATE-GENERAL**
>
> Advocates-General have no comparable counterparts within the United Kingdom, with their closest comparison being an *amicus curiae* (friend of the court, ie counsel appointed separate from the parties to put forward a neutral argument or one in the public interest. It is not unusual for the *amicus* to be the Attorney-General).
>
> Article 252 TFEU makes clear that the role of the Advocate-General is 'to make, in open court, reasoned submissions on cases which...require his involvement'. In other words, the Advocate-General will read the written submissions of both parties and provide an independent viewpoint to the ECJ on what it believes the law is.

Although the ECJ is not bound in any way by the opinion of the Advocate-General it normally carries with it significant weight and it will, in fact, frequently be followed (Fairhurst (2010) 155) and thus the opinion of the Advocate-General can often be an early clue to the parties when identifying how the court is likely to rule.

The appointment of judges and A-G are generally for the Member States but, interestingly, the TL creates a partial appointments commission. Article 255 TFEU creates an ad hoc panel of seven persons 'chosen from among members of the Court of Justice and the General Court, members of national supreme courts and lawyers of recognized competence, one of whom shall be proposed by the European Parliament'. The Council is responsible for the creation and operation of this panel and its purpose is to give an 'opinion on candidates' suitability to perform the duties of Judge and Advocate-General. There is no reference to any power of veto: they may simply discuss their suitability but presumably a negative opinion would be politically embarrassing and thus a Member State may choose to withdraw its candidate although it would seem that it is under no obligation to do so. All judges must swear a judicial oath prior to taking up office (Article 2 of Protocol 3 TFEU).

Court of Justice

The Court of Justice has the power to review decisions of the General Court (Article 256(1) TFEU) and, accordingly, it acts as an appellate court to the GC although this power is exercisable only in respect of points of law.

Article 251 states that the Court of Justice will sit in chambers, a Grand Chamber or, when set out in Statute, a full court. Protocol 3 to the TFEU provides for a 'Statute on the Court of Justice of the European Union', which, in essence, provides further details on how it shall operate. Chambers will ordinarily be divided into divisions of three and five judges (Article 16 of Protocol 3 TFEU) and each chamber will elect one of their number as President. A Grand Chamber shall consist of thirteen judges (Article 16 of Protocol 3) and is presided over by the President of the Court. A matter is heard by a Grand Chamber whenever a Member State or an EU institution so requests it. The full court is heard only when in specific circumstances or where the Court or A-G considers that it raises such a serious point that it should be heard by the full court. Confusingly, whilst the full court should mean that it sits *en banc* (ie all twenty-seven judges) Article 17 of Protocol 3 states that a full court will be quorate with only fifteen judges sitting. The same provision states that a Grand Chamber (which should consist of thirteen judges) is quorate if nine judges sit.

Article 20 of Protocol 3 states that a procedure before the Court of Justice shall consist of two parts: the written part and the oral part. The written procedure involves the usual discovery together with communications from the parties as to the merits of their arguments. The oral procedure involves the reading of documents, the arguments of the lawyers, and any witnesses. Ordinarily the A-G would give a submission as to the law (see above) but Article 20 of Protocol 3 allows the Court to rule that no submission is required so long as it hears from the A-G about whether he should make a submission.

Protocol 3 makes a series of references to witnesses and evidence on oath. The broad effect of these rules is that the Court of Justice has the same power of compulsion as a court of a Member State and that a failure to attend is punishable as though it were a failure to attend a court of the Member State. Similar rules apply to testimony and, in particular, false testimony so that the false testimony by a British citizen at the Court of Justice in Luxembourg would be punishable as perjury in the courts of England.

General Court

According to Article 256 TFEU the General Court has jurisdiction to determine first-instance actions or proceedings under Articles 263, 265, 268, 270, and 272 unless they are expressly reserved by Treaty to the Court of Justice. It also has jurisdiction to hear appeals against the decisions of the specialized courts. It also has a limited role in respect of preliminary rulings under Article 267 (see Article 256(3) TFEU) although most Article 267 rulings will be heard by the Court of Justice (see the discussion at 4.3.4.3).

Whilst the General Court does have an A-G it is notable that Article 49 of Protocol 3 TFEU states that judges of the General Court can be asked to perform the task of an A-G. The duty of an A-G is the same as with the Court of Justice, ie to provide an independent assessment on the merits of the case. Article 50 of Protocol 3 states that the General Court should sit in chambers of three and five and that each chamber shall elect its own President, but the Article also provides that in some instances it is possible that work of the Court can be exercised by a single judge.

Language

Although it will use any of the official languages of the Court, its official working language for historical reasons is French. That said, where a Member State is a defendant in a case then the proceedings must be heard in that state's official language. As French is the official language, the definitive judgment is produced in French although it will ordinarily be transcribed into the parties' natural language and ordinarily an English version will also be produced.

4.3.2.6 Court of Auditors

The last institution to consider is the Court of Auditors. As it acts as only a limited source of law it is mentioned here only very briefly. Article 285 TFEU states that that it shall be responsible for carrying out the Union's audit and that it shall be comprised of a national from each of the Member States. Article 286 TFEU requires the members to be suitably qualified to perform an external audit and they act for a (renewable) term of six years (Article 286(2) TFEU). They themselves elect a President who holds office for a (renewable) term of three years.

A member of the Court of Auditor can only be removed by the Court of Justice of the European Union when it finds that he no longer meets the requisite conditions or meets the obligations of his office (Article 286(6) TFEU). In essence this means that the members have independence of office and only where the Court of Justice finds the members have acted in a manner equivalent to corruption can they be removed from office.

The effectiveness of the Court of Auditors has been the subject of some debate. Under Article 287(1) TFEU it has to examine all accounts of the revenue and expenditure of the Union and must provide the European Parliament and Council with a 'statement of assurance as to the reliability of the accounts and the legality and regularity of the underlying transactions'. Prior to 2008 the Court had never certified the accounts as being fair and accurate although the Commission questioned the belief that this meant that, as some sections of the media reported, that corruption was rife.[5] Instead the Commission argued it was because the standards were too high in that any qualification, irrespective of how minor this was, meant that the accounts could not be fully certified. In 2008 the Court of Auditors issued an 'unqualified (clean) opinion on the reliability of the 2008 EU accounts'.[6]

4.3.3 Sources of EU law

Now that the Institutions have been explained it is necessary to turn our attention to the sources of law. After discussing these sources it will be necessary to consider what impact they have on the law of England and Wales (see 4.3.4). To an extent this section will be considered relatively simple as it is likely that you will receive further instruction on this when you study the law of the EU as a substantive topic on your law degree. Further information on this can also be found in EU textbooks.

The exact number of sources of law is open to debate. One commentator argues that there are three (treaties, legislation, and court decisions) (Weatherill (2010) 27) but others have suggested that there could be up to seven different sources (Fairhurst (2010) 56). To an extent this difference exists because of the position of the EU law in international law. The argument that there are seven includes the possibility that there are a number of sources of law that are commonly found in other international sources of law, eg 'soft' law etc. For our purposes it is really only necessary to consider the three that are identified by Weatherill.

4.3.3.1 Treaties

Arguably the most important source of EU law is the Treaties themselves. An explanation of the Treaties has been given already but it is notable that the TL has created a position whereby the Treaties have now been consolidated into two of relevance, those being the TEU and the TFEU. These treaties are the most important sources and can be classified as the primary source of law for the EU. This includes the protocols to the Treaty, which include, for example, reference as to how the courts work (eg Protocol 3 of the TFEU) and what measures countries have opt-outs for (eg Protocols 15–18 and 20–22).

The TEU and TFEU are automatically binding on all Member States as part of their accession to the EU (save where they have negotiated an opt-out to particular issues: eg the United Kingdom has declined to participate in those areas that relate to freedom, security, and justice: see Protocol 21 TFEU).

Separate to the TEU and TFEU are treaties that are concluded between the EU and another state/organization. This is not a treaty concluded by the individual countries *within* the EU and another country as that would just be an ordinary bilateral treaty. Instead, the EU as a legal entity in its own right has the authority to enter treaties in respect of certain matters and when it does so the Member States are bound to give effect to it as though they have signed it themselves.

Charter of Fundamental Rights

An interesting issue that arises is in respect of the *Charter of Fundamental Rights*. This was originally a stand-alone document agreed in 2000 that was not intended to

---

5. <http://ec.europa.eu/budget/sound_fin_mgt/myths_facts_other_en.htm>.
6. Court of Auditors Press Release 2009/11/10. ECA/09/67.

be legally binding (Fairhurst (2010) 32). A declaration annexed to the *Treaty of Nice* announced that there would be a review as to the legal status of the Charter and this has occurred with it becoming fully incorporated into EU law, with Article 6(1) TEU stating, 'The Union recognises the rights, freedoms and principles set out in the Charter of Fundamental Rights of the European Union....which shall have the same legal value as the Treaties'. Accordingly, the Charter becomes an essential part of the jurisprudence of EU law, although it should be noted that it remains a separate document, it does not form part of either the TEU or TFEU although it has the same legal status. Whilst it is sometimes said that the UK and Poland are not bound by the Charter this is not strictly true since, as noted above, it forms part of the general principles of EU law. Instead the UK has negotiated a 'clarification' of the application of the Charter to it (Protocol 30 TFEU). Article 1 of this Protocol states that it does not extend the ability of the Court of Justice of the EU or any domestic court to decide that the laws or practices of the United Kingdom is inconsistent with the fundamental rights and freedoms and Article 2 states that the Charter applies only to those rights or principles that are recognized by UK law. Quite what the effect of this Protocol is remains questionable. The Charter itself suggests that it does not provide any authority to the ECJ to find that national laws are inconsistent with the rights contained within the Charter. The second Article is also of questionable merit since it, in essence, allows the ECJ to decide what is, or is not, recognized in UK law (for a further discussion see Craig (2008) 163).

European Convention on Human Rights

Article 6(3) TEU states that the *European Convention on Human Rights* shall constitute general principles of the EU law. It will be seen that signing the ECHR is a prerequisite for membership of the EU but the TEU makes clear that the Convention is part of the ordinary law of the EU meaning that, for example, the Court of Justice could rule on whether the action of an institution is contrary to rights contained within the ECHR.

4.3.3.2 Legislation

The EU produces legislation and it was noted above that the Council and Parliament act as the legislatures although only the Commission has the right to initiate legislation. Some students will try to 'map' the legislation of the EU onto the legislation in England and Wales to find comparators but realistically this is impossible to do. EU legislation has its own formulation and it is better not to try to consider it analogous to any other form of legislative act. All EU legislation is delegated to the extent that, as will be seen, the right to enact legislation derives from the Treaties and the legislation cannot be incompatible with the Treaties. The discussion on competences (4.3.1.3 above) is important here. It will be remembered that the TEU states what the EU has competence over and accordingly if it does not have competence then it may not act and, it follows, may not pass legislation in respect of this.

Article 288 TFEU states that there are three forms of legislation: regulations, directives, and decisions. The effects of these are different and are set out within Article 288.

> A regulation shall have general application. It shall be binding in its entirety and directly applicable in all Member States.
>
> A directive shall be binding, as to the result to be achieved, upon each Member State to which it is addressed, but shall leave to the national authorities the choice of forms and methods.

A decision shall be binding in its entirety. A decision which specifies those to whom it is addressed shall be binding only on them.

In addition to these forms are opinions and recommendations (which may be given by the Council or Commission) but these are not binding and are merely advisory, although they may be taken into account by the Court of Justice of the European Union.

It is not always clear which form of legislation should be used. Sometimes the Treaties themselves will make clear which form to take. For example, Article 46 TFEU governs the freedom of movement for workers and it states that the European Parliament and Council may issue legislation through either regulations or directives. Accordingly, the Parliament and Council can decide which form to pass in respect of a measure relating to Article 46 but could not, for example, issue a decision. Sometimes there is no choice. For example, Article 50 TFEU relates to the freedom of establishment as regards economic activity and it states that the European Parliament and Council may make directives to secure this. Accordingly, a measure designed to support Article 50 could only be legislated by directive. Where the Treaty is silent as to which form of legislation should be used then it is up to the institution sponsoring the legislation to decide which form to adopt (Article 296 TFEU). Interestingly, it has been held that it is the substance of the legislation that decides what form it takes and not its label. So, if for example, the Commission issues legislation that it states is a regulation but its substance would appear more akin to a directive then the ECJ can alter its status (see *International Fruit Company v Commission* [1971] ECR 411).

All legislation must be 'reasoned', ie the legislation itself must state what the legal basis for the action is. This includes a statement of which article of a treaty authorizes the legislation to be passed, together with cogent reasons as to why it is being made (Article 296 TFEU). This reasoning will include the objectives of the legislation, why it is necessary, who it is addressed to, and what steps must be taken to comply with the legislation. It is possible to use the reasoning as the basis of a judicial review of the legislation (*Germany v Commission* [1963] ECR 63 and see Fairhurst (2010) 147). All legislation must be published in the *Official Journal of the EU* (Article 297(1) TFEU) and enter force either on the date specified within the legislation or on the twentieth day following its publication.

Regulations

Regulations are arguably the strictest form of legislation. They are primarily issued by the Commission although they are now ordinarily subject to the ordinary legislative procedure (save where the Treaty states otherwise). Regulations are automatically binding on all Member States and they are of general application, ie they do not provide specific details of legislative purpose (Chalmers et al (2006) 133). As they are automatically binding on all Member States then the legislatures of the Member States need not take any executive or legislative action in order to ensure compliance: they form part of the law as soon as the regulation comes into force.

 Example Airline compensation

A good example of a regulation is Regulation 261/2004. This provided for common rules regarding compensation to be paid to air passengers whose flights were either cancelled or subject to long delays. The airline industry did not welcome this regulation although many passenger groups did. As a regulation it was directly effective and thus created an actionable right. During the summer of 2010 a volcanic explosion in Iceland caused widespread air travel disruption. Certain airlines, especially budget airlines, suggested that they would refuse to pay compensation as required by the Regulation because, in their opinion, it was not fair. The airlines, however, backed down when it was realized that the Regulation was automatically in force and the rights contained within it were legally binding.

Directives

Directives are probably the most frequent form of legislation passed by the EU and this position is likely to increase as, for example, legislation is passed in respect of matters relating to freedom and justice. A directive is only binding on the Member States that are mentioned in the directive although it is possible (and indeed usual) to list all the Member States in the directive. Whilst the directive will say what the purpose of the legislative act is and what the eventual aim is, it will leave the precise details of how this will be achieved to Member States (eg they could use primary or secondary legislation, amend existing or introduce new legislation). A directive will normally state how long (from the date when it comes into force) a Member State has to comply with the directive and a failure to legislate by this date will be actionable by the Commission (discussed above).

 Example Data protection

The European Commission issued Directive 95/46/EC which covered the protection of personal data. The UK government was (like those of all Member States) bound to implement this Directive, with the deadline being the end of 1998. The UK government had the choice of enforcement mechanisms and it decided that it would implement the Directive through the use of primary legislation. Accordingly the *Data Protection Act 1998* was passed which met the requirements of the Directive but also dealt with some purely domestic issues too.

Decisions

There used to be two forms of Decisions, those which were simply known as decisions (and which survive) and a second form known as a *Framework Decision* which was introduced by the Treaty of Amsterdam. These were similar to decisions but were instead collective decisions of the European Council and were designed to harmonize laws. They were primarily used in respect of third pillar business and the abolition of the pillar structure has meant that this form of legislation is no longer required and future work in this area will be undertaken by normal legislative means.

 Example Child protection

The European Union passed a Framework Decision on combatting the sexual exploitation of children and child pornography (2004/68/JHA). This was designed to harmonize the laws and to ensure there was a minimum level of protection. The EU had consulted on replacing this Framework Decision with a new Framework Decision but following the Treaty of Lisbon such legislation no longer exists and it currently intends to replace the Framework Decision with a directive (see Memo/10/107 of 29/3/2010). A directive was chosen on the basis that the EU wishes to set down a threshold for laws but wishes to leave the details to the Member States.[7]

Decisions need not be addressed to Member States but could instead be addressed to a particular institution or body within a Member State. Arguably this is most frequently found in respect of competition matters (Mathijsen (2004) 29) where the Commission may require an individual body to take particular action so as to ensure that they are not acting in an anti-competitive way. Decisions are generally used where the action sought is administrative or procedural rather that when the object is to harmonize the laws of any country (Chalmers et al (2006) 134).

4.3.3.3 Decisions of the Court of Justice of the European Union

One of the reasons why some students find EU law complicated is because the approach to case law is different in the EU than that adopted in England and Wales (a point judicially recognized by Lord Denning MR in *Bulmer v Bollinger* [1974] 3 WLR 202 which was one of the first cases in the appellate courts of England and Wales to look at EU law). It was noted in Chapter 3 that the system in England and Wales is based on the common-law approach and that *stare decisis* applies. The same approach is not taken by the Court of Justice. There is no 'common law' or residual power: the authority of the Court of Justice is based solely on the Treaties themselves and this is reinforced by the TL which expressly states that in the absence of any competence, the EU has no power to act (Article 4 TEU). That said, the Court has taken account of general principles such as natural justice (see, for example, *Hauer v Land Rheinland-Pfalz* [1980] 3 CMLR 42) and, of course, this has been expanded by the TL which has incorporated both the ECHR and *Charter of Human Rights* into the general jurisprudence of the EU. The Court of Justice does not operate a formal system of *stare decisis* although it will, so far as possible, try to act in a way that takes account of its previous decisions (Fairhurst (2010) 161).

From a constitutional perspective, the Court of Justice has considerably more powers of review than the courts in England and Wales. This includes not only the right to review any legislation but also the ability to strike down legislation that is incompatible with Community Law (Article 263 TFEU). It will be recalled from Chapter 2 that this is considerably more power than the courts in England and Wales have, a position that has not changed following the passing of the *Human Rights Act 1998* where a declaration of incompatibility will have no effect on the legal standing of an Act of Parliament (see 5.1.2.4).

Judgments

It is often said that the Court of Justice (including the General Court) will ordinarily give only a single judgment and this can be contrasted with, for example, the Supreme

---

7. As this is a matter relating to freedom, justice, and home affairs any directive will not be addressed to the UK (which has an opt-out on such matters) unless the UK asks to be brought within the directive.

Court of the UK where every judge may speak (although there is an increasing tendency in the Supreme Court to produce a single judgment). However this is not necessarily correct. Whilst the Court will *ordinarily* give a single judgment and possibly a single dissenting judgment (where it is not a unanimous decision) it is open to judges to produce individual *assenting* and *dissenting* judgments.

Judgments of the Courts are always reserved although the length of delay between the hearing and delivery of judgment will differ between the courts and the type of case, with some being expedited. The official languages of the court is French although it is customary to also use English and where a Member State is a party to the proceedings then the language of that state will be used. National modes are used for address and the dress of advocates. Accordingly, where a barrister from England and Wales is speaking in the court, the judges would be referred to as 'My Lords' and the barrister will be fully robed in wig, gown, bands, and collar. All judges of the courts will wear the same dress, which is a judicial robe with a single garment around the neck in place of where judicial bands would be worn by members of the English judiciary.

All judgments of the Courts are published in the *Official Journal* and an official law report series (comparable to *The Law Reports* in England and Wales) is also in existence, the series being known as ECR—*European Court Reports*. All judgments should be published in the official languages of the EU, which can occasionally raise issues about translation. Where there is any doubt then French is considered to be the definitive text and reference will be made to the French text. All judgments can also now be found on the Internet and the Online Resource Centre accompanying this book includes a link to judgments.

Interpretation

It is perhaps necessary briefly to consider how the courts interpret legislation. It was noted in Chapter 2 that England has a series of canons of interpretation (see 2.3) and similar rules apply to the Court of Justice of the EU. It has been suggested that there are four methods of interpretation adopted by the Court of Justice:

- literal
- historical
- contextual
- teleological (Fairhurst (2010) 163).

The literal approach is the same as that adopted by domestic courts: the relevant instrument is examined and simply given its ordinary meaning. Of course an interesting question that arises in Union law is which language should be used when deciding a literal interpretation? The meaning of words does differ amongst languages and the slight differences can be problematic. Unlike with English law there is no presumption that the literal rule is the 'ordinary' rule of statutory interpretation and indeed the Court has, in the past, refused to use the rule even where the wording of the instrument in question was clear (*Commission v Council* [1970] ECR 263). The historical approach has been likened to the mischief rule of interpretation (Fairhurt (2010) 164) and is rarely used but it does allow the Court to consider the preliminary debates to identify what the purpose of the instrument was.

The more common rules of interpretation are the contextual and teleological rules. Perhaps the classic definition of the contextual approach was given in the case of *Cilfit* [1982] ECR 3415, a case that will be examined below. In that case, the ECJ stated:

> ...every provision of Community law must be placed in its context and interpreted in the light of the provisions of the Community law as a whole, regard being had to the objectives thereof and to its State of evolution at the date on which the provision in question is to be applied (at [20]).

This is one of the reasons why legislation must be reasoned as it allows the Court to identify the context of the legislation. However, the latter part of the quote demonstrates that a legislative position need not be fixed and where the legislation is a directive this may be particularly true since there will be a period of time before Member States have actually (lawfully) complied with the directive.

The teleological interpretative method is similar to the contextual approach in that it is based on interpreting the instrument in a way that furthers the aims and objectives of the Union as a whole (Fairhurst (2010) 165). Accordingly the emphasis of the Court is, in many instances, less focused on what the words of the instrument are and more on how the Union's policy can be furthered. This is significantly different to how the English courts would interpret legislation.

 QUESTION FOR REFLECTION

Read the *Cilfit* case. At para 18 it was said:

> it must be borne in mind that Community legislation is drafted in several languages and that the different language versions are all equally authentic. An interpretation of a provision of Community law thus involves a comparison of the different language versions.

Is this realistic? How can a lawyer advising a client on a matter of EU law or even a domestic court applying the law (see below) properly consider multiple sources of law in different languages? Would it not be appropriate to limit the number of languages a document is produced in or even suggest that there is only a single authoritative version? One possible advantage of this is that there would be reduced scope for doubt as to the meaning of a word. A possible disadvantage is that each national court would presumably have to translate this meaning into its own language in any event so that the case can be adjudicated domestically. What further advantages and disadvantages may there be to such a proposal? How can the ECJ deal with conflicts between language?

4.3.4 Supremacy of EU law

Arguably the most controversial aspect of EU law to some in the United Kingdom is in respect of its supremacy. The notion of supremacy has already been discussed in this book and it was noted in Chapter 2 that Parliament considers itself supreme and can legislate in any way it sees fit. The Treaty however makes it clear that Member States are bound by EU law. Declaration 17 of the *Declarations annexed to the final act of the intergovernmental conference which adopted the Treaty of Lisbon* states:

> The Conference recalls that, in accordance with well settled case law of the Court of Justice of the European Union, the Treaties and the law adopted by the Union on the

basis of the Treaties have primacy over the law of Member States, under the conditions laid down by the said case law.

This was a political statement agreed by all Member States but the supremacy principle is also contained within the Treaties. It will be remembered that Article 2 TFEU states that where the Union has exclusive competence a Member State shall not legislate in respect of those areas save when permitted by the EU. Also, it will be remembered from above that regulations, directives, and decisions are *binding* on Member States (either in general (regulations) or to the Member States that are named). If they are binding then this means that domestic law must be subservient. This is perhaps most notable in respect of Regulations which, it will be remembered, are of general effect and have direct effect in law (Article 288 TFEU). The ability to make law binding over others must be considered a key factor for supremacy. Of course the counter-argument is that on a purely legal (rather than political) basis, the domestic laws remain supreme because a Member State could choose to withdraw from the European Union (something now expressly catered for under Article 50 TEU). This is undoubtedly true and thus 'ultimate' sovereignty remains with the Member States but assuming that a country (and for our purposes, the United Kingdom) wishes to remain within the EU, who has supremacy?

4.3.4.1 Direct effect

It is important at the outset to differentiate between direct *applicability* and direct *effect*. They are interlinked concepts but are subtly different.

⊙ DIRECT APPLICABILITY/DIRECT EFFECT

The concept of international law has already been discussed and it has been noted that international provisions will not ordinarily become part of domestic law without domestic legislation giving it effect. EU law is however different and applies independently and will involve some laws becoming directly applicable in Member States (most notably 'regulations': see Article 288 TFEU), ie it will become part of the domestic laws without the need for individual legislation to be passed each time EU legislation is passed.

Direct effect is slightly different in that whilst directly applicable laws become automatically part of domestic law, those laws subject to direct effect will be enforceable under the domestic courts but they do not automatically form part of domestic law. In other words the right is recognized as enforceable in the domestic context but it does not become an inherent part of domestic law.

The key to this is the notion of supremacy but what does this mean in terms of its relationship with the United Kingdom? The starting point in understanding direct effect is to examine one of the earliest decisions of the ECJ, that of *van Gend en Loos v Nederlandse Administratie der Belastingen* [1963] ECR 1, which has been described as one of the most important cases the ECJ has adjudicated (Chalmers et al (2006) 47).

🗐 Case box *van Gend en Loos*

In this case, the applicants had attempted to import urea-formaldehyde from Germany into the Netherlands. They were made to pay an import tax which was a direct contravention of the EC Treaty.

They petitioned a court in the Netherlands arguing that the tax should be repaid. There was no provision in domestic law for this and the question that arose was whether the applicants could rely on the EC Treaty in domestic cases. The matter was referred to the ECJ (see 4.3.4.3 below) who stated unequivocally that the Treaty was directly effective and thus became automatically part of domestic law and could be relied upon by citizens.

This answered the question for treaties and marked a significant step in the enforcement of Community law. Prior to this decision only the Commission could attempt to enforce Community law and yet this created a situation where the victim would not be recompensed for their breach as it was dealt with at an international level. By providing direct effect it meant that individual citizens—who were supposed to benefit from the creation of the Community (Union)—could now use EU law as part of a domestic action irrespective of whether domestic law had (previously) recognized these issues.

However, because this in effect permits law to be directly imputed there are basic requirements that must be satisfied to ensure that the law is clearly identifiable (Fairhurst (2010) 267). The conditions set out by the Court can be summarized as requiring a 'clear, unconditional and negative prohibition which was not dependent upon any further implementing measures at either EU or national level' (Chalmers et al (2006) 367) although the requirement that the legislation must create a negative prohibition rather than positive obligation was later dropped (Chalmers et al (2010) 270). The basis of the requirements is that it must create identifiable rights that citizens of the EU should have the right to enforce. Thus clarity becomes the most important part of direct effect and they are relatively uncontroversial.

Treaty articles are, following *van Gend*, classic examples of instruments that are capable of having direct effect but it is important to note that even they must comply with the conditions set out in that case. In *Costa v ENEL* [1964] ECR 585 the ECJ held that (the then) Article 97 did not lead to direct effect. This Article allows Member States to take action to prevent the common economic market from being distorted but their action can only take place after consultation with the Commission, thus it could not be said to be 'not dependent upon any further . . . measures'. Regulations are directly applicable as a result of Article 288 and will ordinarily be directly effective (Fairhurst (2006) 239) subject to the conditions put forward in the *van Gend* case.

The more problematic form of legislation is that of the directive and it is not clear whether they are directly effective or not. In order to understand the basics of this distinction it is also necessary to distinguish between two types of direct effect, known as vertical direct effect and horizontal direct effect.

VERTICAL AND HORIZONTAL EFFECT

Direct effect is considered to have two planes to it. The first is vertical direct effect and this is where the relevant legislation creates a legal obligation between the individual and the Member State. The second plane is horizontal direct effect and creates a legal obligation between an individual and another individual. A simple explanation of this (which will suffice for now) is to think of import taxes and discrimination. Both are central features of EU law.

VERTICAL EFFECT

Nicola wishes to import some pens from Germany. However, the UK law has (fictitiously) decided that the importation of pens should carry an import tax of 25 per cent, which is contrary to EU law. Amy would take action against the UK government in the domestic courts suggesting that the prohibition of import taxes (Article 28 TFEU) has vertical effect, ie it binds the government and allows Amy to seek resolution before the domestic courts.

HORIZONTAL EFFECT

Susie is employed by a firm of accountants. She has applied for promotion to partner but been turned down. The post has been given to a less qualified and less experienced man. Amy believes that she has been discriminated against by sex. Amy could take action against her employers arguing that EU law has horizontal effect, ie that it provides rights that would allow Amy to take action against another private body rather than just the state.

Article 288 TFEU states that directives are binding as to the *result* to be achieved but Member States are left with discretion as to how to implement them. Given that this means that the implementation of the directive will vary between the Member States it can be questioned whether they could ever meet the test set out in *van Gend* that the legislation will be clear. However in *van Duyn v Home Office* [1974] ECR 1299 the ECJ implied that a directive could be directly effective (see, in particular paragraphs [12] and [13]). The ECJ did not go as far as to say that directives *were* directly effective but stated that the *effect* of a measure may be directly effective in terms of providing citizens with a right of redress. Some commentators believe that the case was limited in application because the matter arose as a result of a failure by the United Kingdom to implement a directive (Fairhurst (2010) 273). If a directive was neither directly applicable nor effective then this would have meant a citizen could take no action in respect of this but merely wait until the European Commission took enforcement action. The ECJ appears to be adopting a principle of 'estoppel' (ibid) in that it will not allow non-action to prevent citizens being given the rights the directive was supposed to provide.

It would appear therefore that there was ultimately a recognition that directives could have vertical direct effect if they were sufficiently clear and it was possible to identify what the right provided was, who were entitled to the rights, and who was liable to provide the rights (see *Francovich v Republic of Italy* [1991] ECR I–535 and Fairhurst (2010) 273). What of horizontal effect? In *Marshall v Southampton Area Health Authority* [1986] ECR 723 the ECJ held that directives were not horizontally directly effective and thus could not be used against a private body. This did cause a number of difficulties in identifying precisely what a public body was and the ECJ accepted that it could not just be domestic classification (see Fairhurst (2010) 274–277).

Before ending this brief examination of direct effect, the position of decisions must be noted. These were discussed above and they are directly effective in respect of the body they were addressed to (Article 288 TFEU) so long as they meet the *van Gend* principles. It will be remembered that this could (theoretically) involve an element of horizontal effect in that a decision can be made in respect of either a Member State or a private or public body but it is important to note that it is not possible for a decision to be used against someone other than to whom it is addressed. In those circumstances alternative action would need to be taken.

4.3.4.2 European Communities Act 1972

It has been noted above that certain EU law will be directly effective but how is that achieved in the United Kingdom? Although the United Kingdom joined the (then) EEC in 1973, it was necessary that the laws of the United Kingdom were prepared for accession and thus the *European Communities Act 1972* (ECA) was passed. This Act was passed in the traditional way by Parliament and it should be noted at the outset that both Houses of Parliament passed the legislation.

Arguably the most important provision within the ECA 1972 is s 2(1) which provides:

> All such rights, powers, liabilities, obligations and restrictions from time to time created or arising under the Treaties, and all such remedies and procedures from time to time provided for by or under the Treaties, as in accordance with the Treaties are without further enactment to be given legal effect or used in the United Kingdom shall be recognised and available in law, and be enforced, allowed and followed accordingly.

This is not the most user-friendly provision within a statute but it is possible to identify certain key phrases that demonstrate what the purpose of the Act was. One of the key phrases is 'in accordance with the Treaties' which makes it clear that Parliament is accepting that it is to be bound by the Treaty negotiated by the executive (in this case the Treaty of Rome and all subsequent treaties). Its reference to 'all such remedies and procedures' demonstrates that the Act was contemplating a procedural shift: domestic law would have to recognize EU law and the procedures governing its legislation.

Perhaps the most important words are, however, 'without further enactment to be given effect…in law'. This demonstrates that Parliament was stating unequivocally that not only was the Treaty of Rome to be binding on domestic law but that any laws that were made as a result of the Treaty, eg regulations, would automatically apply. This is then followed by s 2(2) which gives effect to legislation that is not automatically applicable (eg directives) and provides that these can be achieved through secondary legislation although there are limits on this in that it is not possible to act retrospectively or to create a term of imprisonment of more than two years. The argument is that such matters would require the full consent of Parliament and should be dealt with purely as an Act of Parliament. Of course this is not the *only* way that EU law can be given effect and it has already been noted that, for example, the *Data Protection Act 1998* was a response to an EC directive and yet took the form of primary rather than secondary legislation.

The source of most controversy in the debate over EU law is as regards supremacy and yet this is something that the 1972 Act expressly refers to:

> Any such provision…as might be made by Act of Parliament, and any enactment passed or to be passed, other than one contained in this part of the Act shall be construed and have effect subject to the foregoing provisions of this section…(s 2(4))

This clearly refers to s 2 as a whole (Foster (2009) 149) but the wording of this section is quite important. Section 2(4) is making it absolutely clear that not only does the ECA 1972 alter legislation that has previously been passed (in that it must now be read as though it were compatible with EU law) but that the Act has *prospective* effect in that future legislation must also be construed in a way that is compatible with EU law. The law is quite clear as to this and one commentator has suggested that this will be achieved by 'denying effectiveness to any national legislation passed later which is in conflict [with EU law]' (Foster (2009) 149).

It is important to note that the wording of s 2(4) is considerably stricter than the equivalent adopted under the *Human Rights Act 1998* (see 5.1.2.2 below). The HRA 1998 empowers courts to interpret legislation in a way compatible with the Convention 'so far as it is possible to do so' (s 3(1)), ie recognizing that there will be circumstances when this is not possible (and would lead to a declaration of incompatibility: see 5.1.2.4 below). The ECA 1972 on the other hand states that legislation, including future legislation, 'shall be construed' in a way to give effect to EU law, ie there is no discretion and where there is conflicting wording EU law must take precedence.

Parliament still possesses the ultimate power in that it could decide to repeal s 2(4) but s 2 would appear to suggest that it is not possible to implicitly repeal s 2(4); merely legislating in a way contrary to s 2(4) (which would ordinarily lead to the repeal of the original legislation) would have to be construed according to s 2(4), ie in a way that does not offend EU law. However, if Parliament wished, it could pass a piece of legislation that stated *either* that s 2(4) is repealed or that s 2(4) does not apply to this particular piece of legislation. However, either situation would almost certainly cause conflict with the EU and could be taken to be a breach of the obligation under the Treaty. This would make the UK subject to enforcement proceedings which would ultimately lead it to either changing the law or (ultimately) withdrawing from the EU.

 Case box *Thoburn v Sunderland City Council*

The issue of implicit repeal was considered expressly in the case of *Thoburn v Sunderland City Council* [2002] EWHC Admin 195. The EU passed two directives (80/181/EEC and 89/617/EEC) which effectively harmonized the system of weights and measurements and required loose goods to be sold in metric rather than imperial measurements. This caused considerable political dispute with many newspapers, particularly the 'right-wing' newspapers, suggesting that it was an inappropriate interference with UK law. The United Kingdom had implemented this measure through the creation of a criminal offence for failing to display metric information.

Thoburn was a market trader who refused either to sell or display anything other than imperial measurements. Sunderland City Council, as the appropriate prosecuting body, prosecuted him under the domestic legislation. Thoburn attempted to argue that as the *Weights and Measures Act 1985* was passed subsequently to the ECA 1972 and was arguably in conflict with s 2 he should not be convicted as s 2 was implicitly repealed by this Act. The High Court rejected this argument holding that implied repeal was not possible.

 QUESTION FOR REFLECTION

Foster suggests that there are two possible interpretations of s 2(4). The first is that it is a rule of construction and is, therefore, simply a further rule of statutory interpretation, albeit one stricter than the HRA 1998. The second possibility is that although we traditionally decide that there is no such thing as entrenchment in the United Kingdom, s 2(4) does create an element of entrenchment. This argument is based on the premise that only the express repealing of s 2(4) would permit Parliament to legislate in a way incompatible with EU law and that stating 'This Act of Parliament is not subject to s 2(4)' would not be permissible because this itself would infringe s 2(4).

Having read the text above do you think that s 2(4) is de facto entrenchment? Now read *Thoburn* [2003] QB 151 at 181–185. Is EU law entrenched subject to the ultimate power of withdrawing from the European Union?

LISTEN TO THE PODCAST

For guidance on how to answer this question and a discussion of the main issues, listen to the author's podcast on the Online Resource Centre:
www.oxfordtextbooks.co.uk/orc/gillespie_els3e/

Perhaps the most significant jurisprudence that examined the issue of the supremacy of EU law and the place of s 2 was the *Factortame* litigation which (eventually) resolved the question and held definitively that EU law was supreme.

Case box Factortame

The facts of the *Factortame* litigation need only be summarized as they are complex. The EU has a fishing policy that is designed to control the fishing that is permitted by each Member State. Each state had a quota of fishing rights but foreign fishermen could take advantage of this if they registered themselves in a Member State country. Factortame was a large Spanish fishing firm who registered themselves in England and sought to use the British quota. As a result of protests the UK government passed the *Merchant Shipping Act 1988* which altered the status of shipping registration and would have limited foreign ownership of fish quotas.

Factortame believed that the Act was incompatible with EU rules on the basis that it was discriminating solely on grounds of nationality. It sought to challenge the decision of the government to introduce the Act through judicial review. The matter proceeded to the High Court who referred certain questions to the ECJ (see 4.3.4.3 below for details of this procedure) but this would take time. The question arose whether interim relief (ie a temporary injunction pending the conclusion of the litigation) could be given in the meantime. The House of Lords held that under English law that it could not (*Factortame v Secretary of State for Transport (No 1)* [1990] 2 AC 85) but referred a separate question to the ECJ as to whether interim relief should be possible. The ECJ responded that the obligation under the Treaty was for Community law to be given immediate effect (*R v Secretary of State for Transport, ex p Factortame* [1990] ECR I–2433) meaning that interim relief should be permissible.

The House of Lords, when it received this reply, indicated that as they were so bound s 2 could be used to create an interim relief even though no such domestic remedy existed elsewhere (*R v Secretary of State for Transport, ex p Factortame (No 2)* [1991] 1 All ER 70) and Lord Bridge importantly stated that EU law was supreme and that domestic law would have to be modified to take into account this supremacy. His Lordship also gave short shrift to the argument that this was not known at the time of accession by stating that supremacy had been established by the ECJ before the time the United Kingdom joined the (then) EEC (see Foster (2009) 154).

An interesting issue arose in 2010 over the compatibility of EU law with domestic law. This time the challenge was not that UK law was not compatible with EU law but rather it was suggested that UK law was void where EU law had not been complied with. In the 1980s the EU passed a directive on technical standards (Directive 83/139/EEC) that required Member States to notify to the European Commission all 'technical regulations' in respect of the sale of certain goods. The United Kingdom had passed the *Video Recordings Act 1984* which was designed, in part, to restrict the sale of video recordings unless they had been certified for release. The VRA 1984 was undoubtedly a technical regulation within the meaning of the 1983 Directive. Rather surprisingly it took until

2009 for anyone in government to realize that the Act had never been notified to the EU and, accordingly, the VRA 1984 was technically in breach of the Directive.

Three defendants who had been convicted of various offences under the VRA 1984 sought to argue that their convictions should be quashed since the VRA 1984 was in breach of EU law and should be considered void. In *R v Budmir and Rainbird; Interfact Ltd v Liverpool City Council* [2010] EWCA Crim 1486 the Court of Appeal rejected this contention. The Court agreed that the Act was in breach of EU law but it noted that there was nothing within EU law that required the conviction to be quashed in such circumstances. They noted that the defendants had been properly convicted under English law and their conviction should only be quashed where there was an injustice, and no such injustice arose here.

The decision of the Court of Appeal is somewhat complicated (for an interesting discussion on its merits see Madhloom (2010)) but it is perhaps notable that here any breach or incompatibility was simply technical. There was no doubt that the VRA 1984 performed an appropriate function, the only breach of EU law was that the law had not been notified. It is difficult to believe that any notification would have made any difference, perhaps something made clear when Parliament repealed the VRA 1984 and enacted the exact same provisions (this time notifying the measure to the EU) (see *Video Recordings Act 2010*).

Sovereignty Act

It was reported in late 2010 that the Foreign Secretary of the coalition government was to propose a 'sovereignty Bill' to be placed before Parliament this year. The legislative measure would, apparently, make clear that EU law only takes effect by the will of Parliament and this will can be withdrawn. This presumably must be an exercise solely in political presentation since it has been seen that the ECA 1972 provides for this position. It is difficult to know what substantive legal purpose such a Bill would have and it is submitted that it is highly unlikely to have any real impact on s 2, ECA 1972 and thus the position will remain the same. The Westminster Parliament is sovereign in that it can ultimately decide to withdraw from the EU. However the Westminster Parliament, as do all other EU Member States, agrees to surrender some sovereignty to the EU to the extent that it voluntarily decides that some EU law will take direct effect into UK law and takes precedence. The TL arguably clarifies this in a way that previous treaties did not, thus rendering any sovereignty clause by the Westminster Parliament somewhat moot.

4.3.4.3 References to the Court of Justice of the EU

It has been seen so far that EU law can be directly applicable and effective; that is to say, that some law will slot into domestic law without the Member States having to do anything, and in some other instances the principle will be set out in EU law but domestic law will implement it. In both situations the EU legislation has now become part of domestic law and, through the ECA 1972, it takes precedence over conflicting domestic legislation unless expressly revoked. Accordingly, a person wishing to rely on EU law would bring an action in the domestic courts using domestic procedures as their legal right now exists under domestic law.

What happens where the litigation raises questions as to the interpretation of EU law? Does this remain a matter solely for the domestic courts or is it something that the Court of Justice of the EU should rule upon and, if so, how? Article 267 TFEU states:

> The Court of Justice of the European Union shall have jurisdiction to give preliminary rulings concerning:
> (a) the interpretation of the Treaties;
> (b) the validity and interpretation of acts of the institutions, bodies, offices or agencies of the Union.

It is notable that the TFEU refers to the 'Court of Justice of the EU' as it will be remembered that this comprises both the *General Court* and the *European Court of Justice* and it is clear that both courts have jurisdiction to give preliminary rulings (Article 256 TFEU) although only in the circumstances set out in that Article.

Article 267 TFEU states that there are two types of preliminary reference requests: a discretionary system and a mandatory system. The discretionary system is explained as:

> Where such a question is raised before any court or tribunal of a Member State, that court or tribunal may, if it considers that a decision on the question is necessary to enable it to give judgment, request the Court to give a ruling thereon.

Thus *any* court may refer a question to the Court of Justice although the procedures of the domestic courts may limit this to the extent that it is not incompatible with the Treaty. For example, it is unlikely that in England and Wales it would be desirable for a magistrates' court to decide that they should refer a question to the Court of Justice and procedures could be put in place to ensure that, for example, the High Court makes the ultimate decision (this could, for example, be through judicially reviewing a decision to refer or not to refer a question).

The mandatory system is explained as:

> Where any such question is raised in a case pending before a court or tribunal of Member State against whose decisions there is no judicial remedy under national law, that court or tribunal shall bring the matter before the Court.

Thus whilst any court has discretion as to whether to refer a matter to the Court of Justice, a court of final resort would theoretically have no discretion to refer and *shall* refer the matter. Of course this is premised by the first part of Article 267 which is premised on the basis that a question arises. A key issue is under what circumstances a domestic court believes that a question arises and is not, for example, already settled.

Article 267 refers to a preliminary reference procedure because, contrary to what is often said in the media and even some textbooks, it is not possible to 'appeal' to the Court of Justice. Instead the domestic court has to decide whether, and if so to what extent, EU law resolves the dispute before it. This is part of the principle of direct effect: EU law forms part of the national law and thus it is for the national courts, and not the Court of Justice, to resolve this. The preliminary reference procedure however recognizes the fact that the Court of Justice is the ultimate arbitrator of EU law and thus where a point of EU law is not settled, the domestic court can seek an opinion of the Court of Justice. Theoretically the Court of Justice does not have the jurisdiction to discuss the compatibility of domestic law with EU law (*Costa v ENEL* [1964] ECR 585) but the obvious solution to this is to ensure that the question is phrased in such a manner that the query is over the application or interpretation of the EU legislation.

In *Irish Creamery Milk Suppliers v Ireland* [1981] ECR 735 the (then) ECJ discussed the purpose of the preliminary reference procedure and stated it established 'a framework for close co-operation between the national courts and the Court of Justice based on the assignment to each of different functions' (at [5]). The different roles can be seen from the fact that the Court of Justice simply answers the questions posed and does not adjudicate on the actual case. The matter is then referred back to the domestic court who must apply the ruling of the Court of Justice to the facts as identified by the national court. The Court of Justice does not make findings of fact; only the domestic courts do this, and accordingly the reference is preliminary to the final adjudication, that being given by the domestic court.

Article 23a of Protocol 3 states that the rules of procedure can ensure that preliminary references can be sent to the relevant court under an expedited procedure and where the matter relates to the area of freedom, security, and justice that the reference can be sent under an urgent procedure. This is presumably because the latter could involve significant infringements on the liberty of an individual and thus time will be of the essence in deciding on the legality of any instrument or procedure. This is supported by Article 267 TFEU itself which states, 'if such a question is raised in a case pending before a court...with regard to a person in custody, the Court of Justice of the European Union shall act with the minimum of delay'.

Must or should refer?

The Court of Justice has been clear that it is ordinarily for the national court to decide when a preliminary reference should be made (*Irish Creamery Milk Suppliers v Ireland* [1981] ECR 735) although it did suggest that it would be preferable for the factual basis of the case to have been adjudicated so that the questions can be placed into a proper context (at [6]) and in recent years this 'preference' has become more substantial (see, for example, *Bacardi-Martini SAS, Cellier des Dauphins v Newcastle United* [2003] ECR I–905). However, setting aside this issue of timing, it is relatively clear that the Court is comfortable with the idea of the national court deciding whether to refer a matter or not.

Where issues become slightly more complicated is in respect of when a reference *must* be made. The third paragraph of Article 267 states that a reference must be made where there is no appeal against a decision, but what does that mean and does this interfere with the general principle that it is for the domestic courts to interpret legislation? Within England and Wales it may appear obvious that the House of Lords is the court from which there is no appeal but appeal opportunities are restricted from other courts. For example, an appeal from the magistrates' court to the Divisional Court will only be subject to another appeal in extraordinary circumstances (see 13.2.2 below)—is the Divisional Court required to make a reference?

The position becomes even more complicated when one notes that it may not be possible to identify the last court until it is too late. Foster provides the example of a case litigated in the Court of Appeal and where the Court of Appeal and House of Lords (now Supreme Court) both refuse to give leave to appeal. The Court of Appeal—which was not the lowest court—had *discretion* to refer the matter to the Court of Justice (and let us assume it decided not to) whereas the Supreme Court would *have* to refer it. However, by denying leave the Court of Appeal became the last court but the matter has already been resolved so there is no mechanism for now petitioning the Court of Justice (for a discussion on this see Fairhurst (2010) 187).

Even though Article 267 talks about mandatory referrals this is not strictly correct as there are many instances when a referral need not be made. Perhaps the classic example of this is when the same question has already been adjudicated by the Court of Justice. In those circumstances there is no need to refer the matter again and the final appeal body can just take judicial notice of the original judgment. This was developed into a process known as *acte clair* where national courts would not have to refer where the law is particularly clear (Tridimas (2003) 12). However could this be abused by the courts?

> ### Case box *Three Rivers*
>
> In *Three Rivers District Council v Governor of the Bank of England* [2000] 2 WLR 1220 the House of Lords was called upon to consider the applicability of an EC directive. As the House of Lords is a court from which there is no appeal they should have theoretically referred the matter to the ECJ. However, they did not do so arguing that they were capable of considering Community law with a small risk of them reaching the wrong verdict. No case had previously gone to the ECJ on this exact issue although similar decisions had. The House believed that the disadvantages entailed in a reference were not outweighed by the benefits. Tridimas suggests that this is a liberal interpretation of *acte clair* although he does not expressly suggest that it is wrong (Tridimas (2003) 42).

There must be concern that since it is for the domestic courts to decide whether a reference shall be made, they could simply choose not to refer in cases arguing, like in *Three Rivers*, that the matter was wholly within their competence. This, however, arguably fails to take account of the cooperative procedure that the ECJ sees Article 267 bringing. There is no identifiable sanction against a court that adopts this approach although presumably the Commission could take action against the Member State arguing that the application of the law by that Member State (through the rulings of the domestic courts) is wrong. Whether such powerful action would be taken over minor issues of Community interpretation is more questionable.

4.4 European Convention on Human Rights

The second European Treaty that is of direct importance to domestic law is the *European Convention on Human Rights* (ECHR). Its importance has grown since 2000 when the *Human Rights Act 1998* came into force and this instrument has already been discussed in Chapters 2 and 3 and we will return to it in Chapter 5. However in this part of the chapter it is intended to demonstrate where the source of ECHR jurisprudence arises. The use of this law in the domestic context is explained in the other chapters.

4.4.1 Background to the Convention

The ECHR was created in the aftermath of the Second World War and was designed to ensure that some of the atrocities that preceded and occurred during the war could not happen again. That said, it is important to realize that the Convention is not a treaty governing war but rather the treatment of citizens in general. A significant number of the lawyers who drafted the Convention were British and the United Kingdom was the first country to sign the Treaty in 1950 (see Bingham (2000) 134). Although the Treaty came into force in 1953 and some countries directly incorporated it into their domestic law, the United Kingdom did not do anything that would lead to it being used by the individual citizen, believing that this was unnecessary as the Treaty simply gave effect to freedoms already secured by the common law. However in 1966 the United Kingdom accepted the right of individual petition allowing UK citizens the right to petition the European Commission on Human Rights (ECmHR) alleging a breach of the Convention and since 1981 citizens of its territories (excluding Hong Kong[8] and the Isle of Man). Since that time a significant number of cases have been brought and Bingham (2000) argued that the high number of cases was one reason to incorporate the Convention into a domestic setting (at pp 135–136).

The Convention itself consists of sixty-six Articles but of these the most important are Articles 2–18 which create the human rights and fundamental freedoms that citizens of the Council of Europe have as protection. The remaining Articles create the machinery by which the rights and freedoms will be protected. Existing alongside the Convention itself are a number of protocols. The protocols can be divided into two classes. The first are those protocols that amend the Treaty (eg Protocols 3, 5, 8, and 11) and the second are those that create additional rights and freedoms (eg Protocols 1, 4, 6, 7, and 12). Where the protocols create additional rights then Member States are not obliged to safeguard these rights and freedoms unless they agree to be bound by the protocol or some parts of the protocol.

⊃ PROTOCOLS

Article 1 of Protocol 6 abolishes the death penalty subject to a reservation under Article 2 of the Protocol permitting the penalty to continue in time of war for certain offences. The Protocol was created on 28 June 1983 but the United Kingdom did not ratify this protocol until 1 June 1999 (see s 1(1)(c) HRA 1998 and associated delegated legislation). Protocols 4, 7, and 12 have not been ratified by the United Kingdom and accordingly the additional rights set out in those protocols are not afforded to citizens of the United Kingdom or its territories.

4.4.2 The institutions

When the Treaty was first ratified there were three bodies that were relevant to the Convention:

- Committee of Ministers
- European Commission on Human Rights
- European Court of Human Rights.

Protocol 11 to the Convention altered this to abolish the ECmHR and to remove the judicial function of the Committee of Ministers. The ECtHR is now the pre-eminent body and a Commissioner for Human Rights has been created although the commissioner has, in effect, a political rather than a purely legal function.

---

8. This was, of course, prior to Hong Kong return to Chinese rule in 1997.

4.4.2.1 The Committee of Ministers

The Committee of Ministers was, as its name suggests, a body constituted of relevant domestic ministers of the contracting states. It served as the 'executive' to the Council of Europe and was responsible, therefore, for proposing amendments to the Convention and monitoring that the ECtHR was functioning correctly (Harris et al (1995) 691). Perhaps its most controversial purpose, however, was that it had the right to adjudicate on disputes that were not referred to the ECtHR (Article 32). It has been argued that, in reality, decisions only went to the ministers where it was a minor issue that had already been resolved by the ECtHR in other cases or where the contracting state admitted that there was a breach of the Convention but had indicated that it would not change the domestic provision that infringed the Article (Harris et al (1995) 693). This latter point is an interesting one because although the ECtHR provides declarations of illegality and can order a contracting state to issue compensation (Article 50) its judgments are decisions of an international body and accordingly are not binding on any state. If a state wishes to ignore the law then there is little that can be done about this; unlike the Treaty of Rome, the ECHR does not provide an enforcement mechanism and instead enforcement is left with the Committee of Ministers. This means that a political resolution would need to be sought and, in practice, that has led to some accusations that countries have been able to ignore decisions of the ECtHR although in reality compliance has been 'exemplary' (Harris et al (1995) 702) and this is in part because of the diplomacy of the Committee.

Article 32 of the Convention has now been modified to remove reference to the Committee of Ministers and the ECtHR now has jurisdiction over all cases. The Committee continues, however, to supervise the execution of the Court's judgments.

4.4.2.2 The European Commission on Human Rights

It is perhaps understandable that some students get confused between the Council of Europe and the European Union given that both had Commissions and Courts. However the bodies were significantly different from one another with the European Commission on Human Rights (ECmHR) acting as a de facto filter for cases before the ECtHR (before its abolishment).

The Commission was constituted, under Article 20, as including one member from each contracting state, thus mirroring the position in respect of the judges. Article 25 of the Convention stated that all applications had to be referred to the Commission who would then decide whether they were admissible. If the Commission decided that a case was not admissible then the matter could not proceed further. If, however, the Commission considered it admissible then it had to decide whether to refer the case to the Committee of Ministers or, more commonly, the Commission would produce an opinion on the case.

The opinion appeared to be a judgment although it had no legal status and was merely an indication as to what the Commission believed the law to be, including reference to previous decisions of the ECtHR. The Commission would make findings of fact and law, identify whether it thought there was a prima facie breach and ultimately decide whether it was admissible. The ECtHR was not bound by the opinion and in a number of situations the ECtHR would depart from the Commission; but in the majority of cases the opinion of the ECmHR was a good indication of how the case would progress and there were instances where countries had settled the dispute before it reached the ECtHR as a result of the opinion.

Some argue that the Commission acted as an effective filter for the ECtHR (Harris et al (1995) 574) but there was no doubt that it was an extremely costly and time-consuming process. As the Council of Europe increased in size so the number of cases continued to rise and the delay between an application and eventual resolution by the ECtHR grew. It was therefore decided that the ECmHR should be disbanded and a new system of deciding admissibility would be introduced.

4.4.2.3 The European Court of Human Rights

The role of the ECtHR has grown as a result of the abolition of the ECmHR and the reduction of the jurisdiction of the Committee of Ministers. The Court now has responsibility for deciding the admissibility of decisions and then, separately, the resolution of the case. Article 27 states there are three divisions of the Court:

* Committees: a panel of three judges
* Chambers: a panel of seven judges
* Grand Chamber: a panel of seventeen judges.

In addition there is the Plenary Court which consists of all judges. The Plenary does not sit judicially but exists to elect the President and Vice-Presidents of the Court together with deciding rules of court etc (see Article 26). More than one type of division outlined above can sit and indeed the expectation is that there will normally be more than one Committee and Chamber sitting to increase the number of cases heard. Importantly, Article 27(2) states that whenever the Court is sitting in either a Chamber or Grand Chamber, the defendant Member State must be represented as a judge, either through the ECtHR judge appointed for that Member State or, if that person is unable to sit, an ad hoc judge proposed by the Member State. It may seem unusual for, in effect, the defendant to be represented on the bench but this is a standard feature of international tribunals and is designed to ensure that the judge can guide the other judges through the relevant domestic laws and procedures.

Committees normally sit to consider cases that appear to be manifestly ill-founded and can be withdrawn from the list. Article 28 provides Committees are to rule matters inadmissible where the three judges agree unanimously and expressly states that no right of appeal exists from such a decision. Where no decision is made under Article 28 (ie it is not struck out by the Committee) then the matter proceeds to a Chamber which will then consider the admissibility and merits of the decision (Article 29). According to Article 29(3) the merits of the case should normally be heard separately from admissibility although this need not occur in exceptional circumstances, eg where there is a particularly pressing need.

Where a matter involves a particularly complicated interpretation of the Convention or where the ECtHR wishes to depart from its previous decisions then Article 30 allows the Chamber to surrender its jurisdiction to the Grand Chamber, thus permitting a much more authoritative analysis of the case to be made. However this is comparatively rare and the usual expectation is that the matter would be heard by the Chamber.

A decision of a Chamber is normally final but either the applicant or the defending country can petition the Grand Chamber within three months of the judgment of the Chamber (Article 43(1)). The Grand Chamber shall form a Committee of five judges to consider whether they should entertain this petition, the decision being whether it is a matter of general importance (Article 43(2)). If they decide to allow the petition then the matter proceeds to the Grand Chamber for a full rehearing. If they refuse the petition then the judgment of the Chamber is automatically final (Article 42). Decisions of a Grand Chamber are always final (Article 44(1)) and are not subject to any appeal.

4.4.3 Identifying the law

It can be seen from the above that the principal sources of law are the Convention itself and the decisions of the ECtHR. Although the ECmHR has now been abolished, its decisions remain important as they assist in identifying the boundaries of admissibility. That said it must be remembered that the ECtHR is not bound by the ECmHR and accordingly they amount to a persuasive secondary source of law.

4.4.3.1 The Convention

A background to the Convention is provided above and an overview of Articles 2–14 is given in the next chapter which details the importance of the HRA 1998. However, it is important to note that the ECtHR has consistently stated that the Convention is not a static document but that it progresses with society:

> That the Convention is a living instrument which must be interpreted in the light of present-day conditions is firmly rooted in the Court's case law…It follows that these provisions cannot be interpreted solely in accordance with the intentions of their authors as expressed more than 40 years ago. (*Loizidou v Turkey* (1995) 20 EHRR 99 at 133)

This has implications for the way in which the Convention is to be interpreted. It follows, for example, that a literal interpretation (see 2.3.1 above) will not be adopted as the meaning of words rarely change. Instead the ECtHR considers the Convention to safeguard society and the passage above demonstrates that as society grows and develops the rights of an individual will also adapt.

 Example Transsexuals

One of the most obvious examples of the Convention acting as a living instrument can be seen from the treatment of transsexuals. In *Rees v United Kingdom* A 106 (1986) the ECmHR rejected the suggestion that a ban on transsexuals marrying was an infringement of Article 12 (the right to marry) and this was later confirmed by *Cossey v United Kingdom* A 184 (1990). Yet in *Goodwin v United Kingdom* [2002] IRLR 664 the ECtHR changed its mind and held that a bar was a breach of Article 12 and argued that society had moved on since the earlier stages and that it was no longer appropriate to keep an absolute bar.

The rejection of a literal approach can also be seen from the manner in which the ECtHR approaches its use in the context of the wider international law. In *Fogarty v United Kingdom* (2002) 34 EHRR 12 the ECtHR said:

> The Convention…cannot be interpreted in a vacuum. The Court must be mindful of the Convention's special character as a human rights treaty, and it must also take the relevant rules of international law into account. The Convention should, so far as possible, be interpreted in harmony with other rules of international law…(p 314)

This reinforces the fact that the Convention is a set of *minimum* safeguards and that where other international instruments discuss the concept of rights, eg the *United*

Nations Convention on the Rights of the Child, then the ECtHR will try so far as possible to construe the ECHR to take account of these instruments.

European or domestic context?

At the time of writing there are forty-seven countries that are a signatory to the ECHR and each has its own legal system. It has been seen in Chapter 2 that language is important when construing instruments and the question must arise therefore whether the Convention is construed in a pan-European way or in respect of each signatory's construction.

The answer to this question is not particularly clear as sometimes the ECtHR will arrive at an autonomous meaning and at other times it will permit the individual signatories some latitude. Some commentators argue that an autonomous meaning is only given to words where there is the capacity for misunderstanding as a result of the way in which words are interpreted (Harris et al (2009) 16).

 Example Autonomous meaning

It may be thought that we understand what the term 'criminal charge' means (see Article 6(1)). However not every country may necessarily have a clear divide between criminal and civil law. Indeed in England and Wales this issue could still raise a problem. We may think of a matter being of a criminal nature where a penalty is imposed but this need not be the case because of regulatory frameworks. A good example of this is tax. If a person is obliged to complete a self-assessment as part of their tax affairs there is a deadline by which the forms must be received by the Inland Revenue. If a person does not meet that deadline then a £100 fine is imposed. Is this a criminal penalty or a regulatory penalty? Certainly someone so fined would not have to declare it as a 'criminal conviction' in any job application so does that mean it is not a criminal charge?

Providing autonomous meanings to words should provide a level of consistency across jurisdictions, including in domestic settings. Of course the position is not immediately clear as questions will arise as to whether a domestic instrument necessarily equates to the autonomous meaning but it does mean that a contracting state could not circumvent human rights by using words that appear to take a matter outside the remit of the Convention.

However it could also be argued that the Council of Europe is certainly not one homogeneous body and that society in each country could be different to another, especially as the bulk of the ECtHR's work is now in respect of emerging democracies (Woolf (2005) 9). The ECtHR has recognized this and in respect of certain convention rights will allow domestic institutions latitude in respect of the way that rights and freedoms are secured, this latitude being known as the doctrine of the margin of appreciation.

This doctrine, which first appeared in the leading case of *Handyside v United Kingdom* (1976) 1 EHRR 737, recognizes the fact that the domestic institutions (courts and executive) are best placed to understand the requirements of society and accordingly the ECtHR will sometimes defer to their finding that a measure is necessary for the protection of society (Harris et al (2009) 11–14). Loveland expands on this point and notes that a justification for its use is that the ECtHR is not an appellate court per se in that it is not involved with resolving individual cases (as appellate courts are) but rather it has a supervisory role whereby it ensures that national institutions give effect to the rights and freedoms of the Convention (Loveland (2009) 596). This supervisory role can be seen from the fact that although the ECtHR is happy to extend a margin of appreciation in respect of some matters, it will decline to do so in others and even where the margin is extended it reserves the right to supervise the margin of appreciation (see *Handyside*).

Positive or negative rights

Another feature of the Convention that must be understood is that although many of the Articles are framed in the negative—ie institutions shall not do something—the ECtHR has stated that many of the Articles also have positive obligations. A positive obligation in this sense means that not only must a state not infringe the relevant Article, it must put in place a framework by which a person's right is protected, including preventing other people (including private citizens) from infringing their rights.

 Example Rape

In *MC v Bulgaria* (2005) 40 EHRR 20 the ECtHR held that there was a positive obligation under Article 3 of the Convention to ensure that domestic laws protected women from rape and that such acts were investigated and prosecuted properly. This case followed the earlier decision of *X and Y v Netherlands* (1986) 8 EHRR 235 which held that Articles 3 and 8 had positive obligations in respect of ensuring that the criminal law protected the vulnerable from sexual offences.

4.4.3.2 The European Court of Human Rights

The second source of law for ECHR matters is, of course, the ECtHR and it has already been noted above that this is an important source as the manner in which they interpret the Convention can lead to an extension of rights. For example the plain words of Article 3—'No one shall be subjected to torture or to inhuman or degrading treatment or punishment'—would ordinarily lead one to believe that this was a negative obligation, ie the state should not torture or subject someone to inhumane or degrading treatment. However the ECtHR has made clear that Article 3 also contains positive obligations and so the impact of Article 3 is significantly wider. Arguably, therefore, whereas in the United Kingdom the judiciary is a secondary source in terms of its relationship to Acts of Parliament the same cannot be said for the ECtHR where its decisions are arguably as important as the Convention itself.

Article 45 of the Convention states that the ECtHR must give reasons for its judgments and reasons and Article 45(2) expressly provides for the right to give a dissenting or partly dissenting judgment. Reference to 'decisions' includes admissibility decisions and normally, therefore, each case will contain at least two decisions; the first will be given when admissibility is decided and the second, usually much later, is when the merits of the case are given—the judgment. Admissibility decisions are an important source of law as the reasons given for non-admissibility will frequently identify common legal principles and the limits of the Convention Articles.

When giving judgment, the ECtHR, like the Supreme Court of the United States of America, will normally only give a single judgment and, where it is not unanimous, normally a single dissenting judgment.[9] This position can be contrasted with the Supreme Court or English appellate courts where it is arguably more common for each judge to give a judgment. There are good reasons for giving a single judgment especially where it involves a Grand Chamber, not least efficiency and time, but the disadvantage is that sometimes it is not always clear precisely what the Court means whereas with individual judgments it is possibly easier to identify the reasons.

Another feature of judgments of the ECtHR is that they will rarely contain the equivalent of *obiter dicta* and certainly not *per curiam* comments. The ECtHR limits its jurisdiction upon applications to real problems and will not answer hypothetical questions except when requested to do so by the Committee of Ministers under Article 47 although it has never been called upon to do so.

Precedent

The ECtHR has, over the past fifty years, decided on a large number of cases and the question then arises as to how the court considers its past decisions. In Chapter 2 it was noted that the courts in England and Wales adopt the doctrine of *stare decisis* believing that certainty and predictability of the law is important. In *Goodwin v United Kingdom* [2002] IRLR 664 the ECtHR discussed the issue of precedent:

> While the Court is not formally bound to follow its previous judgments, it is in the interests of legal certainty, foreseeability and equality before the law that it should not depart, without good reason, from precedents laid down in previous cases . . . (at para 74)

Thus the ECtHR considers precedent a desirable object but it does not feel itself to be formally bound by itself. It may seem that this is comparable to the House of Lords (see 3.2 above) but arguably the position is slightly different since the House starts with the proposition that it *is* bound but that in exceptional circumstances it can depart or overrule its own decisions. The ECtHR differs in that it does not have this initial presumption but rather just thinks it is desirable to follow previous cases. In part this rule is necessary because of its belief that the Convention is a 'living instrument'. It was noted that some believe that rigid adherence to the doctrine of precedent can restrain the development of law and the ECtHR clearly believes that this would be a mistake in this field. However the importance of not departing from previous decisions too easily can be found in the fact that a significant departure is one reason for a case being referred from a Chamber to the Grand Chamber (see 4.4.2.3 above).

◆ Summary

In this chapter we have examined the sources of international law that may have an impact on the English Legal System. In particular we have noted:

- International law ordinarily governs states not individuals.

---

9. Although it is perhaps increasingly common to see individual dissenting judgments, in part because sometimes the dissenters disagree with one another.

- The primary sources of international law are conventions and treaties. Treaties are agreements between two or more countries and conventions are international documents where countries agree to be bound by a system of rules or goals.

- International law also relies on custom, that is to say informal rules that have been commonly agreed over a period of time.

- A particular problem with international law is its enforceability. Sometimes the treaty will state how the law will be enforced. The United Nations may become involved to assist in implementing it.

- The United Kingdom joined the (then) EEC in 1972. As part of the conditions for joining we agreed that EEC (now EU) law would become automatically part of the law of the United Kingdom.

- The principal treaties governing the EU are the *Treaty on European Union* and the *Treaty on the Functioning of European Union* and disputes are adjudicated by the *European Court of Justice*.

- The EU has its own executive which is divided between two bodies, the *Commission* and the *European Council*.

- The *Council* and *European Parliament* constitute the legislature of the EU. The powers of the Parliament have been strengthened by the *Treaty of Lisbon* and Parliament now has broadly the same powers as the Council.

- Legislation can be proposed by either the *Council* or the *European Parliament* or by the *European Commission* itself. Only the *European Commission* can initiate legislation.

- After *Lisbon*, the judiciary is represented in the *Court of Justice of the European Union* which is divided into two standing courts (the *European Court of Justice* and the *General Court*) and specialist courts. Each court currently consists of one judge from each Member State and a President of each court is elected by its judiciary. Both courts ordinarily sit in divisions known as chambers.

- The *European Convention on Human Rights* was written in the aftermath of the Second World War. It is controlled by the *Council of Europe* and is enforced by the *European Court of Human Rights*.

- Any country that wishes to join the *European Union* must first join the *Council of Europe* but the Council also includes countries who have no desire to join the EU.

- The Convention is considered to be a 'living instrument' meaning that it changes with society.

- There is no sanction for failing to implement a decision of the *European Court of Human Rights* but most countries will voluntarily adhere to its decisions in order to discharge their international obligations.

? End-of-chapter questions

1. A potential difficulty when considering vertical effect is deciding what amounts to a public body. In some countries the energy supplier will be public (ie state-owned) and in other countries (eg the United Kingdom) it will be a private body. However, do they do anything different and should they be treated any differently in terms of EU law?

2. Read Wade (1996) and Eekalaar (1997). In the first article Professor Wade argues that the decision in *Factortame* has effectively abrogated parliamentary sovereignty. Professor

Eekalaar disagrees. Do you think the position is as simple as Wade suggests or can there be a 'temporary' ceding of sovereignty but with the ultimate right to act in the national interest?

3. Read Beernaert (2004). Does the increasing number of states joining the Council of Europe mean that the European Court of Human Rights will effectively concentrate on the new 'emerging democracies' rather than developing human rights in the original Member States? Is there not a danger, therefore, that citizens in the United Kingdom and other states will not have adequate protection for a breach of their rights?

 ## Further reading

Read the text of the Attorney-General's advice on the legality of the invasion of Iraq. A copy can be found at (2005) 54 *International and Comparative Law Quarterly* 767–778.

The Attorney-General considers many aspects of the applicability of international law to English law and also potential remedies that may be used against the government if it had been proven to be illegal.

Boyron S (2002) 'In the name of European law: The Metric Martyrs case' 27 *European Law Review* 771–779.

This article considers the implication of the judgment in *Thoburn v Sunderland City Council* (2002) and considers the place of European sovereignty in England and Wales.

Craig, P (2008) 'The Treaty of Lisbon, process, architecture and substance' 33 *European Law Review* 137–166.

This article provides a very readable and comprehensive analysis of the principal changes brought about by the *Treaty of Lisbon*.

 For multiple choice questions, updates to this chapter and links to useful websites, please visit the Online Resource Centre at

www.oxfordtextbooks.co.uk/orc/gillespie_els3e/

5

Human Rights Act 1998

By the end of this chapter you will be able to:

- Identify the principal Articles of the ECHR.
- Discuss which bodies are bound by the HRA.
- Assess how the HRA has been used in domestic contexts.
- Understand its impact on the domestic legal system.

Introduction

In 1997 a Labour government was elected to power in the United Kingdom under the leadership of Tony Blair. One of the manifesto commitments of that administration was to incorporate the *European Convention on Human Rights* (ECHR) into domestic (UK) law. It was seen in the previous chapter that the Convention had been drafted in the aftermath of the Second World War but that the United Kingdom had traditionally decided that there was no need to incorporate it into domestic law arguing that its protections were all to be found in the common law.

By the 1990s there was a growing recognition that this was not true and Labour, who traditionally had been against incorporation, decided that the Convention should be given domestic force. The *Human Rights Act 1998* (HRA) is one of the most important pieces of legislation to have been passed in recent years but its impact was arguably overstated at the time.

This chapter will examine the HRA and discuss some of the important issues that arise from its use. An overview of the relevant Convention articles will also be given.

5.1 The Human Rights Act 1998

The HRA itself is a short piece of legislation containing only twenty-two sections but this disguises its importance. In Chapter 2 the changes the Act has made to statutory interpretation were considered and it has been seen that there was a definite change of mindset when human rights issues were involved. However, it is important that we recall that the HRA does not completely rewrite statutory interpretation and that it only applies where the normal rules of interpretation would lead to a conflict with the ECHR (see 2.3.4 above).

5.1.1 The decision to incorporate

Bingham, speaking extrajudicially at the time he was Master of the Rolls, stated:

> I would suggest that the ability of English judges to protect human rights in this country and reconcile conflicting rights...is inhibited by the failure of successive governments over many years to incorporate into United Kingdom law the European Convention on Human Rights and Fundamental Freedoms. (Bingham (2000) 131)

This was not a universally popular opinion but by the time the speech was given a significant debate had arisen as to the need to incorporate the ECHR into domestic law. There had been three attempts to incorporate the Convention into domestic law, once in 1987 by Sir Edward Gardiner QC, a conservative MP, and twice in 1994 and 1996 by Lord Lester of Herne Hill QC, a Liberal Democrat peer.[1] The attempts had been resisted because it was thought that the rights were to be found already in domestic law through the common law. Since 1966 UK citizens had the right to petition the European Court of Human Rights (ECtHR) where they believed the state had breached their rights[2] but the decision of the Court was theoretically unenforceable although successive governments had voluntarily acceded to judgments even when they disagreed with them.[3] By the 1990s there was 'an ever-lengthening list of occasions…[when] the Commission or the Court have found the United Kingdom to be in breach of its obligations' (Bingham (2000) 135), which appeared to contradict the traditional opinion that the domestic courts were equally able to give force to the Convention rights.

A matter is only admissible before the ECtHR where domestic remedies have been exhausted (Article 35(1)) so where the ECtHR had ruled against the United Kingdom these matters had already been adjudicated on domestically without any such finding. The inconvenience of obtaining such a declaration was (and still is) great with the average delay in the mid-1990s being between six and eight years (Bingham (2000) 135) and the cost being upwards of £30,000.[4]

The new Labour government argued that it would be more appropriate to allow the Convention to be litigated domestically and issued a white paper (*Rights Brought Home*) setting out its proposals. The long title of the Act is: 'an Act to give further effect to rights and freedoms guaranteed under the European Convention on Human Rights' and it does not therefore make reference to either incorporation or domestic authority. The Lord Chancellor argued that this phraseology was correct because the Convention was already being complied with and the Bill (now Act) was simply extending this compliance (Cooper (1998) 4), and another commentator argues that the true position of the HRA can be described thus:

> The Human Rights Act 1998 maintains the dualist distinction between the United Kingdom's obligations in international law and the provisions of domestic law. The United Kingdom's international obligations under the European Convention are not directly applicable in domestic law. Instead, the Human Rights Act 1998, s 1 and s 2, makes a list of 'Convention rights'…available as rights before the domestic courts. (Dwyer (2005) 362–363)

It is for this reason that the term 'incorporation' would be inappropriate not least because the Convention has not become a full part of the English Legal System. The HRA, as will be seen, only directly applies in respect of actions against the state and not against private disputes although it may exist through 'horizontal effect'[5] because courts are classed as public bodies.[6] Dwyer argues that the HRA is designed to establish this domestic framework and not to minimize the international obligations of the United Kingdom which can only be regulated by treaty. Fredman suggests that its summary could be:

---

1. *Rights Brought Home: The Human Rights Bill*, October 1997, Cmnd 3782, para 1.5.
2. Bingham (2000) notes that the decision to grant a right of petition to the ECtHR was extremely controversial at the time (p 134).
3. *Rights Brought Home* (n 1 above) para 1.10.
4. Ibid para 1.14.
5. Horizontal effect in this context means the adjudication between two private parties as distinct from the 'vertical effect' of adjudicating between the state and private citizen.
6. For a summary of the arguments surrounding 'horizontal effect' see Wade (1998) 524–525 and Beyleveld and Pattinson (2002).

[The Act] simply…empower[s] United Kingdom judges to adjudicate in an area that was formerly the exclusive preserve of the European Court of Human Rights. (Fredman (1998) 538)

Other commentators agree, noting that nothing in the HRA stops someone from petitioning the ECtHR save that, since the Court itself requires domestic options to have been exhausted, petitioners will have to try domestic proceedings first (Feldman (1998) 709–711). It is quite possible that this could have a beneficial impact on the Court itself and Bingham, when arguing for a scheme similar to that created by the HRA, suggested that a full reasoned examination at domestic level could help influence law at the ECtHR (Bingham (2000) 137, 140).

5.1.2 The basic framework

The HRA is designed to ensure that public authorities act compatibly and to this extent s 6, which imposes such a duty, is central to the Act. Following this duty the Act sets out how the Act can be used in litigation (ss 7, 8, and 10) and how the courts should approach their duty (ss 2–4). Other parts of the Act cover derogations and the appointment of the judiciary to the European Court of Human Rights but these are outside the scope of this book and readers should cross-refer to texts on *Public Law* or *Human Rights Law* for further details.

5.1.2.1 Duty to act compatibly

Section 6(1) HRA states:

It is unlawful for a public authority to act in a way which is incompatible with a Convention right.

This simple phrase acts as the keystone to the Act. Whilst it refers to a public authority acting 'unlawfully' it is important at the outset to note that this is in its civil context and not the criminal one: no criminal sanction is imposed by breaching the HRA. Subsection (1) creates a number of pertinent questions that need to be resolved, most notably:

- Who is a public authority?
- What does 'acting' mean?
- What does 'incompatible' mean?
- What remedies arise from this illegal act?

The final question is considered elsewhere as it is contained within other statutory provisions.

Public authority

The Act applies only directly to public authorities and s 6(3) states:

'public authority' includes–

    (a) a court or tribunal, and

    (b) any person certain of whose functions are functions of a public nature,

but does not include either House of Parliament or a person exercising functions in connection with proceedings in Parliament.

Parliament is exempted because the Act does not contradict parliamentary supremacy and accordingly the legislature reserves the right to Act in a way incompatible with the Convention. Section 6(4) distinguishes between the House of Lords sitting in its judicial and legislative capacities with the former being expressly exempted from the protection afforded under s 6(3) and it must implicitly come within s 6(3) as a public authority.

The definition of public authority was always going to be crucial to how the Act works in practice (Klug and Starmer (2005) 723). It is commonly said that there are two forms of 'public authorities' created by the Act (ibid) but realistically there are three, with Klug and Starmer's two being in addition to 'courts or tribunals'. They label their two forms as being 'pure' public authorities (ie those authorities that have public functions, eg the police) and 'hybrid' authorities (ie those who sometimes act in a public capacity and at other times in a private capacity). The latter arises because the Act itself recognizes that sometimes a public authority can act in a private way (s 6(5)).

The leading decision on the definition of 'public authority' is *Aston Cantlow and Wilmcote with Billesley Parochial Church Council v Wallbank* [2004] 1 AC 546. The House accepted the distinction between 'core' and 'hybrid' authorities and Lord Nicholls noted that one difficulty of being classified as a 'core' public body is that it would not be possible for that authority to seek to rely on Convention rights itself (p 554). Whilst this is almost certainly an *obiter* comment it is likely to be correct when one recalls the relationship that exists under the Convention (and therefore by implication the Act). The purpose of the Convention was that the state should uphold the rights and freedoms and not infringe them. The Act extended this principle to public authorities but they continue to relate to the state and thus one 'core' public authority cannot sue another as this would be the state suing itself. Lord Nicholls, again almost certainly correctly, argues that 'hybrid' bodies can themselves use the Convention, at least when acting in their private capacity (p 555).

The Court of Appeal in *Aston Cantlow* had argued that a body is a public body if it has powers that a private body or citizen would not normally be able to acquire ([2002] Ch 51), but the House of Lords rejected this approach arguing it was too simplistic. Lord Hope argued that a parallel could be drawn to Article 34 of the Convention and that a distinction should be drawn between those which are obviously governmental organizations and those which are not (p 565). His Lordship, with whom a majority of the Lords agreed, stated that these would be 'core' or 'pure' public authorities. The 'authority' at issue in the *Aston Cantlow* case was the Wilmcote with Billesley Parochial Church Council. Parochial Church Councils (PCCs) are a creature of the Church of England and, because it is an established church, have a public status in so far as legislation creates and defines their authorities.[7] However Lord Hope, and a majority of the House of Lords, argued that this was not sufficient to make them a public authority as they could not realistically be said to have any governmental function and could not, therefore, be a 'core authority' (pp 569–570).

Lord Hope argued that deciding whether a body was a 'hybrid authority' required an examination of the facts in each case and identifying what it was precisely that amounted to a 'public function'. In the circumstances of this case the House held that

---

7. This ecclesiastical jurisdiction arises from the Synod which passes legislation known as 'Measures'. A Measure then proceeds to the Houses of Parliament and if they assent to it (and normally they will do so almost automatically) it is then given Royal Assent and has the same status as an Act of Parliament but is not an Act of Parliament (for general details of this see: <http://www.cofe.anglican.org/about/churchlawlegis/legislation/>).

the PCC did not have any public functions in the circumstances of this case, which concerned the recovery of land charges (see, in particular, the comments of Lord Hobhouse at pp 576–578).

Klug and Starmer argue that the test adopted by the House of Lords is correct. They characterize it as a very narrow approach to deciding who is a 'core' public authority (in effect only those who are governmental agencies) together with a wide definition of 'hybrid' bodies (those who undertake a public function) (Klug and Starmer (2005) 724). They suggest this approach is flexible and ensures that rights will be protected without denying rights to bodies that exercise some public functions.

❓ QUESTION FOR REFLECTION

Read Klug and Starmer pp 723–725 and *Aston Cantlow and Wilmcote with Billesley Parochial Church Council v Wallbank* [2004] 1 AC 546. How should a 'public body' be defined? Think of a university. Is this a public or a private body for the purposes of human rights? What would the implications be for plagiarism hearings (see, for example, 5.2.3.4 below).

🎧 LISTEN TO THE PODCAST

For guidance on how to answer this question and a discussion of the main issues, listen to the author's podcast on the Online Resource Centre:
www.oxfordtextbooks.co.uk/orc/gillespie_els3e/

Horizontal effect

Separate from the discussion as to what is, or is not, a public authority is the question of horizontal effect. Section 6(3)(a) makes clear that a court is a public body. Accordingly a court must act in a way compatible with the Convention. If this is taken literally then it must mean that the HRA can have a horizontal effect between two private parties because whereas the parties will not be bound by the Convention, a court when adjudicating on it must give effect to the Convention and act in a way compatible with it.

 Example Horizontal effect

Amy is suing Mandy alleging that she is playing her music too loud. This could be said to infringe Article 8 of the ECHR (right to respect for private and family life) but Mandy is not a public authority and not bound by the HRA.

When the matter gets to court Amy argues that there is a positive obligation (see below) to uphold her Article 8 rights. As the court is a public body it must act in a way compatible with the Convention, ie securing the Article 8 rights of Amy. Accordingly Amy has still managed to use the ECHR even though neither party to the litigation is a public body.

The notion of horizontal effect is quite controversial because if it is taken too literally then it could lead to a situation where the ECHR does become fully incorporated into UK law because the courts will always be bound to uphold someone's rights. Given the wide meaning that Article 8 and Article 10 (freedom of expression) have been given by the ECtHR, it is likely that most issues could interact with either Article.

The courts have, so far, managed to sidestep the issue of horizontal effect by relying on existing legal positions when they arise. In the example above the courts could as easily use the domestic law of nuisance in preference to the ECHR. Perhaps the most illustrative example of this sidestep was in *Campbell v Mirror Group Newspapers Ltd* [2004] 2 AC 457. The case in the *Daily Mirror* newspaper concerned reports that Naomi Campbell, a well-known supermodel, was attending meetings of Narcotics Anonymous. The story included details of when the meetings were, what was said, and photographs of her leaving the meetings. From a human-rights standpoint the issues were a prima facie breach of Article 8 balanced against the newspaper's Article 10 rights. It had long been thought that this would be one of the battlegrounds of the HRA and indeed parliamentary concern led to s 12 HRA being enacted which provides for various procedural and doctrinal findings in respect of the freedom of expression including the statement in s 12(4) that 'the court must have particular regard to the importance of the Convention right to freedom of expression' although in *Douglas and Others v Hello! Ltd* [2001] QB 967 Sedley LJ stated that all of Article 12 is of particular regard and therefore Article 12(2) is as important as Article 12(1) (p 1004).

In *Campbell* the House of Lords sidestepped the human-rights issues by relying on the domestic doctrine of confidence, a common-law tort. Morgan (2004) notes that this sidestepping is somewhat unconvincing as many of the features of this case would not fall within the tort of confidence as previously understood (p 564). Morgan correctly identifies that the judges were reluctant to tackle the issue even if only in *dicta* and questions whether the courts will ever tackle the issue directly (p 566). Until such time the question of horizontal effect is confined to academic circles although it is notable that the government-published *Study Guide* to the HRA does include reference to this doctrine so there appears to be official acceptance that at some point the question will need to be tackled (see Allen and Hill (2002) para 2.12).

Acting

Section 6(1) talks about 'acting' incompatibly but s 6(6) makes clear that a failure to act is also actionable unless the failure is in respect of parliamentary material (s 6(a)–(b)). The latter provision was required because although s 6(3) exempts Parliament from the provisions of the Act, without s 6(a)–(b) it would have been possible to bring an action against the relevant government minister alleging that he *should* have brought legislation before Parliament or exercised authority delegated to him by Parliament.

The inclusion of omissions is important because, as will be seen, a number of Articles in the ECHR include positive obligations—ie a duty is imposed on the state to secure the Convention by not merely refraining from interfering with the right itself but also to provide assistance to ensure that the right is not interfered with by others (see 5.2.2 below and also the discussion of individual rights).

Incompatibility

The requirement is that the public body must not act (or fail to act) in a way that is incompatible with the Convention. This simply means that it must act in accordance with the Convention and ensure, where relevant, that it respects a person's rights and freedoms including facilitating this where a positive duty is imposed. The courts must decide whether an action is incompatible and it will be seen below that the HRA permits the courts to look towards the jurisprudence of the ECtHR in deciding the meaning of these rights and freedoms.

5.1.2.2 Interpreting the Convention

Central to any decision as to whether the duty under s 6(1) has been complied with is an understanding of what the relevant Convention Articles mean. Section 3, which governs how the courts must interpret domestic statutes, has already been considered in Chapter 2. However in order to interpret the statute it must be possible to identify the relevant Convention right.

Section 2 HRA expressly deals with interpretation and s 2(1) states that a court must take into account any decision, inter alia, of the ECtHR or the Commission.[8] There had been concerns that whilst the language appears mandatory the Act then states that the court must decide how relevant it is to proceedings, thus providing a degree of flexibility which may mean the court could decide not to follow it (Masterman (2004) 725).

It is perhaps something of a surprise that the matter did not become in issue to any degree of prominence until 2009 when the Supreme Court ruled on whether domestic courts were obliged to follow decisions of the ECtHR. In *R v Horncastle* [2010] 2 WLR 47 the Supreme Court was asked to rule on an evidence case. The appellant had been convicted of causing grievous bodily harm with intent (s 18 *Offences Against the Person Act 1861*) and whilst the victim had given a statement to the police, the victim had (for unconnected reasons) died before the matter came to trial. The statement was read out in court and, whilst there was other evidence, the Court of Appeal (Criminal Division) had ruled that it was 'to a decisive degree' the basis upon which the appellant had been convicted.

The appellant sought to argue that the admission of the statement breached Article 6 of the ECHR as he was unable to cross-examine the victim: the jury therefore only heard one side of the story. Reliance was placed on *Al-Khawaja and Tahery v United Kingdom* (2009) 49 EHRR 1 where the ECtHR had held that where a statement of a person not able to be cross-examined was 'the sole, or at least, the decisive basis' for a conviction then Article 6 was breached.

The Supreme Court refused to follow the decision of *Al-Khawaja*, in part because Article 43 of the ECHR allows a party to a decision to petition that the matter is heard by the Grand Chamber of the ECtHR (discussed in Chapter 4). This had happened in this case although the matter had not been resolved. The Supreme Court held that whilst s 2(1) meant that ordinarily a decision would be followed, the Supreme Court reserved the right to rule that certain decisions of the ECtHR did not sufficiently appreciate or accommodate particular aspects of the UK domestic process. In such circumstances it could refuse to follow the Strasbourg court.

The decision is perhaps surprising given that the relevant case before the ECtHR related to the UK. Whilst there may be decisions of the ECtHR that do not recognize the subtleties of UK law it should not be in those cases where the ECtHR has had UK law specifically brought to its attention.

Can the decision be justified? It will be remembered that Dwyer argued that it creates a dualist approach to human rights and the jurisprudence of the ECtHR is central to the international context rather than being fundamental to the domestic context. Nothing within the Convention requires the domestic law to mirror exactly the Convention and indeed it has already been noted that states are only required to 'take account of' decisions of the ECtHR so it could be argued that it would be unusual to bind domestic

---

courts in a way that they are not so bound at international level. The dualist approach also, of course, means that if an aggrieved person believes the domestic interpretation is wrong they could petition the ECtHR alleging that the state (through the judiciary) has failed to secure their human rights or freedoms.

A principal reason why s 2 does not require the courts to be bound by decisions of the ECtHR is that it relies on a different legal premise. As was seen in Chapter 3, the English Legal System is based on the premise of *stare decisis* and yet the ECtHR does not recognize such an approach. Whilst the ECtHR will take into account its previous decisions it does not feel that it must be bound by them, in part because it has consistently argued that the Convention is a 'living instrument' that changes to take into account the progress of society (see Masterman (2004) 728 who discusses this). It was thought that a danger in making all courts bound by the ECtHR could undermine *stare decisis* in this country leading to uncertainty.

The final reason is one articulated by Lord Irvine and returns us to the dualist approach when he said: 'our courts must be free to try to give a lead to Europe as well as to be led'. The logic behind this comment is that cases will inevitably continue to proceed to the ECtHR and that Court will benefit from a full examination of human-rights issues at the domestic level. This is something that was raised in *Horncastle* where the Supreme Court noted that if the matter proceeded to the Grand Chamber it would have the benefit of the Supreme Court's analysis ([2010] 2 WLR 47 at 124) meaning that the domestic courts can contribute to the evolution of Strasbourg jurisprudence.

⮑ PRECEDENT VSECTION 2

It has been noted that s 2 requires the courts to take account of ECHR issues and there has been some discussion as to what this means in terms of precedent. How has this resolved itself in practice? In *Kay v Lambeth London Borough Council* [2006] 2 AC 465 the House of Lords stated that the rules of precedent should be followed and that where a binding precedent is incompatible with a decision of the ECtHR the matter should be sent to appeal, even invoking the 'leap-frog' procedure that allows decisions of the High Court to be appealed to the Supreme Court where a matter is of public importance.

An example of this in practice can be found in *R (on behalf of Purdy) v DPP* [2008] EWHC 2565 where the Divisional Court was asked to rule on an assisted suicide issue. The claimant suggested that the DPP should have to publish a specific policy in respect of when he would prosecute people for assisted suicide. This raised a similar (but sufficiently distinct) point from the 'Diane Pretty' litigation. An issue arose as to whether Article 8(1) was engaged. The House of Lords had held in the *Pretty* case that it was not (*R (on behalf of Pretty) v DPP* [2002] 1 AC 800) but Diane Pretty had then taken the matter to the ECtHR who held that it had invoked Article 8 (although deciding it was a justifiable interference) (*Pretty v United Kingdom* (2002) 35 EHRR 1).

The Divisional Court had to decide whether it was bound by the House of Lords decision in *Pretty* or whether it could follow the ECtHR (which s 2 would seem to imply). They held that the ruling in *Kay* was clear and that they were bound by the House of Lords and that only the House (now Supreme Court) could alter this precedent (see para 46 of *Purdy*). The decision in *R v Horncastle* [2010] 2 WLR 47 would lend support to this argument as the Supreme Court was, in that case, expressly stating that it had the right to depart from Strasbourg and that other courts must follow the ruling of the Supreme Court.

Margin of appreciation

The ECtHR does not, in connection with certain rights or freedoms, always adopt a uniform approach to the meaning of rights and freedoms but instead extends a 'margin of appreciation' to the states. A margin of appreciation is, in effect, latitude in terms of the implementation of rights whereby it recognizes that society in some states will differ from others. Perhaps the most illustrative example of the margin of appreciation is to be found in the field of obscenity legislation. Different countries adopt different rules to the criminalization of obscenity and although any rule will interfere with the right to freedom of expression (Article 10) this can be justified for, inter alia, the protection of morals (Article 10(2)). In *Handyside v United Kingdom* (1979) 1 EHRR 737 the ECtHR made clear that the protection of morals is an area where a margin of appreciation must be extended as each country has a different approach to morality and pornography (pp 753–754). The ECtHR refused to set down a rule that would be relevant to all societies but said that morality in different states should be taken into account and that the state should have the right to protect society. The margin is not unlimited however and the ECtHR can curtail the margin where it believes a state has gone too far in its restrictions.

It is less clear whether the margin applies to the HRA. Lord Hope in *R v DPP, ex p Kebilene* [2000] 2 AC 326 thought it did not as it was a matter of international law whereby an international court showed deference to a state in terms of its individual society (p 380) but Lord Irvine, the then Lord Chancellor, has argued that the courts have adopted their own version of this test (Irvine (2003) 315). He argues that this version is where the courts defer to Parliament and the executive over some issues surrounding society on the basis that certain areas are political rather than purely legal (ibid). It has been said that this deference began with judicial review (Leigh (2002) 266) and has become an established part of HRA actions with the concept being the courts will defer to the executive where there is a 'fair balance' between the interests of society as a whole and the individual's human rights (p 276). However, Leigh argues that it should be restricted solely to qualified rights (ie Articles 8–11) and not to absolute rights, for example Articles 2 and 3 (p 277).

Others disagree with this proposition and suggest that there is no reason why deference should not occur in absolute rights too (Atrill (2003) 44). This argument is based on the premise that there is no such thing as a 'qualified' right and that Articles 8–11 are erroneously so called because, in essence, the first part of each Article provides only a prima facie right or freedom and it is only when the derogation (the second paragraph of each Article) is applied can it be decided whether the right applies or not (pp 44–45). Accordingly, Atrill argues that all rights are unqualified and that there is no difference between the Articles themselves. Certainly it is true to say that the rights and freedoms traditionally labelled as qualified are not subservient to the absolute rights, with the ECtHR itself arguing that Article 10 (freedom of expression) is an essential foundation for democracy (see, for example, *Hertel v Switzerland* (1999) 28 EHRR 534) which suggests that it recognizes this as one of the more important rights. However, this would also be slightly misleading in that the ECtHR itself has adopted a strict interpretation to Articles 2 and 3 with any margin of appreciation being highly restricted.

Atrill argues that the domestic equivalent to a margin of appreciation—judicial deference—is required for all rights and that not doing so would restrict the development of rights (Atrill (2003) 51). Lord Irvine appears to believe the correct approach is somewhere between these two polarized opinions. He recognizes that there is a need for the courts to hold the executive and legislature to account and that proportionality (see below) is a powerful tool in checking the validity and extent of any deference (Irvine (2003) 316) but he also argues that there are some situations where the courts need to defer to the executive and legislature, as bodies with democratic authority. A good example of this, he suggested, was terrorism (pp 317–318) although others would undoubtedly argue that this is a situation where the courts need to be active in order to ensure the executive does not gain draconian powers to the detriment of society. However, the two need not be mutually exclusive since the ECtHR itself has stated that deference does not exclude its jurisdiction and the same would be true here. A domestic margin of appreciation means that the courts will ordinarily be slow to act in certain situations but that they continue to reserve the right to act where they believe that the powers of even the elected authorities are disproportionate to the threat they seek to combat.

Necessity and proportionality

Central to many of the Convention rights, but in particular the qualified rights under Articles 8–11, are the concepts of necessity and proportionality. Arguably this is a little simplistic as proportionality is referred to in many Convention Articles, particularly Article 6 (right to a fair trial), and necessity is also a flexible concept. Some argue that necessity is part of proportionality as at its simplest it can be argued that necessity means that just because a public body has the right to do something does not mean that it should. A public authority should only interfere with someone's rights when it has to, not just when it wants to: in other words it is when it *has* to—not when it would be *merely convenient* to do so.

In *Soering v United Kingdom* (1989) 11 EHRR 439 the ECtHR explained the principle of proportionality:

> inherent in the whole of the Convention is a search for a fair balance between the demands of the general public interest of the community and the requirements of the protection of the individual's fundamental rights. (p 469)

Thus proportionality is remembering that although a person has a right, this right must be kept in the context of society's rights and should not create a position whereby it causes undue problems for society. In respect of the qualified rights (see below) proportionality will often mean that the extent of a right should be limited so as to ensure that the public are not unduly constrained. Arguably proportionality has two dimensions to it. The first is whether a right should be interfered with (and this will incorporate the idea of necessity) and the second is how far the interference should go. It is, in particular, this latter dimension that is particularly relevant to the qualified rights.

⊙ PROPORTIONALITY

In Northern Ireland there is a 'Parades Commission' that seeks to adjudicate on disputes arising from marches that occur each year in the Province. The marches are normally undertaken by Protestant organizations (eg the Orange Order) and commemorate historic battles. The battles were part of a series of campaigns between Protestant and Catholic monarchs that sought control of Europe, the United Kingdom, and Ireland. Many marches throughout the island of Ireland take place peacefully but the march in Belfast has often been controversial and has, on a number of occasions, led to violence between Republican and Loyalist factions hiding under the cloak of Protestant and Catholic allegiances.

Articles 10 and 11 provide the right to freedom of expression and freedom of assembly and, taken together, could provide a right to march. However both are qualified rights and the state (through the Parades Commission in this instance) can interfere with the rights so long as it is for a legitimate aim and proportionate.

In recent years the Parades Commission has banned the march from passing through Catholic areas of Belfast City and instead re-routed it through Protestant areas. Although this is highly controversial to the Orange Order (who claim the right to walk down the Queen's Highway) the decision is arguably proportionate as it seeks a balance between the right of people to march (and indeed the parades and marches do occur) but also between the wider members of certain sections of society who consider the marches offensive. Finding the balance is not easy and it is this tension which the ECtHR was considering (albeit in a different context) in *Soering* and its later pronouncements on proportionality.

When considering whether a public body acted appropriately the concept of proportionality was alien to the English courts with the traditional view being taken that the courts would only interfere when a decision was illegal, procedurally improper, or irrational (see, for example, *Associated Provincial Picture Houses Ltd v Wednesbury Corporation* [1948] 1 KB 223 and Loveland (2009) 456–482). However, proportionality arguably differs considerably from these traditional grounds as the latter examined whether a decision was wrong and yet proportionality is suggesting that there are competing rights. In *R (on behalf of Daly) v Secretary of State for the Home Department* [2001] 2 AC 532 Lord Steyn summarized what he believed were three differences:

> First, the doctrine of proportionality may require the reviewing court to assess the balance which the decision maker has struck, not merely whether it is within the range of rational or reasonable decisions. Secondly, the proportionality test may go further than the traditional grounds of review inasmuch as it may require attention to be directed to the relative weight accorded to interests and considerations. Thirdly, even the heightened scrutiny test . . . is not necessarily appropriate to the protection of human rights. (p 547)

His Lordship certainly believed that the intensity of the review of a decision-making process under proportionality is greater than in traditional reviews (ibid) presumably because of the balance required: ie the courts must look at the rights of both the claimant and society in deciding where the balance is to be struck and not just at whether the decision was wrong. However, it should be remembered that this only applied where a Convention right is in issue; if the matter is purely one of domestic law then the traditional grounds of review continue to be used.

5.1.2.3 Litigating the Act

Section 6 provides a duty on public authorities to act in a way compatible with the Convention but how is this to be enforced? It was noted that it is a civil rather than criminal liability but as will be seen that does not necessarily mean its use is restricted to civil matters. Section 7 HRA deals with the use of the Act and it provides that it can be used both as the basis of an action (s 7(1)(a)) and in defending an action (s 7(1)(b)). In other words the Act can be used as both a 'sword' and a 'shield'. However, its use is restricted to a 'victim', the definition of which has caused some difficulty.

Victim

To an extent it can be argued that domestic English public law has adopted a reasonably inclusive approach to permitting people to challenge the actions of public authorities. The concept of 'judicial review' grew significantly in the twentieth century and whilst its boundaries are the cause of some controversy (see Stevens (2002) 129–136) it is an established doctrine that permits a wide range of people to challenge the actions of a public body.

The courts have developed a doctrine known as 'standing' (sometimes referred to as *locus standi*) in respect of deciding who is able to bring actions under judicial review although this is now, to an extent, consolidated in Parts 8 and 54 of the *Civil Procedure Rules* which govern civil litigation.[9] The basis for 'standing' is that a person can show sufficient interest in the matter that is to be challenged (s 31 *Senior Courts Act 1981*). It is not necessary for them to show an actual infringement of their legal rights and it allows, for example, campaign groups to access judicial review (Loveland (2009) 551–557).

The ECtHR on the other hand has always adopted a strict approach to who can bring an action. In part this is because the Convention itself states that only a victim or a state can petition the Court (Articles 33–34) and the ECtHR has ensured that the definition of 'victim' will not include hypothetical cases (see Nicol and Marriott (1998) 735). Controversially the government, when enacting the HRA, decided to adopt the ECHR definition of a victim rather than the domestic public law meaning used for judicial review.

It is important to note that this restriction only applies where s 7 is to be used; where no human-rights issues are involved and the matter proceeds under administrative law, the courts continue to adopt the domestic approach. Some argue this limits the application of the HRA to protecting only those who can demonstrate a real personal detriment (Fredman (1998) 542) rather than adopting a more flexible approach that permits bodies to challenge the wider actions of a public body. This is certainly a landmark change and argues that it is a rare example of when '[ECHR] law is less generous than our own' (Wade (1998) 532). No clear rationale was put forward for this restriction although others suggest the whole issue is a distraction since, if a victim cannot be found, then it is probably a purely hypothetical argument and the courts should not be troubled (Cooper (1998) 2). This supposition is probably correct as at the time the Act was being debated there was a widespread fear that the courts would be 'clogged' with challenges under the Act, including vexatious ones. In fact this did not materialize, a point made by Lord Irvine (2003) pp 312–313.

To some degree the government was right to believe that it will be relatively easy to find a victim because although a campaigning group might not bring an action, one of their members could and the campaign group could fund it.

 Example Campaign groups

Townsville Water, a (hypothetical) water authority, has decided that they are going to discharge lightly treated sewage off the coast of Townsville. Greenpeace may wish to challenge

---

9. The rules governing civil litigation are considered in Chapter 14.

this decision but could not do so under the HRA as they themselves would not amount to a 'victim'. However Gordon, one of their members who surfs off Townsville beach, could bring an action as he is a victim but Greenpeace can fund the action.

However, this is a less than ideal situation as the individual victim is taking a risk as the courts will impose personal liability so if the campaign group renege on their promise to fund the litigation then the individual victim is liable for the costs. Also, given that it relatively simple to adopt such an approach it must be seriously questioned whether the restriction can achieve its 'aim' of restricting vexatious challenges. The better approach might have been to recognize the role of campaign groups and to adopt the traditional doctrine of 'standing' and trust the courts to ensure that leave is not given to vexatious or purely theoretical challenges.

Sword

Assuming that a person can demonstrate that they are a victim then s 7 of the Act permits the victim to bring an action against the public authority citing breach. The breach need not have happened as s 7(1) expressly states that an action can be in anticipation of the breach.

> **Example** Anticipated action
>
> Robert is organizing a protest march against capitalism. The police do not wish the route of the march to proceed through the city centre. They plan to use their powers to order the route to be re-routed through outlying areas.
>   Prima facie this is a breach of Articles 10 (freedom of expression) and 11 (freedom of assembly) and Robert, as a direct victim, could bring an action against the police before the march takes place alleging the actions of the police, a public authority, will interfere with his rights.

The HRA does not itself create any new form of litigation but instead states it can be used as a basis of action under existing procedures. This will normally be a form of judicial review given that it is the actions of a public authority, but it may also take the form of an action in other forms of law, for example tort (nuisance, negligence, wrongful imprisonment, etc). Normally proceedings should be instigated within one year of the alleged breach occurring (s 7(5)) although the courts do have discretion to extend this where they believe it is fair to do so. Where the HRA is used then the Act itself provides for additional remedies (see below).

Shield

Section 7 does not just provide for the right to take action against a public authority but also permits a victim to rely on the Convention as a defence to proceedings brought against them by, inter alia, a public body. In the civil sphere this may, for example, include a situation whereby a local authority seeks to enforce planning rules and the victim states that this enforcement interferes with their right to respect for private and family life (Article 8).

Where the shield is arguably more frequently employed (albeit not necessarily successfully) is in criminal trials. Whilst s 6 HRA does not create any criminal liability, s 7 of the Act does permit someone to raise a Convention right as a defence in any proceedings, including criminal cases. The usual claim under these circumstances will be that the prosecuting agency has breached its right to a fair trial (Article 6).

5.1.2.4 Remedies under the Act

Assuming that it can be demonstrated under s 7 that an individual's rights have been infringed then the next question that arises is as to what remedy the court will grant in respect of this breach. The Act states:

> [A court] may grant such relief or remedy, or make such order, within its powers as it considers just and appropriate. (s 8(1))

A number of issues arise here including declarations and compensation. The first matter, however, is whether there is a right to any remedy.

Article 13: The missing Article

Article 13 of the Convention provides that everyone whose rights are breached under the Convention has the right to an effective remedy. However, Article 13 has, controversially, not been included within the HRA. In part, this is because the government argued that the HRA itself was the realization of Article 13 and that, whereas before a remedy could only be obtained by petitioning the ECtHR itself, the HRA allows for domestic remedies (White (1997) 517). Given that the HRA does not create any new procedures it was also thought that a remedy will always be granted but this misses the point that damages and relief are often discretionary.

One argument, however, is that the courts will have to interpret the Convention to take account of Article 13 ensuring that where a breach is detected then a remedy is granted (Feldman (1998) 692). Whilst this should be unproblematic in many situations (see below) it does arguably create a difficulty where a statute is contrary to the Convention and cannot be interpreted in such a way to make it compatible. In these circumstances the only option a court has is the declaration of incompatibility but, as will be seen, this cannot be said to be an effective remedy.

Declarations of incompatibility

It was noted in Chapter 2 that the courts have a duty to attempt to construct primary legislation in a way that is compatible with the Convention (para 2.3.4) but there may be circumstances when this is not possible. Unlike in some jurisdictions, most notably the United States of America, the courts have no power to 'strike down' any law, with s 4 HRA setting out what should happen when the courts are presented with a scenario where an Act of Parliament clearly contradicts the ECHR.

Section 4 gives the higher courts the power to impose a declaration of incompatibility. The expectation was few declarations would be either sought or made (Feldman (1998) 698) and the early years of the Act's implementation did appear to show this. That said, the position is perhaps more complicated by an absence of central statistics on the matter. Prior to 2006 the Ministry of Justice kept a publicly available database of final declarations made, but it has since stopped updating this database, something decried by the *Joint Committee on Human Rights* in its thirty-first report (para 81).

A crucial feature of a declaration of incompatibility is that it does not affect the legality of the relevant Act. Indeed, at its most basic, a declaration under s 4 is just that, a mere statement from the court that a person's Convention rights have been breached. The actions of any public servant need theoretically not change when a declaration of incompatibility is made. Some have therefore questioned whether a declaration is of any use (Feldman (1998) 699) and certainly the *Joint Committee on Human Rights*, in its thirty-first report, questioned whether they afforded sufficient protection. The Committee noted that, of course, remedial action need not be required in each occasion, but it concluded that the government should be required to state, within a defined timescale, whether and, if so, how it would remedy any breach.

The fact that a declaration of incompatibility carries with it no direct action means that it can be argued it is itself incompatible with Article 13. It is perhaps for this reason that the government did not want to include Article 13 in the HRA as if it were then the courts might be obliged to provide a remedy to the person suffering breach which would directly challenge the supremacy of Parliament. Given that a declaration of incompatibility is, in effect, a finding of breach then it would seem likely that anyone who suffers loss or damage arising from this breach could petition the ECtHR as it would be somewhat difficult for the government to contest such an action. The ECtHR can award compensation in such circumstances as Article 13 is binding on the Convention in its international guise.

A declaration of incompatibility does, however, have wider implications beyond the dispute between the parties. Where a court is contemplating making a declaration of incompatibility it must serve notice on the government so that it can be joined as a party (s 5). If a declaration is given then s 8 HRA grants the government remedial powers to remedy this breach. This is known as a 'Henry VIII order' and it means that the government may amend primary legislation via secondary legislation. At least one commentator believes that this is a curb on the supremacy of Parliament in that the executive is altering laws passed by the legislature (Fredman (1998) 542).

REMEDIAL CORRECTIONS

In *R (on the application of H) v Mental Health Review Tribunal (North and East London Region)* [2002] QB 1 the Court of Appeal made the first declaration of incompatibility when it held that s 73 *Mental Health Act 1983* was incompatible with Article 5 (right to liberty) of the ECHR. Section 73 stated that where a person had been detained under the *Mental Health Act* then the burden of showing that the detention was no longer justified was on the patient rather than on the health authority. The government sought to use its powers under s 8 and the *Mental Health Act 1983 (Remedial) Order 2001*, SI 2001/3712 was made which amended s 73 to place the burden on the authority.

Remedies against judicial acts

Where the allegation is that a court (which is expressly a public authority by virtue of s 6(3)(a)) has acted contrary to the Convention then the only remedy that lies is a right of appeal or judicial review (s 9). This is to ensure that people do not re-litigate their disputes by suing individual judges when they believe that the judgment of the court has infringed their Convention rights. This is a necessary step and has led to little dispute.

Judicial immunity (see 7.5.2.4 below) is also expressly contained in the Act when it states that damages may not be awarded when a judicial act has been undertaken in good faith (s 9(3)). The only exception to this rule is in respect of Article 5 of the ECHR (right to liberty). Article 5(5) expressly states that where a person has been detained unlawfully by the state they have an automatic right to compensation. Section 9(3) HRA makes clear, therefore, that the rule against damages does not extend to breaches of Article 5 although the government (via the appropriate minister) must be made a party to the proceedings when any court believes that it will be necessary to award damages under that section (see s 9(4)).

Remedies in civil matters

The full range of remedies can be found in connection with civil matters. The range of remedies is very wide and ranges from a simple declaration through prerogative orders to financial relief.

A simple declaration may be used where someone has used the Act in respect of an anticipated breach. If we refer back to the example on p 157 it is possible that Robert would be satisfied with a simple declaration that his rights would be infringed by detouring the route as the police are unlikely to act in a way that has been declared unlawful.

Alternatively Robert may ask for a prerogative order (so called because the historic justification for these orders derives from the sovereign), most likely a *mandatory order* (formerly known as a *mandamus*)[10] which would compel the police to allow Robert's protest to proceed down the route they wish. Other prerogative orders include *quashing orders* (formerly *certiorari*) which would quash an unlawful decision and *prohibiting orders* (formerly *prohibitio*) which prohibits a public body from doing a particular act that would lead to a breach. The latter is used where it is anticipated that a breach may occur.

In other situations the applicant may seek financial compensation. To an extent the Act restricts the availability of this remedy in certain ways. The first is that only a court or tribunal that has the power to provide financial compensation may do so. In the vast majority of situations this will be unproblematic as most courts have the right to provide compensation but some tribunals do not. The second restriction is that the HRA states that the courts must apply the reasoning of Article 41 of the ECHR and the ancillary jurisprudence. Article 41 governs when the ECtHR may award compensation and it, in effect, restricts compensation to situations when it will provide 'just satisfaction'. In a number of cases the ECtHR has stated that a declaration of breach is sufficient satisfaction and it has been questioned whether the domestic courts are likely to adopt a similar approach (Fairgrieve (2001) 703). Even where the ECtHR does decide that damages are required they tend to be compensatory damages and not punitive or exemplary damages (p 704). It is likely that it is this aspect of Article 41 that the government was intending when it was drafting s 8. However, this could cause confusion and other commentators have argued this could arise where an action could proceed either under a human-rights head or through domestic liability, since damages under domestic law (eg tort) will be unconstrained whereas damages where a breach is found will be subject to Article 41 (Fredman (1998) 703).

---

10. The Latin terms *mandamus*, *certiorari*, and *prohibitio* were renamed by the *Civil Procedure (Modification of Senior Courts Act 1981) Order 2004*, SI 2004/1033, para 3.

Remedies in criminal cases

It was noted above (5.1.2.3) that it is possible to use the HRA in criminal proceedings. Where a person is charged with a criminal offence what is the remedy for a breach of a Convention right? The HRA makes clear that it is possible to rely on the Convention as a defence and accordingly it may be possible, in extreme situations, to argue that a defendant should not be convicted as a result of the breach of the Convention but these will be relatively rare examples. More likely is that a serious breach of the Convention could lead to a successful argument that prosecuting the defendant would amount to an abuse of process and, accordingly, the prosecution should be halted. The House of Lords accepted that this could be the case, albeit *in obiter* and *per curiam* in the conjoined cases of *Attorney-General's Reference (No 3 of 2000); R v Looseley* [2001] 1 WLR 2060 where they accepted that the abuse-of-process doctrine was compatible with the ECHR. However in a later decision the House stated quite clearly that it would be exceptional for breaches to halt criminal proceedings.

In *Attorney-General's Reference (No 2 of 2001)* [2004] 2 AC 72 the House of Lords was called upon to consider the appropriate remedy in situations where there had been excessive delay in prosecuting defendants and bringing them before the courts for trial. Article 6(1) states a defendant has the right to a trial 'within a reasonable time' and the judge at first instance had stayed the trial arguing this was the appropriate remedy. The Attorney-General referred the matter to the appellate courts[11] and it eventually reached the House of Lords.

The House agreed that undue delay could breach Article 6(1) and argued that the 'clock' will normally start when a person is charged or summonsed before the court although this was not always the case as excessive delay between a formal interview and a charge may also be relevant (p 91). However, the House was dismissive of the idea that the only 'effective remedy' for undue delay is a stay of proceedings. Lord Bingham argued that remedies such as an acceleration of the timetable, the granting of bail, or even financial compensation might suffice (p 89). His Lordship suggested that a stay should only be granted if the delay was so long that it would no longer be possible to guarantee a fair trial. The rationale behind this is that of proportionality: society has the right to expect protection from those who commit crimes and that where it is possible to do so fairly then a trial should continue. Lord Nicholls went further and argued that a stay would not be an effective remedy because it was against the wrong breach. His Lordship argued that normally the breach is not holding a trial after an excessive delay but rather not holding a trial in sufficient time (pp 93–94). If, as the House believed, it is the latter then the trial is not unfair even if there has been a breach of Article 6. If the trial is not unfair then it cannot be an effective remedy to stay the trial. The House was leaving open the possibility that there could be circumstances in which holding a trial after excessive delay would be unfair (but that it is likely to be as a result of other factors, eg witness availability etc) and in those circumstances the effective remedy *may* be the stay of a trial.

It would seem therefore that the opportunities to use the HRA as a defence in criminal trials is now somewhat restricted although it has been suggested that this is not yet settled law and that the ECtHR itself has been taking a stricter line on procedural

---

11. An *Attorney-General's Reference* in this context is a hypothetical appeal whereby the appellate courts are asked a point of law that arises from an acquittal. It proceeds as though it were an appeal but the decision of the appellate courts does not alter the acquittal, it simply forms a precedent for future cases (see 13.4.2 below).

defects in trials, especially improper delay (Ashworth (2004) 576). Ashworth appears to be arguing, therefore, that the ECtHR may suggest that delay may by itself lead to an unfair trial which would, following Lord Nicholls' argument, lead to the only effective remedy being a stay. It is notable that in the *Attorney-General's Reference* Lord Hope gave a strong dissenting judgment where he argued that it is not possible to detach the timing of the trial from the fairness of its execution (p 110) and that any delay that takes place after undue delay is necessarily a breach of the right to a fair trial. Lord Hope was alone in his views but if Ashworth is correct his analysis may find favour in the ECtHR. Given that Article 13 is not within the HRA it is conceivable to see that a person convicted after undue delay but within Lord Bingham's reasoning could petition the ECtHR alleging a breach of Article 6 *and* a breach of Article 13. The ECtHR has no power to quash convictions but it could, presumably, state whether it thought that financial compensation or the granting of bail is an 'effective remedy' for the purposes of Article 6. Whether a domestic court would then follow that decision is perhaps more moot.

❓ QUESTION FOR REFLECTION

What do you think the remedy should be for a breach of human rights in a criminal case? Just because a right has been infringed does not necessarily mean that the defendant did not commit the crime he is accused of. Should a conviction be quashed or a prosecution halted simply because there has been a violation of human rights? Read the next section (5.2); do you think the remedy should differ depending on which right has been infringed?

🎧 LISTEN TO THE PODCAST

For guidance on how to answer this question and a discussion of the main issues, listen to the author's podcast on the Online Resource Centre:
www.oxfordtextbooks.co.uk/orc/gillespie_els3e/

5.2 The individual rights

In this section a very brief examination will be made of the key Convention rights. Not all rights will be discussed here but rather the ones you are most likely to read about. This section is designed to help you understand the basic principle of the Convention rights and how it may be used in practice. In a departure from the usual style of this book, further reading will be given to you after each right in case you wish to consider the rights in more detail.

5.2.1 Absolute and qualified rights

It is sometimes said that Articles can be divided into absolute and qualified rights, the latter being Articles that can be interfered with under certain circumstances. The ECtHR itself uses this language when referring to Articles 8–11, each of which is in two parts. The first part sets out what the right or freedom is, and the second part sets out the circumstances under which the state can interfere with this right.

However, some have suggested that this is too basic an analysis (see, for example, Atrill (2003) 44) and that all rights are subject to some qualifications. Certainly, as will be seen, there is an argument that this may be true. Article 2, the right to life, is often referred to as an 'absolute' right and yet on the face of the Article it states there are circumstances under which the state can kill and not infringe this right. Is this not a qualification? Similarly other Articles do not appear to contain any qualification, eg Article 6 (right to fair trial) and yet the ECtHR has stated that this is not an absolute right (see, for example, *Condron v United Kingdom* (2001) 31 EHRR 1). That said, this is perhaps merely a recognition that there is no 'binary divide' between absolute and qualified rights but that each exists alongside other laws.

The term 'qualified right' will continue to be used in this text especially in relation to Articles 8–11 as this is the wording used by the Strasbourg authorities. This will be discussed further below.

5.2.2 Positive and negative obligations

Article 1 of the ECHR requires states to 'secure to everyone in their jurisdiction the rights and freedoms [of the Convention]' and this has been construed to mean that some Articles will have a positive obligation on the state to secure the right. A negative obligation is quite standard and merely means that the state (in our case the United Kingdom) must not infringe the rights under the Convention. For example, therefore, this means that the state must not use torture on someone. However certain Articles (most notably Articles 2, 3 and 8) also place a positive obligation on the state to *protect* a citizen from receiving such treatment (see, for example, *Osman v United Kingdom* (2000) 29 EHRR 245). Thus a state will not only be liable for actually infringing a right but also for allowing a private citizen to be harmed by another. That said, the positive obligation is not absolute and merely requires the state to take reasonable action and this includes, for example, ensuring that there are effective laws protecting an individual (see, for example, *X and Y v Netherlands* (1986) 8 EHRR 235). To this extent it can be said that there is a limited 'horizontal effect' to the ECHR and, therefore, the HRA 1998.

5.2.3 Principal Convention rights

5.2.3.1 Article 2: Right to life

The first substantive right to examine is Article 2 which states:

1. Everyone's right to life shall be protected by law. No one shall be deprived of his life intentionally save in the execution of a sentence of a court following his conviction for a crime for which this penalty is provided by law.

2. Deprivation of life shall not be regarded as inflicted in contravention of this article when it results from the use of force which is no more than absolutely necessary:

   (a) in defence of any person from unlawful violence;

   (b) in order to effect a lawful arrest or to prevent escape of a person lawfully detained;

   (c) in action lawfully taken for the purpose of quelling a riot or insurrection.

In England and Wales Article 2(1) could, in fact, be shortened by the deletion of the second sentence (beginning 'No one shall...') because the United Kingdom has also signed the Sixth Protocol to the Convention which abolishes the death penalty (Article 1) although in time of war it may be reintroduced to a limited extent (Article 2). Whether this is more than a moot point however is somewhat questionable since the United Kingdom has never declared war since the Second World War and thus, despite fighting numerous conflicts, it has never been in a state of war since 1945.

Article 2 is one of the classic examples of a positive obligation (see 5.2.2 above) and the words 'everyone's right to life shall be protected by law' has been interpreted to mean that the public have the right to be protected by the state where an identifiable danger exists (see, for example, *Osman v United Kingdom* (2000) 29 EHRR 245). Controversially, it has also been used to state that any operation by state authorities which could lead to the use of lethal force must be carefully planned and the risk of using lethal force considered and minimized (see *McCann v United Kingdom* (1996) 21 EHRR 97) and Article 2 has also been used to state that there should be the right to an independent and effective investigation after a death inflicted by the state (*Jordan v United Kingdom* (2003) 37 EHRR 2). This has become increasingly important in recent years with cases discussing whether investigations into shootings by police officers conducted by the Independent Police Complaints Commission satisfy the requirements of Article 2 (see, for example, *Saunders and another v IPCC and others* [2008] EWHC 2372 (Admin) which raised questions whether the practice of allowing police officers to confer before making their statements may infringe the procedural safeguards guaranteed by Article 2).

It can be seen, therefore, that Article 2 is a wide-ranging power. The main purpose of Article 2(2) is paragraph (a) and the courts have suggested that this is roughly equivalent to the domestic law under s 3 *Criminal Law Act 1967* although there is a subtle difference of wording between s 3 and Article 2(2)(a).

Further reading

Ni Aolain F (2002) 'Truth telling, accountability and the right to life in Northern Ireland' 5 *European Human Rights Law Review* 572–590.

This is an interesting article on the use of Article 2 within the context of the anti-terrorist operations in Northern Ireland.

Rogers J (2005) 'Shoot, identify and repent?' 155 *New Law Journal* 1273–1274.

This is a controversial article that examines the potential liability of the police regarding the shooting of Jean Charles de Menezes, the innocent Brazilian who was wrongly shot by the Metropolitan Police in July 2005. Note, however, you should also read the Crown Prosecution Service report on this case (a link can be found on the Online Resource Centre accompanying this book) as this demonstrates why no officers will be prosecuted for this.

Wadham J (2004) 'Investigations into deaths in police custody and the Independent Police Complaints Commission' 4 *European Human Rights Law Review* 353–361.

This looks at how the IPCC investigates deaths allegedly caused by the police.

5.2.3.2 Article 3: Prohibition of torture

Article 3 is the shortest of all the Convention articles:

No one shall be subjected to torture or inhuman or degrading treatment or punishment.

This is another absolute right and one that contains a positive obligation on states, ie not only must it not subject somebody to torture, inhuman or degrading treatment, it must protect the person suffering this from others. Some uncertainty arose as to what the difference in wording was but in *Ireland v United Kingdom* (1979–80) 2 EHRR 25 the ECtHR defined the terms. The case followed accusations of mistreatment by the security force in Northern Ireland of suspected terrorists. The Court found that whilst no suspect had been tortured, they had suffered inhuman and degrading treatment, the Court believing that torture involved 'deliberate inhuman treatment causing very serious and cruel suffering' (p 80).

In order for a treatment or punishment to amount to either degrading or inhuman treatment it must pass a minimum threshold of severity (see *Costello-Roberts v United Kingdom* (1995) 19 EHRR 112) since not every type of shameful treatment will amount to a breach of Article 8. That said, this is not to say that it is not actionable since it is possible action could be brought under the right to personal integrity under Article 8 (see 5.2.3.6 below). One of the principal battlegrounds in relation to Article 3 is the concept of corporal punishment with the European Court reaching different conclusions as to its compatibility with Article 3 (see *Costello-Roberts v United Kingdom (1995) cf A v United Kingdom* (1999) 27 EHRR 611).

Outside of corporal punishment it has been suggested that a respective imbalance in power may lead to the threshold being passed, and accordingly abuse that takes place by law enforcement agencies whilst a suspect is within their custody is likely to constitute a breach of Article 3 (see, for example, *Selmouni v France* (2000) 29 EHRR 403).

Sexual assault will almost certainly pass the threshold for Article 3, not least because of the psychological issues that arise in respect of any sexual assault. This is most relevant in the context of the positive obligation placed on states and means that they must have appropriate and effective laws in place to criminalize sexual assaults and ensure they are appropriately investigated (see *X and Y v Netherlands* (1986) 8 EHRR 235). In the (hopefully exceptional) circumstances where a prisoner is sexually assaulted by a state agent this will almost automatically lead to a breach of Article 3 (see *Aydin v Turkey* (1998) 25 EHRR 251).

 Further reading

Feldman D (2002) *Civil Liberties and Human Rights in England and Wales*, 2nd edn (Oxford: OUP), Ch 5.
   This examines the right to bodily integrity

Ireland v United Kingdom (1979) 2 EHRR 25.
   This remains the leading case on the infliction of inhuman and degrading treatment and continues to provide the definitions in this area.

Smith RKM (2004) ' "Hands-off parenting?": Towards a reform of the defence of reasonable chastisement in the UK' 16 *Child and Family Law Quarterly* 261–272.
This discusses the recent debate over the place of corporal punishment by parents.

5.2.3.3 Article 5: Right to liberty

Article 5 is an important Article within the ECHR as it governs protection from arbitrary arrest. Its form is as follows:

1. Everyone has the right to liberty and security of person. No one shall be deprived of his liberty save in the following cases and in accordance with a procedure prescribed by law:

    (a) the lawful detention of a person after conviction by a competent court;

    (b) the lawful arrest or detention of a person for non-compliance with the lawful order of a court or in order to secure the fulfilment of any obligation prescribed by law;

    (c) the lawful arrest or detention of a person effected for the purpose of bringing him before the competent legal authority on reasonable suspicion of having committed an offence or when it is reasonably considered necessary to prevent his committing an offence or fleeing after having done so;

    (d) the detention of a minor by lawful order for the purpose of educational supervision or his lawful detention for the purpose of bringing him before the competent legal authority;

    (e) the lawful detention of persons for the prevention of the spreading of infectious diseases, of persons of unsound mind, alcoholics or drug addicts or vagrants;

    (f) the lawful arrest or detention of a person to prevent his effecting an unauthorised entry into the country or of a person against whom action is being taken with a view to deportation or extradition.

2. Everyone who is arrested shall be informed promptly, in a language which he understands, of the reasons for his arrest and of any charge against him.

3. Everyone arrested or detained in accordance with the provisions of paragraph 1.c of this article shall be brought promptly before a judge or other officer authorised by law to exercise judicial power and shall be entitled to trial within a reasonable time or to release pending trial. Release may be conditioned by guarantees to appear for trial.

4. Everyone who is deprived of his liberty by arrest or detention shall be entitled to take proceedings by which the lawfulness of his detention shall be decided speedily by a court and his release ordered if the detention is not lawful.

5. Everyone who has been the victim of arrest or detention in contravention of the provisions of this article shall have an enforceable right to compensation.

It can be seen that this is a very long Article and accordingly we will be only examining certain aspects of this Article. It is likely that you will spend considerable time on this Article during a module on *Civil Liberties* and possibly *Public Law*, especially when you examine the regulation of the police power of arrest.

Article 5 provides the circumstances in which a person can be deprived of liberty. It is sometimes said that it provides protection from arbitrary arrest but this is not necessarily true since Article 5 will be engaged only if the arrest leads to a person's liberty being removed, although this could include being prevented from leaving the scene of arrest. Also, Article 5 does not necessarily provide administrative safeguards after arrest as certain aspects (eg police interviews) are to be found in other Convention Articles (eg Article 6).

That said, arrest is arguably the most important frequently used part of Article 5, and Article 5(1)(c) provides that this may be lawful but only where a person is brought before 'the competent legal authority'. It is not immediately clear from the face of Article 5 what this means but in England and Wales the first person a suspect will face is a custody sergeant, a police officer, who will decide whether to authorize his detention (s 37 *Police and Criminal Evidence Act 1984*). An inspector will then decide whether to continue detention after eight hours (s 40) and finally a superintendent can take the decision to extend the time, for certain offences, to thirty-six hours in exceptional circumstances (s 42). After this time has elapsed the police have two options open to them. They either release the offender or they bring the offender before a magistrate. It is clear that this is the competent authority to whom Article 5(1)(c) refers. Article 5(2) and 5(3) then provide additional safeguards such as knowing why a person has been arrested and that he should be brought before a judge, which would appear to be an overlap with Article 5(1)(c) but it is clear that the primary purpose of Article 5(3) is dealing with securing liberty rather than the purpose of the arrest. Article 5(3) therefore provides that a person should either be brought before a court or granted bail. It is important to note, however, that it is possible for bail to be subject to conditions. In the early days of the HRA 1998 this had caused some difficulties with some lawyers suggesting that conditional bail was an infringement of human rights but this was quite clearly a misreading of the legal position (see Gillespie (2001) 465–466).

An important aspect of Article 5 is to provide a mechanism for securing liberty. This is to be found in Article 5(4)–(5). This provides that everyone shall have the right to petition a court to question the appropriateness of any detention and that where any detention is found to be unlawful there should be an automatic right to compensation. To an extent this may be thought comparable to the procedure known as *habeas corpus* but it is an important safeguard.

 # Further reading

Ashworth A and Strange M (2004) 'Criminal law and human rights' 2 *European Human Rights Law Review* 121.
   Especially pp 128–130 which discusses pre-trial criminal procedure.
Gillespie AA (2001) 'Curfew and bail' 151 *New Law Journal* 465–466.
   This examines the compatibility with Article 5 of a curfew condition imposed on bail.

5.2.3.4 Article 6: Right to a fair trial

One of the most important rights in the Convention and certainly one of the most-quoted is Article 6 of the ECHR. This provides:

1. In the determination of his civil rights and obligations or of any criminal charge against him, everyone is entitled to a fair and public hearing within a reasonable time by an independent and impartial tribunal established by law. Judgment shall be pronounced publicly but the press and public may be excluded from all or part of the trial in the interests of morals, public order or national security in a democratic society, where the interests of juveniles or the protection of the private life of the parties so require, or to the extent strictly necessary in the opinion of the court in special circumstances where publicity would prejudice the interests of justice.

2. Everyone charged with a criminal offence shall be presumed innocent until proved guilty according to law.

3. Everyone charged with a criminal offence has the following minimum rights:

   (a) to be informed promptly, in a language which he understands and in detail, of the nature and cause of the accusation against him;

   (b) to have adequate time and facilities for the preparation of his defence;

   (c) to defend himself in person or through legal assistance of his own choosing or, if he has not sufficient means to pay for legal assistance, to be given it free when the interests of justice so require;

   (d) to examine or have examined witnesses against him and to obtain the attendance and examination of witnesses on his behalf under the same conditions as witnesses against him;

   (e) to have the free assistance of an interpreter if he cannot understand or speak the language used in court.

Entire books have been produced on Article 6 and thus we will be examining the Article extremely briefly, in part because it is an Article that will be examined in other parts of the book and also throughout your legal studies.

The key words of the Article are actually its marginal note, and the ECtHR will frequently consider everything holistically and balance matters against the 'right to a fair trial' rather than focus on the individual rights. It should be noted that Article 6 applies to both civil and criminal matters although from the wording it is clear that most guarantees exist in respect of criminal trials. It is also important to note that 'in the determination of his civil rights and obligations' does not mean every civil matter will come within Article 6 and issues such as the treatment of state employees have been considered to be outside the scope of Article 6 (see, for example, *Lombardo v Italy* (1996) 21 EHRR 188).

In terms of the criminal sphere perhaps the most important aspects of the Article are the 'independent and impartial tribunal' (Article 6(1)), the ability to defend oneself in court (Article 6(3)(b)–(d) inclusive), and an implicit doctrine known as the 'equality of arms'.

Independent and impartial tribunal

It may be thought that in a system of justice this would not be overly problematic but Article 6 has had a significant impact on how decisions relating to individuals are adjudicated. However, this has been an area of fruitful litigation for some time. Reference will be made to *McGonnell v United Kingdom* (2000) 30 EHRR 289 when examining the doctrine of the separation of powers (see 7.2 below). In Scotland the judicial system was placed under severe pressure when it was decided that part-time judges were not independent or impartial because of the manner in which they were appointed (*Davidson v Scottish Ministers (No 2)* [2004] UKHL 34) something that although not directly applicable to England led to the Lord Chancellor deciding that he would alter the way in which Recorders were appointed (see Chapter 7).

The same argument led to fundamental changes in the way that courts martial (ie judicial tribunals set up to adjudicate the law relating to serving members of HM Forces) were administered. The ECtHR has long had difficulties with the system of courts martial, not least because the judge and jury used to be all members of the armed services (*Morris v United Kingdom* (2002) 34 EHRR 52). Eventually civilian judges were introduced to solve this problem (*Cooper v United Kingdom* (2004) 39 EHRR 8) but it eventually culminated in new legislation being required to administer service justice (*Armed Forces Act 2006*).

The most controversial application of this doctrine was, however, undoubtedly in relation to how those convicted of murder were sentenced. There is only one sentence that can be imposed for the crime of murder; that of life imprisonment (adult defendant) or detention for life (young offender). However, the Home Secretary decided how long a person should stay in prison by having the final say over the tariff.

⇄ TARIFF

Although a person is sentenced to life imprisonment it is extremely rare for a person to spend the rest of their life in prison. There is a system of early release which allows prisoners to be released 'on licence' (ie to be on good behaviour). Where a life sentence has been imposed then the minimum period before which a person can be considered for release is known as the tariff. After this period has expired the Parole Board will decide whether a person should be released or not.

The first case to call into question the appropriateness of a politician having this power was that of *T v United Kingdom; V v United Kingdom* (2000) 30 EHRR 121. This was the case concerning the killers of Jamie Bulger. 'T' and 'V' were boys aged ten years when they abducted and killed Jamie Bulger, a two-year-old boy. The crime was controversial for a whole series of reasons but one important aspect of the case was that the ECtHR held that it was wrong for a politician to decide how long the boys should spend in prison, suggesting that this should be a judicial and not political function. This eventually culminated in *R (on the application of Anderson) v Secretary of State for the Home Office* [2003] 1 AC 837 in which the House of Lords held that the Home Secretary should not have any say in the setting of *any* tariff, including those for adult offenders. The decision was hugely controversial with the then current and previous Home Secretaries arguing that it should not be a purely judicial factor as society (through the political process) should also have the right to a say in how long its worst prisoners spend in gaol. However, ultimately the rule of law prevailed and the *Criminal Justice Act 2003* gave ultimate responsibility for the setting of tariffs to the judiciary.

Defending oneself

Article 6(3) provides a series of steps that are designed to allow a person to defend himself when accused of committing a crime. However in certain offences, most notably, sex offences, a tension exists between allowing a person to present a rigorous defence and also ensuring that the victim of a crime is not put through unnecessary distress. This tension has already been examined earlier in this book in the context of statutory interpretation (see *R v A (No 2)* [2002] 1 AC 45 and see 2.3.4 above) and it will also be examined in later chapters when we examine the course of a criminal trial where the issue of 'equality of arms' will be an important feature of the discussion (Chapter 12).

 ## Further reading

Ashworth A and Strange M (2004) 'Criminal law and human rights' 2 *European Human Rights Law Review* 121 at 130–140.

This is an important discussion on the impact that Article 6 has had on the criminal process.

Lyon A (2005) 'Two swords and two standards' *Criminal Law Review* 850–863.

This discusses the changes required to the courts martial system as a result of the ECHR.

Shute S (2004) 'Punishing murderers, release procedures and the "tariff", 1953–2004' *Criminal Law Review* 160–182.

This is an extremely detailed and influential article that discusses the issue of the sentence and release of murderers and the setting of a tariff.

5.2.3.5 Article 7: No punishment without law

Article 7 of the ECHR is particularly important within the criminal context. It provides:

1. No one shall be held guilty of any criminal offence on account of any act or omission which did not constitute a criminal offence under national or international law at the time when it was committed. Nor shall a heavier penalty be imposed than the one that was applicable at the time the criminal offence was committed.

2. This article shall not prejudice the trial and punishment of any person for any act or omission which, at the time when it was committed, was criminal according to the general principles of law recognised by civilised nations.

Whilst there are many issues enveloped within Article 7, the most important is that criminal offences should not be retrospective. It has already been noted that whilst Parliament is competent to legislate as it sees fit, there is a convention that it will not create retrospective criminal offences (see 2.3.6 above). This rule undoubtedly predates Article 7 but following the introduction of the HRA 1998 it continues to be an extremely important principle by which Parliament must be guided.

Although Article 7 prevents retrospective punishment it is important to note that the Article does not prevent the interpretation of the law evolving through time. Perhaps the most important example of this is in respect of marital rape.

Example Marital rape

Historically the law had taken the approach that a man could not be guilty of raping his wife. This approach was based on the fact that the contract of marriage included the right to conjugal relations. The rule was widely condemned and eventually in *R v R* [1992] 1 AC 599 the House of Lords held that the rule no longer had any role in modern society.

This ruling led to the appellant's conviction for rape being upheld along with his custodial sentence. He petitioned the European Court of Human Rights arguing that this ruling contravened Article 7. His argument was that at the time of the rape the law had recognized a marital exemption and that the House of Lords decision had therefore turned a lawful act into an unlawful act retrospectively. In *SW v United Kingdom* (1996) 21 EHRR 363 the European Court of Human Rights dismissed this argument suggesting that all the House of Lords had done was evolved the law and made it applicable to contemporary society. They also held that this evolution was predictable and thus was not retrospective.

Further reading

Ashworth A and Strange M (2004) 'Criminal law and human rights' 2 *European Human Rights Law Review* 121 at 124–127.
This discusses the recent decisions in respect of Article 7.

5.2.3.6 Article 8: Right to respect for private life

Alongside Article 6, Article 8 is one of the more popular rights that is litigated under the Convention. It provides:

1. Everyone has the right to respect for his private and family life, his home and his correspondence.
2. There shall be no interference by a public authority with the exercise of this right except such as is in accordance with the law and is necessary in a democratic society in the interests of national security, public safety or the economic well-being of the country, for the prevention of disorder or crime, for the protection of health or morals, or for the protection of the rights and freedoms of others.

This is the first of the 'qualified rights' and it can be seen immediately that the qualification is contained in Article 8(2). Article 8(1) sets out the right, and Article 8(2) states the circumstances under which the right can be infringed.

As with Article 6, entire books have been produced just on the meaning of Article 8 and this is another right that you will come across throughout your legal studies, including in modules such as *Land Law, Equity and Trusts, Medical Law*, etc.

Not just private life

Article 8 is often referred to as the right to respect for private life yet Article 8(1) makes clear that a person has the right to respect to:

- private life

- family life
- home
- correspondence.

Not infrequently these will be subsumed within the concept of 'private life' but it is important to note that this need not be the case and, for example, correspondence can be a significant issue for prisoners. The ECtHR has held that it is not appropriate for prisoners' correspondence to be routinely intercepted (*Valasinas v Lithuania* (App No 44558/98)) although it does accept that where there is a pressing need to do so, this can be justified (ie it will allow Article 8(2) to apply) although the limits of such interference will be strictly considered (*Foxley v United Kingdom* (2001) 31 EHRR 25).

The ECtHR has consistently stated that the purpose of Article 8 is to protect an individual from arbitrary interference with a person's rights by the state (see, for example, *Glaser v United Kingdom* (2001) 33 EHRR 1 at [63]) and this takes on a series of forms. Perhaps one of the most significant in recent years has been in regulating surveillance. The United Kingdom traditionally operated on the basis that because the law did not state that public authorities could not put somebody under surveillance, they were free to do so (see, for example, *Malone v Commissioner of Police for the Metropolis (No 2)* [1979] Ch 44) whereas the ECtHR argues the opposite is true under the Convention. Accordingly a legal basis must exist under which Article 8 can be interfered with (*Malone v United Kingdom* (1985) 7 EHRR 14) and this law must be readily accessible with appropriate legal (rather than administrative) safeguards against abuse of authorities (*Govell v United Kingdom* (1997) 23 EHRR CD101). Within the context of surveillance this led to the enactment of the *Regulation of Investigatory Powers Act 2000*.

Positive obligation

Article 8, like Articles 2 and 3, contains both a positive and a negative obligation. This means that the state should not only ensure that they do not infringe Article 8 themselves but also ensure that they protect individuals from having their Article 8 rights infringed by others. A good example of this can be seen from *Moreno Gomez v Spain* (2005) 41 EHRR 40 where the ECtHR considered that the positive obligation meant that the impact of noise and smells must be considered when deciding whether to grant a licence to a night club within a residential area.

More significantly the positive obligation also gives rise to the right to physical integrity and accordingly treatment that is below the minimum threshold for Article 3 (see 5.2.3.2 above) may come within Article 8 (see *X and Y v Netherlands* (1986) 8 EHRR 235). In *Pretty v United Kingdom* (2002) 35 EHRR 1 the ECtHR confirmed that 'private life' is a broad concept that cannot be precisely defined but that it covered, in essence, the respect for human dignity. The ECtHR conceded that whilst no right to suicide could be included within Article 2, it may be possible to infer a limited right under Article 8 but it also held that a blanket ban on assisted suicide could be justified under Article 8(2).

Further reading

Fenwick H (2001) 'Covert surveillance under the Regulation of Investigatory Powers Act 2000, Part II' 65 *Journal of Criminal Law* 521–536.
Examines the reasons for the passing of RIPA and questions its compatibility with Article 8.

Rogers J (2003) 'Applying the doctrine of positive obligations in the European Convention on Human Rights to domestic substantive criminal law in domestic proceedings' *Criminal Law Review* 690–708.
This article takes an interesting line on positive obligations and focuses on its application in the criminal law.

5.2.3.7 Article 10: Freedom of expression

Although Article 10 is a qualified right it has been said that freedom of expression is the bedrock upon which a democracy is built (*Bowman v United Kingdom* (1998) 26 EHRR 1) and it is accordingly one of the most important Convention articles. It provides:

1. Everyone has the right to freedom of expression. This right shall include freedom to hold opinions and to receive and impart information and ideas without interference by public authority and regardless of frontiers. This article shall not prevent States from requiring the licensing of broadcasting, television or cinema enterprises.

2. The exercise of these freedoms, since it carries with it duties and responsibilities, may be subject to such formalities, conditions, restrictions or penalties as are prescribed by law and are necessary in a democratic society, in the interests of national security, territorial integrity or public safety, for the prevention of disorder or crime, for the protection of health or morals, for the protection of the reputation or rights of others, for preventing the disclosure of information received in confidence, or for maintaining the authority and impartiality of the judiciary.

Article 10 is, in essence, the Convention equivalent of the right to free speech although it has a much wider remit than this. Together with Article 11 (see 5.2.3.8 below) it is the primary right to allow protests. This is another Article that you will encounter throughout your legal study and particularly in modules such as *Public Law*, *Constitutional Law*, or *Civil Liberties*.

The classic case examining Article 10 was *Sunday Times v United Kingdom* (1992) 14 EHRR 229 which was also known as the 'Spycatcher case'. The ECtHR made clear that Article 10 should be interfered with only when strictly necessary to do so and that where the press were concerned the proportionality was raised further because the press acts as the 'public's watchdog' (at [50]). This is undoubtedly recognition of the fact that totalitarian states will frequently control the press and that one of the easiest ways of controlling the public is to place restrictions on the press.

> ### 👁 Example Spycatcher
>
> In 1985 a former member of MI5 (now the Security Services) sought to publish a memoir of his time within MI5. This was unprecedented as it provided operational details of his work within what was, at that time, still a secret service (indeed MI5 was not officially recognized until the enactment of the Security Service Act 1989). This included allegations that MI5 had bugged embassies, and also allegations that it and its sister service MI6 (now the Secret Intelligence Service) planned assassinations.
>
> The book was immediately banned in the United Kingdom although ultimately certain newspapers, most notably *The Sunday Times*, tried to serialize the book. Injunctions were taken out restraining publication and when these were breached contempt of court proceedings were initiated. *The Sunday Times*, and others, alleged that this was a breach of Article 10 of the ECHR, something that the ECtHR ultimately agreed with.
>
> The book received official clearance in 1988 when it was accepted that it had been serialized and published so widely around the world that it was illogical to ban sale in the United Kingdom especially since many copies had legitimately been imported from abroad.

However, Article 10 should not be considered merely a tool of the press and it is extremely important within the context of personal protests. Perhaps one of the most important statements came in the case of *Redmond-Bate v DPP* [2000] HRLR 249 in which Sedley LJ said:

> Free speech includes not only the inoffensive but the irritating, the contentious and the eccentric, the heretical, the unwelcome and the provocative provided it does not tend to provoke violence. Freedom only to speak inoffensively is not worth having. (at p 260)

This is an important point and one undoubtedly within the spirit of Article 10. That said, however, it is also important to note that Article 10 is not absolute. Sedley LJ expressly considered speech that tended to provoke violence would fall outside of his scope and Article 10(2) expressly considers qualifications in other situations. Perhaps the most controversial is 'morals' since this can be used to disguise a multitude of possibilities.

The leading case on the use of 'morals' as a qualification is *Handyside v United Kingdom* (1979–80) 1 EHRR 737 where the ECtHR stated that it was not possible to identify a single moral basis across all contracting states (at [48]). Accordingly the Court would extend a 'margin of appreciation' to the individual states meaning that they would enjoy discretion to decide the moral standpoint of their society. However, the Court was also clear that the ECtHR had a supervisory role in ensuring that the application of this margin together with any restrictions placed on expression by the contracting states were strictly necessary. In the context of morals this must also take into account that society evolves and that something which may infringe society's standards at one point in time may not do so later.

📖 Further reading

Fenwick H (2007) *Civil Liberties and Human Rights* (Oxford: OUP), Ch 6.

This critiques the decision in *Handyside v United Kingdom* in respect of obscenity and questions whether it is appropriate to allow moral standpoints to interfere with the freedom of expression.

Rowbottom J (2005) 'Obscenity laws and the Internet: Targeting supply and demand' *Criminal Law Review* 97–109.

This is a challenging piece that questions whether and, if so, how the law should tackle online obscenity whilst balancing society's right to freedom of expression.

5.2.3.8 Article 11: Freedom of assembly

Article 11 is another key important provision within the Convention and can be considered a fundamental principle of democracy. Alongside Article 10 it governs the right to protest but it also has a wider remit. The provisions of Article 11 are:

1. Everyone has the right to freedom of peaceful assembly and to freedom of association with others, including the right to form and to join trade unions for the protection of his interests.

2. No restrictions shall be placed on the exercise of these rights other than such as are prescribed by law and are necessary in a democratic society in the interests of national security or public safety, for the prevention of disorder or crime, for the protection of health or morals or for the protection of the rights and freedoms of others. This article shall not prevent the imposition of lawful restrictions on the exercise of these rights by members of the armed forces, of the police or of the administration of the State.

It can be seen that Article 11 is concerned with the right to be associated with others, either by assembly (eg a demonstration) or to join organizations and unions. However, it is important to note that this is a qualified right and that the right to join is not universal. The final sentence makes clear that Article 11 may not extend to agents of the executive, particularly in respect of the police and armed forces. Given the nature of these agencies it is understandable that restrictions may need to be put in place to ensure the smooth operation of these important bodies. In the United Kingdom this exception has been used with the police and members of HM Forces being denied the right to join a union. As regards the police there are other bodies that fulfil some of the responsibilities of unions (the Police Federation for officers up to an including the rank of chief inspector, the Superintendents' Association for officers of the rank of superintendent and chief superintendent, and the Association of Chief Police Officers for those of chief officer rank) but their responsibilities are curtailed and the police are not allowed to strike. This rule has also been used to justify restrictions on political activity for certain posts within local authorities (see *Ahmed and Others v United Kingdom* (2000) 29 EHRR 1).

However, perhaps the more usual manner of engaging Article 11 is in respect of peaceful assembly. It can be seen from the very wording of Article 11(1) that the right only exists to peaceful protest and it follows therefore that where violence is likely then interferences may be possible. That said, issues of proportionality and necessity arise and if at all possible the state should try to minimize disruption rather than prevent assembly as a whole.

Example Parades Commission

We have already discussed the issue of the Parades Commission in Northern Ireland (p 154) but this is also a classic example of the balance to be drawn under Article 11. The parades undertaken by Loyalist members of the Northern Ireland community are extremely controversial especially when routed through or near to Nationalist areas of the Province. There has been a long history of violence breaking out on such parades. However, the Parades Commission does not find it necessary to ban such assemblies but rather it exercises its powers to re-route the parades in order to minimize violence (see *Re Tweed's Application for Judicial Review* [2001] NI 165).

Further reading

'Parades and Freedom of Assembly' (2001) 2 *Human Rights and UK Practice* 19–20.
   Summarizes the activities and decisions of the Parades Commission of Northern Ireland.
Stone (2010) Ch 7, particularly pp 258–259.
   This rehearses the importance of the freedom of assembly in a democracy.

5.2.3.9 Article 17

An important but often neglected Article within the Convention is Article 17 which prohibits abuse of the Convention itself. Article 17 is not an independent Article, in that it cannot be the sole subject of litigation but is instead used in combination with other Articles. It is particularly of importance to Articles 10 and 11. Article 17 provides:

> Nothing in this Convention may be interpreted as implying for any State, group or person any right to engage in any activity or perform any act aimed at the destruction of any of the rights and freedoms set forth herein or at their limitation to a greater extent than is provided for in the Convention.

The essence of this right is that one cannot rely on the Convention in order to undermine the rights of others. The classic example of this would be in respect of Articles 10 and 11 where someone may wish to join a racist organization that has as its purpose the undermining of the rights of others due solely to their colour. The Convention will not allow such matters because the right claimed is an affront to the rights and freedoms contained within the Convention.

Case box *Glimmerveen and Hagenback v Netherlands*

In *Glimmerveen* and *Hagenback v Netherlands* (1982) 4 EHRR 260 the applicants had been convicted under Dutch law of distributing leaflets that were racist in character and called for the creation of a white state. The European Commission on Human Rights said 'the general purpose of Article 17 is to prevent totalitarian groups from exploiting in their own interests the principles enunciated by the Convention' (p 267). It dismissed the applicants' contention that Article 10 protected their right to distribute the leaflets on the basis that they were seeking to use Article 10 in such a way as to undermine the rights and freedoms of others and thus Article 17 applied.

It is right that the ECHR contains such a provision although it is important that those who interpret the Convention do not abuse the power given to them under Article 17 since the rights under Articles 10–11 do include the right to be unpopular and offensive. However, where the rights claimed seek to undermine the rights of others it is quite clear that this should be stopped.

 Further reading

Harris DJ, O'Boyle M, Bates EP (2009) *Law of the European Convention on Human Rights* (Oxford: OUP) 648–651.

This is the most authoritative text on the EHCR and in these pages the learned authors succinctly explain the application and limits of Article 17.

5.3 Repealing the Act

Lord Irvine, writing sometime after the commencement of the Act, stated:

One commentator asked recently why the Human Rights Act is still disliked. It is a good question. (Irvine (2003) 324)

The Act will certainly not receive any prizes for being the most loved piece of legislation to have found its way onto the statute books. The press, especially those that are traditionally considered to be 'right-leaning' (eg *Daily Telegraph*, *Daily Mail*, and *Daily Express*) loathe the Act and they have consistently campaigned to repeal it.

The Conservative party, which had not voted against the 1998 Act, attempted to seize the initiative and propose the Act's repeal. During the general election campaign of 2005 Michael Howard, the then Conservative leader, called for its repeal, and this was repeated in the 2010 election. It has to be said that not every Conservative was necessarily against the proposal. For example, in the 2005 general election, Dominic Grieve, the then shadow Attorney-General (and who became Attorney-General in 2010), was reported as saying:

The Human Rights Act has many benefits which it has conferred...I don't think the...Act has anything to do with fuelling a compensation culture at all.[12]

12. *The Times*, 30 March 2005, news (p 28).

However despite this there has continued to be a campaign to repeal the Act and in the 2010 general election the Conservative party intended to replace it with a British Bill of Rights (not to be confused with the existing *Bill of Rights* which was legislation passed in 1689). The 2010 general election led to a coalition government and the Liberal Democrats were firm supporters of the HRA 1998 and at the time of writing (Autumn 2010) there has been no indication that the coalition government intends to repeal the Act.

Why is it that the Act continues to be controversial? The Act has had a poor reception in terms of public relations and this is in part because from a politician's point of view it is an ideal tool for attack with some suggesting that it damages the balance of power between the holders of elected and unelected power. From a lawyer's point of view, however, the Act appears to be working well. It provides ordinary citizens with the ability to challenge unwarranted intrusion by the state, arguably something that each mainstream political party wishes. In government the position of Attorney-General is almost paradoxical. Whilst the Attorney-General is a politician, he is not political per se as a significant proportion of his work is acting as a legal advisor to the government and accordingly he must be unbiased and apolitical. Shadow Attorney-Generals will often follow a similar reasoning and this is perhaps why Dominic Grieve was reported as saying the things he did; his legal opinion was that the Act was not problematic.

Two principal attacks appear to be advanced against the Act. The first is that it politicizes the judiciary and detracts from the legitimate power exercised by elected politicians. The second attack is the allegation that it promotes a 'compensation' or 'blame' culture whereby society becomes increasingly litigious. In respect of the first challenge the Act has unquestionably changed the relationship between the executive and the judiciary (Feldman (2006) 54) and this has caused some tension but Feldman also notes that there appears to be deference to the executive in respect of some acts. However, whilst the courts are prepared to defer in some instances, the deference is not absolute such as where they believe executive acts, even in respect of terrorists, infringe on fundamental rights such as liberty without due process (see *A v Secretary of State for the Home Department* [2004] UKHL 56). There may be no easy solution to the politicization of judges, not least because it is difficult to identify a demarcation between political and legal decisions (Fredman (2006) 80).

The second attack is that of the blame culture and this was advanced as one of the principal attacks by the Conservatives during the general elections of 2005 and 2010. They alleged that the HRA was responsible for an increase in litigation. Given that the HRA has only a limited horizontal effect (see above) it would appear difficult to believe that this is necessarily the case and it is more likely that the use of contingency fees and specialist accident-claim firms (often not operated by lawyers) are more likely to account for the culture. However, it is quite possible that the HRA could be responsible for the growth in claims against public-sector bodies. The courts have considered this issue but appear somewhat sceptical about the idea that the quest for compensation is necessarily wrong:

> Concerns have been expressed in various quarters about the development of a 'compensation culture'. In my experience in this court, dealing with a wide range of complaints against public authorities, most citizens who have suffered as a result of some bureaucratic error are not motivated, or at least not primarily motivated, by a desire for monetary compensation. (*R (Bernard) v London Borough of Enfield* [2002] EWHC Admin 2282 at [39] per Sullivan J)

This has developed into a doctrine whereby where a public authority acts wrongly but seeks to put matters right promptly and without causing any significant loss or damage to the claimant then monetary compensation should be minimal and instead recourse should be made to alternative remedies such as declarations (see *W v Westminster City Council* [2005] EWHC 102). Some argue that the impact of the HRA has not been as significant as expected with no court being overwhelmed by claims and with the courts being rigorous in rejecting spurious cases (Turner (2004a) 685).

It would appear therefore that the complaint is unfair but this has not stopped the government from legislating to reduce the impact of litigation on the National Health Service. Where there has been political concern for some time about whether compensation is interfering in the front-line operation of the NHS—see the *NHS Redress Act 2006*. However the Act is probably human-rights compliant as it still provides access to a legal resolution of disputes arising from clinical negligence and arguably what the legislation will do is to reduce the legal costs involved.

Would repealing the HRA make any substantive difference? It is submitted that it would not. The Conservative party was not suggesting that the UK would cease to be a signatory of the ECHR (which, in any event, would be difficult to do without withdrawing from both the *Council of Europe* and the European Union). Even if the HRA was repealed the courts would still be called upon to consider whether public bodies have infringed the rights and freedoms of individuals. Many of the rights and freedoms put forward could also be found in the common law. Whilst the HRA specifically requires courts to take account of the jurisprudence of the ECtHR the courts could do so in the absence of any legislative provision: the courts already take account of the decisions of other countries' courts and even the international courts. It is highly unlikely the courts would cease to refer to the ECtHR if the HRA were suddenly repealed. The Conservative party was also suggesting replacing the HRA with a 'Bill of Rights' and it appears that this would include many of the rights and freedoms contained within the ECHR. Indeed it would be difficult to see how one couldn't since the rights contained within the ECHR are quite basic and, in any event, any domestic rights instrument would, by virtue of being a signatory to the ECHR, need to be compliant with it. The suggested alteration was, in essence, a question of political presentation. It was reported that Dominic Grieve, in opposition, stated that the HRA could be amended so that the courts were not bound by the Convention (see Travis and Hirsch (2010)) but as was seen earlier in this chapter the Supreme Court certainly does not consider itself bound by the ECtHR (see *R v Horncastle* [2010] 2 WLR 47). It is submitted that it is unlikely the Act will be repealed and, if it ever were, it is unlikely that much would change. The courts will not suddenly stop recognizing rights; they will just be labelled differently.

◆ Summary

The Human Rights Act 1998 is an extremely important instrument and it is one that you will encounter throughout your law studies and your career. In this chapter we have noted:

- Public bodies have a duty to act compatibly with the Convention. This is a *civil* not *criminal* duty.

- Defining a public authority is not easy although all courts and tribunals are automatically covered.
- Public authorities tend to be divided into 'pure' public bodies (eg the police, prison service, local authorities, etc) and 'hybrid' public authorities (eg universities).
- The courts are given a wide discretion in interpreting legislation to ensure that they are compliant with the Convention and they may also interpret the Convention itself.
- The definition of a victim in the Human Rights Act 1998 is more restricted than, for example, judicial-review procedures but this is in line with the *European Convention on Human Rights*.
- Article 13 (right to an effective remedy) is not contained within the HRA. There are competing arguments as to whether the HRA 1998 is itself a response to Article 13 or whether this means rights in the UK are not as protected.
- Certain rights contain a *positive obligation* on the state. This means that not only must the state ensure that it does not breach the right, it must also ensure that it can protect its citizens from others infringing their right. The most obvious example of this is Article 2 where a state must protect its citizens where it knows there is a risk of harm.

❓ End-of-chapter questions

1. Is it possible to repeal the *Human Rights Act 1998*?
2. Should the *Human Rights Act 1998* be fully incorporated, ie to apply both vertically and horizontally? What do you think the implications of extending the Act horizontally would be?
3. Read the box on page 152 concerning precedent and s 2. Is the decision in *Kay* not in direct contravention of s 2 *Human Rights Act 1998*? Was it not Parliament's intention that the courts follow decisions of the ECtHR and does this not mean that a court of first instance, when faced with such a precedent, will be acting incompatibly with the ECHR, thus breaching s 6?
4. Read Chapter 13 on appeals. If a court, including the ECtHR, considers a trial to be unfair, do you think the conviction should be quashed? Read *R v Rowe, Davis and Johnson (No 3)* [2001] 1 Cr App R 8.

📖 Further reading

Dwyer DM (2005) 'Rights brought home' 121 *Law Quarterly Review* 359–364.
This is a useful article which looks at how the HRA 1998 has been implemented.

Fredman S (1998) 'Bringing rights home' 114 *Law Quarterly Review* 538–543.
This is a very good article which comments on the progress of the Human Rights Bill (as it then was) and discusses some of the issues that were raised at the time.

Fredman S (2006) 'From deference to democracy: The role of equality under the Human Rights Act 1998' 122 *Law Quarterly Review* 53–81.
This is a good article which includes a useful examination of the margin of appreciation.

Irvine of Lairg, Lord (2003) 'The impact of the Human Rights Act: Parliament, the courts and the executive' *Public Law* 308–325.

An interesting article by the then Lord Chancellor who considers the impact the Act has had on the process of governance.

Klug F and Starmer K (2005) 'Standing back from the Human Rights Act: How effective is it five years on?' *Public Law* 716–728.

A good analytical article which examines how the Act has been used in practice.

For multiple choice questions, updates to this chapter and links to useful websites, please visit the Online Resource Centre at

www.oxfordtextbooks.co.uk/orc/gillespie_els3e/

PART II

The Practitioners of Law

6

The Courts

By the end of this chapter you will be able to:

- Identify how the courts in England and Wales are organized and funded.
- Identify the principal courts in England and Wales.
- Discuss the types of cases heard in each court.
- Understand what the other courts do.

Introduction

Of all the institutions within the English Legal System, the courts are perhaps the most recognizable. Most people are aware of what a court is but they perhaps do not know that there are several different types of courts nor fully understand what each does.

This chapter will consider how the modern court structure is organized and what each court does. It will not consider the historical development of the courts but those wishing to understand the evolution of the courts should consult the further reading identified at the end of the chapter.

6.1 The organization of the courts

The first issue to examine is how courts are organized. As will be seen below, there are many different types of court and this raises questions as to how they can be classified and how their day-to-day business is organized.

6.1.1 Classifying the courts

The first issue to examine is how courts are classified. The variety of courts have led some to question whether the courts can be grouped together but, as will be seen, this is not necessarily the easiest thing to do.

6.1.1.1 Civil/Criminal

It may be thought that the easiest way of classifying the courts would be to designate whether they are civil or criminal. In principle this would seem appropriate since it is recognized that there is a civil justice system and a criminal justice system.

The difficulty is that whilst it is easy to designate the Crown Court as a criminal court, it is less easy to categorize any other court. The magistrates' court (see 6.2.1 below), for example, deals with the vast majority of criminal cases but it also has a civil jurisdiction and so it cannot be said to be a purely criminal court. The High Court of Justice (see 6.2.4 below) is predominantly a civil court but it also has a limited criminal jurisdiction. The Court of Appeal (see 6.2.5 below) is divided into two divisions, the civil division and the criminal division, so that is relatively easy but the Supreme Court (see 6.2.6 below) has jurisdiction over both civil and criminal matters in England and Wales.

It can be seen therefore that classifying courts as either civil or criminal courts is impracticable.

6.1.1.2 Original or appellate jurisdiction

Another potential classification system is to examine whether courts have original juris-diction, ie they hear matters of first-instance (eg trials) or whether they hear appeals from other courts.

As an abstract idea this, as with the civil/criminal distinction, seems logical but the existing court structure immediately poses challenges. For example, whilst the magistrates' court and county court only possess original jurisdiction, the Crown Court exercises both an original and appellate jurisdiction. The same is true of the High Court and this is without even considering whether judicial review is original or appellate jurisdiction (something complicated by the fact that certain courts and tribunals may be subject to judicial review).

Accordingly it can be seen that this categorization does not assist either.

6.1.1.3 Superior and inferior courts

One of the most traditional forms of classifying the courts is to examine whether they are superior or inferior courts.

Ascertaining what the superior courts are is not always easy. The starting point is that it includes those courts labelled a superior court by s 1 *Senior Courts Act 1981* (renamed by Sch 11 *Constitutional Reform Act 2005*(CRA 2005)). The courts listed are the *Crown Court, High Court of Justice*, and *Court of Appeal*.

However, other courts are known to be superior courts. For example, the Employment Appeals Tribunal which, as its name suggests, is technically a tribunal is, in fact, a superior court. It is so designated by statute (s 20(3) *Employment Tribunals Act 1996*). The Courts-Martial Appeal Court is considered to be a superior court (s 1(2) *Courts-Martial Appeal Court 1968*) so could it be argued that the superior courts are only those that are so designated by statute? Certainly now the Supreme Court is in being then this may be true (as s 40(1) CRA 2005 states that the Supreme Court is a superior court of record) but it was certainly not true historically since the House of Lords was a superior court and yet this arose not through statute but through the fact that it was an intrinsic part of Parliament.

What of inferior courts? Statute rarely states that they are inferior so perhaps the solution is that where a statute does not state that a court is superior then it should be treated as inferior. Unfortunately this does not appear to be a safe proposition as historically some courts were treated to be superior in the absence of statute (for example, the Central Criminal Court prior to the establishment of the Crown Court). In *R v Cripps, ex parte Muldoon and others* [1983] 3 WLR 465 it was said:

> It is necessary to look at the relevant functions of the tribunal in question including its constitution, jurisdiction and powers and its relationship with the High Court in order to decide whether the tribunal should properly be regarded as inferior...(p 87 per Robert Goff LJ)

The meaning of its relationship with the High Court is taken to mean that where the High Court is able to act in a reviewing capacity over the tribunal, ie it is subject to judicial review, then the court is an inferior court. However, this does not always work since, for example, the Crown Court may sometimes be subject to judicial review (where the matter does not concern its jurisdiction over indictable offences) and yet it has been seen that, by statute, it is a superior court.

6.1.1.4 A need for classification?

It can be seen that it is not easy to identify a classification for the courts. In practice it is rarely necessary to clarify the courts and instead a distinction is drawn between the types of justice. Some would argue that there are three types of justice systems;

criminal, civil, and family but in reality the distinction is between two; civil and criminal. Accordingly, it can be said that the need for classification, at least in practice, is perhaps questionable.

6.1.2 HM Court Service

Setting aside the classification of the courts, how are they organized in practice? The main courts of England and Wales (ie the magistrates' court, county court, Crown Court, High Court, and Court of Appeal) are operated by Her Majesty's Court Service, an executive agency of the Ministry of Justice. The Supreme Court is not operated by HM Court Service but is responsible for its own administration (through its Chief Executive) this status reflecting the fact that it is a court of the United Kingdom and not just of England and Wales. The position of these courts is discussed below (6.1.3).

HM Court Service was administratively created in 2005 when the previous Court Service was combined with the administration of the magistrates' courts (which had previously been a complicated administration based on localities). The Lord Chancellor, as Minister of Justice, is politically responsible for the functioning of the service although it is headed by a chief executive, a senior civil servant. HM Court Service is also overseen by an executive board which includes executive members (ie senior members of HM Court Service including the chief executive or members of the Ministry of Justice), three judicial members, and two non-executive members (including a lawyer). The board is overseen by an independent chairman. The *Courts Act 2003* (CA 2003) provides that the Lord Chancellor has responsibility for appointing court officers and staff responsible for serving the courts, and HM Court Service exercises this power on his behalf.

Previously HM Court Service was organized in forty-two areas corresponding to the previous geographical areas used by the criminal justice areas, but recently this has changed and it is now organized into eight regional areas (seven geographical and one specifically dedicated to the Royal Courts of Justice). Each area has its own director who is responsible to the chief executive and the executive board. The director is also required to work with the Court Boards within their area. HM Court Service itself employs the staff that service the courts, including the administrative staff, the clerks to the courts (or legal advisors), ushers, etc. It does not employ members of the judiciary as they are office holders who, depending on their rank, are appointed either by the Lord Chancellor himself or by the Queen (discussed in Chapter 7).

6.1.2.1 Court Boards

The CA 2003 created Court Boards (ss 4–5 and Sch 1). The country is divided into twenty-three geographical areas, each of which has its own Court Board. Each court board comprises a minimum number of seven persons, who must be:

- one judge
- two magistrates (from within the area of the Courts Board)
- two people with knowledge or experience of the courts in the local area (eg lawyers)
- two lay members who must live in the Courts Board area.

The maximum number of persons on a court board is twelve (reg 3 *The Courts Boards (Appointments and Procedure) Regulations 2004*, SI 2004/1193).

Section 5(1) CA 2003 states:

Each courts board is under a duty...

(a) to scrutinize, review and make recommendations about the way in which the Lord Chancellor is discharging his general duty in relation to the courts with which the board is concerned, and

(b) ...to consider draft and final business plans relating to those courts.

The relevant courts the board is concerned with are the magistrates', county, and Crown Courts within its area (s 5(4) CA 2003). Guidance can be issued to the boards (s 5(5) CA 2003) and the latest version of the guidance makes clear that the functions of the board relate to administration and not any judicial matters, and members cannot use a meeting of the board to criticize a judicial pronouncement or decision.

In essence the boards work with the senior managers of HM Court Service to set budgets for the courts to ensure that they are properly staffed and can operate in an efficient manner. The presence of the judiciary, magistracy, and lawyers means that it will be possible to identify quickly any problems and these can be raised to HM Court Service in an expedient manner.

6.1.2.2 Judicial administration

Aside from the Court Boards, where there is some judicial representation, the judiciary itself is responsible for some parts of the administration of the courts, especially at the regional level.

The courts in England and Wales are divided into six circuits and each is assigned two presiding judges (s 72(1) *Courts and Legal Services Act 1990* (CLSA 1990)). The presiding judges are puisne judges (meaning judges of the High Court: see 7.1.2.3 below) and whilst presiders they have responsibility for the administration of justice on the circuit. A Lord Justice of Appeal (Court of Appeal judge: see 7.1.2.2 below) is appointed as the senior presiding judge (s 72 CLSA 1990) who coordinates the work of the presiding judges.

Having at least two presiding judges for each circuit means that ordinarily one judge will always be on circuit (at least during the legal year). This means that they are in a better position to oversee matters. In the early days it has been said:

In broad principle the Presiding judges were responsible for the judicial or operational side of the circuit, while the Circuit Administrator was responsible for the administrative support. But in practice the two overlapped...(Dunn (1993) 217)

This overlap has certainly continued and by 2008 their administrative responsibilities were being suggested as becoming almost overbearing (*The Daily Telegraph* (2008) 10 January). The principal responsibility of the presiding judge is to assign judges to the relevant cases. It will be seen in Chapter 12 that only certain judges are entitled to sit on certain cases. However, even where a judge is entitled to sit on a case, the presiding judge has to identify who is the most appropriate. *The Telegraph* reported that whilst trying a serious murder, Mr Justice Gibbs (then presiding judge of the Midlands circuit) had to respond in a single week to twenty letters and seventy circuit-connected emails together with various telephone calls and that this, together with the other commitments being a presider brings, led to him working seventy hours per week whilst on circuit.

6.1.3 The Supreme Court

It was noted above that HM Court Service does not administer the Supreme Court.

Section 48 CRA 2005 states that the Supreme Court will have a chief executive who is appointed by the Lord Chancellor after consultation with the President of the Supreme Court. Section 49 permits the President of the Supreme Court to appoint staff to service the court although the chief executive, after consultation with the Lord Chancellor, will decide the number and type of staff. Presumably the President will also be involved in such discussions although it is notable that s 49 does not require this. The Supreme Court would seem to have a larger staff than when it was the House of Lords although this is, in part, because much of the administration of the judicial committees was subsumed within the wider House of Lords administration.

6.1.4 Funding

It will be remembered that HM Court Service is an executive agency of the Ministry of Justice. Accordingly the funding for the courts—except for the salary of the judiciary—comes from the departmental budget of the Ministry of Justice. Prior to the creation of the Ministry, in 2007, the money came from the Lord Chancellor's Department.

The creation of the Ministry of Justice led to considerable tension between the judiciary and executive. It will be seen in Chapter 7 that planned changes to reform the office of Lord Chancellor had also led to concerns and it would have been thought that the government would have attempted to resolve these issues by being careful to keep the judiciary informed of planned changes to the organization of the courts. However, following a series of political difficulties for the Home Office it was decided to separate some parts of the functions of the Home Office and to combine them with the powers of the Lord Chancellor's Department to create the Ministry of Justice. The then Lord Chief Justice commented:

> The first I or the then Lord Chancellor, Lord Falconer, learnt of the creation of the Ministry of Justice was when we were reading our Sunday Telegraphs on the 21 of January 2007 Once again the government had not consulted on a key constitutional change...No guarantees of the protection of the independence of the judiciary were given. There was no promise to protect the administration of the justice within the new Department. (Phillips (2008) 5)

The concern of the judiciary was focused on a number of issues but one of the most important was whether the budgets of the court were separate.

One department was to uphold the rule of law and the independence of the judiciary and yet the same department would also have responsibility for criminal justice. That department would have one pot of money from which to fund the court system, and the prisons. The judiciary was concerned that the department would rob Peter to pay Paul—Peter being the judges and Paul being the prisons. Would the department be able to prioritize the administration of justice whilst dealing with criminal justice policy? (Phillips (2008) 5)

Since the administration of government is a matter of prerogative not statute, no legislative measure was required to establish the Ministry of Justice. This, in turn, meant there were few opportunities to address concerns. The judiciary wished the budget of HM Court Service to be 'ring-fenced', ie it could only be used for the administration of

the courts and not used when other aspects of the ministry's budget is under strain. The government refused this request and the dispute between the judiciary and executive became public.

Eventually a pragmatic solution was created. This was twofold. The first was the establishment of the Executive Council of *HM Court Service* (see 6.1.2 above) which includes representatives of the judiciary. The second was the establishment of a formal *Framework Document*, which was published by the Ministry of Justice in April 2008. This document (a link to which can be found on the ORC) explains that whilst HM Court Service remains an administrative part of the Ministry of Justice, there is recognition that the administration of justice requires cooperation between the executive and the judiciary and, in particular, a commitment to the independence of the judiciary (p 3). The document also notes that all staff of HM Court Service owe a joint duty both to the Lord Chancellor (as Minister of Justice) and the Lord Chief Justice (as head of the judiciary in England and Wales) (p 11).

In terms of funding arrangements, the budget is not formally 'ring-fenced' but the Lord Chancellor and Lord Chief Justice agree a budget that is not ordinarily subject to change. Where the Lord Chief Justice disagrees with the allocated budget he may write formally to the Lord Chancellor or to Parliament stating his objections. The Executive Board monitors the budget and should any change be introduced it should go through the same consultation process as the original budget, including providing the Lord Chief Justice with the opportunity to write to Parliament (pp 14–18). The judiciary seems happy with this arrangement although it perhaps does not bring the same level of protection as 'ring-fencing' but any letter written by the Lord Chief Justice to Parliament would almost certainly be made public which may place pressure on the government.

❓ QUESTION FOR REFLECTION

Were the judges right to be concerned that the budgets for the courts are not 'ring-fenced'? If the prison population continues to rise then pressures on the budget will increase. It is theoretically possible that pressure could then be placed on the judges to sentence offenders in a particular way, potentially compromising their judicial independence.

Do you think a framework document is sufficient or should there be a statutory rule stating that the budget for HM Court Service should be set annually and kept 'ring-fenced'?

6.2 Key courts

So far this chapter has discussed how courts are classified, organized, and funded, but what are the courts in the English Legal System? A number of courts and tribunals exist and so if a detailed discussion of all these were to take place then this chapter would be extremely long! Instead a summary will be given of the key courts that feature commonly within the English Legal System and later (6.4) a brief outline of some other common courts will be made.

The courts that will be considered in this part are:

- magistrates' court
- county court
- Crown Court
- High Court of Justice
- Court of Appeal
- Supreme Court.

Diagram 6.1 shows the approximate structure of the English Legal System. It will be seen that the precise placing of the courts is a matter of debate and also alters depending on the type of work that the court is undertaking.

6.2.1 Magistrates' court

The first court to note is the magistrates' court. This is the lowest of the courts that we are concerned with. Magistrates' courts are local courts. Before the implementation of the CA 2003, the courts were divided into local petty sessional areas and run by local *Magistrates' Courts Committees*. Now, however, they are subsumed within HM Court Service and whilst they continue to sit in local locations, their organization and management is undertaken by the local area and regional offices of the Court Service.

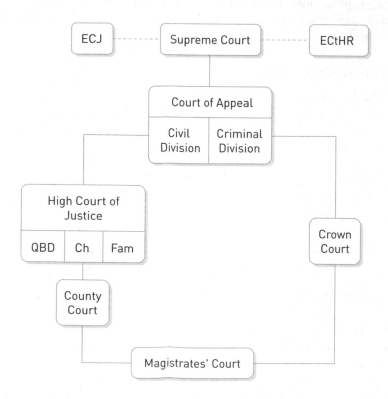

Diagram 6.1 The hierarchy of the courts

Magistrates' courts primarily have a criminal jurisdiction and indeed the vast majority of criminal cases heard in England and Wales take place in the magistrates' court. It will be seen later in this book that criminal matters can be divided into summary matters, indictable matters, and those that can be tried either summarily or on indictment (see 10.7.1 below). Summary trials take place in the magistrates' court before either a district judge (magistrates' court) (see 11.1.1.2 below) or a bench of lay magistrates (see 11.1.1.1 below). The punishment an offender can receive in the magistrates' court is currently limited to six months' imprisonment although, at a time yet to be announced, their powers will be increased to imposing twelve months' custody.

A separate criminal jurisdiction that exists in the magistrates' court is in respect of adolescent crime. Here the court is known as the 'youth court' and whilst they are frequently located in the same building, matters are heard in specific courtrooms that are laid out in a less formal manner and a separate entrance from the adult magistrates' court must be maintained. The youth court has jurisdiction over all but the most serious of adolescent crime, even where an offence is theoretically triable only on indictment for adult offenders. Separate punishments also exist for youth crime, with the overall aim to be preventing reoffending rather than punishing transgressions of the law.

The magistrates' court also has a limited civil jurisdiction. Its largest role is probably in respect of family-law matters, particularly public child-care law. When sitting in this jurisdiction it is known as the 'family proceedings court' although it continues to be staffed by specially trained magistrates. All public child-care proceedings, eg situations where a local authority is seeking to remove a child from care or requires the presentation of a child for assessment purposes, must begin in the family proceedings court although the case may then be transferred to higher courts. Other civil jurisdiction relates to the recovery of certain debts (including, for example, the supply of services such as gas and electricity) and the licensing of gambling institutions.

6.2.2 County court

The second court to examine is the county court. Like the magistrates' court, this is an inferior court (see 6.1.1.3 above). The county court is a purely civil court and its jurisdiction is set out in statute. The original jurisdiction was set out in the *County Courts Act 1846* but such courts had a very limited jurisdiction and the modern version of the courts was established by the *County Courts Act 1984*.

As an inferior court created by statute, the county courts have limited jurisdiction. If a statutory provision does not grant it jurisdiction to deal with the matter, then a judge of the county court has no right to adjudicate on the matter. They are local courts in that they are distributed across the country, with the distribution taking account of population areas. At the time of writing there are 216 county courts although increasingly a number are being housed in combined court centres with the Crown Court. The advantage of this is that the county and Crown Courts share some judicial posts and the administration of the courts can be shared by grouping the courts together. That said, there remain more county courts than Crown Courts. In Autumn 2010 it was announced that to save money from the Ministry of Justice budget approximately fifty county courts could close.

As noted above, the county court has an exclusively civil jurisdiction. Many of the matters relate to types of actions that could also be heard in the High Court but which are considered less serious because either the nature of the claim or the amount of compensation sought is reduced. In terms of general civil jurisdiction the county court deals with matters such as breach of contract, claims in tort (negligence, nuisance, etc), personal injury, certain disputes as to land, and even some admiralty claims. The county court will frequently also deal with contested probate so long as the estate is not more than £300,000 (s 32 *County Courts Act 1984*).

The county court also has a family jurisdiction and the vast majority of divorces are dealt with by the county court, with only complicated and high-value divorces taking place in the High Court. Other family matters, including access to children and some types of public child-care proceedings are also dealt with by the county court.

The county court has exclusive jurisdiction over small claims. It is common to hear of the 'small claims court', a title that has quasi-recognition within HM Court Service. In fact it is an informal part of the county court and proceedings are instituted within the county court. The small-claims procedure is considered in detail within Chapter 14.

The county court originally had its own procedural rules (known as the *County Court Rules* printed in a green volume so colloquially known as 'the Green book') but following a series of reviews it was decided that a single set of procedural rules should exist for the county court, High Court, and Court of Appeal (Civil Division). These rules, known as the *Civil Procedure Rules* were introduced by the *Civil Procedure Act 1997* and the rules continue to be updated. Following Lord Woolf's report on *Access to Justice*, the county court and High Court have similar jurisdictions and except for those cases that are specifically reserved to either, a claim may be made in either court but will be transferred to the appropriate court during case management (see 10.7 below).

6.2.3 The Crown Court

The Crown Court is the first superior court that is to be considered (see 6.1.1.3 above). It is a court of both original and appellate jurisdictions; in other words some trials at first instance take place but it also hears certain appeals. It is often said that it has an exclusively criminal jurisdiction but that is not quite true in that it has a limited civil jurisdiction in its appellate capacity.

The Crown Court is a relatively modern invention although it is a development from the system of assize courts (which were presided over by puisne judges sent on circuit) and quarter sessions which were locally based criminal courts. The fusion retains some elements of the assize system in that today puisne judges will preside in the Crown Court whilst sitting on the circuit they are assigned to. The Crown Court came into being through the *Courts Act 1971* although its jurisdiction is now based on the SCA 1981.

6.2.3.1 Trials of first instance

The principal work of the Crown Court is to deal with trials that take place on indictment, ie involving a trial. The work of the Crown Court in this capacity is discussed in Chapter 12. The Crown Court can currently sit at seventy-seven separate locations although the most famous remains the *Central Criminal Court*, also known as the 'Old Bailey'. Theoretically each Crown Court centre has the same jurisdiction but, in practice, the Crown Court is divided into different types of court centre. The allocation is by tier and there are three tiers:

Tier One. These are courts where High Court judges will regularly visit and preside and in which circuit judges and recorders will also sit for the full range of Crown

Court business. These are also courts where High Court judges will preside over civil High Court business.

Tier Two. Tier-two cases are, in effect, the same as tier-one courts except there is no civil work undertaken.

Tier Three. These are courts where a High Court judge would not normally preside and where only class 3 indictable offences (see 12.1.1.1 below) are heard by circuit judges and recorders.

A contested trial will take place before a judge and jury. The process of the trial is discussed in Chapter 12.

6.2.3.2 Appeals

The Crown Court also has an appellate jurisdiction. It may hear appeals from the magistrates' court. This type of appeal is discussed at 13.2.1 below. Whilst the appeal will ordinarily be for criminal matters, the Crown Court does have a limited civil appeal over some civil orders such as the *Anti-Social Behaviour Order*, *Sexual Offences Prevention Order*, and *Foreign Travel Order*. These are imposed by the magistrates' court sitting in their civil capacity but they are quasi-criminal orders in that they prohibit an offender from doing something contained in the order, and breach of an order amounts to a criminal offence.

6.2.4 High Court of Justice

The High Court of Justice (or High Court as it is invariably known) is probably the most important court in the English Legal System. It has unlimited jurisdiction in civil matters which means that in the absence of a statutory or common-law rule prohibiting a judge sitting on such a case, the High Court has jurisdiction over the dispute. Whilst it is primarily a court of civil jurisdiction, it does have an important appellate and reviewing jurisdiction in respect of criminal matters.

The High Court is based in the Royal Courts of Justice in the Strand although it also sits in twenty-seven first-tier Crown Court centres (see 6.2.3.1 above) outside of London. Each circuit has at least one court exercising High Court jurisdiction.

The High Court is divided into three divisions, into which all business of the court will be assigned. The three divisions are the Queen's Bench Division (King's Bench Division when the monarch is a King), Chancery Division, and the Family Division (s 5 SCA1981). In 1988 the judiciary suggested that the divisions should be abolished[1] and in the mid-1990s a further proposal was brought forward to reformulate the divisions by, for example, merging the Chancery and Queen's Bench Divisions. In his interim report on *Access to Justice*, Lord Woolf rejected this argument (Woolf (1995), Chapter 12, para 17) believing that the specialist jurisdiction of the Chancery Division would be lost in a merger and he noted that, for example, there are only a small number of Chancery puisne judges (in 2010 there are only eighteen judges out of a total of 108) and they work closely together as a team. Lord Woolf, in his final report, did not recommend any changes to the divisional structure and so it continues to consist of three divisions.

---

1. See (1988) *Law Society Gazette*, 25 May.

6.2.4.1 Queen's Bench Division

The largest of the three divisions is the Queen's Bench Division (it currently being staffed by 72 out of 108 puisne judges and with Lords Justice of Appeal sitting in the Administrative Court where required). The principal work of the division can be divided into three distinct areas although, as will be seen, other specialist work also occurs within the division.

General work

The Queen's Bench Division deals with much of the high-value civil work assigned to the High Court. All civil work that falls outside of the Chancery Division or Family Division is heard in the Queen's Bench Division and this includes, for example, most claims from contract, personal injury claims, and libel actions. As will be seen from Chapter 14, much of the classes of work this division hears could also be heard in the county court but the High Court is selected where a matter is particularly complicated or where the amount of compensation sought is high.

Appellate work

The Queen's Bench Division has an appellate jurisdiction. Under the procedure for civil appeals (see Chapter 14) an appeal is ordinarily to the next level of judge. So where a person wishes to appeal against a procedural matter in the county court this will ordinarily be heard by a High Court judge and it will normally be a judge of this division.

The Queen's Bench Division also currently has a criminal appellate jurisdiction. It is possible to appeal against a finding of magistrates by way of case stated (see 13.2.2 below). Such an appeal is brought before this division.

Supervisory jurisdiction

The High Court has always had an important supervisory jurisdiction. This is where it exercises the power of review over inferior courts, tribunals, and some public bodies. It is now commonly referred to as 'judicial review' and it is a jurisdiction that has developed extensively over the past few decades yet can be extremely controversial, especially when it involves the court overturning decisions of ministers. This jurisdiction is discussed at 14.3.

The supervisory jurisdiction is exercised by the 'Administrative Court'. Unlike certain 'courts' within the Queen's Bench Division, this is an administrative title that has no statutory force. It is, therefore, technically just a panel of the Queen's Bench Division although the Civil Procedure Rules set out a separate body of rules for this work (Part 54 of the *Civil Procedure Rules*).

The Administrative Court is headed by a 'lead judge' (currently the President of the Queen's Bench Division) who works with the appropriate administrative staff to administer the working of the court. Other judges of the High Court are designated by the Lord Chief Justice to hear matters in the Administrative Court. Where the judges are not already assigned to the Queen's Bench Division they are considered to be additional temporary judges of that division when hearing the matter.

Specialist jurisdictions

The Admiralty Court and Commercial Court both exist within the Queen's Bench Division. These are statutory courts (s 6 SCA 1981) and deal with specific types of jurisdiction. The Admiralty Court, as its name suggests, exercises particular claims in relation to maritime law, for example, claims relating to salvage or disputes as to the carriage of goods. The Commercial Court is a very specialist jurisdiction and relates to international business law and banking law. The court also has a role in arbitration (a concept discussed in Chapter 16).

The final specialist court is the Technology and Construction Court. Like the Administrative Court, this is not a statutory court but rather an administrative title. The work of the Court is set out in Part 60 of the *Civil Procedure Rules* and its work will cover, for example, disputes as to the supply and installation of computer systems, or disputes in relation to construction or engineering projects. Its work requires specialist judges and outside of London it is not unusual for specially trained circuit judges to sit temporarily as acting judges of the High Court.

6.2.4.2 Chancery Division

The Chancery Division is a specialist division of the High Court and considers work relating to, for example, trusts, wills, companies, certain land claims, and certain claims relating to tax. Its work is technical and the judges of this division are supplemented by masters of the Chancery Division. Masters hold a judicial office similar to that of the district judge (see 7.1.3.3 below) but who exercise jurisdiction in the High Court. Whilst the masters cannot hear full trials, they dispose of much of the procedural matters and frequently their involvement will lead to the case being settled before the matter proceeds to trial.

Within the Chancery Division exists two specialist courts. The first is the Patents Court (s 6 SCA 1981). This court deals with disputes relating to copyright, patents, and intellectual property disputes. The work is very specialist and the judges who sit on these matters are normally given specific training and it is not uncommon for circuit judges to act as an additional judge of the High Court when hearing these matters.

The second court is the Bankruptcy Court. As with the Administrative Court within the Queen's Bench Division, this is an administrative title for convenience. The court, as its name suggests, deals with disputes relating to bankruptcy and insolvency.

6.2.4.3 Family Division

The Family Division is the newest of the three divisions. Prior to 1971 the third division was Probate, Divorce, and Admiralty Division. The probate function was transferred to the Chancery Division and the admiralty work was assigned to the Queen's Bench Division. Wardship—the state's care of children who cannot care for themselves—was exercised by the Queen's Bench Division but this was transferred to the new Family Division.

The Family Division, as its name suggests, deals with most matters relating to divorce, family disputes, and children. Complicated public child-care matters are heard in this division as will complicated or high-value matters relating to private disputes. There are currently eighteen judges of the division (plus a president) but their work is supplemented by specialist district judges who will be responsible for a considerable amount of the work of the division, including some contested trials. In addition, outside of London it is not unusual for a specialist circuit judge to sit as an acting judge of the Family Division, especially where matters are urgent.

Whilst all divisions will have a judge 'on call' the work of this division often means that the court will 'sit' at unusual times. There is always at least one judge who can be contacted at any time, day or night, and hearings can be heard over the telephone. This may occur, for example, where there is a dispute as to whether a child should have urgent medical treatment, or where somebody is seeking to remove a child from the jurisdiction.

6.2.4.4 Divisional Courts

A Divisional Court is when two or more judges sit in the High Court together to hear the same case (s 66 SCA 1981). This will ordinarily happen in their appellate or reviewing capacity. Whilst a Divisional Court can be created of any of the three divisions of the High Court, most Divisional Courts have been of the Queen's Bench Division, especially when it is exercising its powers of judicial review. However, since the establishment of the Administrative Court it is more common for judges to sit individually to hear some matters. Where this happens, it is not a Divisional Court but simply a hearing of the Queen's Bench Division (within the courtesy-titled 'Administrative Court').

6.2.5 The Court of Appeal

The modern Court of Appeal came into existence in 1966 which fused the previously separate Court of Appeal and Court of Criminal Appeal into a single court consisting of two divisions: the Criminal Division and the Civil Division. The Criminal Division is presided over by the Lord Chief Justice and the Civil Division is presided over by the Master of the Rolls. The Lord Chief Justice, as head of the judiciary, can (and has) appointed judges of the Court of Appeal as Vice-President of either or both divisions (s 3 SCA 1981). The judges of the Court of Appeal can sit in either division and in both divisions (but most frequently in the Criminal Division), puisne and even certain circuit judges can sit in the court as additional judges.

The Court of Appeal can sit in panels and in both divisions it is common for a single judge (in the Criminal Division this will normally be a puisne judge) to consider whether leave to appeal should be given and within the Criminal Division to hear applications for bail. The Criminal Division ordinarily sits in panels of three, and it must sit in an uneven number of no less than three judges when determining appeals against conviction (s 55 SCA 1981) and certain other appellate decisions. When it sits in panels of two judges (eg for sentences against appeal) if the judges are divided then it must relist the matter for a hearing before three judges (s 55(5) *Criminal Appeals Act 1968* (CAA 1968)). The Civil Division can theoretically dispose of an appeal by a single judge (s 54(2) SCA 1981) but ordinarily it will sit with at least two judges. As with the Criminal Division, if an even number of judges sit and they are divided as to the outcome, the case should be relisted before a panel of the Court consisting of an uneven number of judges (s 54(5) SCA 1981).

The Court of Appeal ordinarily sits in the Royal Courts of Justice in London and any number of courts can sit at the same time so long as they are properly constituted. In recent years the Court of Appeal has sat in locations outside of London. This originated with the Civil Division but it has included the Criminal Division and the court has sat in a number of locations, including Cardiff, Manchester, and Newcastle-upon-Tyne. Recently the Criminal Division has also begun using live video-links to allow an appellant to see (and participate) in an appeal hearing whilst saving the costs of transporting the prisoner to London.

6.2.6 The Supreme Court

The Supreme Court is the newest court within the English Legal System although, as noted already, it is technically a UK court as its jurisdiction is not restricted to English cases. The Court was established by Part 3 of the CRA 2005 and it came into being in October 2009 (at the start of the legal year). Its jurisdiction, broadly speaking, includes that which the House of Lords exercised but it also assumed responsibility for devolution issues that were previously within the jurisdiction of the Judicial Committee of the Privy Council (6.4.1 below).

The Supreme Court was created as part of wider constitutional changes, and an attempt to lead to the separation of powers in respect of the legislature and judiciary. As part of this process, the Lord Chancellor had his judicial functions removed (see 7.2.1 below) and it was decided to remove the judiciary from the legislature. Members of the judiciary have been debarred from being a member of the House of Commons for some time, but a number of judges, most notably the Lords of Appeal in Ordinary were entitled to sit in the House of Lords and participate both in its judicial and legislative capacity. The CRA 2005 altered this by stating that peers who serve as a judge may not sit in the House of Lords during their employment (s 137 CRA 2005) although they will be free to sit when they have retired (this will be discussed more fully in chapter 7).

Whilst the government was clear that the primary reason for the establishment of the Supreme Court was the separation of powers (Department of Constitutional Affairs (2003) 10), it was suggested that an additional reason was the fact that the work of the Law Lords could not be adequately supported because of the lack of space available in Westminster (p 12). This was perhaps slightly unconvincing reasoning since there is no reason why a separate annexe could not have been created to provide additional support and space. For example, MPs were given an annexe across from the Palace of Westminster (known as Portcullis House) and a similar arrangement could have been established.

Although the separation of the legislature and judiciary was generally welcomed, the Law Lords themselves were divided as to whether the changes were needed or desirable, with some arguing that their presence in the House of Lords was 'of benefit to the Law Lords, to the House and to others including litigants' (Law Lords (2003) at [2]). That said, the argument that the Law Lords could intervene in debates to ensure that errors of law were corrected during the parliamentary process was arguably overstated since in 2000 the Law Lords committed themselves to being bound by two principles:

1. that the Law Lords were supposed to be impartial and accordingly in matters of party-political controversy they would not normally speak
2. participating in parliamentary proceedings may debar them from sitting as judge when a matter relating to the legislation appears before the Appellate Committee.[2]

However, it was only a convention and there were some interventions. For example, Lord Woolf (the then Lord Chief Justice) and Lord Steyn (a then Law Lord) both criticized elements of the (then) *Asylum and Immigration Bill* as it was passing through Parliament, and at the time this was one of the most politically sensitive and partisan pieces of legislation (Windlesham (2006) 40–41).

---

2. *Hansard*, HL Deb, vol 614, col 419 (22 June 2000).

The Law Lords made other contributions to the House. It was reported that twelve places on House of Lords scrutiny committees were taken by serving Law Lords and that one Law Lord had served as the chairman on nine committees (Windlesham (2005) 813). Whilst there may therefore have been a benefit in using the Law Lords for the purpose of scrutinizing legislation it could be questioned whether this was an appropriate use of the most senior judges' time. There are others with legal qualifications in the House, including retired Law Lords, and surely they are as able to identify potential flaws.

The Supreme Court hears only a small number of appeals. During its first legal year (October 2009 through to (approximately) July 2010) the Court received 206 applications for permission to appeal (it granting 69) and it heard 67 appeals, giving judgment in 62 (the remaining 5 being reserved) (see *A Supremely successful first legal year*: Press Notice 08/2010 of the Supreme Court). This can be contrasted with the Court of Appeal. The latest statistics are contained in *Judicial and Court Statistics 2008* (Cm 7697) and for the year 2008, a total of 3,294 applications for appeal were made to the Civil Division and 1,225 appeals were heard. In the Criminal Division a total of 7,240 applications were made and 2,532 appeals were heard. In broad terms this means the Supreme Court hears less than 2 per cent of the number of appeals the Court of Appeal hears. For a matter to be heard by the Supreme Court it must involve a point of public importance and the Court is slow to grant leave, so as to ensure that it is not overwhelmed by cases. The Court of Appeal (and, to a lesser extent, the High Court) are also now very slow to grant leave to the Supreme Court, arguing that it is for that court to decide which cases it will hear.

The Supreme Court, like its predecessor the House of Lords, does not (unlike the Supreme Court of the USA) sit *en banc*, ie together. Instead panels of the Court are established, with each panel being a minimum of three justices (s 42(1)(b) CRA 2005). Ordinarily leave is dealt with by a panel of three justices and ordinarily this will be dealt with on paper without an oral hearing (rule 16(1) *Supreme Court Rules 2009*, SI 2009/1603) although the justices could refer the matter for an oral hearing (rule 16(2)(c)), again usually heard by a panel of three justices. Substantive appeals are usually heard by five justices although it can sit in larger panels (so long as there is an odd number of justices: s 42(1)(a) CRA 2005) and it has done so on a number of occasions, including constitutions of seven (*Re S-B (Children)* [2009] UKSC 17) and nine (*Norris v Government of United States of America*) [2010] UKSC 9). It will normally only do so when a case is of particular importance.

6.2.6.1 The House of Lords

Prior to the establishment of the Supreme Court the highest court was the House of Lords. Traditionally judicial matters were heard in the chamber of the House and any peer could participate, but during the nineteenth century it became clear that a more professional approach should be taken and life barons were created as Lords of Appeal in Ordinary, commonly known as the 'Law Lords'.

The modern House of Lords organized itself into an appellate committee to determine substantive appeals. An appellate committee consisted of a panel of not less than three Lords (s 5 *Appellate Jurisdiction Act 1876*) although it was more usual for a panel of five Law Lords to sit and there were higher panels of seven (eg *A v Secretary of State for the Home Department* [2005] UKHL 71) and even nine Law Lords (eg *Jackson v Attorney-General* [2005] UKHL 56). The appellate committee had to be distinguished from the appeals committee. This was a committee of three Law Lords that sat to decide whether leave to appeal to the House of Lords should be granted. If leave was granted then the matter proceeded to the appellate committee.

As the appellate committee was part of Parliament then technically it could not sit during the prorogation (the period at the end of each parliamentary year before a new Parliament is called by the monarch at the state opening of Parliament) or dissolution of Parliament but the *Appellate Jurisdiction Act 1876* expressly permitted the appellate committee to continue to perform its duties during such times (ss 8 and 9), perhaps reinforcing the fact that the appellate committee was de facto separate from the legislative role of the House of Lords.

6.3 The 'European Courts'

The structure diagram (Diagram 6.1) shows that next to the Supreme Court are two European Courts; the European Court of Justice (which has jurisdiction over matters relating to the European Union) and the European Court of Human Rights (whose primary function is to rule on matters relating to the *European Convention on Human Rights*). Both of these are important courts in their own rights and whilst one will often hear people refer to 'appealing to Europe' this is not technically correct since neither court operates as an appellate court as such.

The detail of these courts and their interrelationship with the English Legal System was discussed earlier in the book (see 4.3.4.3 and 4.4.3.2 above) and rather than duplicate material, readers should cross-refer to these sections for a discussion of these institutions.

6.4 Other courts

Section 6.2 discussed the key common courts within the English Legal System. Among the other courts and tribunals (tribunals being discussed in Chapter 15) three other courts deserve a brief discussion, those are:

- Judicial Committee of the Privy Council
- Court of Protection
- Coroner's Courts.

The discussion of these courts will be much briefer but will allow the reader to understand the broad jurisdiction of each court.

6.4.1 Judicial Committee of the Privy Council

The Judicial Committee of the Privy Council was established by the *Judicial Committee Act 1833* (JCA 1833) although the Privy Council itself is an ancient advisory body to the monarch. Prior to 1833 the Privy Council heard appellate matters and legal petitions from the colonies but it was Privy Councillors rather than judges who resolved the matter. By 1833 this was considered inappropriate and the Act of that year stated that judicial matters were to be heard by the Judicial Committee which would consist of senior judicial officers of the United Kingdom and Commonwealth countries (colonies at that time).

Whilst Court of Appeal judges are appointed to the Privy Council upon appointment (see 7.1.2.2 below) the modern Privy Council ordinarily takes the form of five Justices of the Supreme Court sitting, thus continuing the traditional staffing that saw it having the reputation as being the House of Lords in all but name. That was never quite true since, for example, other judicial officers sit, including a number of Commonwealth judges but it is more common for the Justices of the Supreme Court to sit.

The current jurisdiction of the Judicial Committee can be summarized as follows:

- Appeals to the Queen in Council. A number of Commonwealth countries and British overseas territories continue to have the Privy Council as its head. Under this jurisdiction the Judicial Committee is technically tendering advice to the monarch and their judgment is then given legal standing by an Order in Council.

- Appeals to the Head of State. The Kingdom of Brunei allows an appeal against civil matters to proceed to the Privy Council. By agreement between the UK monarch and the sultan of Brunei the Privy Council tenders advice to the sultan rather than the Queen.

- Appeals to the Judicial Committee. Certain republics within the Commonwealth continue to allow appeals to the Privy Council even though the Queen is no longer head of state. Under this jurisdiction the judgment of the Privy Council is final rather than it being merely advice to the monarch.

- Domestic jurisdiction. Appeals from the Channel Islands are heard by the Privy Council as are appeals from certain disciplinary bodies and ecclesiastical courts. Where the High Court sits as a 'prize court' an appeal lies to the Privy Council rather than through domestic avenues of appeal. Prior to the establishment of the Supreme Court devolution issues (discussed in Chapter 1) were heard by the Privy Council but the jurisdiction to hear these matters was transferred to the Supreme Court (Sch 9 (Part 2) CRA 2005).

In addition, the Queen can refer any matter of law to the Privy Council for its advice (s 4 JCA 1833).

Regardless of which jurisdiction is being exercised only a single judgment is given (in contrast to, for example, the Supreme Court, Court of Appeal, and Divisional Courts where additional assenting and dissenting judgments are presented).

6.4.2 Court of Protection

The *Mental Capacity Act 2005* (MCA 2005) created the Court of Protection as a superior court (see 6.1.1.3 above) in its own right (s 45 MCA 2005). Prior to this, issues concerning those adults who were considered to be unable to act for themselves were dealt with either by the High Court of Justice, usually the Chancery Division or the Family Division. The statute expressly states:

> The court may sit at any place in England and Wales, on any day and at any time.
> (s 45(3))

The implications of this is that the court can sit outside of a formal courtroom and can deal with urgent matters. It will be seen in Chapter 7 that a High Court judge has an inherent power to sit anywhere at anytime (see 7.1.2 below) but this provision is ensuring that there is no doubt that a judge, of whatever rank, has this power when sitting in the Court of Protection.

The court must have a president and vice-president (s 46(3)) and the President of the Family Division is the President of that court and the Chancellor of the High Court (head of the Chancery Division) is the Vice-President. Judges of the High Court, Circuit Court, and district judges can be designated by either the Lord Chief Justice or the President of the court (if the Lord Chief Justice so delegates) to sit in the Court of Protection. A circuit judge or district judge must be nominated by the Lord Chief Justice (in consultation with the Lord Chancellor) to be the senior judge of the Court of Protection (s 46(4)) who is, in essence, in day-to-day administrative charge of the Court.

The jurisdiction of the court concerns the mental capacity of adults and the court can determine whether a person has appropriate mental capacity and, if not, make declarations as to their finances or welfare along with adjudicating on disputes relating to lasting or enduring powers of attorney, including their discharge. Powers of attorney are where a competent adult is assigned to make decisions as to the welfare of the person lacking capacity (see Part 1 of the MCA 2005).

6.4.3 Coroners' courts

Coroners' courts are one of the most ancient forms of court within England and Wales, with the office of coroner dating back to medieval times. The modern coronial system investigates unnatural and violent deaths or those who die in custody together with a specialist jurisdiction relating to buried treasure trove (a rather complicated provision but, at its simplest, it is buried gold, silver, or coins from the same find, that are over 300 years old when discovered). The coronial system will be subject to major changes when the *Coroners and Justice Act 2009* (CJA 2009) comes into effect. There will probably be a phased implementation of the new system but it is likely that the new coronial system will come into effect in late 2011 or early 2012. This section of the chapter will consider the new system.

As with other aspects of the English Legal System (most notably the system of tribunals, discussed in Chapter 15), the changes to the coronial system are designed, in part, to strengthen their accountability and to reform the offices. Traditionally a coroner did not need to be a lawyer and could instead be a medical practitioner (although under s 2(1), *Coroners Act 1988* such persons needed to obtain a specific legal qualification). When the CJA 2009 comes into effect coroners will be judicial appointments (with a five-year period (discussed more extensively in Chapter 7) see Sch 3, para 3 CJA 2009).

Coroners have traditionally been employed by local authorities and this link survives the CJA 2009 reforms. England and Wales is to be divided into coronial areas, each of which will equate either to a local authority or a combination of local authority borders (Sch 2). Each coronial area will have a senior coroner who will be the principal coroner and he will be assisted by area and assistant coroners (Sch 3). Coroners will have the equivalent status to an inferior judge (see Chapter 7) in that they hold office for good behaviour but can be removed administratively by the Lord Chancellor with the consent of the Lord Chief Justice (Sch 3, Part 4).

Coroners' courts differ from the rest of the English Legal System in one very important respect; they are inquisitorial rather than adversarial (see 1.3.2.1 above).

Accordingly, there are no 'sides' to a coroners' court and this can mean that there is difficulty in a family of the bereaved securing legal aid for representation before the coroners' courts. This matter was litigated in *R (on the application of Main) v Minister for Legal Aid* [2007] EWCA Civ 1147. The applicant lost her mother and sister after a railway accident. She claimed for legal aid to provide representation at the inquest and whilst the Legal Services Commission recommended that representation be given, the Lord Chancellor (as minister responsible for legal aid) refused to allow representation. The Court of Appeal, upholding this decision, stated that the coroner was able to identify the issues without representation from the family and placed strength on the fact that the coronial system was inquisitorial rather than adversarial.

❓ QUESTION FOR REFLECTION

The decision in *Main* was that the Lord Chancellor could not be compelled to grant legal aid for representation in an inquest. Had the family been able to fund counsel privately then representation would have been permitted. Does this not show a flaw in the coronial system? Does it mean that justice can be 'bought'?

Why do you think the family wanted their own representative? Was the Court of Appeal right to think that a coroner can identify matters without representation from the family?

🎧 LISTEN TO THE PODCAST

For guidance on how to answer this question and a discussion of the main issues, listen to the author's podcast on the Online Resource Centre:
www.oxfordtextbooks.co.uk/orc/gillespie_els3e/

Coroners' courts are inferior courts and are thus susceptible to judicial review, something that has been exercised numerous times (see, most notably, *R (on the application of Paul) v Deputy Coroner of the Queen's Household and Assistant Deputy Coroner for Surrey* [2007] 2 All ER 509 and *R (on the application of Al-Fayed) v Assistant Deputy Coroner of Inner West London* [2008] EWHC 713 (Admin)). The jurisdiction of a coronial court is now set out clearly in statute. In respect of deaths, a coroner must investigate where:

- the deceased died a violent or unnatural death;
- the cause of death is unknown; or
- the deceased died while in custody or otherwise in state detention (s 1(2) CJA 2009).

The purpose of the investigation is:

- to ascertain who the deceased was;
- how, when, and where the deceased came by his death;
- the particulars (if any) required to be registered concerning the death (s 5(1) CJA 2009).

Interestingly s 5(2) continues by stating that the second element will also require ascertaining in what circumstances the deceased came by his death where this is necessary to prevent a breach of the *Human Rights Act 1998*. This, it is submitted, is a reference to the jurisprudence that has been established under Article 2 (discussed in 5.2.3.1 where it was seen that there are positive obligations in respect of the investigation of any death).

The issue of when a jury should be established has long proven controversial (and was one of the principal reasons for litigation in the inquest relating to Diana, Princess of Wales: see *R (on the application of Paul) v Deputy Coroner of the Queen's Household and Assistant Deputy Coroner for Surrey* [2007] 2 All ER 509: note the office of the Coroner of the Queen's Household has been abolished by s 46 CJA 2009). Statute has now clarified this and stated that a jury should not normally hear an inquest (s 7(1) CJA 2009) save where the coroner has reason to suspect:

- the deceased died while in the custody of the state and the death was violent, unnatural, or unknown;
- the death resulted from an act or omission by a police officer or a member of the armed services police in the purported execution of their duty;
- the death was caused by a notifiable accident, poisoning, or disease; or
- the senior coroner believes that there is sufficient reason for doing so (s 7(2)–(3), CJA 2009).

Where a jury is empanelled then it is a jury of seven to eleven persons (s 8(1) CJA 2009), the exact number being for the senior coroner to decide. A decision of the jury need not be unanimous, but only where only one or two jurors disagree and the jury has had sufficient time to attempt to reach a verdict (s 9 CJA 2009). The CJA 2009 has also strengthened the rules relating to jury service, including providing for criminal penalties for those who act inappropriately in respect of being summoned to attend as a juror (Sch 6 CJA 2009).

The coronial system, whilst locally based, will be under the administration of a Chief Coroner and Deputy Chief Coroner. The Chief Coroner is appointed by the Lord Chief Justice and must either be a puisne or circuit judge (Sch 8, para 1 CJA 2009). The Lord Chief Justice may also appoint such many persons as he deems appropriate to be a Deputy Chief Coroner and these persons must be puisne or circuit judges or a senior coroner (Sch. 8, para 2 CJA 2009).

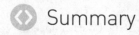 Summary

In this chapter we have noted:

- Classifying the courts is not a simple process since many of the courts have both a civil and criminal jurisdiction.
- The courts in England and Wales (ie excluding the Supreme Court which is a UK court) are now administered by a single agency, HM Court Service.
- The courts of original jurisdiction (ie which hear trials of first instance) are the magistrates' court, county court, Crown Court, and High Court.
- The Crown Court and High Court have both an original and appellate jurisdiction.

- The High Court is divided into three divisions (Queen's Bench Division, Chancery Division, and Family Division) and when two or more judges sit together in the High Court it is known as a Divisional Court.

? End-of-chapter questions

1. Given that the county court and High Court have similar jurisdiction is there any point in keeping them as separate courts? Would it not be appropriate for there to be just one court—a civil court—which could be staffed by different judges? Are there any advantages or disadvantages to this approach?

2. A similar question can be asked in respect of family law matters. Family law, particularly in respect of children, is a specialist area of law. Public and private child-care proceedings can be transferred from magistrates' court to county court or High Court or vice versa. Some have suggested that a single family court should be established (see, for example, Robins above). Consider the arguments in favour of such an approach.

3. Why do we need so many appeal courts? In Chapter 13 it will be noted that it is possible to appeal from the Crown Court to the Court of Appeal and then to the Supreme Court. Is there any need for there to be two appeal courts; should the Court of Appeal not be the final appellate court? In Scotland there is no right of appeal in criminal matters to the Supreme Court, the final appellate court being the Inner House of the Court of Session.

📖 Further reading

Mance, Lord (2006) 'Constitutional reform, the Supreme Court and the Law Lords' 25 *Civil Justice Quarterly* 155–165.

This is an interesting article written by a then Lord of Appeal in Ordinary, discussing the work of the House of Lords and considering ways in which changes might arise as a result of the creation of the Supreme Court. Now the Court has been established it is interesting to compare the current position with that predicted by Lord Mance.

Robins J (2005) 'Strength in unity' 102 *Law Society Gazette* 18–19.

Discusses the possible advantages of creating a single family court.

Samuels A (2006) 'A unified civil court' 25 *Civil Justice Quarterly* 250–260.

This article discusses whether it would be appropriate to introduce a unified civil court to streamline civil proceedings.

You may also find it interesting to read the annual reports of the Court of Appeal (each Division produces a separate report and they are housed on the judiciary website). A link to the publications can be found on the Online Resource Centre at

www.oxfordtextbooks.co.uk/orc/gillespie_els3e/

7

Judges and Judicial Independence

By the end of this chapter you will be able to:

- Identify the key judicial offices, their ranks, and styles.
- Understand how judges are appointed and assess the recent changes.
- Discuss the merits of the current judicial structure.
- Assess the independence of the judiciary.

Introduction

At the heart of the English Legal System is the judiciary, a body of persons often caricatured in the media as doddery old men who are bordering on senile. The truth, however, is that both the full-time and part-time judiciary in England and Wales are extremely professional persons who have come from the very best of the Bar and solicitors. That is not to say that controversy does not surround the judiciary and, in particular, the way that they operate and are appointed to their office. Scepticism also exists as to the role the state has in the execution of the judicial office, ie is there such a thing as judicial independence? In this chapter these issues will be discussed.

As will be seen, there are different types of judges within the English Legal System and these differences are echoed in how they are styled and referred to. The Law Reports, and many other legal publications, will use abbreviations to refer to judges. The following table helpfully summarizes how the different grades of judges are styled, abbreviated, and referred to in court.

Table 7.1 Abbreviations

Judge	Styled	Abbreviation	Referred to in court
President of the Supreme Court	Lord [n] PSC	PSC	My Lord/Lady
Lord Chief Justice	Lord[a] [n] CJ	LCJ (or Lord [n] CJ)	My Lord/Lady
Master of the Rolls	Lord (or Sir[b]) [n] MR	[n] MR	My Lord/Lady
President of the Family Division	Sir[c] [n] P	[n] P	My Lord/Lady
President of the Queen's Bench Division	Sir [n] P	[n] P	My Lord/Lady
Chancellor of the Chancery Division	Sir [n] C	[n] C (formerly V-C)	My Lord/Lady
Justices of the Supreme Court	Lord [n] JSC	Lord [n] JSC	My Lord/Lady
Lords Justice of Appeal	Lord Justice [n]	[n] LJ	My Lord/Lady
Puisne Judges	Hon Mr(s) Justice [n]	[n] J	My Lord/Lady
Circuit Judges	His (Her) Honour Judge	HHJ[d] [n]	Your Honour[e]
Recorders	Mr(s) Recorder [n]	–	Your Honour
District Judges (including magistrates' court)	District Judge [n]	–	Sir or Madam

[a.] Whilst this post is currently (and previously) held by a peer, the provisions of the CRA 2005 mean that in future this may no longer be true. Presumably on these occasions they will be Sir (or Dame) [n].

[b.] The Master of the Rolls was traditionally not a peer although he was frequently appointed a peer after a term of service.

[c.] Where the Master of the Rolls or other ex officio judge is female then she will be Dame [n] rather than Sir [n].

[d.] In Law Reports a circuit judge will normally just be referred to as Judge [n] but technically their title, His or Her Honour Judge [n] is abbreviated to HHJ.

[e.] Where the judge is an Honorary Recorder they are referred to as My Lord or My Lady as are all judges sitting in the Central Criminal Court ('the Old Bailey').

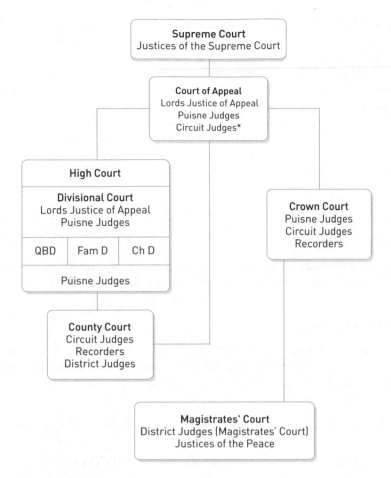

Diagram 7.1 The court and judicial structure

To assist you in understanding where all the judges sit, Diagram 7.1 shows the court and judicial structure.

7.1 The judicial office

The position of a judge is not one that is taken by employment but it is, rather, an office that the holder possesses during his tenure. It is not the place of this chapter to discuss the differences between an office holder and an employee save to say that it normally means an office holder cannot use employment legislation as regards the performance and termination of their office, and the manner in which a person is accountable for disciplinary issues would also differ.

The style, number, and type of judges have differed over the centuries but the modern English Legal System now has a relatively fixed hierarchy of judicial appointments, both full- and part-time. Other people may be titled 'judge' (eg judges of the First-Tier

Tribunal and Upper Tribunal) but for reasons of space this chapter will focus only on those who form the 'mainstream' judiciary, ie those who sit within the courts noted in Chapter 6. This chapter will also not focus on the magistracy as they do not, strictly speaking, hold a judicial office, the office of justice of the peace being a distinct but related office. The appointment of the magistracy is discussed elsewhere (Chapter 11) and in, order to allow a proper contrast to be drawn, the position of the district judge (magistrates' court) is also considered in that chapter. It should be noted, however, that the district judge (magistrates' court) is a judicial officer and is appointed in the same way as an inferior judge (see below).

The judicial hierarchy can be broken down into three principal divisions:

* senior judges
* superior judges
* inferior judges.

The appointment process differs for each division and, to a lesser degree, there are also some differences to reflect the individual office that is being appointed.

7.1.1 Senior judges

The first category of judges to examine are the most senior judges, listed as 'senior judges' in s 60 *Constitutional Reform Act 2005* (CRA 2005) and they are judges who combine not only a judicial post but also an administrative/leadership role. The principal office holders are:

* Lord Chief Justice (who is also the *President of the Courts of England and Wales*)
* Master of the Rolls (who is also normally the *Head of Civil Justice*)
* President of the Supreme Court
* President of the Family Division (who is also the *Head of Family Justice*)
* Chancellor of the High Court (formerly known as the *Vice-Chancellor*)
* President of the Queen's Bench Division.

There is also the power to create a series of deputies and these will be discussed below. Other judges do have administrative roles or titles but they are not considered to be senior office holders and are paid and appointed the same way as the other judges.

7.1.1.1 Lord Chief Justice

The Lord Chief Justice has always been the most senior professional judge but, following the changes to the role of the Lord Chancellor, he became the head of the judiciary with the title *President of the Courts of England and Wales*. Section 7(4) CRA 2005 defines the courts as:

* Court of Appeal
* High Court
* Crown Court
* county court
* magistrates' court.

The Supreme Court is not listed because this is not a court of England and Wales but of the United Kingdom. The Lord Chief Justice was, by tradition, given a peerage upon appointment but following the constitutional reforms to the House of Lords and the removal of the Lords of Appeal in Ordinary from the House of Lords it is highly unlikely that this position will remain. However, by statute, the title remains Lord Chief Justice regardless of whether he has a peerage or not.[1]

The Lord Chief Justice was traditionally the head of criminal justice and the CRA 2005 makes him titular *Head of Criminal Justice* (s 8). The Act does, however, provide for a deputy head in order to allow the Lord Chief Justice to delegate some of the administrative authority and this person will be someone who is a Lord Justice of Appeal (see s 8(4)(b); the current holder is Lord Justice Thomas).

7.1.1.2 Master of the Rolls

The Master of the Rolls, along with the President of the Supreme Court, ranks joint second to the Lord Chief Justice in precedence and is traditionally the head of the Court of Appeal (Civil Division) and, following the *Courts Act 2003* (CA 2003), was created the *Head of Civil Justice* (s 62(1) CA 2003). The 'Rolls' in his title reflects the fact that historically the Master of the Rolls was the clerk responsible for maintaining the rolls and records of the Chancery Court. This responsibility was later transferred to the Public Records Office under ministerial responsibility but the ancient title remains.

The CA 2003 permits a Deputy Head of Civil Justice to be created in order to assist the Master of the Rolls in his work (currently Lord Justice Moore-Bick).

7.1.1.3 President of the Supreme Court

Historically the House of Lords, the predecessor to the Supreme Court, did not have a dedicated president: the judge who had served the longest was considered the 'senior' and thus administratively responsible for the allocation of judges to individual cases.

This changed on 6 June 2000 when Lord Bingham was 'promoted' to the House of Lords to become Senior Law Lord (the promotion carrying with it a pay cut). It was said at the time that creating a Senior Law Lord would bring a more professional management approach to the judicial committee with someone being designated as its head. This was important in its preparatory work for its transformation into the Supreme Court.

The CRA 2005 formalized this approach, creating a *President of the Supreme Court* (s 23(5): currently Lord Philips) and a deputy (currently Lord Hope). The President and Deputy President have administrative responsibilities over, for example, the judicial operation of the Supreme Court and the President superintends the Chief Executive for the administrative operation of the Supreme Court (s 48,CRA 2005). The President also has the power to issue rules and practice directions (s 45 CRA 2005) and these regulate the proceedings of the Supreme Court. The President and Deputy President are responsible for allocating the justices to each case but there is no requirement that they preside over every case and indeed there are a number of occasions when they do not sit, even where the Court constitutes a bench of seven (eg *R v Rollins* [2010] UKSC 39).

---

1. A comparison could perhaps be drawn to Northern Ireland where the Lord Chief Justice is so called but is actually a knight (the current holder being Sir Declan Morgan).

7.1.1.4 Heads of Division

In Chapter 3 it was noted that the High Court is divided into three divisions (Queen's Bench, Family, and Chancery). Each division has a Head of Division although prior to the 2005 Act only the *President of the Family Division* was a Head of Division as of right. The President of the Family Division is now also the Head of Family Justice and a Deputy (who must be a Lord Justice of Appeal, currently Lord Justice Thorpe) can be created.

The 2005 Act created the new offices of the *President of the Queen's Bench Division* and the *Chancellor of the High Court*. Prior to the 2005 Act the Lord Chief Justice was President of the Queen's Bench Division but this new office recognizes the fact that now the Lord Chief Justice is the head of the judiciary, a new Head of Division is required to oversee the work. Lord Justice Judge (as he then was), who previously held the honorific title of *Deputy Chief Justice* (which was neither a statutory office nor remunerated differently to a Lord Justice) became the first holder of this post (in 2008 he was subsequently promoted to be Lord Chief Justice). The Lord Chancellor was also the President of the Chancery Division but there existed a *Vice-Chancellor* who was a de facto Head of Division. The 2005 Act has renamed this office the *Chancellor of the High Court* to reflect the fact that the Lord Chancellor no longer has any judicial responsibilities.

7.1.2 Superior judges

Those judges who are considered to be superior judges are:

- Justices of the Supreme Court
- Lords Justice of Appeal
- puisne judges.

These are judges who sit, as of right, in the higher courts—the High Court and above. Superior judges have unlimited jurisdiction in that their jurisdiction is not limited specifically by statute. In practice this means that they can use something called the *inherent jurisdiction*, ie the common-law powers, and unless a rule of law or statute limits the jurisdiction of the courts in a particular way the judges have the right to act as they deem fit.

 Example Unlimited authority

A simple, but perhaps illustrative, example of the difference in authority can be seen by where a judge sits. An inferior judge can only sit in a designated court—ie one that has been approved by the Department of Constitutional Affairs (DCA) as a court. However in *St Edmundsbury & Ipswich Board of Finance v Clark* [1973] Ch 323 Megarry J decided that he had an inherent power to sit anywhere (p 327). The use of the inherent power was permitted because the judicial authority for a superior judge arises from his office whereas the judicial authority for an inferior judge arises from the court. The judge therefore sat in Iken village hall to hear the evidence of a witness. The judge also, as a safeguard, asked the Lord Chancellor to designate the town as a place where the High Court could sit (p 328) but Megarry J was adamant that this was merely a 'fail-safe' procedure and through the use of the inherent jurisdiction he could sit anywhere.

7.1.2.1 Justices of the Supreme Court

The ordinary judges of the Supreme Court are referred to as the *Justices of the Supreme Court* (s 23(6) CRA 2005) and their number is currently fixed at twelve (s 23(2) CRA 2005) which was the same number as the Law Lords (see below).

The first justices of the Supreme Court were the existing Law Lords at the time of its creation (s 24 CRA 2005). At the time the Court was created Lord Scott was due to retire and Lord Clarke, the then Master of the Rolls, became the first Justice of the Supreme Court to be appointed direct to the Supreme Court. Law Lords were peers and thus upon their appointment they became Lord or Lady [*n*]. Lord Clarke had been given a peerage (which was customary to long-serving Masters of the Rolls) and so he, and the other eleven Justices, are all peers. The most recently appointed member of the Court, Sir John Dyson JSC, was not ennobled on his appointment. This is perhaps because the CRA 2005 prevents serving judges from sitting in the House of Lords (s 137 CRA 2005) although it should be noted that it merely prevents them from *sitting* in the House and not being a member of it.

Some criticized the fact that Sir John Dyson was not ennobled (Morgan (2010)) and said that all the justices should bear the same title. It would have been impossible and unfair to have stripped the existing justices of the Supreme Court of their peerages but to do otherwise would have meant that Justices would continue to be automatically ennobled even though they could not take their seat in the House until after retirement, something that would seem peculiar. A better solution would be to adopt an honorific title. In Scotland the superior judges are known as Lord [*n*] even though they are not ennobled. The same system has now been adopted for the Supreme Court and Sir John Dyson is now referred to as Lord Dyson without being formally appointed to the House of Lords. Being the only knight amongst peers could have suggested that he was inferior to the others, something that was clearly not true. The change to an honorific title must therefore be welcomed.

Lords of Appeal in Ordinary

Whilst they no longer exist, it is of historical interest to note that the judges of the House of Lords were known as the Lords of Appeal in Ordinary, although they are often referred to as the Law Lords. The 'in ordinary' meant they were remunerated for their work. Each judge was granted a life peerage upon appointment, becoming *Baron* or *Baroness X* upon appointment. Technically any judge who held, or had held, a high judicial office within the meaning of the *Appellate Jurisdiction Act 1876* and who was also a peer could sit in the House of Lords. This included retired Law Lords, the current and retired Lord Chief Justices, and certain Masters of the Rolls.

7.1.2.2 Lords Justice of Appeal

The ordinary judges of the Court of Appeal are known as a Lord or Lady Justice of Appeal (s 63 CA 2003). Prior to the 2003 Act the statutory title for a judge of the Court of Appeal was a Lord Justice of Appeal (s 2(3) *Senior Courts Act 1981* (SCA 1981)) and this meant that when Dame Elizabeth Butler-Sloss became the first female member of the Court of Appeal she was officially known as Her Ladyship, Lord Justice Butler-Sloss. Sometime after her appointment, the Lord Chancellor and Lord Chief Justice issued a practice direction (*Practice Note (Mode of Address: Lord Justice Butler-Sloss)*

[1994] 1 FLR 866) which stated that for informal purposes she was to be known as Lady Justice Butler-Sloss but it took until 2003 before the feminine alternative was formally permitted.

Upon appointment to the Court of Appeal a person is sworn in as a member of the Privy Council and is thus entitled to the prefix 'Rt Hon' and is styled *Lord/Lady Justice X*.

7.1.2.3 Puisne judges

Puisne judges (pronounced 'puny') is the formal name given to the ordinary judges of the High Court although in practice they tend to be referred to as 'High Court judges'. The term 'puisne' means lower rank and means that they are the lowest rank of the superior court judges. That said, all puisne judges rank above the inferior judges.

Puisne judges are given the honorific 'Honourable' whilst they hold that rank and are referred to as Mr or Mrs Justice X—the full title, therefore, being the *Honourable Mr(s) Justice X*. Upon appointment they are also knighted or made Dames, something that happens in a private audience with the Queen rather than at a traditional investiture (see Dunn (1993) 184).

7.1.3 Inferior judges

The inferior judges are so called because they do not exercise unlimited jurisdiction but instead their powers are defined by statute. Accordingly, if the statute does not prescribe any authority then they may not exercise any jurisdiction. The principal inferior offices are:

- circuit judges
- recorders
- district judges (including district judges (magistrates' court)).

Tribunal judges are also inferior judges as their power arises from statute but their jurisdiction will be considered elsewhere.

7.1.3.1 Circuit judges

The office of circuit judge is relatively modern, being created by s 16 CA 1971 although prior to this other judicial appointments did exist, including the county court judge although this was a civil judge. The office of circuit judge now spans both civil and criminal work and a judge can expect to sit on both types of work. When a judge is appointed he is assigned to one of the six circuits and he will, especially when quite junior, spend time sitting at the various courts within the circuit. As a judge becomes more senior it is more likely that he will sit primarily in one or two courts although he can, at any time, be asked to sit in other courts within the circuit where it is necessary to do so.

Each court centre has a resident judge, who is in administrative control of the criminal list and that judge will normally be the senior judge of that centre. Some resident judges (in the largest court centres) are paid extra for this role and are designated as senior circuit judges: the other resident judges are not paid extra and the role tends to rotate according to seniority. The resident judge has recently been joined by the designated judges who have similar responsibility for the civil work. There are two types of designated judge: the designated family and designated civil judge. Along with the administrative responsibilities, the designated judges will frequently hear High Court-level work. As with resident judges, at the major court centres the designated judges will be paid as senior circuit judges.

Some circuit judges also bear the title Recorder. This can be a source of confusion for law students as a recorder can be either one of the most junior judicial roles or the title given to the most senior circuit judges, and it is best not to confuse the two! Where it is the senior circuit judge, the term is honorary recorder and it is an office that has existed for many years although traditionally only three full-time posts existed: those of London, Manchester, and Liverpool. These recorderships are substantive posts (ie the posts are specifically advertised as such) and they are automatically senior circuit judges.[2] In the passing of the CA 1971 Parliament had specifically retained the power of local authorities to grant an honorary recordership of the borough (s 54). Theoretically this power was vested in the local authority (because the holder of the office becomes a borough dignity, second only in precedence to the lord mayor) but in practice it is made in consultation with the Department for Constitutional Affairs. No increase in pay is given to the (local) honorary recorders but those appointed have all tended to be the senior judge in the larger court centres (eg Middlesbrough, Bristol, Plymouth) and so were all paid as senior resident judges in any event. The local honorary recorder is not, however, a substantive post and it lapses upon the retirement of the resident judge and it is for the local authority to decide if, and when, it should be granted again.

All circuit judges are styled *His (or Her) Honour Judge X* and upon retirement are entitled to the honorific His or Her Honour. Honorary Recorders wear a different robe (it is red) and are referred to as 'My Lord' or 'My Lady' in court although upon retirement they keep only the honorific His or Her Honour.

7.1.3.2 Recorders

The second type of recorder is the more common and is a part-time judicial role held by practising lawyers. The office, like the circuit judge, is relatively modern and was created by s 21 CA 1971 although part-time roles previously existed,[3] including those bearing the title recorder and assistant recorder. A recorder can be appointed to hear either civil or criminal cases but they are restricted to the circuit-bench work.

A recorder is styled as *Mr or Mrs Recorder X* when in court but is given no style or title when they are not sitting as recorders. They are referred to in court as 'Your Honour' since they are sitting as de facto circuit judges. They may continue to practise in private practice.

7.1.3.3 District judges

The most junior judicial rank is that of the district judge. It is important at the outset to distinguish the district judge from the district judge (magistrates' court) with the former acting solely as a civil judge. Part-time district judges are also permitted and those appointed are known as deputy district judges.

The district judge will normally hear procedural and interlocutory matters but they also hear nearly all of the claims heard in the small claims court and some divorce matters.

2. By tradition the Recorders of London, Liverpool, and Manchester are knighted on appointment.
3. These tended to be criminal-only appointments and were deputy judges of the assizes or Deputy Chairman of the Quarter Sessions.

District judges are styled *District Judge X* for the duration of their appointment and are not given any honorific. They are referred to as 'Sir' or 'Madam' in court.

7.1.4 Judicial dress

One of the more distinctive elements of the English court system is the dress worn in courts. The dress of lawyers is discussed elsewhere (Chapter 8) but what of the judiciary? Traditionally the judiciary, particularly puisne judges, had a wide range of judicial robes to wear but recently there has been a simplified system of robes.

Leaving aside the formal state robes a judge possesses (which are really only used for the ceremony at the start of each legal year) what is the working dress of the judiciary? The simplest of them all are the Justices of the Supreme Court. The Justices do not sit in robes although they do have ceremonial robes that were newly created for the Court. The robes are only worn at the opening of the court and at other ceremonial occasions. The Justices of the Supreme Court are following the tradition set by the House of Lords where no robes were worn, in part because the appellate and appeals committees were, in essence, comparable to other committees where no robes are worn.

Judges of the Court of Appeal used to sit in the Court of Appeal wearing a silk black robe (similar to that worn by Queen's Counsel) and a judicial wig. Following the *Practice Direction (Court Dress)(No 5) and Amendment No 20 to the Consolidated Criminal Practice Direction (Court Dress)* [2008] 1 WLR 1700 judges in the Civil Division of the Court of Appeal will now wear a new civil gown (discussed below) and no wig. The practice direction states that there is no change in the Criminal Division (at [5]) so presumably wigs and the black silk gown are worn. It will be interesting to see how long it will be until the new robe is worn in the Criminal Division too.

Puisne judges' dress now differs according to their work. In civil matters, the new civil gown will be worn but the President of the Family Division has stated that no gown should be worn when sitting in family proceedings (*Practice Note (Family Proceedings: Court Dress)* [2008] 1 WLR 1701). In criminal matters, puisne judges used to wear a series of robes depending on the season. Puisne judges in criminal matters will now only wear the 'winter' robe, which consists of a red robe, black scarf girdle, and a scarlet casting-hood or tippet worn with a judicial wig.

Circuit judges have a lilac robe. Even for civil cases they will not wear the new civil robe because, during the consultation they indicated a preference to retain their robe. Quite why this was permitted is open to question since it would have made more sense for a single civil robe to be used rather than accede to the sartorial preferences of the circuit bench. However, wigs and collars will no longer be worn and, as noted above, no robe is to be worn in family matters. When sitting on criminal business, a circuit judge wears the lilac robe, a judicial wig, and a red tippet (sash) over their left shoulder.

District judges will ordinarily not sit in robes but when they sit in open court in the civil courts they will wear the new civil robe and no wig. District judges (magistrates' court) will not wear a robe whilst in the magistrates' court but if they sit in the Crown Court (for example, when exercising the jurisdiction of recorder or acting circuit judge) they will wear a black silk gown and judicial wig.

For completeness it should be noted that recorders, as part-time members of the judiciary, wear their practitioners robe and a practitioners wig (when sitting in criminal matters) or no wig (when sitting on civil matters).

Civil robe

The civil robe is a simple black robe that is worn without wig, band, wing collar, or a collarette. The 'rank' of the judge is set out on colour tabs worn at the neck of the gown as follows:

- Court of Appeal (inc Heads of Division)–Gold
- High Court–Red
- District Judges–Blue.

Members of the High Court Masters Group (which are analogous to district judges but for High Court civil work) wear pink tabs.

7.2 Constitutional reform

It was noted above that the Lord Chief Justice is the *President of the Court of England and Wales* and is the head of the judiciary. Prior to the implementation of the CRA 2005, which brought about this change, the Lord Chancellor was the head of the judiciary but why was this change brought about?

In order to understand the reasons it is necessary to be able to identify between the three organs of state, those being:

- legislature (ie in the United Kingdom, Parliament)
- executive (ie the government)
- judiciary.

Montesquieu, an eighteenth-century jurist, called for the separation of powers suggesting that man cannot be free without this and that the most important freedom was the independence of the judiciary. Whilst some jurisdictions take a strict approach to this doctrine (most notably the United States of America where the US Constitution clearly prescribes the limits of the respective organs of state) others are less clear. Montesquieu lived in England during some of his life and the separation of powers both then and now is less clear than in other jurisdictions, eg the United States. The most notable conflict is with the legislature and executive since in the United Kingdom the executive (government) tends to be drawn from the party with a majority in the legislature.

The modern encapsulation of this rule has been suggested as meaning that absolute power should not reside in one person or organ of states, that power should be shared between the bodies with checks and balances included to prevent abuse (Barnett (2011) 82). The doctrine will be explored in more detail in other subjects, most notably either *Constitutional Law* or *Public Law* but it is wise to note that its application in the United Kingdom has always been considered problematic (Barendt (1998) 14–17) and Lord MacKay, the former Lord Chancellor, even argued the doctrine had no direct application in the United Kingdom (MacKay (1991) cited in Bingham (2000) 56) something supported by at least one other commentator (Windlesham (2005) 812). However, this argument is based, in part, on the belief that a strict interpretation of the separation-of-powers doctrine requires the elements of state to be equal, something that they are not in the United Kingdom. However, the United Kingdom is not alone in this and indeed there is nothing to suggest that the limbs must be equal and even in the United States of America there is inequality since Congress can overrule a decision of the President and even legislate to reverse a decision of the US Supreme Court. It has been noted that in England and Wales the legal presumption tends to be that Parliament is sovereign, the argument being therefore that this is the 'heavier' branch. This need not necessarily displace the application of the doctrine so long as there is distinction between the branches.

7.2.1 Lord Chancellor

Where the issue was problematic however was in the application of the doctrine to the Lord Chancellor since he, prior to the implementation of the CRA 2005, belonged to all three branches.

7.2.1.1 Background to the office

The Lord Chancellor (more formally the Lord High Chancellor of Great Britain) is an historic office and was primarily designed as the Keeper of the Great Seal (the stamp by which formal documents were sealed by the monarch). The Lord Chancellor is, in the order of social precedence, outranked only by the Royal Family and the Archbishop of Canterbury. He was until the CRA 2005 also paid more than the prime minister although the latter by convention assumed more powers.

The office was therefore an important one historically but even in its modern guise it was one of the most important appointments. The constitutional ambiguity that was debated until the inception of the CRA 2005 was the fact that the Lord Chancellor was a member of all three branches of the government.

Executive

As a political appointee he was a senior member of the cabinet and accordingly a member of the executive. In historic times the Lord Chancellor was not alone in being so since it was not unusual for the Lord Chief Justice to be a member of the cabinet, and occasionally the Master of the Rolls was an MP (Bingham (2000) 229) but in modern times this practice ended and no 'career' judge sat in the cabinet.

Legislature

Along with sitting in the cabinet the Lord Chancellor was also the 'speaker' of the House of Lords and thus sat in the House of Lords. As 'speaker' the Lord Chancellor did not have the same powers as the Speaker of the House of Commons as the House of Lords traditionally regulated itself but he was an important member of the House. Obviously the Lord Chancellor was not alone in being a member of the judicial and legislative branches as the Lords of Appeal in Ordinary also sat in the House (see 7.2.2. below) as did the Lord Chief Justice and some Masters of the Rolls, who whilst not receiving a peerage automatically on appointment would customarily be given one after some years of service.[4] Membership of the House of Commons has also been an issue of controversy, whilst a serving full-time judge is barred from sitting in the House of Commons (s 1 when read in conjunction with Sch 1 *House of Commons Disqualification Act 1975*) no such bar exists for part-time members of the judiciary. It

---

4. Of the last ten Masters of the Rolls all were made peers although two (Lord Denning and Lord Phillips) were already peers when appointed to the office.

has been noted that it was not unusual for MPs to be elevated to judgeships upon their retirement from the House (Griffith (1997) 16) although this practice fell out of favour from the 1970s onwards.

Judiciary

Finally, the Lord Chancellor was the head of the judiciary and could sit in the appellate committee of the House of Lords where he would preside. Although not every Lord Chancellor sat as judge, the majority of modern Lord Chancellors did so even though they frequently had no judicial experience before being appointed Lord Chancellor.[5] Lord Falconer[6] refused to sit as a judge, in part because he was by then committed to altering the office and partly because of concerns about human rights.

 Case box *McGonnell v United Kingdom*

The issue of judicial independence arose in the case of *McGonnell v United Kingdom* (2000) 30 EHRR 289. The facts of the case are relatively complicated but can be summarized as the chief judge of the island of Guernsey (known as the Bailiff) had presided over the legislature when he was the Deputy Bailiff and this had involved steering some legislation through their parliament. When Bailiff he was asked to adjudicate on a case that related to the legislation and did so. The European Court of Human Rights held that this amounted to a breach of Article 6 in that it denied the applicant the right to a fair trial before an impartial tribunal. Some commentators have suggested that this could have implications for the Lord Chancellor and Law Lords if they participate in debates within the legislature (see, for example, (2000) 4 EHRLR 423–425).

7.2.1.2 Reforming the office

Although the office was controversial because it appeared to be a direct contravention of the doctrine of separation of powers, this debate tended to be a theoretical rather than pragmatic argument as noted by Lord Bingham, a strong supporter of constitutional reform:

> I know of scarcely any suggestion that any Lord Chancellor since [World War II] has not honoured the convention...[that] when acting as head of the judiciary...the Lord Chancellor acts without any regard at all to political considerations. (Bingham (2000) 229)

This proposition is supported by the fact that a Lord Chancellor, as the head of the judiciary, was required to take the judicial oath. This, it was thought, would demonstrate the independence that should arise in judicial matters. Whilst in practice this may

---

5. The exception being Lord MacKay who was a Lord of Appeal in Ordinary before being appointed Lord Chancellor.

6. Who was never intended to be Lord Chancellor. When Lord Falconer replaced Lord Irvine it had been intended that he would become a mere Secretary of State (for Constitutional Affairs) but it was discovered that ending the post of Lord Chancellor required legislative action and could not be undertaken by the prerogative and so he became the Lord Chancellor *and* Secretary of State for Constitutional Affairs. Although Lord Falconer preferred to style himself as Secretary of State the post of Lord Chancellor takes precedence over all other cabinet ranks (including the prime minister) and so he was correctly known as the Lord Chancellor.

have been the case it cannot be doubted that the appearance of partiality would arise and few would probably regard an oath as a sufficient constitutional safeguard.

Yet at the same time paradoxically it has been thought that the Lord Chancellor could be the guardian of judicial independence, with senior judicial figures arguing that as a 'cabinet heavyweight' he could put forward the concerns of the judiciary to cabinet and ensure the rule of law is upheld (Stevens (2004) 8). Indeed Lord Bingham argued that the Lord Chancellor was a key figure because he had no 'political ambition' (cited in Stevens (2004) 9), presumably the argument being that the only office which is de facto higher than the Lord Chancellor was the prime minister (although as a matter of precedence it was lower) and as a peer this avenue of progression would be denied to him.[7]

This constitutional paradox made constitutional reform difficult with it being reported that Lord Woolf, the then Lord Chief Justice, postponed his retirement until he could be certain that a constitutional settlement had been put forward that would guarantee the independence of the judiciary. The first steps for this were put forward in a document known as the Concordant which existed between the executive (through the then Lord Chancellor) and the judiciary (through the Lord Chief Justice) which set out what the rights and responsibilities of the executive and judiciary would be for the future (Windlesham (2005) 820). At the heart of this Concordant was the proposition that the executive would be bound by a statutory duty 'to respect and maintain judicial independence' (ibid) meaning that the focus of judicial independence would broaden from the Lord Chancellor to all members of the government.

Whilst the original intention was to abolish the post of Lord Chancellor the CRA 2005 has, in fact, kept the post but it does not appear that it will necessarily be the preserve of lawyers. Section 2 CRA 2005 states that the Lord Chancellor must be qualified 'by experience' and this includes legal practice (s 2(2)(c)–(d)) but it need not and can include experience as a minister, member of either House of Parliament, or 'any other experience that the Prime Minister considers relevant'. Precisely what this means in practice is not clear but it does presumably mean that there will be a divorce between the modern and historic offices. Since the Lord Chancellor is neither the head of the judiciary (since s 7 of the CRA 2005 states that the Lord Chief Justice takes on this mantle) nor the speaker of the House of Lords (s 17 provides for a speaker to be created and the House of Lords decided that there would be 'Lord Speaker' with Baroness Hayman being the first elected speaker) then this presumably means that the Lord Chancellor may return to being merely a counsellor and Keeper of the Great Seal.

That said, however, the Lord Chancellor will continue to be a focus for the law since the person appointed to the post must swear an oath in the following terms:

> I [name] do solemnly swear that in the office of Lord High Chancellor of Great Britain I will respect the rule of law, defend the independence of the judiciary and discharge my duty to ensure the provision of resources for the efficient and effective support of the courts for which I am responsible. (s 6A *Promissory Oaths Act 1868*)

In effect this ensures that the Lord Chancellor will, as now, also be the Secretary of State for Constitutional Affairs with political responsibility for the running of the justice system. This is certainly advisable and beneficial but the changes do mean that, in

---

7. This convention effectively being cemented by the fact that the Earl of Home renounced his peerage to become Sir Alec Douglas-Home when invited by the Queen to become Prime Minister in 1963.

effect, the department is in the same position as other departments and accordingly the Lord Chancellor need not be a lawyer in the same way that the Secretary of State for Defence need not be a former or serving member of the armed services.[8] Whoever is appointed, however, has the political responsibility to secure judicial independence, this sitting alongside the more general governmental duty imposed under s 3 CRA 2005.

7.2.2 Removal of judges from legislature

All full-time judges are prohibited from sitting in either House of Parliament (s 137 CRA 2005). Whilst this primarily affected the Law Lords and Lord Chief Justice it does have an impact on certain other members of the judiciary. Once a judge has retired he may sit in either House if entitled to do so.

7.3 Judicial appointments

The process of choosing judges has been the source of some debate for many years and has recently changed to reflect the constitutional changes of the late 1990s and early 2000s. Traditionally judicial appointments, particular of superior judges, were clouded in mystery and secrecy with 'secret soundings' akin to that of the QC system (see 8.4 below) being normal. Lord Elwyn-Jones, the former Lord Chancellor, explained the process:

> When a vacancy had to be filled, the heads of the Divisions...were invited into my office to consider likely names. Usually we agreed as to the one most meriting appointment. Occasionally two names were equally supported. Then the choice was left to me. (Elwyn-Jones (1983) 265)

When the Lord Chancellor had decided on the appropriate person he would invite him in for a chat and ask whether they would accept a seat on the bench. It was comparatively rare for a person to refuse an appointment (Pannick (1987) 9) although some did, either because they did not wish to cease to be an advocate or because they did not want the inevitable drop in pay.

The traditional system of appointing judges was increasingly said to be untenable, not least because of concerns that the 'old boys' network' was creating a non-diverse and non-representative judiciary. In recent years two significant changes occurred. The first was the introduction of advertising for inferior judges, this being extended in 1998 to include the first advertisement for a High Court judge.[9] However this, and subsequent, advertisements were only to create a 'long list' of suitable people from whom the Lord Chancellor could select a judge. Additionally the Lord Chancellor retained the right to invite someone who had not applied to take up a judgeship. The second important step towards accountability was the appointment of the Judicial Appointments Commissioners who had the responsibility for auditing the appointment process. The Judicial Appointments Commission (JAC) is independent of the government and publishes annual reports on the appointment process, the most critical of which was probably its first annual report (CJA (2003)) although the 2003 review of the High Court

---

8. That said, the two Lord Chancellors who have been appointed from the ranks of the Commons (Rt. Hon. Jack Straw MP and Rt. Hon. Kenneth Clarke QC) have both been members of the Bar.

9. The advertisement was placed on 24 February.

Table 7.2 Membership of the Judicial Appointments Commission

Lay members	Chairman of the Commission
	5 additional members
Judicial members	5 members consisting of:
	• 1 Lord Justice of Appeal
	• 1 puisne judge
	• 1 judge who is either an LJ or puisne judge
	• 1 circuit judge
	• 1 district judge
Professionals	2 members:
	• 1 solicitor
	• 1 barrister
Lay magistrate	1 member
Tribunal member	1 non-lay member (either member or Chair)

competition (CJA (2004)) is also critical and specifically stated the idea of having a mix of invitations and advertisements was unfair (pp 23–27).

Eventually the Department for Constitutional Affairs published a consultation paper on the appointment of the judiciary, something that one commentator described as both 'logical and disappointing' (Stevens (2004) 22). Stevens argues that it is logical because the pressure for the reform of the judiciary has been building for a considerable time, and disappointing because, in his opinion, it has led to a fudge whereby the integrity of the system is not as guaranteed as in other states, most notably through a lack of majority of lay persons. The counter-argument, of course, is that whilst it is essential to have lay persons on a panel to ensure there are no deals being done, it would obviously be sensible for the panel also to contain professionals who know the system.

The CRA 2005 placed judicial appointments onto a statutory basis. Two schemes apply for constitutional reasons. The first applies to members of the Supreme Court and the second applies to all judicial appointments. The systems are actually comparable but the principal distinction is that the former is an ad hoc commission that is constituted when a member needs to be nominated whereas the latter will be a permanent body.

7.3.1 Judicial Appointments Commission

Focusing on the appointments in England and Wales, the CRA 2005 created the JAC which, unlike the first commission, has a role in the appointing of persons instead of just auditing the process. Schedule 12 of the Act states that the JAC consists of fifteen members with quite specific details as to who can sit.

No member can be appointed if they are employed in the civil service (para 3) which reinforces the fact that this system is designed to be completely independent. This list is intended, presumably, to ensure that the JAC is competent to deal with all possible appointments. The commissioners are appointed for a term of office no longer than five years at any one time and may not serve a total of more than ten years (para 13).

The JAC creates its own rules and processes and a link to these is to be found on the ORC. The CRA 2005 lists three different types of selection procedures depending on grades.

7.3.1.1 Lord Chief Justice and Heads of Division

The first process is designed to select either the Lord Chief Justice or a Head of Division. Except where the vacancy is for the Lord Chief Justice, the Lord Chancellor must consult with the Lord Chief Justice to discuss the timing of the referral to the JAC, which then decides the process by which it will appoint a member, and a panel will be created which consists of (s 71 CRA 2005):

- The most senior Supreme Court judge who held a judicial office in England and Wales prior to his appointment to the court.[10]
- The Lord Chief Justice (or where this is the vacancy a person nominated by the Supreme Court judge above).
- The Chairman of the JAC or his nominee.
- A lay member of the JAC nominated by the Chair.

This will normally mean the panel is evenly split between lay and professional members as the Chair of the JAC is a lay member. The panel must also consider the selection process it wishes to use which could theoretically mean therefore that the panel decides that open competition is not required and an alternative approach could be adopted.

In 2008, Sir Igor Judge (now Lord Judge) became the first Lord Chief Justice to be appointed under this new process. The person nominated in the absence of the Lord Chief Justice was Sir Anthony Clarke MR.

The statutory qualification for a Head of Division is to be qualified as a Lord Justice of Appeal (see below) or that the person is a judge of the Court of Appeal (s 10(3)(a) SCA 1981) and the latter includes Lords of Appeal in Ordinary (see s 2 SCA 1981). In practice the Lord Chief Justice tends to be appointed from either the House of Lords or the Court of Appeal. Before Lord Judge CJ was appointed, the previous two (Lord Woolf CJ and Lord Philips CJ) were both Master of the Rolls prior to their appointment. Lord Judge was the President of the Queen's Bench Division before appointment and it would seem, therefore, that modern Lord Chief Justices will have held one of the senior judicial posts before appointment.

The process for appointing a Head of Division is that the panel will nominate a single person and forward that name to the Lord Chancellor (s 70 CRA 2005) who has three options:

1. accept the recommendation
2. reject the recommendation
3. ask the panel to reconsider the selection (s 73).

The difference between option 2 and option 3 is that with the former the nominee cannot be nominated again (s 75(2)) whereas the latter simply requires the panel to consider whether they have appointed the correct person. When the panel reconvenes following a rejection or reconsideration the Lord Chancellor has the same three options

---

10. In other words, if the President of the Supreme Court is a Scottish judge, the next most senior judge who is a judge in England and Wales will be nominated.

open to him. If the matter reaches stage 3 (ie the nominee was rejected at stage 2 or the panel asked to reconsider) then the Lord Chancellor must accept the recommendation (s 73(4)) although where the panel was asked to reconsider at either stages 1 or 2 and the panel nominated a different person the Lord Chancellor could appoint the original nominee (s 73(5)). In 2010 it was reported that the then Lord Chancellor (Jack Straw MP) exercised his right to ask the panel to reconsider its selection when it proposed Lord Justice Wall as the new President of the Family Division (Gibb, 2010a). The panel reconsidered and put forward Wall LJ again, with the Lord Chancellor deciding not to reject the appointment and Sir Nicholas Wall was then appointed President.

7.3.1.2 Lords Justice of Appeal

The CRA 2005 also specifies a separate, yet similar, system for the appointment of Lords Justice of Appeal. The principal difference is in the constitution of the panel which becomes:

- the Lord Chief Justice or nominee (who must be a Head of Division or LJ)
- a Head of Division or LJ nominated by the LCJ
- the Chairman of the JAC (unless he is unavailable when it is another lay member of the JAC)
- a lay member of the JAC (s 80).

When a person is nominated the Lord Chancellor has the same options as before (s 82) and the process continues until a nomination is accepted (no later than stage 3). The statutory qualification for an LJ is possession of a ten-year High Court qualification (which means rights of audience to advocate in the higher courts, ie a solicitor–advocate or a barrister) or being a judge of the High Court (s 10(3)(b) SCA 1981). In practice, a Lord Justice of Appeal is always appointed from the ranks of the puisne judges.

7.3.1.3 Puisne judges and other judicial appointments

The CRA 2005 creates a single scheme for all judicial appointments for or below the grade of puisne judges (although this does not change the distinction between superior and inferior judges). The process differs in that there is no statutory panel but, rather, it is for the JAC to decide how it will fill the vacancies and, presumably, constitute panels from the members within the JAC. The Lord Chancellor still has the same three options as above (s 90) but an additional option arises because the JAC could decide that none of the applicants was suitable for appointment and decline to make a recommendation (s 88(2)); however, the Lord Chancellor can ask the JAC to reconsider that decision (s 93).

Whilst it is not possible to consider the statutory qualification process for all the potential judicial appointments, the criteria for the judges discussed are as given in Table 7.3.

7.3.2 Supreme Court appointments

Appointments to the Supreme Court have to be kept separate because it is a court of the United Kingdom and not England and Wales and the Acts of Union creating the United Kingdom guaranteed that the legal systems of Scotland and Northern Ireland would be preserved as sovereign systems in their own right, so the United Kingdom court cannot be under the direction of English procedures.

Table 7.3 Judicial appointments criteria

Puisne judge	Ten-year High Court qualification or being a circuit judge for two years (s 10(3)(c) SCA 1981)
Circuit judge	Ten-year Crown or county court qualification;[a] sits as a recorder or holder of a designated judicial appointment for at least three years[b] (s 16(3) CA 1971)
Recorder	Ten-year Crown or county court qualification (s 21(2) CA 1971)
District judge[c]	Seven-year general qualification[d] (s 9 County Courts Act 1984)

[a] Which means the right to conduct advocacy in the Crown Court (solicitor–advocates and barristers) or county court (solicitors or barristers) (s 71 CLSA 1990).

[b] CA 1971 para 1A, Sch 2. The offices are certain tribunal judges, district judges (including district judge (magistrates' court)), masters of the High Court etc.

[c] Not including a district judge (magistrates' court).

[d] This is a right of audience in all matters in the Crown, county or magistrates' court, ie a solicitor or barrister (s 71 Courts and Legal Services Act 1990 (CLSA 1990)).

The criterion for appointment to the Supreme Court mirrors that of the House of Lords and is either holding high judicial office for a period of at least two years or having higher rights of audience for fifteen years (s 25(1) CRA 2005). In recent times nobody has been appointed direct from practice and the members appointed from the English courts are usually Lords Justice of Appeal although 'high judicial office' includes puisne judges. In 2010 it was reported that Jonathan Sumption QC was asked to apply to become a Justice of the Supreme Court and had done so. Jonathan Sumption QC is one of the best members of the Bar but has never held a full-time judicial post. It was reported that many members of the judiciary were angry about the attempt to appoint him, suggesting that only a full-time senior judge should be appointed (Gibb (2010b)). Jonathan Sumption QC eventually withdrew from the process and Sir John Dyson was appointed. It would seem therefore that irrespective of the statutory requirements, we have a de facto career judiciary and that Justices of the Supreme Court will only be filled from the senior judiciary.

By convention two members are from Scotland and one from Northern Ireland. The CRA 2005 does not enshrine this convention into the statute although s 27(8) hints at it by stating:

> In making the selections for the appointment of judges of the Court the commission must ensure that between them the judges will have knowledge of, and experience in, the law of each part of the United Kingdom.

It is regrettable that this language should be employed as it would have been better to use precise language requiring a judge from each of the legal systems within the United Kingdom but perhaps this phrase is sufficient to ensure the convention remains.

The prime minister recommends to the Queen who will be appointed to the Supreme Court (s 26(2)) but the Lord Chancellor will provide only one name to the prime minister for recommendation and the prime minister may not decline the name (s 26(3)) which is a significantly different position to the previous position where prime ministers had the ultimate patronage. Lord Hailsham, Conservative Lord Chancellor between 1970 and 1974 and again between 1979 and 1987, makes clear in his autobiography that Mrs Thatcher, the then prime minister, ensured she was involved in the discussions and that a list of possible names was submitted although he is careful to note that she did not appoint anyone that was not on the list (Hailsham (1990) 427).

No process is prescribed in statute and accordingly it will be for the JAC to decide the nature of any competition, which may mean that in order to comply with the convention noted above, the JAC may decide to restrict an appointment to members of a particular jurisdiction. The statute does state (s 27 CRA 2005) that part of the process includes consulting:

- senior judges who are not members of the JAC nor have any interest in being appointed to the Supreme Court themselves (presumably for this appointment)
- the Lord Chancellor
- the First Minister of Scotland
- the First Secretary of the Assembly of Wales
- the Secretary of State for Northern Ireland.[11]

A panel, similar to that used for senior judicial appointments in England and Wales, is created (Sch 8, para 1 CRA 2005), the members being:

- President of the Supreme Court
- Deputy President of the Supreme Court
- one member each of the JAC for England and Wales, Scotland and Northern Ireland.[12]

Where the post of President or Deputy President is vacant then the next senior ordinary judge of the court will join the panel instead (para 2). The panel is chaired by the most senior judge on the panel, with the President and Deputy President of the Supreme Court having precedence (para 7).

When the JAC has nominated a person then the Lord Chancellor has the same three options open to him as exist for judicial appointments in England and Wales and eventually, therefore, a nominee will be recommended to the Queen for appointment to the Supreme Court.

The President and Deputy President of the Court are selected by the same process and this would appear to suggest therefore that the tradition of seniority by appointment ended by the appointment of Lord Bingham is unlikely to return as the JAC could decide to appoint someone from outside the Supreme Court to either position.

7.3.3 Appointment Commissions: the solution?

The JAC is certainly a marked contrast to the way in which judges have traditionally been appointed but is this the way forward and will it lead to perceived improvements? Not everyone was supportive of the idea of a commission, including those senior judges who believed that the wider constitutional reform process (including the creation of the Supreme Court) was correct. It has been noted that both Lord Bingham and Lord Woolf have argued that one person is better placed to decide on the suitability of a candidate

---

11. Matters relating to justice were not until recently devolved in Northern Ireland but now they are it is not known why the discussion cannot be devolved to the First and Deputy First Ministers.

12. At least one of these must be a non-judicial member and all must be nominated by the Chair of the respective commissions (para 6, Sch 8).

than a committee which, Lord Woolf argues, could lead to a system of 'Buggins' turn next' (Stevens (2004) 23).

An independent appointments commission should, at least, remove the potential for bias or partisan politics to play a role. Even in the most recent times there have been allegations that judicial appointments have been made not on the basis of merit but on connections to the government.

◉ Example President of the Family Division

When Lord Falconer, the then Lord Chancellor, appointed Potter LJ to the position of President of the Family Division in 2005 the media instantly referred to him as a 'crony' because he was the pupil-master to both Lord Falconer and Lord Goldsmith, the Attorney-General. Did that mean the appointment was wrong? The professionals working in the Family Division (ie solicitors and barristers) were surprised as custom appeared to indicate the President would come from within the division whereas Potter LJ was a Chancery Division judge (see, for example, Langdon-Down (2005) 22), but others believed that it was a welcome appointment as it was thought that the Family Division was becoming a little too inward-looking and needed an outside manager to ensure efficiency and a fresh look at the issues (see Hoult (2005) 10).

However others would suggest that Lord Chancellors have proven themselves to be extremely robust when making appointments that may appear controversial. Perhaps the classic example of Lord Chancellors ignoring political issues occurred in 1979 when Lord Hailsham decided to recommend to the Queen that Elizabeth Butler-Sloss, then a registrar of the Principal Registry of the Family Division (which is comparable to, but slightly higher than, a district judge), be elevated to the High Court bench. Civil servants were concerned because she was the sister of the Attorney-General (Lewis (1997) 268) but such concerns were brushed aside as it would be 'wrong in principle to discriminate against her' (p 269). Butler-Sloss became one of the most popular and respected judges on the bench, including being made the first Lady Justice of Appeal and first female President of the Family Division.

The Lord Chancellor has not, of course, been removed from the decision-making process and some may have concerns as to whether this underpins the integrity of the appointment system. A former Permanent Secretary of the Lord Chancellor's Department disagrees however and he states that the appointment of the judiciary is an executive act and should therefore be undertaken by a minister accountable to Parliament (Legg (2004) 52–53). It was unclear how this accountability would arise but in 2010, when the then Lord Chancellor asked the JAC to reconsider the appointment of Wall LJ as President of the Family Division, it was stated that if he had rejected the nomination he would have had to publicly state the reasons why (Gibb (2010a)). Any public statement would almost certainly require a statement to Parliament where the matter could be debated. On that basis there is perhaps a degree of accountability remaining within the system.

The constitution of the panels has also led to some concern. The Commission for Judicial Appointments strongly argued that lay members should constitute a majority of people appointed to the JAC (CJA (2004) para 3.4) and yet this is not the case. Indeed when one focuses on the panels created to appoint the senior judiciary, lay members will have no power of veto. The panels have four members, two of whom are lay, but the chair of the panels is the most senior judge on the panel and the chair has a casting vote where the panel is deadlocked (see ss 71(12), 80(12)–80(13)) which means that the lay members could object to a candidate being rejected but this could be overruled by the professional members. This is not the case with the new system of appointing QCs (see 8.4 below) and it may seem somewhat strange that lay members should have a veto on senior advocates but not senior judges. However the counter-argument is why is there a need for lay members to have a majority? Whilst it is perfectly understandable for lay members to become involved and act as an independent voice on the interview panel, it is slightly less clear why a non-lawyer would be any better at appointing judges.

7.3.4 Diversity

Perhaps one of the key areas of controversy of the judiciary is their diversity. A long-held criticism of the judiciary is that they are all from the same mould: white, male, middle-class, privately educated Oxbridge graduates (Griffith (1997) 18–22). This position is perhaps exemplified by the current senior judiciary. The five most senior judges (the Lord Chief Justice and the four Heads of Division) list their educational backgrounds. All were educated at either the University of Oxford or the University of Cambridge. Four of the five list their school education and all four were privately educated. All five are white and male.

Speaking in 1992, Lord Taylor the then Lord Chief Justice said:

> The present imbalance between male and female, white and black in the judiciary is obvious...I have no doubt that the balance will be redressed in the next few years...Within five years I would expect to see a substantial number of appointments from both these groups. This is not just a pious hope. It will be monitored. (Taylor (1992))

7.3.4.1 Current statistical position

What is the position now, nearly two decades later?

Gender

The number of female students entering university to read law has been increasing since 1970 and since 1988 there have actually been more female entrants than male (Rackley (2002) 605) and since 1992 there have been marginally more newly qualified female solicitors than male solicitors (ibid). The last census reported that there was a population in England and Wales of just over 52 million people, of which approximately 26.7 million (51 per cent) are female and approximately 25.3 million (49 per cent) are male. It can be seen, therefore, that in both society in general, law schools, and newly qualified lawyers there are slightly more females than males.

However if the judicial statistics are examined it can be seen that the position in terms of gender is extremely poor. There is (at the beginning of the judicial year 2009/10) currently no female Head of Division and there has only ever been one (Lady Justice Butler-Sloss was President of the Family Division between 1995–2005). Of the twelve Justices of the Supreme Court only one (8.3 per cent) is female. Lady Hale was appointed a Lord of Appeal in Ordinary in 2005 and prior to that there had been no female Law Lords. There are four (10.5 per cent) Lady Justices of Appeal, admittedly a slightly higher percentage than previously. There are sixteen (14.95 per cent) female puisne judges. This means of the senior judiciary as a whole, there are twenty-one (12.3 per cent) female judges.

Of the more junior ranks of the judiciary the position is only marginally better. There are eighty-seven (14.5 per cent) female circuit judges, and 37 (30 per cent) district judges and district judges (magistrates' court) (the most junior branch of the judiciary). Of the part-time judiciary, there are 185 (15.78 per cent) recorders (ie part-time judges of the circuit bench) and 76 (37.8 per cent) deputy district judges and deputy district judges (magistrates' court) (ie part-time district judges).

Overall this means that only 17 per cent of the judiciary are female. Why is this? The usual reason was that put forward by Lord MacKay, the then Lord Chancellor:

> As more women progress through the profession, it is to be expected that the numbers of women within the judiciary will increase. (McGlynn (1999a) 89)

However, this misses the point that women have been members of the profession for a considerable period of time and defies the statistics discussed above. It has been noted that historically the judiciary has been recruited from the Bar and females have, despite their representation more generally, suffered, in the words of one commentator, 'institutional discrimination' at the Bar (McGlynn (1998) 89). By the end of the calendar year 2009 women accounted for 3,860 (31.5 per cent) of the 12,241 barristers practising in independent practice (the traditional route for members of the judiciary). In employed practice the position is better with 1,399 (46.2 per cent) of the 3,029 employed barristers but such members rarely progress to the judiciary.

There does not appear to be much evidence for the idea that the numbers will eventually increase (in line with the optimism of Lords Taylor and MacKay.) There is an expectation that full-time members of the judiciary will be drawn from part-time members of the judiciary yet it was seen the representation of women in the part-time judiciary is still below that which can be legitimately expected.

Ethnicity

The position in respect of ethnic representation is even worse. The last census suggests that approximately 7.9 per cent of the population consider themselves to be a member of the ethnic minorities. However the latest judicial statistics demonstrate that no Head of Division belongs to an ethnic minority nor are there any Justices of the Supreme Court or Lords Justice of Appeal. Since the first edition of this book, the number of puisne judges from a minority ethnic background has tripled. There are now three (2.7 per cent) judges, which means there has been no change between the second and third editions. This means that of the senior judiciary as a whole there are only three minority ethnic judges which accounts for 1.8 per cent of the senior judiciary.

Of the junior judicial ranks, there are sixteen (2.63 per cent) circuit judges who belong to an ethnic minority, which is more than that reported in the first edition of the book but less than in the second edition. There are twenty-two (3.7 per cent) district judges. Of the part-time judiciary, there are 62 (6.6 per cent) recorders and 32 (4.0 per cent) deputy district judges. As a whole, only 4.8 per cent of the judiciary would consider themselves as belonging to a member of the ethnic minorities. Admittedly and the situation has improved since the first edition which may provide hope that this means that the prognosis for future appointments is good, and the latest figures for barristers practising in independent practice show that 20 per cent of the profession are members of the ethnic minorities.

7.3.4.2 Extending diversity

Despite these figures it can be seen that the professions and senior members of the judiciary argue that they are trying to make the judiciary more diverse. The question is perhaps whether these are mere words or whether there is a true move towards the diversification of the judiciary.

Perhaps the first point of note is that whilst recent statutory reforms allowed feminine judicial titles to be used (eg Lady Justice of Appeal instead of Lord Justice of Appeal and even provision for a Lady Chief Justice; see s 64(2) CA 2003) the title of the Law Lords did not change and thus Lady Hale stated that when she was introduced to the House of Lords by letters patent she was introduced as a Lord of Appeal in Ordinary (Hale (2005) 72; and see s 6 *Appellate Jurisdiction Act 1876*). At a simplistic level this can be dismissed as irrelevant, with everyone knowing that Lady Hale is female, but it does demonstrate what could be perceived as an inherent male bias within the judiciary and prior to appointment she noted that such matters were 'trivial but...annoying manifestations of the assumption that this is a male profession which women are allowed to join provided that they pretend to be men' (Hale (2001) 497).

When thinking about this whole area, one commentator asks quite a pertinent question: '*Why* [*sic*] should we want a more representative judiciary? Is it simply that there *ought* to be more women judges...?' (Rackley (2002) 609). Presumably this could be extended further, ie to ask why should we want more female judges and members of the ethnic minorities. It could be argued that we expect our judiciary to be representative of society but is that really what is desired? It is unlikely that in terms of socio-economic factors there would be a desire or expectation for representation and surely the public would wish the best members of the legal profession to become its judges—so why diversity? It has to be something more than just 'to make up the numbers' (Rackley (2002) 610) but Hale, speaking extrajudicially, argues that it is about 'individuals and their rights' (Hale (2001) 489), ie the right to progress within a profession and not to be discriminated against.

❓ QUESTION FOR REFLECTION

Do you think the judiciary should be diverse? What about representative? What does judicial representation actually mean? Think about *why* you want a more representative judiciary; what are the advantages that this would bring to the justice system?

It could be suggested that it is a matter of public confidence. How can a white male bastion inspire confidence in the justice system? Whilst one should be wary of looking to the media where attacks are often intemperate, inappropriate, and frequently completely wrong, it is not difficult to think that the judiciary currently make themselves difficult to defend against accusations that they do not know the 'real world'. If they cannot even recognize a multicultural society how can they possibly adjudicate on such matters?

Appointment on merit

One commentator notes that the current system of diversity and appointment has been summarized accurately by Lord Lloyd of Berwick, a Lord of Appeal in Ordinary:

> I would like, obviously, the judiciary to be as diverse as we can get it. But that must not interfere with the fundamental principle that we have got to choose the best man for the job. (Malleson (2006) 126)

One cannot help but focus on the last words of this quote. Although, as has been noted, the convention within law is to refer to the masculine and indeed this book follows the convention because to use 'he or she' or the even worse '(s)he' is awkward prose, one cannot help but think that there are times when the inclusion of the words 'or woman' or the substitution of 'person' would be appropriate. Arguably the quote of Lord Lloyd is such an example.

The justification for the slow progress of diversity is that only the best are appointed to be judges and that any move towards positive assistance would be contrary to this rule and could even dilute the quality of judges. Deciding who the 'best' candidate is can always be difficult because if one gets the best schooling and education it can be easy to be the 'best' especially if those choosing you meet the same profile, but what does that mean here?

In a review of the appointments system, it was noted that whilst there is almost unanimity in accepting that judges should be appointed on merit but interestingly there was no clear consensus on what 'merit' actually means (Legg (2004) 49). However, the report differentiated between two types of merit, namely 'maximal merit' where only one candidate is judged suitable for appointment as he is the best person available (p 50) or 'minimal merit' where the selected panel identifies a number of people who are qualified for the appointment and then a person is chosen from that pool on the basis of policy decisions (p 51). The implication of this argument is that the latter approach is an inferior way of appointing members of the judiciary even though it can be justified on policy grounds, not least the fact that a more diverse judiciary may assist in securing public confidence.

However is it this simple? Part of the difficulty of locating the maximal best candidate is the advantages that arise from the status quo. During the early 2000s considerable debate ensued as to whether those educated in the public schools were being over-represented at the very best universities, particularly Oxbridge. Those who qualified at Oxbridge were certainly well represented in the major law firms and at the Bar. Did it mean that those who were educated at public schools were more intelligent than those at state schools or did it reflect the fact that public schools, because of their teaching patterns and staff/student ratios, are better able to devote more time and attention to their students thus allowing students to demonstrate their full potential? If it is the latter, as many believe, then simply selecting the maximal merit candidate each time will mean that the cycle could become self-sustaining with those who had the best opportunities becoming the best candidates. The minimal merit scheme (although I dislike the term) has the advantage of setting out the competencies of the judges allowing a broad analysis to be made of their qualities and then deciding how someone fits into the wider considerations. This is not the same as positive discrimination and is no different to many companies who will state that they 'particularly welcome applicants from the ethnic minorities'. This is not watering down quality but ensuring that all applicants have the same opportunities.

Malleson, probably the most authoritative commentator on the area, argues that there need not be a binary system where it is either the maximal or minimal system but rather that the maximal system could be altered through the provision of a 'tie-breaker' system (Malleson (2006) 129). The basis of this argument is that there will not necessarily be 'one' candidate that appears best but there may be a number of applicants who are equally qualified. In those circumstances it is suggested that there should be a 'tie-break' feature whereby those who come from an under-represented group should be given the position (ibid). This is arguably distinct from the 'minimal' system in that the minimal system looks solely at the criteria and ranks the person thereafter whereas the 'tie-break' system is a derivative of the maximal system because it looks at persons but where there is difficulty in deciding between two or more persons, the 'tie-break' is under-representation.

Malleson notes that the 'tie-break' situation was not supported particularly widely even when the then Lord Chief Justice, Lord Taylor, attempted to introduce the system on a limited scale (Malleson (2006) 132). The argument appeared to be that any interference with a strict application of the 'merit' system is unwelcome. Yet this stance ignores the reality that this means that those who have come from a privileged background can continue to claim that they are the 'better' candidates as a result of their education and career. The link between the Bar and the judiciary is perhaps a handicap in this context in that there are certain chambers which have a 'well-worn path' between Bar and Bench in part because of the inevitable contacts that are propagated (see Hale (2001) 490 for a useful criticism of this).

❓ QUESTION FOR REFLECTION

What do you think of the 'tie-break' proposal? Is this a sufficient compromise between the need to appoint judges by merit but also to create a 'level playing field' upon which under-represented groups of society can compete for judicial appointments?

🎧 LISTEN TO THE PODCAST

For guidance on how to answer this question and a discussion of the main issues, listen to the author's podcast on the Online Resource Centre:

www.oxfordtextbooks.co.uk/orc/gillespie_els3e/

Family-friendly policies

It will be seen that it is unusual for a circuit judge to be promoted to the High Court bench or beyond (7.5.2.3 below) and therefore if women are to become members of the senior judiciary they will ordinarily begin their full-time career as a puisne judge. The difficulty with the role of a puisne judge is that judges in the Queen's Bench and Family Divisions (and to a lesser extent the Chancery Division) will spend a considerable time 'on circuit', ie sitting away from their home. Life on circuit is not, as the media sometimes present it, a luxurious exercise since QBD judges will normally act as the 'single judge' of the Court of Appeal during that time and thus work on papers. High Court judges also hold an important social rank and thus there is a considerable amount of entertaining that must be done in the evening, together with work on papers etc.

Until recently a judge 'on circuit' was *required* to stay in judge's lodgings even if his home was within commutable distance. Other circuits will (not infrequently) be a significant distance away from their home so that the judge will spent four to six weeks away from home three, and possibly four, times a year (Auld (2001) 238). This can hardly be described as 'family friendly' and is undoubtedly a disincentive to both male and female judges but, arguably, a greater disincentive to female judges who do not wish to be away from what might be young members of a family (Malleson (2006) 131). McGlynn, citing Sandra O'Connor—the first woman to be appointed to the US Supreme Court—noted that a significant issue may be that a woman may wish to have a child and that the judicial structure should be able to take this into account (McGlynn (1999b) 97–99). This should not just be in respect of a 'pregnant judge' but should also take account of the fact that if a female lawyer takes time out to raise a family this should not prejudice an application for a judgeship later.

Family-friendly policies are commonplace in society and it should not be difficult to identify ways that such policies could be adopted to the judicial system. This is as big an issue as the diversity of the professions since a more diverse application system will only be achieved if people apply for judicial appointments. If they believe the conditions of the post are not suited to their lifestyle they will simply not apply for them regardless of how open the system becomes.

❓ QUESTION FOR REFLECTION

Is it realistic to suggest that the legal system can adopt 'family-friendly' policies for puisne judges? The nature of High Court work is that it can be long and complex. How does one provide for 'family time' around such (serious) commitments?

7.3.4.3 The Bar's grip

A particular difficulty in diversification is the fact that there is an undisputed link between the Bar and the Bench and arguably this creates a situation whereby significant numbers of persons are not considered. The reforms of the CSLA 1990 (see s 71) altered the Bar's exclusive privilege of putting forward candidates for the senior judiciary but doubts continue to exist as to whether the gap has truly narrowed. The first solicitor to be appointed to the High Court bench was Mr Justice Sachs although he was appointed via the circuit bench (to which solicitors had been appointed for some time). The first solicitor to be appointed direct from practice was Lawrence (now Lord) Collins. However the third appointment, (Sir) Henry Hodge, was a circuit judge prior to appointment as was the latest appointment, (Sir) Gary Hickinbottom (now Mr Justice Hickinbottom). Indeed as of 2010 only a single puisne judge (Hickinbottom J) is a former solicitor. Lawrence (now Lord) Collins, in January 2007, became the first solicitor to be appointed a Lord Justice of Appeal and, in 2009 became the first solicitor to be appointed a Lord of Appeal in Ordinary and subsequently a Justice of the Supreme Court

One reason why the grip has not yet been broken is that the primary criterion for a judgeship was 'visibility' meaning appearing or at least interacting with senior members of the judiciary frequently (Hale (2001) 492). The Bar, as will be seen in the next chapter, traditionally had exclusive rights of audience in the higher courts and even today barristers continue to undertake the bulk of the work there. In addition to this, the Inns of Court are extremely vital and again this lends assistance to the Bar. The Inns are governed by Masters of the Bench who are ordinarily either senior members of the judiciary or Queen's Counsel. A prospective puisne judge who is also a barrister will almost certainly be trying to ingratiate himself to his Inn by undertaking extra work etc which brings him to the attention of the senior members of the profession, an advantage that solicitors simply do not have.

Whether the JAC will break this has yet to be discovered, in part because it is believed that 'references' will continue to play an important part in any judicial appointments process. However the signs are not good since, as noted already, the number of High Court judges who are former solicitors has actually reduced.

Other professions

The then Labour government suggested that restricting the judiciary to the two principal professions was not appropriate and in 2005 suggested that legal executives should be eligible to become members of the judiciary,[13] albeit in the more junior positions, eg deputy or full district judges. However, such a system would potentially provide access to other benches since appointment as a district judge can act as a 'threshold' for appointment for the Circuit Bench (see 7.3.1 above).

The judiciary were not happy with the proposal but Fennell, a legal correspondent for *The Times*, argues that the concerns may be misplaced stating, 'I imagine that the proposal to allow legal executives to become judges should do a lot to enhance the quality of common sense on the bench',[14] although his point then becomes confused as the basis of his premise is that ILEX provides the opportunity to become qualified as a solicitor. This, as we shall see, is perfectly true (see 8.7.1.3 below) but theoretically such persons are not disqualified from judicial appointments since when they are made solicitors they will have a general qualification (and thus the most junior positions will be available after a number of years) and if the higher advocacy examinations were taken then all appointments would be open.

The government argued that allowing ILEX members to access judicial appointments would bring more diversity to the bench but there are significant numbers of solicitors and barristers who are from diverse social, ethnic, and sexual backgrounds and it is difficult to see why the judicial members could not be drawn from these ranks. Also is the quest for diversity or representation? The Law Society and Bar Council have both argued that judicial appointments should reflect society rather than represent it; by this they mean that class, gender, ethnicity, religion, and sexual orientation should not be a bar to any appointment and that a diverse bench would enhance merit and the judiciary but that appointments should not be made on a quota basis (Baksi (2005)). The proposals have gone forward and certainly now a Fellow of ILEX is entitled to apply for a position of district (or deputy district) judges and certain tribunal judges. It will be a considerable wait to see whether any ILEX-qualified district judges will then become circuit judges.

❓ QUESTION FOR REFLECTION

Read CJA (2004) para 3.4 where it is argued that lay members should form a majority of the panel and contrast this with Legg (2004) p 53 who suggests the opposite and is of the opinion that a judge should be a chair. Why do you think there need to be lay members on a panel that is deciding whether to appoint (or promote) members of the judiciary? Will lay members understand the subtleties of the judicial office? Who should chair the panels?

---

13. 'Judges to Come from Wider Pool of Applicants' DCA Press Release 181/05.
14. 'Wider Bench', *The Times*, 19 July 2005, Law Supplement.

7.4 Judicial training

When judges are appointed should they be trained? It may seem a peculiar question to ask yet traditionally training was not offered and a lack of experience was certainly no barrier to appointment:

> Lord Devlin recalled that when he was appointed to the High Court in 1948, 'I had never exercised any criminal jurisdiction and not since my early days at the Bar had I appeared in a criminal court…Two days after I had been sworn in, I was trying crime at Newcastle Assizes.' (Pannick (1987) 69)

Dunn notes that when he was appointed it was a case of speaking to other members of the judiciary to understand the principles of giving judgment and discovering the usual awards for compensation etc (Dunn (1993) 181–183). The Lord Chief Justice began to operate 'sentencing conferences' for members of the circuit judiciary and this was eventually extended by the President of the Family Division to include training on family work.

The ad hoc approach of judicial training needed reform however and in 1979 the *Judicial Studies Board* (JSB) was created to have an oversight of judicial training, and it has been suggested that the board 'discharges an ever more important function' and that as it is operated by the judges it contributes to judicial independence (Bingham (2000) 67; and see below). The JSB was originally restricted to criminal law but it now operates a comprehensive service to all members of the judiciary.

The JSB is headed by a judge of the court of appeal (currently Hallett LJ, the first woman to be appointed as head of the JSB) and has an executive board as its governing body. This currently consists of the Chair of the JSB, the Directors of Training, the Director of Studies (who has day-to-day control of the JSB and who is always a circuit judge), two non-executive directors, and two executive directors. The JSB is divided into committees and area-specific training. Its current principal offices are:

- Director of Crime Training
- Director of Civil Training
- Director of Family Training
- Magisterial Committee
- Tribunals Committee
- Senior Judiciary Committee
- Equal Treatment Advisory Committee.

Each Director of Training or head of committee is a puisne judge save for the senior judiciary committee which is headed by a Lord Justice of Appeal (currently Sedley LJ although a Director of Senior Judiciary Training has also been appointed and its holder is a puisne judge). It would appear that the judiciary, or at the very least the senior judiciary, consider judicial training to be important and appointing a senior member of the judiciary to oversee each part of its work demonstrates this.

The creation of a Senior Judiciary Committee is an interesting development since traditionally the JSB would be responsible only for the training of the inferior judiciary. There was recognition however that the senior judiciary could also benefit from training and, to be fair to the various judges, many of the senior judiciary did voluntarily attend training programmes. The commitment to senior training is also evidenced from the fact that all puisne judges have protected training days in which they can attend training programmes. In the first two years of appointment they will have five protected days and subsequently they will have two days (JSB (2010) 36). That said there is still work to be done and, for example, there is little reference to the training needs of Lord Justices of Appeal and it is notable the training needs analysis programme for this rank has been delayed (JSB (2010) 36).

The JSB now provides a prospectus of training (JSB (2010) 9) which is similar to the prospectus that can be found in colleges or universities. In essence it lists all the training courses that are to be performed and judges are asked to indicate which courses they wish to attend. That said, some training is compulsory. For example, recorders are required to attend a criminal induction course so that they are aware of the responsibilities of a judge and how to manage a criminal trial. Similarly as part of the training programme there is a *serious sexual offences seminar* and judges must attend this seminar before they are allowed to sit on trials relating to rape or serious sexual offences involving children (JSB (2010) 17).

Even with the new JSB programme the training is still relatively limited. One commentator has suggested that judges should attend a 'judicial college' for a period of up to two months, with lectures and seminars being supplemented with mock trials (Pannick (1987) 71). He rejects the idea that because a judge comes from practice there is an inherent ability to cope with the work of a judge, pointing out that the difference between practice and the bench are significant. The JSB has never gone this far although the need for such work is perhaps mitigated slightly by the fact that full-time members of the judiciary are now chosen from the part-time judiciary and the part-time judiciary must receive training as part of their appointment. The possibility of a unified judicial college however has raised its head once more (JSB (2010) 10) in part because there is now recognition that all levels of judiciary should be trained and that it would make sense for this training to be done by one body. Certainly the JSB has become more professional and the creation of a college may well be the next natural step.

❓ QUESTION FOR REFLECTION

Pannick has suggested that those wishing to be judges should be 'trained' before becoming full members of the judiciary. Do you think this is now unnecessary since full-time judicial appointments will ordinarily come from the part-time judiciary?

7.5 Judicial independence

Judicial independence is an important concept that is often discussed and yet there is very little literature that attempts to provide a definition (Stevens (1993) 3). It is frequently suggested that the classic definition is that judges should be independent from the executive but this is not possible in the most literal sense:

> Judges sit in courts provided by the state, they have offices provided, heated and lighted by the state, they have clerks paid by the state, they use books and computers mostly provided by the state, they are themselves paid by the state. (Bingham (2000) 57–58)

This is an astute point and demonstrates that full independence is neither practicable nor particularly desirable but what does independence mean and why should judges be independent?

7.5.1 Independent from whom?

The first issue to examine is who judges should be independent from. The law dictionary defines judicial independence as:

> The practice in the UK whereby judges are freed from outside pressure...(Curzon (2002))

The notion of 'outside pressure' is significantly wider than simple independence from the executive although the definition continues by stating:

> [It is] secured by, eg the charging of judges' salaries on the Consolidated Fund, separation of judiciary from Parliament, security of tenure of office, judicial immunity.

This demonstrates that independence will ordinarily mean independence from the other arms of the state (executive and legislature) but that it need not be restricted to this, and the opening sentence of the definition—'outside pressure'—does suggest that it could be wider than this.

7.5.1.1 Independence from the state

It has already been noted above that complete independence from the state would be extremely difficult because the operation of the judiciary is a state responsibility, hence the reason it is considered to be one of the three arms.

Legislature

It will be recalled that all full-time members of the judiciary are now excluded from sitting in either House of Parliament (s 137 CRA 2005) and to this extent there is independence from the judiciary.

Judicial independence from the legislature is also provided for in parliamentary rules. A good example of this is *Erskine May* (which sets out the rules and protocols of Parliament), which states that a Member of Parliament should not criticize a judge by name in Parliament (McKay (2004) 439). Interestingly, of course, this does not stop a Member from criticizing a judge *outside* Parliament and it will be seen that this has happened on a number of occasions. However if it is outside Parliament then it could be suggested that this was not the *legislature* but merely someone who is a member of the legislature criticizing a judge.

Executive

The principal challenge for judicial independence is normally its relationship with the executive. Lord Bingham has already noted that pragmatically there will always be a degree of interrelationship between the executive and the judiciary but the nature of the interaction is crucial to independence. The position of the Lord Chancellor has been discussed already (see 7.2.1 above) and to an extent it can be suggested that this is a step towards independence but it will be remembered that some commentators have argued that the Lord Chancellor acted as a constitutional safeguard. Independence will also involve the appointment, promotion, and discipline of judges but it has been noted elsewhere in this chapter that the executive now takes little part in these issues following the reforms of the CRA 2005.

Independence from the executive will include reference to their work. Lord MacKay, a former Lord Chancellor, noted that judges required administrative freedom and control, most notably in the selection of cases and listing of matters (Bingham (2000) 56). In essence this protects against the 'Judge Deed' type situation where there is a perception that the government 'picks' the judge that will sit on a case. Although much of the listing is dealt with by court administrative staff, who are employed for HM Court Service (part of the executive), they may only do so in conjunction with the judiciary since the resident judge and presiding judge can provide guidance in relation to how cases are assigned to judges. There is also the ultimate sanction in that a judge (usually the resident or presiding judge as senior judge in a particular court) can transfer a matter from one list to another or reserve the case for himself. In this way it would suggest that it is possible to demonstrate independence over cases.

What of attacks from the executive? It was noted above that Members of Parliament may not criticize a judge by name in Parliament, and in the United Kingdom ministers are drawn from members of either House. The executive should not ordinarily criticize the personal decisions of a judge and yet this has happened on a few occasions. One judge has argued that the relationship between executive and the judiciary is 'fraught and imbalanced' (Wilson (1994) 1454) although the then Lord Chief Justice, Lord Woolf argued that the relationship was 'based on a satisfactory working relationship…probably, it is much better than ever before' (Woolf (2001) 5). That is not to say there have not been tensions, however, in part demonstrated by the fact that Lord Woolf had postponed his retirement because he believed there was a danger that judicial independence might be undermined (see 7.2.1.2 above).

Occasionally highly personalized attacks are made in contravention of the principles enshrined above. Perhaps the most notable of these in recent years was the campaign by David Blunkett when he was Home Secretary. In interviews he suggested 'it was time for judges to learn their place' (Bradley (2003) 402). This comment followed the judgment of Collins J in respect of the treatment of asylum seekers (*R (on behalf of Q) v Secretary of State for the Home Department* [2003] EWHC 195) which the Home Secretary saw as undermining his campaign to regulate illegal immigration. In an interview with the BBC he named Mr Justice Collins as being responsible for undermining Parliament and suggested that he would continue to do so (Bradley (2003) 400). In fact, despite the highly personalized comments and briefings by the government against the judge, the Court of Appeal largely upheld the ruling ([2003] EWCA Civ 364) and yet this latter ruling did not meet with any criticism (Bradley (2003) 405).

Did the criticisms of the Home Secretary undermine judicial independence? It could be argued that they did in that they could be viewed as an attempt to put pressure on the judiciary to rule a particular way. However the counter-argument is that the Home Secretary was a litigant and was, in effect, suggesting unease at a particular decision, albeit in intemperate terms. When the appellate courts ruled (in effect terminating further legal resolution) the government accepted the matter.

❓ QUESTION FOR REFLECTION

Should the government be able to criticize members of the judiciary? Does it matter which member of the government it is? For example, if the Lord Chancellor or prime minister was to criticize a judge *by name* would that be more serious than a Secretary of State doing so?

🎧 LISTEN TO THE PODCAST

For guidance on how to answer this question and a discussion of the main issues, listen to the author's podcast on the Online Resource Centre: www.oxfordtextbooks.co.uk/orc/gillespie_els3e/

7.5.1.2 Independence from the media

Judicial independence need not necessarily be restricted to the state and it has been noted that:

> One of the most dramatic changes that has taken place over the past thirty years or so has been the increasing freedom felt by newspapers, in particular, to attack judges with a vigour…that was formerly quite unknown. (Oulton (1994) 569)

In the sixteen years since this was written the position has arguably become even more vociferous especially by the tabloids with the *Sun*, supposedly the most popular newspaper in the country, consistently referring to Lord Woolf, the then Lord Chief Justice, in derogatory terms and in September 2004 asking readers to sign a petition requiring him to be sacked[15] and even sending 'removal men' to the Royal Courts of Justice and his private residence.[16] This was followed in 2006 with a campaign to 'out' judges that the *Sun* believed had imposed unduly lenient sentences. The names of the judges were given together with derogatory comments made about the sentences that they had passed.

It is not just the criminal justice system that has incurred the wrath of the media. Perhaps the most notable attack by the media in recent times has been over the contested issue of the right to privacy. In a speech to the Society of Editors in November 2008 Paul Dacre, the editor-in-chief of the *Daily Mail* specifically accused Mr Justice Eady of 'arrogant and amoral' judgments and of trying to introduce a right to privacy through the granting of injunctions against the publication of stories relating to celebrities' private lives. The attack was unprecedented although it was, in part, an attack on the *Human Rights Act 1998* as much as on Eady J (the media's attitude to the HRA 1998 was discussed in 5.3 above). Not all of the media agreed with the attack and the response of the legal profession was interesting. Four eminent QCs wrote to *The Times* stating that Mr Dacre was wrong (*The Times*, 11 November 2008) and Lord Falconer, the former Lord Chancellor, also stated the attack was wrong.

Mr Justice Eady did not formally respond and the Judicial Communications Office (which has responsibility for issuing press notices on behalf of the judiciary) released a short statement that said, 'Judges determine privacy in cases in accordance with the law and the particular evidence presented by both parties. Any High Court judgment can be appealed to the Court of Appeal' (*Press Release* 10/11/2008). It did lead to a discussion as to what the response should be to media attacks. Some judges have, when the media comment has been particularly unpleasant, resorted to the laws relating to

---

15. 'The *Sun* Calls on Lord Chief Justice to Quit', *Sun*, 22 September 2004.
16. *Sun*, 23 September 2004.

defamation and some judges have even suggested that derogatory press comments could amount to contempt of court (Dunn (1993) 182). This argument would only work with superior courts but even then it would be a complete overreaction and Lord Bingham has stated that the contempt laws should ordinarily have no place in such battles (Bingham (2000) 61). Indeed His Lordship suggests that judges should be 'thick-skinned' enough to ignore press comments. The response to the Paul Dacre attack led Pannick to question who should respond to attacks? He suggested that it should not be for the Lord Chancellor (Pannick (2008)) since although he is protected with upholding judicial independence, this is primarily in respect of attacks by the executive and indeed it could compromise independence if the executive responds on behalf of the judiciary. The answer is perhaps not easy and Lord Bingham's suggestion to leave well alone appears to be the default position. Interestingly the effect of this is that the legal profession will come to the aid of the judiciary through comments being made by senior solicitors or members of the Bar.

❓ QUESTION FOR REFLECTION

Do you believe that judges should have a remedy against the media if they make unjustified personal attacks? Should the press not have the right to comment on the administration of justice? Read Article 10 of the ECHR (see 5.2.3.7 above). Does this have any impact on your answer?

7.5.1.3 Independence from each other

Perhaps one of the most unusual examples of judicial independence relates to the judges themselves. The courts in England and Wales adopt a hierarchical structure and it has been noted already in this chapter that there are different ranks within the judiciary and this means that, potentially, there may be situations where a judge tries to interfere with another. The DCA, when discussing judicial independence, notes this possibility:

> Judicial independence does not just mean independence from outside influence, but also that of one judge from another...[N]o judge, however eminent, is entitled to tell another judge how to exercise his or her judgment in any individual cases. (DCA website, August 2005)

Obviously judicial independence from each other does not extend to ignoring the principles of *stare decisis* as this would cause confusion and end certainty within the English Legal System. It will also be seen that the hierarchical structure has led to quasi-disciplinary measures being adopted by the higher courts, but the principle is just as important. Traditionally this approach has led to judges adopting an extremely independent system whereby they act in isolation and rarely look at each other's work (although they may discuss cases during lunch or after sitting with other judges as any visitor to the judge's dining room can attest) but Lord Woolf, the then Lord Chief Justice, suggested that perhaps judges should look at each other's performance on the bench (Woolf (2001) 7) although he rejects the idea of it becoming even a peer-review appraisal system (p 8) and expressly states the principle of annual reflections would not compromise the independence of the judiciary (ibid).

7.5.2 Securing independence

If judicial independence exists how is it secured? The CRA 2005 attempts to encapsulate the protection in statute but other factors are equally important. Some forms have already been discussed but the key issues of securing independence would include salary, tenure (including promotion and discipline), and immunity.

7.5.2.1 Statutory independence

It has been noted that the judiciary was keen to ensure that with the abolition of the Lord Chancellor there would be provision to guarantee the independence of the judiciary. It was seen above that one of the principal responsibilities of the Lord Chancellor was to act as a 'buffer' between the executive and the judiciary (see 7.2.1.2 above and see Elwyn-Jones (1983) 267). Arguably the Lord Chancellor may still have this responsibility since his oath says, inter alia, 'I will…defend the independence of the judiciary'. In addition to this the CRA 2005 (s 3(1)) places a statutory duty on the government:

> The Lord Chancellor, other ministers of the Crown, and all with responsibility for matters relating to the judiciary or otherwise to the administration of justice must uphold the continued independence of the judiciary.

This includes (s 3(6)):

(a) the need to defend that independence

(b) the need for the judiciary to have support necessary to enable them to exercise their functions

(c) the need for the public interest in regard to matters relating to the judiciary or otherwise to the administration of justice to be properly represented in decisions affecting those matters.

These duties are imposed primarily on the Lord Chancellor. Yet how will this be achieved?

One commentator has suggested that Lord Irvine, whilst Lord Chancellor, did not have the confidence of the judiciary or professions in his ability to uphold the independence of the judiciary (Malleson (2004) 126), yet another commentator suggests that the judiciary appeared to have more confidence in Lord Irvine than Lord Falconer (Dyer (2005) 6). It could be inferred that neither presumably inspired confidence in safeguarding judicial independence and this may, in part, be as a result of them being considered two of the more 'political' Lord Chancellors. It is notable that when the media launched their attack on the Lord Chief Justice (see 7.5.1.2 above) nothing was heard from the Lord Chancellor and it was left to the Attorney-General to intercede.[17] The Attorney-General is a legal officer and titular head of the Bar, it is not his primary responsibility to safeguard the independence of the judiciary: this should be the responsibility of the Lord Chancellor.

However the ability of the Lord Chancellor to intercede is perhaps demonstrated by other examples. In 2006 there was considerable controversy over the sentence imposed in relation to Craig Sweeney, a convicted paedophile who abducted and sexually abused a very young girl. The media were extremely critical of what they saw as an extremely lenient sentence and John Reid, the Home Secretary, was also critical of the

---

17. 'Plea for End to Attacks on Woolf', *Guardian*, 13 November 2004.

sentence making comments that were probably comparable to those of David Blunkett (see Gillespie (2006) 1153). The Lord Chancellor publicly stated that it was not the fault of the judge that the sentence was wrong but the legal framework. However, Vera Baird QC, a junior minister in the Department for Constitutional Affairs, criticized the judge by name on BBC Radio 4 suggesting that the judge had personally got the matter wrong (Gillespie (2006) 1154). Interestingly, there was then a public exchange of letters between the Lord Chancellor and the junior minister whereby Vera Baird formally withdrew her remarks. This was followed by further public confirmation by the Lord Chancellor that the judge had not erred, even though this implicitly criticized the Home Secretary for making his comments. The media were very much against this sentence and thus the easy political decision would have been either to stay silent or support the Home Secretary but Lord Falconer did not do this and, in effect, met his statutory obligations.

❓ QUESTION FOR REFLECTION

It was noted above (7.2.1.2) that the Lord Chancellor need not, following the CRA 2005, be legally qualified. Could someone without a background in the law be able to safeguard the independence of the judiciary?

7.5.2.2 Salary

At first sight judges would appear to be very well paid, with the Lord Chief Justice receiving £239,845 and a circuit judge receiving £128,296[18] but this should be placed into context when many practitioners will earn several times this (for an interesting analysis on this see Genn (2009)). Yet salary is important, as has been noted by Lord Bingham:

> There is of course, a close connection between judicial salaries and judicial independence...if a judge's salary is dependent on the whim of the government, the judge will not have the independence we desire in our judiciary. (Bingham (2000) 65)

In recognition of this, in England and Wales where there has been concern about the salary levels of the judiciary it has been suggested that the government has listened to the judges and acted accordingly (Pannick (1987) 13–14) although other commentators point out that in 1991 the government rejected the report of the Top Salaries Review Board (which makes recommendations as to the salaries of civil servants, ministers, and senior public figures) and imposed a lesser salary increase (Griffith (1997) xiv–xv).

The current position as regards judicial salaries is that they are undoubtedly less than an applicant for a judgeship earns in practice (for an analysis see Genn (2009)), but that there are alternative benefits. The judges are paid out of the consolidated fund (s 12 SCA 1981) which means that there is no parliamentary debate on their salaries. The government continues, however, to influence the salary levels because although the *Senior Salaries Review Body* (SSRB), an independent body, recommends the salary levels, it is for the government of the day to decide whether they will accept the recommendations or not. The decision as to whether to accept the recommendation is reported to Parliament who are entitled to question the relevant ministers as to the reasons for this.

---

18. The Online Resource Centre provides the latest salary details.

In 2005 the SSRB published a consultation paper on whether the judicial salaries bands were correct and how they should be 'pegged' to comparable posts (SSRB (2005)).

7.5.2.3 Tenure, promotion, and discipline

Three directly related issues that could conceivably interfere with judicial independence are the tenure of judges, any promotion they receive, and how they are disciplined. In order to discuss these issues it is necessary to distinguish once again between superior judges and inferior judges as the manner in which they are treated is significantly different. The position of judges of the Supreme Court, although obviously superior judges, will also be considered separately because of the changes introduced by the CRA 2005.

Superior judges

Superior judges enjoy significantly stronger protections than members of the inferior judiciary. Puisne judges and Lords Justice of Appeal hold office until retirement age (currently seventy (s 11(2) SCA 1981))[19] 'during good behaviour, subject to a power of removal by Her Majesty on an address presented to her by both Houses of Parliament'. In other words, subject to an additional power of removal through disability, a superior judge may only be removed if both Houses of Parliament pass a resolution requiring them to go. Only one judge has ever been removed in this way, in 1830 (see Pannick (1987) 90) and it would be extremely rare for anyone to achieve this 'distinction', not least because most judges would probably prefer to resign rather than be subjected to such an approach.

Where a superior judge is incapacitated by illness or disability then the SCA 1981 provides that the Lord Chancellor may remove him (s 11(8)). To ensure that this power cannot be abused, subsection (9) requires judicial consent to this procedure. Where the incapacitated judge is a Head of Division then at least two other Heads of Division must agree, where it is a Lord Justice of Appeal the Master of the Rolls must agree and where it is a puisne judge the appropriate Head of Division must agree. Given that all of the judges who must agree with this are all superior judges holding similar security of tenure, it should ensure that the measure can never be used by a Lord Chancellor in an inappropriate manner.

The CRA 2005 has, however, provided additional disciplinary procedures that may be exercised by the Lord Chief Justice, as head of the judiciary. These powers apply to all levels of judges and are considered in further detail below.

Promotion for the superior judge is a controversial area. Lord Denning once wrote that a judge when appointed had nothing to gain from promotion and did not seek it (Denning (1955) 17) and at the time this was probably true because there were so few posts in the Court of Appeal. However this may no longer necessarily be true and Bingham concedes that there may have been a concern that some judges would tailor their judgments in such a way to gain judicial advancement although he states that he cannot think of any examples of this and it would amount to a violation of the judicial oath (Bingham (2000) 60). It is certainly not possible to identify any candidates where

---

19. It is not known whether this will continue to be the case given that the government is considering abolishing the retirement age for ordinary workers. In 2010 it was noted that Lord Collins, a Justice of the Supreme Court, could be required to retire after only 18 months in the Court because he will then turn 70. There has been some suggestion that the age should revert to 75 (as it used to be) but it is less than clear that the government will legislate to allow this.

it might be thought that their decisions had denied advancement although some may argue that it is possible to identify the opposite where judges who may have appeared controversial have gained advancement. The changes made by the CRA 2005 have essentially meant that such tailoring would not bring any advantages since appointment to the High Court, Court of Appeal, and Supreme Court will be made by independent appointment commissions. The appointment of Sir Nicholas Wall as the President of the Family Division (discussed at 7.3.1.1) perhaps illustrates this. There were some who argued that the Lord Chancellor did not want Wall LJ appointed because of his pronouncements but the independent Appointments Commission led to this issue being resolved in a fair and transparent way.

Inferior judges

The security of tenure for a circuit judge is significantly different from that of a superior judge. Circuit judges must retire at the age of seventy but they are also subject to removal by the Lord Chancellor 'on the ground of incapacity or misbehaviour' (s 17(4) CA 1971). Neither incapacity nor misbehaviour as a cause for removal requires the consent of any other judge (in the same way as with superior judges). The CRA 2005 states that where this is to be undertaken then 'prescribed procedures' must be followed which suggests that there will now be a statutory scheme that will lead to dismissal (s 108(1)).

In recent times only one circuit judge has been removed by the Lord Chancellor, and Hailsham, the Lord Chancellor who was responsible for the dismissal, makes it clear in his autobiography that he would have preferred the judge to resign but, at that time, a pension would not be payable to someone who resigns whereas a part pension would be paid to someone who was dismissed (Hailsham (1990) 429). That said, there have been two occasions when dismissal could have occurred. One case arose under the 'old' system and one under the 'new' system of judicial discipline. The difference between the cases is perhaps instructive.

The first of these two cases was referred to Lord Hailsham for consideration of removal and senior judges again asked for removal (Hailsham (1990) 430). Lord Hailsham does not mention the judge by name but Judge James Pickles names himself in his own autobiography (Pickles (1992) 175–196). Judge Pickles was perhaps one of the most controversial judges in modern times and, by his own admission, was something of a maverick. Hailsham describes him as:

> [an] obscure and absurd judge whose only real claim to fame was the number of times when his behaviour had been criticized and his judgments [*sic*] reversed by the Court of Appeal...(Hailsham (1990) 430)

Part of the controversy of Pickles was his unconventional views of sex crimes, something that led to him being denied the right to sit on such cases. In his own autobiography he discusses the dress of women and says:

> If [a woman] seems to want sex but does not, a man who tries to grab it from her cannot be excused but she must share the blame. (Pickles (1992) 138)

Sadly such pronouncements were also uttered on the bench and he appeared to ignore sentencing precedents, passing sentences that were frequently anomalous and led to him being criticized in the Court of Appeal, most notably in *R v Scott* [1990] Crim LR 440. Judge Pickles reacted to these developments by discussing matters with the press and, rather famously, provided an interview on television where he referred to the Lord Chief Justice as 'an ancient dinosaur living in the wrong age' (Pickles (1992) 180). Lord Hailsham declined to dismiss him because he felt it was unfair that he acted as prosecutor, judge, jury, and executioner (Hailsham (1990) 430). Later when Lord MacKay informed Judge Pickles that he was contemplating dismissing him, Pickles used this argument as a defence to the charges (Pickles (1992) 185–195). In the end, the position led to a public letter of rebuke by the Lord Chancellor and Pickles eventually retired.

The second case was more recent. His Honour Judge Gerald Price QC was a circuit judge assigned to the Welsh circuit. He was the subject of a tabloid investigation where he was accused of having an affair with a male sex worker. His conduct was investigated by the *Office of Judicial Complaints* and the Lord Chancellor and Lord Chief Justice had decided that he should be removed from office although he resigned before the disciplinary process could be completed.

The cases of Judges Pickles and Price demonstrates a difference between the way in which inferior and superior judges can be dismissed. For example, it would be extremely difficult to control administratively the type of cases a puisne judge can sit on (as there is no requirement of 'ticketing') although the Lord Chief Justice could re-assign the judge to a different division of the High Court. A puisne judge accused of the same conduct as Judge Price would have required an address of both Houses of Parliament to dismiss. One circuit judge has publicly suggested that it is inappropriate for the distinction to remain, not least because circuit judges spend a not inconsiderable period of their time doing High Court work (Wilson (1994) 1454).[20] The reception to the call has not been unanimous with Lord Bingham suggesting that the risk of inappropriate dismissal is theoretical and with little practical consequence (Bingham (2000) 59).

❓ QUESTION FOR REFLECTION

It has been suggested by Wilson that judges of all ranks should receive the same security of tenure. Is there any justification for allowing more junior judges to be dismissed by the executive, even where it is supported by the senior judiciary? If not, how does one deal with a problem like Judge Pickles or Judge Price? Had either judge have been a puisne judge could either the judiciary or executive have done anything about him?

🎧 LISTEN TO THE PODCAST
For guidance on how to answer this question and a discussion of the main issues, listen to the author's podcast on the Online Resource Centre:
www.oxfordtextbooks.co.uk/orc/gillespie_els3e/

Promotion for the circuit bench has traditionally been extremely limited. It has already been noted that some may be eligible to become a senior circuit judge through the assumption of administrative responsibility for which they are remunerated for, but access to the senior judiciary is normally denied to them. Some circuit judges are appointed to the High Court bench but as has been noted already this is quite rare. Given the statutory qualification for a puisne judge is appointment as a circuit judge

---

20. Some work can be released to a circuit judge and in other cases a circuit judge can sit as a High Court judge (s 9 SCA 1981) and whilst doing so he has all the powers of a puisne judge.

(s 10(3)(c) SCA 1981) it may mean that with a fully open and independent appointments commission that there could be more progression.

Extending disciplinary measures

Judge Pickles, in his autobiography, states:

> It is absurd that the Lord Chancellor has no effective control except the power to remove circuit (not High Court) judges for 'misbehaviour'...(Pickles (1992) 196)

This, of course, misses the point that the presiding judge and Lord Chief Justice had the power to make directions restricting the types of cases a judge could hear (used against Pickles) but there is some truth to this point, that the only disciplinary measure was dismissal. The CRA 2005 provides a solution to this although the power now rests with the Lord Chief Justice as head of judiciary. The provisions do not differentiate between inferior and superior judges and empower the Lord Chief Justice, after following due process, to issue 'formal advice, a formal warning or reprimand' (s 108(4) CRA 2005). It is not clear what the effects of such measures are but, presumably, they could be used in conjunction with directions to ensure that judges are limited to the types of work that they carry out if this is appropriate.

The Act also gives the Lord Chief Justice the power to suspend someone from being a judge where a judge is subject to criminal proceedings, serving a sentence, or where the action that led to the criminal proceedings taking place is being used to begin dismissal proceedings (s 108(4)). The Lord Chief Justice may also suspend someone who has been convicted of an offence, but where it has been decided not to dismiss the person, if the LCJ believes it is necessary to do so in order to maintain the confidence of the judiciary (s 108(5)) or where a judge is being investigated for misbehaviour other than a criminal offence (s 108(6), (7)).

Perhaps the most notable example of the new powers of censure is that of Mr Justice Peter Smith, a puisne judge of the Chancery Division. The judge acted in an unprofessional way towards a barrister who had suggested he should recuse himself from a case concerning a legal firm where the judge had attempted to seek employment (the full details are set out by the Court of Appeal in *Howell and others v Millais and others* [2007] EWCA Civ 720). Following his rebuke from the Court of Appeal he issued a somewhat bizarre and argumentative public statement, after which he was reported to the Office of Judicial Complaints. After the investigation it was decided that his behaviour amounted to misconduct and he was formally reprimanded by the Lord Chief Justice.

Although Peter Smith J is probably the most high-profile judge to have been disciplined, the annual report for the OJC 2009/10 notes that across the judiciary, twenty-eight judicial office holders were removed from office following a complaint into their behaviour, with a further eighteen resigning (OJC (2010) 14). Of the twenty-eight removed the vast majority (twenty-five) were magistrates although two were members of the mainstream judiciary and one was a tribunal judge. Of lesser punishments it is notable that eleven office holders (including two members of the mainstream judiciary) received formal advice or a warning and eighteen (including ten members of the mainstream judiciary) received formal guidance.

7.5.2.4 Judicial immunity

In the next chapter it will be noted that advocates have lost their immunity for negligence but the judiciary have traditionally been immune from actions arising out of their judicial actions. Immunity apparently dates back to the seventeenth century and acts as a privilege to any words that a judge utters within a case (Pannick (1987) 95). However there continues to be a distinction between inferior and superior judges in that the latter have immunity from all actions even when acting outside their jurisdiction so long as the words or actions were done in good faith whereas an inferior judge's immunity is restricted to actions within their jurisdiction.

The argument advanced for judicial immunity is that it protects judges from vexatious litigants and an attempt to try and re-litigate each matter, and it has been suggested that in order for the immunity system to work properly the privilege must be absolute: including acts where a judge acts negligently or inappropriately (Pannick (1987) 98). The same reasons were advanced in support of the immunity of advocates (see 8.8.1.4 below) and yet this has been ended so why should judges continue to have absolute immunity? At least one commentator believes they should not and that it would not contravene the independence of the judiciary to allow judges to be sued for misconduct in their office (Pannick (1987) 99). However it seems unlikely that the judges themselves would ever end their own immunity (through the appellate courts so ruling), nor is it likely that Parliament would do so either; indeed s 9 of the HRA 1998 expressly preserves judicial immunity.

7.6 Judicial ethics

Sir Thomas Bingham (as he then was) wrote extrajudicially:

> Judicial ethics...appears to have been largely neglected in this country in recent years. (Bingham (1995) 35)

This is a fair comment but indeed the position is arguably replicated by the whole legal profession, which barely touches upon ethics from education through to practice (see, for example, Boon and Levin (2008) 153). Yet ethics are an essential part of the administration of justice and, although a significant amount of attention is placed on the ethics of the legal profession, this applies equally to judges.

The ethics of judicial office are arguably based on the judicial office which requires the judge to try cases 'without fear or favour, affection or ill-will'. Certain aspects of this will be discussed elsewhere in this book, most notably in relation to the conduct of judges within a trial but the issue that should be discussed here is the idea implicit within the oath, that a judge should not be biased or compromised.

7.6.1 Financial issues

If judges are to try cases 'without fear or favour' then their financial interests may well become relevant. It has been noted above that their salary tends to be less than that which they received in practice and accordingly it is likely that they may be in possession of various investments. It is clear, however, that judges must ensure that their investments do not conflict with their role as a judge. It has been suggested that whilst a judge could, theoretically, be a 'name' for Lloyds of London,[21] if they sat in

---

21. Lloyds of London is one of the principal insurance markets in the world. It is not an insurance company but rather facilitates its members (known as 'names') to underwrite insurance policies. If nothing happens then the 'names'

the Commercial Court (which principally deals with high-value commercial transactions such as insurance claims) then they would ordinarily relinquish this (Bingham (1995) 41) to save an appearance of bias (see below). Many Lords Justice of Appeal will similarly relinquish their status since the Court of Appeal (Civil Division) will not infrequently deal with such matters.

Judges, especially members of the senior judiciary, are frequently asked to undertake extrajudicial work. What should the position be in terms of remunerating such work? If, for example, a judge is asked to provide an after-dinner speech, can he ask for money?

The rules are not set down but it is implicit within the judicial oath and office that a judge will not bring the office of judge into disrepute. Commanding significant fees for outside work would almost certainly do so. It has been suggested:

> it would [not] be generally regarded as improper for a judge to accept a modest honorarium for a lecture or address which he had given, although most would perhaps decline or ask that the sum be paid to charity: a gift of wine or a book a judge might, properly in my view, accept, but the identity of the donor and the value of the gift would plainly affect his decision. (Bingham (1995) 41)

Most members of the judiciary would probably agree with this statement and from the occasions when I have organized a judge to speak at functions this does appear to be the rule, with judges simply accepting the offer of a dinner and specifically rejecting any suggestion of an honorarium.

7.6.2 **Politics**

By convention judges must be apolitical and the Lords of Appeal in Ordinary and other senior members of the judiciary when they were entitled to sit in the House of Lords sat on the cross-benches of the House of Lords, ie they were 'independent' members. Whilst there were a number of judges who were appointed from the ranks of Members of Parliament (Griffith (1997) 16) this 'tradition' appeared to have happily faded out in recent years but in 2007 (Sir) Ross Cranston, a former Labour party MP and former Solicitor-General was appointed a puisne judge. That said, his appointment was not the source of any political controversy. The establishment of the independent JAC should prevent any future appearance of political bias. A judge should not become involved in any party political issue once appointed and should ordinarily resign from any political party they may belong to. In July 2008 Cranston J recused himself from a case in the High Court because it raised issues about hunting and he had, whilst an MP, made comments about hunting when the *Hunting Act 2004* was proceeding through Parliament. His Lordship (correctly) considered that it would be inappropriate for him to preside (in part, because it was thought there was a risk of the appearance of bias, see 7.6.3.2 below).

⮌ RETIRED JUDGES

Whilst there is no rule to suggest that retired judges cannot become political it appears customary for retired Law Lords to sit on the cross-benches whereas retired Lord Chancellors

can achieve significant gains; if there are many disasters they can lose a lot of money. In the early 1990s there was considerable controversy when a number of 'names' faced bankruptcy as a result of many natural disasters.

(as political appointees) will ordinarily continue to sit with their party. It appears the same rule applies to retired judges who succeed to peerages. A good example of this is Baroness Butler-Sloss who was elevated to a life peerage in 2006 after retiring in 2005 from her position as President of the Family Division. Baroness Butler-Sloss sits on the cross-benches.

7.6.3 **Appearance of bias**

Perhaps the most important aspect of judicial ethics is in respect of bias or, perhaps more correctly, the appearance of bias (as it is difficult to know whether a judge has truly been biased: see *Locabail (UK) Ltd v Bayfield Properties Ltd* [2000] QB 451 at 472). The issue of bias is undoubtedly central to the judicial oath and it is also one of the areas where there has, in recent years, been considerable debate.

It has been suggested that bias can be divided into two forms: automatic disqualification and disqualification for apprehended bias (Olowofoyeku (2000) 456). Automatic disqualification will normally follow when a judge has an interest in the case that creates a situation where the judge appears to be sitting in his own cause. Apprehended bias exists where there is some other reason to believe that there is a 'real danger' that the judge will not consider the matter independently.

7.6.3.1 **Automatic disqualification**

A judge should never judge his own cause, in other words if the judge has an interest in a case then he should not sit as judge. In *Locabail* it was held that a *de minimis* principle existed within this rule meaning that minor or inconsequential interests could be ignored (p 473).

👁 **Example** Rental income

The case of *Locabail* was actually a series of conjoined appeals and one of the appeals was known as *R v Bristol Betting and Gaming Licensing Committee, ex p O'Callaghan*. The facts of this case are not strictly relevant and can be summarized as the appellant had attempted to judicially review the Committee's decision to grant an extended gaming licence to a branch of Corals, a national bookmakers' firm. The judge in the case was Mr Justice Dyson. It transpired that the family of Dyson J owned a property investment company and that some of their property was rented to branches of Corals. The actual amount disputed was calculated at £5,000 and the Court of Appeal dismissed the suggestion that if a national company the size of Corals was ordered to pay £5,000 it might jeopardize its ability to pay rent on one of its shops—in effect the only interest that Dyson J could have had. This was clearly within the *de minimis* principle and the appeal was dismissed (see pp 498–500).

Precisely what is significant would depend on each individual case but the benchmark is ensuring that the law is not brought into disrepute. *De minimis*, when translated, means 'minimal things' and thus it is not 'small' or 'reasonable' but 'minimal', meaning, in effect, that anything not trivial would lead to automatic disqualification.

The concept of 'cause' had been restricted in effect to pecuniary or propriety interests (Jones (1999) 385) but this was to change in the most dramatic way.

Pinochet

In the late 1990s significant controversy existed over the case of Senator Pinochet, the former dictator of Chile. Senator Pinochet had been visiting the United Kingdom for many years for treatment but he was considered a 'war criminal' by many and a Spanish judge had issued an extradition warrant for his arrest. As a result of bilateral EU extradition treaties, extradition had to be contemplated and a stipendiary magistrate issued two provisional arrest warrants, both of which were executed.

Senator Pinochet claimed diplomatic immunity and sought to judicially review the decisions claiming both warrants should be quashed. The Divisional Court held that both warrants should be quashed but stayed this until an appeal was heard by the House of Lords (the quashing order needed to be stayed otherwise Senator Pinochet could have left the country which would have rendered any appeal moot). Before the matter reached the House of Lords the campaigning group *Amnesty International* sought, and received, leave to intervene in the proceedings (meaning they could make representations as an 'interested party'). The House of Lords ruled by a majority of 3:2 that the appeal should be granted ([2001] 1 AC 61) and thus the arrest warrant was upheld.

However shortly after the hearing, Senator Pinochet's solicitors were contacted with the allegation that Lord Hoffmann, one of the Law Lords who heard the case and who had voted with the majority, was a director of the charitable arm of *Amnesty International*. The legal team for Senator Pinochet petitioned the House of Lords to overturn the decision arguing that it was procedurally flawed since Lord Hoffmann was party to the proceedings and therefore was automatically excluded from the case.

The House of Lords had never been asked to overturn one of its previous decisions in this way before, but held unanimously that it did have jurisdiction to do so (*R v Bow Street Metropolitan Stipendiary Magistrate and Others, ex p Pinochet (No 2)* [2000] 1 AC 119). Further, the House held that the decision did have to be set aside because Lord Hoffmann was automatically disqualified from sitting in judgment on the case because one of the parties to the case (albeit simply as an intervener) was *Amnesty International*. There was no suggestion that there was any financial or propriety interest in this case, Lord Hoffmann was not paid for his role as director and chair of the charity but it was stated that he did have an interest. The organization *Amnesty International* is unincorporated but the activities of its headquarters are divided into two companies; the first is an ordinary limited company which deals with the non-charitable aims of the organization, and the second was the charitable company that Lord Hoffmann chaired.

The charitable arm of *Amnesty International* had provided funding for a report into the activities of the Chilean government which had concluded that breaches of human rights had occurred and that nobody had ever been held to account for these. Whilst it was *Amnesty International* that intervened (and Lord Hoffmann was not a member of *Amnesty International*) the House of Lords held that though it was not possible to say that Lord Hoffmann was a party to the proceedings—in that *Amnesty International* and the charitable organization were theoretically separate entities—the charitable arm did have an interest in the outcome because its founding documents stated it was, inter alia, incorporated to 'procure the abolition of torture' (p 135). Given that it had an interest in the proceedings it then followed that Lord Hoffmann, as one of its directors, also had an interest in the matter and so should have been automatically disqualified.

The decision was unanimous and there were some concerns as to its effect. Lord Hutton had said that the links between Lord Hoffmann and *Amnesty International* were 'so strong that public confidence in the integrity of the administration of justice would be shaken if his decision was allowed to stand' (p 146) which is a damning indictment of the position. Lord Irvine, the then Lord Chancellor, reportedly argued that it had undermined justice (Jones (1999) 398) and it was reported that some members of the judiciary believed Lord Hoffmann should have resigned.

The decision of the House of Lords was largely welcomed but at least one commentator has noted that the decision has led to a 'growth industry' of lawyers attempting to find interests that debar a judge from sitting (Philips (2004) 113). The vast majority of these challenges are doomed to fail however since the House of Lords was quite clear as to why Lord Hoffmann should have disclosed his interest. The facts of that case were unusual in that *Amnesty International* had intervened in the case: had the charity not intervened then the issue would not have arisen.

7.6.3.2 Apprehended bias

The other significant manner in which a judge can be asked to stand down is in respect of apprehended bias. This remains an ethical issue not least because it is apprehended bias—ie there is some factor that makes people believe that there could be the appearance of bias rather than the fact that the judge is *actually* biased.

Precisely what would meet this criteria will differ according to different sets of facts but in *Locabail* the Court of Appeal was quite clear about what would *not* ordinarily give the appearance of bias, including 'religion, ethnic or national origin, gender, age, class means or sexual orientation' (p 480) and this has to be right. Perhaps more controversially they stated: 'the judge's social or educational or service or employment background or history...membership of sporting or charitable bodies' would not lead to the appearance of bias. This may, at first sight, appear to be surprising because it would be relatively easy to think of situations when these factors could lead to the suggestion of bias.

The House of Lords has recently considered similar issues in *Helow v Secretary of State for the Home Department* [2008] UKHL 62. This was a Scottish case where the appellant, a Palestinian, had sought leave to remain in the United Kingdom but her rejection, and subsequent appeals, had been rejected and she was to be deported. She complained that Lady Cosgrove, a member of the Court of Session (in this context this is roughly the equivalent of the High Court) who had adjudicated on the final appeal was a member of the *International Association of Jewish Lawyers and Jurists* and had been the founder member of the Scottish branch of this organization.

The appellant sought to argue that the association had a strong commitment to causes and beliefs at odds with the appellant, and she specifically contended that the organization was anti-Palestinian. To support this she adduced speeches by the President of the Association.

The House of Lords rejected her appeal stating that mere membership of the organization was insufficient to show the appearance of bias, and that some stronger connection would need to be shown, for example a link between the President and the judge. This is certainly consistent with *Locabail* but this decision, and the comments from *Locabail* identified above, need to be put into context, in that in the vast majority of times where they would be relevant it would not be through the appearance of bias but because of an automatic disqualification. This would apply equally to the employment context. If a judge had worked for a considerable period of time in a firm that was party to the proceedings then it is likely that this would be covered by automatic disqualification and not appearance of bias.

The test for disqualification for appearance of bias is whether there is a 'real danger of bias' (*Helow* at [14]) and this should be considered through the eyes of a 'fair-minded and informed observer'. In essence this means questioning whether a reasonable person would perceive the risk of bias. If they do then the judge should step down.

> ### Case box *AWG Group Ltd v Morrison*
>
> A good example of this test can be seen from the case of *AWG Group Ltd v Morrison* [2006] EWCA Civ 6. The judge assigned to the case was looking through the papers when he saw that he recognized one of the directors to be called as a witness. This was someone well known to him and the judge would not have wanted to preside over a case which necessitated him deciding whether the witness was telling the truth or not. The response of the respondents to this dilemma was to remove the director from the list of witnesses and replace him with another director.
>
> The Court of Appeal held that this was not an appropriate response. If there was the appearance of bias then the judge was disqualified from trying the case; a discretionary case-management decision could not remedy this appearance of bias. The director the judge knew was involved in the case even if he was not (now) giving evidence and a reasonable person would perceive a real risk of bias in such a situation.

Solicitors

Where life becomes slightly more interesting is in respect of part-time judges. The rule as to automatic disqualification applies to all judges. Barristers are, as will be seen, technically self-employed and thus are, or should be, aware of those who they are currently acting for. It is irrelevant whether another barrister within a particular set of chamber is appearing before the judge because as self-employed persons they are not in partnership so the judge is not acting as one of the parties. In *Locabail* it was noted that the position for solicitors is different. A partner in a solicitor's firm is legally responsible for the professional acts of all other partners and employees (p 478). Accordingly it would, in the opinion of the Court of Appeal, be inappropriate for a part-time judge to sit on a case where his firm has an interest. This will be relatively easy when the representative of one of the parties is the judge's firm but what about the position whereby the firm used to act for a party? The solution, according to the Court of Appeal, is for the solicitor who is sitting part-time as a member of the judiciary should, when invited to sit on a case, undertake a careful conflict check to ensure that the firm has never acted for either party in the past (p 479).

❓ QUESTION FOR REFLECTION

The House of Lords were undoubtedly correct to state that apparent bias can undermine the integrity of the justice system but is it realistic to expect a solicitor to check all clients in order to decide whether they can sit on a case? To take an example, Allen & Overy are one of the largest legal firms to be based in the United Kingdom. They operate worldwide and have over 4,900 staff including in excess of 450 partners. How easy would it be for a solicitor to check that no work had been undertaken? Or should firms who allow their staff to sit as judges have sufficient systems in place to ensure that there can be no conflict of interest?

7.7 Restrictions on practice

Where a person is elevated to a full-time judicial position then they must cease to practise (s 75 CLSA 1990), something that is quite reasonable as it ensures that there is no conflict of interest. Is the decision to become a judge irrevocable however? Those who are elevated to the bench will normally consider it to be their last employment with the intention of serving until retirement. However this need not be the case and in 1970 a puisne judge, Mr Justice Fisher, decided to resign from the bench and work in the city instead. This decision was greeted by outrage (Pannick (1987) 7) as the expectation of the public was that judges would accept a judgeship and sit for the duration of their appointment.

Fisher J did not return to practice but is it possible? It has always been assumed that it is not possible (see Pannick (1987) 7) but very recently this assumption has been challenged by the resignation of a puisne judge (Laddie J) and the retirement of a circuit judge (HHJ Cook).[22] Both indicated that they wished to be involved with practice, with HHJ Cook joining a solicitors' firm as a partner and Laddie J joining a senior solicitors' firm as a senior consultant. HHJ Cook was reported to have commented that whilst the Bar traditionally refused to allow a former judge to return to practice, the Law Society had no such ethic[23] which demonstrates an interesting division between the professions.

Should judges be permitted to return to practice? It is widely reported that the senior judiciary do not believe that it should be possible, with the suggestion that it undermines the appearance of judicial impartiality and, potentially, their independence. However, one argument is that the previous rules have never been more than conventions (Pannick (2005)) and questions whether some practitioners may be more ready to join the bench if they believe it is possible eventually to return, but this misses the point that they could accept a part-time judicial appointment such as Recorder or Deputy High Court Judge.

◆ Summary

This chapter has introduced the judiciary and the concept of the judicial office. It has also discussed the independence of the judiciary. In particular it has:

- Identified that there are different levels of judges, with the senior judiciary comprising the Lord Chief Justice and Heads of Division.

22. *The Times*, 28 June 2005, Law Supplement.
23. 'Lord Chancellor Reviews Ban on Judges Returning to Practice Law', *The Times*, 23 June 2005.

- Noted that the Lord Chief Justice is now the Head of the Judiciary.
- Noted that there are part-time members of the judiciary known either as district judges, recorders, or Deputy High Court Judges depending on which court they sit in.
- Identified that superior judges (puisne judges and above) have unlimited authority whereas the inferior judiciary (circuit and district judges) are limited to the jurisdiction provided by statute.
- Discussed how the CRA 2005 has amended the role of the judiciary.
- Considered how appointments to the judiciary are made and discussed how to make the judiciary more diverse.
- Noted that a fundamental constitutional principle is that judges are independent and that securing the independence of the judiciary is not easy and involves not only separation from the legislature and executive but also from each other and the media.
- Discussed the tenure of the judiciary and identified that inferior judges can be more readily dismissed than superior judges.

End-of-chapter questions

1. It has been seen in this chapter that there remains a significant difference between the superior judiciary and the inferior judiciary. In a modern legal system is there any need for such a distinction to remain?

2. Read Windlesham (2005). It can be seen from this reading that removing the Lord Chancellor from his judicial duties has necessitated a constitutional concordant between the executive and judiciary supplemented by a statutory duty to uphold judicial independence. Would it not have been better to simply leave the Lord Chancellor alone? If Lord Bingham, an ardent supporter of constitutional change, agrees that there was no real bias by the Lord Chancellor has this not just been change for change's sake rather than a significant shift in responsibilities?

3. The new independent appointments scheme could lead to an increase in the number of circuit judges being raised to the High Court bench. Is this desirable? Is there not a danger that this could undermine the circuit bench by making it a 'training ground'? Yet the circuit bench is important in its own right.

4. Read Pannick (2005) and compare and contrast Bingham (1995) pp 50–51. Given the importance of judicial independence (above) is there not a danger that by allowing judges to move between practice and the bench a judge may be influenced by an advocate appearing before him who he may wish later to apply for a job?

Further reading

Bingham T (2000) 'Judicial independence' in *The Business of Judging* (Oxford: OUP).
This is an essay written by Lord Bingham who discusses the concept of judicial independence and places it in the context of the modern judiciary.

Masterman R (2005) 'Determinative in the abstract? Article 6(1) and the separation of powers' 6 *European Human Rights Law Review* 628–648.

This article discusses the doctrine of the separation of powers and considers how the ECHR impacts upon it.

Rackley E (2007) 'Judicial diversity, the woman judge and fairy tale endings' 27 *Legal Studies* 74–94.

This fascinating article tells the story of some female members of the judiciary and discusses how to obtain a diverse judiciary.

Stevens R (2002) *The English Judges: Their role in the changing constitution* (Oxford: Hart Publishing) 129–136.

Wilson H (1994) 'The county court judge in limbo' 144 *New Law Journal* 1453.

This article discusses the different ways that superior and inferior judges can be dismissed and questions whether this means that the independence of inferior judges is not secured.

You should also familiarize yourself with the consultation papers on the *Supreme Court* and the *Judicial Appointments Commission*.

 For multiple choice questions, updates to this chapter and links to useful websites, please visit the Online Resource Centre at

www.oxfordtextbooks.co.uk/orc/gillespie_els3e/

8

The Legal Professions

By the end of this chapter you will be able to:

- Identify the various branches of the legal profession.
- Understand the differences between the two principal professions.
- Discuss whether the professions should fuse into a single profession.
- Understand how a person qualifies as a member of the professions.
- Identify ethical issues relating to the practice of law.

Introduction

Many of you will start your studies in law with the intention of becoming a lawyer although by the end of their studies only 50 per cent of law students will actually seek a position as a member of the legal professions. In this chapter we will discuss what the legal professions are, what they do, and how it is possible for someone to qualify as a member of the professions. The chapter will also examine the rules governing practice as a member of the professions and, in particular, the issue of ethical behaviour.

8.1 Defining the professions

The term 'lawyer' has become an almost standard term that is heard in daily use and the *Oxford English Dictionary* defines it as 'a member of the legal profession' but this masks the point that there is no single legal profession but instead there are two principal professions and some secondary ones. It is for this reason that most law dictionaries will not define 'lawyer' because it is a colloquialism that is used as shorthand but does not describe anyone in particular, as nobody in the United Kingdom is a 'lawyer' per se but has a more specific title.

It is often said that England and Wales is one of three countries to continue to have separate legal professions[1] with the vast majority of countries having a single profession but this is not necessarily correct in that a distinction must be drawn between qualified members of the legal profession and non-qualified members of the profession. In England and Wales there are commonly thought to be two branches of the qualified legal profession: barristers and solicitors. In other countries, for example the United States of America, there is one, commonly known as an attorney. However other people will consider themselves to be a 'lawyer' and in other jurisdictions, and increasingly within England and Wales, they are an important part of a functioning legal system. In England and Wales the two principal professions are joined by two other types of 'lawyer', those being legal executives and increasingly 'paralegals' (who may also be known by other terms, for example, fee-earners etc), a species of lawyer that has been largely imported from America. These lawyers and certainly the Institute of Legal Executives (ILEX) which governs legal executives view themselves as a branch of the legal profession so perhaps the reality is that there are now three, or possibly even four, branches to the profession.

The main focus of this chapter will be on solicitors and barristers, as these remain the principal branches of the profession and the ones most people are familiar with. However, towards the middle of this chapter the other two branches will be discussed briefly.

---

1. The others being Scotland and the Republic of Ireland, both of which obviously have strong links to the English Legal System.

8.2 Barristers

The first group to examine are barristers, who are also referred to as 'counsel' and are frequently thought to be the specialist advocates although, as will be seen, this is not necessarily accurate.

⊃ 'COUNSEL'

Barristers, especially those who practise as advocates, are often referred to as 'counsel' and may sometimes style themselves as 'of counsel', eg Martin Squires of counsel. When a solicitor instructs a barrister, he will usually summarize the case and the action requested by preparing a document known as 'instructions to counsel' which is also called a 'brief to counsel'. Precisely why barristers are also called counsel is lost in the mists of time but it is important to recognize their dual title.

8.2.1 History of the Bar

Barristers collectively are known as 'the Bar' for reasons that will become clear later. The profession is the older branch, with the term barrister existing as far back as the thirteenth century and until recently they had the sole rights of audience in the higher courts. Whilst there is in existence the Bar Council (more properly known as the General Council of the Bar for England and Wales) which acts as the 'trade body' of barristers, their responsibility is to their Inns of Court, to which all members must belong.

⊃ RIGHTS OF AUDIENCE

'Rights of audience' is a specific legal term. A person does not automatically have the right to appear in the courts and perform advocacy, the rules on when a person may do so differ depending on the profession, the court, and the type of case. The ability to act as an advocate in a court is known as 'rights of audience' and so if one is said to have rights of audience in the High Court, it means that the person can appear in the High Court as an advocate and represent his or her client.

8.2.1.1 Inns of Court

There are now four Inns of Court, all of which are honourable and learned societies, which is why barristers are referred to as *learned* whereas solicitors are not. The Inns are Middle Temple, Inner Temple, Gray's Inn, and Lincoln's Inn. Traditionally each Inn was slightly different and the choice of Inn to some degree was a conscious choice for a barrister's career. Lincoln's Inn was primarily considered to be a Chancery-based Inn, ie its members would specialize in Chancery matters and to an extent this has remained, although its members are certainly more general practitioners now. Gray's Inn traditionally had a provincial focus, again something that has been retained to an extent with many members of the North-Eastern Circuit belonging to this Inn but realistically the modern Inns no longer act as specialists and the choice of an Inn is now one of pure personal preference rather than any career choice.

Traditionally the Inns of Court were responsible for the training of barristers and all education took place within their own Inn. From the mid-nineteenth century, however, the four Inns decided that it would be best to cooperate in the education of barristers and they established the Council of Legal Education and the Inns of Court School of Law which took over the education of student members of the Inns. However, the importance of the Inns to education remains and even today a student member of an Inn is (theoretically) restricted to his own Inn and may only use its facilities until he has become a barrister at which point the facilities of all four Inns become available. The Bar Council has taken over as the main body with the day-to-day responsibility of regulating barristers but the Inns of Court continue to have the sole right to call members to the Bar and they execute any punishment arising out of disciplinary hearings, including the ultimate sanction of removing a barrister. Clementi (2004)[2] argues that the division of responsibility between the Bar Council and the Inns of Court is not clear (pp 31–32) and to an extent this has been clarified with the creation of the Bar Standards Board (8.8.1.1).

In recent years there has been some discussion as to the purpose of the Inns with one eminent QC describing them as 'self-perpetuating geriatric oligarchies' (Robins (2005) 19) and another describes them as a glorified private club (something that Dunn (1993), a former Court of Appeal judge, agrees with (p 186)). However others disagree and Robins (2005) reports the words of a junior barrister who joined the Inn during his vocational training year and says, '[my time] made me feel included in the inn [*sic*] and the workings of the inn, and it gave me a sense of professional history' (p 21).

8.2.1.2 Masters of the Bench

The Inns of Court are presided over by a series of senior members of the Inns known collectively as the 'Masters of the Bench' and colloquially referred to as 'benchers'. Most members are elected by benchers of the Inn, although some are, by tradition, ex officio benchers, most notably the senior judiciary. All High Court judges are automatically made a bencher if they have not already been elected (and Rothwell (2005) notes that this applies to High Court judges who used to be solicitors (p 23)). Clementi (2004) has questioned whether it is correct for members of the judiciary to take an active role in the running of the Inns (p 31) although he did not take his questioning to the extent of recommending any substantive change and any change would undoubtedly be resisted by the judiciary who consider their membership of the Inns as advantageous, particularly to student members who will come into contact with members of the judiciary at an early stage of their careers and in a friendly place.

⮎ MASTERS OF THE BENCH

Regardless of what title a Master of the Bench holds (eg a judicial office such as Lord Justice of Appeal, Mr Justice, etc) when they are performing their role as a Master of the Bench they are referred to as 'Master [*n*]' and referred to simply as 'master' (even if they are female). This can cause some confusion to junior members who, for example, see one of their Masters sitting in the House of Lords (where he will be referred to as 'My Lord') and in the evening be calling him 'Master'. The purpose of the rule is to ensure that all realize that they are all members of the same Inn and, therefore, part of the same community.

---

2. In 2003 the government ordered a review on the regulation of the legal profession under the chair of Sir David Clementi. His report, produced in 2004, includes reference to the structure of the professions.

The head of the Inn is the Master Treasurer and he is appointed for a one-year term. Whilst it is not a full-time position, it is not far from it and the person appointed will normally undertake less professional work (even judicial work if they are a judge when appointed) during their year of office. The next senior member is known as the Master Reader and he will normally become the Master Treasurer the following year. The person who is in day-to-day control of the Inns is the Under Treasurer (sometimes called Sub-Treasurer) who are not infrequently former senior members of the Armed Forces[3] and they will lead the team of employees of the Inns. A crude, but somewhat accurate, analogy to explain the relationship between the Master Treasurer and Under Treasurer is that between the chairman (Master Treasurer) and chief executive or director of operations (Under Treasurer) of a company, this reinforcing that the post of Master Treasurer is not a ceremonial one, but one that carries with it executive responsibilities (Dunn (1993) 186–188).

8.2.1.3 The 'Bar'

When a person becomes a barrister he is said to have been called to the Bar. This term is another that has historical significance. Before the Inns of Court School of Law was established, the training of barristers took place in the Inn and by members of the Inn. The students and instructors (senior members of the Inn) would sit in the centre of the room set out like a courtroom. The students would sit in the middle of the court, within the bar, and when they were called to 'the utter bar' which means 'outer' they left the middle of the court and took their places outside the bar signifying they were no longer students. When a barrister is called they become a junior barrister and they remain a junior for the rest of their careers unless they opt to 'take silk' and become a Queen's Counsel (QC). This process is discussed below but is mentioned here because when a member of the Inn is appointed a QC they are called 'into' the bar (as distinct from 'to the bar').

⊕ SITTING IN COURT

In many of the old courts the status of a barrister will be reflected in where they sit. In the older and more important courts the first row of the advocates' benches will be separated from the rest by a gate or bar. Only those who have been called into the bar, ie QCs, may sit in that row of benches, with junior barristers having to sit in the row behind. In more modern courts where no gate exists barristers will sit in any row except when a junior barrister is being 'led' by a QC in which case the junior will ordinarily sit behind the QC.

It had been planned that in 2008 the system of calling people to the Bar would change with the introduction of deferred call. In essence this would have meant that a person would not be called to the Bar nor entitled to refer to himself as a 'barrister' until after the completion of pupillage. This would have been a major difference from the current position where anyone who meets the criteria set down by the Inns can be called. However, following consultation, the Bar Standards Board in 2007 announced that it was abandoning the proposal to defer call believing that it would cause confusion.

---

3. In the Middle Temple, for example, the current Under Treasurer is a retired Air Commodore and before that there were two Rear Admirals.

Instead it is intended to produce an online register of those who hold a practising certificate and are entitled therefore to practise.

8.2.2 Education and training

The way that barristers were historically trained has been discussed but how are they trained now? Training prior to full qualification is divided into three parts:

- academic stage
- vocational stage
- pupillage.

Once qualified, a practising barrister also has a responsibility to undertake continuing professional development, ie to maintain their training throughout their career.

8.2.2.1 Academic stage

The academic stage for those who wish to become solicitors or barristers is now the same. The length it takes depends on the educational background of the candidates. Direct entry is only available to graduates but it remains the case that for both solicitors and barristers there is no requirement for them to complete a law degree. If, however, the candidate is not a law graduate then they can undertake a conversion course that was once referred to as the Common Professional Examination (CPE) and is now increasingly being referred to as the Graduate Diploma in Law (GDL), this being the preferred name as it recognizes that students are already graduates and also because it tends to suggest a formal qualification (a graduate diploma) whereas the CPE suggested it was just an internal examination, something it most certainly was not! Some universities also allow graduate entry to law degrees which is a 'fast-track' law degree on the basis that it is not necessary to develop undergraduate learning techniques as the entrant is already a graduate, which means that the programmes can focus purely on the law.

During the academic stage, regardless of which route is taken, the candidate must, as a minimum, receive education in the following:[4]

- Constitutional Law
- Contract Law
- Criminal Law
- Equity
- Law of the EU
- Land Law
- Law of Tort.

It is also expected that students will receive a good understanding of how to research law and acquire the general skills required to study law. The GDL programmes will normally focus solely on these exemption subjects whereas a law degree will generally allow the student to undertake a series of optional subjects which provide a slightly wider grounding in law.

---

4. Note, some of the names may change between institutions.

The minimum requirement for acceptance onto the vocational stage for the Bar is a lower-second-class honours degree.

8.2.2.2 Vocational stage

After the completion of the academic stage a candidate must choose which branch of the profession he wishes to pursue. This is not an irrevocable decision as it is possible to change between the professions; in recent years the number of barristers qualifying as solicitors has increased whereas traditionally it was more common for the transfer to be in the opposite direction.

The vocational stage of training is now called the Bar Professional Training Course (BPTC). Prior to the academic year 2010/2011 the course was known as the Bar Vocational Course (BVC) and before that the 'Bar Finals'). Until comparatively recently a student who wished to study for the Bar had to study at the Inns of Court School of Law in London. This had a number of advantages, not least the proximity to the Inns of Courts, but it was thought that the monopoly was bad for student access so, following the lead of the Law Society, the Bar Council allowed universities to offer the course and currently eight institutions do so, with the Inns of Court School of Law itself being taken over by City University, London and the title eventually passing away.

Technically when one is called to the Bar, it is to the degree of the Bar and this is recognized as a postgraduate-level course. However the BPTC is primarily vocational in nature, although academic knowledge is required of the rules of litigation, evidence, and ethics. The major focus of the course is the application of legal knowledge to situations and a number of practical training exercises are used which take the form of 'mock' briefs where the student is expected to undertake work that is likely to occur in the early years of practice. The course remains a foundation of skills, however, since pupillage is considered to be the appropriate place of the completion of the acquisition of practical skills. In comparison to the Legal Practical Course (see 8.3.1.1 below) the BPTC concentrates more on advocacy, drafting legal documents, and legal research. Advocacy remains one of the most important skills of a barrister and this is accordingly an important acquisition. The importance of ethics is also highlighted in the course and indeed ethics is a strand that flows throughout the course and it is possible for a student to fail the entire BPTC if they act in an unethical manner.

Students on the BPTC may have an opportunity to begin actual casework during their course. Some institutions have developed law clinics whereby the students work on live cases (under the supervision of academics who are professionally qualified) as part of their curriculum.

8.2.2.3 Pupillage

Perhaps the most important part of the training for becoming a barrister is pupillage. It is perhaps the most difficult to secure as Mason (2004) notes that there are over three times the number of would-be pupils as there are pupillages. Although the pupil will have (currently) been called to the Bar, during pupillage he will refer to himself as a 'pupil barrister'. Pupillage will normally last for twelve months but exceptionally it is possible that it could last up to eighteen months. Pupillage is broken into six-month blocks referred to as the first six and second six (and exceptionally a third six) and although some chambers will offer twelve-month pupillages these are, in fact, two separate six-month arrangements.

The Bar Standards Board refers to pupillage as:

the final stage of the route to qualification at the Bar, in which the pupil gains practical training under the supervision of an experienced barrister.

It is, therefore, the first time when the responsibility for the training passes from universities to the practitioners. A barrister of at least ten years' experience can apply to become a pupil-master, ie someone who is entitled to train pupils and accordingly it can be seen that it is very much practitioner-led.

In the first six months the pupil barrister is restricted as to what he can do, and realistically this work amounts to a 'shadowing' operation in which the pupil will observe the work of the master. That said, behind the scenes the pupil will begin to develop many of the 'unseen' skills of a barrister; although Pannick (1992) argues that traditionally this part of the pupillage was considered a waste of time (pp 208–209) the modern position is arguably different. Although a first-six pupil will not be allowed to perform advocacy or meet with a client alone, he will begin to work on paperwork relating to legal cases, including claim forms, defences, and particulars of claim. All of this documentary work will, of course, be under the supervision of, and probably corrected by, the pupil-master but it is the first steps into practice.

In the second six months a pupil barrister gains limited rights of audience and the ability to undertake legal work, albeit under the (loose) supervision of his master. A pupil in the second months may well begin to undertake advocacy work, probably in the magistrates' court (crime) and county courts (civil) and is entitled to meet clients in the same way as fully qualified barristers will. It should be emphasized, of course, that the pupil is not yet fully qualified and he can anticipate a lot of questioning from his master as to how he intends to undertake the advocacy etc.

Traditionally pupils were never paid and indeed in historical times (until the early to mid-twentieth century) it was expected that pupils would pay barristers for acting as their masters. In modern times it has been recognized that this is unacceptable and the Bar Council has now stipulated that pupillages, subject to a small number of limited exceptions, must be remunerated. Given the headlines in the tabloid newspapers that scream of 'fat cat' lawyers it may be expected that a pupil's award would be substantial, but in fact the current minimum is £833.33 per month which equates to an annual stipend of £10,000, although travelling costs and training courses must also be met by chambers (Annex R, *Code of Conduct*). Whilst it is true to say that some chambers offer in excess of this amount, with some awards being in excess of £40,000, a significant number are set at this modest level and there may be limited opportunity to earn additional money.

Status of pupillage?

An interesting issue that arose when awards became compulsory was what the employment status of a pupil barrister is. It will be seen that fully qualified barristers are actually independent practitioners and accordingly are self-employed. A pupil barrister, however, is not entitled to practice without limitations and is under the supervision of his pupil-master so does this change their status? The matter was put to the test in *Edmonds v Lawson and Others* [2000] QB 501 where the claimant attempted to sue the respondents (who were the head of chambers and her two pupil-masters) claiming that pupillage was either employment or apprenticeship and, accordingly, she was entitled to the statutory minimum wage. The litigation was unusual in that it was completely friendly—it was a test case that was brought not only with the consent of the Bar Council, but actively encouraged by it, both sets of counsel who appeared in the case were actually instructed by the Bar Council themselves (p 507).

The Court of Appeal accepted that the offer, and acceptance, of a pupillage does amount to a legal contract. However, it rejected the idea that it was either a contract of employment or a contract for apprenticeship. Their reasoning for this was that the binding duties of a pupil do not include anything that would not be conducive to the pupil's own education whereas an employee or apprentice must do anything that can be reasonably asked of them (pp 517–518). The court also noted that in the second six months of pupillage, the pupil barrister is able to earn money in their own right and that this method of earning money is no different to the way that full practising barristers earn remuneration (p 518). Accordingly, no contract of employment or apprenticeship existed and thus the provisions of the *National Minimum Wage Act 1999* did not apply. It is clear, therefore, that a pupil barrister must, like with those barristers who practise independently, be regarded as being self-employed.

❓ QUESTION FOR REFLECTION

Consider *Edmonds v Lawson* (2000): is the decision of the Court of Appeal not simply wrong? Why should a pupil barrister not be entitled to the national minimum wage? Is there really any distinction between a pupil and an employee?

🎧 LISTEN TO THE PODCAST

For guidance on how to answer this question and a discussion of the main issues, listen to the author's podcast on the Online Resource Centre:
www.oxfordtextbooks.co.uk/orc/gillespie_els3e/

8.2.2.4 Continuing Professional Development

In common with the other professions the Bar now requires practitioners to continue to develop their legal knowledge. As all law students know only too well the law changes all too often and it is thought, therefore, that it is appropriate that practising barristers should keep up to date with general legal knowledge in ways other than just by preparing cases. The Bar Council introduced the concept of Continuing Professional Development (CPD) in a staged way, with new practitioners having had a responsibility since 1997 but it was not until 2005 that all practising barristers were required to undertake CPD work. The current requirements are that those who have been qualified for less than three years must undertake 45 hours of CPD (including nine hours of advocacy and three hours of ethics) and those qualified for over three years must undertake twelve hours of CPD.

The Bar Standards Board, like other professional bodies, permits CPD to accrue in a number of ways, and whilst they themselves will arrange some training sessions they will 'accredit' other training seminars offered by external agencies. Robins (2005) notes that an advantage of the Inns organizing the sessions is that, if they use their own members' high-quality training, they can be produced for a fraction of the cost that commercial firms would charge (p 20). The process of accreditation is basically a system whereby the Bar Council assures itself that the agencies will provide an appropriate level of training and awareness and an agreement as to how many hours each seminar will count for. There is also flexibility for those who mix teaching and practice, with teaching on undergraduate-level programmes (including CPE or GDL) being able to count this as part of their CPD requirement, presumably because the nature of an academic post is to maintain awareness of key current issues in the law. Breach of the CPD requirements amounts to a disciplinary offence and there have been a number of instances when the Bar Standards Board has fined barristers for failing to adhere to this requirement.

8.2.3 Practice

Once a barrister has fully qualified how do they practise? The rules differ between those who serve as employed barristers and those who act in private practice.

8.2.3.1 Private practice

Perhaps the recognizable type of barrister is that in independent (private) practice.

Chambers

After pupillage it is necessary for a person to find a place from where he can practise, known as a tenancy. Barristers are all self-employed and until 2010 they were not allowed to establish a legal partnership with each other but instead they joined together in loose associations known as chambers (also known as 'sets') in order to pool resources (something that continues to be the norm subject to the rules relating to *Legal Disciplinary Practices* discussed below).

Each barrister (known as a tenant within chambers) will pay rent and a proportion of their income to cover the expenses of chambers. Chambers itself will employ some staff; some will include administrative assistants, but the most important of the employees are the clerks. The clerk to a barrister is an unusual position and has often been likened to the 'pimp' of a barrister. It is not possible for individual barristers to tout for business and, accordingly, the clerk is responsible, in part, for bringing work into the set. Many briefs will be for specific barristers but some will be chambers briefs where a firm of solicitors is happy to deal with anyone within the set and it will then be for the clerk to decide who gets the brief. Where a trial overruns and this prevents a barrister from starting another case the clerk will also redistribute the work. Traditionally a clerk was given a percentage of the brief fee but in modern times it is now more likely that clerks will be on a salary with bonuses paid depending on performance. The attraction this brings is that clerks will concentrate on all barristers whereby when it was a percentage system there was always the risk that the clerk would concentrate on the more experienced practitioners for whom he could attract a higher fee. Chambers normally has a team of clerks, with one being the senior clerk who has ultimate responsibility for supervising the rest and the general operation of clerking. Increasingly in modern times the senior clerk is being called the 'practice manager' or even 'chambers manager'. Good clerks are extremely useful to chambers and there is a strong market in poaching the best. The very best senior clerks can expect high six-figure salaries and the vast majority of senior clerks will earn significant salaries, quite frequently more than what many of the barristers within their chambers will earn.

Once a person is of at least three years' call he is entitled to work without being a member of chambers, ie from home if he so wishes, or he can establish chambers himself. There does appear to be an increase in the number of sole practitioners and some clever clerks have created schemes whereby they will perform an agency-type clerking service for these persons. Acting as a sole practitioner does bring the advantages of more control over work and is undoubtedly cheaper (no chambers expenses, rent, etc) but there is the difficulty that if a sole practitioner's source of work is not strong it is unlikely that they would pick up briefs from others within a set when they become available because of overrunning trials etc.

Court work

The stereotypical view of a barrister is that they spend most of their time in court; in part because once they are qualified a barrister has rights of audience in every court. However, this general impression is not strictly accurate. Whilst it is true to say that barristers specialize in litigation and advocacy it does not mean that all their time will be spent in court, indeed this depends on their area of practice. Whilst criminal and family practitioners will spend the majority of their time in court, other practitioners will not and for those with a primarily civil practice, especially Chancery matters, court is the measure of last resort and they will feel that they have almost failed if it gets to court (because of the costs of litigation) in that most matters can be settled before trial.

It is, however, true to say that advocacy is the most important tool of a barrister but it need not be restricted to oral advocacy and a considerable amount of written documentation will be prepared by barristers. One of the most important aspects of the work of a barrister is the provision of counsel's opinion. This normally takes place at the beginning of litigation and it is the time when a barrister will assess the likely success of any litigation, and identify the key evidential difficulties. The preparation of counsel's opinion will normally require the barrister to undertake research on a specialist area and then to present this advice to the solicitor and those instructing them. If, after considering the advice of counsel, it is decided to proceed with litigation it is likely that the barrister will also be involved in the drafting of the various documents that are needed for litigation, including the claim form, particulars of claim, defences, and questions between all the parties. All of these are a specialist skills and training is developed during the Bar Professional Training Course.

When a barrister does appear in open court he appears in the full rig that the public know so well. Except for tribunals and the magistrates' courts where no robes are worn, all barristers must wear a gown, wig, and bands. The robes of QCs will be discussed below, but junior barristers wear a stuff gown, bands (which are the white tails that are worn around the neck—ladies have a wrap-around version which includes a collar whereas male barristers' shirts have detachable collars and they replace the normal collar with a winged one), and the infamous wig. There has been a debate for many years as to whether this costume should remain and in 2003 the government issued a consultation paper which suggested a number of options, the most simple of which being that advocates (of all grades) should only wear a gown.

Despite the fact that civil judges have now abandoned their wigs (see 7.1.4 above), it has been decided that barristers will continue to wear wigs and gowns in open court except where the judge does not wear robes, in which case the barrister will wear only a suit too. The vast majority of these occasions involve hearings not heard in open court.

The retention of wigs and gowns was considered an important matter for the Bar when consulted although this was perhaps more relevant in criminal matters where it has been suggested that they provide a degree of authority and anonymity (Megarry J in *St Edmundsbury & Ipswich Board of Finance v Clark* [1973] Ch 323 made *obiter* comments that discussed the merits of judicial and advocates robes (p 330)) although the degree of safety this brings is perhaps slightly questionable. In any event it must be seriously questioned whether advocates will continue to wear wigs in civil matters now that judges do not. It would seem inevitable that a practice direction will ultimately follow that counsel follow the lead of the judiciary and abandon wigs, at least for civil matters.

The 'cab rank rule'

Solicitors, to an extent, have the right to pick and choose their clients (although it will be seen later that they tend not to exercise this right). Barristers in independent practice, on the other hand, are bound by their Code of Conduct to adopt something which is called the 'cab rank rule' which is described as:

> A self-employed barrister...must in any field in which he professes to practise in relation to work appropriate to his experience and seniority and irrespective of whether the client is paying privately or is publicly funded...[accept a brief]...and do so irrespective of:
>
> (i)   the party on whose behalf he is instructed,
>
> (ii) the nature of the case, and
>
> (iii) any belief or opinion which he may have formed as to the character, reputation, cause, conduct, guilt or innocence of that person. (rule 602, *Code of Conduct*)

Pannick (1992) quotes Lord Irvine QC (later a Lord Chancellor) who describes the rule as:

> the duty to appear for the Yorkshire Ripper or any other defendant against whom there may be a hostile climate of public opinion. In civil cases, it is also his duty to appear not only for a particular interest group with which he might prefer to identify but for every interest group...(p 136)

In other words personal preference cannot decide what case a barrister takes. A criminal practitioner cannot, for example, decide that he will only defend cases and will never accept a prosecution brief as this would breach the cab rank rule. Similarly, a barrister could not decide that he will refuse to take briefs from companies that trade with a particular country because such personal ethics infringe the rule.

👁 **Example** Cab rank rule

Arthur Hoskins has been charged with two counts of robbery. The Crown Prosecution Service approaches the clerk to Rhiannon Holloway, a barrister who practices in criminal law. The cab rank rule states that if it is possible for Rhiannon to do this case (ie there is no conflict of interest and she is available during the likely time that this will come to court) then she must accept the brief. Rhiannon could not reject the brief in the knowledge that the defence solicitors, who regularly instruct her and other members of the set, may well approach her and she could get more money acting as the defence. The prosecution came first and therefore that brief has to be taken.

The rule is not universally approved of. Williams (2000), a practising barrister, argued that it was a restriction on freedom and that it cannot be justified but Pannick (1992) states: 'any lawyer who does not understand [the purpose of the rule] really has no business being an advocate' (p 145). The basis for this statement is Pannick's belief that to remove the rule would be to prejudice the impartiality of the advocate and would cause people no longer to understand that an advocate's arguments are not necessarily his own belief but rather the instructions of his lay client (p 140). Whether society fully understands this distinction is perhaps somewhat questionable but the essence of the point is almost certainly true and it undoubtedly makes it easier for an advocate to perform his duty without needing to like or approve of his client.

❓ QUESTION FOR REFLECTION

Williams (2000) argues that the cab rank rule is anarchistic; do you agree? If yes, how would people who are suspected of the most serious crimes (eg child abuse or murder) ever be represented? Read 8.9.2.1 below which discusses how a lawyer should deal with defending someone they believe guilty. Is there not a danger that by abandoning the cab rank rule the jury will become superfluous with defence counsel deciding whether someone suspected of committing a serious crime is guilty or not? (On this point see *Ridehalgh v Horsefield and another* [1994] Ch 205 at 234.)

🎧 LISTEN TO THE PODCAST

For guidance on how to answer this question and a discussion of the main issues, listen to the author's podcast on the Online Resource Centre:
www.oxfordtextbooks.co.uk/orc/gillespie_els3e/

Is the rule enforced? The Bar Standards Board does attempt to uphold it and breach of this rule is considered to be a serious disciplinary offence but Pannick noted that, even in the early 1990s, there was concern that the rule was being avoided through, for example, instructing the barrister's clerk to pretend that the barrister is already committed (p 144) and a suggestion that a barrister would only act for certain parties (eg trades unions) or would never defend a rapist (ibid). Clementi (2004), when discussing the merits of the rule, notes that one submission by a barrister stated:

> any reasonably successful barrister will be able credibly to assert that his current professional and private commitments preclude him or her taking on a case that is unattractive to him or her—until the next interesting case comes along which they would rather do. (p 131)

It would appear that the rule can be obscured but whether this should justify the end of the rule is perhaps more questionable. Whilst some, such as Williams, believe it is a restriction on practice, to others it is an inherent protection to the vulnerable that no matter how unpopular they are, or how abhorrent an allegation against them is, they can ensure that they are provided with access to the law.

The barrister's client

In the example used immediately above, let us assume that the Crown Prosecution Service (CPS) did not brief Miss Holloway first, the solicitors for Mr Hoskins offered the brief to Miss Holloway first and this was accepted. Who is the client of the barrister? It may be thought that given Mr Hoskins is the person who has been charged with the crime and who will ultimately appear in court it will be him but this would be wrong. In fact the client of the barrister is the solicitor, and the relationship that exists in respect of this case is between solicitor and barrister not between Mr Hoskins and Miss Holloway. The ultimate client, Mr Hoskins, will be referred to as the 'lay client'.

This 'third party' approach can cause difficulty in terms of payment. Historically a barrister was not able to sue a solicitor for fees because it was considered that the relationship between solicitor and barrister was not a contractual one (see, for example, *Kennedy v Broun* (1863) 143 ER 268) and this led to a position whereby barristers incurred a significant amount of 'aged debt', ie debt where a solicitor refused to pay for the barrister's service or held on to the money for a longer period of time (thus recouping the interest). There were undoubtedly tensions that existed between the professions on the subject of late or delayed paying (see Hailsham (1990) 440–441), with solicitors frequently (and perhaps from their point of view somewhat understandably) using a finite amount of money to pay their expenses first and then paying the remainder to the barrister even if this was less than the agreed fee. The Law Society has always maintained that the proportion of late or non-payment was small whereas barristers disagreed and pointed out that it was difficult to establish a precise figure since barristers were unlikely to complain as this could lead to firms no longer instructing them. The historical position was removed by s 61 *Courts and Legal Services Act 1990* (CLSA 1990) which stated a barrister and solicitor could enter a contractual relationship, but left it for the Bar Council to decide when this occurred. The status quo remained for many years but in 2004 the Bar Council changed its position from presuming that the relationship between solicitor and barrister was *not* contractual to presuming it *was* contractual and accordingly the position is now that a barrister can sue a solicitor for reduced or non-payment of fees.

The other historical feature of the third-party rule was that a lay client could *only* access the services of a barrister via a solicitor, and indeed at one point a barrister was never allowed to meet with the lay client without the solicitor being present. Some argued that this was a costly rule that meant that a person would always have to pay for two lawyers where one would suffice and eventually the rules were relaxed in 2004, with the latest version being known as *The Public Access Scheme Application*. Barristers who wish to have direct access to the public must attend a one-day training course. The status of the client in direct access work differs and, as with solicitors, fees can be reclaimed by litigation.

8.2.3.2 Employed practice

Whilst the majority of barristers will remain in independent practice a significant number of barristers are now employed. The numbers have increased in recent years because of a change as to the rights of audience such barristers have. Traditionally only barristers in independent practice had unlimited rights of audience and a barrister who became employed lost their rights of audience in the higher courts and were restricted to those courts that solicitors could appear in. Until comparatively recently this caused problems for agencies such as the CPS where the Director of Public Prosecutions (DPP), usually a senior barrister, would lose his rights of audience upon taking up his employment. It also meant that those agencies who did seek barristers, eg CPS, Government

Legal Service, could not attract the best barristers because the loss of the rights of audience meant their opportunities were somewhat reduced.

The CLSA 1990 reforms, together with the Bar Council relaxing its Code of Conduct does, however, now mean that the opportunities for barristers in employed practice are quite good. Access to the higher courts is now possible and this means that some companies are creating in-house legal services sections that include barristers. The employed Bar can be quite attractive to barristers, especially newly qualified barristers, because there is not the problems that arise out of self-employment in that an employed barrister will get paid leave, capped working hours, and a regular salary.

Historically the limitations and prohibitions of practising barristers forming partnerships applied to the employed Bar too, and thus barristers working in-house could not own shares in the practice (effectively barring them from being a partner). The *Legal Services Act 2007* (LSA 2007) reforms have relaxed this and as from 2010 it is possible for barristers to own shares in *Legal Disciplinary Practices*, something discussed below.

8.3 Solicitors

The second principal branch of the legal profession is solicitors who are regulated by the *Law Society for England and Wales*, often referred to as the *Law Society*.

Solicitors are, compared to barristers, relatively modern creatures. Until the mid-nineteenth century, non-barristers were split into different types of lawyers, including attorneys, proctors, and solicitors, the latter being principally Chancery specialists. In 1831 an amalgamating body was granted its Royal Charter under the name of the *Society of Attorneys, Solicitors, Proctors and others not being Barristers, practising in the Courts of Law and Equity of the United Kingdom* which hardly trips off the tongue! In 1903 the name was (thankfully) changed to the *Law Society* and at around that time the term 'solicitor' replaced the other forms of address as the accepted title for this branch of the profession.

The Law Society is governed by an elected president, vice-president, and Council. The day-to-day operation of the Law Society is the responsibility of the chief executive who is a non-legally qualified person who is responsible for the general operations of the organization. The chief executive is, as one might expect, assisted by a number of non-legally qualified staff who undertake administrative responsibility for the work of the society.

When contrasting solicitors and the Bar people are often tempted to make the analogy that solicitors are the equivalent of GPs, with barristers being akin to consultants. The nature of this analogy is supposed to demonstrate that barristers are more likely to specialize than solicitors but it contains two critical flaws. The first is that consultants tend to be considered a promoted post whereas a would-be lawyer makes the decision as to which branch before commencing training. The second flaw is that it is not actually true to suggest that solicitors do not specialize. Whilst those within a small high-street firm may undertake a variety of work there is still the ability to undertake a degree of specialism with one solicitor perhaps focusing on crime and another on family etc. Within large firms there is arguably even more scope to specialize with many firms being dedicated to one form of work, most usually company or commercial law, and specialisms existing within that field. More than this, however, solicitors are entitled to be employed by other firms and most medium-sized companies will have a legal department, and this allows specialisms through, for example, employment law. Solicitors are also employed by the Crown and this allows for specialist areas to be created; can it be said that a solicitor employed by the CPS is any less specialist in crime than a barrister in a set of chambers dedicated to criminal work?

8.3.1 Education and training

There are now four stages to qualifying as a solicitor:

- academic stage
- vocational stage
- training contract
- Professional Skills Course.

There is also an expectation to undertake Continuing Professional Development (CPD); indeed the Law Society introduced compulsory CPD attendance before the Bar Council did. The academic stage is exactly the same as for those wishing to join the Bar, the decision being made at the end of the degree, CPE, or GDL.

8.3.1.1 Vocational training

Everyone who wishes to qualify as a solicitor, including those who wish to qualify via the ILEX route (see 8.7.1), must currently undertake a vocational training course known as the Legal Practice Course (LPC). There has, for some time, been a debate as to what the status of the LPC is, with many believing that it is at undergraduate rather than postgraduate level but this is somewhat irrelevant and, indeed, the Law Society sets out minimum standards and many universities will now offer a postgraduate qualification to those students who successfully complete the course.

Like the Bar, the Law Society used to have its own training provider, the *College of Law*, but this was granted its independence significantly before the Inns of Court School of Law. The Law Society also opened up the provision of LPC courses significantly earlier than the Bar and there are currently twenty-seven institutions at which the LPC can be studied, and given that that the *College of Law* and *BPP* have a number of sites, this leads to over thirty locations where the course can be completed.

The modern LPC has many similarities to the BPTC in that there are a lot of practical exercises involved in the scheme and whilst there is a core of subjects that must be studied by all students, including conveyancing, accountancy, etc there is also the opportunity to study a series of electives, helping to demonstrate to potential employees the type of work the applicant is interested in. A considerable period of time is spent on preparing the student for the type of work and forms that they are likely to encounter in their early years of practice and thus the preparation of court forms and instructions to counsel follow, together with advocacy skills since it is a myth to say that solicitors do not perform advocacy—many do although it tends to be restricted to the more junior courts (albeit those where the bulk of the work is heard, eg magistrates' courts).

As with the BPTC, some institutions have established legal clinics where students can begin to work directly with the public during their vocational training stage. Gaining such experience at an early stage can be a valuable way of learning the skills necessary to complete the LPC together with the opportunity to meet relevant people who could assist in identifying a training contract.

8.3.1.2 Training contract

The third stage of qualification is the training contract and, like with the vocational stage, unless someone is qualifying via the ILEX route then the training contract must be completed. The training contract is similar to the pupillage stage for barristers in that it is 'hands-on' and is the first opportunity where pure practitioners are involved in the training rather than those who are also academics. The training contract lasts two years and could involve working in more than one body as some firms do form loose partnerships that give a wider experience to the trainees. It is also worth noting that whilst competition for training contracts is intense, especially in the larger city firms, it is not quite as competitive as that for pupillage.

Unlike the position that currently exists for barristers, a person is not entitled to call themselves a 'solicitor' until they have signed the Roll of Solicitors and this will only take place where all the requisite stages have been completed. A person undertaking a training contract will be referred to as a 'trainee solicitor' but they must not hold themselves out as a full solicitor.

The training contract must involve the trainee experiencing at least three types of law (eg personal injury, family law, crime, etc) although some firms will provide a broader base and others will provide different experiences between a particular broad specialism (eg litigation, company formations, etc). The trainee must be quite closely supervised and unlike at the Bar where there is normally a single person for each part of the pupillage (eg first six months, second six months) a trainee solicitor may, and probably will, be under the supervision of a team.

Trainee solicitors are paid throughout their training contract and this has been the norm for many years, certainly long before the Bar decided that it was necessary. The minimum starting salary of a trainee solicitor is set by the Law Society and is currently set at £18,590 pa for those employed within Greater London and £16,650 pa for those outside London. However, it appears that the *Solicitors Regulation Authority* will allow the minimum salary to be waived by a trainee, which seems an unusual stance since it means the minimum is not actually a minimum and some trainees have had to apply for waiver in order to get a training contract. That said, many firms will provide a higher training salary, particularly the larger firms. As trainee solicitors are employed (unlike barristers) they are also entitled to paid holidays. The minimum is twenty days per year (the statutory minimum) and the Law Society set the maximum at twenty-five days per year during the training period.

Throughout the training contract a trainee solicitor will be completing a portfolio-type document that demonstrates the skills and experiences of their practice. Those responsible for supervising the trainee solicitors must ensure that this is kept up to date and is an accurate record of what happens.

8.3.1.3 Professional Skills Course

The final, and most recently introduced, part of the training to become qualified as a solicitor is completing the Professional Skills Course. This course must be completed by all would-be solicitors regardless of what route they take to qualification. The course is the equivalent of twelve full-time days, although it can be done either in a block or part-time, and takes place at the same time as the training contract and it is the employer, not the trainee, who pays for the costs of the course. There are three core modules on the course:

- advocacy and communication skills
- financial and business skills
- client care and professional standards.

Other modules designed to examine specific areas of law or practice can also be undertaken. The course is designed to allow a trainee solicitor to receive further vocational training (akin to the LPC) whilst at the same time being linked to the practice that they are experiencing through the training contract.

8.3.1.4 Admission to the Rolls

A person formally becomes a solicitor when they are admitted to the Rolls. A practising certificate must be obtained from the Law Society, for which an administration charge (currently £100) is made. The admission can take place either in the person's absence or at a ceremony that takes place twice a month. This used to be before the Master of the Rolls, who was responsible for admission to the Rolls, but the *Solicitors Regulation Authority* has now assumed this responsibility.

8.3.2 Practice

Some aspects of the solicitors' practice have already been discussed and it has been noted that they have a more flexible practice than barristers, there being those who practise in a law firm and those who are employed in a non-law firm to undertake legal services. Like at the Bar, it is not possible for a newly qualified solicitor to set up immediately as a sole practitioner; this is a protection on the basis that newly qualified solicitors still require an element of training and development. It would be naive to suggest that a person at the end of their training contract is fully able to undertake all aspects of legal work.

Before starting a practice (be that as a sole practitioner or in a partnership) there must be at least one person who is entitled to supervise others, and the Law Society define this as being someone who has held a practising certificate for at least three of the last ten years, and who has completed management CPD.

Promotion for a solicitor can arise in a number of ways. Because solicitors have always been able to form partnerships (and indeed frequently do so) the promotion path normally involves someone progressing to a partnership, even though in major firms the partnership may still involve a salary rather than equity share.

8.3.2.1 Rights of audience

When a solicitor first qualifies he has very limited rights of audience, generally restricted to the junior courts and tribunals. A solicitor's rights of audience encompass all matters in the magistrates' court and county court. Within the Crown Court a solicitor may only appear for preliminary matters following a transfer for trial (see 10.7 below) or for appeals against the decisions of magistrates where their firm was involved at first instance. In the High Court a solicitor has no automatic rights of audience in open court but can be heard in chambers although this would normally be for preliminary matters.

A solicitor can, however, gain higher rights of audience by taking additional training.

8.3.2.2 Solicitor–advocates

Historically the Bar had exclusive rights to the higher courts (defined as the Crown Court, High Court (in open session), the Divisional Courts, Court of Appeal, and House of Lords) but in recent times this caused considerable disquiet from solicitors and certain governmental bodies (eg Office of Fair Trading). It was argued that denying higher rights of audience to solicitors raised costs for a litigant because he needed to brief both a solicitor and a barrister even if the matter was relatively simple.

The then government decided in the late 1980s that it was necessary to break the traditional monopolies held by the professions and the CLSA 1990 permitted, for the first time, solicitors to appear in the higher courts. However the statutory authority was only the first step and it was necessary, before any solicitor advocates were created, for the Law Society and senior members of the judiciary to agree on a system of authorizing such advocates. It took until 1994 for the agreement to be reached and the first solicitor–advocates to be appointed.

Qualifying

In order to qualify as a solicitor–advocate a person must have been a solicitor for at least three years and to have actual experience of advocating in the junior courts. This is a particularly important part of the process and initially this had caused difficulty in some areas of law (eg high-money commercial contracts) where a case would never reach the lower courts and so a solicitor had no opportunity to undertake the normal advocacy.

There are three types of licence that can be sought:

- all proceedings (ie a solicitor–advocate so licensed can appear in both the civil and criminal courts)
- civil proceedings (ie a solicitor–advocate would be able to appear in the higher courts for civil matters but not the Crown Court)
- criminal proceedings (ie a solicitor–advocate could appear in the Crown Court and higher courts for criminal matters but not for civil matters with the exception of the Crown Court where all business is licensed).

It may seem strange to have different types of licence but it makes sense given the type of practice that solicitors may have. A solicitor who is employed by the CPS will not appear in civil matters so why should they need to learn the civil litigation rules etc? Similarly a solicitor who works for a commercial law firm will never undertake criminal work so why should they learn the specific rules of evidence and court rules governing criminal trials? The combined licence does, however, at least mean that someone in a general firm can gain rights of audience for all of their work.

From November 2005 a solicitor who wishes to gain higher rights of audience must undertake a development route which requires CPD work, formal assessments on the procedure, ethics, and evidential rules relating to the relevant litigation. A portfolio is also kept and the would-be advocate is nominated a mentor who will assist in the process.

Court work and dress

Once the higher rights of audience have been granted a solicitor–advocate is entitled to serve in all higher courts relevant to their licence, including the House of Lords. A solicitor–advocate is entitled to appear in all matters that counsel can and may appear as though counsel. A solicitor–advocate remains subject to the Law Society's regulations, including further regulations on the conduct of litigation, and does not become subject to the Bar Council's regulations.

Traditionally a solicitor–advocate was not able to wear the wig and simply wore the gown and bands but eventually the judiciary brought about equality and in *Practice Direction (Court Dress)(No 4)* [2008] 1 WLR 357 it was stated that solicitor–advocates may (which implies that, unlike counsel they do not have to) wear wigs.

8.4 Queen's Counsel

The highest branch of advocates in England and Wales are called Queen's Counsel (QC).[5] Traditionally this was restricted solely to barristers but in 1996 the system was changed and solicitors were entitled to become QCs, although before 2006 only twelve solicitors had ever been given this distinction, and the vast majority of applicants continue to be barristers. Indeed in the 2009/10 competition only ten solicitors applied to become QCs and only one of these was successful.[6] The process of becoming a QC is known as 'taking silk', the name coming from the fact that the court dress of a QC is a silk rather than stuff robe, worn over a court coat (a long, formal frock coat that is worn instead of a suit jacket). The robe and process has also led to QCs being called 'silks'.

8.4.1 Appointment

The appointment process for QCs has proven to be very controversial and it was suspended from 2003 till 2005 whilst a new process was established. Before the new system, the Lord Chancellor (as chief legal advisor and representative of the Queen) had absolute control over who was allowed to take silk and this undoubtedly led to a number of silks being created for political reasons (see Hailsham (1990) 386). A junior barrister would apply to the Lord Chancellor for silk and would nominate two friendly judges for their application and the Lord Chancellor would then confidentially ask senior judges and barristers what they thought of the candidate (this being later extended to include major law firms). The Lord Chancellor could also take into account any other issues he believed were relevant (see, for example, the description of the process put forward by Lane (1985) 100–101) and thus the process was far from transparent. Unsurprisingly, in 2002 Sir Colin Campbell the Commissioner for Judicial Appointments suggested that the system was deficient and this led to the suspension of the scheme.

The new scheme begins with an application form which includes the provision of a 'self-assessment' scheme where a person is asked to evaluate themselves against a series of competencies. An application can be made by either a barrister or a solicitor–advocate and the same system applies to both. The application forms are then sifted and those who pass the sift stage are sent to the senior judiciary to assess whether there are any issues of integrity. On the application form the candidate must list all those

5. When the Sovereign is a King then an order of the Privy Council translates all QCs into KC's (King's Counsel).
6. *Report of the Queen's Counsel Selection Panel for England and Wales, 2009–10 Competition Awards.*

judges who he has appeared before in a matter of substance (ie a trial rather than pre-liminary matter) in the past two years. The candidate identifies one judge from that list who would provide a reference and the selection committee chooses three others from the list provided. All four judges are approached to provide a commentary on the competence of the applicant. In addition to this, six practitioners (normally already QCs) must be listed and four of these will be approached by the panel for a reference. Those who are considered suitable after this stage will be interviewed by a panel nine strong. The panel will be chaired by a distinguished lay (ie non-lawyer) person; the remaining eight will consist of:

- three lay members
- one senior retired judge
- two senior barristers
- two senior solicitors.

The names of those candidates who are selected by the panel are then passed to the Lord Chancellor and then to the Queen where the letters patent appointing the person a QC will be made. Traditionally new QCs were announced on Maundy Thursday but this practice appears to have (regrettably) failed to survive the new arrangements with the first silks appointed under the new scheme being appointed in July 2006 and the 2010 competition being announced in February.

It has to be accepted that this new process bears little resemblance to the old system and is certainly more transparent. Indeed it could actually be argued that it is too transparent and that the Bar Council and Law Society may have created a beast that is too burdensome. In 2003, the final year operated under the old scheme, 394 applicants applied for silk (see *Commissioners for Judicial Appointments Audit Report 2003*) and whilst there was a modest fall in 2010 to 275 applications this continues to be a significant number. Even if only half of these applicants passed the sift stage then this means that there would be over 1,000 individual references sought, an administrative nightmare and a serious imposition on judicial time (with four judicial references being required for each applicant). The Judicial Appointments Commissioners were already concerned at the bureaucracy involved in the old system and whether this could lead to references being missed or mislaid (ibid, annex c, para 3.7) and this new scheme does not appear to resolve these issues. The cost of the process must also be of concern. Previously the Department for Constitutional Affairs (DCA) administered the process but it has now been accepted that this is wrong and it is now administered by an independent body created by the professions. The suggestion was that it should be self-funding yet the appointment commissioners have previously argued that the scheme is not sustainable (ibid, paras 3.2–3.4). Indeed they argued that not accounting for consultees' time, the cost per applicant was £1,150 and yet now a panel interview will be undertaken. The panel members are paid and this inevitably increases the costs. Self-funding has been introduced and for the 2010–2011 application period, the application fee was £2,200 (excluding VAT) with an additional fee of £3,500 being payable for successful applicants. In 2010 the number of applicants was 275 (a smaller number than, for example, the first competition in 2007 where 333 applications were made) with 129 (47 per cent) of applications being successful. It would seem that notwithstanding the cost of a (successful) application being £6,000 practitioners still wish to be elevated to the dignity of QC.

8.4.2 Practice

A person who is appointed QC will see a dramatic shift in their practice with the real possibility that their fees will rise because silks are paid higher than juniors. However, it is a gamble because a silk should only undertake work that is suitable for them and thus it is possible that someone may have a thriving junior practice but a less stable practice as a silk actually earning less money (see the cautions of Elwyn-Jones (1983) on this matter (p 153)).

A silk is sometimes also known as a 'leader' because in many cases the QC will appear with other counsel to conduct the litigation, and the QC, as the senior advocate, would normally lead this team (although increasingly, particularly in legally-aided criminal appellate work, a QC may appear alone). Unlike in America where huge teams of lawyers are engaged, it is more normal in England and Wales for a team to involve two, and sometimes three, advocates led by one silk. The junior barristers on the team will normally have been involved in the case before the silk is appointed and will conduct much of the preliminary work. However the junior barristers will also normally be involved in the litigation, not only in reading the papers and deciding on tactics but also normally conducting the examination of more junior witnesses.

When a QC appears in court, he should wear a silk robe over a court jacket (a long formal buttoned jacket that is worn instead of a suit jacket) and a wig. A solicitor who is appointed QC was entitled to wear a wig even before the changes made to the court working dress for solicitor–advocates. Upon being appointed a silk, the QC will purchase a full-bottomed wig (similar to the ones judges possess) but these are never worn in court.

8.5 Fusion

The preceding sections of this chapter should have demonstrated that traditionally the two sides of the profession (barristers and solicitors) were quite separate and that each performed a specific task. The reforms of the CLSA 1990, and subsequent statutes, have meant that the distinction between the branches is no longer quite the same as it once was. England and Wales is one of three jurisdictions to retain a two-branch profession, and in Scotland it is more usual for a person to become a solicitor first before applying to join the *Faculty of Advocates* (as the Scottish Bar is known) although this is no longer essential and it is theoretically possible to qualify direct from university. The system in Ireland is roughly the same as in England and Wales but with barristers having slightly more freedom. In most other jurisdictions, including in common-law jurisdictions[7] there is no formal distinction between advocates and non-advocates and increasingly the question has been asked whether the professions in England and Wales should fuse?

8.5.1 Advantages of fusion

There are undoubtedly some advantages to a fused profession, both from the individual lawyer's point of view and the general public. The usual arguments advanced include:

- common training programme

---

7. This is the expression normally given to those countries whose legal system is historically based on UK principles. It generally includes former and current colonial or Commonwealth countries.

- costs
- efficiency.

8.5.1.1 Common training

Although the academic stage for both professions is now the same, the vocational and professional training requirements do differ in both content and time. This, in effect, means that someone who wishes to become either a solicitor or barrister must decide early in their career which path to follow. The decision is not irrevocable as it is possible to transfer between the professions but recognizing that one has proceeded down the wrong track could lead to disenchantment and, at the very least, a considerable amount of wasted time. One of the more common forms of fusion that is discussed is that everyone would start as a solicitor and only the best would be given advocacy rights in the higher courts after career development. This would ensure that everyone had the same starting point but it would, however, mean that people who were interested in advocacy might have to wait several years before demonstrating their aptitude. An advantage of fusion to the would-be lawyer is that it is likely to ensure that everyone would have employment rights and a minimum level of salary.

8.5.1.2 Costs

Except for those few situations when either a solicitor–advocate is engaged or where a person contacts a barrister direct, a person wishing to litigate in the higher courts will often have to engage both a solicitor and barrister and, therefore, there is a suggestion that costs would be reduced as only one lawyer would be required rather than two.

However whilst the argument probably has an element of truth to it, the position is not necessarily as simple as many may think. Whilst there will be a degree of overlap between the work of the solicitor and barrister much of the work is separate and thus even if a single lawyer is engaged then it is likely that much of the work will still be done and payment required for it. It also does not naturally follow that only a single lawyer will work on the case and many large firms currently have litigation departments where a case will be passed and the lawyer working in the litigation department may have a higher rate than the other. Finally, in respect of some simple work it is quite possible that costs could rise. In preparatory or simple matters (eg plea and directions hearings, guilty pleas, etc) an advocate may only be required for an hour, or even less. A barrister will undertake the work for a set fee and hope that he can pick up more than one on a day. A solicitor on the other hand will probably only have the one case and will charge by the hour. If, therefore, the case is listed first this may mean that the costs are less but if the solicitor has to wait at court all day until his case is heard the client will undoubtedly be charged not only for the time when the solicitor was actually advocating but also the time spent waiting, this would be quite costly.

8.5.1.3 Efficiency

Closely related to the issue of costs is efficiency. Where more than one lawyer is involved in a case there is likely to be scope for inefficiencies to be created, especially where they are in different locations. A solicitor and a barrister may have very different diary commitments and thus finding a time when both are available for consultations etc could take longer than for a single practitioner. However this difficulty is eased by the fact that barristers are now able to see lay clients with a representative from the solicitor's firm rather than the solicitor themselves, or indeed in certain circumstances to see the lay client alone. Where paper and documentation is being sent between individuals there is also the scope for it to be lost etc. Against this argument, however, there is the rather obvious argument that large companies are quite inefficient themselves and having a single firm acting is no guarantee that paperwork will not go missing etc.

8.5.2 Disadvantages of fusion

Not everyone is in favour of fusion and there are a number of reasons why fusion should not occur, the most notable being:

- loss of specialist expertise
- reduction in the standard of advocacy
- loss of the 'cab rank rule'
- loss of professional detachment.

8.5.2.1 Expertise/advocacy

The most common argument against the fusion of the professions is the belief that it could lead to a loss of specialist expertise, particularly the art of advocacy. It has been noted already that a barrister is more likely to specialize in a particular area of the law and it may be thought that fusing the professions may lead to a loss of such expertise. To a degree it could be argued that this would not happen because if the demand for work exists then the same number of experts are going to be required but if, as would seem likely, most would be employed by firms there is likely to be pressure on people to have a wider form of expertise and instead of being briefed nationally it is quite possible that people would try to find more local contacts, perhaps localizing expertise.

The other argument is that the expertise of the art of advocacy itself could be damaged. Certainly in 1977 the *Royal Commission on Legal Services* argued that fusion could lead to a reduction in the standard of advocacy. It could be argued that, following the right of solicitors to gain higher rights of audience, and indeed the ability of solicitor–advocates to take silk, that this is no longer strictly true. However, there are a relatively small number of solicitor–advocates and compared to the Bar they arguably undertake less advocacy work than some barristers, especially in respect of common-law and criminal litigation. Firms may create specialist advocacy departments whose members concentrate on advocacy but it is also quite likely that the fused lawyer would be required to do a lot of other work and thus spend more time out of court than they currently do perhaps leading to a reduction in their skills.

8.5.2.2 Cab rank rule

The cab rank rule has been set out above (see 8.2.3.1) and it is considered to be an important rule in the provision of legal services. Alongside ensuring that a person can be provided with legal services regardless of their character or the allegations made against them (which is not necessarily a difficulty since although general solicitors are not bound by the rule it is difficult to identify a person who has been denied access to legal advice because members of that profession, quite rightly, note that even those who society may find repugnant are able to access impartial legal advice) the rule is supposed also to protect someone from being held to ransom in terms of fees. The clerk and those instructing the barrister will agree an appropriate fee and then that case must be dealt with by the barrister and not returned if a more lucrative case arises later.

The cab rank rule is often cited as an argument against fusion, in part because the solicitors' code of practice does not include an ethic for its solicitors requiring them to uphold the principle and so it is arguably for the individual conscience of a solicitor whether to accept instructions. When the LSA 2007 reforms (see 8.5.3 below) are introduced it would appear likely that the cab rank rule will be relaxed for those who operate within a Legal Disciplinary Practice (LDP), in part because the LDP will now be regulated by the *Solicitors Regulatory Authority* and not the *Bar Standards Board*.

However it is likely that a modified form of the rule will remain in force. Section 17(3)(c) CLSA 1990 requires professional bodies that are to permit the right to advocate in the courts to establish rules guaranteeing a modified version of the cab rank rule (most notably, the right to an advocate regardless of the advocate's personal opinion on the client or the client's business etc). The Law Society has, in its rules governing solicitor–advocates, included a provision satisfying s 17(3)(c) and so there is no reason why a fused profession would not continue to abide by s 17(3)(c) and thus maintain a version of the cab rank rule.

8.5.2.3 Professional detachment

It is often said that a barrister tends to be more remote than a solicitor when it comes to dealing with the lay client, but many barristers, particularly those with a criminal practice, may contest this especially in relation to the longer trials. It is also somewhat naive to suggest that because solicitors are with the lay client longer than a barrister they will somehow lose the professionalism that is inherent within the legal profession.

Perhaps the more significant issue however is the loss of the 'second opinion' that is currently undertaken. When a solicitor briefs a barrister on a particular case he will inevitably ask counsel's opinion on the matter. It is quite possible that the barrister will identify something that the solicitor has not or disagree with him over the chances of successful litigation. Where the barrister is a specialist advocate this latter possibility becomes slightly more important. If, in a fused profession, a single lawyer was to follow the case from start to finish then it is possible that this would end.

This problem would only exist in the completely fused model whereas others have suggested that an alternative model would be for everyone to enter the profession as a solicitor and for those with an interest in advocacy to become a barrister when their career has progressed. Arguably this could solve many of the difficulties outlined above.

8.5.3 The beginnings of fusion?

The LSA 2007 will, when fully implemented, transform the provision of legal services. Whilst lawyers will continue to belong to one of the professions, the rules relating to who may be part of a legal firm or, indeed, whether non-legal firms can offer legal services will be transformed. The LSA 2007 promises to radicalize the provision of legal services and it could mark the beginnings of fusion.

The LSA 2007 defines what are 'reserved legal activities' and 'legal activities' and these are crucial to its later changes. A reserved legal activity is:

(a) the exercise of a right of audience

(b) the conduct of litigation

(c) reserved instrument activities

(d) probate activities

(e) notarial activities

(f) the administration of oaths (s 12(1) LSA 2007).

These are, in essence, the type of activities that are currently reserved to the current legal professions. A 'legal activity' is defined as:

(a) a reserved legal activity, and

(b) anything which constitutes one or both of the following:

> (i) the provision of legal advice or assistance in connection with the application of the law or the resolution of legal disputes,

> (ii) the provision of representation in connection with any matter concerning the application of law or the resolution of legal disputes. (s 12(3))

This is obviously much wider and must, for example, include the provision of certain advice by the Citizens Advice Bureau and a considerable amount of the advice and representation that takes place in tribunals (see Chapter 15). A person may only carry out a reserved legal activity if he is authorized to do so (s 13 LSA 2007) and it is an offence to do so without authority (s 14 LSA 2007: the offence is punishable by a maximum sentence of two years' imprisonment) or to pretend to be so authorized (s 17).

This is largely uncontroversial and, in essence, is simply the codification and clarification of existing rules. However, the LSA 2007 goes much further by altering the very structure of the legal profession. The two issues of interest are Legal Disciplinary Practices and Alternative Business Structures.

8.5.3.1 Legal Disciplinary Practices

The LSA 2007 produced an 'interim' step which is that known as the Legal Disciplinary Practice (LDP) which allows lawyers and, to a limited extent, non-legally qualified persons to come together as equals. It will be remembered from the discussion above that, traditionally, independent barristers could not enter into a partnership and only solicitors could be equity partners in their firms. The LDP shreds these rules by allowing lawyers of all descriptions to act as equity partners and permitting non-legally qualified persons to become managers of a business.

The LSA 2007 introduces this through a 'backdoor' mechanism in that an LDP does not feature in the main body of the Act but rather it is permitted through amendments to other legislation, most notably the *Solicitors Act 1974* and *Administration of Justice Act 1985* to permit (principally) the *Solicitors Regulatory Authority* (SRA: see 8.8.1.2 below) to recognize LDPs and permit alternative business models.

An LDP has its statutory foundations in s 9A *Administration of Justice Act 1985* which does not, interestingly, refer to an LDP but rather to a 'legal services' body. According to the Act a legal services body is a body corporate or unincorporated that meets the 'management and control condition' and the 'relevant lawyer condition' (s 9A(1) AJA 1985).

The management and control condition requires:

(a) at least 75 per cent of the body's managers to be legally qualified;

(b) the proportion of shares in the body held by persons who are legally qualified to be at least 75 per cent;

(c) legally qualified persons must have 75 per cent of the voting rights of the body;

(d) all the persons with an interest in the body who are not legally qualified are managers of the body; and

(e) all the managers of the body who are not legally qualified are individuals approved by the SRA as suitable. (s 9A(2) AJA 1985).

The requirement is therefore in essence that those who are legally qualified must account for 75 per cent of those who exercise management of the company (in essence meaning those who hold equity in the firm). At least one of the managers must be a solicitor or a registered European lawyer (s 9A(4) AJA 1985) but the remaining lawyers can be more diverse and can include solicitors, barristers, legal executives, licensed conveyancers, patent clerks, etc. In other words a legal firm can now involve solicitors, legal executives, and barristers in its management (including equity partnership).

This is a major change and some believe that it could radically alter the way that, for example, solicitors interact with legal executives and barristers. It has been noted already that increasingly barristers are being employed 'in house' as advocates. The LDP, when implemented, will allow barristers to be not only employed but co-owners of the firm. It is believed that this could lead to some of the larger firms of solicitors perhaps taking on significant number of barristers as 'partners' so as to ensure that they can offer a 'one-stop shop'.

The fact that only 75 per cent of managers must be legally qualified does allow for other professions, for example, accountants, human-resource managers, etc to be managers of a company which could be attractive to niche firms. For example, a company that specializes in fraud may well wish to set up a firm that involves accountants, auditors, solicitors, and barristers to produce a 'one-stop shop'. The requirement for 75 per cent of managers to be legally qualified answers the criticisms of some who were concerned that commercial pressures may conflict with a lawyer's duty to the court (see, for example, McVea (2004) 574). However, it should be noted that an LDP must remain a legal firm, ie one that primarily offers legal services, and therefore the other professionals who may join them (eg human resources, accountants, etc) are there to assist in the provision of legal work by, for example, bringing their expertise in relation to dispute resolution.

The uptake on LDPs was relatively modest (Robins (2009)) with two of the original three LDPs simply allowing for a non-lawyer to become an equity and managing partner, and the third allowing a legal executive to hold an equity stake in the firm. That said, it is likely that over the coming years the numbers of LDPs will increase, particularly those that involve members of the Bar forming partnerships with solicitors.

8.5.3.2 Alternative Business Structures: 'Tesco Law'

When fully implemented, Part 5 of the LSA 2007 will permit the so-called 'Tesco Law'. The term is used to describe the fact that Tesco, and other major-brand supermarkets, have diversified in recent years to provide lots of services other than the sale of goods. The most notable examples are banking and insurance services which most major supermarket chains now provide. 'Tesco Law' is designed to explain the fact that the alternative business models put forward by the LSA 2007 will allow, for example, supermarkets to operate legal services.

At the time of writing it is expected that Part 5 will not come into existence until towards the end of 2011, and this means that much of the detail on how this will be implemented is now yet known. The delay is to allow the Legal Services Board (LSB) time to understand how Alternative Business Structures (ABS) are to be regulated.

ABSs will be remarkably different to LDPs in that whilst an LDP, as noted above, has limitations as to who may own and manage the firm (75 per cent must be lawyers) and the work they can do (they must be primarily a legal firm), ABSs will not be under any such restrictions. This will mean, for example, that non-lawyers will be able to own and manage firms that undertake reserved legal activities and ABSs will be able to offer alternative work, for example, financial advice. The reserved legal activity will continue to be undertaken by an appropriate legally qualified person but the firm can be owned and managed by non-lawyers. How does this differ from 'in-house lawyers'? The key to an in-house lawyer is that he is only offering legal advice to his employers: an ABS will be able to offer legal services to the public. Of course part of the tension that exists in respect of ABS is over concerns that a commercial enterprise would place pressure on lawyers to cut corners in order to save money, or that managers will not understand the ethical requirements of lawyers. The regulation of ABS will therefore be important and it is believed that such regulation will expressly include references to the fact that the duty of a company to its shareholders are subordinate to the duty to comply with the regulatory environment (Heslett (2010)).

A lot of attention in relation to ABS has focused on the large-scale firms (Tesco et al) but it could, of course, be a smaller scale. For example, a firm of accountants and lawyers could combine to provide a niche firm. Under existing laws this is not possible because the non-lawyers could not be equity owners but an ABS will permit this. However the additional regulatory burden may mean that many firms choose not to do this (Mayson (2007)) because the benefits are perceived to be outweighed by the disadvantages of excessive regulation. What of larger companies? They are likely to have bigger pockets. Is it likely that supermarkets and others would be interested in offering legal services? It would seem that the answer is 'yes'. The offering of insurance policies, for example, demonstrate how supermarkets and other consumer services are trying to offer 'services' to their customers, those services being considered to be part of their wider 'lifestyle' branding.

The likelihood of expansion in this area is perhaps demonstrated by the fact that some large brands are already purporting to offer legal services, albeit through subcontracting to legal firms. Perhaps the classic example of this is 'Halifax Legal Solutions' which is a subscription system for customers of Halifax Bank of Scotland. Halifax Legal Solutions provides a subscription-based service which allows subscribers to have free conveyancing and will-writing services together with a 24/7 hour legal helpline. Although the branding is Halifax, the service is actually operated by a legal firm on behalf of Halifax. However both companies obviously believe that there is an advantage to brand-recognition and the advent of 'Tesco Law' is likely to build on this by allowing major brands to run the company rather than having to subcontract them.

❓ QUESTION FOR REFLECTION

Think about ABSs. Whilst some (for example the Consumer Association, 'Which?') believe that the changes are to be welcomed as it will make it clearer who can provide legal services, others believe it is a step too far and that lawyers are officers of the court and should not be interested in just making money (McVie (2004) 567–571). Are there any dangers with ABS? Will lawyers be under pressure to act unethically if they are employed by large commercial organizations?

🎧 LISTEN TO THE PODCAST

For guidance on how to answer this question and a discussion of the main issues, listen to the author's podcast on the Online Resource Centre:
www.oxfordtextbooks.co.uk/orc/gillespie_els3e/

8.6 Diversity in the professions

The legal profession is considered to be quite a conservative profession and suffers from a stereotypical view of its members. Many believe that its members are white, middle-class, Oxbridge-educated persons (normally male) and that success within the profession is based on who one knows rather than aptitude. This would be a largely inaccurate reflection but, sadly, one with a degree of truth within it.

In terms of gender, changes are occurring. Most law schools are beginning to note that there are more female law students than males (Rackley (2002) 605). Progress is being made within the professions too, with the pace increasing. In 1992 26.3 per cent of solicitors were female and by 2003 this had risen to 38.6 per cent (Rose (2003) 20) and by 2009 (the latest year for which statistics are available) this had risen to 45.2 per cent. The position at the Bar is no better although the Bar Council is actively seeking women to gain access to all positions and women have previously been chair of the Bar Council.[8] The current position (2009) is that women account for 31.5 per cent of practising barristers in independent practice and 44.5 per cent of the employed Bar. The difference in figures is perhaps understandable when it is remembered that those in independent practice are, in essence, self-employed and thus it may be less attractive for a woman who wishes to start a family since there is no maternity leave or pay.

There is some concern that the statistics presented above obscure a glass ceiling, with one commentator noting that the vast majority of partners continue to be men, including those who are recently appointed (Abel (2003) 134). Similarly, another commentator has suggested that there has been 'institutional discrimination' at the Bar (McGlynn (1999a) 89). Certainly this would seem to be supported by the applications for QC. In the 2009/10 competition only 46 (17 per cent) of applications were by women, although this was an increase from the 2008/09 competition where only 29 (12 per cent) of applications were made by women.

What these statistics do mask is the question of whether women are to be found in higher numbers outside of private practice, for example in public-sector employment, where employment conditions are normally better in terms of maternity leave, career breaks, etc. This is potentially a factor with many private practice firms not even allowing part-time work (Abel (2003) 129).

---

8. The first being Heather (now Lady Justice) Hallett QC.

Another failure of the statistics is that they do not appear to focus particularly well on the social backgrounds of lawyers (as distinct to judges) although a considerable amount of work has been undertaken at the academic stage which appears to demonstrate that those from the 'new' university sector,[9] whose student members tend to be from more diverse socio-economic backgrounds than the 'traditional' universities, are gaining employment (see Cuthbert (2003) although questions have been raised as to whether this is necessarily correct in terms of the Bar (Mason (2004) 1602)) but more has to be done to examine whether they are managing to progress to all levels. However the high costs of training to be a lawyer must be considered a barrier to access and it has been questioned how realistic it is to suggest that vocational training is anything other than the preserve of the middle classes (Abel (2003) 121).

The position as to the representation of the ethnic minorities is slightly less optimistic. It is possible to identify some progress, as in 1992 only 2 per cent of solicitors were from the ethnic minorities whereas by 2002 this had risen to 8.4 per cent but they appear to be in the more junior positions within the profession or are sole practitioners (Rose (2003)). As of 2009 (the latest figures) the proportion had risen to 9.8 per cent of solicitors in private practice and 10.6 per cent of all solicitors. Accordingly the rate of increase has certainly slowed. David Lammy MP, a then junior minister in the Department for Constitutional Affairs and himself a black lawyer, stated that there remained 'glass ceilings, glass corridors, titanium ceilings [and] dead-ends' (Lammy (2004) and see Abel (2003) 136). The position at the Bar is approximately the same with 10.8 per cent of those within independent practice identifying themselves as belonging to an ethnic minority although the position in the employed Bar is slightly better with 15.6 per cent identifying themselves as an ethnic minority. This latter figure is perhaps notable as it appears to replicate the position with women, with minorities believing that employed practice is a safer option as they obviously consider that it is easier to access such positions (perhaps because employment legislation protects against discrimination) than independent practice even though the rewards of the latter are arguably better.

It is suggested that the two principal disadvantages to ethnic minority students are financial and contacts. Finance is always a thorny issue but it is frequently stated that those from the ethnic minorities are frequently less affluent than those from non-ethnic minority backgrounds. Lammy notes that the professions have attempted to use their funds to create scholarships, with the Law Society (then) providing £150,000 but he states:

> I have to say, as a minister, that £150,000 when students have debts of £35,000 to £40,000 is not going to reach the sorts of numbers we need.

Whilst this is undoubtedly correct it does perhaps miss the point that the debts are accrued because of the government's policy of introducing tuition fees for higher education courses and replacing university grants with loans. In the 1960s and 1970s it was possible to get a grant from some local education authorities to study for the equivalent of the LPC or BPTC and yet now just the fees for these courses can be in excess of £10,000. This is undoubtedly causing difficulties in terms of encouraging access to the legal profession. In an age where the average student will be expected to have debts of at least £25,000,[10] a law student, having completed the LPC or BPTC, can expect to

9. That is to say, those institutions that were formerly known as polytechnics and which were given university status in 1992.

10. 'Student debt to reach £25,000 for 2010 intake' BBC News Online, 13 August 2010.

have £20,000–25,000 more debt than this. The common response to this of course is that lawyers can expect high salaries but it has been noted in this chapter already that a barrister will start on a minimum of £10,000 and a solicitor on just over £18,000 whereas the starting salary for a trainee (graduate) manager at McDonalds restaurants is £21,500 plus private healthcare benefits.

The second issue raised by Lammy is contacts. Whilst the era of the 'old boys' club' is probably gone, it is still necessary to maintain contacts in order to progress within the profession and he notes that without the contacts it is difficult to get work experience and then the necessary pupillage or training contracts. The position is, according to Lammy, particularly severe within the major city firms where he alleges black and ethnic minority members are under-represented at management level. The response to this has come from the ethnic minorities themselves through the formation of official associations, most notably the *Black Solicitors' Network*. The position is arguably no better at the Bar where few Masters of the Bench are members of the ethnic minorities and where the criteria for appointment as a Master of the Bench continue to relate to factors that are more likely to favour white, middle-class members than members of the ethnic minorities (see Abel (2003) 129).

8.7 Other legal professions

It was noted above that although it is often considered that the legal profession is divided into two branches; there is an argument that two further branches are developing and these will be discussed briefly.

8.7.1 Legal executives

Legal executives belong to the Institute of Legal Executives (ILEX). Traditionally they were used principally as assistants to solicitors but the CLSA 1990, which reshaped much of the legal profession, provided them with additional opportunities and they can, realistically, now be considered the third branch of the legal profession. There are approximately 22,000 legal executives but more will be in training to become a legal executive. There are a number of different stages to qualifying as a member of ILEX and only when a person has become a Fellow of the Institute can a person truly refer to themselves as a 'legal executive', although before then they can refer to themselves as a member of ILEX.

8.7.1.1 Training

Unlike solicitors and barristers, legal executives need not be graduates when they commence their training and indeed the minimum academic qualifications are merely GCSEs. However more recently, a graduate entry scheme has begun and, as with the other principal branches, where a person is a graduate in law an exemption from the academic stage can be granted. It is fair to say, however, that the vast majority of entrants to ILEX continue to be non-law graduates. An attraction of becoming a legal executive is that, unlike for solicitors and barristers, all the training can take place alongside work. Accordingly instead of accruing debts by attending university, a prospective legal executive will be paid from the moment that he starts with a firm.

The training comprises three elements:

Stage 1: Student. This is the initial training and consists of a series of papers, with an ILEX Professional Diploma in Law being studied which provides general guidance on the law, and the Higher Diploma in Law providing specialist papers for the area of practice a person intends to practice in.

Stage 2: Membership. It normally takes approximately four years to complete stage 1 (possibly longer if the person was not a graduate). At that point they are eligible to become a Member of ILEX.

Stage 3: Fellowship. A person will be upgraded to 'Fellow' after completing at least five years' qualifying employment under the supervision of a solicitor, at least two years of which must have occurred after completing stage 1.

Like members of the other branches of the legal profession, a legal executive is expected to continue to develop his education and training through CPD (Continuing Professional Development) and the minimum requirement is for eight qualifying hours per year, half of which must be in the specialist area that the person is working, and the other half will be in general legal updates.

8.7.1.2 Practice

Whilst both barristers and solicitors will frequently specialize, they need not and a number remain as general practitioners who will undertake a variety of work. Legal executives, on the other hand, will tend to specialize in an area and remain in that area of work. Legal executives will tend to practice only in civil law although there is no reason why they could not, for example, also qualify as accredited police-station representatives but their practice will tend to be civil-orientated. Legal executives will choose their specialism whilst training and in order to get the qualifying employment experience required to become a Fellow, they will focus on that area. That said, although they tend to specialize, it can be in a reasonably broad way and could encompass subject headings (eg family law, company law, etc).

A significant part of their work will be assisting a solicitor, and it is worth noting that legal executives do not have independent practising rights; that is to say, they must be supervised by solicitors and cannot create a firm that exists solely of legal executives although following the reforms of the LSA 2007 it is now possible for a legal executive to own shares in a practice. Much of the work of a legal executive will be quite similar to the provision of legal advice by solicitors and will frequently involve dealing with clients direct. Following the reforms of the CLSA 1990 legal executives are now entitled to have limited rights of audience. All Fellows have rights of audience in chambers for pre-trial procedural issues but they are entitled to undertake further training and seek rights of audience in open court. Very few legal executives have successfully qualified as advocates, but once granted, it permits a Fellow to conduct advocacy in the county court, magistrates' courts and certain non-trial litigation in the Crown Court (such as bail applications).

8.7.1.3 Qualifying as a solicitor

Although ILEX is keen on its standing as a profession in its own right, a significant incentive for those who join ILEX is that it is also a path to becoming a solicitor. The normal route for qualifying as a solicitor is to study law at undergraduate or graduate level, then undertake a vocational training course and finally undertake a training contract. However the Law Society will also allow ILEX Fellows to qualify as a solicitor once they have the requisite experience and have passed the conversion course. Once qualified, an ILEX Fellow need not undertake a training contract because the minimum of five years' experience that has been undertaken to become a Fellow acts as the equivalent of a training contract.

The advantage of an ILEX Fellow converting includes less restriction on their practice, including the ability to become sole practitioners or to set up their own practices, and also to study for wider rights of audience in the higher courts. It is not known precisely how many ILEX Fellows convert to solicitors, and there are some anecdotal comments about how well their future careers compare to traditionally qualified solicitors, but within a small to medium-sized firm it would be an attractive method of qualifying, not least because of the fact that from the very earliest stage the legal executive will have been earning money.

8.7.2 Paralegals

One of the more recent developments of the legal profession is the so-called 'paralegal'. This was originally an American term, but has become an established part of the English legal framework. Traditionally the paralegal was a euphemism for someone who would photocopy documents and prepare extremely basic documentation but over recent years there has been an expansion in the number of non-qualified people who assist in the execution of legal work.

Within the United States a paralegal is a separate profession in its own right (although it bears some similarity to our legal executives) but in the United Kingdom this has not yet taken place. That said some bodies are trying to create a fourth branch to the profession, with a company creating a national association to provide training for paralegals. The emphasis on this group is on those who have no formal legal education and, to an extent, it can be seen that this is attempting to compete with legal executives, but whereas the latter have statutory recognition, paralegals currently have none and so it has to be questioned why someone would wish to progress through this route.

The more usual type of paralegal within England and Wales is someone who does have a legal background. A person in this group will normally become a paralegal at one of two points in their life. The first is after the completion of their law honours degree and before going on to do either the LPC or BPTC, or the second point is after completing the LPC or BPTC but where they have not secured a training contract or pupillage. For those in this group, it is likely that the post of paralegal is viewed as a temporary one, with the intention of using it as a stepping stone to a position as a solicitor or barrister. The logic behind this is sound in that as a paralegal one will be meeting members of the profession every day, and where the post sought is in a firm of solicitors is quite possible that the company that hires the person as a paralegal may, when they recruit a trainee solicitor, look favourably upon someone who has proven themselves already.

Since there is no single definition of a paralegal it is not really possible to say what their duties would be, since they will inevitably differ between the firms and organizations that use them. The common theme is that in private practice they will normally act as 'fee earners', that is to say they will conduct a limited caseload for which the company will be able to bill the client. Precisely what work is undertaken will depend on the qualifications and experience of the paralegal but it is likely to include document preparations (witness statements, claim forms, defences, etc) and may even include limited advocacy work in tribunals and non-contested issues.

Paralegals are not restricted to the private sector although they may not be known by this title within the public sector. However if one were to consider the work of caseworkers within, for example, the CPS and the Criminal Cases Review Commission it could be argued that these are undertaking comparable work. Caseworkers will undertake much administrative and quasi-legal work on a live case and will often help instruct counsel, attend court, and provide summaries of evidence etc. The work is vital to the smooth operation of these organizations and can provide an interesting career for those who have not sought to become professionally qualified or who have not been able to access the relevant training elements to qualify.

8.8 Complaints and discipline

Lawyers, like any professions, will include a mixture of people, including some who undertake their work inappropriately. The professions must have a system in place that allows for investigations to be undertaken in respect of malpractice.

8.8.1 Codes of conduct

Both barristers and solicitors are bound by (separate) codes of conduct. It has been suggested that one of the purpose of Codes is they 'educate both legal neophytes and qualified lawyers as to how they should behave' (Nicolson and Webb (1999) 96) although they also act as a statement of standards that the professional bodies indicate to the wider community they will adhere to. They are a relatively recent invention (Nicolson and Webb (1999) 98) in part because prior to this it was thought that the professions should be able to regulate themselves in looser forms; the difficulty this brings, of course, is a complete lack of transparency and accountability.

The Codes operated by the Law Society and Bar Council are significantly different, with the former being almost four times longer than the latter (Nicolson and Webb (1999) 99) although this is in part because of the nature of the professions. Since barristers cannot form partnerships there is no need for detailed description of the circumstances of when partnership may be formed and how. Barristers will not 'hold' money for a lay client, this is done by the solicitor, and accordingly there is no need for significant sections of rules that relate to the transparency of lay funds. However, this need not explain all issues and it can be questioned whether the two Codes take a different approach, with the Bar Code taking a 'purposive' approach which seeks to set out the parameters by which a barrister shall practise and the Law Society taking in a 'literal' or 'prescriptive' approach whereby the Code operates as a series of specific rules governing the practice of law.

8.8.1.1 Barristers

Discipline is, strictly speaking, a matter for the Inn of Court that a barrister belongs to but all four Inns have established common procedures to ensure that complaints and action are dealt with appropriately. Until comparatively recently, the Bar Council dealt with matters of discipline through its *Professional Conduct and Complaints Committee* but recently this was replaced by the *Bar Standards Board* (BSB).

The BSB is an arms-length organization of the Bar. Whilst it is funded by the Bar Council and half of the board is from the Bar (although its chair and seven other members are lay members), it is considered to be independent from the Bar Council and no member of the BSB is part of the Bar Council.

In October 2010 the *Legal Ombudsman* (see below) came into effect and now lay complaints (ie those from a lay client) will be made to that organization which includes the right to order compensation. The *Legal Ombudsman* does not have jurisdiction to consider allegations of professional misconduct and such matters continue to be within the jurisdiction of the BSB. If the BSB believes that a barrister has breached the Code of Conduct then the matter is sent to the Complaints Committee.

The Complaints Committee includes both barristers and lay members. They can dismiss an appeal but this may only be done where a majority of the lay members agree to this course of action. Otherwise the Complaints Committee has to decide to send the matter to one of two disciplinary panels:

- Summary Procedure Panel. This concerns action where the facts are not in dispute and where the disbarment of the barrister will not be ordered.
- Disciplinary Tribunal. This is a formal hearing which deals with the most serious complaints or situations where the facts are in dispute. The powers of the Disciplinary Tribunal include the power of fine, suspension, or disbarment.

Each panel is constituted by the Council of the Inns of Court and includes at least one judge or QC (normally a judge in a Disciplinary Tribunal), one junior barrister, and one lay member. The Disciplinary Tribunal takes place in open and takes the format equivalent to a court hearing, including the calling of evidence and cross-examination of witnesses. Its findings are published on the website of the BSB.

8.8.1.2 Solicitors

Traditionally the Law Society regulates the activities of all solicitors, including solicitor–advocates, although solicitors are technically officers of the Supreme Court (something that barristers are not) and so the court theoretically has the power to regulate solicitor's conduct too although it would be rare for it to do this except through, for example, wasted costs orders.

The Law Society, like the Bar Council, has created an arms-length organization for its regulation, known as the Solicitors Regulatory Authority (SRA). The SRA, like the BSB, created an independent system for dealing with complaints from the general public which was known as the *Legal Complaints Service* (LCS). From October 2010 the *Legal Ombudsman* assumed direct responsibility for complaints received from members of the public.

Where there has been professional misconduct by a solicitor then this remains a matter for the SRA, and this will include matters relating to, for example, continuing professional development or the misappropriation of client funds.

Adjudicating on disciplinary matters relating to solicitors is the responsibility of the *Solicitors Disciplinary Tribunal* (SDT). This is a statutory tribunal established under s 46 *Solicitors' Act 1974*. The members of the tribunal are appointed by the Master of the Rolls[11] and include solicitors and lay persons (who may not be barristers or solicitors).

---

11. It has been noted already that the Master of the Rolls traditionally had responsibility for the management of the Rolls of Solicitors and whilst this obligation has been transferred to the SRA the Master of the Rolls continues to exercise certain administrative regulatory functions.

The tribunal sits in divisions of three; two solicitors (one of which will chair) and one lay member. The tribunal is formal and takes the format of a court trial. Ordinarily the SRA will 'prosecute' the matter and it is empowered, in very serious matters, to instruct counsel where appropriate. The tribunal has significant sanctions including:

- striking a solicitor from the Roll
- suspending a solicitor from practising
- reprimanding a solicitor
- fining a solicitor[12]
- banning the person from working as a solicitor.

The tribunal will also consider requests from solicitors suspended (or struck) from the Roll to resume practice.

8.8.1.3 Independent oversight

Although both the Bar and Law Society have attempted to show independence through the creation of arms-length regulatory bodies, there has long been concern about the regulation of lawyers. In 2003 the Lord Chancellor created a review of the regulation of the legal profession and chose Sir David Clementi as its chair, the report being delivered in 2004. Whilst Clementi was broadly sympathetic to some parts of the regulatory systems he did believe it was necessary to increase the accountability of the professional bodies, especially in connection with the complaints procedures.

The government responded in the LSA 2007, which has transformed the oversight of the professions. The Act has two principal issues of relevance here. The first is the creation of an *Office for Legal Complaints* (OLC) (s 114 LSA 2007) and the second is the establishment of the *Legal Services Board* (LSB) (s 2 LSA 2007).

The LSB has a statutory responsibility, inter alia, to ensure standards of regulation, training, and education. Whilst therefore the LSB does not replace either the BSB or SRA it will hold those bodies to account on matters such as educational requirements (including both the academic and vocational stages), continual professional development, and the regulation of lawyers. The LSB is chaired by a lay person and consists of the chair, the Chief Executive, and between seven and ten persons appointed by the Lord Chancellor. A majority of the LSB must be lay (Sch 1, para 2, LSA 2007) meaning not qualified as lawyers.

The LSB must create a 'consumer panel' (s 8 LSA 2007) which will include representation from those who seek the work of lawyers. The panel cannot include a member of the LSB (other than who is appointed to chair the panel, who will be a member of the LSB), a member of the OLC, a lawyer, or member of a regulator of lawyers. The panel will provide advice to the LSB as to the functioning of the provision of legal advice and, presumably, issues such as whether regulation is working.

The primary responsibility of OLC is to create the *Legal Ombudsman* (s 115 LSA 2007). The Ombudsman will assume responsibility from the BSB and LCS for complaints brought about by lay members of the public. The Ombudsman is independent of the professions, consumer protection groups, and the government. Its principal aim is to investigate complaints about the work undertaken by barristers, solicitors, legal executives and certain other legal professions. If it considers that the work undertaken

---

12. Any fine is payable to HM Treasury not to the Law Society.

was inappropriate then it has the power to order the relevant legal professional to pay compensation, this obligation being enforced by the relevant professional body (usually the BSB or SRA). Whilst the Ombudsman has no power to rule on matters relating to breaches of the professional codes of conduct, it can bring allegations of such breaches to the attention of the BSB or SRA who may then decide to action it themselves.

The scheme became operational in October 2010 and so at the time of writing the scheme has only just started and it is not possible to identify whether it brings any advantages over the previous schemes. Presumably the principal advantage is that of transparency, in that whilst the BSB and SRA are arms-length organizations, they are ultimately part of their parental bodies (the Bar Council and Law Society) whereas the same is not true of the Legal Ombudsman.

8.8.1.4 Immunity

Those of you who are also studying the *Law of Tort* at the same time as the module you are currently on will be familiar with the idea of negligence. For those of you who are not currently studying *Tort*, the law recognizes that where someone holds themselves out as a professional in an area of service, they should be accountable if they fail to meet a basic standard of care in the discharge of their duties, known as being negligent (see, for example, *Hedley Byrne & Co v Heller & Partners* [1964] AC 465). Should an advocate be liable in law for the negligent handling of cases?

Traditionally the answer was 'no'—a lay client could not sue an advocate on the basis that they lost a case because of their advocate's negligence (see, for example, *Rondel v Worsley* [1969] 1 AC 191) but eventually this immunity began to become restricted solely to negligence in court or litigation papers (the case of *Saif Ali v Sydney Smith Mitchell & Co* [1980] AC 198 comprehensively discussed the immunity) and where a lawyer gave advice negligently an action could arise. There were a number of reasons why this was so, perhaps the most commonly cited being that it could lead to re-litigation. If a person charged with a crime is convicted then the way to challenge this decision is by way of an appeal. If, the argument went, an advocate could be sued for negligence then when the appeals were exhausted a person would have nothing to lose by suing his advocate for negligence. If he won this action then would this grant him the right to another appeal?

In *Hall v Simons* [2002] 1 AC 615 the House of Lords was called to re-examine whether there was a justification for advocates to have an absolute exemption from negligence and they decided there was not. The House carefully considered every possible reason why the immunity should remain and decided each was unconvincing and that it was against public policy to exempt one profession from litigation when others, arguably with a higher stake for public policy exemptions (eg doctors), have no exemption. The House did not believe that their decision would 'open the floodgates' as they pointed out that the rules of civil litigation permit a judge to strike out vexatious proceedings at an early stage (ibid at 681–683 per Lord Steyn). The House also argued that criminal practitioners would have an additional protection in that using civil negligence laws to challenge convictions would almost certainly be viewed as an abuse of process by the courts and the action quickly stayed (ibid at 679–681).

The decision in *Hall v Simons* was eminently sensible: it is difficult to justify granting immunity to one profession when real harm could be caused by the negligent actions of an advocate. There is not one standard of negligence and since the case there have been few cases alleging negligence perhaps demonstrating that the fears of the profession were unfounded.

8.9 Legal ethics

The issue of discipline was discussed immediately above and it was suggested that the Codes governing the professions in effect set out the standards by which a barrister or solicitor should conduct himself. A central part of this conduct can be summed up as ethics and yet it is comparatively rare for students to be introduced to legal ethics during an undergraduate course (Boon and Levin (2008) 159). However it is important that you are able to understand some of the ethical issues that lawyers encounter.

8.9.1 Responsibility to clients

Some of the more significant ethical issues relate to what a lawyer can, and cannot, do in respect of their clients (normally meaning their 'lay client' when it is a barrister). Complete books have been written about the issue of ethics but in this section some of the main ethical duties that arise will be discussed.

8.9.1.1 Providing advice not seeking control

Lawyers provide advice but one of the questions that arises is how far they may go in terms of encouraging people to act on that advice. In the criminal context this will ordinarily take place in the context of a 'plea bargain' and this is discussed in more depth in Chapter 10. However the concept is wider than this and needs to be outlined here.

A lawyer is supposed to serve his client's best interests but also allow the client to act autonomously so that they are making decisions on the basis of advice. However concern has been raised as to whether the actions of lawyers seek to push this envelope and actually control or manipulate the decisions of the clients (Nicolson and Webb (1999) 123). Perhaps one of the classic examples of this is where a lawyer 'misleads clients in personal injury matters by playing down expectations as to likely compensation so as to encourage earlier settlement' (p 137). It has been remarked that the advantage of this is that there can be a high turnover of work through the processing of more cases (Boon and Levin (2008) 361). However it could equally work in reverse whereby for a high-value claim it may be in the interests of a lawyer to raise expectations so that early settlement offers are rejected, thus prolonging the litigation and increasing the costs.

It is essential that lawyers simply set out the legal position and put forward options to the client, but ultimately it must be for the client to decide which option to take. The possible tactics are for the lawyer to explain but it is important that a client is not 'bounced' into accepting something that he does not wish to do. This is particularly true in respect of plea bargains where there is some evidence to suggest that some people will feel pressurized by the lawyer to plead guilty even though they believe they are innocent (Phillips (2004) 145–146). This simply cannot be justified and it is a particular duty of a judge to ensure that any guilty plea is being tendered correctly and not simply for the sake of convenience (Otton (2002) 326).

8.9.1.2 Client confidentiality

One of the most important ethical issues is that of client confidentiality. Yet interestingly it is a duty that could involve a lawyer in other ethical difficulties, for example when a client plans to commit a crime (Nicolson and Webb (1999) 248). The justification for the rule is that a person must be entitled to be able to engage a lawyer to seek advice without worrying whether he will inadvertently disclose something that would undermine his own case (Nicolson and Webb (1999) 249).

Some have, however, criticized the rule in that whilst it does protect both the individual and lawyer it does nothing to assist third parties or society who may be affected by that individual's actions (Nicolson and Webb (1999) 253). Indeed the rule could even cause significant harm to society or an individual since client confidentiality will not be waived even where to do so would protect an innocent person going to prison (Nicolson and Webb (1999) 254).

> 👁 **Example** Client confidentiality
>
> Wendy has been accused of the murder of Vanessa. Trevor has been accused of theft but when talking to his counsel, John, he indicates that he was the person who actually killed Vanessa not Wendy. John is bound by client confidentiality and cannot tell anyone what Trevor has said even though Wendy may be sentenced to life imprisonment as a result of this.

The only exceptions to this rule are where someone is at risk of serious harm or where a lawyer is being used to facilitate a crime (Boon and Levin (2008) Chapter 11) but the circumstances surrounding these exceptions are somewhat confused, not least because the suggestion is that it is only against *serious* harm, so what happens where less serious harm is to be inflicted? Also, what does facilitate a crime mean? It appears to include crimes in the future (ibid) so that, at least, a person cannot go to a lawyer and ask for advice on how to commit 'the perfect murder'.

Money laundering

In recent years some of the most controversial aspects of the rule governing client confidentiality is in respect of money laundering which is described as:

> the process by which 'dirty money'—the proceeds of crime—is changed so that the money appears 'to originate from a legitimate source'. (Law Society Guidance reproduced in Boon and Levin (1999) 259)

Solicitors are arguably a target for such behaviour since they hold money for clients and can make transactions on behalf of their clients (including investments, property deals, etc). In recent years the government has attempted to ensure that the proceeds of crime are recovered and this culminated in the *Proceeds of Crime Act 2002* (PoCA 2002) which has led to a statutory exception to the rule of confidentiality.

The Act creates a positive duty on persons to report money laundering, including 'reasonable suspicions' (s 330 PoCA 2002) and the fact that it was given in confidential situations is no defence. Further offences are created to deal with situations where, for example, a solicitor tips off his client that money recovery procedures have begun (s 333) or where a person becomes involved in a transaction that he knows, or suspects to be, involving money laundering (s 328). It has been suggested that all solicitors must be fully familiar with the money laundering regulations (Phillips (2004) 79). However recent decisions have cast doubt on this, with the suggestion that legal professional privilege may 'trump' PoCA.

Legal professional privilege is something that you will study in more depth during a course on *Evidence* but is an offshoot of the confidentiality regime. In essence, anything said to a lawyer in contemplation of, or during, judicial proceedings is privileged—ie it may not be disclosed and is not admissible in court.

Case box *Bowman v Fels*

The principal decision in this area is *Bowman v Fels* [2005] EWCA Civ 226. This was a family case. The solicitors acting for one party received documents that made them believe that repairs to the matrimonial property had been included (illegally) in the business accounts of that party. This could amount to money laundering (although not exactly the typical scenario) and the solicitors believed that they needed to make a disclosure to comply with PoCA and prevent them from committing an offence.

The Court of Appeal decided that if something arose in the course of ordinary proceedings then there would be no duty to disclose this to the authorities as it would be privileged information. The Court suggested that privilege would override PoCA except when the solicitor was deliberately trying to act dishonestly, ie by facilitating money laundering with the knowledge that he was so doing.

It is easy to overestimate the importance of *Bowman v Fels*. Although it is an important case (see Pace (2005)) it does not state that lawyers are exempt from PoCA but only decides that if they become suspicious of activity *during the course* of litigation then they do not need to report the matter. Accordingly if the suspicions arise outside of litigation or if it is more than suspicion—ie direct knowledge—then presumably the matter must be reported.

8.9.1.3 Conflicts of interest

Another significant ethical issue that arises in respect of lawyers is that there must not be a conflict of interest when representing a party. To an extent this has been discussed already in respect of part-time judges who sit on cases where a client of the firm is a party to the proceedings (see 7.6.3.2 above). A similar position arises in respect of representing clients, ie a firm should not represent more than one person in the same or similar proceedings. However there are multitude of different guises to this head of ethics including, perhaps most notably, where the proposed transaction or litigation has an impact on the lawyer's personal interests (Phillips (2004) 294 provides a useful summary of possible conflicts of interest).

PERSONAL CONFLICTS

There are numerous examples of when there may be a personal conflict with the solicitor. Perhaps the classic example is where a client wishes to make a will but wishes to leave a substantial amount of money to the solicitor. It would not be appropriate in those circumstances for the solicitor to act unless the client took further independent legal advice. Arguably this could also apply where, for example, the interest is personal but slightly detached. For example, if the solicitor is the Treasurer of a local charity and the client wished to leave a substantial amount of money to that charity, there would still almost certainly be a personal conflict of interest.

Perhaps the most common (potential) conflict of interest is that which arises between clients. The rule appears quite clear here: if there a dispute arises between two people who are clients of the lawyer then he must not act for either (Boon and Levin (2008) 340). This rule is not a personal one and so it does not just apply to the individual solicitor dealing with the matter but the whole firm. Accordingly this does mean that where a firm is engaged by a party they must undertake a careful check of existing clients to ensure that they will not create a conflict of interest.

❓ QUESTION FOR REFLECTION

Is it realistic to suggest that a large firm will have no conflicts of interest? For example, if a firm has offices across the United Kingdom is it a conflict of interest if their Birmingham office takes a client who is in conflict with a client serviced by the Exeter office? However is geography a sufficient 'wall' in the era of the Internet and global communication systems?

There is an exception to the rule (ibid) and this is where a lawyer does not have any 'confidential information' in respect of the other party. In those circumstances it is possible to act although it may be unwise to do so. However some argue that this is not sufficient protection and that the mere fact that they used to be a client should prevent the law firm acting for the new client (Boon and Levin (2008)). This is justified on the basis that although there may be no confidential information in existence, the solicitor may have knowledge of their anxiety or how they react to stress etc which could provide a tactical advantage. Similar issues were raised in *Re Z* [2009] EWHC 3621 (Fam). A husband and wife were involved in high-value divorce proceedings that had taken over a decade because of reconciliations. The wife was being represented by Mr A from F & Co, the senior partner of which was Mrs F, who used to represent the husband when she worked with the firm G & Co.

The husband sought an injunction preventing F & Co from representing the wife. The High Court applied the ruling of the House of Lords in *Prince Jefri Bolkiah v KPMG* [1988] 2 AC 222 which had said that an injunction can be granted where the claimant can show a real risk that confidential information could be disclosed, however slight that risk is, unless the respondent solicitors can show that they have taken steps to remove the risk. The High Court in *Halewood International Limited v Addleshaw Booth & Co* [2000] Lloyds LR 298 ruled that confidential information may continue in memories and that whilst a person may not recollect something, this may alter as circumstances change and memories are prompted.

Brodey J ruled in *Re Z* that because Mrs F had acted for the husband for over a year it is likely that she would continue to be aware of some of the circumstances and possibly also the manner in which he conducted himself and business, which could be relevant. Whilst F & Co had undertaken to ensure Mrs F was not involved in the case, the fact that she was the 'hands-on' senior partner of a small firm meant that there was a real risk that confidentiality could be breached. This case perhaps demonstrates how seriously the courts take potential breaches of confidentiality.

8.9.2 Practical ethical issues

Alongside the particular relationship with a client other ethical issues arise in respect of those who seek to practise law. Two of the more commonly raised ethical issues will be discussed in this area: defending the guilty (which is inevitably linked to the 'cab rank rule') and whether those who have been convicted of crimes should be allowed to become lawyers.

8.9.2.1 Defending the guilty

If you qualify as a lawyer then when you attend dinner parties and other social functions you will probably stop telling people that you are a solicitor or a barrister and start to make up another profession because one question is asked above all others: 'How can you represent somebody you know is guilty?'

Suspected guilt

The answer to this question depends on whether a lawyer suspects that the client is guilty or whether he has been told by the client that he is guilty. Initially let us concentrate on the first possibility. The answer to the question in this case is quite complicated and an entire book could be produced discussing the answer. The brief answer, however, is part practical and part philosophical.

The philosophical answer can be simplified to asking the question, who says a person is guilty? The law provides for three mechanisms by which a person is to be found guilty (depending on the court):

- the client pleads guilty
- at summary level, either a majority decision of three justices of the peace or a single district judge (magistrates' court) must declare guilt
- at Crown Court level, at least ten members of the public sitting as jurors must declare guilt.

If for the moment we leave aside the first method and assume the client is saying that he is not guilty but the lawyer believes that he is, then in either situation is it open to a single lawyer to decide guilt or innocence? The state has set down the rules by which a person is to be tried and someone who agrees to work in the legal system must adhere to this principle. If it were to be otherwise then why have a trial? If the lawyer is to decide guilt or innocence then we could save a lot of taxpayers' money by having all cases brought before lawyers who could dispense summary justice on their beliefs. The system would break down and thus it must remain with the duly constituted tribunals of fact. This simple philosophical argument can be easy when one is discussing the theft of a bar of chocolate or a basic assault case but what about cases of child abuse, rape, or murder? Arguably the rule applies even more to these cases as due process is most important in the worst cases. A barrister does not have to like his client but by entering criminal practice he is saying that he is prepared to conduct criminal litigation and unless he withdraws from private practice then this means both prosecuting and defending cases. If someone does not believe that they can defend a rapist then they should not work in independent practice.

Client confirms guilt

What happens in the alternative scenario, where a person tells his lawyer that he is guilty? The Code of Conduct for barristers states that one of the most important principles for a barrister is the duty not to mislead the court (see para 302 of the Code) and this means that a barrister may not suggest in court that his client is not guilty if he has been *told* by his client that he is guilty. Does this mean that a guilty person cannot be represented? It certainly does not mean that where a person intends to plead guilty as the guilty person has the right to make representations to the court as to sentence and, accordingly, a lawyer may be engaged to do this. Can a guilty person ever legitimately plead 'not guilty'? The answer, perhaps surprisingly, is 'yes' and *Written Standards of Work* exist for this.

In England and Wales the law states that a person is to be found guilty by the courts only where the prosecution can prove beyond all reasonable doubt that the accused committed the crime. Accordingly it has been decided that it is possible for a barrister to 'test' the prosecution evidence of a guilty client to see whether this threshold has been passed. The written standards state:

> While...it would be right to take any objections to the competency of the Court, to the form of the indictment, to the admissibility of any evidence or to the evidence admitted...a barrister must not (whether by calling the defendant or otherwise) set up an affirmative case inconsistent with the confession made to him. (*Written Standards for the Conduct of Professional Work*, para 12.4)

The position is normally, therefore, that a lawyer can act for the defendant up until the point of the close of the prosecution case but cannot put forward a defence case as this would tend to suggest that a person is not guilty which would be misleading the court.[13]

8.9.2.2 Criminals as lawyers

Whilst it may seem a strange issue to discuss, can a person who has been convicted of a crime become a member of the professions? The answer is yes although they have additional hurdles.

In order to gain entrance to the Law Society or Inns of Court a student must demonstrate that they are of good character. Both professions define this in a subjective way, ie they will look at individual applicants rather than create an overarching rule that would apply regardless of the specifics of a case. It is important to note that it is not only criminal convictions that could affect the ability of a person to join the professions but also disciplinary and other matters. For example, findings of plagiarism and examination irregularities at undergraduate level are considered to be extremely serious and have stopped people from joining the professions.

Both professions will call applicants who are not of good standing before special committees. For the Law Society this is likely to include a member of the Council and members of the profession whereas for the Bar Council it is likely that the Masters of

---

13. It should be noted that the Law Society maintains similar rules—see rule 21.20.

the Bench of the Inn that the applicant is applying to will hear the matter. The circumstances of the reasons for the bad character will be discussed together with any relevant information on rehabilitation etc. The decision whether to admit will be based purely on whether the panel believes that it would cause professional embarrassment to the profession if such a person is admitted.

 Example Louise Woodward

Perhaps the most infamous example of this rule is that of Louise Woodward who was convicted in America of the manslaughter of a child whilst acting as an au pair after her A levels. Upon returning to the United Kingdom she read for a law degree and, upon its completion, applied to the Law Society for permission to join them as a student lawyer and begin studying the LPC. Her application was considered by a special panel of lawyers and they allowed her to commence studies and a firm of solicitors in Manchester (who did not undertake criminal work) provided her with a training contract. Many people felt uncomfortable about this decision, not least because there was doubt as to whether other people convicted of homicide would be allowed in. The Law Society itself said that it was a unique case and at the time of the trial there was a perception in the United Kingdom that she had been treated unfairly in America (although little authority was adduced for this) and this may have swayed its decision.

QUESTION FOR REFLECTION

Do you think there are any crimes that should lead to a person not being fit to practice as a lawyer? How do you think the general public would react to a lawyer who has a history of fraudulent or violent offending? Do you think that Louise Woodward should have been able to practise as a lawyer? Imagine that the crime had taken place in this country: would the parents of the child believe that the law was being brought into disrepute?

LISTEN TO THE PODCAST
For guidance on how to answer this question and a discussion of the main issues, listen to the author's podcast on the Online Resource Centre:
www.oxfordtextbooks.co.uk/orc/gillespie_els3e/

 ## Summary

This chapter has examined the legal profession and identified who is entitled to practise law in England and Wales. In particular it has noted:

* There are two principal branches to the legal profession in England and Wales. The first branch consists of barristers and they continue to have automatic higher rights of audience. The second branch consists of solicitors who are now entitled to receive higher rights of audience.

- Barristers tend to practise independently but they form loose associations known as chambers where they will share clerks and administrative staff. Chambers will also have a 'head of chambers' who chairs policy discussions.

- Whilst traditionally barristers were not legally able to form partnerships they may now own shares in an LDP.

- Solicitors are allowed to form partnerships and it is unusual for them to practise independently.

- There are three stages to qualifying as a member of either profession. The first is the academic stage and involves passing either a qualifying law degree or the Graduate Diploma in Law. The second stage is vocational education and is either the Bar Professional Training Course (for barristers) or Legal Practice Course (for solicitors). The final stage is work-based training and consists of either pupillage (for barristers) or a training contract (for solicitors).

- Existing alongside these principal branches are other forms of lawyers. The Institute of Legal Executives is probably the next biggest branch. Legal executives work under the supervision of solicitors and can eventually qualify as solicitors themselves.

- Concern continues to exist over the diversity of the legal professions although the position appears to be changing, albeit slowly.

- A number of ethical challenges exist to the work of the professions and the traditional regulatory role of the professions is being challenged. In recent years, independent oversight of the regulatory process has been introduced to install public confidence in the system.

❓ End-of-chapter questions

1. Pannick (1992) states: 'any lawyer who does not understand [the purpose of the cab rank rule] really has no business being an advocate' (p 145) yet others disagree and Clementi (2004) appears to question whether the rule has any modern application (pp 130–132). Should the cab rank rule be abolished?

2. Robins (2005) reports that the Law Society are pleased with the new process of appointing QCs with the suggestion that it could lead to more solicitors being awarded this distinction. In the same article, however, Andrew Dismore MP refers to QCs as 'a price-fixing cartel to defraud the public'. Should we have a system of QCs and if so, should it apply to all lawyers or only to advocates?

3. Read Myers and Flannery (2004) pp 1698–1699 where two solicitor–advocates are interviewed about their job. One suggestion put to them is that they should become barristers. Is this not the crux of the matter? Why should solicitors be given higher rights of audience when they are not constrained by the regulations governing barristers (eg prohibition of partnerships, cab rank rule etc)? If we are going to allow solicitors to have higher rights of audience then should the distinction in dress and mode of address be removed?

4. Stephen Irwin QC, the chair of the Bar Council during 2004, argued that Clementi was wrong to suggest that a central regulatory system was required saying: 'the Bar regulates itself very successfully and very cheaply because we have high degree of commitment from barristers who are pretty tough on their own colleagues.' Why should lawyers be investigated or regulated by outside bodies rather than their own internal systems?

Further reading

Nicolson D (2005) 'Demography, discrimination and diversity: A new dawn for the British legal profession?' 12 *International Journal of the Legal Profession* 201–228.

This article discusses whether enough is being done to make the legal professions more diverse.

Robins R (2005) 'Inn a time warp?' 102 *Law Society Gazette* 19–20.

This article questions the relevancy of the Inns of Court in the modern legal practice and questions whether they hold the profession back as 'gentlemen's clubs'.

Webb J (2005) 'Legal disciplinary practices: An ethical problem in the making?' 8 *Legal Ethics* 185–194.

This article considers whether the disciplinary changes proposed by the Clementi report will in fact raise greater ethical dilemmas.

 For multiple choice questions, updates to this chapter and links to useful websites, please visit the Online Resource Centre at

www.oxfordtextbooks.co.uk/orc/gillespie_els3e/

9

Funding Legal Services

By the end of this chapter you will be able to:

- Identify the background to legal aid.
- Understand some of the controversies that exist over state funding of legal action.
- Identify how state funding is provided.
- Consider the merits of 'conditional fees' and assess whether they are an alternative to state funding.

Introduction

One of the most controversial aspects of the legal process is how lawyers should be paid, in particular by the state. The concept of 'legal aid' is relatively new in this country but is now well entrenched. However, recent reforms have ensured that it is a ghost of what it once was and further curbs are planned. In this chapter the key issues surrounding the funding of litigation are considered.

9.1 Background to legal aid

Legal aid is a comparatively modern concept within the English Legal System and in effect traces its history to the Second World War. But it has expanded to the point where it is considered to be an everyday feature of the legal process. Since the 1980s, however, it has become an incredible political 'hot potato' with Conservative, Labour, and coalition governments suggesting that 'fat cat' lawyers have abused the system although at least one commentator argues that the latest attacks are arguably just more noticeable since legal aid has always had a troubled existence (Flood and Whyte (2006) 80). It has been suggested that the principal justification for legal aid is that failing to assist the poorest in society accessing the law is a 'significant denial of justice' (Zander (2007) 585). This is a particularly strong argument since it is frequently the very poor who are most in need of the law's protection as they can be readily exploited by those who know they are unable to take action. Within the sphere of employment law this was one of the reasons why unions became important since they would assist with legal proceedings to enforce conditions of employment. A similar rationale lies behind the national minimum wage (see *National Minimum Wage Act 1999*) and here the state, through HM Revenue and Customs, acts on behalf of the low-waged to ensure that they are given an appropriate wage.

It has been suggested that there have been three stages of legal aid in this country (Zander (2007) 586). The first stage was when it was funded directly by the state and administered by the Law Society. This period lasted forty years (1949–1989). The second stage was when the Legal Aid Board (LAB) took over the administration of the scheme from the Law Society, in part because there were concerns at solicitors being responsible for their own payment. This also marked the beginning of the principal political controversy surrounding this area. This second phase is said to have lasted from 1989 to 1999 but realistically it was not until 2000 when the third phase began. The third phase is the creation of the *Legal Services Commission* (LSC) created by the *Access to Justice Act 1999* with a remit to revolutionize the legal aid scheme. However, this is supplemented by the development of the criminal legal aid scheme which will need to be considered separately later since the creation of a new publicly funded defence service has arguably led to a fourth phase in the history of legal aid.

A common aspect within all the phases of the legal aid scheme has been the concept of means-testing. Since legal aid is considered to be a solution for those who cannot access lawyers it was considered appropriate that it should be restricted to those who could prove they were of low income. This was particularly true in respect of representation at court but was also supposed to happen at the pre-trial hearings. However there has, for many years, been suspicion about how high-profile figures have managed to obtain legal aid, including key businessmen who lived in houses worth millions. Some have suspected that it is possible to 'hide' money by ensuring that income and assets are held elsewhere.

Linked to the concept of means was the recovery of legal aid. As will be seen later in this book, the general rule in civil litigation is that the 'loser pays' all the costs. Accordingly, if a person who is legally aided wins then the costs of the litigation should be claimed against the opposing side meaning that the legal aid budget does not suffer. However, there are many exceptions to the 'loser pays' principle (see 14.1.2.2 below) and the legal aid provisions did allow for legal fees to be recovered from any awards that were made to the claimant.

Perhaps the biggest change from the initial legal aid scheme and the current one is that of budgets. Theoretically, throughout all stages of legal aid there has been a budget set but until the most recent set of reforms there was no upper limit on the expenditure set, ie it did not matter if the budget was overspent, often by significant amounts. This led to enormous pressures on the system and transformed the way the practices operated. One commentator noted that the greatest growth was in the period 1975–1984 where the Bar's legal aid earnings rose threefold and accounted for half of the Bar's income (Abel (2003) 241). The rise for solicitors was even more pronounced, rising from £40 million in 1975 to £280 million in 1984, a sevenfold increase (ibid).

The then Conservative government was determined to cut back on legal aid and commented that although it was an important feature of the legal system it 'could not be a blank cheque from the taxpayer' (Abel (2003) 244). One of the strongest criticisms was that it encouraged cases to be dragged out since lawyers were paid by the hour. However the profession's response to this was that this was also true with private cases but they were a professional body and accordingly would not prolong matters that were not justified. However, at the very least the *perception* that this could happen was present and the media appeared to be largely on the government's side, the popular belief being that lawyers are overpaid (Abel (2003) 244–245).

The Conservative government argued that it was necessary to centralize the legal aid system, in part to recognize that it was not just private law firms that provide advice but that other bodies (eg Citizens Advice Bureau, Law Centres, etc) also provided assistance and were supported by the state. The government wished to rationalize this system (Zander (2007) 586) but also ensure that there was a control mechanism on spending. It proposed the creation of the LSC and suggested that it would be operationally independent although funded by the government. The LSC would have the power to decide what areas of law to fund and there was an intention that not every area of law would continue to be funded.

Ultimately the Conservative reforms were left unfinished and the incoming Labour government had to decide what to do. In opposition, the Labour party had been strongly opposed to many of the Conservative measures, arguing that limiting legal aid could be considered a barrier to access (Abel (2003) 293), but this position altered dramatically after it was elected and at least one commentator has suggested that the Labour government has effectively ended 'legal aid as we know it' (Abel (2003) Ch 8) which, whilst dramatic, is undoubtedly correct.

The reality of the system was that legal aid continued to place increased pressure on the government's budget and that it was unsustainable for this to increase whilst the government sought to limit funding on other aspects of the state. The professions reacted badly to the proposals of the government and it culminated in a heated debate between the professions and the government. Perhaps the most notable aspect of the debate was when the government produced a list of the top earners from legal aid which was condemned by the professions as an attempt at humiliating them (Abel (2003) 304, 310). However the government argument was that it demonstrated a problem with the legal aid scheme, that a judge would receive a salary of only £100,000 per year but some lawyers earned £1 million per year from legal aid. However, at the junior end of the profession the position is significantly different with small rewards being given (Abel (2003) 304). Nonetheless, the media debate inevitably focused on the 'high end' of the profession since it was easy to portray lawyers as 'fat cats'. This ultimately turned the tide of the discussion and led to the government winning the battle for legal aid.

9.2 Legal aid today

As noted already, legal aid is extremely controversial and this continues to be the case today. Parts 1 and 2 of the *Access to Justice Act 1999* (AJA 1999) implemented legal aid reforms. Technically legal aid ceased to exist and was replaced by various terms loosely referred to as 'assistance'. However, it is still relatively common to refer to it as 'legal aid' at least in short-hand. The principal provisions of the Act were:

- the establishment of the *Legal Services Commission* to oversee the principal forms of legal aid
- the creation of the *Community Legal Service* which was to have responsibility for civil legal aid work
- the creation of the *Criminal Defence Service* which was to have responsibility for criminal legal aid work
- allowing solicitor firms to undertake conditional fee arrangement work.

Alongside these statutory changes were non-statutory changes that further encouraged users to settle disputes without recourse to litigation. This will be considered in more detail in Chapter 16.

As noted above, the AJA 1999 established the *Legal Services Commission* (LSC) to be responsible for the administration of legal aid. The Commission is slightly smaller than the old Legal Aid Board and its commissioners are both legal and lay persons so that a broad range of views and experience is brought to the Commission. It is broadly divided into two further bodies; the *Community Legal Service* and the *Criminal Defence Service* which administer the civil and criminal legal aid schemes respectively.

9.2.1 Community Legal Service

The Community Legal Service is primarily responsible for administering the civil legal aid work although it does have a 'direct access' scheme where it provides certain information to the public direct. Originally this was a website known as *CLS Direct* but it has subsequently been renamed *Community Legal Advice*.[1] This website offers legal advice for many common everyday legal queries and also provides a telephone helpline to offer people independent legal advice.

The statutory responsibilities of the CLS are:

(a) the provision of general information about the law and legal system and the availability of legal services;

(b) the provision of help by the giving of advice as to how the law applies in particular circumstances;

(c) the provision of help in preventing, or settling, or otherwise resolving disputes about legal rights and duties;

(d) the provision of help in enforcing decisions by which disputes are resolved; and

(e) the provision of help in relation to legal proceedings not relating to disputes (s 4(2) AJA 1999).

The website that it established assists the CLS in meeting its statutory duties but it mainly meets its obligations through the management of the *Community Legal Services Fund* (CLSF) (s 5 AJA 1999) which is, in essence, the civil 'legal aid budget'. The bulk of the money for the CLSF comes from the government but the CLS is also able to charge for some of its services and thus it gains some of its funding from this and some local authorities also provide funding (although in many instances this is through the production of joint ventures known as *Community Legal Advice Centres* (CLACs) discussed below (9.4.3)).

The government is able to state what priorities should be given to applications for funding (s 6 AJA 1999). The primary priorities are:

• special Children Act proceedings

• civil proceedings where the client is at real and immediate risk of loss of life or liberty.

After this the four general priorities are:

• help with social welfare issues that will enable people to avoid or climb out of social exclusion, including help with housing proceedings and advice relating to debt, employment rights, and entitlement to social security benefits

• domestic violence proceedings

• proceedings concerning the welfare of children

• proceedings against public authorities alleging serious wrongdoing, abuse of position or power, or significant breach of human rights (Zander (2007) 590).

The last priority is important because it recognizes that the state should not seek to abuse its position by, in essence, exploiting someone's human rights but then fail to provide access to the courts to challenge such a decision. The issue of the link between human rights and legal aid will be explored further below (9.3).

It should also be noted that the mere fact that something is not listed as a priority does not mean that it will not be funded. A priority is just that; it is something that the CLS should consider first but where there is further resource available it can fund other matters. That said, there are a number of matters where legal aid would not

---

1. <www.communitylegaladvice.org.uk>.

ordinarily be granted (Sch 2 AJA 1999). This includes actions where negligence leads to injury, death, or damage save where it involves medical negligence. These are exempted because it was thought that they would be suitable for *Contingency Fee Arrangements* (CFA) (Zander (2007) 590). The status of CFA is discussed below (9.4.1). Other matters that are excluded include conveyancing, the making of wills, defamation, and matters arising out of company law. These exclusions are perhaps understandable given that, in essence, they are matters relating to finance and the state should not pay for disputes relating to private finance.

9.2.1.1 Contracts

The legal aid system had effectively operated on the basis that the Legal Aid Board would fund individual cases: a person would identify a lawyer and then an application would be made to the Board who would decide whether that particular case was appropriate. Legal aid was, broadly speaking, available through any provider. The AJA reforms changed this and the legal aid budget proceeded on the basis of tenders. Accordingly, providers would 'bid' for a set number of cases, for which they would be paid a rate for the case. A provider would not be able to go above the limit that they had been given. Whilst it is said that this means that there will be more control of the finances (in that there is a finite number of cases that can be funded) it does beg the question about what happens where a firm has achieved its quota of cases, where does this leave the client? It also raises further issues in terms of the type of providers that are awarded the contracts and this is discussed below (9.5).

At the time of the AJA reforms it was estimated that approximately 11,000 firms provided civil legal aid (Zander (2007) 596) but within six years this number had almost halved. It is believed that the number is likely to decrease even further (see the discussion on 'the future' discussed below 17.2). Firms would bid for a contract which can be divided into one of three categories:

- controlled work
- licensed work
- controlled and licensed work.

Separate to this scheme are individual contracts that exist for high-claim litigation and also specialist litigation (eg applications for judicial review or class-based claims) which would not fit within an ordinary contract and would require the CLS to consider separately whether it will fund such matters.

Controlled work is the more 'normal' contact that is sought by providers. It includes a variety of different services, including:

- legal help (this is the initial legal advice that is provided to a client but does not include generic legal advice (ie the operation of a website that provides general legal advice); it could also include the sending of initial letters)

- help at court (this includes basic litigation assistance including the issuing of proceedings and the funding of an advocate to conduct certain proceedings)

- controlled legal representation (this provides free representation before the First-Tier Tribunal in either the Mental Health or Immigration chambers).

The contract awarded to the firm will be for a set number of 'matter starts', ie cases to be opened. The contract can also indicate the type of work that can be provided (ie a firm may hold a contract for 500 matters start but it may state that 50 of these can relate to housing, 300 relate to family, 100 relate to consumer law, and 50 relate to employment). The contract will also state how long a firm can work for before needing additional permission to continue with the work. Where the firm only has controlled work it can seek permission to continue the matter through to litigation and the LSC will provide permission to do this on a case-by-case basis.

Licensed work covers the costs of representing a person before the courts although this does not include the cost of very high-claim litigation or specialist litigation that was noted above. A contract for licensed work will not state how many cases should be undertaken by the provider but rather it is permission for the provider to seek such work. Permission to begin each case must be given by the LSC and this will include an examination of the merits and means tests. Realistically, most legal firms will seek controlled and licensed work but some niche firms that concentrate solely on advocacy may seek only a contract for licensed work.

Quality

To be approved as a provider it is also necessary for the firm to meet certain quality standards and this leads to a quality mark. An interesting feature of the quality standard is that it applies to all providers, including not-for-profit providers. The quality threshold is administered, in part, by peer review, ie engaging lawyers to consider the quality standards of other organizations. The process of peer review will include considering the files, considering whether appropriate advice has been given, and whether, for example, the case has proceeded at appropriate speed.

9.2.1.2 Means-testing

Prior to the AJA reforms a person was automatically entitled to a short period of time in which they could freely consult a solicitor (known as the 'green form' scheme). It was generally no more than two hours although this included any time spent researching and writing a letter so it was, not infrequently, an hour or hour and a half. If further time was required then either an application for full legal aid needed to be made or the client would have to pay. However, the AJA reforms have altered this and virtually all work is now subject to means-testing. That said, there remains a small amount of work that does not require means-testing: legal aid will be provided irrespective of the financial standing of the client. Such exceptions are highly specific and relate to situations where the state is making a significant interference with a person's private and family life. The most obvious examples of open-access legal aid are public child-care proceedings (ie where the local authority is seeking to take a child into care) or proceedings before the First-Tier Tribunal (Mental Health Chamber) (see reg 3 *Community Legal Services (Financial) Regulations 2000*, SI 2000/516 (CLS(F)R 2000)).

The rules for means-testing are set out in the CLS(F)R 2000 although they are regularly amended (two amendments occurring within 2010). Whilst the precise thresholds change depending on the nature of the case, the most usual cases are brought within reg 5 which states the current threshold is based on gross income and disposable income. If a person receives gross income (ie before tax and national insurance is deducted) of more than £2,657 per month then they will not be eligible. If they receive less than this then their disposable income will be calculated (ie their income after certain essential deductions are been made) and they will be eligible if their disposable income is less than £733 per month (subject to the capital requirements). A further complication is that capital will sometimes be taken into account. This includes savings, shares, valuable assets, and the net value of a house although the latter is relatively complicated. The net value of a house is the market value of the house less the mortgage. However only a maximum of £100,000 will be offset for a mortgage irrespective of how much a person actually owes (reg 32(2) CLS(F)R 2000). The resultant amount is then subject to a further offset, which is that the first £100,000 of the resultant capital of the main dwelling is also not counted (reg 32B CLS(F)R 2000). An example may assist here: Robert owns a house worth £225,000. He has a mortgage on the house for £100,000. This means he has capital in the house of £125,000. According to reg 32B the first £100,000 of this capital is disregarded meaning that his disposable capital is £25,000.

If a person has disposable capital in excess of £8,000 then they will not be eligible for legal aid. Including capital is somewhat controversial since it may not be easy for certain people (eg the elderly) to release equity from a house without selling it. However, the counter-argument is, of course, that it would be relatively easy for a person with considerable assets to disguise monthly income meaning that someone able to pay for legal services would be in receipt of inappropriate legal aid. The relatively low threshold of capital does mean that the vast majority of home-owners will not be eligible for legal assistance.

Even if a person is within the thresholds it is possible that they may have to make a contribution to their legal aid (reg 38 CLS(F)R 2000). The contribution would be a fixed percentage of their disposable income. Certain people do not need to make a contribution; this includes a person who is properly in receipt of income support, income-based jobseekers allowance, or a state pension credit (reg 4 CLS(F)R 2000).

The *Community Legal Advice* website includes a calculator that asks a series of questions on a person's income and states whether they are eligible for legal aid. The Online Resource Centre provides a link to this.

9.2.1.3 Merits test

The second test that must ordinarily be satisfied is the merits test. Legal aid is not available to all actions: it would be unreasonable for the state to fund litigation that is hopeless or has a small chance of success or where the result would be academic. The merits test is contained within *The Funding Code*, the document that sets out the rules under which the LSC operates. The actual test differs depending on the various level of assistance being sought. In terms of 'legal help', ie the initial advice, the merits test is simply that 'there is sufficient benefit to the client, having regard to the circumstances of the matter...to justify work' and that it is 'reasonable for the matter to be funded out of the Community Legal Service Fund' (s 5). Where the matter includes representation at court then the following criteria apply:

- Could the matter be funded by an alternative manner (including insurance or another funder (eg union) but this does not include a CFA).
- Could other levels of assistance be offered (eg legal help etc).
- Is it necessary for there to be representation and this will include considering the complexity of the court and the existence of other proceedings.
- If the matter has, or is likely to be, allocated to the small claims track (this is because small claims hearings are usually heard without the use of lawyers: see 14.2).

Where the matter involves 'full representation' (ie the conduct of litigation) then the following circumstances should be considered:

- Could the matter be brought through the use of a CFA.
- The application will be refused if:
  - the prospects are unclear;
  - the prospects of success are borderline and the case does not appear to have a significant wider public interest or to be of overwhelming importance to the client; or
  - the prospects of success are poor.
- Where the claim is for a money claim then the application will be refused unless:
  - the prospects are very good (80 per cent or more) and likely damages will exceed the likely costs;
  - the prospects are good (60–80 per cent) and likely damages must exceed likely costs by a ratio of 2:1;
  - the prospects of success are moderate (50–60 per cent) and likely damages must exceed likely costs by a ratio of 4:1.

This demonstrates the cautious approach that the LSC adopts to litigation.

9.2.2 Criminal legal aid

Perhaps the most controversial aspect of legal aid in recent years has been in connection with criminal matters. The media, in particular, have been concerned at the fact that some high-profile defendants were given legal aid when it would seem that they could otherwise afford to fund their defence costs and this perception arguably increased when three MPs who were charged with criminal offences relating to their expenses were given legal aid. However, this latter example is perhaps unfair because the litigation is complex (including seeking a ruling from the Supreme Court) and thus costly.

A difficulty with criminal legal aid is the dual role of the state. The then Lord Chancellor, Lord Irvine, commented that criminal legal aid was the classic example of 'demand-led' costs but it has been pointed out that this neglects the fact that it is the state itself that creates the demand as it is the state, and not a private citizen, who decides whether to prosecute an offender.

Following the AJA 1999 criminal legal aid is the responsibility of the *Criminal Defence Service* (s 12 AJA 1999) although it is notable that the *Community Legal Advice* website, which is operated by the CLS, includes some generic advice on criminal matters. The CDS operates legal aid in two distinct ways; the public defender service and contract work.

9.2.2.1 Public defender service

The public defender service (PDS) was originally set up as a four-office pilot in Birmingham, Liverpool, Middlesbrough, and Swansea, although four other offices subsequently opened (Cheltenham, Chester, Darlington, and Pontypridd). Currently the number of offices has reduced to four, these being Cheltenham, Darlington, Pontypridd, and Swansea. The other offices closed. Those who staff the PDS are public-sector employees (ie paid for by the state) although operationally they are based in the CDS. A comparison can be drawn to the *Crown Prosecution Service* (CPS) as in effect the PDS was designed to be the mirror of the CPS (see 10.1.1 for a discussion on the CPS).

The concept of a PDS was, and is, extremely controversial not least because it raises questions as to independence (Tata et al (2004) 121). Whilst questions may be raised about the independence of the CPS it is perhaps less troublesome since it is the state bringing a prosecution. The prosecution should not abuse its powers but the state has, in modern times, always prosecuted people. However, defence work is different. If a defence lawyer is being paid by the state will he defend politically unpopular cases to the best of his ability? Anthony Edwards, a respected private-practice solicitor and member of the LSC who had professional responsibility for the PDS, argued that he had not seen any evidence of ethical issues being raised and stated: 'I never bought the idea that just because you're in employment, you're biased' (Rose (2004) 21).

This is almost certainly correct and nobody has raised any evidence to suggest that there has actually been any bias on the part of PDS lawyers but as will be seen later in this book, bias is also about *perceptions* rather than reality and there could be a perception of a conflict of interest. However, to counter this the PDS publishes a Code of Conduct that identifies how their employees are operationally independent, and those members who are legally qualified are, of course, regulated by the professions. Failing to defend someone to the best of one's abilities could only be considered as serious professional misconduct and the professions would have to take the necessary steps to prevent that.

❓ QUESTION FOR REFLECTION

Read Section 7.5, which considers the issue of judicial independence, and Section 8.9, which looked at the ethics of the legal profession. Can a public defender service really be independent? Does this matter?

9.2.2.2 Contract work

The second method by which the CDS operates is through contract work and to this extent it operates in a way very similar to the CLS and so little needs to be said about this. As with civil legal aid the reforms of the AJA have led to a reduction in the number of firms who undertake criminal legal aid work. Whilst it has been noted that the issue of Very High Costs Cases (VHCC) was outside the standard contracts for civil cases, the impact of VHCC has been considerable in the field of criminal law and the rules relating to VHCC continue to be fluid and this will be returned to later in this chapter (9.5.1.1).

9.2.2.3 Legal advice at a police station

Perhaps the first issue to note is in respect of legal advice that is provided to a person who has been arrested by the police (s 58 *Police and Criminal Evidence Act 1984* provides the right to free and impartial legal advice when arrested). Traditionally this has always been an important part of the criminal justice system and it is notable that there has been no serious attempt to alter this position. Technically an offender can choose his solicitor although where he wishes this to be legally-aided advice (ie he wishes the consultation to be free) then he must know that the solicitor has a contract with the CDS (although apparently in two-thirds of cases the suspect's own solicitor is the one who attends (Zander (2007) 611). It is more likely that an offender will be given the 'duty solicitor' a rota of names of solicitors, or other qualified persons, who are 'on call' for arrests.

Traditionally all legal advice was given person face-to-face but recently this has altered and it is increasingly common for defendants to receive telephone advice and indeed this is now the most usual course if the offence is non-imprisonable save where it involves certain driving offences. Where the offence is imprisonable then an attendance allowance is paid as are situations where the offender is to be formally interviewed under caution following arrest.

9.2.2.4 Post-charge advice and representation

Free legal advice at the time of arrest has not proven particularly controversial, what is more controversial is the situation after charge. The rate of pay for such legal work used to be variable, with each solicitor and barrister almost being able to set a price, albeit within a defined range. The AJA 1999 reforms introduced the concept of fixed-price contracts so far as possible. Fixed fees would be paid for attendance at the police station, preparatory work, bail applications, etc. By paying a fixed fee for each stage of proceedings it was hoped that this might lead to a reduction in delays.

As with the civil system, solicitor firms must 'bid' to hold a contract with the CDS. As with the civil legal aid system, this has seen a reduction in the number of firms that operate legal aid. The initial contract is for a solicitor only and this will be sufficient for most summary matters but where the matter proceeds to the Crown Court and it is necessary to engage either counsel or a solicitor-advocate then a separate contract is issued for this although in these circumstances it will frequently be for a fixed fee save for the VHCC regime.

As with the civil system there is a merits test although this is generally easier to satisfy than the civil test as it is based on factors such as a potential loss of liberty, loss of reputation, or loss of livelihood (Sch 3 AJA 1999 and see Zander (2007) 604). Few cases will not meet the threshold and it has been remarked that, for example, in 95 per cent of cases before the Crown Court the defendant will be represented by an advocate who is publicly funded (Zander (2007) 604) and indeed much of the work of the junior Bar is to be found in routine legally-aided work, but even the most eminent QCs at the Criminal Bar will spend a considerable proportion of their work being funded by legal aid (hence the government's 'naming' policy of showing who earned the most money from the criminal legal aid fund (Abel (2003) 310).

9.2.2.5 Means-testing

Perhaps the most controversial aspect of criminal legal aid in recent years is the introduction of means-testing and, most latterly, contributions within the Crown Court. Whilst theoretically criminal legal aid was always subject to a means test and a contribution afterwards where an offender was convicted, the reality is that this rarely occurred (Zander (2007) 606). The government, through the AJA 1999, changed the system so that defendants appearing in the Crown Court were not means-tested prior to their trial or hearing but, once convicted, the Crown Court could decide whether a convicted offender should be required to pay some or all of the costs of his defence (Zander (2007) 606).

The *Criminal Defence Service Act 2006* was designed to alter the manner in which means tests (which had been temporarily abolished) were conducted in the magistrates' court with the intention that those who could afford to pay for their defence should. The current system is explained by the LSC on its website but can be summarized thus:

- **Parachute applicants.** These are applications where no means testing is required because they are in receipt of an appropriate benefit (eg income support, income-based job seekers allowance etc).

- **Initial means test.** The applicant's income (including salary, benefits, and money from other sources) is examined. Where the applicant has income from a partner then this is taken into account. The income is then adjusted to take into account dependants and children (see table below).

- **Full means test.** Where an initial test shows that the applicant's income is more than £12,745 and less than £22,335 before tax then a full means test is undertaken which examines the applicant's disposable income. Where their annual disposable income is greater than £3,398 then they are denied legal aid.

- **Complex means test.** This is a system that is used where a person has a complicated income structure (eg self-employment, company directorships, etc).

- **Hardship.**

The complex means test cannot be explained in this book as it will take into account individual factors.

Initial means test

The initial means test is operated on a series of factors. The whole of the income is taken into account and then adjusted on the basis of weighting. The single person has a weighting of 1 and a couple a weighting of 1.64. A weighting for children is then given according to Table 9.1:

Table 9.1 Weighting for children

Age of child	Weighting
0–1	0.15
2–4	0.30
5–7	0.34
8–10	0.38
11–12	0.41
13–15	0.44
16–18	0.59

The age of the child is calculated by reference to how old it will be at its next birthday. The adjusted income is then calculated by dividing the income by the total weighting. Two examples will assist here.

> **◉ Example**   Example A
>
> Susan is a single mother of two children (aged three and seven). She earns £22,500 from her job. She is given a weighting of 1.0 and her two children have a combined weighting of 0.64 meaning the total weighting is 1.64. Her income is divided by 1.64 producing an adjusted total of £13,719. Accordingly Susan is entitled to legal aid.

> **◉ Example**   Example B
>
> Ben and Paula earn a combined income of £36,500. They have two children (aged one and three). They have a couple weighting of 1.64 and their children have a weighting of 0.45 making a total weighting of 2.09. The £36,500 is divided by 2.09 producing an adjusted total of £17,464, which means Ben is entitled to legal aid.

Unlike with the civil legal aid system, capital is not taken into consideration. If a person receives legal aid in the magistrates' court then they make no contribution, even if they are subsequently convicted. An interesting issue with means-testing, of course, is the likelihood of someone within custody being able to remember all the details of their income and expenditure. How likely is it that someone can remember this precisely when asked and without being able to look at documentation (since a person is in custody). Of course, it is likely that in such circumstances an application for full representation can be deferred but it does raise questions about how a person in custody is treated for the initial proceedings.

9.2.2.6 Crown Court

The most controversial aspect is means-testing in the Crown Court. This was originally a pilot scheme but in 2010 it was rolled out throughout England and Wales. The system in the Crown Court is significantly different to that adopted in the magistrates' court. The government, concerned at the cost of the criminal legal aid budget, suggested that those who were capable of paying towards their defence should do so. This followed a number of high-profile cases where ostensibly rich people were given legal aid (perhaps not helped by the fact that three Members of Parliament who were charged with various offences relating to their parliamentary expenses also received legal aid).

Another difference between the magistrates' and Crown Court schemes is that everyone will be entitled to a publicly-funded lawyer in the Crown Court but people will be expected to pay a contribution to the cost and, potentially, repay the costs if they are convicted. The broad income calculations are the same as with the magistrates' court and thus the various thresholds (initial test, complete test, etc) is calculated as above. The biggest difference is that where a person has a disposal income in excess of £3,398 (which, is effectively, £280 per month so a very low threshold) then the defendant will be required to make a contribution to costs either before or during the trial. The contribution is calculated at 90 per cent of the disposable income per month and is paid for five months from the time it reaches the Crown Court or until the case ends, whichever is the sooner. If a payment is delayed than a sixth payment is required. There is a cap for a maximum contribution although this is complicated in that it depends on the type of case but ranges from £6,731 for an offence of burglary through to £185,806 for murder. The cap means that if 90 per cent of someone's disposable income exceeds the total amount to be paid then they do not pay any more. For example, the cap at £6,731 equates to five monthly contributions of £1,346 and this equates to a disposal income of £1,495. If, for example, someone had a disposable income of £2,000 they would still only pay £1,346 per month for the five months.

If a person is acquitted then they will receive all their contributions back together with interest on the sums. If the person is convicted then if the contributions paid are greater than the actual costs of the case then the balance is returned to them but if the contributions are less than the actual cost of the case then they may be required to pay the remainder of the costs if they have more than £30,000 in capital (including equity within a house).

Means-testing in the Crown Court is extremely controversial (see, for example, Groarke (2010)). Does the fact that a person must pay the full costs of their defence have an impact on others? For example, let us assume that D, a husband, is found guilty of a serious offence and is told to pay £50,000 in costs. He and his wife have equity of £90,000 in their matrimonial home that they share with their two children. Does D have to sell the house in order to pay the costs? The answer is no. There is no requirement to realize the assets although a statutory charge can be registered on the house so that when the house is eventually sold the money would be repaid at that point. The LSC states it will take into account the personal circumstances of the offender and, presumably, this would mean taking into account the values of joint assets. In the example above, the wife would ordinarily be deemed to own half of the equity value (ie £45,000). It may be unreasonable of the LSC to place a charge of £50,000 onto the house as this would mean that the wife would lose out financially even though she may be completely innocent.

9.3 Legal aid and rights

The status of legal aid has proven somewhat controversial over the years and perhaps the most interesting question that should be asked is whether it is a right or whether it is a discretionary measure from the state. Should it also differ depending on whether the matter is civil or criminal?

9.3.1 A human right?

It may appear at first sight to seem extraordinary to suggest that legal aid could be considered a human right since we have an understanding in our minds as to what such concepts could be, but there is at least an arguable case that in some situations a right could exist.

Article 6(3) of the ECHR states:

Everyone charged with a criminal offence has the following minimum rights:

(c) to defend himself in person or through legal assistance of his own choosing or, if he has not sufficient means to pay for legal assistance, to be given it free when the interests of justice so require;

Clearly therefore at least in terms of criminal charges a person does have the right to legal aid albeit in limited circumstances. The first limitation is that the Article is premised as inherently based on means—'if he has not sufficient means to pay for legal assistance'—and, accordingly, if a person can pay for representation then clearly they should. The second limitation is that it is not expressed as an absolute right—'when the interests of justice so require'—although where guilt is contested or where the sentence could lead to a person being sent to gaol it would appear likely that the interests of justice would so require it. Perhaps the most interesting potential qualification is in respect of the choice of advisor.

The first sentence of Article 6(3)(c) is relatively clear and uncontroversial. If a person is able to pay for representation then they should have the right to choose their representative. The second part of the sentence becomes less clear. It could be construed that Article 6(3)(c) is stating that if a person cannot afford legal advice then assistance should be provided to him, ie a solicitor is assigned to him. The second way of construing the sentence is to suggest that it is an extension of the previous words. Accordingly, a person should have the right to choose an advisor and if he cannot afford to pay that advisor then the state should pay for the assistance. It would be extremely controversial to suggest that the second possible reading is correct and the courts have certainly taken the line that the former is more likely to be correct (see, for example, *R v De Oliveira* [1997] Crim LR 600).

Article 6(3) expressly relates to criminal proceedings and there is no comparable right for civil proceedings so it would appear at first sight that there is no right to legal aid for civil law actions. However in *Steel and Morris v United Kingdom* (2005) 41 EHRR 22 the European Court of Human Rights suggested that the right could be based under Article 6(1), the right to a fair trial.

Case box   *Steel and Morris v United Kingdom*: The 'McLibel' case

Steel and Morris v United Kingdom marked the end of one of the most interesting legal campaigns to have been fought in recent times. Steel and Morris were two environmental campaigners who handed out leaflets outside a McDonalds restaurant which made various claims about the nutrition of McDonalds burgers and the way in which the company performed its operations.

McDonalds decided to sue Steel and Morris for libel. They were represented by a high-profile legal team led by Richard Rampton QC whereas Steel and Morris could not afford representation. Legal aid was not available for defamation actions (either as a defendant or claimant) and thus they had to represent themselves. The trial judge (Bell J) assisted them in some of the technical rules relating to the litigation but they were otherwise responsible for their own litigation. By popular assent it was considered that Steel and Morris performed extremely well in court and possibly even better than some lawyers!

However, the absence of funding did cause significant problems. The cost of transcribing each day's proceedings was £750 which they could not afford. Initially McDonalds provided the transcripts to the respondents without charge but this was withdrawn because Steel and Morris refused to provide an undertaking that they would only use it for the purposes of court proceedings and not for publicity etc. There were over 20,000 documents produced and many of the factual and legal issues were extremely complicated. It was suggested that without proper assistance they could not adequately prepare their defence.

The litigation undertaken before the domestic courts was extremely complicated and indeed at the time this was one of the longest cases that had taken place before the courts (although this may in part be as a result of only one side having legal representation) but the quantity of written materials produced together with the number of ancillary proceedings and witnesses examined meant that realistically both Steel and Morris were at a disadvantage compared to McDonalds in the exercise of the litigation. The ECtHR stated that a fundamental part of Article 6(1) is the right to equality of arms; in other words in order for both sides to receive a fair trial they should ordinarily be in roughly the same position in terms of access to the law. The ECtHR stated that during this litigation, because legal aid was not permitted, there was an inequality of arms and that this was caused, at least in part, by the state, thus creating a breach of Article 6.

Whilst this is clearly an extremely significant case in that the ECtHR has, for the first time, accepted that granting legal aid for civil cases may be a human right, it is crucial not to overstate the importance of the case. The ECtHR did not rule expressly that Steel and Morris *had* to be given legal aid; what the Court stated was that the blanket denial of legal aid by the government meant that there was *inevitably* an inequality of arms and thus the state had failed in its obligations to allow a fair trial to occur. This is something subtly different to stating that legal aid should have been given. It has been suggested that the test for inequality is 'whether or not the [party] suffered a substantial disadvantage compared to his adversary' (Shipman (2006) 12) and this must mean taking account of all factors in the case including the parties themselves.

❓ QUESTION FOR REFLECTION

Is there a justification for denying legal aid from a class of civil actions? The ECtHR implied that Steel and Morris should have received legal aid, but why should the state fund an action that was based on their own personal thoughts and actions? However, if no legal aid is given does this mean campaigns etc become the preserve of the rich or those well versed in legal matters?

🎧 LISTEN TO THE PODCAST

For guidance on how to answer this question and a discussion of the main issues, listen to the author's podcast on the Online Resource Centre:
www.oxfordtextbooks.co.uk/orc/gillespie_els3e/

9.3.2 **Fair trial through free representation**

Perhaps the second element of any 'rights-based' argument in respect of legal aid is to consider whether a person receives a fair trial whilst on legal aid. To an extent this was considered in respect of the *McLibel* litigation above, but it is of crucial importance in criminal proceedings. If the state is to pay a fixed amount or even employ lawyers to represent the defendant then it is crucial that this does not interfere with the right to a fair trial.

It has been noted that research from jurisdictions outside the United Kingdom has suggested that publicly paid defenders sometimes pressure their clients to plead guilty in order to maximize the number of fixed-paid clients they can process (Tata et al (2004) 126). Interestingly, research conducted in Scotland suggested that whilst solicitors would strongly contest any allegation of pressure, they suggested that they were more likely to be 'realistic' with their clients because they did not, unlike for privately paid clients, depend on prolonging cases (ibid). Certainly their evidence suggested that state-funded solicitors would 'settle' a case earlier in the process, usually through tendering a plea of guilty (Tata et al (2004) 127). What is less known, however, is which of the two possible explanations above is correct.

Interestingly the same research demonstrated that clients were less likely to have confidence in 'salaried' public defenders than private practitioners (Tata et al (2004) 132) although it is not clear why this is. It is possible that it is because they view the fact that the state pays them as potentially objectionable and this does raise questions as to whether they are being open to them. In Chapter 11 it will be seen that many have suspicions about lay magistrates because there is a belief that they become over-accustomed to the court staff and lawyers and perhaps a similar argument is raised against public defenders, with there being some concern as to whether they are properly distant from the judiciary, justices, and prosecutors. This theory is perhaps substantiated slightly from the finding that the principal reason for disliking state defenders was the absence of choice; that a defendant could not choose a solicitor but one was found for them (Tata et al (2004) 133). Perhaps the reason they thought this is because of the suspicion that a state employee would not do all they could for them.

One question that has not been answered is how clients react to their state-appointed solicitor in terms of openness. If a client has no confidence in his solicitor then it is less likely that the latter will be open with the client and this may inhibit a fair trial. It is unlikely that the courts would entertain such a challenge especially since the professional bodies would regulate state-funded defenders in the same way as with private-sector defenders.

❓ QUESTION FOR REFLECTION

Should the fact that a lawyer within the public defender service is bound by the same code of conduct as a private-sector lawyer mean that doubts as to their independence are no longer justified?

9.4 Alternative funding arrangements

Although so far this chapter has been primarily focused on legal aid it is necessary to consider alternative ways of funding litigation. Three alternative sources can be considered here: conditional fee arrangements (CFAs), law centres, and *pro bono* work.

9.4.1 Conditional fee arrangements

The AJA 1999 reforms realistically brought conditional fee arrangements (CFAs) onto the legal map although they had previously been permitted in a limited capacity through the *Courts and Legal Services Act 1990* (CLSA 1990). The AJA 1999 reforms however made them more attractive to both lawyers and lay clients, not least because the full conditional fee was recoverable from the losing party. At the heart of CFAs is the notion of a 'no win, no fee' arrangement. Ironically this scheme has been enthusiastically supported by professions outside the law, most notably 'claim management companies' who are often insurance bodies seeking easy-to-handle personal injury claims. It is more often the actions of these bodies (who use slogans such as 'Where there's blame, there's a claim') that lead to the belief that the United Kingdom has established a 'compensation culture' with litigation becoming the standard consequence of an accident.

A CFA is where a solicitor agrees to undertake litigation on a contingency basis. Whilst it is often said that this is 'no win, no fee' it is usually not that simple as the losing party would ordinarily be responsible for the costs of the other side. So, for example, A sues B on a contingency fee basis. If A loses then whilst A's solicitors may not charge any fee, the solicitors for B would be allowed to recover their costs of defending the litigation. To protect against this, a litigant would ordinarily take out an insurance policy that would cover these fees in the event that they lose. The incentive for a solicitor (who, in the example above, would not receive any payment from A if they lost the case) to take such cases is that they are able to charge a 'success fee' which is permitted to be up to 100 per cent of the ordinary fee. The AJA 1999 amended the CLSA 1990 to ensure that the insurance premiums paid as part of the CFA and the success fee (sometimes known as 'uplift') should be recoverable from the losing side. Thus the losing side will not only have to pay their own costs but also up to twice the costs the other side incurred and also the insurance premiums etc.

It was noted above that CFAs have been put forward as a primary alternative to legal aid, with many actions for damages now not being funded by the LSC but simply relying on legal aid. However, there are questions as to the fairness of such cases. For example, whilst these cases are often sold as 'no win, no fee' this is, as has been noted, not quite correct and a person may have to pay insurance premiums which could be reasonably costly and which may result in people of low means not wishing to pursue matters. There is also the argument that CFAs encourage litigation only where there is a reasonable prospect of success. Since solicitors run the risk of not being paid for work if they lose the case then it is more likely that they will only take such matters that are likely to succeed, meaning hopeless litigation is unlikely to be pursued. To an extent this has also been considered a disadvantage since it means, in essence, that a person with a lower likelihood of winning may be denied access to the law. Legal aid used to allow some of these cases to be brought but it was noted above that the risk/benefit is now calculated as part of the legal aid test (9.2.1.3) and this must be correct: the state should not fund litigation that has little chance of success and certainly it is open to private practitioners also to decline such litigation.

Most of the arguments against CFA are premised on the basis of the uplift. There have been challenges to the uplift and one of the first cases to consider this matter was in *King v Telegraph Group Ltd* [2005] 1 WLR 2282 where the Court of Appeal was asked to rule that permitting the recovery of the 100 per cent uplift was unfair and, in the context of defamation claims, potentially a breach of Article 10 ECHR. The court rejected these arguments although it did accept that there was potential unfairness but noted that Parliament had provided for these schemes and the courts must acquiesce to this. That said, the courts have noted the potential difficulties of CFAs. In *Campbell v Mirror Group Newspapers (Costs)* [2005] UKHL 61 the House of Lords had warned that CFAs can have a chilling effect on litigation and, in essence, can amount to a weapon in that a litigant may fear defending an allegation for fear of being forced to pay up to twice the level of proportionate costs as part of a 'success' fee (at [31]). The dangers of this combative approach is perhaps heightened when one considers 'claims' firms, ie those firms (often not involving legally-qualified persons) who use the threat of litigation and the CFA costs regime to pressurize a person into a settlement. The balance of power between claimant and defendant can be unbalanced by a CFA.

👁 Example Balance of power

Rachel slips on the floor of her local corner shop. She falls and breaks her arm. It had been raining extremely heavily outside and it is not clear why she fell but Rachel states it is because the floor was wet and had not been adequately mopped by the shop.

Rachel contacts 'Ambulance-Chasers Direct Ltd', a (fictitious) claim management company who take her case on a contingency basis. They contact Sarah who owns the shop. They state that the accident was the result of Sarah's negligence and that she must settle the case by paying compensation or face court proceedings.

Sarah may dispute the nature of the claim but it would be expensive to fight the case. Ambulance-Chasers Direct Ltd, as a large company, however will be able to afford the litigation especially since it is more likely than not that they will succeed. This economic imbalance makes it more likely that Sarah will settle as she knows that Ambulance-Chasers Direct Ltd are able to issue proceedings, causing her increased costs than if she settled now. The economic imbalance may also cause the settlement figure to be higher than it ordinarily would be (as Sarah does not wish to incur litigation fees) meaning that Sarah loses out.

❓ QUESTION FOR REFLECTION

Think about the example above. How else could this be resolved? Rachel in this example probably has a right to claim compensation: it is quite possible that it is Sarah's fault. However, Sarah could well be disadvantaged as a result of the CFA. Even if she did fight the claim and go to court, she would be responsible not only for paying the compensation but also the costs and 'uplift' of the claim management company. Is this arrangement fair to all parties?

The possible imbalance of powers has been recognized by the courts and they do have residual discretion to impose an order for a costs cap. This is a rule whereby the costs payable by the losing side are limited to a prescribed sum, in essence preventing the 'success fee' from being recovered. The right of the court to do this was recognized perhaps most notably in *Henry v BBC (Costs Capping)* [2006] 1 All ER 154 where the Court noted that CFAs could create a situation where the matters were so unequal between the parties that it would be unreasonable to allow the uplift and thus a cap could be imposed (although in that case no cap was imposed because the cap must be prospective rather than retrospective).

The use of CFAs has been particularly controversial in respect of defamation actions and against public authorities. The argument against their use in defamation proceedings is that the CFA regime may mean that the media are reluctant to publish a story where they fear that any subsequent litigation not only exposes them to the costs of defending litigation but also, potentially, up to double the fees of instigating action. Where the law of defamation remains somewhat transient (for example, in respect of what amounts to justifiable comment about a person's private life) this may not be a risk that they are prepared to take and this could therefore stifle the free press. The then Labour government had proposed amending the CFA regime so as to impose a legislative cap on the success rate of 10 per cent (rather than the 100 per cent currently permitted). However, this was abandoned in the face of criticisms that it could mean that lawyers would refuse to take such cases and it could, in essence, mean that a defamed person could never take action (as legal aid is not available in such matters) (see (2010) LS Gaz 9 Apr 2).

Perhaps the more notable criticism is in respect of actions against public authorities, particularly the state. In late 2010 the Metropolitan Police Commissioner wrote to the Home Secretary to complain about the manner in which compensation is awarded for police misconduct. The reaction to this was extremely negative, with it being presented that the police were seeking to avoid responsibility for their errors, but at least some part of their point must be true. The costs of claims against the police may be inflated as a result of conditional fee arrangements. Where, therefore, the police decide to defend a claim or refuse to settle for what the claimant considers reasonable, there is a risk that the police will end up paying the costs of defending the litigation, plus the costs incurred and an additional uplift. To one extent this is uncontroversial: the claimant's lawyers have taken the risk that the litigation may not succeed and thus they should perhaps be entitled to receive a reward for taking that risk (not least because if this was not the case then a lawyer would only take cases that are absolutely guaranteed success: under the present scheme there are at least some cases that they will lose and thus not be paid for their work). There is also the argument that the police, or other public body, should accept liability when they have done something wrong. However, this neglects two principal facts. The first is that sometimes it will be open to debate as to whether a fault exists (and indeed what level of compensation should be awarded) and secondly the fact that public bodies only have finite resources. If, for example, the police or another public body has to pay out up to 100 per cent of the legal fees as an 'uplift' then this could have a significant impact on front-line public services. It is not easy to see how this can be resolved since there is an intrinsic tension within the system. The government, which ultimately controls all public expenditure, does not wish to pay for legal fees from legal aid (even though successful claims would see costs being reimbursed) and it is encouraging private lawyers to take on this responsibility (hence the desire for CFAs). However, this undoubtedly means that it could cost the government more in the long term or means they have to accept reduced service limits.

❓ QUESTION FOR REFLECTION

Should the police, NHS, or other front-line public services be protected from the CFA regime? Requiring such bodies to pay any appropriate damages but also then their own costs of defending the litigation and, potentially, up to twice the costs of bringing the legal action must have an impact on front-line services. Is it right that the number of police officers, doctors, or nurses is affected by the CFA regime? What alternative scheme could be brought however? If CFAs were withdrawn from this action would this not mean that only the rich would be capable of bringing an action against a public authority? How could that be considered fair?

Before leaving CFAs, an interesting compromise should be noted that was first identified in the case of *Gloucestershire County Council v Evans* [2008] EWCA Civ 21. The local authority entered into a CFA with its solicitors. The basic hourly charge was £145 and a success fee under the CFA of 100 per cent would be payable although this would be recovered from the losing side. If, however, the local authority lost then it would pay costs at £95 per hour. Thus instead of this CFA being a 'no win, no fee' it became a 'no win, lesser fee' arrangement. The losing party appealed against the order of the costs judge that they were liable for the success fee arguing that, in essence, the basic fee was £95 per hour and the successful party was therefore trying to recover a success fee well in excess of 100 per cent, something prohibited by the CLSA 1990. The Court of Appeal rejected this and stated that the provisions of the Act were clear. A success fee was payable on the costs incurred by the winning party. The agreement clearly stated that these fees would be £145 and thus a one hundred per cent uplift was permitted. If the solicitors were prepared to accept a lesser amount where they lost (but not the 'no fee' that ordinarily would be given) then this was a matter for them. To an extent this may seem a surprising decision since it would appear to alter the risk/benefit ratio at the heart of CFAs. The solicitors were taking the risk that they would recover a lower fee than their standard charge but this is arguably a lower risk than not being paid at all. Whilst the use of the standard charge for the uplift was undoubtedly correct it must be questioned whether it was fair or reasonable to charge the maximum possible uplift (100 per cent) as the success fee. Where the risk is reduced then it would seem appropriate that the uplift is similarly reduced.

9.4.2 Law centres

Law centres are perhaps closer to legal aid than CFAs in that they are still based on the premise of free legal assistance. Law centres became established in the late 1960s with the first such centre being opened in North Kensington, London. Law centres were considered to be part of social responsibility changes and provided fully qualified lawyers to provide free legal assistance to those within the community. By the end of the 1970s some thirty law centres had been established and by the 1980s there was a further increase to approximately fifty-five. However, since the 1980s there has been no further increase, in part because of different governmental priorities over social responsibility and also because of changes to the legal aid budget.

Law centres are independent and are often managed locally by elected boards of management. As independent charitable-sector bodies, seeking funding has always been difficult; although legal aid (now the CLS) will pay a proportion of the fees, other sources of income are required. Although some local authorities will contribute this will frequently be insufficient and law centres have to try to raise funds themselves.

Ordinarily the work of law centres will be the provision of advice although they will undertake limited advocacy work, most notably in respect of tribunals where it has been otherwise more difficult to obtain representation (see Chapter 15.3.2 for a further discussion on this). Another significant difference between law centres and legal aid is that there is no means-testing for users of their services: they will provide assistance to anyone.

9.4.3 Community Legal Aid Centres

The reduction in Law Centres has been caused, in part, by the LSC and government's plans to reform the way that community-based legal aid occurs. The latest guise of community legal services are known as 'Community Legal Aid Centres' (CLACs).

The first CLAC was opened in Gateshead and was formed by an amalgamation of the pre-existing Gateshead Law Centre, Citizens Advice Bureau, and three private firms of solicitors. Later CLACs were launched with the tendering process in Leicester being somewhat fraught and unsuccessful the first time around. The eventual successful bidder for Leicester CLAC led to the demise of the Law Centre. In 2008 the establishment of the Hull CLAC became politically sensitive when there were fears that long-standing pre-existing providers of free legal advice would lose out from the establishment of the CLAC. That said, these matters were resolved and there are currently eight CLACs in existence with plans for two more to be opened imminently. A significant issue with CLACs is that they become the sole provider of social welfare law services in the area. The LSC will not contract with other bodies to provide such advice. This means that pre-existing contractors (for example, a Law Centre) will cease to be able to undertake such work, possibly leading to their demise. The LSC claims that providing a single point of contact is more efficient and provides for a higher standard of service for the users. Others cast doubt on this believing that it creates a monopoly that survives through meeting appropriate statistical quotas meaning that where a quota is completed there is a risk that a person will not be given appropriate advice. Being the sole provider also causes difficulties where there is either a dispute between user and CLAC or a conflict of interest (Griffith (2008) 6).

9.4.4 *Pro bono*

The final form of funding to consider, albeit briefly, is where work is undertaken *pro bono*, in other words for free. The professions have seen *pro bono* work as part of a social responsibility programme and in recent years it has been encouraged by both professions and large City firms. Some will argue that it is a convenient public-relations exercise to avoid criticism of large fees but it is quite clear that it does assist many individuals who would otherwise want for advice and/or representation.

One of the earliest *pro bono* units was that operated by the Bar Council and this was later joined by the Inns of Court School of Law (now City Law School) Free Representation Unit (FRU). The FRU was an interesting development in that it used trainee barristers to present cases and provide advice, although they were supported by both Inns of Court School of Law staff and practising members of the Bar. The Unit has become increasingly strong and other universities have adopted the model with many now offering legal advice. Perhaps the most notable of these is the Law School Office operated by Northumbria University which undertakes both civil and criminal work and whose activities led to a person's conviction for robbery being quashed.[2]

In recent years the professional *pro bono* units have been cooperating more effectively with each other and the other *pro bono* clinics (eg at universities) and this has led to a situation where in the most deserving cases a full litigation service can be conducted in this way, from initial referral to solicitor through to counsel appearing in court. However, although it is an important part of the professions' work it remains a very small part of the overall provision of legal services.

An interesting change is brought about by s 194 LSA 2007. By that section a civil court may order a person party to proceedings to make a payment to a prescribed

---

2. The appellant was Alex Allan and his conviction was quashed in August 2001. The Court of Appeal praised the work of the students in undertaking this case.

charity. The *Legal Services Act (2007) (Prescribed Charity) Order*, SI 2008/2680, prescribed the *Access to Justice Foundation* as the prescribed charity. This is charity that exists to support *pro bono* schemes. The power under s 194 is designed to presumably reflect the fact that a true *pro bono* case involves no legal fees and therefore there is nothing to recoup from a losing party. This power permits a court to, presumably, order the losing party to make a contribution to the charity although its wording leaves open the possibility that a winning party could also be ordered to make a donation.

9.5 The future of funding

Legal funding remains a topical issue and the Comprehensive Spending Review in October 2010 suggested that the legal aid budget would be reduced by approximately ten per cent. This is on top of previous reductions and it demonstrates that legal aid is being continually squeezed by successive governments. The last major review of legal aid was conducted by Lord Carter who, in 2005, was asked to review how legal aid should be resourced by the state. Whilst he reported in 2006 many of the aspects of his scheme have not yet been implemented.

9.5.1 Criminal legal aid

The primary recommendation of Lord Carter was that a more market-orientated approach should be given to publicly funded criminal cases. In part this is an attempt to align the criminal legal system closer to the civil legal aid system, with the suggestion that a smaller number of firms should be engaged to do the majority of the legal aid work. How this works in terms of firms in small rural locations is perhaps open to debate. The bidding process was controversial as regards civil legal aid but would be extremely controversial in respect of criminal work where concerns as to quality and the right of access to a named solicitor is a much longer tradition. Also if firms bid for a certain number of contracts, what happens where the firm is full. Whilst it may be annoying for a litigant to go to another firm or use a CFA the consequences for a person accused of a criminal offence are considerably more serious. Of course the counter-argument is that if a considerable portion of the current legal aid budget is caused by administrative costs then it would be better for larger firms to take responsibility for such matters so that the administrative costs account for a smaller proportion of the overall budget for a firm. It would seem that competitive tendering is likely to be a key feature of the criminal legal aid budget (see (2010) Law Gaz 21 October) and this will undoubtedly have an impact on the number of firms that will hold a contract and, according to its detractors, an impact on access to justice.

The other principal changes recommended by Carter include moving away from negotiated fees to standardized graduated fees (Carter (2006) 4). In essence this means that a set fee will be given for a set classification of work rather than for the length of time it takes to do so. The claim is that this will encourage efficiency in that lawyers will know they get the same amount of money regardless of the time spent on it. A safeguard against 'sloppy practices' is that there will be a peer review scheme to assess the quality of service provided by firms. Graduated fees have been used for advocacy in the Crown Court since 2005 but Carter believes it should be introduced to litigation work (ie the non-advocacy aspects of a case proceeding, eg disclosure, case management, etc) and that it should also move into magistrates' courts. Again, there are arguments for and against such a move given that it is relatively easy to see that the overall aim is to reduce payments.

9.5.1.1 Very High Costs Cases

One of the principal changes will be to high-cost criminal litigation. Carter argued that this accounted for a disproportionately high part of the legal aid budget (Carter (2006) 4) and that tendering and tighter controls must be used to ensure that costs are kept under control. There is a suggestion that the type of firms that can 'bid' for these contracts should be reduced and they should be able to demonstrate efficiency and an ability to monitor progress. Some (most notably Vos (2006) 433) argue that this could be an opportunity rather than an impediment but only if all the criminal justice agencies work together. This is perhaps the crux of the matter. Whilst it is relatively easy politically to attack lawyers for the increase in legal aid spending, the court service must ensure that it is being efficient. Vos suggests an example of this problem is the listing process which frequently does not take into account the availability of counsel, meaning that the case has to be sent to another barrister, entailing delays and costs.

➲ DISCLOSURE

Geoffrey Vos QC believes Carter could provide opportunities as well as challenges. An example he cites is the disclosure process in long trials. Disclosure is discussed in a later chapter (see p 401) and he suggests that one reform (that was not picked up by Carter) would be to change the way in which disclosure occurs. Let us assume that there are three defendants in a case (X, Y, and Z). Under current rules the prosecution would disclose all the relevant information to each defendant separately. Counsel for each defendant would then examine all the evidence separately and decide what was relevant to their case.

Vos argues that rather than do this they could employ an independent barrister. This barrister would, after discussing the case for each defendant, sort through all of the disclosed material and identify what was relevant for each defendant. This could mean that costs are saved since only one barrister would be reading all the material rather than three.

This approach has traditionally been rejected because of concerns that if counsel for one of the defendants was chosen to do this, there could be a danger that it prejudices the defence of another defendant (especially where defendants were to blame each other). This proposal does not cause such a conflict if it is ensured that the barrister is independent of the parties, so that he would owe a duty to all three defendants.

This is a relatively simple reform proposal that could be easily implemented without the need for legislation. The judges could bring this about in conjunction with the Legal Services Commission through a change to the *Criminal Procedure Rules*.

The initial battleground in reforming VHCC occurred when the CLS sought to limit the pay of counsel conducting complex work. The rates of pay for the Bar would be from £91–£145 per hour for QCs and £79–£127 for a leading junior (where junior counsel leads another junior counsel) and a junior barrister acting alone would be paid £70–£100 per hour. Court fees would be paid at £476 per day for a silk, £390 for a leading junior and £285 for a junior acting alone. It will be remembered from earlier in the book that realistically one-half of such fees is taken up by tax and expenditure etc. The Bar Council notes that some recently qualified juniors who practice in crime can be earning as little as £10,000 per year and even those with established practices may be earning around £40,000 per year. Whilst this may seem a lot of money, if it is compared to other professions it probably reflects poorly.

The response of the Bar to the LSC reforms was one of intransigence. Although over 2,000 members of the Bar were asked to sign up to the revised scheme, it was estimated that less than 200 originally signed up, including only three QCs. The low number of contracted counsel meant that the scheme was in danger of causing severe problems to the criminal justice system. In the autumn of 2008 it was reported that the trial of the persons accused of the murder of the schoolboy Rhys Jones might have had to be postponed because of this stand-off. In the event, the LSC backed down and provided an exemption for this case but it did demonstrate the potential power the Bar had in respect of VHCC.

Eventually a suitable compromise was created but by 2010 it was decided that the idea of establishing a panel of advocates who would be able to conduct VHCC was considered inappropriate. Instead the LSC decided that it would contract individually in respect of each case. That said, the contracts will ordinarily be on graduated (fixed) fees for the work. Also, from 2010 there has been a reduction in the amount that will be paid for this work and it is likely that following the *Comprehensive Spending Review* of 2010 further cuts may be forthcoming. Quite how this will operate in practice is open to question since it could lead to a situation where members of the Bar decline to take a case (but see the rules relating to the so-called 'cab rank rule' at 8.2.3.1) which could have a significant impact on justice.

9.5.1.2 Recovery of costs

It was noted earlier that recent amendments to the legal aid scheme have meant that defendants must make a contribution to their legal aid costs. However, not every defendant seeks legal aid, some pay for their representation privately. Where they are acquitted then ordinarily they can recoup the costs of defending themselves from central funds (s 16 *Prosecution of Offences Act 1985*). This has always been on the basis of actual cost but in 2009 the Lord Chancellor passed regulations limiting the amount of money that could be recouped (*Costs in Criminal Cases (General) (Amendment) Regulations 2009*, SI 2009/2720). The premise of these regulations was that instead of the recovery of costs being based on what had been paid and was reasonable, they would instead be reimbursed on a scale set out by regulations (see Zander (2009)). The intention was that the costs would be set at legal aid rates: ie a person who paid his legal fees would not be able to recover the actual amount he paid but only an amount equivalent to that which would have been paid to the legal team under legal aid rates. In some instances this could have been a significant difference but the government justified it on the basis that it was part of its policy that those who are able to contribute to their defence should do so.

The Law Society sought judicial review of the decision of the Lord Chancellor to pass these regulations and in *R (on the application of the Law Society of England and Wales) v Lord Chancellor* [2010] EWHC 1406 (Admin) the High Court accepted that the fee structure prescribed under the regulations was unlawful. The court stated that it was not proper for it to decide whether it was a legitimate action of the government to make successful defendants pay a higher proportion of costs (at [47]); however, it noted that the Act (rather than the regulations) require the Lord Chancellor to repay sums that are 'reasonably sufficient' (at [48]) and that this must include paying the market rate. The court was concerned that the Lord Chancellor was seeking to control the market (at [50]) and that this would be an inappropriate exercise of his powers. The court then quashed the new scales (at [77]). The government did not appeal against this judgment but it is unlikely that the new government that was elected after this case will leave this matter alone.

9.5.2 Civil legal aid

Civil legal aid was also considered by Carter although the presumption appeared to be that the civil legal aid budget should, subject to certain exemptions, be whatever is left after the criminal budget has been set. One of the primary focuses is the belief that firms who wish to undertake civil legal aid should join together to create community networks (Carter (2006) 4). In essence this may mean combining with the not-for-profit sector or forming an alliance whereby firms decide to specialize in certain types of work and refer this to each other.

One controversial aspect of the Carter reforms that has already been implemented is the fact that the not-for-profit sector is be treated in the same way as commercial firms (Department of Constitutional Affairs (2006) para 2.2.23). Carter appeared to believe that legal aid should be established through a series of community networks (Carter (2006) 4) which would involve forming an alliance between the not-for-profit and with-profit sectors. To an extent this has occurred with the creation of CLACs (discussed at 9.4.3 above) but this can only account for a small amount of the legal aid work and is generally restrictive in the type of work that it can operate.

The additional pressures on the civil legal aid budget mean that it is likely that legal aid will continue to be restricted. There is some concern that pressure will be brought not to offer legal aid in public child-care proceedings or proceedings before the First-Tier Tribunal (Mental Health) Chamber. Currently legal aid is given automatically in these instances because it is viewed as an important principle when deciding the welfare of a vulnerable member of society. However, as costs are stretched then pressure may be put to introduce, for example, means-testing to such cases. Whilst the reality is that this may have a minor impact as a significant number of litigants within such proceedings would come within the means-testing it would mark a major cultural shift and could create a situation where the most vulnerable are not adequately protected.

Legal aid is an area where the government and professions continue to battle. An initial approach by the government to implement some of the Carter recommendations to the civil legal aid budget by altering the civil contract was the subject of considerable debate. The LSC attempted to implement many of its changes through the contract it had with solicitor providers. In 2007 the original contracts would expire and the LSC sent out new contracts that included a term that would allow it to amend any term within the contract if it believed it desirable to do so in order to reform legal aid. Whilst there was provision for consultation in any amendments, the only remedy for a firm who disagreed with the amendment would be to terminate the contract, in essence denying it the right to participate in civil legal aid work.

The Law Society believed that this was giving too much power to the LSC and it would, in essence, mean that the LSC could alter any of the fundamental terms, including (for example) payment as of right. It launched an action for judicial review of the matter and in *R (Law Society) v Legal Services Commission* [2008] 2 WLR 803 the matter came before the Court of Appeal. The case was so important that the Lord Chief Justice presided over the court (even though, as noted in Chapters 6 and 7, the Master of the Rolls ordinarily presides over the Civil Division).

The Court of Appeal ruled that the contract was void. Although it accepted that public contracts could have clauses permitting amendment, they must not infringe the principles of transparency encapsulated within EU law. A fundamental part of that rule was that terms were certain and the parameters of the clause the LSC purported to include were so wide that certainty would not be permitted. Following the decision, the LSC and the Law Society began negotiations as to how civil legal aid work would continue. The court case led to considerable delays in the new contract and it was not until 2010 that the revised contract was published, this time in a manner more acceptable to the Law Society. However, its exact implementation continues to be a matter of debate.

In 2009 a further review was announced by the Ministry of Justice, the Magee Review, which could see the legal aid budget being divided between the CLS and CDS more directly, with the fund being administered differently. Of course this undoubtedly creates a tension between budgets although it could mean that the civil legal aid budget is actually protected more than it is now since de facto the criminal legal aid budget comes first. However, how this will fit into other sources of funding, for example, CFAs is perhaps of a greater challenge. It certainly means that legal aid will remain the subject of some debate for many years to come.

9.5.2.1 Conditional fee arrangements

Lord Justice Jackson was asked to prepare a report on the costs of litigation, in part because there was a belief that the CFA scheme had began to lead to real injustices. His report (Jackson (2010)) has suggested a marked shift in the CFA scheme. Jackson LJ has suggested that there should be a significant shift from the indemnity principle. He believes that where the complainant succeeds then the defendant should be expected to pay the claimant's costs but where the claimant loses then each side should bear its own costs. This would be remarkably different from the current system where whoever loses pays the costs of both sides. More than this, Jackson LJ recommended that allowing for insurance to be recouped should be abolished (although this is, in part, automatic if a losing claimant need no longer pay the costs of the defendant) and said that any success fee should be payable by the defendant but by the claimant out of any damages awarded, with the deductible percentage being a maximum of 25 per cent.

It could be argued that such a scheme could be a useful rebalancing of a CFA. The fact that the claimant himself now pays the success rate means that the balance of power is shifted. A solicitor will still be paid his costs (by the losing defendant) but the maximum success fee would be 25 per cent of the damages awarded. The effect of this could mean that a person who can afford to litigate will receive more compensation than someone who could not.

 Example Defending CFA claims

Arnold and Charlotte are walking along a road when a car, travelling too fast, skids on ice and careers into them. Both Arnold and Charlotte suffer personal injuries, both receiving a broken leg and spinal injuries. Both issue proceedings against Kenneth, the driver of the car. Charlotte has private means and she can afford to engage a solicitor by herself. Arnold enters into a CFA with a solicitors firm. The judge at court awards both £20,000 compensation and awards costs. Charlotte will receive the full £20,000 in compensation but Arnold will receive only £15,000.

It could be argued that the example above is fair. Charlotte was risking her own money: if she had been unsuccessful she would have had to pay the legal costs from her own means. Arnold, on the other hand, would not have had to pay for anything as he was on a CFA. However, in the example above it was always certain that Charlotte and Arnold would win: the only question was quantum (the amount of damages). Should Arnold receive 25 per cent less damages when realistically there was little risk to be run by the solicitor?

The change to the cost regime is perhaps even more unfair. Whilst this is perhaps similar to the scheme operated in civil proceedings assigned to the small claims track (where an unsuccessful claimant does not pay the costs of the defendant: see 14.2.2) that rule applies because the small claims track should not involve lawyers. However much of the litigation considered by Jackson LJ will involve lawyers.

❓ QUESTION FOR REFLECTION

Return to the example of the shop presented on page 320. Sarah may feel that Rachel's injuries had nothing to do with her. However if Rachel secures a CFA then Sarah is left with a potentially unfair situation. If Rachel wins then Sarah needs to pay compensation, the costs of defending the litigation, and Rachel's costs of bringing the action. If, however, Rachel loses then Sarah still has to pay for the costs of defending the litigation. How is that fair if Rachel did nothing wrong? Does this not encourage spurious claims as it will put pressure on defendants to settle?

🎧 LISTEN TO THE PODCAST

For guidance on how to answer this question and a discussion of the main issues, listen to the author's podcast on the Online Resource Centre:

www.oxfordtextbooks.co.uk/orc/gillespie_els3e/

The government has yet to respond to Lord Justice Jackson's report but given the pressures on the legal aid budget it would seem likely that at least some of the recommendations will be adopted, transforming the funding of legal services.

Summary

This chapter has examined the funding of legal services, with particular emphasis on whether the state should fund services. In particular it has:

- Noted that legal aid first started just after the Second World War.
- Identified that the legal aid budget had continued to increase until politicians argued that it was unsustainable.
- Found that legal aid is the cause of extreme controversy between the government and the legal profession, with the former arguing it can be abused by the latter.

- Noted that the most recent reforms have severely restricted civil legal aid and re-introduced a means test to criminal legal matters, including requiring some defendants to make a contribution to their defence at the Crown Court.

- Identified that the European Court of Human Rights believes that in certain circumstances the provision of state assistance is required for a litigant to receive a fair trial.

- Noted that conditional fee arrangements exist and that the legal fees for successful claimants can be up to double what they ordinarily would be but concerns exist as to how fair their use is.

? End-of-chapter questions

1. Read Tata et al (2004) particularly pp 132–133. Their empirical research has suggested that defendants prefer the freedom to choose a solicitor and not have one chosen for them. Do you think that a person should have the right to choose their legal representation even when they are not paying for the service?

2. Cape (2004) p 409 argues that legal aid reforms have had little effect on the practice of barristers specializing in crime because despite the advocacy reforms set out in the AJA 1999 (see 8.3.2.2 above) very few solicitors advocate in the Crown Court. The barrister is subcontracted from the principal contracts between the CDS and solicitors and so both are paid. Is there a case for stating that only a solicitor should be employed for legal aid cases in routine Crown Court matters?

3. Flood and Whyte (2006) state: '[o]ne of the questions that emerges...is about the status of legal aid as a right. Is it one? Or is it something—a boon or a gift—to be given or withdrawn at the whim of the state?' (p 81). Do you believe that legal aid should be considered a right? Do you think it depends on the nature of the case? For example, where the state is involved (eg crime, judicial review, or public care proceedings) should legal aid be given automatically since to do otherwise may limit the right of a citizen to hold the state to account?

📖 Further reading

Cape E (2004) 'The rise (and fall?) of a criminal defence profession' *Criminal Law Review* 401–416.

This is an interesting article that charts the history of legal aid in the criminal justice system over forty years.

Shipman S (2006) '*Steel and Morris v United Kingdom*: Legal aid in the European Court of Human Rights' 25 *Civil Justice Quarterly* 5–19.

This is an interesting article that critiques the case of *Steel and Morris v United Kingdom* and suggests that the European Court of Human Rights has raised many questions that it has not answered.

Tata et al (2004) 'Does mode of delivery make a difference to criminal case outcomes and clients' satisfaction?' *Criminal Law Review* 120–135.
This presents the findings of an empirical study into the changes introduced into Scotland. The changes are comparable to those that took place in England and Wales and the article raises some interesting issues about legal aid and criminal law.

 For multiple choice questions, updates to this chapter and links to useful websites, please visit the Online Resource Centre at

www.oxfordtextbooks.co.uk/orc/gillespie_els3e/

The Criminal Justice System

10

Preliminary Matters

By the end of this chapter you will be able to:

- Understand the different stages in the prosecution process, and identify who completes the steps.
- Identify alternatives to prosecution.
- Identify how prosecutorial decisions may be challenged.
- Understand the concept of bail and identify the legal rules that apply.
- Identify who makes the decisions regarding bail.
- Understand how a case is assigned to an appropriate court and how it is transferred.

Introduction

This chapter is the first of four chapters that will examine the criminal justice system, and it examines preliminary issues, ie some of the issues that take place before the trial begins. It should be noted that this examination will not start at the very beginning of the process, the investigation of crime, as this is ordinarily covered in other subjects (eg Public Law, Constitutional Law, or Civil Liberties). The starting point for this examination will be that the crime has been investigated and the police believe that there is sufficient evidence to suggest that their suspect is the person who committed the crime.

In this chapter there will be an examination of some of the issues that must occur before a trial takes place. Three of the main controversial aspects of the pre-trial criminal process will be examined; that of the decision to prosecute, bail, and transfer for trial.

10.1 Prosecuting agencies

Although this chapter will be focusing on the principal prosecuting agency, the Crown Prosecution Service (CPS), this is not the only body that is allowed to prosecute and it will be necessary to examine some of the other agencies before continuing the analysis of how prosecutions occur.

10.1.1 The Crown Prosecution Service

The CPS is the principal prosecuting agency in England and Wales. It is a relatively modern creature, having been created by the *Prosecution of Offences Act 1985* (PoOA 1985) but it became 'live' in 1986, although its professional head, the Director of Public Prosecutions (DPP) is a historic office (Calvert-Smith and O'Doherty (2003) 384). Before the establishment of the CPS the police would act as both the investigators and prosecutors of crime. There was considerable disquiet over whether the police were capable of exercising this role appropriately (Dingwall and Harding (1998) Ch 2), with the belief that they were prosecuting too many weak cases which has consequences for wasting time, costs, and placing victims and defendants under undue distress (Ashworth and Redmayne (2010) 195).

The Royal Commission on Criminal Justice argued that a central prosecuting authority should be created and this eventually led to the PoOA 1985 and the establishment of the CPS. At the time this was extremely controversial, with the police, in particular, being against the establishment of an independent prosecutor since they believed that prosecuting lawyers were 'theirs' and they should instruct them (Sanders (2002) 156). However, the Act rejected such an approach and the premise of the system is that the CPS independently examines the action of the police and decides whether the full engagement of the law is required. The level of independence the CPS has from the police has been questioned over the years (Zander (2007) 245–246) and although recent reforms could, as it will be seen below, arguably strengthen this independence the contrary could be true since CPS lawyers are sometimes located within police stations, potentially weakening their professional independence (Zander (2007) 264; cf Glidewell (1998) 132).

The Royal Commission believed that a series of local prosecutors should be created, each accountable to the same political authority as the police. However, this was ultimately rejected and the CPS became a national organization under the governance of the DPP. However, recent years have seen this altering, in part because there was a belief that there was insufficient correlation between the CPS and police areas. There was also concern that the national agency was overly bureaucratic and did not properly represent a professional prosecuting agency. Eventually a formal review of the CPS was undertaken, this being chaired by Sir Ian Glidewell, a former Lord Justice of Appeal. His report was damning of the CPS and he found that it had not achieved the goals set out upon its creation (Zander (2009) 247). He argued that the CPS was too centralized and focused on administration. The then DPP, Dame Barbara Mills QC, was blamed for many of these problems although it would perhaps be fairer to argue that they were institutional failings. In any event the DPP (as professional head) had to take responsibility and she resigned from the post of DPP shortly after the report was released which allowed reforms of its structure to be made.

The modern CPS is less centralized and is established into forty-two areas. Outside London, each area corresponds to the area covered by a police constabulary.[1] Each CPS area is headed by a Chief Crown Prosecutor (CCP). Sir David Calvert QC (as he then was),[2] the new DPP, argued that each of the CCPs would become 'mini-DPPs' meaning that they would hold delegated authority from the DPP and would be responsible for making decisions for their area. Sitting alongside the DPP (although in reality slightly below since the PoOA is clear that the DPP is the head of the CPS (s 1(1)(a) PoOA 1985)) is now a chief executive. Sir Ian Glidewell recommended this approach and it allows the DPP to concentrate most of his effort on his legal responsibilities. A parallel approach occurs in the CPS with each area having its own area business manager who acts as a local chief executive, ie assisting the CCP with the administrative responsibilities. With the advancement of statutory charging (see below) the forty-two areas have also been joined by *CPS Direct* which is a division of the CPS which offers twenty-four-hour support to the police. CPS Direct has its own CCP and business manager but its jurisdiction is not territorial but temporal (ie CPS Direct offers services when the main area offices are closed).

January 2010 marked another milestone in the history of the CPS when the *Revenue and Customs Prosecutions Office* (RCPO) came within the CPS. The RCPO was a relatively new organization (it being established by the *Commissioners for Revenue and Customs Act 2005*) which had been set up because of concerns that HM Revenue & Customs, who originally prosecuted in their own name, were not effective (White (2006) 160). This followed a series of high-profile errors in prosecution (White (2006) 162–163) and independence from the investigative side along the model of the CPS was introduced by the 2005 Act. However, to save money it was decided to merge

1. There are forty-three police forces in England and Wales but London has two (Metropolitan Police and the City of London police). The CPS on the other hand simply operates a single area for London.
2. Sir David Calvert QC was the first modern DPP to be elevated to the High Court bench shortly after standing down from the post of DPP.

the RCPO and CPS and as of January 2010 the RCPO is now a division of the CPS ('Revenue and Customs Division') and the DPP is now responsible for their work.

The establishment of the CPS has in effect led to a division in the responsibility for the prosecution of crime. The police (and now Customs) now have responsibility only for the investigation of the crime and indeed no longer have the power to decide whether someone should be prosecuted (see 10.2 below). This was not always the case and for many years there was an 'uneasy relationship' between the police and CPS where the latter did not have the responsibility in deciding the charges but acted only as a 'reversing authority' whereby it could challenge a decision to instigate proceedings but not a decision to decline to instigate proceedings (Sanders (2002) 158). This has now been resolved and the CPS now has responsibility for the disposal of offenders.

How has this change altered the independence argument? Auld, in his review, appeared to suggest that the CPS should become involved at a much earlier stage and that it should adopt a more proactive approach to the pre-trial investigation of crime (Auld (2001) 399). The question that this raises, of course, is whether becoming involved in pre-trial matters will necessarily prejudice its independence. It is certainly known that the CPS will become involved from the very early stages of crime and where there is a particularly large or complicated crime it would not be unusual for the CPS to work alongside the police in the preparation of the case, including advising on the appropriate type of evidence to be gathered. It has been suggested that the division of responsibility has 'now been dismantled' (Ashworth and Redmayne (2010)) although the reasons for this is apparently a belief that the investigation and prosecution of offences will become fairer and easier.

QUESTION FOR REFLECTION

What do you think the role of a prosecuting agency should be? Should prosecutors, who are familiar with the intricacies of evidential rules, be involved in the investigation of crime? Indeed could it not be argued that the lawyer should have overall responsibility for the investigation of serious crimes? What would the implications of such an approach be?

LISTEN TO THE PODCAST

For guidance on how to answer this question and a discussion of the main issues, listen to the author's podcast on the Online Resource Centre:

www.oxfordtextbooks.co.uk/orc/gillespie_els3e/

10.1.2 Other state-funded prosecuting agencies

It has been suggested that up to 20 per cent of crime is prosecuted by agencies other than CPS (Sanders (2002) 159) and these can be very diverse with state agencies including the Health and Safety Commission, Pollution Inspectorate, Post Office, and local authorities who have responsibility for licensing and Trading Standards (see Ashworth and Redmayne (2005) 174–175).

It has been suggested that these prosecuting authorities tend to use prosecutions in a different way to the police, in that a prosecution becomes a measure of last resort (Cownie et al (2007) 323). This argument is based on the premise that the police will ordinarily act on the assumption that their purpose is to establish whether a crime has taken place and, if so, there is an expectation that a prosecution will be brought. This need not occur (see 10.2 below) but it is certainly a presumption. With the exception of the Serious Fraud Office (SFO) this is perhaps less true of the other state prosecuting agencies. For many of these agencies a prosecution is used only where a matter is so serious that it is the only form of disposal or where other forms of disposal have not succeeded. Other (principally administrative) mechanisms tend to be put in place by these bodies in the hope of avoiding prosecutions.

Whether this system is necessarily comparable is perhaps more questionable. It will be seen that the CPS has a non-prosecutorial disposal system (see 10.3.3 below) and this will not infrequently involve minor crimes. However the crimes prosecuted by many of the alternative state-prosecution bodies are not as serious so it is perhaps easier to justify such avoidance.

10.1.2.1 Serious crimes

Where matters become more complicated however is in respect of serious crimes. The Serious Fraud Office (SFO) deals with crimes that involve multi-million-pound crimes and yet its success rate has been seriously questionable (White (2006) 160). The SFO has, as its name suggests, a remit in respect of serious or complex fraud cases (s 1(3) *Criminal Justice Act 1987* (CJA 1987)) and it remains separate from the DPP with its own director accountable to the Attorney-General. The SFO retains a joined-up investigatory and prosecutory system whereby the director of the SFO is empowered to investigate serious fraud and prosecute them where she finds it necessary to do so (s 1(5) CJA 1987). The SFO has a small team of investigators itself but may require the police to assist them. A lawyer heads each investigation and is in charge of the investigation although the practicalities of this will almost certainly be delegated to senior operational investigators. Once the evidence is gathered the lawyer will then decide whether to prosecute the matter.

The integrated process of investigation and prosecution is to be found in regulatory matters (see 10.1.2.2 below and White (2006) 160) but the SFO is not a regulator, it deals with major crime. However, it was argued that creating small multidisciplinary teams headed by a lawyer would ensure that the evidence gathered would be appropriate for prosecution. However the success of the SFO has been somewhat questionable and this has led some to question whether the fact that there is not an independent oversight of the evidence is perhaps leading to weaker cases being prosecuted.

The SFO remains the only 'serious crime' body to continue with the integrated approach. In 2005 the *Serious and Organised Crime Agency* (SOCA) was created. It was popularly dubbed Britain's answer to the Federal Bureau of Investigation (FBI) in that it has a national remit but such comparisons are false. Whereas the FBI deals with Federal matters (ie a separate system of law that coexists with state laws), SOCA does not have a different jurisdictional basis but rather a territorial one: it is allowed to work across force boundaries but only in respect of serious crime. Its agents are not sworn constables although police officers can be seconded and many of its early members were not police officers but civil investigators.

The relationship between investigators and prosecutors would be crucial. Early indications appeared to suggest that an integrated approach would be taken since it was stated that there needed to be a different approach to prosecution of serious crime (White (2006) 177) but in the end the integrated model was rejected on the basis that the prosecutors and investigators needed independence (p 178). It can be legitimately questioned why the same conclusion cannot be drawn in respect of the SFO.

10.1.2.2 Less serious crime

It is not just serious crime that is prosecuted by agencies other than the CPS, indeed this probably accounts for very few of these 'outside' prosecutions. The more likely agencies are those that deal with minor crime or regulatory functions. Classic examples of these bodies are the Health and Safety Commission and most notably local authorities. When one thinks about law enforcement, local authorities are often neglected and yet they are an important part of the process with powers ranging over issues such as trading standards, health and safety, and regulatory compliance. Most local authorities will have a legal department and this department will handle the prosecutions on behalf of the authorities. The departments will also however deal with many other aspects including public child-care law, education law, electoral law, etc.

Members of a local authority legal team are unquestionably employees of the local authority and are certainly subordinate to the chief executive, even in larger organizations where the head of legal services may command an important position within the organization. Is there any independence in prosecutions here? It could be argued that there is internal independence in that the legal team will not normally have line-management responsibility for the operational teams in trading standards etc but ultimately there is no independence since all departments are accountable to the chief executive.

❓ QUESTION FOR REFLECTION

Revisit your previous answer relating to the independence of prosecutors (p 338 above). Do you think it makes any difference that some prosecutors will not be operationally independent from the investigators? Do you think it is easier to justify when the prosecutions are regulatory and used as a matter of last resort?

An interesting question arose in 2010 about what happens where a body does not have any statutory authority to prosecute. The *Financial Services Authority* (FSA) regulates the financial industry in the UK and it has express power to prosecute offences under sections 401–402 *Financial Services and Markets Act 2000*. However it has recently purported to be able to prosecute for offences relating to money laundering even though it has no express power to do so. In *R v Rollins* [2010] UKSC 39 the appellant, who was being prosecuted for money laundering, argued that in the absence of any power to do so the FSA lacked competence. The Supreme Court ruled that the FSA, as a person in being (a registered company has a legal personality), has the right to bring a private prosecution (see below) for any offence not reserved to a particular prosecutor. Accordingly, the FSA did not need any express statutory power to prosecute.

10.1.3 Private prosecutions

Although we think of the state as being responsible for prosecutions this is not always the case and indeed English criminal law is founded on the basis that private citizens (and indeed anyone the law considers to have a legal personality: see the discussion about the FSA above) may launch a prosecution. The creation of the 'principal' national prosecuting agency did not alter this principle and s 6(1) PoOA 1985 expressly reserves the power of a private citizen to bring a private prosecution subject to the caveat that the DPP may take over any prosecution (s 6(2)).

In *Gouriet v Union of Post Office Workers* [1978] AC 435 Lord Diplock argued that the private prosecution was an important constitutional safeguard 'against capricious, corrupt or biased failure or refusal of those authorities to prosecute offenders' (at p 477).

However, this statement was given before the establishment of the PoOA 1985 and although the power of private prosecution was retained by that Act it could be argued that the independent examination of evidence means it is less appropriate for the action to continue.

The retention of private prosecutions remains controversial and in a recent case Lord Bingham, the Senior Law Lord, described its retention as 'anomalous' (*Jones v Whalley* [2006] UKHL 41 at [15]) and part of this controversy is over the fact that a person may be privately prosecuted after being told that the state will not prosecute him. However, it now appears that this depends on what the offender has been told. In *Jones v Whalley* the respondent (Whalley) assaulted the appellant (Jones). The police were informed and they issued a caution (see 10.3.3.1 below) which included a statement to the effect that by accepting a caution no court action would be taken against him. The respondent sought to start a private prosecution at the magistrates' court and the appellant argued that this was an abuse of process and so should be stopped. The justices accepted this but the Divisional Court overturned the decision holding that the right to private prosecution should not be impugned. The House of Lords, however, reversed that decision and decided that the proceedings *would* be an abuse of process and may not occur.

The House of Lords accepted that the police were wrong to give the assurance they provided but argued that this was sufficient to justify a stay for abuse. Lord Bingham even went so far as to state:

> A crime is an offence against the good order of the state. It is for the state by its appropriate agencies to investigate alleged crimes and decide whether offenders should be prosecuted. ([2006] UKHL 41 at [16])

The House declined to consider whether the provision of a caution will *always* amount to an abuse of process but stated that in this case it was because the police had misled the defendant by failing to mention the possibility of a private prosecution. The House argued that the solution to this problem would be for the respondent to judicially review the decision to impose a caution on the basis that its wording was flawed. It will be seen later in this chapter, and indeed in this book, that judicial review is not an easy, cheap, or quick remedy and this suggestion by the House of Lords is somewhat unhelpful. The House clearly finds private prosecutions distasteful but the House has lacked the courage to decide one way or the other whether they should be permitted to continue. Given that Parliament stated that private prosecutions should continue to exist, it is difficult to see how this ruling can be considered compliant with Parliament's intention since the private individual has little or no control over the actions of the police and CPS.

It was noted that the DPP has the right to take over prosecutions and it is submitted that there are two reasons for doing so. The first is, rather obviously, to prosecute the offender rather than require the private individual to do so. If this occurs then the matter ceases to be a private prosecution and it becomes a state prosecution in the ordinary way. The second and more common reason is to discontinue a prosecution. Once the DPP has taken over the prosecution then he can discontinue any action, meaning the proceedings would stop (s 23 PoOA 1985). In *R v DPP ex p Duckenfield* [2000] 1 WLR 55 the Divisional Court held that when deciding whether to exercise his powers to take over a private prosecution, the DPP did not need to refer to the Code for Crown Prosecutors, in part because it would be unusual for a private prosecution to take place where both tests are satisfied (as under those circumstances the CPS would ordinarily prosecute). The decision of the Divisional Court appears contrary to that expressed by Auld who suggested that private prosecutions should adhere to both prosecution tests (Auld (2001) 415) but if this were the case then for what reason would the DPP not take over a prosecution? Indeed it could be argued that if both tests were satisfied then it would be unreasonable of the DPP not to do so and that a judicial review could succeed.

👁 Example Stephen Lawrence

In 1993 Stephen Lawrence, a black teenager, was murdered by a white gang in a racist killing. The police investigation of the crime was handled extremely badly with allegations that the Metropolitan Police Service was 'institutionally racist'. Five suspects were identified but the CPS eventually had to drop any planned prosecutions as a result of a lack of evidence. The Lawrence family decided to launch a private prosecution but in 1996 this collapsed because the evidence (gathered by the police) was insufficient and key parts of it were ruled inadmissible.

In 1998 after further evidence came to light a senior CPS lawyer suggested that the private prosecution had 'wrecked' any chance of bringing the killers to trial (at the time the relaxation of 'double jeopardy' had not occurred (see 13.4.3 below)).

❓ QUESTION FOR REFLECTION

Do you think it is right to allow private prosecutions to occur? Lord Bingham clearly believes that they are anomalous and that it is a public law matter. Consider the arguments for and against abolishing the right (eg if we take the *Lawrence* example, what other solution did the Lawrence family have?).

🎧 LISTEN TO THE PODCAST

For guidance on how to answer this question and a discussion of the main issues, listen to the author's podcast on the Online Resource Centre:
www.oxfordtextbooks.co.uk/orc/gillespie_els3e/

10.2 Decision to prosecute

For the remainder of this chapter, our examination will concentrate on the CPS. The first issue to examine is how the decision to prosecute is made. This is not a decision that should be taken lightly. It is always likely to cause distress to the suspect and possibly other people connected with the suspect (eg partner, children, etc). With some crimes (eg violence, dishonesty, or sexual offences) it can cause a stigma to be attached to the suspect irrespective of whether the matter is even proven. Prosecuting someone will also incur expense, both by the state as prosecutor and the person who has to defend himself. A trial can also be difficult for both witnesses and the victim who are cross-examined over their evidence and it is incumbent on the prosecuting authorities, therefore, to ensure that only those cases where there is a likelihood of success are instigated.

10.2.1 Charging

When the CPS was created the initial decision as to whether a suspect should be the subject of a prosecution was made by the police through a process known as 'charging'.

There were suggestions that the charging system was inconsistent with some people being charged regardless of the strength of the evidence whilst others against whom there was strong evidence would be released or cautioned (Sanders (2002) 154). Indeed there has been some concern over whether ethnicity and socio-economic factors influenced these decisions (see, for example, Sanders (1985) 178–182, Rutherford (2001), and Ashworth and Redmayne (2010) 185–186).

Some argued that one reason for this is that the decision whether to charge and indeed what to charge rested with the custody sergeant and he would be heavily influenced by the arresting officer or officer in charge of the case, especially where that person was senior in rank to him (Sanders (2002) 154). There were also suggestions that policies and practices differed over different types of offences and this all led to a position whereby it was thought that the CPS were being called upon to review prosecutions that were too weak even at the investigation stage let alone the prosecutorial stage.

Auld believed that the disparity between charging and review was stark, leading to a waste of resources in reviewing inappropriate cases (Auld (2001) 399) and he recommended that the CPS and police agree from an early stage what the charge should be.

The eventual response to Auld was the creation of a scheme known as 'statutory charging' which was rolled out as a pilot in 2002, this pilot being extended in 2004 and subsequently extending across all CPS areas with statutory authority under Part 4 of the *Criminal Justice Act 2003* (CJA 2003). This provided for a phased approach but the CPS quickly ensured that all areas were covered by the scheme (CPS (2006) 18).

The essence of the statutory charging scheme is that the CPS and not the police have responsibility in deciding whether an offender should be charged. The police lose their discretion as to whether someone should be prosecuted although some have suggested that they have a residual power to impose simple cautions without reference to the CPS (Brownlee (2004) 896).

10.2.1.1 Action by the police

Section 37 of the *Police and Criminal Evidence Act 1984* (PACE 1984) now states that where someone is being investigated by the police after arrest they may take one of four actions:

1. to release the suspect without charge and on bail for the purpose of enabling the CPS to decide whether to prosecute

2. to release the suspect on bail but not for the purpose of enabling the CPS to decide whether to prosecute (ie to permit further investigations to be made etc)

3. to be released without charge and without bail

4. to be charged.

The custody sergeant has the sole responsibility in deciding which option to take (s 37(7A) PACE 1984) which may lead some to question whether anything has changed from the previous system, especially since they retain the ultimate discretion under option 3. If the police decide not to refer a matter to the CPS then no review by the CPS can take place (see Brownlee (2004) 900) although it is perhaps more unlikely that they would do this where there is evidence that needs to be considered.

It should be noticed that there is a difference between options 1 and 4. The former allows the police to bail a person whilst the CPS *considers* whether to charge somebody, and after that consideration the person may (if the CPS so direct) be charged. After charge the police sergeant will decide whether to grant bail or remand the person in custody until the next available sitting of a magistrates' court (see 10.6.2 below). However, a case does not need to be delayed to consider charge and where the matter is particularly serious it is likely that the suspect will be charged at the expiry of the detention period following arrest.

The CPS has reacted to these changes in a 'twin-track' approach. The first is that there is a duty prosecutor who will ordinarily be available within designated police stations during normal working hours. This means that the investigating officers can have immediate discussions with a prosecution lawyer as to the strength of the case and the appropriate charges to be made. The second approach exists outside working hours and is the creation of CPS Direct, a system of 'on-call' prosecutors who work outside of normal working hours. These prosecutors, who do not work within a geographical context, can provide advice from their home as the CPS has invested in placing specialist communication equipment in the homes of Crown prosecutors (see CPS (2004) 15). This allows the prosecutor to review the evidence in a timely manner and ensure that the charges are accurate.

10.2.1.2 CPS options

Section 37B of PACE 1984 sets out the responsibilities of the CPS when a case is referred to it. The first decision that must be taken is whether there is sufficient evidence to justify a prosecution. If there is sufficient evidence then the prosecutor *must* consider whether to charge him with a particular offence or whether the matter could be dealt with by a caution (s 37B(3) PACE 1984). This latter part of the test is interesting since it means, for the first time, that considering the applicability of a caution is mandatory whereas it was previously discretionary.

The question that this raises of course is what does 'sufficient evidence' mean? The issue of 'sufficient evidence' has been perhaps the most debated and controversial issue since the inception of the CPS. The PoOA 1985, PACE 1984, and CJA 2003 are silent as to what this means but the Code for Crown Prosecutors (CCP)[3] makes it clear that there are in fact two possibilities (CCP para 3.2). Where the intention is to hold the defendant in custody after charge (ie effectively where the advice is 'immediate') then the 'threshold test' applies whereas in all other circumstances (ie where the case has been referred to the CPS whilst the offender is still on bail) the 'full code' test is adopted.

---

3. The Code for Crown Prosecutors is issued under the authority of s 10 PoOA 1985 and details the rules and regulations that supposedly govern the prosecution process.

When the 'threshold test' is used the full prosecution tests will be considered at a later stage: the threshold test is simply an interim stage.

Threshold test

The threshold test is in two parts and is based on the evidence currently available (CCP, para 5.5). The first part of the test is whether the prosecutor is satisfied that 'there is at least a reasonable suspicion that the person to be charged has committed the offence' (CCP, para 5.6). The second part of the test is whether the prosecutor believes 'that there are reasonable grounds for believing that the continuing investigation will provide further evidence...so that all the evidence taken together is capable of establishing a realistic prospect of conviction' (CCP, para 5.9).

It is worth noting that the test is framed on 'reasonable suspicion' which is similar to that required by a police officer to arrest (see s 24(1) PACE 1984) so it is undoubtedly a low threshold and, as has been noted by others, paradoxically lower than that required where the suspect's liberty is not at stake (Brownlee (2004) 902). However, the argument is that this is necessary given the tight timescales and in any event there must be an agreed date by which the full tests will be considered.

10.2.1.3 The prosecution tests

The CCP provides that there are two 'full' tests that must be satisfied before any prosecution may be started: the evidential test and the public-interest test (CCP, Part 4). Both of these are somewhat controversial and there have been doubts raised as to whether this is actually anything more than a paper exercise (Hoyano (1997) 556) with the real analysis being made by reference to confidential prosecution manuals.

Evidential test

The first test that must be satisfied is the evidential test. It was noted immediately above that where the lower 'threshold test' was used at the time of charging, this test must be considered. Where the decision to charge has not yet been made then this will be the first test to use when deciding whether to charge a person with a criminal offence. The CCP defines the evidential test as:

> Crown Prosecutors must be satisfied that there is enough evidence to provide a 'realistic prospect of conviction' against each defendant on each charge. They must consider what the defence case may be, and how that is likely to affect the prosecution case. A case which does not pass the evidential test must not proceed, no matter how serious or sensitive it may be (CCP para 4.5).

The most obvious question that this raises is what is the meaning of 'realistic prospect of conviction'? This is an important issue and it is one that is inextricably linked to the standard of proof in a criminal trial. In order to provide that there is a realistic prospect of a conviction then it must be more likely than not that the evidence supports a prosecution. However, debates arise as to what this means in practice.

❓ QUESTION FOR REFLECTION

Consider the meaning of 'realistic prospect of conviction'. What do you think it means?

If it means that it is more likely than not that the evidence supports a prosecution then does this mean that if there is a 51 per cent chance that the suspect committed the crime the test is satisfied? Or do you think it means that if there is a 51 per cent chance that the evidence gathered is likely to lead to a prosecution that the test is satisfied. Is there any difference between these two statements?

This conundrum has been at the heart of some of the criticism of the CPS particularly by the police where they believe that the CPS is sometimes too cautious in its application and does not let the courts decide on weak cases. In part this was based on the premise that it is thought that the police would use the 'prima facie test' (ie is there evidence that would make the case at least arguable) (see Ashworth and Redmayne (2010) 200). The argument for the CPS test is that a prosecution is an expensive and emotionally challenging business and one that should not be engaged without a realistic prospect of success. What is clear is that the CPS prosecutors must examine *all* the evidence and make judgements as to whether it is likely to be admissible and what weight is likely to be given to the evidence by the tribunal of fact, ie its reliability (CCP para 4.7). The CPS must also consider the evidence the defendant may adduce.

The CCP makes clear the importance of this test. If there is insufficient evidence then a person should not be charged, or if charged then the prosecution should be halted (CCP para 4, 5). Indeed this principle is so strong that the matter will be kept under review throughout the history of the case and if at any stage, including at court, it is believed that the evidential test is no longer satisfied then the case will be halted.

Public-interest test

The second test is whether it is in the public interest for a person to be charged or prosecuted. Statute makes it expressly clear that the CPS may decide not to charge someone notwithstanding the fact that there is sufficient evidence to show that he may be guilty (see s 37B(5)(b) PACE 1984). This is welcome reinforcement to the principle contained in the CCP. The basis of this test is a statement by Lord Shawcross, a former Attorney-General, who stated:

> It has never been the rule in this country—and I hope it never will be—that suspected criminals must automatically be the subject of prosecution. (CCP para 4.10)

In other words, just because someone has committed a crime does not necessarily mean that they should be prosecuted. There could be any number of reasons why a decision is taken not to prosecute even where there is clear evidence to suggest that the law has been broken. The CCP provides a list of factors that make it more or less likely that a prosecution will take place (CCP, para 4.16 et seq) and the public-interest test requires prosecutors to take these into account.

Prosecution policies

The CCP is the overarching prosecution policy but it does not specifically state the circumstances when a person will be prosecuted for a particular crime. This became relevant in the context of those people suffering from permanent debilitating illnesses who wished to commit suicide (which is not illegal) but could not without assistance (which is illegal).

The first case of note was *R (Pretty) v Director of Public Prosecutions* [2002] 1 AC 800 where the House of Lords were asked to rule on a case where a woman wanted her husband to assist her in suicide. Diane Pretty suffered from advanced motor neurone disease and could not therefore take an overdose herself. She wished to die but needed her husband to feed her enough pills to make her die, which would amount to a criminal offence (s 2 *Suicide Act 1961*). A prosecution under s 2 can only be brought if the DPP gives his permission (s 2(4)) and thus the applicant asked for an assurance that he would not be prosecuted. The DPP refused to give this assurance and the applicant (Mrs Pretty) applied for judicial review of that decision.

The main decision of the House was based on the ECHR where it held that the Convention did not provide a right to die (something that was implicitly upheld by the European Court of Human Rights when it declined an application by Mrs Pretty: *Pretty v United Kingdom* (2002) 35 EHRR 1) but of more interest was the court's observations about the DPP's power. The House held that the DPP had no right to confer immunity on an individual person (at [39] per Lord Bingham) although Lord Bingham suggested that he might be able to produce a policy document explaining the circumstances under which someone would be prosecuted for a crime although it was conceded that it may be an unwise action (ibid). Such policies exist in a number of offences (published on the CPS website) but there had been no indication that such policies were required and Lord Bingham did not appear to be going so far as to require them.

The ruling was controversial and at least one academic has suggested that it created an inappropriate state of affairs whereby a person would not know the circumstances in which their planned actions will be culpable (Tur (2003) 10). The matter inevitably returned to the courts and was the subject of the last-ever judgment of the House of Lords.

Debbie Purdy suffers from primary progressive multiple sclerosis and is currently wheelchair bound and will, at some point, be incapable of doing the most basic tasks herself. She has no wish to live in what she believes to be an undignified manner and so, at a time of her choosing, she wanted to be able to travel to another country and commit suicide. In order to do so she would need assistance to travel and she was concerned that if her husband assisted her abroad he would be guilty of the offence under s 2 *Suicide Act 1961*.

Debbie Purdy did not seek to persuade the DPP to provide her husband with immunity (as Dianne Pretty had done) but instead focused on the suggestion by Lord Bingham that additional guidance was required. She argued that the DPP should be *required* to produce guidance indicating the factors that would be considered when deciding to prosecute. The matter proceeded through the courts and in *R (on the application of Purdy) v Director of Public Prosecutions* [2009] UKHL 45 the House of Lords held that the DPP did have a legal obligation to publish advice which indicated the circumstances which would lead them to decide whether to prosecute or not. The House ruled that Article 8 of the ECHR required the law to be clear and accessible and that this required advice on the particular circumstances.

The ruling is important not only for the particular circumstances relating to Debbie Purdy's case but also because it shows that the statutory code (the CCP) is not sufficient by itself to show how prosecutorial discretion will be exercised and it also undoubtedly means that the individual offence policies produced (which are published on the CPS website) must be taken into account.

10.3 Selecting the charges

Assuming that the prosecution tests have been satisfied then the next step is to decide what a person should be charged with. In many cases this may appear simple but need not be because the criminal law is complicated and there are many overlapping offences.

10.3.1 Principles

The CCP details how the CPS should approach the issue of charging. They should:

- reflect the seriousness and extent of the offending
- give the court adequate powers to sentence and impose appropriate post-conviction orders
- enable the case to be presented in a clear and simple way (CCP para 6.1).

These steps may seem relatively ordinary but history suggests that in many cases there has been over-charging (see 10.3.2 below). The conduct element of many crimes will cover many different offences and these guidelines are supposed to ensure that the charge is reflective of the conduct and consequences.

Example Wounding

The *Offences Against the Person Act 1861* (OAPA 1861) provides for a number of non-fatal offences ranging from assault occasioning actual bodily harm (ABH: s 47) to wounding or causing grievous bodily harm with intent (GBH: s 18). Existing alongside this is the crime of common assault (s 39 *Criminal Justice Act 1988* (CJA 1988)). Each has its own definition and sentence. As you will find out in your *Criminal Law* module, the definition of a wound is simply any cut that penetrates all layers of the skin (*Moriarty v Brookes* (1834) 6 C & P 684). Consider the following case:

> Jordan was holding some paper when David came over and ripped it from his grasp. This action caused a paper cut to Jordan's finger.

What should the correct charge be? According to *Moriarty v Brookes* David has caused a wound to Jordan and so is theoretically liable for the offence of unlawful wounding contrary to s 20 OAPA 1861. This is punishable by a maximum sentence of five years' imprisonment and usually tried in the Crown Court (although it may also be tried in the magistrates' court).

Charging s 20 would be a gross overreaction to a simple paper cut however. If any charge had to be laid (and that is perhaps open to question) then it would likely be one of common assault, which is a summary-only offence triable in the magistrates' court.

The second factor listed above is, however, extremely significant. It is important to note that the court must have sufficient powers available to it when dealing with an offence.

10.3.2 Over-charging

A common criticism of the CPS by the police was that the CPS would 'downgrade' charges (Ashworth and Redmayne (2010) 210). In other words, the police would opt for one charge but the CPS would either reduce the charge to a lesser offence or accept a plea of guilty to a lesser charge. Sir Ian Glidewell, in a review of the CPS, was asked specifically to consider whether the CPS was systematically downgrading charges.

The conclusion of Glidewell was that there was no evidence to suggest downgrading although he suspected that it might be (Glidewell (1998) 84). However, this was contested by a report of Her Majesty's Inspectorate of the CPS who, when considering crimes of domestic violence, found that the police were systematically over-charging offenders and was critical of the CPS for not always taking prompt action to remedy this situation (HM Crown Prosecution Service Inspectorate (2004) 96). It would seem therefore that the criticism was actually a mirror of what the true position was: far from the CPS systematically downgrading charges inappropriately it was the correction of an initial mistake by the police.

The changes to charging brought about by statutory charging should mean that this does not occur since the CPS will be the one deciding the charges from the outset. This should mean that there are less pleas of guilty to an alternative charge although at the time of writing there is no evidence to suggest whether this has occurred.

10.3.3 Diversion

Whilst outside the scope of this book it is quite possible that the CPS may decide to divert a person away from the criminal justice system. Diversion works on the premise that although there is sufficient evidence to show that a crime has taken place and that it is in the public interest for formal action to be taken, the offender need not be prosecuted but could be given non-judicial action. The three principal types of diversion are:

* simple cautions
* conditional cautions
* final warnings and reprimands.

Alongside these formal forms of diversion exist the inherent power to take informal diversionary action, ie to warn a person as to their conduct but this would ordinarily take place prior to the CPS involvement. Diversion is controversial with Lord Judge CJ, in his first press briefing in 2009, suggesting that a failure to prosecute individuals could undermine public confidence in the criminal justice system. The DPP agreed and was reported to have said in 2009 he wanted only minor offences to be dealt with by a caution or diversionary scheme but statistics continue to show that this is not always the case and cautions have been imposed for serious offences, including rape and robbery.

10.3.3.1 Simple cautions

Simple cautions were, in effect, the original diversion and it is where the police in effect give a formal warning for an offence. A caution is recorded on the Police National Computer and can, apparently, be discussed in court (see Home Office Circular 30/2005 at [27]) although it does not have the status of a conviction.

A simple (as distinct from conditional) caution does not have any statutory authority. In essence its status derives in part from the statement of Lord Shawcross above (see 10.2.1.3 above) and through non-statutory guidance. The latest guidance is Home Office Circular 30/2005 and it states that a simple caution can only be made where there is sufficient evidence to pass the 'evidential' prosecution test (see 10.2.1.3 above), where there has been a clear and reliable admission of guilt by the defendant, and it is in the public interest for a caution to be given. Given that there is no statutory basis for a caution it could be questioned why a caution should be recorded on the Police National Computer as a disposal. In part this is, presumably, because a person must admit guilt before a caution can be administered and in this way they are accepting the fact that they did break the law.

A particular difficulty with cautions is that their ancillary effect can be not insignificant. In early 2006 there was significant controversy when it was identified that some of those who had been cautioned for a sex offence were teaching in schools (see Gillespie (2006b) 19). It was considered that this was inappropriate, presumably because of their admission of guilt. Similarly, if a person accepts a caution for a prescribed sexual offence they are liable to comply with the sex offender notification regime (most commonly referred to as the 'sex offenders register') for a period of five years (see s 82(1) *Sexual Offences Act 2003*). Given that the evidence is not tested by a court it could be questioned whether this is appropriate. The argument in favour of simple cautions is that one can only be imposed if a person consents but research suggests that such consent will not always be free (Soothill (1997) 484) and could, in fact, result from the person seeking to avoid the publicity of a trial irrespective of its outcome (Gillespie (2006b) 23).

10.3.3.2 Conditional cautions

Conditional cautions are a recent introduction under the CJA 2003 of which s 22 permits a prosecutor to order a conditional caution to be imposed. Whilst the term 'conditional caution' is used it is submitted that the scheme has more in common with a community sentence order than a simple caution. In essence it is a caution that can contain requirements on it. The requirements are such that 'facilitate the rehabilitation of the offender' or ensures that he 'makes reparation for the offence' (s 22(3)) and this potentially could include a wide range of powers although the central ethos is that the conditions must be rehabilitative or reparative rather than punitive.

A conditional caution can only be imposed if five conditions (s 23) are satisfied:

- that there is evidence to show the offender committed the offence
- the prosecutor is satisfied that the evidential test is satisfied and that a conditional caution is appropriate (this would seem to imply the public-interest test)
- the offender admits that he committed the offence
- the offender is warned that breach of the conditions could lead to him being prosecuted
- the offender signs a document that contains an admission, his consent to the caution and a list of the conditions.

As noted immediately above, the 'sting' in a conditional caution is that if the conditions are breached then the person may be prosecuted for the original offence (s 24). This can be contrasted with a simple caution, where there is no penalty for reoffending.

Conditional cautions are undoubtedly controversial since they are bordering on amounting to a punishment (although it is likely that the courts will argue that they do not amount to a punishment because of their rehabilitative purpose; see *Welch v United Kingdom* (1995) 20 EHRR 247; *Ibbotson v United Kingdom* (1999) 27 EHRR CD 332). The principal difficulty with the scheme is that it is administrative. Although a prosecutor must be assured that there is sufficient evidence, no court has tested the evidence or the reliability of the confession. On that basis can it really be justified to impose potentially onerous conditions on an offender?

That said, it is clear that the government believes conditional cautions are an important disposition for offenders, particularly where the conduct is relatively minor. It is notable that the *Criminal Justice and Immigration Act 2008* (CJIA 2008) has introduced a system of conditional cautions (based heavily on the adult system) for adolescents. The system of final warnings and reprimands (see 10.3.3.3 below) continues to exist but the conditional caution, with its ability to control behaviour, is now also an option for prosecutors.

10.3.3.3 Final warnings and reprimands

Final warnings and reprimands were the first form of diversion to be placed onto a statutory footing, with their definition existing under ss 65–66 *Crime and Disorder Act 1998* (CDA 1998). The provisions only apply to juveniles (ie persons under 18 years of age) and are designed to be formal diversions from the criminal justice system. More informal diversions, eg Anti-Social Behaviour Orders (ASBOs: see s 1 CDA 1998) or Acceptable Behaviour Contracts also exist.

For the first offence a person should ordinarily be reprimand (s 65(2)) unless the police believe that the offence is so serious as to warrant a warning (s 65(4)). For a second offence, a person who has been reprimanded should be warned (s 65(3)) but no person may be warned twice, in effect meaning that a subsequent offence should be dealt with by prosecution.

Where a juvenile is warned then he should be referred to a Youth Offending Team (s 66) who will consider whether a rehabilitative programme is necessary, potentially including counselling, treatment, or mediation (Zander (2007) 256). Early research into the use of reprimands and warnings suggested that the powers were not being used appropriately and that they had become de facto punitive (see Evans and Puech (2001)). When first created, a reprimand or warning could only be imposed where sufficient evidence existed for there to be a realistic prospect of conviction if the offender had been prosecuted (although some doubted whether this was adhered to: Evans and Puech (2001) 799–800) and where an admission has been made (again doubt arises as to how strictly this is adhered to: ibid p 799). It was thought that, like adult cautions and conditional cautions, a juvenile would need to consent to being disposed of in this way but in an extremely controversial case, the House of Lords ruled that there was no requirement for a child to consent (see *R v Durham Constabulary and another, ex p R* [2005] 1 WLR 1184).

This decision can be criticized for effectively denying due process to a juvenile (see Gillespie (2005a)). Despite what the House of Lords said, the consequences of a warning are probably punitive and yet there is no judicial oversight of the requirement to impose a reprimand or warning. This cannot be correct yet the European Court of Human Rights rejected an application to challenge the decision (Application No 33506/5) stating that because the police were expressly not prosecuting him, it was not the determination of a criminal charge and thus outside the remit of Article 6. It is unfortunate that the ECtHR ruled this way as it raises questions as to whether adolescent offenders—who may be the most in need of protection—are not protected by judicial or legal oversight.

The CJIA 2008 has amended the CDA 1998 by stating that the evidential test is now that the police must consider whether there is sufficient evidence to charge the offender rather than whether it provides a realistic prospect for conviction (CJIA 2008, Sch 9, para 2). Whether this makes any practical difference is perhaps questionable since the evidential test in the *Code for Crown Prosecutors* (see 10.2.1.3 above) states that a person should only be charged if there is sufficient evidence to provide a realistic prospect of conviction, so the change brought about by the CJIA 2008 may be simply cosmetic.

10.4 Challenging the decision

Eventually a decision will be made as to whether to prosecute an offender and it would be extremely naive to suggest that this decision would be welcomed by all parties. Many people will seek to disagree with this decision but what, if anything, can be done about it? There are, it is submitted, two classes of people who are most likely to be able to justify a challenge: those being the accused and the victim (including the dependants of a murder victim).

10.4.1 The accused

The person most likely to seek to challenge a decision to prosecute is arguably the accused. Should a defendant be permitted to challenge a decision to prosecute? The argument against permitting a challenge is that if the defendant believes that the prosecution is wrong then he can plead not guilty and let the matter proceed to trial. However is it that simple? Lord Shawcross, it was noted above, suggested that not every crime should be prosecuted and accordingly perhaps the decision to prosecute should be open to challenge.

There are a number of reasons why challenges may be brought but they are all likely to revolve around the issues of fairness. Perhaps the most common reason for challenging a decision is that the CPS has made a procedural fault in its decision to prosecute. An example of this would be that some offences require the permission of the Attorney-General or DPP before they can be commenced. If the CPS has failed to obtain the necessary permission then this must mean that the decision is automatically flawed.

Another possible reason for challenging a decision to prosecute may be to argue that the criminal offence itself is contrary to established legal principles or prosecuting a person for that offence is unlawful. If the offence is flawed then it would be perfectly reasonable to argue that a person should not be prosecuted for breaching it. Post-2000 the most likely form of argument under this head would be that either an offence or the prosecution would breach the *European Convention on Human Rights* (ECHR) (see, for example, *R v Dehal* [2005] EWHC Admin 2154). Such challenges are permitted by virtue of s 7 of the *Human Rights Act 1998* (see 5.1.2.3 above).

A third common reason for challenging a decision is that the prosecution is simply unfair. A good example of this would be where the defendant argues that he has been tricked into committing the crime by law enforcement agents. This is commonly referred to as 'entrapment'. However, it is a long-standing rule of English law that entrapment is no defence (see *R v Sang* [1980] AC 402 and in particular *R v Looseley; Attorney-General's Reference (No 3 of 2000)* [2001] 1 WLR 2060) and thus a defendant could not plead not guilty in court and then ask the tribunal of fact to acquit him on the basis of entrapment. Is it fair however for a person to be tricked into committing a crime? It could be argued that it is not and that it would not be in the public interest to prosecute someone under those circumstances. A decision to prosecute under these circumstances could be challenged.

It has been suggested that the number of judicial reviews of prosecutorial decisions has risen in recent years (Sanders (2002) 163) and whilst this is probably true the courts do appear to draw a distinction between the types of challenges.

10.4.1.1 Decisions to prosecute

In *R v DPP, ex p Kebilene* [2002] 2 AC 326 the House of Lords was asked to consider, inter alia, whether it was possible to judicially review the decision of the DPP to give consent to a prosecution. The case concerned a particular terrorist offence which required the DPP's consent before a prosecution could be commenced. Lord Hope argued that judicial review of the DPP's consent should not be permitted, not least because the only remedy would be for the court to ask him to reconsider his position as a court could not order the DPP to give consent (at pp 375–376). Lord Steyn went further and suggested that a decision to prosecute should not be subject to judicial review, in part because alternative remedies exist (at pp 370–371). This principle was strongly reaffirmed in the recent case of *R (Pepushi) v Crown Prosecution Service* [2004] EWHC Admin 798 in which Thomas LJ said:

> we wish to make it clear…that applications in respect of pending prosecutions that seek to challenge the decision to prosecute should not be made to this court. (at [49])

The reasoning of his Lordship was that of Lord Steyn, that alternatives to judicial review exist, but what are these alternatives? The most obvious is to plead not guilty and be the subject of a trial. Where the criticism is based on a flaw in the offence rather than the fact that the defendant did not commit the *actus reus* this would be unlikely to succeed. However, there is the alternative of asking the judge to rule whether the offence is known to the law or if a prosecution is an abuse of process.

The concept of 'abuse of process' is one that has been refined over the years, and is a doctrine that has been developed through the inherent jurisdiction of the courts. The doctrine is based on the fact that proceedings ought to be fair to the defendant and where there are material irregularities that make the process unfair then the trial should be halted irrespective of whether a person actually committed a crime.

ⓠ QUESTION FOR REFLECTION

Let us assume that David has been accused of possession of a class A drug with intent to supply. This is a very serious offence and one that would carry a substantial term of imprisonment if he were to be convicted. However, if the drugs were to reach the streets then a number of people could become addicted to the drugs. David accuses Elaine, a Detective Constable in Anytown Police, of coercing him to get the drugs. He claims Elaine told him where to buy drugs and who he could sell them to. Should David be able to argue that he should not be prosecuted for this crime? What are the arguments for and against requiring David to stand trial? Would it make any difference to your argument if he had previously been convicted of a drug-dealing offence?

🎧 LISTEN TO THE PODCAST

For guidance on how to answer this question and a discussion of the main issues, listen to the author's podcast on the Online Resource Centre:
www.oxfordtextbooks.co.uk/orc/gillespie_els3e/

10.4.1.2 Decision not to prosecute

Although it may appear extraordinary, there may be circumstances when a suspect may wish to challenge a decision *not* to prosecute him, ie he wants the prosecution to go ahead in order to 'clear his name'. There have been reported instances of this but it is submitted unlikely that the courts would entertain such an application. The overriding principle is that a person is innocent until proved guilty and accordingly the courts would almost certainly view the position as being that the suspect has nothing to 'clear'. Where someone is alleging that he is guilty then alternative remedies would exist for this, eg an action for defamation of character.

10.4.2 Victims

The suspect is not the only person who may wish to challenge a decision to prosecute; it is quite possible that a victim would also wish to do so, yet it has been stated:

> The main group concerned with non-prosecution decisions are victims. Their 'stake' in official prosecutions is not formally recognised by the common law. (Sanders (2002) 161)

The place of victims within the criminal justice system has always been controversial and will probably remain so. One of the tensions that exist between the police and the CPS is that the former perceive themselves as assisting the victim whereas the latter cannot. Indeed the Code for Crown Prosecutors makes this quite clear:

> ....the prosecution service does not act for victims or their families in the same way as solicitors act for their clients, and prosecutors must form an overall view of the public interest (CCP para 4.19)

Historically the victim is just one character within the case. Whilst there may be an increasing recognition of victims and the pressures that a criminal case can place upon them (see Fenwick (1997) and de Than (2000) 165) they remain semi-detached from the process, since in England and Wales, unlike in other jurisdictions, the victim does not have any formal prosecuting role (see Gillespie (1998) 1263).

However, it would be naive to suggest that victims have no place within the proceedings or influence in its decisions and the Code continues:

> In deciding whether a prosecution is required in the public interest, prosecutors should take into account any views expressed by the victim regarding the impact the offence has had. (CCP para 4.18)

This suggests that victims have a say but not a veto in decisions. However, some have argued that this is not necessarily reflective of the position and that the particular views of an individual victim should not be taken into account when deciding whether to bring a prosecution as it is purely a matter of the public interest (Ashworth and Redmayne (2010) 218).

 Example Domestic violence

Perhaps the classic example of a situation where the victim's wishes may be controversial is that of domestic violence. It is not uncommon for victims of domestic violence to retract an allegation made against their partner (Ashworth and Redmayne (2005) 200). If this happens, should a prosecution be stopped? Domestic violence is a particularly brutal form of assault because of the psychological abuse it entails. Society should try to stamp out such violence and thus there is a significant public interest in a prosecution proceeding. There is also evidence to suggest that a victim of such violence suffers cognitive distortions as a result of their treatment and thus a withdrawal of complaint need not be in the best interests of the victim or indeed their true wishes. Alternatively, however, if a prosecution does go ahead there may be difficulties in establishing the evidence (will the victim testify?) and it could in fact cause the victim hardship. The victim may need to leave the house (and possibly her children) or if the man is the main earner then the victim may be placed in a position where she has no money.

How should the wishes and interests of the victim be treated?

10.4.2.1 Decision not to prosecute

The most likely challenge that would be brought by a victim would be against a decision not to prosecute. The House of Lords in *Kebilene* (see 10.4.1.1 above) was careful to ensure that they limited their denial of judicial review to decisions *to* prosecute. Lord Steyn expressly stated that a judicial review of a decision not to prosecute is possible (p 369). His Lordship noted that the main justification for permitting a review of a decision not to prosecute is the absence of any alternative options. Strictly speaking this is not technically true since private prosecutions exist (see 10.1.3 above) but this is not a particularly realistic alternative, something noted by the Court of Appeal:

> only the most sardonic could regard the launching of a private prosecution (a process which, incidentally is become regarded with increasing disfavour in this country) as being equally convenient, beneficial and appropriate [as judicial review]. (*R v Metropolitan Police Commissioner, ex p Blackburn* [1968] 1 All ER 763 at 777 per Edmund Davies LJ)

In *R v DPP, ex p C* [1995] 1 Cr App R 136 the Court of Appeal was asked to consider the principles under which judicial review could begin and Kennedy LJ stated:

> [Judicial review can occur] if and only if it is demonstrated to us that the Director of Public Prosecutions acting through the Crown Prosecution Service arrived at the decision not to prosecute:
>
> (1) because of some unlawful policy...
>
> (2) because the Director of Public Prosecutions failed to act in accordance with his or her own settled policy as set out in the Code; or
>
> (3) because the decision was perverse. It was a decision at which no reasonable prosecutor could have arrived. (p 141)

In essence this statement reflects the traditional grounds of judicial review but the one that may be of most interest is ground 2 which refers to the Code. The CCP has been discussed above but there is considerable doubt as to how it is used:

> Most prosecutors regard the Code as a very basic document to which they saw no need to refer on a regular or even occasional basis...The Code is a Noddy's guide to the principles on which the CPS operates. (Hoyano et al (1993) 558)

Their argument is that prosecutors will ordinarily make a reference to the confidential prosecution manuals that will detail individual factors to be taken into account.

However, even if the Code is rarely used this should not detract from the second point since the Code does represent the minimum statement of policy in relation to prosecutions. Accordingly, if a case fails to adhere to the Code, regardless of whether the Code was actually examined, then a judicial review should arise.

Permitting a judicial review to be brought is only one part of the story, however. Whilst there are a number of remedies open to the High Court when disposing of a judicial review, no court has stated that it has the right to order the CPS (or more realistically the DPP) to prosecute but has instead limited itself to quashing the decision of the DPP not to prosecute. In *ex p C* it was made clear by Kennedy LJ that this did not mean that a prosecution *must* occur because it remained at the discretion of the DPP, and simply entailed the DPP reconsidering the decision albeit this time in the correct way (p 144).

10.4.2.2 Decision to prosecute

It may seem extraordinary but there may actually be circumstances when a victim may wish to challenge a decision *to* prosecute. Perhaps the most obvious example of this would be when it is believed that a prosecution is not in their interests and a good example of this could be in cases involving children.

> It may well be safe to assume that it is in the public interest that child abusers should be prosecuted... Yet, in many cases, once the child's protection has been assured, there may well be a conflict between the public interest in pursuing a prosecution and the child's best interests in having the case dealt with in a manner which causes the least stress and disruption. (Cobley (1995) 160)

This is an interesting issue as it demonstrates that there could be tension between the public interest and the victim. The principal issue will always be the strength of the public interest:

> [A] decision not to prosecute may indicate to the abuser that, so far as the community is concerned, he did not commit the offence. (Fortin (2009) 656)

In other words, whilst prosecuting may not be in the interests of the victim and could even be contrary to the best interests (and/or wishes) of the victim, not prosecuting may cause more harm to the public interest. What should be the position here? Some have suggested that the law should accept a challenge to a decision to prosecute as this would require the judges to consider the rights of each individual victim (Gillespie (1998)) but others argue that society would probably prefer the prosecution to continue.

10.5 Immunity

There has, over many years, been a debate as to how persons who assist the prosecution are treated by prosecutors. As a minimum it would normally lead to a reduction in their sentence (see, for example, *R v A (Informer: Reduction in Sentence)* [1999] 1 Cr App R(S) 52) but there has always been doubt as to whether prosecutors had given de facto immunity to someone cooperating by testifying. In essence such an approach could probably have been justified on the basis of the public-interest test: that it is in the public interest to encourage people to inform against serious crime and that this may have overridden the competing interest that someone who has committed a (minor) crime should be prosecuted.

No formal basis existed for deciding immunity—it was simply a matter of prosecutorial discretion—but this has now changed with the passing of the *Serious Organised Crime and Police Act 2005* which permits immunity to be granted. Section 71 permits, inter alia, the DPP or a prosecutor designated by himself (ie any Crown Prosecutor if he so wishes) to grant total immunity for *any* offence other than an offence under s188 *Enterprise Act 2002* (which deals with cartels and which is subject to immunity provisions within the 2002 Act). Immunity is conferred by a notice and this allows the prosecutor to set out the limits of the immunity (presumably the obligations of the subject) and if these are breached then the immunity may be lifted (s 71(3)).

10.6 Bail or remand?

It was noted above that the police have a number of options open to them when dealing with an offender, two of which are to bail an offender (either for further investigation or to consult with the CPS) or to charge an offender. Where a person is charged then the police have the option of either releasing the person on bail or to remand the offender in custody until the next available meeting of the magistrates' court (s 47(3A) PACE 1984). When the matter is brought before the magistrates (and ultimately, if appropriate, a judge) then the court decides whether to remand the offender into custody or whether to release him on bail. In this section the rules regarding bail will be examined, albeit briefly.

10.6.1 Bail and human rights

Before considering the legal provisions in respect of bail it is worth pausing to discuss the implication of denying bail. If a person is to be remanded in custody then it is, in essence, the only time a person would ordinarily be denied his freedom without being convicted of any crime. The consequence of denying bail is to cause a person who has only been accused of a crime to be sent to prison whilst awaiting the trial. In these circumstances it is clear that denying bail should be an exceptional matter and one that considers the human rights of the suspect.

The main article of relevance here is Article 5 of the ECHR which provides the right to liberty and security of the person. Article 5(1)(c) provides the right to restrict a person's liberty by the lawful arrest or detention of a suspect for the purpose of bringing him before a competent legal authority. This power is then subject to a further restriction in Article 5(3) where it is said that somebody arrested in accordance with Article 5(1)(c) must be brought before a judge and tried within a reasonable period of time or released pending trial. Importantly the Article expressly states that any release can be subject to guarantees to appear for trial. Article 5(4) and (5) state that a person arrested or detained is entitled to challenge his detention and, if it is found to be illegal, is entitled to compensation for the breach.

Article 5 creates a powerful regime and holds states to account for the manner in which they detain subjects. Its justification for this is, of course, that the person being denied bail is merely a suspect until such time as he is convicted by a court. The Law

Commission, in an extremely detailed report, examined the compliance of the domestic bail regime and concluded that bail could be denied if he would:

- fail to attend trial;
- interfere with evidence or witnesses, or otherwise obstruct the course of justice;
- commit an offence whilst on bail;
- be at risk of harm against which he or she would be inadequately protected; or
- where a disturbance to the public order would otherwise result. (Law Commission (2001) para 2.29).

It is important to note that all of these come with the proviso that it must be necessary (and not just desirable) to detain the suspect.

It has been argued that Article 5 is met, in part, by the fact that there is a presumption in favour of bail, both at the police level and by the courts (s 38(1) PACE 1984; s 4 *Bail Act 1976* (BA 1976)). The importance of this presumption can be seen from the fact that previous attempts by governments to deny bail automatically have been rejected by the courts. The Conservative government had intended, in 1994, to refuse bail where a person was charged with certain specified serious offences and had been previously convicted of a like offence (s 25 *Criminal Justice and Public Order Act 1994* (CJPOA 1994)). The provision did not simply state that there would be a presumption against bail but provided for the fact that bail could *not* be granted. The ECtHR was not impressed by the provisions and ruled that they were a contravention of Article 5 (*Caballero v United Kingdom* (2000) 33 EHRR 643). The government response was to amend s 25 to allow bail in exceptional circumstances, something that has been copied by successive governments. However, doubts continued to arise over its compatibility (Leach (1999) 304–305; Law Commission (2001) 57–59) and eventually the courts were called upon to rule on the matter.

In *R (O) v Crown Court at Harrow* [2006] UKHL 42 the House of Lords upheld the previous decision of the Divisional Court ([2003] EWHC Admin 868) that s 25 needed to be interpreted in such a way as to make it compliant with Article 5. The Divisional Court disagreed over whether the interpretation required the use of s 3 *Human Rights Act 1998* with Hooper J arguing that it did and Kennedy LJ arguing that the matter could be dealt with according to ordinary domestic canons of interpretation. The House of Lords ultimately agreed with Hooper J and suggested that the provision needed to be 'read down' so that there is an evidential burden on the defendant to prove 'exceptional reasons' (see, for example, at [12]). In essence this means that the defendant must prove, to the civil standard of proof (preponderance of probabilities) that he has exceptional reasons for s 25 not applying to him.

The decision in *R (O)* confirms that the presumption in favour of bail is robust and it becomes even stronger when one recalls that it is possible to add conditions to bail. In other words, magistrates and judges must, before remanding somebody in custody, decide that unconditional and conditional bail cannot, inter alia, protect the public or guarantee the appearance of the defendant at trial.

10.6.2 Police bail

The first opportunity for bail to be considered is in respect of police bail. It will be remembered that there are three possible times when the police may bail a suspect (two before charge and one at the time of charge) and it is the custody sergeant who has the legal responsibility to decide whether a person is bailed or not. There is considerable debate as to how many suspects are denied bail, although it is not thought to be any higher than 25 per cent and official figures commonly cite the figure of 15 per cent (Hucklesby (2002) 118). Thus the vast majority of suspects are bailed but concerns have also been raised as to whether there is a consistent approach to the granting of bail, especially when ethnicity and socio-economic issues are considered (see, for example, Shute et al (2005) 36).

Section 27 of CJPOA 1994 permitted, for the first time, police officers to grant conditional bail to someone charged (previously this was restricted to the courts) but concern has been raised as to how the police have used their powers. Whilst the purpose of the extension was probably to grant more offenders bail there is some evidence to suggest that conditional bail is being imposed on people who would, under the old system, have been granted unconditional bail (Hucklesby (2001) 441). However, a note of caution should be raised here since this research predated (although was published after) the implementation of the *Human Rights Act 1998*.

The police are entitled to review the conditions of bail and this power is vested in custody sergeants not just the particular sergeant who imposed bail. Where the conditions have been imposed post-charge then there is also a right to petition the magistrates' court to review the conditions and to vary or discharge them (s 3 BA 1976).

10.6.3 Court bail

Whilst the police may make the original decision in respect of bail, it is the courts who will be ultimately responsible for these decisions when a person has been charged. That said, however, research suggests that the police still have a heavy influence on court decisions, at least in the initial stage, as the CPS is more likely to seek the denial of bail for those who were remanded in custody by the police (Hucklesby (2002) 119). To an extent, however, this is perhaps self-explanatory since the police should ordinarily be denying bail only to those who have committed serious offences and/or are at risk to themselves or others or are likely to fail to attend a court hearing.

Where an offender has been denied police bail then the magistrates' court will be the first court that a suspect is brought before, even when the matter is a serious case and one that will automatically be transferred to the Crown Court (see 10.7.2 below). Whenever a custody sergeant denies bail the suspect should be brought before the next available sitting of the magistrates' court and it is for this reason that magistrates will often sit on Saturday mornings or on Bank Holidays. Anyone arrested after that hearing, however, will need to wait until Monday as magistrates' courts never sit on Sundays.

It has been noted already that s 4 BA 1976 creates a presumption in favour of unconditional bail, but what are the circumstances under which bail can be refused? Assuming that a person has been charged with an imprisonable offence (which nearly all offences are) then the court can deny bail if it believes that there substantial grounds for believing that the defendant would:

(a) fail to surrender to custody; or

(b) commit an offence whilst on bail; or

(c) interfere with witnesses or otherwise obstruct the course of justice. (para 2, Sch 1 BA 1976)

It is also possible to deny bail where a person has been charged with an indictable offence (including either-way offences; see 10.7.1 below) and it appears the crime was committed on bail (para 2A) although this must be read in conjunction with the *R (O)* case above. Bail can also be withheld if it is necessary for a person's own protection (para 3).

10.6.3.1 Conditional bail

Where a court decides to grant bail it can either bail the defendant conditionally or unconditionally. Conditional bail should act as an alternative to custody and the court should always consider conditional bail before remanding someone into custody (s 4 BA 1976). Conditions may be imposed by virtue of s 3(6) BA 1976 and are:

such requirements as appear to the court to be necessary to secure that–

(a) he surrenders to custody,

(b) he does not commit an offence whilst on bail,

(c) he does not interfere with witnesses or otherwise obstruct the course of justice...

(d) he makes himself available for the purpose of enabling inquiries or a report to be made to assist the court in dealing with him for the offence,

(e) before the time appointed for him to surrender to custody, he attends an interview with an authorised advocate...

The requirements a court can impose when one of these grounds is established are wide and can include a direction to live at a particular location (including, for example, a bail hostel), to impose a curfew on the offender, or to require him to report to a police station at set times. The requirements must only be included where necessary (although it has been doubted that this occurs, in part because defence solicitors suggest a package of measures in the hope of persuading a court to grant bail; see Hucklesby (2002) 129) and the extent of the conditions must also be considered carefully (see Gillespie (2001)).

> **◉ Example** Sion Jenkins
>
> Sion Jenkins was accused of killing his foster-daughter. After a high-profile trial he was convicted of murder and sentenced to life imprisonment. The Court of Appeal quashed his conviction and ordered a retrial. Jenkins was granted bail but one of the conditions of his bail was that he lived in Wales whereas the murder (and trials) took place in Kent. Sion Jenkins was formally acquitted of the murder after two retrials failed to reach a verdict.

The CJA 2003 introduces a new ground for imposing conditions, that being for the protection of an offender (s 13 CJA 2003). This is a welcome step and brings to an end a lacuna identified by the Law Commission whereby bail could be denied in order to protect an offender, but no conditions could be imposed for this purpose even if this granted liberty (see Law Commission (2001) 70).

10.6.4 Breach of bail

Perhaps the most politically controversial aspects of the bail regime is that of breach, and this is perhaps one of the reasons why s 25 CJPOA 1994 (now a de facto presumption against bail) was brought into force. Every year a debate ensues as to whether enough is done to prevent breaches of bail and 2005 was no exception with the announcement that a 'national blitz on defendants skipping bail' was to be undertaken. The idea behind the operation was that all aspects of the criminal justice system, including the police, CPS, and the courts, would target those who were not fulfilling their bail requirements and take strong action against them.

What can be done about breaches of bail? Perhaps the most notable aspect is the power of arrest under s 7 BA 1976 which permits a court to issue a warrant where an offender fails to surrender to the custody of the court at the date he was supposed to. There are two types of warrant, one backed by bail and one not backed by bail. This is, in essence, a direction to the police on how to handle a suspect when eventually caught. If a warrant is backed by bail then the police should release the bailee once arrested whereas if the warrant is not backed by bail then the bailee should be kept in custody and brought before the appropriate magistrates' court the next day. Despite warrants being issued there is significant concern as to whether absconders are appropriately dealt with. Some figures suggest that 15 per cent of defendants fail to appear on at least one occasion and that fewer than 50 per cent of those who failed to appear are brought before a court within three months of the breach.[4] Penalties for breach are only useful if the police and other agencies seek to use their powers to find abscondees and this is an area that needs addressing.

Section 7 also provides a wider right of arrest to the police, including circumstances when the police have reason to believe that the bailee has either breached, or is likely to breach, the conditions imposed on their bail (s 7(3) BA 1976). When a police officer exercises this power the issue of bail is considered by the custody sergeant in the usual way although it is more likely that a suspect will be remanded in custody until the next sitting of the magistrates' court since they have, at least prima facie, failed to adhere to the previous conditions.

One issue of relevance is when to deal with breach of bail. Absconding whilst on bail (ie failing to answer bail) is a criminal offence in its own right (s 6 BA 1976) and can lead not only to bail being reconsidered in the matter at hand but also to separate proceedings in respect of the breach. The custom has been to defer sentencing of the breach until the end of the proceedings (Turner (2004b) 81). However, the Lord Chief Justice has suggested that this is the wrong approach and that proceedings for breach should be dealt with as soon as practicable (*Consolidated Practice Direction* para I.13.5). This is a welcome instruction since the culpability of the defendant in breaching bail cannot rest on whether the defendant is ultimately convicted or acquitted. Similarly the sentence of the court at the time of disposing of the bail issue may resolve the issue of how bail should be treated in the meantime.

The CJA 2003 introduced a new system of dealing with breaches. Previous legislative solutions dealing with breach had suggested that the presumption in favour of bail did not apply to a person who breached bail (para 6, Sch 1 BA 1976) but the Law Commission argued that this was incompatible with the Convention and argued that the High Court had previously accepted this (see Law Commission (2001) 42–51, esp 48–51 and see *R (DPP) v Havering Magistrates' Court* [2001] 1 WLR 805 at 819–820 per Latham LJ; note, however, the decision, at least in respect of paragraph 6 of that judgment, is almost certainly *obiter dicta*). Section 15 of the CJA 2003 alters this to

4. *Hearing Failures* (2004) 25 LSG 5(4).

state that a court must not release the offender on bail unless 'the court is satisfied that there is no risk that, if released on bail…he would fail to surrender to custody'. This is comparable to the earlier provision but at least leaves, in theory, a possible exception and it is submitted that this should be construed in a similar way to paragraph 2A and that the ruling in *R (O)* should be followed here.

❓ QUESTION FOR REFLECTION

Research appears to suggest that there is a considerable amount of crime committed whilst someone is on bail (see below). Given this, do you think the decision in *R (O)* is justified? What do you think the term 'exceptional circumstances' means and how would a defendant prove these?

10.6.5 Appeals in respect of bail

The *Auld Report* indicated that the appellate system in respect of bail decisions was somewhat unwieldy (Auld (2001) 431–433) and this has now been tidied up by the CJA 2003. The position is now relatively simple. Where a suspect is denied bail by the magistrates' court he will normally be able to apply to the Crown Court. Technically it is not correct to state that this is an appeal because it is not listed as such nor is it heard as one, not least because it is dealt with by a single judge. In reality it is an application to the Crown Court for bail but the fact that the Crown Court can overturn the decision of the magistrates' court does lend itself to the appeal analogy.

The right exists only where bail has been refused and not, therefore, to conditional bail but s 16 CJA 2003 permits a limited right of appeal where it is a condition of residency, surety, curfew, or electronic monitoring. This is dealt with as an appeal and no other application can be entertained in respect of a bail. Since the magistrates' court is an inferior body it is theoretically possible for a judicial review to be brought in respect of a bail decision but realistically this would only occur where the decision of a magistrates' tribunal was perverse and even then the more appropriate remedy may be to apply to the Crown Court.

The prosecution now also have rights of appeal in respect of adult defendants granted bail. Section 18 CJA 2003 permits the prosecution to appeal to the Crown Court where a person is charged with, or convicted of, a crime punishable by imprisonment and who is granted bail. The right is exercised by providing an immediate verbal indication at the conclusion of the hearing and by written confirmation within two hours of the conclusion (s 1(4)–(5) *Bail (Amendment) Act 1993* (B(A)A 1993)). In those circumstances the defendant must be remanded in custody pending the appeal by the prosecution and this appeal will be expedited and normally heard within forty-eight hours of the notice being served (s 1(8) B(A)A 1993).

❓ QUESTION FOR REFLECTION

Do you think it can be justified to deny a person bail because the prosecution disagree with the decision? It is to be remembered that a court has made the decision to grant the subject liberty and yet the suspect can be kept incarcerated for up to forty-eight hours before a circuit judge may rule on the appropriateness of bail. Do you think a suspect wrongly denied bail in these circumstances should be entitled to compensation? Do you believe that it is compatible with Article 5 of the ECHR?

10.7 Transferring the matter to court

Once the decision has been made to prosecute an offender how does the case arrive in court? There are two courts of first instance that hear criminal matters; the magistrates' court and the Crown Court. In the subsequent chapters the trials that take place in these courts will be discussed but it is first necessary to consider how the cases arrive at each court.

10.7.1 Classification of offences

All criminal offences can be classified into one of three ways:

- summary-only matters
- those triable only on indictment
- either-way offences.

Summary matters are those that are heard only in the magistrates' court. Offences triable only on indictment are those that are heard only in the Crown Court and either-way offences are, as their name suggests, heard in either court. Identifying what classification an offence is can be quite simple. Common-law offences are triable only on indictment unless the alternative is stated.

⮕ COMMON-LAW CRIMES

The offences of assault and battery are defined in the common law but s 39 CJA 1988 prescribes their mode of trial as summary only. Murder, on the other hand, is a common-law crime and one that has not been prescribed and accordingly it is triable only on indictment.

The vast majority of crimes are, however, created by statute and the Act will ordinarily state what the classification is.

⮕ CLASSIFICATION OF OFFENCES

The following are examples of how to discover the classification of offences.

SUMMARY-ONLY OFFENCES

(4) A person guilty of an offence under this section is liable on summary conviction to a fine not exceeding level 5 on the standard scale.

TRIABLE ONLY ON INDICTMENT

(4) A person guilty of an offence under this section is liable, on conviction on indictment, to imprisonment for a term not exceeding 10 years.

TRIABLE EITHER WAY

(4) A person guilty of an offence under this section is liable–

    (a) on summary conviction, to imprisonment for a term not exceeding 12 months or to a fine not exceeding the statutory maximum or both.

    (b) on conviction on indictment, to imprisonment for a term not exceeding 10 years.

Unfortunately this rule does not apply to all historic crimes. A classic example of this is theft where s 7 of the *Theft Act 1968* gives the penalties for those convicted of theft. The section states:

> A person guilty of theft shall on conviction on indictment be liable for imprisonment for a term not exceeding seven years.

This would appear to create an offence triable only on indictment and yet theft is, in fact, triable either way. The reason for this change was that the *Criminal Law Act 1977* (CLA 1977) downgraded many indictable-only offences to permit a more balanced approach to be taken to the court system. Some offences became summary-only but many became triable either way. Schedule 1 of the *Magistrates' Court Act 1980* (MCA 1980) produces a consolidated list of offences that have been re-categorized and accordingly where an offence is contained in a statute prior to this it is wise to check Sch 1 to assess how it is to be tried.

10.7.1.1 Summary matters

Approximately 97 per cent of all crime is tried summarily (Darbyshire (1997) 627) and the bulk of this work is summary-only offences. An offence can only be triable summarily if the statute expressly states so, and the CJA 2003 has increased the maximum punishment the magistrates' court can pass to twelve months' imprisonment (s 154) (although this is not yet in force). Whether this means that there may be further 'reordering' of offences is more questionable but this increase in penalty probably has more impact on either-way offences.

Traditionally a magistrates' court only had jurisdiction to deal with summary matters that took place within its own county (s 2(1) MCA (1980)) but s 44 of the *Courts Act 2003* (CA 2003) extended its jurisdiction and it can now hear summary matters irrespective of wherever the crime took place. This brings summary-only offences into line with either-way offences where magistrates' courts always had the power to try crimes regardless of where they had taken place. This could be advantageous when a crime takes place in one county and ends in another.

10.7.1.2 Indictable-only offences

Indictable-only offences were relatively few in number but the *Sexual Offences Act 2003* has increased their number considerably. However, it is still true to state that offences that can only be tried on indictment are comparatively uncommon and are normally reserved to the most serious offences. As noted, above, common-law crimes are indictable only although the number of common-law crimes has decreased since the certainty of statutory law is to be preferred.

Example Conspiracy

Section 1 *Criminal Law Act 1977* repealed, in part, the common-law crime of conspiracy and replaced it with a statutory crime of conspiracy which is triable only on indictment. The offence is committed when two or more persons agree to commit a criminal offence, including a summary-only offence. Accordingly as a quirk of the mode-of-trial proceedings a conspiracy to commit a summary offence is triable only on indictment whereas if the offence were actually to be completed it would be triable only summarily. The punishment for the conspiracy is the maximum that could be passed for the substantive offence.

10.7.1.3 Either-way offences

The largest grouping of criminal offences are those triable either way and most new offences appear to come within these offences. This category of offences has caused the most debate over the years and two particular offences appear to be at the heart of this debate: theft and criminal damage.

Theft

In 1977 consideration was given as to whether the theft of a small amount of money or goods of low monetary value should be classified as a summary-only matter. The argument was that the low monetary value meant that the offence was quite trivial and should, therefore, be disposed of summarily. This proposal was fiercely contested however since theft is a crime of dishonesty and accordingly a finding of theft is a finding that a person has acted dishonestly.

? QUESTION FOR REFLECTION

Why would a conviction for theft be considered any more serious than, for example, a crime of violence? Yet common assault is triable only summarily. What reasons are there for resisting the reduction to summary-only status? (For example, think about the occupation of the offender: would it make any difference if it was a police officer who was charged with the theft of a bar of chocolate rather than a cleaner?)

In the 1990s when mode-of-trial decisions were the subject of some debate in Parliament (see 10.7.2.2 below) the issue was revisited but the position remained (and still remains) the same: theft is an either-way offence.

Criminal damage

At the same time as theft was being debated, an argument arose whether modest criminal damage should be reclassified as a summary matter. The argument differed slightly, in that criminal damage is not a crime of dishonesty and accordingly fewer objections were raised. The CLA 1977 did lead to a partition in the way criminal damage is tried. The modern distinction is that if the damage is to goods of a value of less than £5,000 then the offence is triable only summarily (s 22 MCA 1980; in *R (Abott) v Colchester Magistrates' Court* [2001] EWHC Admin 136 the Divisional Court held that this meant the value of the damage and not the value of any compensation claimed). Where the damage is for more than £5,000 then the offence is triable either way and can, therefore, be tried summarily or on indictment.

When criminal damage was reclassified the sentencing powers of the magistrates' court was also restricted so that damage to property less than £5,000 is punishable by a maximum of three months' imprisonment rather than the usual maximum for summary matters (s 154 CJA 2003).

10.7.2 Transferring the matter

Now that classification has been discussed, how is a case transferred to the correct court? The principal distinction is, in effect, between either-way offences and the others.

10.7.2.1 Non-either-way offences

Trial on indictment gets its name because the accused is asked to plead to an indictment, ie a formal document that lists the charges for which the person is to be tried. The equivalent document for a summary trial is called the 'information'. Where a person has been charged by the police the charge sheet will be sent to the magistrates' court. Where the offender is not arrested and charged (as not everyone will necessarily be arrested, the classic example of this perhaps being speeding offences or a failure to pay a TV licence) then a form listing the charges is prepared by the prosecutor and this is laid before the magistrates' court.

The information must be listed within six months of the crime being committed (s 127 MCA 1980). If the information is out of time then ordinarily no action can be taken against the person. This, however, only applies to summary-only offences and not to either-way offences.

Once the information has been laid before the court, a summons will be delivered to the defendant and this is the court to which he will appear. The course of a summary trial is discussed in the next chapter.

Indictable-only matters

The pre-trial procedure for those crimes that are triable only on indictment is now simple. Historically, persons were sent to the Crown Court from the magistrates' court by way of committal. This required the magistrates to decide whether there was a case to answer. The original form of committal was that all the evidence was heard and it became, in essence, a 'mini-trial'. Eventually this was changed to permit 'paper' committals where only documentary evidence was required. The principal advantage of this was a reduction in time and costs but it also meant that the defendant did not have to disclose his or her defence until the time of trial, something that could be tactically advantageous.

❓ QUESTION FOR REFLECTION

Why would not disclosing the full defence evidence be advantageous to the defendant?

The CDA 1998 introduced a new 'fast-track' approach to transferring cases to the Crown Court, often referred to as 'Narey transfers' since the initial idea arose from the *Narey Report* on delays within the criminal justice system (Narey (1997) Ch 6).

Section 51 of the 1998 Act ensures that where an offender is charged with an indictable-only offence this matter is sent directly to the Crown Court and there is no requirement, or indeed power, for magistrates to review the case save for issues of bail etc. Where the offender has been charged with either-way offences and summary-only offences at the same time as indictable-only offences then, so long as the charges are 'related' (meaning 'it arises out of circumstances which are the same or connected with those giving rise to the indictable only offence', s 50(12)) then they may also proceed directly to the Crown Court.

Committal was, in essence, the opportunity for the defendant to challenge the prosecution case and argue that there was insufficient evidence to convict (although research suggested that only 0.2 per cent of cases were ever dismissed at committal stage: CPS (2004) 29). In order to permit a challenge to be brought under the new scheme the statute permits a defendant to make an application to a Crown Court judge for the matter to be dismissed for lack of evidence (para 2, Sch 3 CDA 1998). If the judge, after reviewing the evidence before the court, does not believe that there is sufficient evidence for a jury properly to convict the defendant then the matter must be dismissed (para 2(2)).

10.7.2.2 Either-way offences

It has been stated that the debate as to who decides the venue of the trial has been one of the most contested issues within the criminal justice system (Ashworth and Redmayne (2010) 328–330). During the period 1998–2000 there was a concerted effort by the newly elected Labour government to abolish the defendant's de facto veto. It is important, when considering this debate, to ensure that the language is correct. Whilst many will talk about the right of a defendant to elect his or her trial venue, this is not strictly true. A defendant could elect trial on indictment and veto a summary trial but could only ask for a matter to be tried summarily. If the magistrates disagreed with his request and thought that a trial on indictment would be more suited then the defendant had no veto.

The debate was long and became quite intemperate at times but ended with the government conceding that the defendant's veto should not be removed. Why does this debate arise? The Home Office, in 1999, argued that during 1998 some 18,500 cases were sent to the Crown Court and that 75 per cent of offenders pleaded guilty at Crown Court. The implication was, therefore, that this was wasting Crown Court time since if defendants were to plead guilty then they could have done so at magistrates' court level. However, it has been suggested that these figures were slightly misrepresentative in that the 75 per cent included those who were sent to the Crown Court on matters that were triable only on indictment and where the magistrates had decided that the case was too serious for the offence to be heard as a summary matter (Choongh (1998) 936). The then Attorney-General appeared to recognize this when, in the House of Lords debate, he argued that 60 per cent of those who elect trial in the Crown Court pleaded guilty,[5] although these figures continued to be controversial.

The principal justification for attempting change was undoubtedly costs. There is a significant difference between the costs of a summary trial and a trial on indictment, in part because there are a greater number of lawyers and a professional judge together with a jury. Whilst members of a jury are not paid, they do receive expenses, but it

5. Lord Williams of Mostyn, *Hansard*, HL Deb, col 1292 (20 January 2000).

appears that they add to the length of the trial, with jury trials taking significantly longer than those in magistrates' courts. The government estimated in 1999 that the changes to mode of trial would have saved it approximately £100 million per year.[6]

Despite these perceived advantages, the attempts were rejected after two separate government Bills were introduced to bring about this change. In part it can be explained by comments of the then Lord Chief Justice, Lord Taylor, who stated, 'in our culture and perception trial by jury is a fundamental right' (Ashworth (1993) 832). Whilst this may be true it is slightly less obvious than it may seem. Many at the time argued that trial by jury was a historic right, even tracing it back to the Magna Carta; however, this is simply not true. The Magna Carta did provide for trial by one's peers—it meant just that a peer (Lord) could be tried by other peers (Lords) and it did not apply to the ordinary citizens. However, Lord Taylor was almost certainly correct when he argued that in recent times the choice has taken on the mantle of a right.

❓ QUESTION FOR REFLECTION

Why should the right to a jury trial be considered a fundamental right? If anything other than a jury trial is not as 'fair', why do we allow other courts to hear matters?

The *Criminal Justice and Public Order Act 1996* (CJPOA 1996) heavily altered the mode-of-trial position but left the right of veto intact. The principal changes were to allow for a smoother transfer to the Crown Court where both parties wished the matter to proceed there, and also for the defendant to provide an early indication as to how he was likely to plead before the decision as to mode of trial was taken.

The first edition was written with the expectation that amendments put forward by the CJA 2003 would be shortly in force. In fact, the government has consistently postponed their introduction and indeed the CJIA 2008 has reversed one principal change contained within the CJA 2003.

It will be necessary briefly to summarize the current position and identify what changes may (in the fullness of time) occur. The 'plea before venue' system introduced by the CJPOA 1996 remains in force. In essence this requires that the charge is put to the defendant in words of ordinary language and he is asked to indicate how, if the matter proceeds to trial, he is likely to plead (s 17A MCA 1980). The defendant should be warned that if he indicates that he would plead guilty then the matter will proceed at summary level but that the court can commit him to the Crown Court for sentence where it believe its powers are inadequate. If he does indicate that he would plead guilty then this is then taken to be his plea and the court proceeds to a sentencing hearing.

If the defendant indicates that he is likely to plead not guilty then the matter proceeds as a mode of trial. The magistrates ask the prosecution and defence for their views on whether a summary trial or trial on indictment would be most suited. The court must take into account the nature of the case, whether the circumstances appear to make the offence serious, whether the powers of punishment following a summary trial would be adequate, and any other circumstance the court feels relevant (s 19(3) MCA 1980). When the allocation guidelines are produced (see below) the court will have to take these into account as an 'other circumstance'.

---

6. Explanatory notes to the Mode of Trial (no 1) Bill 1999, para 15.

If the magistrates believe that the matter should be tried on indictment then the matter proceeds to committal. Where, however, the magistrates believe that the matter is suited to summary trial then they must explain this to the defendant, explain (once again) that he could be committed to the Crown Court for sentence if the court finds the matter serious and then ask whether he consents to be tried summarily (s 20 MCA 1980). If he does not consent to a summary trial then the matter is sent for committal whereas if he does consent, the matter is heard as a summary trial.

Schedule 3 to the CJA 2003 will (when finally implemented) introduce a number of significant changes to the process. One of the most notable is that it would allow a single lay magistrate to decide mode of trial rather than the current bench of three. Another key change was that the prosecution would be able to adduce previous convictions at the mode-of-trial hearing—currently the magistrates are not told this. The essence of the change would be to allow the court, at the earliest stage, to identify whether its powers of sentencing would have been adequate. To counter any unfairness it had originally been intended to restrict the ability of the magistrates to commit the defendant to the Crown Court after conviction at summary trial except where it was thought he was dangerous. However the CJIA 2008 has reversed this change and when the CJA reforms come into force the magistrates will still be able to commit a defendant where they believe the matter is so serious that the Crown Court's sentencing powers should be available.

The other significant change would be to permit the defendant to ask for an indication of sentence when asked to indicate his intended plea. An indication of sentence will allow a court (although it will not have to do so) to inform the defendant of the type of sentence that is likely to be imposed if they try the matter summarily (eg custodial, non-custodial, financial penalty, etc). Draft guidance suggested that where a matter is obviously custodial or obviously non-custodial then it would be helpful to provide the indication unless there are good reason for the contrary (SGC (2006) 7). Where, however, the matter is less clear, then a court may need to be more careful since the court will not be able to go against this indication.

QUESTION FOR REFLECTION

Should a court be able to give an indication of sentence? Why would a court decide *not* to grant an indication?

The changes introduced by the (amended) CJA 2003 are undoubtedly an attempt to simplify the procedure and bring about a more sensible approach to elections. Permitting the magistrates to know the previous convictions of the defendant is a welcome step and one that is probably overdue. There existed a debate over the appropriateness of permitting a defendant's previous convictions to be known by the tribunal of fact, but it did not necessarily follow that the magistrates deciding mode of trial would also try the defendant. Previous convictions do influence a sentence and for this reason it would have been preferable for this change to have occurred sooner. However, it is perhaps more difficult to justify the CJIA 2008 amendment to still permit committal for sentence. If the magistrates are now to know the offender's previous convictions then they should be able to determine whether the case (taken at its highest, ie if what the prosecution say can be proven) is too serious for them. If it is then it should go to the Crown Court. If it is not then it should be dealt with at summary level, including sentence.

It is not known why the government has not introduced the CJA 2003 reforms and at the time of writing they have not indicated when the amended provisions will come into force although the CJIA 2008 amendments have (in their view) made it more likely they will be triggered. At that time the Sentencing Guidelines Council (SGC) intends to produce its definitive version of the allocation guidelines which will detail the factors a court must take into account when deciding mode of trial.

◆ Summary

In this chapter we have examined three of the main aspects of the pre-trial criminal justice system. In particular we have identified that:

- A prosecution begins at the earliest stage through a defendant being charged by the police but under the authority of the Crown Prosecution Service (CPS). The CPS, if it has not already done so, must then review the decision to prosecute and, in particular, this requires the CPS to have reference to two prosecution tests (evidential and public-interest tests). If the decision to prosecute is made then the appropriate forms are laid before the court and transfer or mode of trial takes place.

- A prosecution need not take place and if an offender admits his guilt it is possible that diversion from prosecution may occur. The most notable formal diversionary procedures are cautions and conditional cautions (for adults) and reprimands and final warnings (for children).

- A decision not to prosecute can be challenged by way of judicial review in the courts. The courts are less sure about permitting a decision to prosecute to be subject to judicial review because they argue that this is a matter for the trial judge to resolve.

- There is a presumption of bail and that Article 5 of the ECHR provides a strict test for interfering with this presumption. There have been a number of instances where the government has sought to restrict bail but in each case it has had to (reluctantly) agree that an absolute prohibition is not possible and that bail can be provided where the circumstances permit it.

- There are different types of bail, including police bail and bail from a court. In both situations there can be unconditional bail or conditional bail. A court ultimately has the final say over what type of bail should be made and there is only a limited right of appeal against such a decision.

- Crimes are divided into three categories: summary, indictable-only, and either-way. There are two courts where criminal matters are heard (magistrates' court and the Crown Court) and the categorization of offences has an impact on where the matter should be heard. The most controversial category is the either-way offence where currently the defendant has a veto over a trial being heard in the magistrates' court. Where a matter is to be heard in the Crown Court, the case now proceeds directly there without the magistrates considering the strength of prosecution evidence.

End-of-chapter questions

1. Read Evans and Peuch (2001) and Gillespie (2005a). Juveniles are, potentially, more vulnerable than adults so is it correct that they can be dealt with in a way that is arguably less transparent than adults? Do you think it is right for requirements to be imposed on juveniles without a court having an opportunity to test the evidence?

2. Read Gillespie (1998). If there is evidence to demonstrate that prosecuting a parent for neglect or physical abuse could damage the best interests of the child should the prosecution go ahead?

3. Why should the defendant be allowed to veto summary trial? Does this not suggest there are doubts as to the fairness of proceedings in the magistrates' court (if we are saying that a defendant can choose to be tried elsewhere)? If so, why have summary trial for any matters?

4. If a person has been convicted of breaching a bail in the past should they be granted bail when accused of crimes again?

 # Further reading

Ashworth A and Strange M (2004) 'Criminal law and human rights' 2 *European Human Rights Law Review* 121–140.

This is a comprehensive article that examines many of the key issues relating to how human rights legislation has impacted upon the criminal justice system.

Cammiss S (2006) 'I will in a moment give you the full history' *Criminal Law Review* 38–51.

This is an interesting empirical study that discusses the decision-making process in mode of trial decisions.

Hoyano A (1997) 'A study of the impact of the Revised Code for Crown Prosecutors' *Criminal Law Review* 556–564.

This is an interesting article that discusses whether the Code for Crown Prosecutors is followed in practice.

 For multiple choice questions, updates to this chapter and links to useful websites, please visit the Online Resource Centre at

www.oxfordtextbooks.co.uk/orc/gillespie_els3e/

11

Summary Trials

By the end of this chapter you will be able to:

- Identify the difference between lay magistrates and district judge (magistrates' court).
- Understand how magistrates are appointed.
- Understand how decisions of law and fact are taken in the magistrates' court.
- Identify the course of a summary trial.

Introduction

The previous chapter examined three key pre-trial issues where a person is suspected of committing a criminal offence. The chapter ended with an examination of how a case arrives at either the magistrates' court or Crown Court for trial. In this chapter an examination of what happens during a summary trial will be made and in the next chapter the course of a trial on indictment will be given.

It will be remembered from the previous chapter that magistrates have the power to try two types of offences: summary-only matters and offences triable either way where the defendant elects trial summarily. A wide range of offences can be heard in the magistrates' court. In this chapter an examination of who magistrates are and how a summary trial proceeds will be made.

11.1 Those in court

The logical place to start any examination of the summary trial is to identify those persons who will feature in any trial. Whilst the precise number and types of people will vary depending on the nature of the trial and, in particular, the seriousness of the offence, the following are likely to be present:

- magistrates
- lawyers
- court clerk
- the defendant
- witnesses
- probation officers.

Whilst it is not necessary to consider each of these persons, it will be necessary to make a comment on some of these, in particular those who 'staff' the court.

11.1.1 Magistrates

The most obvious group of people to examine is the magistrates. Who are magistrates and what is the role that they perform? Magistrates are also known as Justices of the Peace (JP) and this is an ancient office that was used by the monarch to designate certain people who were responsible for keeping the King's Peace for a defined area. The office has changed significantly over the years and now, rather than being directly responsible for the arrest of persons and the investigation of crime, modern magistrates keep the peace by sitting in judgment on those who are brought before them.

It is necessary at the outset to draw a distinction between different types of magistrate. The first, and more common type, are lay magistrates and these are people with no formal legal qualification who discharge the office of Justice of the Peace. The second type is the professional magistrate who is legally qualified and paid to sit on cases. These used to be known as stipendiary magistrates but since 2000 they have been known as district judges (magistrates' court) (see s 78 *Access to Justice Act 1999* (AJA 1999)). Whilst both species of magistrates sit on a summary trial they are very much separate creatures in their appointment and work.

11.1.1.1 Lay magistrates

Unlike with the judiciary, it does not appear precise statistics are held in relation to the lay magistracy. As of 1 April 2010 there were 28,607 lay magistrates in England and Wales,[1] meaning numbers have been maintained at approximately 28,000 for at least a decade. It can be seen that the lay magistracy is therefore the largest 'judicial' grouping. Apart from certain preliminary matters, lay magistrates do not sit alone and they are therefore assigned to a local justice area which is often known as a 'bench'. Each year they elect a lay magistrate as the Chairman of the Bench (s 17 *Courts Act 2003* (CA 2003) when read in conjunction with the *Justices of the Peace (Size and Chairmanship of the Bench) Rules 1990,* SI 2005/553), who acts as the senior magistrate for that area. This is an unpaid administrative role that involves the person being 'their leader, representative and spokesperson' (Department for Constitutional Affairs (2006) 1). It also involves the chair (and nominated deputies) convening the training and ensuring that, in conjunction with the Clerk to the Justices (see below), that the operation of the bench runs smoothly.

The organization of magistrates' courts used to be rather complicated with benches being accountable to *Magistrates' Courts Committees* (MCCs) but from April 2005 the system was simplified with *Her Majesty's Court Service* (HMCS) assuming responsibility for all courts in England and Wales (ie not including the Supreme Court). The HMCS now divides itself into twenty-five areas each of which has a director accountable to the chief executive. Each area also has a 'court board' which consists of representation of the judiciary, magistracy, and court users to ensure the smooth running of the court system.

Appointment

As might be imagined from the term, lay magistrates are not legally qualified although, interestingly, neither is legal qualification a barrier to appointment and there have, in the past, been lawyers and legal academics who have sat as lay magistrates. However, the vast majority of lay magistrates have no legal knowledge other than that gained through their training. Lay magistrates are also so styled because, unlike their professional brethren (see below), they are unpaid. Lay magistrates are volunteers although they are eligible for expenses (s 15 CA 2003) to cover loss of wages (although this amount is 'capped', meaning some justices will actually sit at a loss), travelling expenses, etc. Obviously using volunteers can be extremely cost-effective, a point demonstrated by the fact that in 2003/4 expenses amounted to £15 million[2] and yet with 30,000 magistrates this equates to an average of only £500 per magistrate.

To be appointed a lay magistrate, a person must either reside in the petty sessional area that they wish to sit in, or live within fifteen miles of this area. This is, in part, because it has always been thought that a significant advantage of the magistracy is that

---

1. 'Magistrates in post 2010' Judiciary website.
2. *Hansard*, HC WA, vol 425, col 773W (20 October 2004).

they know the local area. That said, whilst magistrates were traditionally not allowed to sit outside of their petty sessional area, this is no longer true and there is now a mechanism that permits magistrates to sit in other areas (s 10 CA 2003). This change was recommended as it was believed it could be useful for justices to assist neighbouring benches to tackle any delay that might accrue because of a reduction (temporary or otherwise) in the number of justices sitting in that area (Auld (2001) 100). To an extent it can be argued that this is not dissimilar to the way that circuit judges can be moved around a circuit, although on a much smaller scale. That said, it does appear to conflict with the idea of the magistracy bringing local representation.

The maximum age for appointment to a magistrate is sixty-five on the basis that they must retire at the age of seventy and accordingly the Lord Chancellor will not appoint someone over sixty-five since by the time the training programme has been completed effectively there will be little time left for the justice to sit. The minimum age for appointment is eighteen although the Lord Chancellor used to state that it would be exceptional for a person to be appointed under the age of twenty-seven. However, the Lord Chancellor has withdrawn this comment and there has been a concerted effort by the government to appoint younger magistrates. The rule was effectively relaxed in 2003[3] and in 2004 and 2005 two people aged twenty were appointed to the magistracy. In 2006 Lucy Tate, a nineteen-year-old law student, became the youngest person to be appointed to the magistracy although this attracted a significant amount of criticism.

❓ QUESTION FOR REFLECTION

Is it realistic to suggest that a magistrate can be appointed at the age of eighteen? Would they command the required respect of defendants, lawyers, and fellow magistrates?

🎧 LISTEN TO THE PODCAST

For guidance on how to answer this question and a discussion of the main issues, listen to the author's podcast on the Online Resource Centre:
www.oxfordtextbooks.co.uk/orc/gillespie_els3e/

Certain persons are automatically disqualified from being a magistrate, the most notable being those listed in Table 11.1.

There is also, of course, the proviso that individuals may not be suitable depending on their own circumstances. The *Department for Constitutional Affairs* has listed the principal qualities of a magistrate:

- good character
- maturity and sound temperament
- understanding and communication
- sound judgement
- social awareness
- commitment and reliability.

3. 'Younger Magistrates Wanted', DCA Press Release, 27 October 2003.

Table 11.1 Automatic disqualification

Serving or recently retired police officers (including Special Constables)	Full-time member of HM Forces
Traffic wardens or civilian employees of police forces	An undischarged bankrupt
Spouse of the above	Anyone who has, or whose partner has, been convicted of a serious offence or number of minor offences
Close family relative of the above if they work in the petty sessional division	A Member of Parliament, a parliamentary candidate, or an election agent
Those whose work or community activities make being appointed a magistrate inappropriate (eg CPS, Probation Service, etc)	

Diversity

Successive governments have attempted to broaden the magistracy because there is a perception that the magistracy is a white, middle-class male bastion. Traditionally it was difficult to challenge such perceptions because there was an absence of statistics but this is no longer true. The latest statistics show that as of 1 April 2010 there are more female magistrates (50.8 per cent) than there are male (49.2 per cent).

What of ethnicity? There have been a number of campaigns to widen the ethnicity of the magistracy and it would seem that this is beginning to achieve results. Information from the 2001 Census suggests that ethnic minorities accounted for 7.9 per cent of the UK population and the latest statistics show that 7.7 per cent of magistrates identify themselves as belonging to an ethnic minority. Of course that does not mean that the campaign can rest since the ethnic minority population is increasing but in any event the quest should not be about achieving a mirrored representation of society but ensuring that ethnic minorities are an accepted part of the judicial system. Certainly the magistracy compares extremely favourably to the judiciary (see Chapter 6) but statistics by themselves do not assist and it is notable that there is still a perception that the magistracy is a white, male bastion and research consistently suggests that ethnic minority defendants would like to see more ethnic minority magistrates (see Shute et al (2005) 118–119) and a clear desire for each bench within a court to include a member of the ethnic minorities (p 120).

❓ QUESTION FOR REFLECTION

Were you surprised by the figures above? Before reading this page what were your views on how diverse the magistracy was? Do you agree with the suggestion that if a defendant is a member of an ethnic minority then at least one member of the bench should be a member of the ethnic minorities? What are the advantages and disadvantages of such a proposal?

Apart from the ethnicity of the magistracy, the other issue that is often discussed is their socio-economic backgrounds with the belief that they tend to be middle-class (Darbyshire (2008) 262). Certainly Auld accepted, without adducing any modern evidence to support this, that magistrates were not necessarily representative but that this did not prevent them from discharging their duties (Auld (2001) 98). Identifying the socio-economic background of the magistracy is not easy since the government does not apparently collate such information.[4] This is perhaps unfortunate as producing an analysis of ethnic minority diversity was one way of tackling diversity in this area (including correcting misperceptions) and it may be advisable for the same to occur here.

Another possible reason for the socio-economic background of magistrates is that they tend to be appointed from professional backgrounds (Darbyshire (2002) 296), in part because of the sitting requirements. Unlike with jury service there is no obligation to let an employee have time off to sit as a magistrate although there are benefits in doing so. Public bodies will consider it a civil obligation and will normally therefore give the time off without a requirement for leave. The same could be true of medium to large-scale professional firms but how easy would it be for a builder or decorator to take a day off?

Controversy exists over whether the quest for full representation could be in danger of creating a sterile bench. Representation now includes political allegiance and it has been argued that it has been very difficult to separate politics from the lay magistracy and that Conservatives are over-represented on the bench (Darbyshire (2002) 298). However, it is not clear why this is the case and Darbyshire suggests that this could either be because Conservatives are more likely to wish to sit on the bench or that Conservatives are more likely to be appointed (ibid).

Trevor Grove, who wrote a book describing his appointment as a magistrate, notes that at interview he was asked who he supported and difficulty arose when he considered himself to be a floating voter and yet was told that he had to choose a party (Grove (2002) 14–15). This perhaps demonstrates the excesses of the quest for pure representation especially during times when it appears there is a decrease in identifiable political allegiances. Interestingly, Grove also makes another comment regarding professions. He notes that a friend of his applied to become a magistrate but was turned down. The reason was, apparently, because she was a teacher and the bench already had a number of teachers on the bench (p 9). The fact that she was a teacher (as were others) perhaps strengthens the note about public and private bodies above, but again it must be questioned why a common application would lead to a rejection as it appears to focus not only on the qualities of the candidate but also on external factors.

 QUESTION FOR REFLECTION

Should it matter what the background to the magistracy is? Would it not be better to concentrate on whether the candidate is capable of judging evidence dispassionately or do you think representation is important?

Post-appointment

Once appointed, magistrates must undertake training because although they are not expected to be experts in law they need to be familiar with court processes, sentencing decisions, etc. Continual training is the key to their magisterial career and will continue throughout their time as an active magistrate. Most of the training is developed locally

4. *Hansard*, HC WA, vol 434, col 638W (9 June 2005).

and the first stage for someone recently appointed is to be assigned a mentor. The mentor is an experienced justice of the peace and can introduce the new magistrate to the bench and the procedures involved. Much of the early training involves a 'shadowing' process whereby the magistrate can see the court process and reflect upon its execution. Whilst the training continues to be delivered primarily locally the material has now been standardized and the responsibility has been handed to the *Judicial Studies Board*, which has the responsibility for training the professional and lay judiciary.

Magistrates must sit for a minimum of twenty-six times per year, each sitting normally lasting a half-day, although research commissioned in 2000 reported that the average magistrate sat forty-one times (Morgan and Russell (2000) 13, 18). Initially newly qualified magistrates are appointed as 'wingers'. Lay magistrates normally sit in benches of three. Only the chair of that bench of magistrates will speak; the other two are fully involved in the decision-making process but must feed questions and comments through the chair. In this context chair of the bench means the panel of three hearing the case and not the more formal 'Chairman of the Bench' that was discussed at the beginning of the chapter. Becoming a chair of a bench in court requires additional training and progression is ordinarily made after a person has accrued significant experience.

11.1.1.2 District judges (magistrates' court)

Whilst the clear majority of magistrates are lay magistrates, there is another breed of magistrates who are paid and were, until recently, known as stipendiary magistrates but are now known as district judges (magistrates' court). Historically, the only area of the country where stipendiary magistrates have been used for a considerable period of time was Inner London. The *Middlesex Justices Act 1792* created stipendiary posts and it was not until the 1940s that lay magistrates (who had been principally dealing with quasi-administrative matters such as licensing etc) became more involved with some of the London courts. As of April 2010 there are 143 district judges (magistrates' court) and 151 deputy district judges (part-time appointments akin to a recorder in the Crown Court).[5] Under s 23 CA 2003 there is provision to create the senior district judge (chief magistrate) and a deputy. The Act is silent as to what responsibility the holders of these offices have but they are, as their title suggests, the leaders of the district judge magisterial bench and accordingly take on added administrative responsibilities to ensure that district judges operate effectively.

Appointment

As would be expected, the duties and appointment of these district judges differ radically from lay magistrates. It is important to note at the outset that this is a judicial post and in order to be appointed as either a district judge or deputy district judge a person must have a seven-year general qualification (s 22 CA 2003) which means that they must have had a right of audience to appear in the Supreme Court, county court, or magistrates' court (s 71(3)(c) *Courts and Legal Services Act 1990*). This, in effect, means a solicitor or barrister who has been qualified for seven years. Realistically, however, a person would have to be qualified for a longer period than this to be appointed. Before being appointed a district judge it is expected that a person will have served as a deputy district judge first. The expectation for deputies is that they will sit for a

---

5. *Hansard*, vol 430, col 432W (26 January 2005).

minimum of fifteen days per year although it is possible that they will sit for more. A deputy will be superintended by a full district judge but it is quite possible that they will be sitting in different petty sessional areas and thus the deputy may be the senior judge in a petty sessional area. A district judge (magistrates' court) is currently paid £102,921.[6] Deputy district judges are paid a daily rate which is currently £468.

Diversity

It was noted that the lay magistracy is, at least in terms of gender and race, relatively representative although there is perhaps still work to be done. District judges are, however, drawn from lawyers and it will be noted elsewhere that lawyers and the judiciary are not particularly representative of society. Are district judges (magistrates' court) diverse?

The most recent statistics (April 2010) demonstrate that 26 per cent of full-time district judges (magistrates' court) are female (an increase from the 2008 statistics where the figure was 23 per cent) but that only four judges (3.77 per cent) are of an ethnic minority. Of the part-time district judges (magistrates' court) 27 per cent are female and 5.88 per cent identify themselves as being of an ethnic minority.

It can be immediately seen that these figures reflect extremely poorly compared to the lay magistracy, especially in respect of gender where a near 50:50 ratio is achieved for lay magistrates.

A more accurate reflection may be to compare the position to that of the circuit bench. In effect district judges (magistrates' court) are comparable to circuit judges although the latter rank higher. The latest statistics show that of the circuit bench (ie circuit judges and recorders) 302 (15.8 per cent) are female and 78 (4 per cent) are from an ethnic minority. It can be seen, therefore, that in terms of gender the position is arguably better for district judges (magistrates' court) than it is for the circuit bench but the same is not true of the representation of ethnic minorities. However, the current position cannot be considered to be particularly appropriate and the government is keen for the judiciary to become more representative although appointments are now independent of the government (see 7.3 above).

The implications of having an unrepresentative judiciary are relatively clear in that it tends to undermine the public's confidence in the fairness of proceedings (Shute et al (2005) 64–70). However, quickly altering the constitution of the district judge bench would not be easy and perhaps not desirable (as some may argue that it goes away from the principle of appointment through merit) but a key test for the *Judicial Appointments Commission* will be to see if the bench becomes more representative (or at least not chronically unrepresentative) and it will be for the courts and government to tackle any perception that the current composition does not undermine fairness for members of an ethnic minority.

Jurisdiction

District and deputy district judges have, since 2000, been able to sit nationally and, unlike lay magistrates, they tend to sit outside their 'base' court more frequently. This is particularly important because district judges will frequently sit on complicated or lengthy trials, in part because they can sit alone (s 26 CA 2003). One of the difficulties

---

6. And is classified as a group 7 appointment. The deputy senior district judge (magistrates' court) is a group 6.2 appointment and is paid £112,116 and the senior district judge (magistrates' court) is a group 5 appointment and paid £125,803.

traditionally with lay magistrate trials is that the justices will only sit in a half-day block which means they can only conduct short cases. Where a trial is likely to take longer than this then a district judge can hear the case as he will sit either permanently or, where he is a deputy, in a block of time. This type of case may not arise in one single petty sessional area so a national jurisdiction allows the district judges to try matters in other areas in a way analogous to how circuit judges move around the circuit.

There is, to an extent, a tension that exists between district judges and lay magistrates and there have been anecdotal stories about situations when district judges who have started sitting in a petty sessional area for the first time have been shunned by the lay magistrates. It has been suggested that this tension was because there is a perception amongst the lay magistracy that there is a national policy to replace lay magistrates with district judges (Auld (2001) 98). This suggestion was rejected by Auld and whilst there has been an increase in the district judge bench it is unlikely that it will ever replace in its entirety the lay magistracy, in part because of the cost, and in part because of the longstanding tradition of lay justice being administered in England and Wales.

Case-hardened?

Padfield (2003) argues that district judges are more likely to become 'case-hardened' (meaning they become less convinced by arguments since they see the same excuses being used in each case) and 'judicially burnt out' than lay magistrates (Padfield (2003) 277) although no conclusive evidence is shown for this. There has always been some concern as to whether magistrates become 'case-hardened' and thus less inclined to acquit a suspect. Certainly it was found that district judges were more likely to remand a person into custody rather than provide bail (Morgan and Russell (2000) 50) and significantly more likely to impose a harsher punishment (p 52). However this by itself does not necessarily mean that district judges are more 'case-hardened' because these judges tend to get the more serious and complicated cases and this may explain the distinction. Morgan and Russell were unable to compare a trial by a lay bench with a trial by a district judge because the number of trials observed was so low that any comparison would be meaningless (ibid).

Some have argued that a solution to any case-hardening would be to provide for a mixed bench, ie a district judge sitting with two lay magistrates. Liberty (2002) is strongly in favour of such a move arguing that it could bring certainty to the bench. Others are less convinced by this move suggesting that the lay magistrates are more likely to be dominated by the district judge (Darbyshire (2002) 292–293), perhaps leading to the position where the lay magistrates are, in effect, puppets of the district judge. Liberty agrees that this could be a problem and therefore suggests that the tribunal should be one of four justices not three. The district judge would act as the tribunal of law and the lay magistrates as the tribunal of fact (Liberty (2002) 10–13), in essence creating a 'mini' judge and juror system. The immediate difficulty with this is that lay magistrates sit for half-days and thus complicated or longer trials would not be able to cope with this system. The solution that Liberty proposes is that lay magistrates sit in blocks of time (Liberty (2002) 12) but this itself carries with it disadvantages, not least the fact that it may put off more employers from releasing their staff, potentially increasing the reliance on magistrates drawn from the public sector.

Liberty's proposal has not been accepted and the position remains that district judges tend to sit alone. Auld argued that this was the preference of both the lay magistracy and the district judges (Auld (2001) 102) with the former liking the ability to chair their own courts[7] and the latter not seeing any real purpose in using lay magistrates. That is not to say that mixed sittings do not occur because sometimes they do, although it is more often to assist in the training of lay magistrates as they (and the *Magistrates Association*) recognize the experience that sitting with a district judge can bring. An important omission is that there is no clear guidance as to when a district judge should be used and when a case should be heard by a lay bench. It has been noted that the suggestion has always been that a district judge should be used for the more serious and complicated cases but lay magistrates would be unhappy about any formal propagation of that rule because it could undermine their own position (Ashworth and Redmayne (2010) 338). However is this sufficient reason not to? It has been noted that the Sentencing Guidelines Council has produced a draft guideline on allocation and it may have been prudent to suggest when a district judge (magistrates' court) should be used or indeed when a mixed bench could be used.

The use of district judges is likely to continue and indeed it would appear that their numbers are increasing (from a total of 257 of deputy and full district judges (magistrates' court) in 2002 to 294 by 2009). One reason for this is that trials proceed significantly quicker when district judges preside. However, although Morgan and Russell (2000) argue that one district judge could replace thirty lay magistrates (p 85) the expense caused by proceeding to a fully stipendiary bench would be significant and it would end the tradition of lay participation in summary matters. All governments have reaffirmed their commitment to the lay magistracy, as have senior members of the judiciary, and it is likely that district judges will, therefore, continue to act alongside, rather than replace, lay justices.

11.1.2 Justices' clerk

One of the most important positions in the magistrates' court is that of the justices' clerk. The position of the clerk is particularly important where lay magistrates sit in judgment. Yet despite its importance it has been suggested that it is a role that is hidden from the consciousness of those who use the court (Darbyshire (1984) 1)—in other words most 'lay' users of the court would not guess that the clerk is a central player in proceedings.

Before examining the duties and responsibilities of the clerk it is important to differentiate between the various terms. Every local justice area will have at least one justices' clerk and this is a person appointed to the area by the Lord Chancellor after consultation with the Lord Chief Justice (s 27 CA 2003). The justices' clerk will frequently not be located in just one building and could be responsible for servicing numerous benches within the local justice area (Darbyshire (2000) 183). They are assisted by deputies or assistant clerks who are more properly known as 'assistant to a justices' clerk' (s 27(7)) but who are sometimes referred to as 'court clerks' or 'legal advisors'.

11.1.2.1 Appointment

It will be seen below that the principal purpose of the clerks is to advise the magistracy on matters of law and therefore it would be expected that the clerks would be legally qualified but this is not necessarily the case. Traditionally, whilst a justices' clerk would ordinarily be qualified, an assistant or court clerk need not be and indeed in 2000 there

---

7. Obtainable from the Judicial Communications Office.

were approximately 640 assistants who were not a member of the professions (although they would either be law graduates or have undertaken a Diploma in Magisterial Law (Darbyshire (2000) 184)).

The government is committed to altering this and any new clerk or assistant clerk must have a 'a 5 year magistrates' court qualification' (meaning a right of audience in the magistrates' court for a period of at least five years. However for existing clerks the position is slightly different. Anyone aged over forty was exempt from the requirement to be professionally qualified and those below forty are entitled to seek professional qualification whilst acting as a clerk so long as they had been a clerk for at least five years (Darbyshire (2000) 190). It should also be noted that certain local justice areas now offer 'trainee legal advisor' posts to graduates of the LPC or BPTC programmes, the intention being that a person would after qualification become a court clerk.

11.1.2.2 Responsibilities

The principal duty of a clerk is to advise the magistrates on matters of law (s 28(4)). This is because justices sitting in the magistrates' court are responsible for deciding decisions of both fact and law. In the Crown Court this responsibility is split with the judge being solely responsible for decisions of law and the jury being solely responsible for decisions of fact.

 Example Fact and law

Suzy is charged with criminal damage contrary to s 1 *Criminal Damage Act 1971*. The damage is spray-painting pink paint onto a tank destined for service in Iraq. The estimate of the damage is £450 (cost of removing the paint) hence it is a summary-only matter.

Suzy does not deny that she was responsible for the damage to the tank but she argues that it was justified because the war in Iraq is illegal. If this defence is to be effective then two decisions must be made. First, there is a matter of law as to whether this justification is capable of amounting to a defence to a criminal charge. Second, if it can amount in law to a defence, does it, as a matter of fact, arise here?

In a trial on indictment the first decision would be made by the judge, and the second decision would be a matter solely for the jury. In a summary trial both matters are decisions for the justices.

It has been suggested that mixing law and fact in this way is 'peculiar' since although justices are entrusted with the decisions of law, lay justices rely wholly on their (subordinate) clerk to advise them on what the law is. This leads to the position where:

> legal argument takes place in court, the argument [being] addressed to the justices who may hardly follow a word of it; in reality, however, it is intended for the ears of the clerk. Rulings...are supposed to be made by the justices...in practice, however, the decisions must be taken by the clerk...(Williams (1955) 290)

It could be argued that this is a justification for either abolishing lay magistrates or requiring them to sit with district judges but as was noted above this was rejected. Similarly an attempt by clerks, at the time of the Narey review of delays in the criminal justice system, to be 're-badged' as district judges and to chair panels was opposed by lay magistrates and ultimately rejected by the government. Certainly such a proposal could be seen as undermining the principle of lay justice (see above) but would, at least, lead to certainty. Currently (theoretically) a justice makes the decision having simply received advice, ie something that can be rejected although it will be seen that it is not necessarily as straightforward as this.

A more recent extension of their purposes is to undertake quasi-judicial work. The CA 2003 permits the Lord Chancellor to prescribe other duties for clerks and *The Justices' Clerks' Rules 2005*, SI 2005/545 prescribe duties that could previously have been exercised by a single justice of the peace and include primarily case-management responsibilities, but also include the issuing of summonses and warrants for arrest and granting adjournments or extensions of bail. This is extremely controversial with some suggesting that it confuses the judicial and advice roles:

> justices' clerks are essentially legal advisers, hired and fired by [the Court Service]. They are not judges. They are meant to serve judges. The justices and district judges are the judges. (Darbyshire (2000) 186)

This concern was shared by the then Lord Chief Justice, Lord Bingham, who when the proposal was first raised, suggested that it could undermine the lay magistracy (Darbyshire (2000) 188).

The counter-argument of course is that the extra duties are designed to reduce delays and allow for matters to proceed to trial in a more expeditious way. It could even be argued that lawyers are more suited to dealing with some of these matters given their legal training. However this is an argument for professionalizing the magistracy, not for permitting clerks to exercise judicial control. The issuing of summonses, warrants, and the granting of adjournments cannot be considered anything other than judicial actions and it is unhelpful and, it is submitted, inappropriate for the distinction between judges and their advisors to be blurred.

11.1.2.3 Provision of advice

It has been noted that the primary role of the justices' clerk is the provision of advice and, interestingly, the statute states that the justices' clerk has this responsibility even when he is not 'personally attending them' (s 28(4)), ie not present in court. The *Consolidated Practice Direction* translates this into meaning 'ensuring there is competent advice is available to the justices when the justices' clerk is not personally present in court' (V.55.1(c)). Given that some court clerks are not legally qualified it may be questioned whether this will necessarily be achieved, but it could be as simple as having a fully qualified 'clerk' on call (something implicit within the next paragraph: see V.55.2).

Where a clerk is sitting in court, the statute (s 28(5)) makes clear that they can be proactive:

> The powers of a justices' clerk include, at any time when he thinks he should do so, bringing to the attention of any or all of the justices of the peace to whom he is clerk any point of law...that is or may be involved in any question so arising.

In other words, the clerk does not have to wait until the justices ask for advice but can, if he so wishes, provide advice whenever he believes it is necessary to do so. The *Consolidated Practice Direction* goes further:

> A justices' clerk or legal advisor may ask questions of witnesses and the parties in order to clarify the evidence and any issues in the case. A legal advisor has a duty to ensure that every case is conducted fairly (V.55.5).

In other words, not only can a clerk give advice but he can ask questions of the witnesses and arguably must do so if he believes that it is necessary for the trial to be fair. However, allowing a clerk to intervene does raise questions again about what the comparative status is between the justices and the clerk. The clerk may raise issues but what if the justices believe the advice was not, or is not, required? Nothing in statute requires them to take the advice although the statute arguably implicitly states that they should not try to prevent the advice from being given to them.

Status of advice

The statute and other official documents refer to the clerk providing *advice* so what is its status? Is it possible for the justices to ignore that advice? As a matter of law, it is the justices who are responsible for decisions of law and fact so theoretically the answer must be yes. However in *Jones v Nicks* [1977] RTR 72 the Divisional Court, with the then Lord Chief Justice presiding, argued that if the justices rejected the advice of the clerk they could be personally liable for any costs incurred during an appeal by way of case stated. The argument is presumably that ignoring the advice is unreasonable and not something that justices would ordinarily do.

However, blindly following the advice will not necessarily assist the justices either since in *R v Lincoln Justices, ex p Count* [1995] COD 351 the Divisional Court warned that where a decision was perverse costs might be incurred even if they were advised by a clerk. Admittedly this was an unusual case in that the court held that the magistrates should have been aware that the advice was wrong, but the precedent is set.

Perhaps the key to understanding this area is to deciding what advice is. If a clerk simply sets out the legal framework then it would be difficult for the justices to ignore this advice. If, however, the clerk goes further and suggests how the law should be applied then this potentially encroaches upon the jurisdiction of the justices and perhaps this can be rejected. To an extent this may be similar to a judicial summing up (see 12.3.6 below) in that a judge directs a jury that they can ignore anything he says about what the facts may mean, but the analogy is not a strong one since in the Crown Court the jury is only the tribunal of fact.

11.1.3 Lawyers

To some it may appear somewhat obvious that lawyers would be involved in a summary trial but as will be seen this is not necessarily the case and it is now perfectly possible for a trial to take place without a lawyer being present.

11.1.3.1 Rights of audience

The magistrates' court is the lowest court in the English Legal System and the rights of audience are generally considered quite wide. The general rule is that all solicitors and barristers have automatic rights of audience for summary trials and this was the position prior to the extension of rights under the *Access to Justice Act 1999*.

11.1.3.2 Defendant in person

The defendant himself may wish to represent himself in court and in common with other trials this is to be permitted. There is no rule in the magistrates' court that requires an offender to be represented legally and the court cannot order representation in the absence of a request by the defendant. A defendant can be accompanied by someone who is not legally qualified. These have, in the past, been referred to as a 'McKenzie friend' (*McKenzie v McKenzie* [1970] 3 WLR 472) although the Court of Appeal has strongly disapproved of this term as it suggests that this is a special class of persons when, in fact, any person has the right to lay assistance and that it does not matter what their qualifications are (*R v Leicester City Justices, ex p Barrow* [1991] 3 WLR 368 and see Thomas (1992) for a critique of this case). That is not to say that an assistant would ordinarily advocate on behalf of the defendant but would, instead, assist in the preparation of the case and make suggestions as to the questioning of witnesses etc.

11.1.3.3 Lay prosecutors

Section 55 of the *Crime and Disorder Act 1998* inserted a provision within the *Prosecution of Offences Act 1985* (PoOA 1985) (s 7A) to permit non-legal staff to be designated as 'crown prosecutors' (formerly they were called 'designated caseworkers' but have since been renamed 'associate prosecutors' (CPS (2007)) perhaps to reflect their changing role) and to exercise the powers of this post for matters relating to, inter alia, bail and the conduct of criminal proceedings in magistrates' courts other than trials, including sentencing matters following a guilty plea (s 7A(2) PoOA 1985).

Whilst controversial, it could be argued that this is a beneficial system in that it allows lawyers to concentrate on those matters where liability is to be contested or where a difficult issue arises. In part this is undoubtedly true and there are only a finite number of lawyers employed by the CPS. The counter-argument, however, is that a prosecution is always so central that a lawyer should be involved in the process.

In 2003/4 there were 254 designated caseworkers but by 2010 this had risen to 446 associate prosecutors (*CPS Annual Report*), which demonstrates the commitment the CPS had to their use. Indeed the CPS argued:

> [A] review of the role of designated caseworkers recognised the vital advocacy role that they undertook and that there was scope and potential...to extend that role (CPS (2004) 22).

A review did, in fact, take place and the *Criminal Justice and Immigration Act 2008* (CJIA 2008) has widened the scope of their use. Under the revised s 7A it is possible for an associate prosecutor (note that term is an administrative one used by the CPS, the Act simply refers to the ability of the DPP to designate persons) to deal with:

- applications for, or relating to, bail in criminal proceedings
- the conduct of trial in the magistrates' courts other than trials of offences triable either-way or offences which are punishable with imprisonment in the case of persons aged twenty-one or over
- the conduct of applications or other proceedings relating to preventative civil orders
- the conduct of proceedings (other than criminal proceedings) assigned to the Director of Public Prosecutions.

The rule that prevented associate prosecutors from dealing with offences triable only on indictment has also been abolished (s 55(4) CJIA 2008) which means that an associate prosecutor could, for example, deal with bail in respect of an offence triable only on indictment.

The extension of these powers is significant. In essence it means that whereas associate prosecutors could previously only deal with uncontested matters, they can now conduct prosecutions in contested summary-only matters that do not carry a sentence of imprisonment.

The legal profession was not wholly supportive of this change (Ward and Bettinson (2008) 14) in part because it was concerned about the absence of a lawyer in the conduct of trials. This difficulty is perhaps accentuated by the fact that, as noted above, the clerk of the court need not be currently qualified and the magistrates frequently are not. Where a defendant is also unrepresented this means it is quite possible that pleas of guilty could be tendered, or even a contested case take place, on evidence that no lawyer has ever seen. Potentially this could lead to a situation where someone pleads to, or is found guilty of, an offence either not known to the law or in circumstances where evidential issues have been compromised.

The extended powers make it inevitable that the use of associate prosecutors will continue to expand. Perhaps the easiest way to allay fears such as those discussed above would be to ensure that where a matter is being dealt with by an associate prosecutor (especially when it is a trial) the matter is heard either before a district judge (magistrates' court) or, and perhaps more likely, that the lay bench is clerked by someone who is legally qualified and can ensure that there is no abuse of process in these matters.

QUESTION FOR REFLECTION

Prosecutors are often considered to be 'Ministers of Justice' meaning that they are not ordinary lawyers within a court: they have a duty to ensure the proper working of the criminal justice system through, for example, correcting apparent errors of law. Can it be right under these circumstances to have a lay person representing the Crown since he will not necessarily be able to discharge that duty?

LISTEN TO THE PODCAST

For guidance on how to answer this question and a discussion of the main issues, listen to the author's podcast on the Online Resource Centre:
www.oxfordtextbooks.co.uk/orc/gillespie_els3e/

11.2 The trial

Summary trials, as was noted in the previous chapter, tend to be quicker than jury trials. Magistrates tend to sit in half-days although it is not unusual for them to sit in two half-day blocks, ie a full day. Many trials will be disposed of in a single day whereas this is perhaps extremely unusual in the Crown Court. However, many of the steps of the trial process are very similar.

11.2.1 Preliminary matters

Certain preliminary matters were considered in the previous chapter, including the provision of the 'plea before venue' in either-way offences (see 10.7.2.2 above). However where a defendant accepts summary trial or where the offence is summary-only the defendant will not actually have pleaded (it will be remembered that in the plea before venue scheme the defendant merely indicates his plea). The first stage, therefore, is to obtain a plea.

Depending on the complexity of the matter it is quite possible that the plea will take place at a time separate to the trial but alternatively (especially where it is an either-way offence and the indication was a not-guilty plea) the defendant must tender a plea to each charge in the information. Unlike in the Crown Court, it is not possible to include alternative charges unless expressly provided for (cf 12.2.1 below).

👁 Example Alternative charges

Caroline has been accused of attacking Victor. The prosecution allege that the attack was unprovoked and caused scratches and a bruise to Victor's arm. Technically speaking, this could amount to an assault occasioning actual bodily harm (s 47 *Offences Against the Person Act 1861*) which is an either-way offence punishable by five years' imprisonment. The prosecution and Caroline accept that the matter should be tried summarily.

It is also possible that because the injuries are slight it could also amount to common assault contrary to s 39 *Criminal Justice Act 1988,* which is triable summarily only and accordingly punished considerably less.

If the prosecution wish Caroline to consider whether to plead guilty to the less-serious charge then they must charge both ss 47 and 39, with it being clear that these are alternative charges (ie she would be guilty of one or other but not both). If the prosecution do not do this then not only can Caroline only plead to the single charge but the justices can only find Caroline guilty of the single charge. Accordingly, if they find that Caroline is not guilty of causing actual bodily harm they must acquit even when they think she should have been guilty of common assault. It is therefore a tactical decision for the prosecution as to whether to include alternative charges.

If the defendant pleads not guilty then the matter will proceed to trial whereas if the plea is guilty then the matter goes straight to the sentencing stage. The more complicated position is where there is a plea to an alternative charge since the prosecution must consider whether they wish to accept the plea of guilty to the lesser charge. There have been allegations that this can amount to 'plea bargaining' but these will be discussed in the next chapter where it is more relevant (see 12.2.1.1 below). Realistically, in the magistrates' court it is more likely that the plea will be accepted since the alternative charge would not otherwise be included.

11.2.1.1 Presence of the defendant

It may be taken for granted that a defendant should be present during a trial but this is not necessarily the case. There are two issues to discuss here: an authorized absence and an unauthorized absence.

Pleading guilty by post

The first and perhaps more frequent circumstance in which the hearing takes place in the absence of the defendant is where the defendant pleads guilty by post. It is possible to plead guilty by post to any summary-only offence regardless of the penalty that can be imposed (s 308 *Criminal Justice Act 2003* (CJA 2003)). When a summons is issued to the defendant a brief summary of the prosecution facts is also sent and details of the postal procedure is given (s 12 *Magistrates' Court Act 1980* (MCA 1980)).

If the defendant chooses to plead guilty by post then the prosecution are not allowed to expand on the facts given in the statement (s 12(8)); this is to ensure that the prosecution do not try to allege it is a more serious offence following a guilty plea. The defendant has the right to make written representation putting forward any mitigation and the magistrates must take this into account when deciding a penalty.

A person cannot be sentenced to prison in his absence under this procedure and accordingly if the magistrates are minded to impose a custodial sentence they must adjourn the matter and summon the defendant to court. In reality the system tends to be only used for minor offences and therefore this issue never arises but it is a useful system and one that does allow for a quicker disposition of cases.

Defendant failing to attend

The second possible reason for a defendant not being present is that he has failed to attend court when told to do so. Traditionally the magistrates, in these circumstances, have discretion as to how to proceed although amendments by the CJIA 2008 have altered this. The usual first step was to adjourn the proceedings and attempt to secure the attendance of the defendant at the next hearing, something they continue to have the right to do. The most likely method of securing attendance is to issue a warrant for his arrest. If the offender was already on bail then the magistrates may impose a bench warrant (s 7 *Bail Act 1976*) but if he was not then an arrest warrant can only be issued if the justices are satisfied that the summons was served appropriately or that the non-appearance arises from a previous adjournment where the accused was present (s 13).

The magistrates had the discretion to try an offender in his absence (s 11 MCA 1980) although they must be sure that the summons and/or the date of any adjourned hearing has been properly served on the defendant. The CJIA 2008 has amended s 11 by stating that where the defendant is an adult, the court 'shall proceed in his absence unless it appears to the court to be contrary to the interests of justice to do so' (s 11(1)(b) MCA 1980, as amended). Section 11(2A) states that where the court believes there is an acceptable reason for the defendant not appearing then it should not proceed in his absence.

If the justices proceed in the defendant's absence then a not-guilty plea is recorded and the prosecution then proceed to outline and prove their case. Whilst it is unlikely that the prosecution would be unable to prove their case given that there will be nobody available to cross-examine their witnesses it is not to be taken for granted. If the prosecution case is not sufficient for them to demonstrate guilt (because their witnesses did not give appropriate evidence or there was some other fatal flaw) then the justices must acquit the defendant in the same way that they would do so had the defendant been present.

Where a person is sentenced to prison in his absence then he must first be brought before the court before being taken to prison (s 11(3A), MCA 1980). Presumably this is to provide an opportunity to explain himself and for the court to explain why they imposed the sentence of imprisonment on him, and what duration that sentence is.

❓ QUESTION FOR REFLECTION

In *Lala v Netherlands* (1994) 18 EHRR 586 the European Court of Human Rights held that it was 'of utmost importance' that a defendant should be present at his trial.

Do you think it can ever be fair to trial a defendant in his absence? (Also see *R v Jones* [2002] UKHL 5.)

 LISTEN TO THE PODCAST
For guidance on how to answer this question and a discussion of the main issues, listen to the author's podcast on the Online Resource Centre:
www.oxfordtextbooks.co.uk/orc/gillespie_els3e/

11.2.2 **The prosecution case**

In any trial the prosecution always go first. This is because of the presumption of innocence. Probably the most important rule in the criminal justice system within England and Wales is the presumption of innocence, ie a person is innocent until proven guilty. The trial is not about determining innocence but rather proving guilt: if the prosecution cannot prove (to the requisite standard) that the defendant committed the crime then the defendant is entitled to be acquitted even if it is likely that he committed the offence.

The prosecution therefore have to establish that there is a case to answer, ie they need to be able to prove that there is sufficient evidence to show that the defendant did commit the crime. Only once that case has been established (see 11.2.3 below) will the defence then attempt to demonstrate that the person is *not* guilty.

In order to prove the case the prosecution must adduce evidence. Many things constitute evidence and many universities now offer the *Law of Evidence* as an optional module in your second and third year. As a brief summary, the most common forms of evidence are real evidence (including physical objects and certain documents) and witnesses. However not every piece of evidence is necessarily admissible. There are a number of legal rules that govern the admissibility or non-admissibility of evidence.

Example Telephone taps

You will probably be familiar with the concept of 'telephone taps' as most criminal investigation TV shows will discuss them. The more proper name for a telephone tap is an 'interception of communication' and Part 1 of the *Regulation of Investigatory Powers Act 2000* (RIPA 2000) regulates their use by law enforcement agencies. Whilst many law enforcement agencies (including the police and security services (ie MI5)) are able to use telephone taps to gain intelligence the product of a tap (ie the original recording or a transcript of the conversations) is not admissible as evidence (s 17 RIPA 2000). Accordingly no matter what the law enforcement agencies hear being said nothing is admissible in court.

In the Crown Court admissibility is relatively simple because the tribunal of fact (the jury) are removed from the courtroom whilst the tribunal of law (the judge) decides whether the evidence is admissible. The difficulty that exists in respect of the magistrates' court is that justices are the tribunal of both fact and law. In order to decide the admissibility the prosecution will almost certainly explain what the evidence is and what it shows. The justices are then expected to rule upon it, and if it is *inadmissible* then they are expected to ignore what they have heard. The criticism of the current system of summary trials is that this may simply not be realistic: how do you forget something that you have heard?

11.2.2.1 Witnesses

As in most trials, a significant proportion of the case is likely to come from witnesses. In summary matters it is quite possible that there may only be a small number of witnesses (for example in a speeding case only the police officer may be called) but most trials will involve their use in some ways.

Where a witness provides testimony in court then the order of testimony is as shown in Table 11.2.

Table 11.2 Order of evidence

Examination-in-chief	Prosecution ask questions
Cross-examination	Defence ask questions
Re-examination	Prosecution ask questions but only on matters asked before
Questions from the bench	Magistrates have the opportunity to ask questions

There is no obligation for any part of the witness testimony to proceed and it is relatively common for there to be no re-examination or questioning from the bench. Some argue that district judges are more likely to be proactive during the trial, including asking more questions (Morgan and Russell (2000) 46). This is because district judges are thought to be able to understand the evidential issues better than their lay colleagues and accordingly are aware of the questions that they are interested in to aid in their deliberations. Where lay magistrates sit then, by convention, only the chair speaks and those who sit with him (colloquially known as 'wingers') must pass questions through the chair. This undoubtedly slows proceedings down slightly and could possibly confuse witnesses who do not understand why questions proceed through the chair. However, the advantage of such a system is that it is possible to maintain consistency and order and there is no danger that the justices will ask contradictory questions or bombard a witness with questions.

Not all witnesses have to give evidence in person and a witness statement can be read out in court where the person states that it is the truth and made in connection with proceedings and where the defence has been given the opportunity to object to this procedure (s 9 *Criminal Justice Act 1967*). If the defence do object and wish the witness to be present then the statement can still be read out and this can stand as the examination-in-chief but the witness must still be brought to court to be subject to cross-examination.

Normally the prosecution will call the witnesses whom they wish to rely upon but the magistrates themselves have the power to call a relevant witness even if neither party does (*R v Haringey Justices, ex p DPP* [1996] QB 351). This is because the magistrates are the finders of fact and accordingly have the right to ensure that all relevant evidence that they require to assist in their deliberations is heard.

Witnesses are obliged to attend court but if either party has reason to believe that a witness will not turn up voluntarily they can ask the justices to issue a witness summons (s 97 MCA 1980) which if disobeyed can lead to an arrest warrant being issued to bring the witness to court. A witness who fails to turn up is also liable to a summons and/or arrest warrant if the justices are satisfied that they were provided with the appropriate details and date of the case.

11.2.3 Submission of no case to answer

After the conclusion of the prosecution case the defence case does not necessarily immediately begin. As was noted earlier, the burden of proof is on the prosecution to prove that the defendant is guilty and not for the defendant to prove his innocence. Accordingly at the end of the prosecution case the defence could ask the justices to rule on whether the prosecution have adduced sufficient evidence to prove guilt; this is known as a submission of no case to answer and, more colloquially, as a 'half-time submission'.

The magistrates must halt the case if they are satisfied that no reasonable tribunal could convict the defendant on the evidence adduced, either because one of the constituent elements of the offence has not been proved or because the witness testimony has been discredited (see *Practice Note* [1962] 1 All ER 448). It is not open to the justices to consider what the defence *may* do, but simply examine the prosecution evidence. Unlike a judge in the Crown Court, who cannot consider his own opinions of the evidence adduced (see the next chapter for more on this), the justices, because they are the tribunal of both facts and the law, can consider how the witnesses have given their evidence and what their credibility is.

If the submission of no case to answer succeeds then the defendant is acquitted of the charges. If the submission fails then it proceeds to the defence case.

11.2.4 Defence case

To an extent the defence case does not differ too much from the prosecution case. The defence have the right to either an opening or closing speech and they will usually choose the closing speech where there will be more opportunity to comment on the evidence that has been adduced rather than discuss what *might* be adduced.

The defence call witnesses in the same way as the prosecution with the roles being reversed (see Table 11.3).

Table 11.3 Order of evidence

Examination-in-chief	Defence ask questions
Cross-examination	Prosecution ask questions
Re-examination	Defence ask questions but only on matters asked before

The defence need not give evidence because, as a matter of law, the defendant is competent to give evidence (ie he is legally capable of being heard) but he is not compellable to give evidence (ie he cannot be forced to give evidence). Whilst this is true, if a defendant does not give evidence in court, the justices may draw an adverse inference against the defendant (s 35 *Criminal Justice and Public Order Act 1994*). Precisely what an adverse inference means is more open to question, but it is clear that it cannot by itself lead to a conviction or be the main reason for a conviction (s 35(3)).

If the defendant does intend to give evidence in trial he should normally give evidence first. This is because the accused, unlike other witnesses, is present in court before he gives evidence. On that basis he could hear the evidence of his witnesses and then alter his evidence to ensure that there is consistency between them. Of course, if a defendant was intending to do this, he could as easily discuss the testimony with witnesses outside the court, but the risks within court are more profound especially when a witness can never be quite sure of the questions that they will be asked, in particular during cross-examination.

After the defence have called their witnesses they will normally give their closing speech. When a district judge is sitting it is likely that the speech will be quite short whereas it may be longer to lay justices. The closing speech can include suggestions as to the legal implications of the evidence, together with interpretations of what the evidence meant. The prosecution do not automatically have the right to give a closing speech but where a matter of law is raised they should have the right to comment on it, regardless of whether it is a bench of lay magistrates or a district judge sitting.

11.2.5 **The verdict**

After the submissions the bench will decide whether the defendant is guilty of the charge laid against him. Where the bench consists of lay justices it is likely that they will retire to consider their verdict, ie they will leave the courtroom to discuss their decision. Where it is a district judge sitting alone, he will normally give instant judgment.

11.2.5.1 **Clerk retiring with the justices**

The position of the clerk to the court was discussed above and it was noted that he has a responsibility to provide advice. In the past it was not uncommon for the clerk to retire with the justices but should it happen? The clerk of the court is not supposed to have any role in respect of decisions of fact but if he retires with the justices then there is the appearance that the clerk almost becomes the 'fourth justice'.

The *Consolidated Practice Direction* makes it clear that advice should ordinarily be given in open court (V.55.7) and in *R v Birmingham Magistrates' Court, ex p Ahmed* [1994] COD 461 the Divisional Court heavily criticized the practice of one chairman who would always invite the clerk into the retiring room so that he knew the verdict before it was returned in open court. This practice could inevitably raise concerns that if the clerk disagreed with the justices he might try to persuade them to reconsider the matter. In *R v Eccles Justices, ex p Fitzpatrick*(1989) 89 Cr App R 324 the Divisional Court was clear that the clerk should not retire with the justices unless clearly asked to do so. However, despite these cases some clerks have continued to retire with the justices and, as has been noted, the *Consolidated Practice Direction* merely *presumes* that advice should ordinarily be given in open court and expressly states that a legal advisor can enter the jury room. That said, a crucial difference now is that where legal advice is given in the retiring room it should be considered provisional (V.55.7) and it must be repeated in open court, providing an opportunity to the legal representatives for the prosecution and defence to comment on the advice.

Given this, and because it is submitted that Article 6 of the *European Convention on Human Rights* requires any advice to be given in open court, it must be questioned whether there is any purpose in allowing a clerk or legal advisor to enter the retiring room. If the justices wish legal advice there is no reason why they cannot return to open court in the way that a jury asking the judge a question of law does so. In this way any advice will be transparent.

❓ QUESTION FOR REFLECTION

Is there any real difficulty in the justices retiring with the clerk? Clerks and justices are required to take oaths of offices and have clearly defined roles and responsibilities. Is it not a little simplistic to suggest that a clerk will, when retiring with justices, decide to go beyond his powers and influence the decision? Or is there a real danger of bias when a clerk retires? Read *ex p Eccles* and see what the Divisional Court thought.

11.2.5.2 Conviction rates

One of the issues frequently discussed within the criminal justice system is whether the conviction rate in magistrates' courts is higher than in the Crown Court and, if so, what that means. The first point to note is that research appears to suggest that in both the magistrates' and Crown Courts the overwhelming position appears to be the processing of people pleading guilty (McConville et al (1994) 212 but cf Padfield (2003) 286) and in the magistrates' court trials are relatively rare (ibid). That said, however, there does appear to be quite clear evidence that the conviction rate in magistrates' courts is higher than in the Crown Court (see [2006] Crim LR 1–2).

The higher conviction rate has been used in the past to suggest that magistrates are more 'hardened' than juries and that they are more prepared to convict (Sanders and Young (2010) 542–544). This suggestion then transforms into a question about whether the magistrates' court is fair. However, conviction and acquittal rates cannot necessarily be this simple. For example, does it automatically follow that if more people are acquitted in the Crown Court the jury system is fairer? It may be that juries are acquitting too many people which could be considered equally problematic. The truth of the matter is that there is no clear understanding of whether magistrates convict too many or juries acquit too many but there does appear to be a perception of mistrust with lay justices.

11.2.5.3 Pronouncement

The verdict of the court will always be given in open court. The justices are allowed to decide by majority but in open court there will never be an indication as to how justices voted—the decision is a collective one and ordinarily a magistrate should not state that he disagreed with the others. Only the chairman will speak and he will state the verdict in respect of all the charges. Where there were alternative charges a verdict on the lesser charge will not be returned if the more serious charge was proven.

In the magistrates' court the usual way of pronouncing guilt or innocence is to say whether the case has been 'proved' (ie guilty) or 'not proved' (ie not guilty). The justices must follow the same rules as a jury in the Crown Court, ie if there is any doubt as to the guilt of an offender they must acquit.

If the defendant is acquitted then he is free to go. If he is convicted then the court will proceed to the sentencing stage.

11.2.6 Sentencing

Where the defendant either pleaded guilty or was found guilty then the justices will be required to sentence the offender. Where the matter is particularly minor it is likely that sentencing will immediately occur. A good example of this is road traffic offences that tend to attract 'standard' penalties and thus, unless there are exceptional circumstances, it is likely that sentencing would occur immediately. Where the offence is more serious it is also possible that the court will wish to sentence immediately and this could be where, for example, a custodial sentence is inevitable.

The CJA 2003 provides the power to increase the maximum sentence of magistrates' courts to twelve months' imprisonment instead of the current six months (s 154 CJA 2003). However, at the time of writing, this power has not been activated by the government.

Custodial sentences are less likely in the magistrates' court than in the Crown Court, in part because the court will often deal with the less serious crimes. That said, custodial sentences do still occur and research suggests that district judges are more likely to impose an immediate custodial sentence than a lay bench (Morgan and Russell (2000) 52). Whether this means that district judges are 'tougher' sentencers than lay magistrates is perhaps more open to question since district judges do tend to sit on the more serious offences where, perhaps, custody is more likely.

 ## Summary

In this chapter we have examined some of the key issues surrounding a summary trial and in particular we have noted that:

- The main 'judges' in the magistrates' court are known as lay justices or justices of the peace.
- A lay magistrate is not legally qualified and sits in a voluntary capacity.
- There are increasing numbers of paid, professional magistrates known as district judges (magistrates' court) or deputy district judges if they sit part-time.
- District judges are legally qualified and may also sit in the Crown Court as a recorder. They are paid for sitting.
- Lay magistrates sit in benches of three whereas district judges will normally sit alone. If a district judge sits with lay magistrates he (the district judge) will preside.
- Although not qualified, lay magistrates remain responsible for decisions of both fact and law. They are assisted with the law by the clerk to the justices who must provide legal assistance when he believes it is in the interests of justice to do so.
- Lay magistrates should be slow to disregard the advice of the clerk.
- The prosecution always give evidence first. They must prove beyond all reasonable doubt that the defendant committed the crime. If they cannot show this by the end of the prosecution case then the defendant must be acquitted.
- If the defendant is not acquitted after the conclusion of the prosecution case then the defence will give evidence, with the defendant giving evidence first.
- At the conclusion of the trial the lay justices will retire to consider their verdict and the clerk should not ordinarily retire with the justices.

- The justices will return the verdict and sentence, with only the 'chairman' speaking. If the defendant is guilty they will say the case is 'proved' otherwise they will say the case is 'not proved'.

 End-of-chapter questions

1. Read Liberty (2002) and Darbyshire (2002) 292–294. Why do you think we continue with the idea of lay benches? Would it not be advisable for at least one justice to be a judge and therefore familiar with the law? Can a trial before lay persons be considered truly fair?

2. Read Darbyshire (2000) 186–193. Should the distinction between 'judge' and 'advisor' remain? What is the objection in giving a professionally qualified clerk some quasi-judicial powers? Read the section on judicial independence (see 7.5 above). Is there an argument that court clerks could be less independent?

3. How representative should a bench be? If the defendant is a member of the ethnic minorities should the bench also contain a member of the ethnic minorities?

 Further reading

Darbyshire P (1997) 'For the new Lord Chancellor: Some causes for concern about magistrates' *Criminal Law Review* 861–874.

This is an interesting article that summarizes some of the key issues for concern that are often raised against the idea of lay magistrates.

Darbyshire P (2000) 'Raising concerns about justices' clerks' in S Doran and J Jackson (eds) *The Judicial Role in Criminal Proceedings* (Oxford: Hart Publishing).

This is one of the few commentaries that examines the issue of justices' clerks. It raises some interesting points about their role within the summary system.

Davis G and Vennard J (2006) 'Racism in court: The experiences of ethnic minority magistrates' 45 *Howard Journal of Criminal Justice* 485–501.

This is an interesting study that interviews magistrates who come from an ethnic minority background and assesses how they are treated by fellow magistrates and those within the system.

Grove T (2002) *A Magistrate's Tale* (London: Bloomsbury).

Ordinarily I would be loath to suggest reading an entire book but this is an extremely easy read and absolutely fascinating. His previous book, *A Juryman's Tale*, is required reading for would-be judges and I would not be surprised to find that *A Magistrate's Tale* is not required reading for magistrates.

 For multiple choice questions, updates to this chapter and links to useful websites, please visit the Online Resource Centre at

www.oxfordtextbooks.co.uk/orc/gillespie_els3e/

12

Trials on Indictment

By the end of this chapter you will be able to:

- Understand what an indictment is.
- Identify who is involved in a trial on indictment and what they do.
- Differentiate between the roles of the judge and the jury.
- Identify the format of a trial on indictment.
- Appreciate how jurors make their decisions.

Introduction

The last chapter examined the procedure of a summary trial, that being a trial that takes place in the magistrates' court. This chapter examines the other principal type of criminal trial which is known as trial on indictment and which takes place in the Crown Court. It was seen in Chapter 10 that only a small percentage of trials will take place in the Crown Court but that they are generally for the more serious crimes. Despite the fact only a relatively small number of cases are heard in the Crown Court it is perhaps the mode of trial that people are most familiar with because it is the one that is portrayed widely in the media.

12.1 Those in court

As with the previous chapter, it will be necessary initially to examine who will become involved in the trial. Some of the people mentioned in this part of the chapter are explained in more detail in other chapters and thus reference will need to be made to those chapters.

The key people are:

- the judge
- the jury
- lawyers
- court clerk
- stenographer
- the usher(s)
- the defendant
- witnesses.

It can be seen that there are slightly more people than in the magistrates' court and additional people would include security guards and probation officers, etc.

12.1.1 The judge

Perhaps the key difference between a summary trial and trial on indictment is the presence of a judge and jury. The judge has ultimate responsibility for the proceedings and has sole responsibility of the law. The judge is always a legally qualified paid person. The judges who are entitled to sit in the Crown Court for a trial are:

- any judge of the High Court
- any circuit judge (including deputy circuit judges)[1]

---

1. These are persons who retired as a Lord Justice of Appeal, puisne judge, or circuit judge but who are still under the age of 75 (s 24 *Courts Act 1971* (CA 1971)).

- a recorder
- a district judge (magistrates' court).[2]

The appointment and qualifications of judges other than district judges (magistrates' court) are set out in Chapter 7, and district judges are outlined in Chapter 11. In addition to this, the Lord Chief Justice has the inherent right to sit in the Crown Court as an ex officio judge, this right accruing from his status as President of the Courts of England and Wales (s 7 *Constitutional Reform Act 2005* and see Chapter 7.1.1.1). Recent Lord Chief Justices have exercised this right occasionally although they have tended to sit only on sentencing matters or short trials. Other members of the judiciary may only sit in the Crown Court when they have been invited to do so by the Lord Chief Justice (s 9(1) *Senior Courts Act 1981* (SCA 1981)) and if they are not so invited then they have no jurisdiction to act in the Crown Court regardless of the seniority of their office (*R v Lord Chancellor, ex p Maxwell* [1997] 1 WLR 104).

12.1.1.1 Allocation of the judge

In the review of the criminal justice system it was said:

> One of the greatest ills of the system is its lack of flexibility in the matching of judges, courts and cases (Auld (2002) 226).

The decision as to how a judge is appointed to a particular case is relatively complicated and arguably a matter of chance in the majority of cases, but with some there is a defined procedure that must be followed. Not every judge is permitted to hear every case and, for example, in cases of murder and sexual offences a judge below the rank of puisne judge must receive additional training before he can hear such cases. This system is known as 'ticketing' and is designed to ensure that only experienced judges hear sensitive cases (IV.33 of the *Consolidated Practice Direction*). It had been suggested that the system of ticketing should be removed (Auld (2002) 237) but as of yet this does not appear to have been acted upon, not least because there is a danger that removing the ticketing system could undermine the confidence of the public in the judicial system.

👁 **Example** His Honour Judge Pickles QC

One of the most controversial judges in modern times was HHJ Pickles QC who was a circuit judge who attracted significant controversy, particularly in respect of sex crimes (see 7.5.2.3 above). Following a series of incidents, including a rebuke in *R v Scott* [1990] Crim LR 440 Pickles was informed that he would no longer be sitting on further sex offence cases. In effect his 'ticket' was removed.

The presiding judge identifies judges who have the appropriate seniority or skills to undertake specialist trials (eg rape)[3] but the decision is ultimately one for the Lord Chief Justice. If selected, the judge has to attend an appropriate training programme and will then be 'ticketed' and permitted to try sensitive cases. It is relatively rare for

---

2. District judges (magistrates' court) sit as recorders when in the Crown Court (s 65 CA 2003).
3. HC WA, vol 434, col 143W, Harriet Harman MP, *Hansard*, 25 May 2005.

'tickets' to be removed (indeed in 2003 and 2004 no 'ticket' was removed)[4] but as was seen from above it is possible. Removal is by the Lord Chief Justice, ordinarily on advice of the presiding judges.

The *Consolidated Practice Direction* (III.21.1) states that allocation will depend on how the offence is classed. There are currently three classes of offences (Table 12.1).

Table 12.1 Classification of offences

Class 1	(a)	Treason
	(b)	Murder
	(c)	Genocide
	(d)	Torture and offences under the *War Crimes Act 1991*
	(e)	Offences under the Official Secrets Acts
	(f)	Manslaughter
	(g)	Infanticide
	(h)	Child destruction
	(i)	Abortion
	(j)	Sedition
	(k)	An offence under s 1 *Geneva Conventions Act 1957*
	(l)	Mutiny
	(m)	Piracy
	(n)	Inchoate offences related to the above.
Class 2	(a)	Rape
	(b)	Sexual intercourse with a girl under 13
	(c)	Incest with a girl under 13
	(d)	Assault by penetration
	(e)	Causing a person to engage in sexual activity, where penetration is involved
	(f)	Rape of a child under 13
	(g)	Assault of a child under 13 by penetration
	(h)	Causing or inciting a child under 13 to engage in sexual activity, where penetration is involved
	(i)	Sexual activity with a person with a mental disorder, where penetration is involved
	(j)	Inducement to procure sexual activity with a mentally disordered person where penetration is involved
	(k)	Paying for sexual services of a child where a child is under 13 and penetration is involved
	(l)	Committing an offence with intent to commit a sexual offence, where the offence is kidnapping or false imprisonment
	(m)	Inchoate offences related to the above.
Class 3		All other offences not listed in classes 1 or 2.

The rules (IV. 33) then state which type of judge should hear a case depending on the class of the offence (Table 12.2).

4. HC WA, vol 434, col 142W, Harriet Harman MP, *Hansard*, 25 May 2005.

Table 12.2 Allocation of judiciary

Class 1	(1) a High Court Judge, or
	(2) a Circuit Judge...provided (a) that in all cases save attempted murder, such judge is authorized by the Lord Chief Justice to try murder cases, and (b) the Presiding Judge has released the case for trial by such a judge.
Class 2	(1) a High Court Judge, or
	(2) a Circuit Judge...or Recorder, provided that in all cases the judge is authorized to try class 2 cases by the Lord Chief Justice and the case has been assigned to the judge by or under the direction of either the Presiding Judge or Resident Judge in accordance with guidance given by the Presiding Judges.
Class 3	Cases in class 3 may be tried by a High Court Judge, or in accordance with guidance given by the Presiding Judges, a Circuit Judge....or a Recorder. A case in class 3 shall not be listed for trial by a High Court Judge except with the consent of a Presiding Judge.

It should be noted that the release in class 1 is specific—ie the presiding judge (unless he designates this responsibility to a senior circuit judge) shall examine each case and state that it can be released to a particular judge. The release in class 2 is more general and is a statement that particular crimes could be released to particular types of judges (eg senior circuit judges, resident judges, deputy circuit judges, recorders, etc). The role of the presiding judge is, therefore, an important one but also a time-consuming one. It is an onerous job and perhaps this is why it is held only for a short time.

❓ QUESTION FOR REFLECTION

Why should there be such a complex way of allocating judges to cases? If a person is appointable as a judge then why should he not be able to sit on any crime? If a judge has particular expertise in a particular area in practice should he not be able to sit on those trials without added experience? Are there any safeguards in allocating trials in this way?

Whilst a different judge may be responsible for the pre-trial arrangements (see below), once a judge has begun to hear a case then it is not possible to change the judge and if, for some reason, the judge must retire from the case (eg sickness etc) then the trial ends and it must begin again. An unusual issue arose in 1996 with the long-running fraud trial of the Maxwell brothers. The trial judge, Phillips J, had decided to sever the indictment meaning that in effect there would be two trials, each dealing with some of the charges against them.[5] Midway through the first trial he was appointed by the Queen to be a Lord Justice of Appeal. Accordingly he no longer had jurisdiction to sit in the Crown Court as of right (see above). The Lord Chancellor designated him a judge of the Crown Court for the completion of the first trial but when the matter proceeded to the second trial (to consider those charges that were severed) he refused to designate the judge. The Court of Appeal held that Phillips LJ (as he then was) had no automatic right to sit in the Crown Court and that the decision of the Lord Chancellor to designate

---

5. This is sometimes done where there are a large number of complicated charges as it simplifies matters for the jury.

judges under s 9(1) SCA 1981 was not subject to review (*R v Lord Chancellor, ex p Maxwell* [1997] 1 WLR 104).

12.1.1.2 Responsibilities of the judge

In the previous chapter it was noted that magistrates have responsibility for both fact and law (see 11.1.2.2 above). It is often said that in the Crown Court this responsibility is divided between judge and jury but in fact that is an oversimplistic distinction because there are numerous situations when a judge will have to make findings of fact (Doran (2000) 5). Examples of where decisions of fact will need to be made include preliminary matters and admissibility decisions, and where a guilty plea is tendered the judge may actually become the sole tribunal of fact (in a procedure known as a *Newton hearing*; see 12.2.1.2 below).

Although a civil case, the leading statement of what the responsibilities of a judge in an adversarial trial are was set out by Lord Denning MR:

> [He] is to hearken the evidence, only himself asking questions of witnesses when it is necessary to clear up any point that has been overlooked or left obscure, to see that the advocates behave themselves seemly and keep to the rules laid down by law. (*Jones v National Coal Board* [1957] 2 QB 55 at 65)

And his Lordship warns that the principal danger for a judge is dropping 'the mantles of a judge and assum[ing] the robes of an advocate'; in other words the judge has to rise above the cut and thrust of advocacy and assure that the rules are followed. The role of a judge is often given a sporting analogy:

> The judge is not an advocate. Under the English and Welsh system of criminal trials he is much more like the umpire at a cricket match. He is certainly not the bowler, whose business it is to get the batsman out. (*R v Gunning* (1994) 98 Cr App R 303 at 306 per Cumming-Bruce LJ)

Case management

Perhaps the most important duty of a judge is to control proceedings. The judge has ultimate responsibility for proceedings including the order of witnesses and evidence that may be adduced (Otton (2002) 327). The *Criminal Procedure and Investigations Act 1996* (CPIA 1996) marked a significant change in the way judges controlled proceedings through the provision of formalized pre-trial hearings (McEwan (2000) 172). These hearings are known as Plea and Directions Hearings (PDH) and some of the key issues are discussed below (see 12.2 below).

A significant part of the case management procedure in the Crown Court is the process known as disclosure. Whilst the detailed mechanics of the disclosure regime are outside the scope of this book, the broad thrust is that the prosecution have a legal obligation to disclose their evidence to the defence prior to the beginning of the trial (see McEwan (2000) 177–180 for a useful background to why these rules were established). There is supposed to be a reciprocal duty by the defence (s 33 *Criminal Justice Act 2003* (CJA 2003)) although this tends to be minimal at best, in part because there are doubts as to the propriety of penalizing a defendant for failing to disclose his or defence (McEwan (2000) 178).

The basis of disclosure is that although a trial is adversarial it should still be considered a search for truth and a defendant should be aware of the case against him, something that is reinforced by Article 6(3)(a) of the *European Convention on Human Rights* (ECHR) (Leng (2002) 208). The prosecution must disclose not only evidence they are going to rely upon (eg the witness statements of those people they wish to call) but also on so-called 'unused evidence', ie evidence that the prosecution will not be relying upon. The justification for this is that it is possible that the prosecution may have gathered evidence that is helpful to the defence.

Example Fingerprints

Laura is accused of unlawful wounding, the alleged facts being that she stabbed Wayne. The prosecution say that they have found her fingerprints on the knife which stabbed Wayne. They will wish to adduce this evidence and will call a Scenes of Crime Officer (SOCO) to give testimony to this effect.

The SOCO also found two other fingerprints on the knife, one of whom they have not yet traced and the other is a man called Terry who it is known Wayne owed money to. The prosecution are unlikely to want to adduce the evidence of the other fingerprints because it does not help their case. However, it possibly assists the defence case (two other possible suspects, one of which has a motive) and so this should be disclosed.

The test enshrined by statute (s 3(1) CPIA 1996) is therefore that the prosecution must:

> disclose to the accused any prosecution material which...might reasonably be considered capable of undermining the case for the prosecution against the accused or of assisting the case for the accused...

It can be seen that it is phrased as either helping the defence or undermining the prosecution case. The reason for this is that undermining the prosecution can, in effect, assist the defence since if the prosecution cannot prove beyond all reasonable doubt that the defendant committed the crime then he is entitled to an acquittal.

What should the position be when there are sensitivities surrounding the disclosure of the information that the prosecution holds? The law recognizes a doctrine known as *public interest immunity* (PII) whereby the prosecution are allowed to withhold certain information from the defence with the approval of the trial judge (see Ashworth and Redmayne (2010) 268–278 for a useful summary of this doctrine).

Example Observation posts

A good example of the type of sensitive information is an observation post. Let us assume that the police suspect someone in 11 Acacia Avenue, Anytown of dealing in drugs. They need to mount covert surveillance on the house to try to gather evidence. 8 Puddle Lane, one street back, has a perfect view of 11 Acacia Avenue and the owner of number 8 allows the police to use her house.

Are there any risks to the owner of number 8? Quite possibly. If the people in number 11 are dealing in drugs then it is quite possible that they would try to take revenge on the persons at number 8. For this reason the court will ordinarily try to protect the identity of the observation post from being disclosed (*R v Johnson* (1989) 88 Cr App R 131).

There are three levels of public interest immunity (Table 12.3):

Table 12.3 Public interest immunity

Level 1	**Inter Partes Hearing**. The parties are both in court explaining why the evidence should, or should not, be disclosed.
Level 2	**Ex Parte with Notice**. The defence are told that an application for PII is to be made but not what it concerns. They are not in the courtroom when the application is made although the judge will speak to them afterwards.
Level 3	**Ex Parte**. The defence are not told that an application has been made.

The judge *must* be involved in the decision to withhold material and ultimately the judge has to decide whether to order the disclosure of the evidence or not (*Jasper v United Kingdom* (2000) 30 EHRR 441 cf *Rowe and Davis v United Kingdom* (2000) 30 EHRR 1). If the judge decides that disclosure is necessary because, notwithstanding the risks to the person or interest being protected, it is necessary for a fair trial to be achieved then the prosecution must either comply with that direction or (and more likely) halt the prosecution.

Although the prosecution will apply for the evidence to be kept secret at a pre-trial hearing, the decision is constantly revisited (*R v H and C* [2004] UKHL 3). If the judge believes at any point in time that it is necessary to revisit the PII ruling then he is obliged to do so and so evidence will not necessarily be kept secret all the time.

 **Example** Revisiting PII

Let us take the example above slightly further. For whatever reason, a police officer called to give evidence suggests that observations were carried out not from 8 Pudding Lane but from a van parked outside 11 Acacia Avenue. The fact that a police officer is not telling the truth could be an important issue in the case. However, how will the defence know that he is not telling the truth since the judge has kept the observation post secret? In these circumstances the judge would have to indicate to the prosecution that they have to disclose the identity of the post to the defence so that the police officer can be cross-examined.

PII is undoubtedly controversial but is almost certainly a necessary part of the current criminal justice system. As law enforcement techniques become more sophisticated (through the use of covert surveillance, electronic monitoring, etc) it will become increasingly frequent for the police to wish to keep their tactics secret on the basis that if they are discussed publicly in court criminals will be able to circumvent them through the use of anti-surveillance techniques. The key to PII is the judge as he must constantly bear in mind the fundamental principle that the defendant is entitled to a fair trial.

Halting a case

Perhaps one of the least well-known duties of a judge is to halt a case. Although the Crown Court is often thought to be a 'jury court' only about 1 per cent of defendants dealt with through the criminal justice system will actually be placed in the hands of a jury (Sanders and Young (2010) 554). This may seem surprising but it is indicative of the system: 97 per cent of defendants are dealt with summarily. Of the 3 per cent who will go to Crown Court, a significant number will plead guilty and others will be acquitted without the jury deliberating. Up to two-thirds of those ultimately acquitted in the Crown Court are actually acquitted on the direction of the judge (Sanders and Young (2001) 555) meaning that the jury have no option but to acquit and do not retire to consider their verdict.

Why should a judge intervene? If a defendant pleads not guilty then is it not for the jury to decide guilt or innocence? The answer lies in the fact that a conviction is both a matter of law and fact. In its most understandable guise it is a matter of fact: the jury decide that a person has in fact done the crime that he was accused of. It is also a matter of law, however, in that a person can only be convicted if there is proof beyond all reasonable doubt that he committed the offence. Whilst it will normally be for the jury to decide whether that proof exists, there may be circumstances when a judge concludes that there is insufficient evidence to go before a jury and that it is simply not possible for them to convict. In those circumstances there is no point in asking the jury to deliberate because, as a matter of law, their decision can only be not guilty. Under those circumstances the judge would step in and direct a jury to acquit. The mechanics of this is the judge will choose a person as the foreperson (usually it is the person in the front row of the jury box sitting closest to the judge) and tell the foreperson that as a matter of law they can only acquit the person. He will then require the foreperson to say that the jury find them 'not guilty'. It could be argued that this last bit is an unnecessary piece of stage management: if the jury cannot convict then the judge should be able to acquit the defendant but the law requires that in the Crown Court a jury must deliver the verdict once a trial has begun so this unnecessary farce is played out.

12.1.2 The jury

The jury has undoubtedly an important status within the criminal justice system with Lord Devlin, a onetime Lord of Appeal in Ordinary, commenting that it is 'the lamp that shows freedom lives' (Devlin (1956) 164) a statement approved of by Lord Taylor, a previous Lord Chief Justice, who said: 'in our culture and perception trial by jury is a fundamental right' (Ashworth (1999) 258). Both are therefore of the opinion that juries demonstrate democracy in action, something that the House of Lords affirmed:

> The institution of jury trial, with all its imperfections, is still trusted by the public as a method of determining the guilt of persons charged with criminal offences. (*R v Smith (No 2)* [2005] UKHL 12 at [7] per Lord Carswell)

What is interesting from this quotation is that there is recognition that trial by jury is arguably not a perfect way of dealing with trials, indeed it can be argued that it is quite flawed. If you ever speak to a lawyer or judge who specializes in criminal law you will always find that they have at least one story to tell about a jury who managed to reach the wrong verdict or who approached their task in an unprofessional manner etc. Yet these same practitioners will almost certainly state that the jury system retains their confidence (Auld (2002) 135).

Juries are often quoted as being a historic guarantee of the rights of the common man to sit in judgement on his fellow citizen; however, this is not strictly true and until 1972 property was a primary factor in the eligibility of people to serve on a jury, meaning that juries tended to be men of a certain economic status (Zander (2007) 486). However, the use of lay members is often cited as being an important part of the democratization of the justice system (see, in particular, Devlin (1956)) and the fact that a jury consists of twelve members is often cited as being reason to ensure that the decision is fair as the prejudices or lack of interest shown by an individual juror can be counterbalanced by the others. However, this point is somewhat weakened when one examines the rules as to majority verdicts (see below) and does not take account of the strength of character of some individuals.

12.1.2.1 Trial by judge alone

Although trial by jury is considered to be part of a democracy, it is now possible for a judge to hear a trial that would otherwise be heard by a jury alone. In such circumstances the judge is both the tribunal of fact and law. Outside of England and Wales trial by judge alone is not unusual, with many trials being heard in Scotland by a Sheriff (the equivalent of a Circuit Judge) and in Northern Ireland terrorist-related crimes (including murder) were heard by a judge alone (known as a 'Diplock court' after the report by Lord Diplock, a then Lord of Appeal in Ordinary, who recommended that trial by jury be suspended for terrorist-related crimes).

In England and Wales the possibility of abolishing trial by jury has long been controversial but the CJA 2003 allowed the Crown Court to rule that it is permissible for a trial to be heard without a jury (s 44 CJA 2003). The first approval for this trial took place in *R v T* [2009] EWCA Crim 1035 which concerned the trial of a number of defendants for an alleged large-scale robbery that took place at Heathrow Airport. After several previous cases collapsed, the Court of Appeal agreed that there was a real risk of jury tampering and that those risks could not be adequately minimized by the police. The trial began in January 2010 and led to the conviction of four men. The trial was extremely controversial with many lawyers arguing that trial by jury was an inherent human right (but see *R v Tuomey* [2011] EWCA Crim 8).

It had been thought that *T* would lead to a number of judge-alone trials but the Court of Appeal has shown that it is willing to approve such trials only where a trial by jury is unfeasible. In *R v J* [2010] EWCA Crim 1755 the Court of Appeal quashed the decision of a judge to order trial by judge alone where it believed that preventative measures could be taken. The court emphasized that trial by judge alone was a last resort and the strong presumption is that a jury should hear a matter. The court noted that a trial could take place and if jury tampering took place then the judge could always discharge the jury and hear the remainder of the matter alone (s 46 CJA 2003) although such a course of action is likely to be controversial since it is likely that counsel would prepare and conduct a trial differently where a jury is absent.

12.1.2.2 Eligibility for jury service

Those who are prima facie eligible for jury service (s 1 *Juries Act 1974* (JA 1974) as amended by the CJA 2003) are:

- registered on the electoral roll and between the ages of 18 and 70
- ordinarily resident in the United Kingdom, Channel Islands, or Isle of Man for the last five years
- not a mentally disordered person and
- not disqualified from jury service.

These criteria mask a more significant change which is that previously a wider range of persons were either able to ask for excusal or were disqualified from sitting as a juror. Those who were eligible for excusal (and thus it was a matter for them as to whether to seek an excusal) included those between the ages of 65 and 70, Members of Parliament, members of the medical profession, and members of HM Forces (s 9(1) JA 1974 and Sch 1, Part III as originally enacted). However, the new scheme removes this excusal system other than for members of HM Forces where their commanding officer certifies that it would be 'prejudicial to the efficiency of the service' for them to serve, although even then normally a deferral rather than full excusal should be permitted (ss 9(2) and 9A JA 1974 as amended by the CJA 2003).

What the Act does not do, of course, is to tackle the issue of under-representation identified by Auld. It is accepted that the turn-out for elections is very low, especially amongst the younger members of society and the ethnic minorities. Given their apathy towards voting it is not unreasonable to assume that they have neglected to register themselves with the appropriate authorities. The suggestion of Auld to use alternative methods of identifying those eligible to serve was worthy of more consideration and its rejection should be reviewed by Parliament.

❓ QUESTION FOR REFLECTION

Do you agree that alternative databases should be used to widen the jury pool? What databases do you think should be used? How important is it that the potential pool contains representatives of as many sections of society as possible?

🎧 LISTEN TO THE PODCAST

For guidance on how to answer this question and a discussion of the main issues, listen to the author's podcast on the Online Resource Centre:
www.oxfordtextbooks.co.uk/orc/gillespie_els3e/

12.1.2.3 Disqualification

Alongside the changes to the excusal from jury service, the CJA 2003 dramatically alters the range of those who are disqualified from serving. Previously those whose occupation, or whose spouse's occupation, was allied to the criminal justice system (eg judiciary, lawyers, police, etc) were disqualified from sitting on a jury as were members of the clergy. Auld had argued that this was a historical irrelevancy and he spent a considerable time noting that in the United States of America it was not uncommon for members of the legal profession, including members of the judiciary, to be called to serve (Auld (2002) 140–141, 146–149). This proposal caused much controversy but it was accepted by the government and the list of people who are disqualified (ie may not sit on a jury regardless of whether they wish to or not) is now restricted to those who are convicted of a crime and may be summarized as follows (Table 12.4).

Table 12.4 Disqualification from jury service

Life imprisonment (or equivalent)	Disqualified for life
Imprisonment for public protection	Disqualified for life
Imprisonment for a term of five years or more	Disqualified for life
Any term of imprisonment (including suspended)	Disqualification for ten years
Community sentence	Disqualification for ten years

Nobody is now automatically excused as a result of their occupation and since the CJA 2003 has come into force two Lords Justice of Appeal, Dyson LJ (as he then was) and Tuckey LJ, have served on a jury along with numerous other judges and lawyers. Whether this is correct remains a topic of heated debate. Auld clearly wished to widen the pool of available juries but the use of judges, particularly senior judges, does appear slightly at odds with the overriding principle of the review which was to quicken up the criminal justice system. Jury trials are longer than summary trials and although a juror will often sit for only a two-week period, that is two weeks when a court, including the Court of Appeal (which suffers from delays), will be without a judge; is this necessarily in the best interests of the criminal justice system?

More serious, however, is the issue of bias. It was noted in Chapter 7 that the issue of perceived bias is something that needs to be guarded against (7.6.3.2) and this must be true of juries too. Whilst it may be unproblematic if a judge—who is supposed to be impartial—sits, what signal does it send if a police officer or prosecutor sits on a jury? The matter inevitably led to litigation. The first, and most important, case is *R v Abdroikov* [2007] 1 WLR 2679. Abdroikov and two other appellants (from different trials) appealed to the House of Lords complaining about the composition of the juries hearing their trials. In Abdroikov, the foreperson of the jury was a serving police officer, and in another appellant's case a member of the jury was employed by the CPS although the juror did not know anyone connected to the case.

The House of Lords noted that the law had changed and it was quite clear that the range of people *entitled* to sit on the case had been widened but Baroness Hale makes the pertinent point that just because a person *can* be summoned for jury service does not mean that they should sit on the case they have been summoned for (pp 2696–7). Her Ladyship noted that whether they can sit depends on whether it would render the trial unsafe.

In respect of the police officer sitting, the House noted that there was no real dispute between the evidence of the police and defendant and there was no link between the station in which the police officer was based and the police witnesses in the trial. The House concluded there was no risk of prejudice. However, it reached a different conclusion in respect of the CPS employee. Lord Bingham noted that it was doubtful it was ever intended for a crown prosecutor to sit on a jury brought by their agency since that would appear to have the appearance of bias since a juror is employed by the prosecutor.

This ruling was explained by the Court of Appeal in *R v Khan* [2008] 2 Cr App R 13 which concerned similar issues. The court in that case indicated that the mere fact that a police officer works in the same locality as a witness does not provide evidence of bias, nor does the fact that he works on similar types of cases. The court also noted that the limitation on CPS employees sitting on juries was limited to those trials where the CPS was the prosecutor. Where an alternative prosecuting agency brought the prosecution (in this case the Department of Trade and Industry) then being the employee of a prosecution service would not show bias.

❓ QUESTION FOR REFLECTION

Do you think the House of Lords and Court of Appeal were right to say there is no appearance of bias where a police officer on a jury is in the same police force as a police witness? Is there realistically any difference between this and the CPS employee? Should police officers only be permitted to sit on jury cases which involve police witnesses from outside their police area (eg a Warwickshire police officer could sit on a case involving Leicestershire police but not Warwickshire police)? Could that cause any practical difficulties?

LISTEN TO THE PODCAST

For guidance on how to answer this question and a discussion of the main issues, listen to the author's podcast on the Online Resource Centre: www.oxfordtextbooks.co.uk/orc/gillespie_els3e/

Bias is not restricted to those who come within the criminal justice system. What happens where someone has made public statements in respect of law and justice issues? Does this raise the possibility of bias? In *R v Cornwall* [2009] EWCA Crim 2458 a juror was a well-known columnist for *The Sun* who had made a series of pronouncements about knife crime, drugs, and immigration. The appellant was a drug dealer who was accused of stabbing a person to death. The Court of Appeal rejected an argument that the juror was biased and noted that there was no evidence that he had not tried the case in accordance with his oath. The court noted that a jury may well have people with strong views on the criminal justice system but that will be one person amongst twelve. The court accepted that public pronouncements could lead to an allegation of bias but they would need to relate specifically to issues before the jury and in this particular case they did not and there was no risk that an independent observer would consider the juror to be biased.

12.1.2.4 Enforcing jury service

Jury service is a civic responsibility and accordingly when a potential juror is summoned to court he is expected to attend. However Auld noted that 15 per cent of jurors refused to answer the juror summons. It is a criminal offence to fail to answer a jury summons, theoretically as contempt of court but more frequently as a summary-only offence punishable by a fine (s 20 JA 1974). However Auld noted that it was comparatively rare for courts actually to pursue those who neglect a jury summons, and accordingly this had created a position whereby significant numbers failed to meet their civic duty. Arguably the position may be somewhat better now since a central jury-summoning bureau has been established so instead of individual courts being responsible for deciding the eligibility or otherwise of jurors a central bureau does this. Accordingly, if courts make the appropriate returns to this system they could be charged with pursuing those who neglect their service.

However, some disagree with this policy, and Auld himself noted that the difficulty with enforcement is that it could clog up courts with a relatively trivial matter. Auld suggested the imposition of a fixed penalty notice (Auld (2002) 145) although that does raise the question why it is that Auld believes that someone who fails to respond to a jury summons would respond to a fixed penalty notice; presumably a significant proportion would fail to pay the ticket necessitating enforcement proceedings at this stage. However Auld is undoubtedly correct in deciding that something has to be done since the jury system is based upon the premise that citizens will do their part and accordingly those who neglect this duty should be held to account.

Employers

Some jurors may not wish to attend jury service because they are concerned as to whether their employer will allow them time off. An employer is legally obliged to release an employee for jury service and a refusal to do so amounts to contempt of court for which the employer could be fined or even imprisoned. An employee has the right not to be subjected to any detrimental treatment as a result of being a juror (s 43M *Employment Rights Act 1996*) and a person who is dismissed for serving as a juror will be considered to have been dismissed unfairly (s 98B ERA 1996).

An employer does not need to pay an employee who is serving as a juror. This potentially can cause financial hardship (which may be a reason for excusal) since whilst a juror is paid expenses, they are subject to fixed limits. Financial loss (which includes loss of earnings, child minding fees, etc) is limited to £64.95 per day for the first ten days of a jury trial (two working weeks) and then £129.91 for days between the 11th and 200th day of jury service.[6] The ordinary payment of £64.95 translates to just over £320 per week, which produces a salary of £16,887. Many employees will receive more salary than this and it must be remembered that this allowance includes payment for child care which may account for a considerable amount of this daily allowance. This may mean that some employees actually lose money for serving on a jury and so it is perhaps unsurprising that some people try to avoid it.

12.1.2.5 Vetting

It has been noted that jurors are disqualified, either temporarily or permanently, if they have been convicted of a criminal offence (see 12.1.2.3 above). It would not be a surprise therefore to know that jurors are often checked against the computer record system to identify those who have a previous conviction. This is relatively uncontroversial and is indeed probably quite sensible.

What is perhaps more surprising is the fact that it is possible for jurors to be vetted. This can involve the names of potential jurors being passed to the police (special branch) or security services (MI5) in order for an analysis to be made as to their background (Doran (2002) 389). This practice has a long history although the first identifiable case of jury vetting took place in relation to a trial under the Official Secrets Act where the prosecution had vetted 'for loyalty' the jury pool but had not removed three potential jurors, two of whom had signed the Act in question and one of whom (who became the foreperson of the jury) was a former member of the Special Air Service (SAS) (Sanders and Young (2010) 562). The result of this disclosure was significant criticism and the Attorney-General agreed to produce guidelines that would limit when any vetting could occur. These guidelines are published and the latest version can be found on the CPS website.[7]

The guidelines make clear that vetting should only occur where the trial concerns a matter of public interest or in a terrorist case. The vetting takes place only with the authorization of the Attorney-General[8] and is designed to allow the prosecution to exercise their power of 'stand by' (see 12.3.1.2 below), the reason presumably being something in the juror's background that is cause for concern.

---

6. HMCS Website. A link to the allowances will be contained on the Online Resource Centre.
7. The Online Resource Centre provides a link to the guidelines.
8. In this context this means the personal authority of either the Attorney-General or the Solicitor-General. It is not possible to delegate this power.

A particular difficulty with this whole exercise is that although the guidelines are published they are not particularly clear and are open to interpretation in a way that would allow the state to 'rig' a jury if it so wished. It has been noted that the guidelines do not place an obligation on the prosecution to 'stand by' a juror who would be biased against the defendant and yet the defendant would have no real way of knowing that they were (Sanders and Young (2010) 563). It also goes against the rule that a jury should be drawn randomly and that the specific characteristics of jurors should not ordinarily be taken into account (Doran (2002) 390).

Article 6 of the ECHR is commonly said to have an 'equality of arms' dimension to it, that is to say that both parties should be operating at roughly the same strength. Whilst it is never possible to obtain absolute parity (in either direction) the rule is based on the fact that one side should not be able to abuse its own position to the detriment of the opposing party. The system of jury vetting would appear to be a classic example of an inequality-of-arms position since the defence do not have the resources or contacts to be able to vet potential jurors. The complete absence of independence and the inevitable security that accompanies the vetting system also leads to the conclusion that there is no transparency within the process. It is difficult to see how this would not amount to a breach of Article 6 but perhaps its limited scope may save it. The European Court of Human Rights (ECtHR) has stated before that Article 6 is not an absolute right and that issues of national security may mean that some aspects of a fair trial may need to be balanced against important state interests.

For the moment the position of vetting appears settled but this is, in part, because the defence will not always know when jury vetting has taken place. Challenges for cause can be made at any stage and could theoretically be made to the judge without the defence knowing (on the basis that their objection might lead to the jurors never being included in the 'jury in waiting'). This makes the possibility of challenging the regime somewhat difficult.

12.1.3 Lawyers

Unlike in the magistrates' court, matters dealt with in the Crown Court are normally dealt with by professional lawyers. The use of associated prosecutors, permitted in summary matters (see 11.1.3.3 above), is not permitted in the Crown Court; the prosecution must *always* be represented by a professional lawyer. No such rule applies to the defendant but because of the seriousness of the charges normally heard in the Crown Court it is more common for the defendant to be represented.

The Crown Court is part of the Senior Courts of England and Wales and, accordingly, the rights of audience differ from those in the magistrates' court and county court. Solicitors do not have any automatic right to appear in the Crown Court, but barristers do. The distinction in the rights of audience is discussed elsewhere (Chapter 8) but historically the Bar had the exclusive rights to advocating in the higher courts. The *Courts and Legal Services Act 1990*, as is well known, extended the rights of audience in the higher courts to solicitors on completion of an additional course. Accordingly, solicitor-advocates can appear in the Crown Court although solicitors by themselves cannot.

12.1.3.1 Prosecution counsel

Counsel for the prosecution has a specific role in these cases. Whilst they do represent the Crown in order to try and achieve a conviction, the overarching position is contained in an often cited statement that prosecutors are 'to regard [themselves] as ministers of justice' (see *R v Paddick* (1865)). This means that prosecuting counsel is not to consider his duty as having the responsibility of securing a prosecution at all costs but of presenting an impartial view of the prosecution case. This, it has been argued, extends to how counsel should present his argument:

> It is important that a prosecution advocate avoids the use of emotive language or any words which will inflame an already tense situation. (Solley (2002) 317)

Viewing prosecution counsel in this way can be contrasted with other jurisdictions, most notably America, where prosecutors frequently deal with the victim on a one-to-one basis and can be seen in front of the media holding hands with the victim or, in homicide cases, the victim's family. This is, in part, because it will be remembered from Chapter 10 that in England and Wales prosecutions are not brought on behalf of the victim but of society as a whole.

An important part of the 'ministers of justice' role is that prosecuting counsel has a particular duty to the court. It has previously been noted that all advocates have a duty not to mislead a court (see 8.9.2.1 above), but prosecuting counsel has a duty actively to assist the court in the application of the law, even when this may mean a ruling prejudicial to the prosecution case. The other implication of this role is to be found in the duties of disclosure, including potentially any adverse issues in respect of the witnesses they are calling (eg any previous convictions of their witnesses etc).

12.1.3.2 Defence counsel

Counsel for the defence does not operate any function equivalent to that of the 'ministers of justice' expected of prosecuting counsel. However, it is important to note that they are bound, like all advocates, by the general rules of conduct and, in particular, the duty not to mislead the court. Bearing that in mind, however, defence counsel does have a much wider scope to advocate the matter and this may mean not always bringing legal technicalities harmful to their case to the attention of the court, unless not to do so would mislead the court (Blake and Ashworth (1998) 23–24); however, the Court of Appeal has, subsequently, decided that counsel do have a duty to bring obvious errors to the attention of the judge at trial and not reserve them for a decision to terminate the case or even as a ground of appeal after conviction (*R v Gleeson* [2003] EWCA Crim 3357). The scope of the freedom is even more obvious when one looks at errors of law where, as Blake and Ashworth note, there is no duty to bring factual errors to the attention of the court even though the corresponding duty exists for prosecutors (pp 24–25).

12.1.4 Court clerk

Each court centre has a court clerk but their role is one of administration rather than legal advice since judges are professionally legally qualified. The clerk has no statutory qualification and assists the resident (or senior resident) judge and the senior administrative grade in the smooth operation of the courts.

12.1.5 Stenographer

The Crown Court, as a superior court of record, has all its proceedings recorded. Historically this was completed by a stenographer who used to type out the proceedings using a shorthand-enabled typewriter but in more modern times they have been recorded using either tape recorders or solid-state recording equipment. The stenographer need not now appear in court at all times but, rather, is responsible for ensuring that the recording equipment is working. In many Crown Court trials the stenographer is absent except for the beginning and end of each session.

12.1.6 Ushers

The usher is a visible symbol of the court and yet has no statutory or formal authority except when a jury retires; however, he is present throughout the trial. The usher assists the clerk in the smooth running of a trial and normally identifies which witnesses are within the court building. The primary purpose of the usher, to assist the jury, will be discussed below (see 12.3.7.2 below).

12.2 Pre-trial matters

Whilst some of the pre-trial matters were discussed in Chapter 11, the vast majority of these matters actually take place in the Crown Court itself and need to be discussed here. Until recently the main format for pre-trial matters was the Plea and Directions Hearing (PDH) although recently this has been replaced, in some courts, by plea and case management hearings (PCMH) although these need not be hearings per se and could, conceivably, be conducted by directions.

12.2.1 The plea

It will be remembered from Chapter 11 that a defendant in an either-way offence will indicate whether his plea will be guilty or not guilty in the magistrates' court and should (theoretically) not proceed to the Crown Court unless he pleads not guilty. Despite this it has been noted above that the vast majority of defendants in the Crown Court will plead guilty, although this will of course include those who have been accused of an indictable-only offence.

One reason for late guilty pleas is that the prosecution must undertake full disclosure for Crown Court trials and thus it is possible that at magistrates' court level the defence did not believe the prosecution case to be as strong but once receiving the full details of the prosecution case through disclosure it may become apparent that it would be difficult to fight the case and accordingly they plead guilty. There is now an incentive to encourage early guilty pleas (ie in either-way offences in the magistrates' court) which is by providing a discount of up to one-third from the sentence imposed (SGC (2004) 5). Where the plea is left to the last minute then a discount of only 10 per cent can be expected (ibid).

The defendant will be asked to plea at the time of his arraignment. This is the time when the charges that he has to answer are formally put to him through the clerk of the court reading aloud the indictment. The arraignment is also the time at which the trial on indictment is deemed to begin and after this point any decisions of a judge sitting in the Crown Court are not liable to judicial review but only to a formal appeal (see s 29(3) SCA 1981 as interpreted by *R v Maidstone Crown Court, ex p Clark* [1995] 1 WLR 831).

The indictment is the formal document that lists the particulars of each offence the defendant is charged with. There are two parts to an indictment: the statement and the particulars. The former is the offence which the defendant is charged with and the latter provides an extremely brief summary of when the law was breached. Each offence is known as a 'count' and a typical indictment will be like that which is displayed below. Each count of the indictment is read to the defendant by the clerk of the court and a plea must be made against all those offences unless they are 'alternative counts', ie those which are expressly alternative offences (one a 'major' and one a 'minor' offence, in which case a plea of guilty to the 'major' offence will mean that there is no point in pleading to the 'minor' offence). A typical indictment is shown in Diagram 12.1.

There are four possible pleas and so the plea is not necessarily as straightforward as may at first be thought.

Where the plea is a simple plea of guilty, ie to the charge proffered, then the matter proceeds to sentencing. Where the plea is one of not guilty then the matter proceeds to trial and the other pre-trial mechanisms are undertaken (see below). Where a defendant refuses to tender a plea then the correct procedure is to treat this as a plea of not guilty and this verdict is recorded by the clerk of the court, with the trial proceeding as though the defendant had said 'not guilty'. The more complicated situations are when there is a 'conditional' plea or one that involves *autrefois convict* or *acquit*.

Autrefois

Along with pleading guilty or not guilty there are two other possible pleas which are known as *autrefois* and they can be summarized thus:

Autrefois acquit—previously been acquitted of the charges.

Autrefois convict—previously been convicted of the charges.

The general rule is that a person should only be tried for the same facts once and, accordingly, if they have been previously acquitted or convicted then the prosecution should not proceed and the matter ends. In recent years there has been a significant shift from this initial position with two statutory changes. The first was the abolition of the year-and-a-day rule in murder cases (*Law Reform (Year and a Day Rule) Act 1996*) which abolished the common-law rule that for a person to be convicted of murder, the death must occur within a year and a day of the actions of the defendant. The extent of this rule was that somebody could, conceivably, be convicted of murder after they had been tried for an assault.

 Example Keith Stephenson

Keith Stephenson was originally charged with grievous bodily harm when he attacked his victim in a public park. He was sentenced for that crime. His victim died three years later from an epileptic fit brought on by the original injury. The Attorney-General consented to a manslaughter charge being brought and, in April 2005, Stephenson pleaded guilty to this charge before Newcastle Crown Court and was sentenced to three years' youth detention.

IN THE CROWN COURT AT ANYTOWN   No 0432101/A

INDICTMENT

The Queen

v

PAUL JONES

PAUL JONES is charged as follows:

Count 1   Statement of Offence

Theft contrary to s.1 of the Theft Act 1968

Particulars of Offence

PAUL JONES, on the 2nd day of February 2010, did steal a pen belonging to GILLIAN FOXGROVE.

Count 2   Statement of Offence

Burglary contrary to s.9(1)(b) of the Theft Act 1968

Particulars of Offence

PAUL JONES, on the 5th day of February 2010, having entered as a trespasser a building, being a dwelling known as 11, Acacia Avenue, stole therein a ruby necklace.

Diagram 12.1 An example of a typical indictment

The second, and perhaps more significant change to this rule, is that introduced by the CJA 2003 which amends the rule of *double jeopardy*, the rule that says a person should not be tried for the same offence twice. Part 10 of the CJA 2003 permits those who have been acquitted of certain serious offences to be retried but only if the Court of Appeal (Criminal Division) allows this. This rule is explored in more depth in the next chapter (see 13.4.3 below) but it is important to note the rule has not been abolished completely. Unless the Court of Appeal quashes the acquittal then the principle of *autrefois acquit* still applies and the defendant cannot stand trial again.

12.2.1.1 Plea bargaining

Otton suggests that there are four forms of plea bargaining:

- an agreement between the judge and accused that if the accused pleads guilty to an offence the sentence will take a particular form
- an agreement between the accused and the prosecutor that if the accused pleads guilty to some offences the prosecution will leave the other offences off the indictment and/or ask the judge for a lighter sentence

- an agreement between the prosecution and defence that they will accept a plea of guilty to a lesser offence than the offence charged

- an agreement that the accused will plead guilty to some of the counts upon the indictment but not to others and the prosecution will not seek a trial for the remaining counts (Otton (2002) 326).

The first two of these examples are, theoretically, illegal under English law whereas the latter two are accepted parts of the criminal justice system. The position has become slightly more complicated by the *Serious Organised Crime and Police Act 2005* (SOCPA 2005) which attempts to regulate certain arrangements between the prosecutors and defence. The position in England and Wales can be contrasted with the position in other jurisdictions, most notably the United States of America, where all four forms of plea bargaining identified above are commonplace (McConville (2002) 353).

The most common form in England and Wales is the reduction in charge, in part because so many acts can be covered by different offences. Perhaps the most usual are those shown in Table 12.5.

Table 12.5 Alternative charges

Murder	Manslaughter
Grievous bodily harm with intent	Grievous bodily harm
Actual bodily harm	Common assault
Burglary	Theft
Robbery	Theft and separate assault offence

Otton argues that it is important that the judge is involved in this process although concern has been raised as to whether this invariably happens. A judge has the power to reject a plea bargain and perhaps one of the most famous examples of this is when the judge refused to accept a plea of manslaughter in respect of Peter Sutcliffe, the so-called 'Yorkshire Ripper'. The Attorney-General of the day, leading for the prosecution, had been prepared to accept this plea but the judge's veto meant that the matter proceeded to trial. Sutcliffe was convicted of murder by the jury. In the majority of situations, however, it is more likely that the judge will approve the bargain because it will save on costs and, in certain cases, prevent vulnerable witnesses from the need to testify (Otton (2002) 326).

The position in England and Wales is governed by a series of rules put forward in the case of *R v Turner* [1970] 2 QB 321 and the essence of the rules is that any discussion between counsel and the judge should be given in open court and no undue pressure must be placed on the defendant to plead guilty. However, this no longer means that a person should not necessarily be told the likely type of sentence (ie non-custodial or custodial) if they were to plead guilty to an offence (*R v Goodyear* [2005] EWCA Crim 888) but it is at the discretion of the judge to decide whether to provide an indication.

It is perhaps this latter point that is the most difficult in the area of plea bargaining. There are undoubted cost benefits in trials resulting in guilty pleas but a person should only plead guilty when they are and should not be influenced by the threat of a loss of liberty if they do not do so. However, research appears to suggest that quite often defendants will consider themselves to be under significant pressure, including from their own lawyers (McConville (2002) 369). Indeed some commentators argue that there is a cultural belief that this is an acceptable way of dealing with a criminal case (Ashworth and Redmayne (2010) 299).

The more difficult spin on this therefore is whether an innocent person is forced to plead guilty because of this pressure or incentive. There appears to be almost unanimous support by commentators that some innocent people will succumb to the pressure (Ashworth and Redmayne (2010) 311; McConville (2002) 369; McConville (2000) 71) but there is some dispute as to the role of defence counsel. It has been seen that some believe that counsel actively encourage such deals whereas others argue that it raises an interesting ethical problem for defence counsel if he suspects his client is innocent but nonetheless decides to tender a plea in the hope of getting a reduced sentence (McConville (2000) 72; but cf Blake and Ashworth (1998) 25 who note that the American Bar Association goes as far as to say that 'reasonable persuasion' may be used to induce a defendant to plead guilty if it is in his best interests).

Plea bargaining, although never referred to as that in court, appears to be here to stay and indeed it even seems to be becoming more formalized. Recent legislation has confirmed in statute the principle that cooperation between defendants and prosecutors should lead to a reduction in sentence (s 73 SOCPA 2005) and this is undoubtedly, perhaps for the first time, the introduction of the second tier of Otton's plea bargaining being introduced into the English Legal System. That said the limits of this section should be appreciated. In *R v Dougall* [2010] EWCA Crim 1048 the Lord Chief Justice noted that it is not open to prosecutors and defence to agree what the sentence of a court would be (at [19]). Whilst s 73 will allow prosecutors to state the extent to which a person has cooperated in the investigation it remains a matter solely for the judge what the sentence, and indeed type of sentence, would be. In *Dougall* the Director of the SFO purported to tell the court not to sentence the offender to a term of imprisonment and the Court of Appeal was adamant that this was inappropriate and is an interference with the powers of a judge.

The CJA 2003 has formalized the previous common-law rule that a person who pleads guilty should receive a reduction in sentence (s 144 CJA 2003), with the Sentencing Guidelines Council (SGC) stating that this should be up to one-third for an early plea. Some, as noted above, do question whether this places a degree of pressure on an offender to plead guilty even where they believe they are innocent. The formalization of plea bargaining is perhaps also to be found in the fact that the PCMH forms used in the Crown Court at the beginning of the trial process expressly ask:

> Might the case against a defendant be resolved by a plea of guilty to some counts on the indictment or to a lesser offence? (PCMH form, question 2)

The PCMH forms are issued by the court and thus instead of the traditional practice of counsel initiating the process it would now appear that the court is entitled to, and indeed ordinarily will, initiate the idea of a plea bargain being reached. Whether this is advisable is perhaps more questionable as it could lead to additional pressure being placed on a defendant.

12.2.1.2 Newton hearings

Another possible form of plea may be where a defendant agrees to plead guilty to the charge but challenges the prosecution facts presented. This could be significant because with some offences the factual basis for the conviction may have an impact on the sentence (eg in an assault case stamping on the head of the victim would be significantly more serious than punching someone). What happens in these situations? In *R v Newton* (1982) 77 Cr App R 13 the Court of Appeal stated there are three potential options:

- accept the defence version of the facts and proceed to sentence on that basis
- decide that the plea is actually one of not guilty and, accordingly, proceed to trial
- the judge could hear evidence to decide the factual basis of the plea and sentence accordingly.

The final stage of this is known as a *Newton hearing* and involves the judge sitting as the tribunal of fact and determining the factual basis upon which to sentence. This could, potentially, involve a full trial with the prosecution and defence providing witnesses to this fact. This demonstrates the point made above that judges in the Crown Court can act as tribunals of fact. There is no need to empanel a jury because guilt is not in issue but clearly the facts do need to be ascertained.

 Example Newton hearing

Gary is accused of actual bodily harm (s 47 *Offences Against the Person Act 1861* (OAPA 1861)). The prosecution allege that he got into a fight with the victim and after punching him in the head several times, caused the victim to fall to the floor and then stamped on his head three times causing severe internal bruising.

Gary admits to the assault but denies stamping on the victim's head saying that after he punched him he fell onto the pavement and hit his head. Stamping on someone is a serious aggravating offence and therefore the sentence that Gary would receive for an actual bodily harm without stamping would be substantially different from one where he was found to have stamped on the victim. Accordingly the judge or prosecution may ask for a Newton hearing to ascertain the true position.

The second option in *Newton*, empanelling a jury, is used where the plea actually amounts to the tendering of a defence or the suggestion that the charge is wrong. Under those circumstances it is only fair that the matter is considered to be a not guilty plea so that the prosecution version can be properly tested.

 Example A (partial) defence

Gail is accused of wounding with intent contrary to s 18 OAPA 1861. She admits that she did stab the victim but says it was accidental. In those circumstances Gail is actually saying that she is not guilty of an offence under s 18 but guilty of an offence contrary to s 20. If the prosecution fail to accept this alternative plea then a jury should be empanelled to try her for the s 18 offence.

12.2.2 Listing

The process by which a case is assigned a date for trial is known as 'listing', the case being placed in a respective 'list' for a court. The resident or senior resident judge (as appropriate) has ultimate responsibility for ensuring that the listing system works. There are three types of lists:

Fixed. These are cases where the date of the trial is fixed in advance and known to all parties.

Warned. These are cases where the trial is placed on a list and when it is likely that space is to be found for the case all parties will be 'warned' of the period it will be heard in and then, ultimately, its date. Less precision is, therefore, given than fixed trials.

Floating. These are placed in a list where the parties are told which date and court centre the matter will be heard in but not which particular court or judge. Whichever judge is free takes the case. If a floater is not heard on a particular day it returns to the list.

There is a commitment to moving away from floating trials, especially when they involve non-professional witnesses, because of the wasted time that can be involved in such matters. There is also the stress to consider with all parties (particularly the defendant, victim, and witnesses) having to contend with not knowing whether the matter is to be heard.

12.3 The trial

Eventually after all the pre-trial matters have been dealt with the trial itself will begin. In this section of the chapter it is intended to walk the reader through the principal steps and focus on some of the more controversial aspects that arise.

12.3.1 Empanelling the jury

The first step, assuming that the defendant has pleaded not guilty, is to empanel a jury. This used to be a reasonably complicated procedure but in recent years it has become simpler although debate has begun again as to how representative juries should be.

The eligibility for jury service was discussed above (see 12.1.2.2 and 12.1.2.3) and those that are summonsed are not called to a particular case but rather to form a large pool from which the usher brings twenty potential jurors into court and they become known as the 'jury in waiting'. The potential jurors will normally be told the name of the defendant and asked if they know him. If they do then they will leave the court and return to the jury pool to be used by an alternative court. The names of the individual potential jurors are on cards and handed to the clerk. The clerk of the court then shuffles the cards and calls twelve names out. In *R v Comerford* [1998] 1 Cr App R 235 the Court of Appeal upheld a policy adopted by the judge of assigning numbers to jurors instead of calling their name out. However, in that case there was a real risk of jury intimidation and accordingly it was accepted as an exception to the general rule.

Where a trial is going to be lengthy or complicated the *Consolidated Practice Direction* states that judges should ask the jury whether they have any personal commitments that may affect their service (IV.42.2). This is purely discretionary and the judge can decide not to waive the summons. In certain traumatic cases jurors have been excused because it may have been difficult for them to concentrate on the case but this is again highly exceptional because arguably the more traumatic a case is, the more important an independent jury is.

12.3.1.1 Ethnicity

Perhaps one of the most controversial areas surrounding the use of jurors is their ethnicity. It is recognized that there can be a problem with the ethnicity of jurors, in part because the primary database that is used is the electoral role and yet it is known that many members of the ethnic minorities simply do not register themselves on the roll (Auld (2001) 155). This has led to a situation where there is doubt as to whether juries are representative. On the one hand it has been suggested that looking at the panels as a whole they may be representative, particular in the cities (Ashworth and Redmayne (2010) 335) but on the other hand when it comes to individual panels statistical probability by itself will ensure that a majority of panels will be all-white regardless of the ethnic origin of the defendant (Sanders and Young (2000) 564). This position is likely to continue since the recommendation of Auld to use alternative lists of persons does not appear to have been acted upon.

This has led to a situation whereby there is discussion over whether a panel should be artificially altered to ensure representation. Research demonstrates that the ethnicity of the jury is a factor of some concern to defendants from an ethnic minority with 20 per cent of black defendants in a study alleging racial bias by the jury (Shute et al (2005) 40). The Royal Commission on Criminal Justice argued that there may be circumstances when jury manipulation may be advisable (Sanders and Young (2010) 565) and Auld also recommended a limited right to alter the representation of the jury (Auld (2001) 159) where race may be a significant issue in the case. However the support for implementing such a change is certainly not universal, with some commentators suggesting the arguments in favour of altering the racial profile of a jury are 'not convincing' (Ashworth and Redmayne (2010) 315). Their argument is based on the premise that the system of 'trial by peers' is misunderstood. Why, they ask, should it be thought that our peers are any better placed to judge us than a random selection of society?

Ashworth and Redmayne suggest that the strength of a jury is in the fact that each member is different and each, therefore, brings a different set of experiences to the jury. This is often cited as the principal point in favour of the jury and also cited as the principal reason why the jury pool should be widened as much as possible, including limiting excusals and deferrals (Auld (2001) 140). Interestingly although the research of Shute et al has demonstrated that there is a belief that juries may not necessarily be fair; they also found that when ethnic minority defendants were tried by ethnic minority magistrates they also perceived bias with the suggestion that they would sometimes be 'tougher' on them (Shute et al (2005) 51, 69, and 119). This demonstrates that there is no easy answer, not least because it is often perceptions that are being dealt with rather than any proof of bias.

The proposals of Auld and the Royal Commission were neither welcomed nor implemented by the government and the courts have also reacted negatively to any suggestion that profile could or should be altered. In *R v Smith* [2003] 1 WLR 2229 the appellant was a black man who had been accused of seriously assaulting the white victim. There appeared quite conclusive proof that the appellant and his companions had been racially abused in the nightclub, possibly by the victim (pp 2332–2333). The jury were all white and the defendant stated that he had suffered racial discrimination in the local area before and believed that the local area was racist (p 2333). The appellant had submitted that it was wrong to leave this matter to an all-white jury and suggested that doing so amounted to a breach of Article 6 of the ECHR (right to a fair trial). The Court of Appeal rejected this argument and stated that whilst it accepted that a racially diverse jury would add to the broad spectrum of the jury's experience (p 2238) it rejected outright any suggestion that only a jury with ethnic minority representation within it would be fair and suggested that the random nature of a jury was a key safeguard against the possibility that a juror might be prejudiced (p 2239). The position appears, therefore, to be clear and a judge has no power to empanel anything other than a random jury.

❓ QUESTION FOR REFLECTION

Was the Court of Appeal right to think that altering the racial profile of a jury is wrong? Is there not an argument for suggesting that the racial profile of a jury may be a relevant factor in some cases? In a previous edition Sanders and Young quote the example given by the Royal Commission who said:

> A black defendant charged with burglary would be unlikely to succeed in such an application. But black people accused of violence against a member of an extremist organisation who they said had been making racial taunts against them and their friends might well succeed. (Sanders and Young (2000) 565)

Is this not similar to the facts in *Smith*? Would it not be relevant to have a member of the ethnic minorities on the jury sitting in a case such as this where racist comments preceded the violence? What are the implications of altering the racial profile of a jury and how far should it go? Is there not a danger that Auld and the Royal Commission's suggestions could almost lead to 'tokenism'?

12.3.1.2 Challenging a juror

In the United States empanelling a jury can take a considerable period of time because both parties have the right to object to a juror. In Northern Ireland the right to peremptorily challenge a juror (ie to object to a juror without having to give any reason) still exists but in England and Wales this right was abolished in 1988 (s 118 *Criminal Justice Act 1988*). That is not to say that there is no opportunity to challenge a juror but the defence can now only challenge for cause although the prosecution have the additional ground of asking a juror to 'stand by'.

Challenges for cause exist for both parties and the challenge is made by counsel (or the defendant himself if unrepresented) who says 'Challenge' immediately before the juror takes the oath. The party who makes the challenge has the burden of proving, on the balance of probabilities, the unsuitability of the juror. The normal reason is bias but there must be proof of the appearance of bias, something that is not easy when, as Doran notes, it is not possible to ask questions of jurors in the way that is common in America (Doran (2002) 388). It is relatively uncommon for challenges to be made.

The other possible method of objecting to a jury is when the prosecution use their power of asking a juror to stand by. Theoretically this just means that the person does not automatically become a member of the jury and returns to the jury in waiting. If enough potential jurors were unable to be sworn in then this could mean that the person stood by could be sworn in but this would be highly unlikely and, in fact, it would mean that the person is not used. Indeed it has been stated that:

> The guidelines [of the Attorney-General] restrict the exercise of the right of stand by to two situations; first, where a juror is clearly unsuitable and the defence agrees that the juror should be excluded, for example where it becomes apparent that a juror selected to try a complex case is in fact illiterate; secondly, where jury checks reveal information justifying the exercise of the right to stand by. (Doran (2002) 388)

The first ground is relatively uncontroversial but the second undoubtedly remains controversial. That said, the concept of jury vetting (see 12.1.2.5 above) appears to be something that is here to stay.

The judge also has an inherent power to stand down a juror and the usual reason for this use would be when the judge realizes that the person is not sufficiently literate to serve on the jury (Sprack (2004) 310) or where disability or infirmity may make the person unsuitable to sit as a juror.

Disabled jurors

The previous sentence noted that a judge may ask a person to stand down if they are disabled but what are the rules regarding the use of disabled jurors? Section 9B JA 1974 states that there is a clear presumption in favour of disabled jurors being able to sit but that where a judge is of the opinion that the person could not, as a result of his disability, act 'effectively' as a juror he should be stood down. In *Re Osman* [1996] 1 Cr App R 126, His Honour Judge Verney, the Recorder of London, stood down a juror who was profoundly deaf and who could only follow the proceedings if a sign-language interpreter was used. The principal reason for this ruling was that the interpreter would have to attend the jury room and would, therefore, become a thirteenth person when only twelve are permitted (p 128). The fact that the interpreter would not be expressing personal opinions was not considered sufficient safeguard. This case was followed in 1999 when a Mr McWhinney was called to the jury. Mr McWhinney was also profoundly deaf and required the services of an interpreter and he was similarly stood down (Majid (2004) 278).

These cases were controversial and there was a commitment to review the matter (Majid (2004) 279 and Auld (2001) 153) but no change in the law has yet occurred. The then Lord Chancellor has argued that he sees no reason why a deaf person should not serve on a jury (Auld (2001) 153) but he left open the argument as to the effect of a thirteenth person being in the jury room.

Where a third person is not needed then there is no significant objection and it is notable that, for example, there have been cases where a blind juror has sat although there may be objections if evidence at a trial is particularly focused on visual evidence. Where it is not (and a significant proportion of trials will not require visual evidence to be shown, as distinct from it merely assisting a jury) then there is no reason why a blind person should not sit. Indeed it is submitted that it is a matter of disgrace that the de facto presumption against deaf jurors still appears to be in existence. There is no reason why a qualified interpreter could not be appointed by the judge and such interpreters be given training as to the limits of their duties (ie not to enter into personal discussions within a jury room). There are currently approximately 9 million people who are deaf or hard of hearing although only approximately 700,000 of them are severely or profoundly deaf. However in an era where we are trying to expand jury service it is nonsensical not to permit deaf people to sit on a jury.

? QUESTION FOR REFLECTION

Do you agree that deaf and blind jurors should be able to sit on juries? Are there any reasons why they should not be permitted? Are these reasons that would stop a juror sitting in a *particular* case or such that it justifies a blanket ban?

12.3.1.3 Taking the oath

A juror in waiting becomes a juror when he is selected and takes the oath. The *Consolidated Practice Direction* (IV.42.4) states that the person taking the oath must say:

> I swear [by Almighty God] that I will faithfully try the defendant and give a true verdict according to the evidence.

Where the person does not wish to swear an oath then they may affirm instead, the wording being:

> I do solemnly, sincerely and truly declare and affirm that I will faithfully try the defendant and give a true verdict according to the evidence.

At this point the person is a juror and he will take his seat in the jury box. When all twelve jurors have been sworn in then the jury is complete.

12.3.1.4 Judicial direction on behaviour

The *Consolidated Practice Direction* (IV.42.7) states that a judge must now direct the jury about their behaviour and expectations:

> Judges should take the opportunity, when warning the jury of the importance of not discussing the case with anyone outside the jury, to add a further warning...The effect of the further warning should be that it is the duty of jurors to bring to the judge's attention, promptly, any behaviour among the jurors or by others affecting the jurors, that causes concern...

The reason for this is that there have been a number of situations when jurors have acted in a way that could prejudice the trial and/or the rights of the defendant. The House of Lords, in *R v Mirza* [2004] 1 AC 1118, stated that it is not possible to investigate the reasons why a jury reached their verdict (see below) but where jury impropriety does occur during the trial, the judge can (and often has a duty to) investigate and deal with any misconduct. This may include, for example, racist comments being made in the jury room or ignoring the judge's direction not to discuss the case outside of the courtroom or bringing external material into court. An unusual incident occurred in 2010 at the Crown Court in Hull where a juror in one trial (trial A) sent a text to a juror in another trial (trial B) alleging the defendant in that case was a paedophile. The juror who received the text reported the matter (as she was obliged to do) and the other juror was found to be in contempt of court.

12.3.1.5 Discharging a juror

The final aspect to discuss concerning the empanelment of a jury is that of their discharge. Of course this is unlikely to take place immediately after their empanelment but it is discussed here for convenience. This section will examine the discharge of the entire jury (which if it takes place before the jury retire to consider their verdict would normally be as a result of an irregularity in the trial) or the discharge of an individual juror.

In respect of discharging the entire jury, it is always a matter for the trial judge to decide when this is necessary although he should discuss this with counsel and not infrequently the decision will be made after a submission from (defence) counsel to invite the discharge of the jury. The normal reason for this is if significant inadmissible evidence is given to the jury but it could also be as a result of an external factor and, in the past, cases have arisen where the jury has been discharged because of media comments. Where the latter occurs it has normally resulted in contempt proceedings being instigated.

Case box R v McCann

R v McCann (1991) 92 Cr App R 239 is an interesting example of this. This case concerned a terrorist case and in the middle of the trial the Home Secretary announced the end of the automatic right to silence, something widely reported. Commentators in the media noted the comments that this could have a particular impact on terrorism cases. The Court of Appeal ruled that the jury should have been discharged when it was apparent that the suspects would not be testifying. This is an example of an innocent external factor that still necessitated the discharge of a jury in order to ensure that the defendant received a fair trial.

It is not always necessary to discharge the whole jury but it is sometimes necessary to discharge a single juror. This is permissible under s 16 JA 1974 and the provision states that when this occurs it need not lead to the discharge of the whole jury, although this is something that a judge will have to take into account. The discharge need not arise as a result of misconduct and could, for example, be as a result of personal circumstances (eg illness) but misconduct is certainly a significant factor in discharges.

The key test in all of this is whether the juror is biased. What does bias mean, however? Traditionally it was thought that it meant bias from a subjective point of view, ie was the juror biased, but in *Sanders v United Kingdom* (2001) 31 EHRR 44 the ECtHR said that bias had to be looked at objectively not just subjectively, that is to say whether a reasonable person would believe that the juror is biased. Arguably this is a wider test and could lead to more jurors being discharged. This test also has a wider implication in that it may lead to the discharge of the entire jury. If there is a risk that the bias of one juror has contaminated the others in the jury then the whole jury should be discharged. Ultimately it is for the judge to decide whether this has happened, although his ruling would almost certainly provide a ground of appeal.

Where the entire jury is discharged for whatever reason then the defendant is not acquitted and is liable to a retrial. Two possible impediments stand in the way of a retrial. First, the prosecution must choose to bring a retrial. The circumstances that led to the original discharge will be considered, as this could affect the evidential or public-interest test which could mean that the decision to prosecute will change and the prosecution could decide not to progress a retrial. The second possible impediment is the judge. It is possible that the judge may decide that it is not possible to have a fair retrial and he has an inherent power to order that proceedings are stayed. In *R v Taylor* (1994) 98 Cr App R 361, the Court of Appeal adopted this discretion after they quashed the conviction of two teenage sisters accused of murder, in part because of pre-trial publicity. The court stated that the publicity was so prejudicial that a retrial would not be possible.

12.3.2 **The prosecution case**

As in a summary trial the prosecution will go first. This is because the prosecution have the burden of proving the guilt of the defendant; if the prosecution cannot adduce sufficient evidence by the end of their case then the defendant is to be acquitted.

The prosecution will normally give an opening speech where they will outline their case to the jury. This will probably mean explaining the charges to the jury and any relevant law that applies. Prosecuting counsel will almost certainly explain to the jury that they must take the law from the judge and that anything he (counsel) says is subject to correction by the judge. By convention prosecuting counsel does not mention any evidence that is going to be contested by the defence although this is not always possible (eg a confession). What should never be mentioned is any evidence of which the defence is going to question the legal admissibility. Normally the admissibility would have been dealt with at the pre-trial hearings but this is not always the case and in some situations a judge will defer a definitive ruling until later in the case to see how other evidence is presented in order to assess its admissibility.

The case then proceeds with witnesses being called. It has already been noted that a witness will be subject to examination in the following order (Table 12.6):

Table 12.6 Order of testimony

Examination-in-chief	Prosecution
Cross-examination	Defence
Re-examination	Prosecution
Judicial questions	Judge

Where there is more than one defendant then each defendant has the right to conduct cross-examination. Theoretically if the judge asks a question then the prosecution have the right to put an additional question of clarification forward (further re-examination) but this is normally never exercised on the basis that the judge should only ask questions that clarify matters rather than controversial ones. Whilst it rarely happens, the jury can sometimes ask questions of witnesses although this is not done directly. The juror passes a note to the judge who reads it and decides whether the question should be put; if it should be, then the judge asks the question. It has been noted that the courts try so far as possible to deter such notes being passed (Doran (2002) 395) and this creates, in the words of one observer, the rather strange position whereby the tribunal of fact takes a 'very passive role in the course of the trial' (Doran (2002) 394). This is undoubtedly true but what is the alternative? The idea of allowing twelve jurors the opportunity to ask questions, even through the judge, could be a recipe for disaster and could lead to extra time or indeed confusion.

Not every witness need give testimony. Sometimes the defence will concede that the evidence of a witness is true—where this is a factual concession (ie they concede that a fact is true) then it is known as an admission and prosecution counsel explains this to the jury (normally after the judge explains the significance of an admission) and the fact is then told to the jury, normally by reading the written statement of the witness to the jury. The other possibility is that the statement of a witness who cannot be found or who will not attend because they are in fear of intimidation can, with the consent of the judge, be read to the jury (ch 2, Part 11 CJA 2003).

12.3.3 Submission of no case to answer

It was noted in the previous chapter that before the defence begins they may (but do not have to) submit that there is no case to answer. The close of the prosecution marks the point at which the prosecution should have adduced sufficient evidence to demonstrate that a person is guilty. If they have not done so then there is no point in proceeding through the defence case because it will inevitably lead to an acquittal. If, on the other hand, sufficient evidence has been adduced then the defence have the opportunity to weaken the prosecution case in their attempt to achieve an acquittal.

It is for the judge to decide whether the prosecution have discharged the burden of proving their case and it is solely a matter of law. Unlike in a summary trial, where the justices are both the tribunal of fact and law, the jury (as the tribunal of fact) are not in court during this submission and ruling. The principal reason for this is that they may become prejudiced by the finding that the case can continue, mistakenly believing that the judge is ruling that the accused is guilty.

The principle behind the submission was set out by the Court of Appeal in *R v Galbraith* (1981) 73 Cr App R 124. The basic test is:

> if the judge comes to the conclusion that the prosecution evidence, if taken at its highest, is such that a jury properly directed could not properly convict upon it, it is his duty...to stop the case. (p 127)

This proposition involves the judge considering the evidence before the court but does this mean that the judge is usurping the function of the court? The Court of Appeal continued by stating that where the evidence involves making an assessment of the reliability or credibility of a witness then the case should continue as the judge should not replace the jury, ie the submission should be rejected.

It is important to note that the submission is not an 'all or nothing' situation. The judge could decide that the submission succeeds for some counts on the indictment but not for others. On those counts for which it does succeed the judge directs the jury to acquit the defendant of those charges and the case proceeds on the others, normally following a judicial direction on the meaning of what has just happened in the context of the continuing trial.

The latest figures available (CPS Annual Report 2009/10) show that in 1,048 cases the judge accepted a submission of no case to answer. The CPS states that this amounts to only one per cent of defendants who are committed for trial and it only accounts for five per cent of all acquittals in the Crown Court. It would seem therefore that whilst the submission is an important aspect it leads to very few cases being stopped.

12.3.3.1 Jury stopping the case

At common law it appears that the judge had the right to invite the jury to acquit an offender after the close of the prosecution case. In *R v C* [2007] EWCA Crim 854 the Court of Appeal questioned whether this was compatible with Article 6, ECHR and, in any event, argued that the courts had no longer approved its use. Instead the court noted that if the judge felt the prosecution case was terminally weakened then he should exercise his discretion to stop the case (see 12.3.3 above). This has to be a sensible ruling since inviting the jury to consider a verdict (albeit only one of acquittal) after the prosecution case could be confusing for them and may lead them to think the defence case (see 12.3.4 below) is to prove innocence, something it is not.

12.3.4 The defence case

The next stage in the trial is the defence case. Assuming that at least one witness other than the accused himself is to testify then the defence has the right to make an opening speech. Where there is more than one defendant then each defendant's case proceeds in turn although sometimes the judge will ask all speeches to be made at the same time. The speech is similar to that of the prosecution although there is more latitude here since it is less likely that the counsel for the prosecution will object to defence evidence. Another distinction is that counsel for the defence may use the opening speech as an opportunity to criticize the prosecution evidence so far adduced, thus providing an opportunity to show how the flaws in the prosecution case will be highlighted by the defence case.

The defence have the right to call witnesses in exactly the same way as the prosecution, with the parties reversing their roles in the examination (Table 12.7):

Where there is more than one defendant then each co-defendant has the right to cross-examine the other defendants' witnesses. Note that the entitlement is to cross-examination and not examination-in-chief because the witness does not belong to that party.

Table 12.7 Order of testimony

Examination-in-chief	Defence
Cross-examination	Prosecution
Re-examination	Defence
Judicial questions	Judge

It should be noted that the judge does have the discretion to permit witnesses to be called before the accused (s 79 *Police and Criminal Evidence Act 1984* (PACE 1984)) but the discretion would only be exercised in exceptional circumstances.

12.3.4.1 Defendant testifying

For the same reason as above the rules of evidence governing the defence case will not be dealt with in detail but one aspect does need to be considered briefly, that of the testimony of the accused. Where the accused is going to testify then he should give evidence before any other witness, the reason being that he is always in court and can, therefore, hear the evidence of the other witnesses and conceivably adapt his evidence accordingly. Whilst the accused cannot be forced to testify (in that he is competent to give evidence but not compellable), if he does not the jury are permitted to draw an adverse inference from his silence (s 35 *Criminal Justice and Public Order Act 1994* (CJPOA 1994)). Any inference cannot be used as the sole or main basis for convicting the accused (see, in particular, *Murray v United Kingdom* (1996) 22 EHRR 29) but it can be used by the jury as a factor in deciding the guilt or innocence of the accused.

In *R v Cowan* [1996] QB 373 the Court of Appeal gave guidance on what should happen if the defendant does not wish to testify. Assuming that the defendant is legally represented then the judge should ask counsel, in open court and in the presence of the jury, whether he has advised his lay client of the consequences of not testifying. Assuming that the answer to this question is 'yes' then the matter proceeds with the defence case and the judge, at the appropriate time, directs the jury as to the implications of this. If the accused is not legally represented then the judge must explain the consequences of failing to testify to the accused and then ask whether he still intends not to testify. A fuller set of instructions, including suggested wording, has now been included in the *Consolidated Criminal Practice Direction* (IV.44).

12.3.4.2 The unrepresented defendant

There is no legal obligation on the accused to be legally represented although given the serious nature of Crown Court proceedings it is clearly desirable and funding will normally be given for this purpose; but sometimes defendants will wish to defend themselves in person.

The judge does not, unlike the clerk of the court to the magistrates, act as a surrogate counsel for the defence, although he should try to ensure that there is a fair trial by explaining the court processes to the defendant and suggesting possible lines of cross-examination, but the judge must not substitute himself as counsel for the defence.

Where problems can arise, however, is in respect of sexual cases. Historically sexual cases and those against children were not considered any different to other cases and, accordingly, the accused could personally cross-examine his accused regardless of the effect this could have on the victim.

Example Ralston Edwards

Ralston Edwards had been charged with the rape of Julia Mason (Julia bravely waived her right to anonymity to highlight her case) and he represented himself. His defence was not clear but he made her describe the attack and his genitalia in detail. He also went through her entire sexual history, ie asking questions about every sexual partner she had ever had. The cross-examination lasted for six days and Ms Mason said it felt as if she had been raped again. The judge felt unable to end the ordeal although this is perhaps highly questionable since controlling cross-examination and the protection of witnesses is undoubtedly a role of the judge (Otton (2002) 327).

The criticism of Ms Mason's treatment was immense and the government eventually acted by restricting the right of a defendant in person to conduct cross-examination of a victim when charged with a sexual offence (s 34 *Youth Justice and Criminal Evidence Act 1999*). Where a person is restrained from personally cross-examining a witness, how will the defendant's case be put to him? There had been a ban on the cross-examination of child witnesses that pre-dated the 1999 Act and under those circumstances the judge would cross-examine the child (McEwan (2002) 247) but this was unsatisfactory, not least because it is the classic example of a judge assuming the 'robes of an advocate', to borrow Lord Denning's phrase (see 12.1.1.2 above). The 1999 Act created a more acceptable system when it decided that the court, when denying the opportunity to a defendant to cross-examine, could appoint counsel to conduct the cross-examination even if the defendant did not request one (s 38).

This provision is undoubtedly controversial for a number of reasons. First, it can be argued that it could place the defendant at a disadvantage since, in effect, any counsel will be appointed late in the day and the person appointed will not necessarily be counsel for the defence, meaning that issues arise as to cooperation and indeed privilege (McEwan (2002) 248). Second, it could be argued it is contrary to Article 6 of the ECHR. Article 6(3)(c) states that everyone has the right to:

> defend himself in person or through legal assistance of his own choosing or, if he has not sufficient means to pay for legal assistance, to be given it free when the interests of justice so require.

It could be argued that preventing personal cross-examination is not allowing the defendant to defend himself in person but the syntax of Article 6(3)(c) does not appear to require that absolutely and does provide for the right of assistance. Admittedly it does appear to suggest that ordinarily the defendant should be able to choose his own counsel but this is then qualified by the final sentence which implies that it may be possible to provide alternative counsel. Similarly any challenge under Article 6(3)(d) which provides the right to examine or have witnesses examined would fail since the court-appointed lawyer can examine witnesses. It should also be noted that the ECtHR has on occasions said that Article 6 is not an absolute right and it needs to be placed into context. In this situation, other Convention rights are in play because the victim almost certainly has rights under either Article 3 (prohibition of, inter alia, degrading treatment) and Article 8 (right to respect for private life).

12.3.5 Closing speeches

In general both the prosecution and defence have the right to a closing speech. However, just because the parties have the right to make a speech does not mean that they must make one and there are times when counsel will decide not to. If speeches are to proceed then counsel for the prosecution goes first and the restrictions as a 'minister of justice' applies; the closing speech is to be relatively staid. Counsel for the defence follows the prosecution and where there is more than one defendant they go in the order they appear on the indictment.

An important restriction on closing speeches is that although they can comment on the evidence that has been adduced, they cannot introduce any evidence that has not been adduced at trial or make assertions that were not put to witnesses during the trial. This is because it is important that everyone should have the right to defend themselves. Even if the accused is not represented he is entitled to a speech.

12.3.6 Judicial summing up

In other jurisdictions the closing speech of counsel for the defence is the last word in a trial but in England and Wales the judge speaks last, his speech being known as the 'summing up'. There are two primary functions of the summing up; first to direct the jury as to the law; and second to remind the jury of the facts and evidence of the case.

Nowadays most of the directions to the jury are set out in specimen directions created by the *Judicial Studies Board* and they are available online (the Online Resource Centre accompanying this book provides a link to them). Whilst these directions have no formal legal status, any deviation from them will frequently form a ground of appeal (Otton (2002) 328). That is not to say that judges are expected to repeat the directions verbatim but they should certainly ensure that the spirit of the directions is adhered to.

Some question why a judge should sum up, given that, in essence, the summing up not infrequently leads to a ground of appeal. However, others believe that reminding the jury of the evidence they have heard and possible links between the issues is helpful. They do not, however, explain why it is that Scotland, for example, manages to do well without a full summing up (the judge merely provides legal directions to a jury) and so does America where, in effect, they do not allow the judge to sum up (Sanders and Young (2010) 576).

Another problem with the English summing up is that it is often far too long and it has been suggested that it could either be summarized or even handed to the jury in written form (Auld (2001) 534–535). Whilst this has not yet been accepted in practice, the Court of Appeal in *R v Sanghera* [2005] EWCA Crim 1248, stated that a short summing up was possible and that it was not necessary to go through each evidential point but merely to provide a summary of the points for and against the defence although it is imperative that important points favourable to the defence are included.

12.3.7 Jury retirement

Assuming that a judge has not directed that the defendant be acquitted then eventually the matter will be passed to the jury to consider its verdict.

12.3.7.1 Immediate steps

The first step is that the judge directs the jury that they should elect a foreperson of the jury. The person who is elected becomes, in effect, the chair of the jury and will help structure their deliberations. The foreperson is the only member of the jury who will speak in court.

The second step is that the jury are told to ignore anything they have heard about majority verdicts. A judge must explain that initially at least a unanimous verdict must be reached, this being to comply with the requirements of s 17 JA 1974. The judge will explain when a majority verdict is appropriate (see 12.3.8.2 below).

12.3.7.2 Jury bailiff

The jury is placed in the charge of a jury bailiff who is an usher and swears an oath to keep the jury in their charge, not to discuss the case with them nor to allow anyone to talk to the jury. The oath is not mere words and the bailiff is the only person who can speak to the jury outside of the courtroom whilst they are in considering their verdict. This means that he should be in a position to stop anyone speaking to the jury, ie stay outside the deliberating room.

The bailiff is, in essence, the conduit between the jury and the judge and if questions arise (see below) it is the bailiff who alerts the judge and carries the question from the jury to the judge. In *R v Anderson and Mason* (1990), unreported, the Court of Appeal stated that the jury bailiff must pass on all communications to the judge and not screen them.

Whilst the bailiff is not entitled to be inside the room, he does have some responsibility for ensuring that the deliberations occur at the correct time. In *R v Hastings* [2003] EWCA Crim 3730 a juror was always late to court after retirement. The Court of Appeal stated that the bailiff should have reminded the jury not to deliberate until all twelve jurors were present although the ultimate responsibility for this lay with the judge.

12.3.7.3 Questions

The jury are not cut off from all contact and they have the right to ask questions if they wish clarification of either the law or evidence, or if they want to be reminded of evidence. The jury (normally the foreperson) will write the question and hand it to the bailiff. The bailiff will then pass the note to the judge who will normally convene the court and ask counsel for their opinion on the answer although the decision is ultimately for the judge. The jury will then be brought into court and the answer given to them. No discourse is entered into and if this does not answer their question then the process is repeated.

12.3.7.4 Improper considerations

The most controversial aspect of the jury considerations process is when something goes awry and the jury acts in an improper way. The position is complicated by the fact that s 8 *Contempt of Court Act 1981* makes it clear that it is a criminal offence to seek information about, or to disclose information, about the deliberations. The courts have been careful to ensure that the jury deliberations remain secret and thus will not normally entertain any challenge based on what might have happened in the jury room (see, for example, the recent House of Lords decision in *R v Mirza* [2004] 1 AC 1118).

A key exception to this would be where the irregularities come to the attention of the court before the verdict has been reached, ie when something can be done about it. To an extent this has been discussed already in connection with jury misconduct and discharge (see 12.3.1.5 above). Does this mean that after the verdict has been delivered the court will never consider how a jury has reached their verdict? The courts will never countenance receiving evidence that suggests how a jury has reached its verdict (an extreme example being *R v Mickleburgh* [1995] 1 Cr App R 297 where the foreperson of the jury visited the defendant in prison to comment on how the verdict had been arrived at; the Court of Appeal refused to hear any evidence as to this visit and rejected it as a ground of appeal). Where, however, an irregularity can be shown without it revealing the manner in which a verdict had been arrived at then the courts are more likely to intervene.

> **Case box** *R v Young*
>
> Perhaps one of the strangest examples of this was *R v Young* [1995] QB 324 where, in the days when a jury would be sent to a hotel overnight (see below) the Court of Appeal accepted evidence that certain members of the jury had used a ouija board to 'contact' one of the murder

victims. The Court of Appeal quashed the conviction on the basis that the jury should not have been deliberating outside the jury room and accordingly this conduct was against s 8. This does raise the rather interesting question, of course, as to what would happen if the ouija board were used inside the jury room!

A slightly less unusual example is to be found in *R v Karakaya* [2005] EWCA Crim 346 where, after the verdicts had been returned, the court usher who was clearing out the jury room found material that had been downloaded from the Internet and obviously brought in by a juror. The accused had been charged with rape and the material downloaded was material that inaccurately portrayed the position of rape within the legal system, including making errors about how a defendant arrives at court. The Court of Appeal quashed the conviction on the basis that it was not necessary to know whether the material had been taken into consideration by the jury (and given s 8 it would not be possible to identify their reasoning) as its presence showed a real risk of prejudice and, accordingly, the conviction was unsafe. The growth of the Internet and its ease of access (including by mobile telephone) has led the Court of Appeal to suggest that juries should be warned not to look for material relating to the case and to try the matter only in respect of the evidence before it (*R v Thompson* [2010] EWCA Crim 1623).

❓ QUESTION FOR REFLECTION

Is it realistic to expect members of the jury not to use the Internet and related resources to consider issues relating to the case? Given witnesses give their name out in court, is there a danger that the jury could try to look up the witnesses and defendant on the Internet or social networking sites (eg Facebook)? Can this be stopped? Do you think it makes any difference to the effectiveness of the criminal justice system?

🎧 LISTEN TO THE PODCAST
For guidance on how to answer this question and a discussion of the main issues, listen to the author's podcast on the Online Resource Centre:
www.oxfordtextbooks.co.uk/orc/gillespie_els3e/

Karakaya, when read in conjunction with *Mirza* (2004), appears to show that it is not possible to question the jury as to why a verdict was reached but if external evidence is present to show objectively that the process may have been compromised then the Court of Appeal can take this into account on appeal.

12.3.7.5 Deliberating for more than a day

Until 1994 a jury, once sent out to begin its deliberation, had to be kept together until they reached their verdict. In cases where the jury could not arrive at a decision on the first day this meant that they would be sequestered and taken to a hotel overnight. Section 43 CJPOA 1994 abolished the automatic application of this rule although it is important to note that a judge still has the discretion to order a jury to stay in a hotel overnight. Where the jury are permitted to disperse and go home for the night, the judge must warn them not to talk to anyone about the case.

One point to note about this direction is the swearing of the jury bailiff. The bailiff must be sworn each day because in order to permit the jury to be dispersed then the usher must be released from his oath, and accordingly each new day involves the usher being sworn in as jury bailiff in open court.

❓ QUESTION FOR REFLECTION

Reconsider the issue about the use of the Internet above. If juries are now allowed to go home does this make it more or less likely that they could access the Internet for issues relating to the case? Also, is there a danger that the jury could talk about the case on, for example, Facebook or instant-messenger services?

12.3.8 **The verdict**

The verdict will ultimately be up to the jury to decide. Whilst it has been noted that a judge has the right to order the acquittal of a person the converse is not true and it is *never* permissible for a judge to direct a jury to convict (*R v Wang* [2005] UKHL 9).

12.3.8.1 Unanimous verdict

Ideally the jury will return with a unanimous verdict. If they do so then the clerk of the court asks the foreperson to stand and asks them whether they have reached a verdict upon which they all agree. Assuming that the answer is 'yes' then the clerk reads each count aloud and asks whether the jury finds the defendant guilty or not guilty. The verdict is then recorded.

12.3.8.2 Majority verdict

It was noted above that when a jury is first asked to retire to consider their verdict they are told that only a unanimous verdict will be permitted. However, it is also known that this is not always true and s 17 JA 1974 permits a majority verdict to be reached. Majority verdicts are controversial because some argue that it contradicts the burden of proof—if some of the jury cannot agree the guilt of the defendant then surely there must be some doubt and yet the standard of proof is 'beyond all reasonable doubt' (see Doran (2002) 396). The counter-argument, however, is that it is an insurance policy against intransigent jurors or 'nobbling' a jury by bribing a single juror (ibid).

It is for the judge to decide when a majority verdict should be permitted but s 17 states that the minimum period of deliberation is two hours since they originally retired. The *Consolidated Practice Direction* repeats previous practice directions, which adds ten minutes to this time to ensure there is no doubt as to compliance with the statute. The argument is that the deliberation does not start until they reach the jury room and not when they leave the court; the extra ten minutes is supposed to account for the time it will take to walk to and from the courtroom etc (IV.46.2). However it is important to note that this is merely a *minimum* time and in complicated cases this period of time may not be sufficient and in very serious cases judges have been known to continue with the requirement of a unanimous verdict for two or three days. Indeed nothing in the statute requires a judge to permit majority verdicts and the judge could, theoretically, decide that a case was not suited to one.

Section 17 states that the permissible majority depends on the size of the jury (bearing in mind that jurors can be discharged). The rules are (Table 12.8):

Table 12.8 Permissible majority jury verdicts

Twelve jurors	11–1; 10–2
Eleven jurors	10–1
Ten jurors	9–1
Nine jurors	Must be unanimous

Receiving a majority verdict is quite complicated and it is set out in the *Consolidated Practice Direction* (IV.46.3–4). The process can be summarized as follows:

- The jury is brought back in and the foreperson stands.
- The clerk of the court asks, 'Have at least ten [nine] of you agreed on your verdict. Answer "Yes" or "No".'
- If the answer is 'No' then the judge sends them out again (or considers discharging them).
- If the answer is 'Yes' then the clerk says: 'What is your verdict?' Where there is more than one count on the indictment this process is repeated for each count.
- If the foreperson says 'Not guilty' then the verdict is so recorded.
- If the foreperson says 'Guilty' then the clerk asks: 'Is that a verdict of you all or by a majority?'
- The foreperson will (presumably) reply 'Majority'.
- The clerk then asks: 'How many of you agreed to the verdict and how many dissented?'
- The foreperson provides the numbers but not the names.

This convoluted process is designed to ensure that if an acquittal is reached nobody knows whether it was a majority verdict or not (see IV.46.6) whereas if it is a guilty verdict a check is built in to ensure that it is a valid majority verdict (and not, for example 7–5).

QUESTION FOR REFLECTION

Not every jurisdiction will allow a majority verdict, perhaps the most obvious example being America. Is it right to allow for a majority verdict? The argument against such a verdict is that the prosecution must prove guilty beyond all reasonable doubt. If one or two jurors do not believe he is guilty but the other ten do, how can that be said to be beyond all doubt?

Are there any consequences to only allowing a unanimous verdict?

12.3.8.3 Inability to reach a verdict

It is quite possible that a jury will not be able to reach a verdict no matter how long they are given. The judge should give them as much time as possible to reach a decision but eventually there may come a time when the judge needs to ask whether, even if more time was given to the jury, they would be capable of reaching a verdict. At this time the judge will give what is known as a *Watson direction*[9] which states that part of the jury oath is that if they are not able to reach a verdict they should say so. If the foreperson of the jury states that the jury is deadlocked then the jury can be discharged and a retrial is considered.

12.3.8.4 Perverse verdicts

It has been noted that each juror must swear 'to faithfully try the defendant and give a true verdict according to the evidence' (see 12.3.1.3 above). In the review of the criminal justice system, Lord Justice Auld believed this did not always happen and that jurors would return what he categorized as 'perverse verdicts' (Auld (2001) 173ff).

Auld admits that:

> there are many, in particular the Bar, who fervently support what they regard as the right of the jury to ignore their duty to return a verdict according to the evidence and to acquit when they disapprove of the law or the prosecution in seeking to enforce it...(Auld (2001) 173)

This is an interesting dimension of a jury trial. Nobody can order a jury to convict (a principle most recently forcibly restated in *R v Wang* [2005] UKHL 9) and thus a jury could, if they so wished, decide to ignore the law and bring in a verdict for whatever reason they wish. Indeed the fact that juries do not have to give reasons for their verdict (something Auld noted was in itself extremely controversial: Auld (2001) 168–173) means that it is sometimes impossible to decide why a jury reached a particular verdict. When the defendant is convicted this is something that can be corrected on appeal, especially where the verdict is inconsistent or clearly against the evidence (see the next chapter for further details on this) but what troubled Auld more was where the perverse verdict was an acquittal.

Auld noted that: 'although juries may have the ability to dispense with or nullify the law, they have no right to do so' (Auld (2001) 174), and suggested that it was 'an affront to the legal process' (p 175). One reason for this statement was that since only one per cent of crime was heard by a jury, why should it be entitled to disapply the law when those subject to summary trial will not receive such favour (ibid). On the other hand, this ability of the jury has long been considered a notable feature of the system and has attracted the label 'jury equity' (Ashworth and Redmayne (2010) 325).

⊙ CLIVE PONTING

Perhaps one of the most famous examples of 'jury equity' is the case of Clive Ponting who was charged with breaching the *Official Secrets Act 1911*. Ponting was a senior civil servant in the Ministry of Defence and came across material that related to the sinking of the General Belgrano, an Argentine cruiser which was sunk during the 'Falklands War'.[a] The official version of events was that the Belgrano was a threat to the Royal Navy Task Force and was sunk near an exclusion zone. The documents that Ponting identified demonstrated that it had been sighted a day earlier and was steaming away from the Task Force.[b] Ponting passed these papers to a Labour MP who had been critical of the execution of the campaign.

---

9. JSB Specimen Direction 58.

As a matter of law this was a simple breach of the *Official Secrets Act 1911* yet the jury acquitted him. The defence was, in essence, that it was in the public interest and yet this would not afford any defence in law. However this did not stop a jury from acquitting him.

a. The campaign colloquially known as the 'Falklands War' took place in 1982 when Argentinian military forces invaded the disputed Falkland Islands, a British colony. In fact although known as the 'Falklands War' this is not strictly accurate since war was not declared by either the United Kingdom or Argentina. Instead the military action took place under the auspices of the United Nations Convention.

b. Not that this would mean that it could not be counted as a threat to the Task Force. Whilst the sinking of the Belgrano remains controversial most military observers believe it was a legitimate military tactic but politically the sinking was handled badly. The definitive statement of the sinking is given in Freedman (2005) Ch 21.

The difficulty with this 'jury equity' power is that in effect it means that the law laid down by Parliament is circumvented and observers have even suggested it 'undermines the rule of law' (Ashworth and Redmayne (2010) 325) and others agree that it does have serious implications for the administration of justice (Doran (2002) 399); but alternatively it can be argued that this is society deciding whether it wishes its laws (for laws are made on behalf of society) to be enforced in circumstances where they believe the 'greater good' should prevail. Mischievously a comparison to the public-interest prosecution test (see 10.2.1.3 above) could be drawn. At the pre-trial procedure the prosecution may halt some crimes stating it is not 'in the public interest' for them to be prosecuted. One way of looking at 'jury equity' is to suggest that it is the jury saying that it is not 'in the public interest' for a person to be convicted. If the prosecution can decide it is not in the public's interest not to prosecute, why cannot the public decide that it is not in the public interest to convict?

It should be noted, finally, that the government has not acted upon Auld's recommendation and thus the principle of 'jury equity' is alive and well although its controversiality remains untouched.

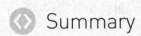 Summary

In this chapter we have examined the key aspects of trial on indictment, including critically examining the institution of the jury. In particular during this chapter we have noted that:

- An *indictment* is a formal document that lists the crimes a person has been accused of. Each crime is known as a *count* and along with the specific offence charged it also details a brief summary of the allegation.

- The principal characters in a trial on indictment are the judge and the jury. The judge is a professionally qualified salaried judge and has many responsibilities in a trial, most notably controlling the proceedings and making decisions in respect of the law.

- Although the Crown Court is often thought to involve a jury, the majority of cases do not proceed to a full jury trial, the rest being disposed of either through guilty pleas or judge-ordered acquittals.

- Jurors are randomly selected and recent changes to the law have enabled a wider range of people to sit on juries.

- The ethnicity of jurors is extremely controversial but the law does not allow a judge artificially to alter the profile of a jury to include, for example, a member of the ethnic minorities.

- The pattern of a trial on indictment is not substantially different from that of a summary trial but it is normally longer and can involve more witnesses. The judge can order an acquittal if he believes there is insufficient evidence to convict the defendant.

- As in a summary trial, the defendant should normally give evidence first because the defendant is always in the courtroom so can hear other evidence.

- The defendant need not be represented but if he does decide to represent himself then he will be precluded from personally cross-examining the victim in sex offences. A barrister will be appointed to him for this purpose.

- Juries are initially told to reach a unanimous verdict but after a minimum of two hours and ten minutes the judge may allow them to bring back a majority verdict.

- Theoretically juries are entitled to return a verdict according to their conscience even if this is contrary to what the law says. This is known as jury equity.

❓ End-of-chapter questions

1. It has been seen that the primary role of the judge is to ensure that there is a fair trial and that the judge should not adopt the mantle of an advocate. However an important aspect of that role is to allow advocates to put forward their case. Read *R v Lashley* [2005] EWCA Crim 2016 which is an extraordinary case where a judge becomes hostile to counsel. What do you think the jury and defendant would have made of this? Was there a fair trial?

2. Read Doran (2002) 289–390. Do you believe that jury vetting can be justified? How can safeguards be built into the system to ensure that the information is not misused by the state?

3. Read Ashworth and Redmayne (2010) 308–310. Can the plea bargaining regime be justified? What are its advantages and disadvantages? Should plea bargains be restricted to the SOCPA 2005 regime, ie only serious crimes?

4. Read Doran (2002) 398–399. Do you think it is right that a jury should be able to disapply the law, or is Auld LJ correct to say that it is an 'affront to justice'?

📖 Further reading

Auld Rt Hon Lord Justice (2001) *A Review of the Criminal Courts of England and Wales* (London: HMSO), Ch 5.

This is the chapter in the report by Auld LJ that discusses the use of juries and their constitution.

Corker D (2002) 'Trying fraud cases without juries' *Criminal Law Review* 283–294.

This provides a critique of the proposals by Auld LJ to abolish jury trials in respect of serious fraud trials.

Doran S (2002) 'Trial by jury' in M McConville and G Wilson (eds) *The Handbook of the Criminal Justice Process* (Oxford: OUP).

This is an intelligent essay that highlights some of the controversial aspects of a trial on indictment.

Ponting C (1987) '*R v Ponting*' 14 *Journal of Law and Society* 366–372.

This is an unusual article in that it is written by a defendant. It is a summary of the case against him when he was charged under the Official Secrets Act. Whilst (obviously) partisan it is interesting nonetheless.

Thornton P (2004) 'Trial by jury: 50 years of change' *Criminal Law Review* 683–701.

This is an interesting piece that demonstrates how far trial by jury has altered in fifty years, particularly in respect of those who are entitled to sit on a jury.

For multiple choice questions, updates to this chapter and links to useful websites, please visit the Online Resource Centre at

www.oxfordtextbooks.co.uk/orc/gillespie_els3e/

13

Criminal Appeals

By the end of this chapter you will be able to:

- Identify where appeals following summary trials and trials on indictment are heard.
- Distinguish between interlocutory and final appeals.
- Discuss the circumstances in which the prosecution may make an appeal.
- Explain how appeals are heard.
- Identify the powers an appellate court has.

Introduction

The previous chapters have identified how criminal trials take place. We have noted that there are two forms of trial: the summary trial which takes place in the magistrates' court and the trial on indictment which takes place in the Crown Court. However, the trial does not necessarily end the matter since in certain circumstances it is possible for either the defendant or prosecution to appeal against rulings of the judge.

This chapter will examine under what circumstances someone is entitled to appeal and how that appeal is heard. It completes our examination of criminal trials and will help place the duties and responsibilities of the appellate courts into context.

13.1 Summary trials or trials on indictment

It has been seen from the previous chapters that the law differentiates between summary trials and trials on indictment and this distinction continues with appeals. It will be seen that there are completely separate ways of dealing with appeals depending on the mode of trial, this distinction including even whether it is possible to appeal against matters of fact.

Diagram 13.1 demonstrates the different paths that can be taken depending on the type of trial and these will be explored in the remainder of this chapter. The dotted line demonstrates the path an appeal from a summary trial takes and the solid line demonstrates the path an appeal following a trial on indictment takes. It can be seen that although some courts share jurisdiction the processes are quite distinct and accordingly will be discussed separately.

13.2 Appeals from a summary trial

Diagram 13.1 presents the appellate structure for summary trials and it can be seen that there are two possible avenues for an appeal from the magistrates' court: either to the Crown Court or to the Divisional Court. A third possibility also exists, that of judicial review, since the magistrates' court is an inferior body but the courts prefer the matter to proceed on the basis of appeal by way of case stated as they argue that this is the more appropriate avenue (*R (on behalf of Stace) v Milton Keynes Magistrates' Court* [2006] EWHC 1049 at [13]). That said, it remains an important method of appeal and the decision over which method to adopt is not always easy (at [15]).

13.2.1 Appeal to the Crown Court

The first appeal route is an appeal to the Crown Court. This is an opportunity that is restricted to the convicted defendant and is unique within the appellate system in that its form is not that of a legal argument but rather a complete rehearing. The appeal can be against sentence or conviction.

The appeal is permitted under s 108 *Magistrates' Courts Act 1980* (MCA 1980) and does not require leave (permission) to be granted: the appeal exists as a matter of right. The composition of the court when hearing the appeal is that a Crown Court judge (normally a circuit judge or recorder but theoretically a puisne judge could sit) presides with usually two lay justices. The judge is the tribunal of law and accordingly the lay justices must take the law as directed by the judge. However, the judge has no veto in respect of decisions of fact where only a simple majority is required.

As noted above, the appeal takes the form of a complete rehearing, with all evidence being reheard (including the witnesses) and the decision made at the end of the trial. Theoretically, the Crown Court could decide to remit the matter to the magistrates' court for another hearing or for disposal regarding sentence but usually the matter is dealt with by the Crown Court but with the proviso that the powers of the Crown Court are the same as in the magistrates' court. However, that does not mean that a sentence cannot be increased: since it is a rehearing a person challenging his conviction could find that his appeal is dismissed and his sentence is actually increased. Ashworth and Redmayne (2010) argue that the ability to increase the sentence is unfair (p 374) and certainly it is not comparable to the position that exists in respect of appeals from trials on indictment where the Court of Appeal has no such power (see below). Sprack (2004) argues that the provision is probably a tool by which appeals are discouraged but it is submitted that this is an inappropriate way of doing it: a person should not feel unable to challenge a conviction because they are afraid their sentence could be increased. A better approach would be to impose a leave requirement (see below) whereby someone must convince a judicial officer that there is merit in an appeal.

Auld disagreed with this right of appeal to the Crown Court. He argued that it historically arose because there was suspicion about the competency of the magistracy (Auld (2001) 617) but he argued that this was no longer true, although it was seen in Chapter 11 that the position is arguably not so straightforward. A further argument advanced is that ordinarily the magistrates will provide reasons for their decision and thus if there is a perception that they have acted in a way contrary to the law then an appeal by way of case stated could be brought (p 620). This last point does have some weight to it. The existence of the right to a complete rehearing purely on the basis that the defendant disagrees with the decision of the magistrates would appear somewhat anomalous, and is certainly not comparable to an appeal following trial on indictment.

Auld suggested restricting appeals to matters of law and before a single judge (pp 621–622) which would have been controversial and somewhat unprecedented; appeals normally take place in respect of at least two judges and this should (except for issues of leave) be retained for confidence. In any event the government rejected this proposal, or at the very least did not act upon it, and thus the current position is that the appeal to the Crown Court continues in the way that it always has. It is also undoubtedly the most popular method of appeal. The 2009 *CPS Annual Report* notes that 14,221 appeals were heard in the Crown Court.

13.2.1.1 Subsequent appeals

For sake of completeness it should be noted that for matters of fact there is no appeal from the Crown Court when sitting in its appellate capacity but where either the

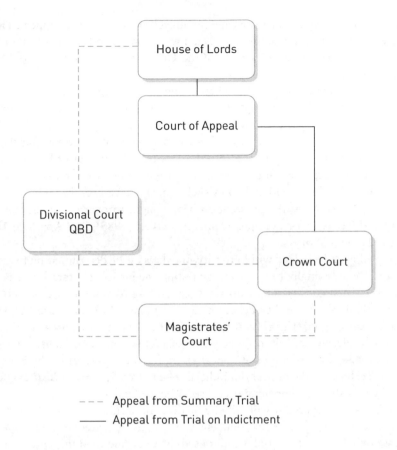

Appeal from Summary Trial
Appeal from Trial on Indictment

Diagram 13.1 Appellate structure of the Criminal Justice System

prosecution or defence wish to argue that they have made an error of law when determining the appeal then they can currently appeal by way of case stated (s 28 *Senior
Courts Act 1981* (SCA 1981)). The matter would be heard in the same way as though
it was being stated by the magistrates' court, see below.

The Law Commission has argued that the right to appeal by way of case stated to
the Crown Court in this matter should be removed.[1] The Law Commission argued that
removing appeal by way of case stated from the Crown Court would simplify criminal
procedure although it noted that it is relatively rare for such appeals to be made and,
in any event, judicial review of the decision of the Court (when acting in its appellate
capacity) would still exist.

13.2.2 Appeal by way of case stated

The second form of appeal is to appeal to the Divisional Court by way of case stated.
This, as it will be seen, is a different species of appeal from appeal to the Crown Court
and has more in common with other appeals. The first point to note is that both the
prosecution and the defence can appeal by way of case stated (s 111(1) MCA 1980)

1. *The High Court's Jurisdiction in Relation to Criminal Proceedings* (Law Comm Report No 324).

and accordingly an acquitted person can find himself the subject of an appeal. This is an important distinction and it can be contrasted with appeals following a trial on indictment, even with recent changes set out in the *Criminal Justice Act 2003* (CJA 2003) (see 13.4 below).

An appeal by way of case stated is where either party is arguing that the magistrates have made an error of law and requires the magistrates to identify the case upon which they based their decision, ie the reasons for their finding. It is for this reason it is known as 'case stated'. Along with this, they will identify a series of questions that they want the High Court to answer. Since the appeal arises out of a matter of law it is unusual for an appeal to relate to a sentence passed, as it would be rare for a court to pass an illegal sentence, but in exceptional cases such appeals have been brought, most notably in driving cases where the prosecution have sought to overturn a decision not to disqualify a driver (see, for example, *Haime v Walkett* (1983) 5 Cr App R(S) 165 and Sprack (2004) 539–540).

Any appeal must be lodged within twenty-one days of the determination by the magistrates and should initially be made by requesting the justices to state a case (s 111(2) MCA 1980). Theoretically the magistrates' can refuse to state a case (s 111(5)) but they may only do so where they believe it to be frivolous. In *R (on behalf of Miller) v Redbridge Justices* [2002] EWHC Admin 1579 the Divisional Court held that frivolous meant 'futile, misconceived, hopeless or academic' (at [14]). Where the justices do refuse to state a case, a right of appeal exists from this refusal to the High Court (s 111(6)). Technically the appeal is a judicial review (see *Redbridge Justices*) not least because the remedy is a compelling order (see 14.3.1.4 above).

Where a case is prepared it will initially be done in draft and this draft sent to both the appellant and respondent[2] for comment and, ideally, an agreement as to the nature of the case (ie what questions of law are raised) is made and then this case proceeds to the High Court for hearing (see rule 64.2 *Criminal Procedure Rules 2005*). The hearing is heard in the Administrative/Divisional Court and normally takes place before at least two judges.[3] It is usual for at least one judge to be a Lord Justice of Appeal but it has become increasingly common for two puisne judges to sit and there does not appear to be any requirement for a Lord Justice to sit, although where he does he will chair the court (unless the other judge is the President of the Queen's Bench Division or Lord Chief Justice). It is not unusual in these cases for the judgment to be handed down immediately after the hearing although the court can, of course, adjourn and give judgment later. There are three options open to the court:

- dismiss the appeal
- allow the appeal and direct that the magistrates should convict or acquit the defendant[4]
- allow the appeal and remit it back to the magistrates' court for a rehearing before either the same or a new bench (see *Griffith v Jenkins* [1992] 2 AC 76).

---

2. The term 'respondent' continues to be used to indicate the party in the original proceedings (eg where the prosecution are appealing the defendant and vice versa) whereas technically, of course, it is the justices themselves who are responding to the appeal. However, the term probably continues out of ease of use and certainly both the original parties are represented at court whereas the justices ordinarily are not.

3. Technically, following the *Access to Justice Act 1999* any appeal by way of case stated does not have to go to a Divisional Court because the statute simply refers the matter to the High Court. However, as a matter of custom it will normally proceed before a divisional court and thus be heard by more than one judge.

4. This can be a partial appeal, ie the court could decide to vary the order of the magistrates.

A peculiar difficulty with an appeal by way of case stated is that as the constitution of the High Court in these matters is ordinarily a Divisional Court of two members it is quite possible that the judges could be divided. Technically in these circumstances the rule is that the appeal fails although this appears somewhat harsh, especially to a convicted (and possibly imprisoned) appellant and it would appear that the court does have the discretion to relist the matter in front of a three-judge panel (see *Cambridgeshire County Council v Associated Lead Mills Ltd* [2005] EWHC Admin 1627).

A further right of appeal exists from a decision of the High Court by way of case stated but only to the Supreme Court and only when it involves a point of public importance (s 1 *Administration of Justice Act 1960*). It is extremely rare for such appeals to be brought and in essence therefore the appeal by way of case stated will usually be the last stage of any appeal.

The *Judicial and Court Statistics* for 2009 shows that there were 76 appeals by way of case stated heard from the magistrates' court of which 44 (58 per cent) were successful. Whilst the success rate would seem quite high, the total number of appeals by way of case stated is small in comparison with the number of appeals brought before the Crown Court.

13.2.3 Judicial review

The third appellate route from the magistrates' court is to petition the High Court for a judicial review of the decision of the justices. This route arises because magistrates' courts are inferior bodies and thus subject to the supervisory function of the High Court (eg *R (on behalf of Stace) v Milton Keynes Magistrates' Court* [2006] EWHC 1049) although, as will be seen, the courts prefer the matter to be heard by one of the other routes. This is perhaps set out most notably in *R (on the application of Clark-Darby) v Highbury Magistrates' Court* [2001] EWHC Admin 959 where the court held that unless the matter was one where an allegation of natural justice was raised (eg a magistrate was biased and should have excused himself) then the normal recourse should be to appeal by way of case stated since that allowed the full reasoning of the magistrates to be set out before the appellate court for examination. In 2009 a total of 305 applications for leave to judicially review a summary trial decision were received but only 66 (21.6 per cent) were granted leave. Of those, thirty-three (50 per cent) were successful. The fact that there are a large number of applications suggest that counsel still prefer judicial review to, for example, case stated but the low success rate of being given leave demonstrates that the Administrative Court is careful as to those cases it will hear.

13.3 Appeal from a trial on indictment

Perhaps the more notable appeals are those that arise from a trial on indictment as these invariably concern the more serious offences. These appeals have also been the more prominent because the miscarriages of justice scandals that encompassed the 1980s and 1990s all concentrated on appeals from the Crown Court. Apart from matters that do not relate to a trial on indictment, which will be discussed below, all appeals from the Crown Court proceed to the Court of Appeal (Criminal Division). This was created in 1966 and is a creature of statute (ss 2 and 3 SCA 1981) although it recognizes a progression from the original Court of Criminal Appeals.

The Lord Chief Justice is the President of the Criminal Division and this has remained true even after the reorganization of the judiciary following the constitutional changes (see s 7 CRA 2005). In 1997 an honorary title of Vice-President of the Criminal Division was created and Lord Justice Rose assumed this position. The *Courts Act 2003* (CA 2003) formalized this arrangement, albeit implicitly, by recognizing the term 'Vice-President' of either Division (s 64) but it remains, in effect, an honorary title and the holder is still formally styled a Lord (or Lady) Justice of Appeal (s 63) and does not receive any additional pay for the duties he discharges, nor is he classed as a 'Head of Division' (see 7.1.1 above). That said, the Vice-President has important delegated authority given to him and is in de facto day-to-day charge of the Court of Appeal (Criminal Division). Apart from the Lord Chief Justice and Vice-President, the court is staffed by Lords Justice of Appeal and puisne judges asked by the Lord Chief Justice to sit (normally these will be judges of the Queen's Bench Division but they need not be and where the matter raises welfare issues it is possible a Family Division judge will be appointed). Since 1995 certain circuit judges have also been eligible to sit in the Criminal Division (s 9 SCA 1981 and s 52 *Criminal Justice and Public Order Act 1994*) although currently only twenty-six circuit judges are so authorized. Previously they were restricted to sitting on appeals that were not heard at first instance by a puisne judge but this was abolished by the CA 2003 although as a matter of listing it appears to have been de facto retained with most circuit judges continuing to sit solely on matters that did not involve a High Court judge. Also in any bench of the Court of Appeal only one circuit judge may sit (s 55(6) SCA 1981) although there is no restriction on the number of puisne judges who may sit.[5]

The Court of Appeal will normally sit in panels of three but can sit in panels of five (known as a 'full court') for significant matters (normally reserved for the issuing of practice directions or where they seek to depart from precedent—see *R v Simpson* [2004] QB 118) and it may also sit in panels of two although not where this involves the determination of an appeal against, inter alia, a conviction or unduly lenient sentence (s 55(4) SCA 1981). Auld argued that extending the power of a panel of two judges to include the determination of appeals against convictions could lead to greater efficiency in the court (Auld (2001) 646–647) but this was rejected in part because of the dangers of a two-judge panel being divided. Whilst, as a matter of statutory law, such a split decision would lead to the rehearing before a three-judge court (s 55(5) SCA 1981) this would lead to problems of delay, costs, and indeed added stress to a convicted appellant, especially where he is held in gaol.

13.3.1 Leave

There is no automatic right to an appeal to the Court of Appeal, one must get permission first. Two routes exist for the granting of leave to a convicted defendant who wishes to appeal against his conviction. The first is to seek permission from the Court of Appeal and the second is for the judge at first instance to give leave (s 1 *Criminal Appeal Act 1968* (CAA 1968)). It must be noted at the outset that the latter course

---

5. In other words, theoretically at least, a Division of the Court of Appeal could be constituted solely with puisne judges.

of action is extremely unusual and indeed the Court of Appeal itself has stated that it should only be in the most exceptional circumstances that a judge certifies a case as fit for appeal, arguing that it should normally be for the judges of the Court of Appeal to grant leave (see, for example, *R v Bansal* [1999] Crim LR 484).

The most usual route, therefore, is to ask the Court of Appeal for permission. The first stage in this process is deciding whether it is possible to appeal. Section 1 CAA 1968 makes clear that a right exists against a conviction and this has led to the question over in what circumstances, if any, an appeal may be brought when a person has pleaded guilty, and thus has not been *convicted* per se. The Court of Appeal has adopted the approach of permitting an appeal to be brought where the plea of guilty was equivocal, ie where the defendant thought there was no other option but to plead guilty. This can arise from two principal reasons; the first is where the plea was made under duress (*R v Turner* [1970] 2 QB 321) and the second is where a judge has made a ruling in law which leaves the defendant with no other option but to plead guilty (*R v Clarke* [1972] 1 All ER 219 and see Sprack (2004) 495–497 for a discussion on when a defendant will be considered to have no other option).

Petitioning the Court of Appeal will normally lead to a 'single judge' considering whether to give leave. The single judge is actually a puisne judge and Auld notes that each puisne judge of the Queen's Bench Division will be allocated a set of appellate applications to consider, normally amounting to approximately fourteen a month (Auld (2001) 639). All of the applications are on paper without any hearing. Auld notes that whilst some applications may be easy to dispose of, others will take a considerable period of reflection (ibid) and yet no time is specifically allocated to the judges to undertake this task, with the vast majority of the applications being undertaken in the evenings or at weekends. This has led some to question the consistency of single-judge decisions with the implication that pressure could lead to a cursory inspection (Ashworth and Redmayne (2010) 376). That said, however, a right of appeal does exist from a refusal by the single judge and this is to the Court of Appeal, normally sitting as a bench of three but occasionally of two, but note that only a minority of applications will be accepted (p 343). In 2009 a total of 1,435 applications for leave to appeal against conviction were made. Of those, 22 per cent were granted by the single judge and 477 refused appeals were renewed before the full court, of which 117 (24.5 per cent) were granted leave to appeal. Of those appeals against conviction brought, 38 per cent of appeals against conviction were successful.

13.3.2 **The hearing**

Assuming that leave is granted then the matter will proceed to a full hearing. Before arriving at the court a lot of procedural issues will have occurred, most notably (and recently) counsel will be required to prepare 'skeleton arguments'. Despite their name, skeleton arguments are comprehensive documents that set out the arguments of both the appellant and respondents. The appellant will prepare their skeleton argument first and this will be served upon the respondents who will then have the opportunity to comment on it. This therefore forms the basis of the arguments although it is not unusual for skeleton arguments to be sent in late or amended (Auld (2001) 643) and indeed it is possible for counsel to depart from the skeleton arguments because the basis of the trial remains the oral argument.

That said the practice of the modern Court of Appeal differs from what it used to be. Dunn, himself a former Lord Justice, comments that the traditional practice propagated by a senior court of appeal judge was:

> I like to come with an open mind to each case. So I never read anything about it, except glance at the judgment and the notice of appeal, before I go into court (Dunn (1993) 234).

This was a not uncommon feeling but nowadays it has changed and the judges will normally have read the documents, with one judge (the one that will eventually be assigned to write the principal opinion) normally reading every document and considering the authorities cited by counsel. The amount of work is increased where the judgment of the court is reserved (that is to say, instead of judgment being handed down immediately at the end of the case the judges adjourn for a period of weeks to allow them to conduct research and produce a written judgment that is now handed down).

Unlike an appeal by way of case stated, which is purely an argument as to law, the Court of Appeal has discretion to hear evidence although it is rarely exercised (see Ashworth and Redmayne (2010) 378). The principal reason why evidence is rarely heard is that the role of the Court of Appeal is not to conduct a trial but rather to review the trial at first instance and this should not require them to hear much evidence. Indeed their power to hear evidence is effectively restricted to 'fresh evidence' which is defined as evidence that could not have been adduced at the original trial (see s 23 CAA 1968 and Sprack (2004) 516–518). Where evidence is heard then the courts have to be careful as to what the purpose of the evidence is; it is not to assist the court in determining whether the appellant is guilty or not but rather whether his conviction is safe (p 517). It will be seen below that it does not necessarily follow that someone whose conviction is quashed did not necessarily commit the crime for that is a matter that only a trial at first instance, usually through the provision of a jury, can decide. Instead the purpose of the appellate court is to decide whether the conviction is safe or whether there is any doubt as to the guilt of a person; this will usually be found where the court finds that some evidential or legal rule would have affected the jury's deliberations, as at that point it cannot be predicted what the jury may have done.

➔ WITNESS TESTIMONY

One interesting issue of distinction in the Court of Appeal is that where it decides to hear witness testimony it is quite possible that the court rather than any party will call the witness. In this case a member of the court will examine the witness (although this will not adhere to the principles of examination-in-chief) and then the person will be tendered for cross-examination (see Sprack (2004) 518). If the court decides that it does not want to call the witness but permits a party to adduce the evidence then the traditional pattern arises.

13.3.3 Decision

It has been noted already that the purpose of the appellate court is *not* to decide the guilt or innocence of the appellant although that is how it may be interpreted by some. The basis upon which the court should exercise its powers is to be found in s 2 CAA 1968 which states that the court shall:

allow an appeal against conviction if they think the conviction is unsafe...and shall dismiss such appeal in any other case.

This simplified test was introduced in 1995 to replace a previous test that permitted a conviction to be quashed when the conviction was unsafe, unsatisfactory, based on an error of law, or where there was a material irregularity. Whether the change in test means anything substantively different or whether it was simply codifying the original tests into one overarching test has been the subject of debate since it was introduced. At the heart of the discussion is whether the Court of Appeal is able to act as suitable guarantor to prevent miscarriages of justice. In the 1970s to 1990s it would appear the answer was 'no' and some argue that the court was too ready to accept police evidence and too slow to accept allegations of corruption (Ashworth and Redmayne (2010) 384), something that other authors have previously commented upon (for an illuminating potted history of how the miscarriages of justice in the 1980s led to a 'crisis' for the criminal justice system read Nobles and Schiff (2000) 117–149 esp 124–128).

At its most basic, the new test shares with the old test the notion of the safety of the conviction and the Court of Appeal in *R v Graham* [1997] 1 Cr App R 302 stated:

> [The test] is plainly intended to concentrate attention on one question: whether, in light of any arguments raised or evidence adduced on appeal, the Court of Appeal considers a conviction unsafe. If the Court is satisfied that, despite any misdirection of law or irregularity in the conduct of the trial or any fresh evidence, that the conviction is safe, the Court will dismiss the appeal. (p 308 per Lord Bingham CJ)

Notwithstanding this, it is apparent that the conduct of the trial will be a central feature in any appeal and in *R v Togher* [2001] 1 Cr App R 33 the Court of Appeal decided that the new test effectively encapsulated the old tests and that where there was a material irregularity this may lead to the safety of the conviction being undermined and requiring the appeal to be allowed. This case was distinguished in *R v Llewellyn* [2001] EWCA Crim 1555 although only to the extent that it was said that if the procedural error forming the basis of the appeal was known at the time of trial but not the subject of any objection then it should not normally form the basis of an appeal. To an extent this is an application of the usual rule that the Court of Appeal will not revisit issues that *should* have been addressed at first instance but it can be argued that this is slightly harsh as there may be tactical reasons why counsel does not raise an objection at first instance.

In 2006 the government consulted on changing s 2 to prevent it quashing a conviction where the evidence suggested that the defendant was guilty despite any errors of law that had been made by judges (Home Office, 2006). The proposals were not welcomed but the government sought to introduce the change in the (then) *Criminal Justice and Immigration Bill*. The proposed clauses would have prevented the Court of Appeal from quashing a conviction where there was no reasonable doubt as to guilt. The clauses were not, however, supported in Parliament and they were withdrawn before the Act received Royal Assent.

13.3.3.1 European Convention on Human Rights

In Chapter 5 it was noted that the courts are expressly considered public authorities within the meaning of s 6 *Human Rights Act 1998* (HRA 1998) and accordingly this means they must give effect to the Convention rights of an individual. Article 6 of the *European Convention on Human Rights* (ECHR) provides that everyone has the right to a fair trial. Whilst it was noted that Article 34 does not expressly form part of the 1998 Act (Coppel and Supperstone (1999) 307) this is, in part, because the HRA 1998 is considered to be the practical application of Article 34 and s 8 states that a court may provide 'such relief or remedy... within its powers as it considers just and reasonable' for a breach of the Convention. What should the remedy be for someone who has suffered an unfair trial? Should it quash the conviction even if the court considers that the person was, in fact, guilty? In other words, should a finding of a contravention of Article 6 automatically lead to a finding that a person's conviction is unsafe?

The answer appears to be a qualified 'yes'. In *Togher* the Court of Appeal considered the impact of the HRA 1998 and was clear that unfairness could undermine the safety of a conviction, something that the court had earlier stated in *R v Rowe, Davis and Johnson* [2001] 1 Cr App R 115 which was an appeal that considered the safety of a conviction after the European Court of Human Rights (ECtHR) had considered that there had been an infringement of Article 6 rights (see *Rowe and Davis v United Kingdom* (2000) 30 EHRR 1). However, the position cannot be that simple and the example of Robert Thompson and Jon Venables, two schoolboys who were convicted for the murder of a toddler known as Jamie Bulger. The ECtHR held that there had been a breach of Article 6 in respect of their trial (see *T v UK; V v UK* (2000) 30 EHRR 121) but it had never been seriously argued that they were *not* the killers or that the breach of Article 6 cast doubt on the safety of their conviction. Quashing a conviction therefore need not be the appropriate remedy and the courts have accepted this logic and in *R v Williams* [2001] EWCA Crim 932 the Court of Appeal accepted this logic when it held that a breach of Article 6(2), breach of the presumption of innocence, would not automatically undermine the safety of a conviction. The submission of Ashworth and Redmayne together with the decisions of the Court of Appeal must be correct and are probably compatible with s 8 HRA 1998, which states that a court must provide the most effective remedy. Not every breach of Article 6 may necessarily require a conviction to be quashed in that this may not be the effective remedy where the safety of the conviction is not compromised; alternative remedies (eg financial compensation or a declaration that a person's rights have been infringed) may be more appropriate and in line with s 8. However, a finding of a breach of Article 6 (the right to a fair trial) must at least lead to the investigation of whether an appeal should be allowed given that the procedural process would appear relevant to the safety of any conviction.

13.3.3.2 'Lurking doubt'

It would be thought that s 2 CAA 1968 was quite specific and that given that the Court of Appeal is a statutory body it should not be able to go beyond the remit of its statutory jurisdiction. However, recently the court has begun to accept that it does have residual power and brought into effect a remedy previously used by the court for Criminal Appeals, that of quashing a conviction as a result of a 'lurking doubt'. In *R v B* [2003] 2 Cr App R 13 the court explained it thus:

> there remains in this Court a residual discretion to set aside a conviction if we feel that it is unsafe or unfair to allow it to stand. This is so even when the trial process itself cannot be faulted. (p 204 per Lord Woolf CJ)

Thus the court is stating that even though statute sets out its jurisdiction it can continue to access the inherent jurisdictions of the court, in part because of its role as a senior court. This was not always the view it took and in *R v F* (1999) *The Times*, 20 October a different constitution of the court held that the concept of 'lurking doubt' was no longer applicable following the change to the single test for appeals. Smith, in an insightful commentary, questions the decision in *F* arguing that the single appellate test was simply codifying existing legislation and accordingly the 'lurking doubt' concept remained (Smith (1999) 307). Certainly there is no reason why the single test should have abolished the 'lurking doubt' concept as the argument is that if the court has a doubt as to whether a person is guilty then his conviction cannot be safe. In *R v B* [2005] EWCA Crim 63 the Court Martial Appeals Court[6] stated:

> There can be no doubt that the lurking doubt notion...continues to be a tool available to this Court. It is plainly an application of the test of unsafety of a conviction, as it is now expressed in splendid isolation in section 2 of the Criminal Appeal Act 1968 as amended. ([at 19] per Auld LJ)

This is the most accurate position and accordingly a court, even when faced with no apparent procedural impropriety, can set aside a conviction where it believes that it is in the interests of justice to do so.

13.3.4 Frivolous appeals

It was noted above that at Crown Court a person who appeals against either his conviction or sentence can have his original sentence increased (see 13.2.1 above). The Court of Appeal does not have this power as the ability to increase a sentence was abolished in 1966 with the formation of the Court of Appeal (Criminal Division). However, the court can order that time spent in gaol pending an appeal can be disregarded for the purposes of early release, in other words ensuring that a sentence is de facto increased as a result of appealing. This process is known as the 'loss of time' provisions (s 29 CAA 1968).

Zander notes that these provisions were used in the 1970s by the Lord Chief Justice to ensure that frivolous appeals were not brought (Zander (2007) 674). There was an impression that the appellate rules were so relaxed that nothing was to be lost by appealing against a conviction, especially where the defendant had been imprisoned. If the gamble paid off the person would be released, whereas if it did not the person continued his or her sentence in prison. The use of the 'loss of time' provisions ensured that those in prison were more careful in bringing hopeless appeals as their sentence was, in effect, frozen during the appellate process even though they continued to be incarcerated. In the immediate years following the *Practice Note* the number of appeals almost halved (ibid) but some question whether it is appropriate to use this power. Ashworth and Redmayne argue that the provisions serve as a de facto deterrent to an individual exercising their legal right (Ashworth and Redmayne (2010) 374) although the court would almost certainly contest this allegation noting that, in effect, no loss of time would be ordered where an appeal was brought on the advice of counsel (see

---

6. In effect the Court of Appeal sitting under another name: the Court Martial Appeal Court hears appeals from courts martial, ie courts that try members of HM Forces for breaching laws whilst in service.

Practice Direction (Crime: Sentence: Loss of Time) [1980] 1 WLR 270), the argument being that such appeals are not frivolous.

The loss of time provisions appear to have the usual rule of a loss of twenty-eight days' time (Ashworth and Redmayne (2010) 373) but the court can, and does, provide for additional loss of time (see, for example, *R v Sanderson* [2003] EWCA Crim 2945) where the single judge ordered a loss of time of sixty days because of an 'impertinent application' (ibid, at [7]). In *R v K* [2005] EWCA Crim 955 the Court of Appeal noted, however, that the provisions are actually rarely invoked, with only four orders being made in 1998, two in 1999, none in 2000, and two in 2001 (at [18]). It is unlikely that there were no frivolous appeals during those years but rather that the single judge and Court of Appeal did not avail themselves of the powers. However, this small number of orders does not detract from the point made by Ashworth and Redmayne, ie that the existence of the power may lead some to be reticent to launch an appeal. The ECtHR has held that the 'loss of time' provisions do not breach either Articles 5 or 6 (*Monell v United Kingdom* (1988) 10 EHRR 205), although it should be noted that the ECtHR accepted that Article 6 was engaged and, accordingly, representation as to the loss of time should be permitted. Ashworth and Redmayne disapprove of this decision (Ashworth and Redmayne (2005) 342) but the decision appears to be a common-sense approach to the issue and recognizes that the courts should have the right to impose a 'sanction' on those who try to abuse the provisions.

13.4 Appeal following an acquittal

Until recently the prosecution had extremely limited options open to them when faced with an acquittal at the Crown Court. To an extent it was thought that this was less problematic because of the usual rule of criminal justice that it is better for a guilty man to be acquitted than for an innocent man to be convicted and gaoled. There was also the additional issue that the vast majority of acquittals arise not from any error of law but as a result of a jury acquitting the defendant and it was thought that the jury had the right to acquit even when they thought, in law, a person is guilty because society has the right to decide when acts should be punished.

However, some trials will lead to an acquittal not because the jury have acquitted the defendant but because the trial judge has made a ruling of law that has the effect of terminating the case. It will be seen that there are two types of rulings: first, when a judge decides that the trial should be halted (eg upon a submission of no case to answer: see 12.3.3 above) and the second when a ruling by the judge as to the admissibility of evidence is such that the prosecution decides that it is no longer able to continue with the prosecution (and the prosecution are under a legal duty to continue to review the decision to prosecute during the course of the trial). It will be remembered that although the Crown Court does not create precedent, where a High Court judge sits his rulings of law can form persuasive precedent (see 3.4.1.4 above) and clearly there is a danger that if such a judge does make an error of law and this is cited to other Crown Court judges then a series of acquittals will arise with little opportunity for the appellate courts to correct this error of law.

Eventually, therefore, it was decided that there should exist a system of referring matters to the Court of Appeal and in 1972 the system of Attorney-General's References was created (s 36 *Criminal Justice Act 1972*). However, pressure grew for the system to be extended and the *MacPherson Report* into the tragic death and subsequent investigation of the murder of Stephen Lawrence recommended that consideration should be given to whether prosecutions should be permitted after appeal and identified two distinct areas of concern: the first is the notion of 'double jeopardy' which prohibits a defendant from being retried for the offence he is acquitted of even if fresh evidence of his guilt comes to light. The second, and for our immediate purpose more relevant, was the notion of an appeal which could take place immediately after the acquittal in the same way as with appeals from convention, a successful application for which would lead to an immediate retrial. The government asked the Law Commission to consider this and in a report (Law Commission (2001)) it recommended there should be a partial relaxation of both rules. Lord Justice Auld, in his report, followed this up by suggesting that the rules should be relaxed but he went further since here the Law Commission thought the rule should be restricted to murder alone. Auld argued for a more widespread relaxation (Auld (2001) 633–634).

Eventually the government legislated to introduce a (limited) right of appeal through the CJA 2003 although at the time of writing it has not yet been brought fully into force. However the right of appeal has not interfered with the right of the Attorney-General to bring a reference to the Court of Appeal and thus both will be considered.

13.4.1 Reference to the Court of Appeal

As noted above, the Attorney-General has had the right to refer a matter to the Court of Appeal since 1972. This type of reference differs quite radically from the sentencing reference in that although both require a specified offence and the personal approval of a Law Officer, the reference following acquittal takes the form of a de facto hypothetical appeal.

The outcome of the reference will make no difference to the acquittal of the defendant; even if the Court of Appeal agrees that the judge made an error of law and that he should never have been acquitted, the person will remain acquitted and protected from any subsequent trial for the same offence. Although the statute does not expressly say so, it is submitted that where the prosecution refer a matter to the court rather than use their new powers under the CJA 2003 it would be unjust to allow the prosecution subsequently to use their powers to apply for the removal of the restriction of double jeopardy (see below) unless new issues are raised that could not have been considered at the time of trial because to do so would be unjust since the prosecution could have appealed instead of referring the matter to the court.

What is the point of a referral to the Court of Appeal if it does not lead to any change in the status of the acquittal? The simple answer is one of precedent: whilst the ruling of a High Court judge may be persuasive for other judges, a ruling of the Court of Appeal is binding on the trial courts and it can thus ensure that any error of law can be corrected. This is, therefore, an important way of correcting the law following a dubious decision of first instance. It is important to note that the problem must be real, ie arising from a case, and it has been held that there is no power for the Attorney-General to refer a purely hypothetical point of law (*Attorney-General's Reference (No 4 of 1979)* (1980) 71 Cr App R 341).

Auld believed that even the extension of prosecution rights of appeal would not remove the justification for s 36 (Auld (2001) 637) and this must be correct. There will be any number of reasons why an appeal from an acquittal may not be possible, not least the safeguards built into the system (see below) and the impact it could have on an *individual* defendant. It may be, therefore, that the Director of Public Prosecutions (DPP) does not believe that an appeal should be made against the decision of a trial judge and yet the prosecution would not wish the ruling to be extended and the *Attorney-General's Reference* system continues to be the most appropriate system for dealing with such matters.

13.4.2 Prosecution rights of appeal

Granting prosecution rights of appeal has been somewhat controversial even though it has long been accepted for those tried summarily. One objection to the granting of such a right is because of the distress that could be caused to a person acquitted to then have the possibility of a conviction held over him, but this is to an extent a false argument. Notwithstanding the point about magistrates' courts it completely ignores the reality of the pre-CJA 2003 appellate system. If a person had been convicted at the end of his trial and imprisoned but successfully appealed to the Court of Appeal he would have his conviction quashed and be released from prison. If, however, the prosecution appealed to the House of Lords (something they were entitled to do; they were simply not permitted to appeal to the Court of Appeal) and the House overturned the acquittal then the defendant was obliged to surrender himself to custody and serve his sentence.

The new scheme contained within Part 9 of the CJA 2003 marks a radical departure from the current position although not as radical as had been suggested. Auld was concerned with the issue of 'perverse acquittals' which he took to mean those where a defendant was acquitted in circumstances that were clearly contrary to the evidence presented (Auld (2001) 636). However, this was denounced by many groups, not least because juries represent society and have the right to decide whether people deserve punishment (see Liberty (2003) 94) and the government rejected this proposal. Part 9 contains two distinct appeals: appeals against terminal rulings and appeals against evidential rulings. The Act also expressly states that no appeal can be brought against a decision of the judge to discharge a jury or against any ruling where a right of appeal exercisable by the prosecution already exists (s 56).

13.4.2.1 Terminal rulings

The first, and perhaps most controversial, change brought about by the CJA 2003 is the fact that the prosecution can appeal against certain terminal rulings. Dennis notes that the term 'terminal ruling' has always been used as regards this provision but in fact the CJA 2003 does not use this specific term (Dennis (2004) 624). However, it is a good summary of what the position is as s 58 permits an appeal to be brought against a decision to accept a submission of no case to answer or a ruling that would lead to the acquittal of a person. This latter ground is brought about by s 58(8)-(9), which state that if leave to appeal or the appeal is abandoned or unsuccessful then the defendant will be formally acquitted. The essence of this condition is that the prosecution would only appeal against a ruling that leaves them in the position of offering no evidence because of the effect of such a ruling.

The prosecution must not only apply for leave to appeal (although leave can be granted by the trial judge, it is likely that the same 'exceptional' rule will be adopted as with defence appeals), they must also, at the time of the ruling, either indicate that they are going to appeal or request an adjournment so as to consider an appeal (s 58(4)).

An interesting question arises where a court refuses to grant leave to consider the issue (ie can the prosecution then later announce they wish to appeal) but in *CPS v C* [2009] EWCA Crim 2614 the Court of Appeal held that the requirement was mandatory and thus if the prosecution are denied an adjournment to consider their options they must *immediately* indicate to the judge that they intend to appeal *and* must also indicate under s 58(8) that they agree that if the appeal is unsuccessful then the defendants are to be acquitted. If either of these steps does not occur then there is no jurisdiction to hear the appeal (see also *R v LSA* [2009] EWCA Crim 1034).

If an appeal is to be brought then it is possible that the appeal could be expedited (s 59). The Act suggests that only when an appeal is not to be expedited can a jury be discharged (s 59(3)) but it is submitted that this must be read in the context of the general powers of trial judges which include the dismissal of a jury when it is not possible for a person to gain a fair trial. The purpose behind this is no doubt to ensure that lengthy trials are not started again if the prosecution appeal succeeds (if the appeal fails then, of course, no jury will be required as the defendant is acquitted) but it must be seriously questioned whether a jury could continue. Whilst they cannot, presumably, be told that an appeal has been lodged (as that would appear to be highly prejudicial) the Act does not make clear what an 'expedited' appeal is. If the expedited appeal takes longer than a few days (somewhat likely) then it is submitted that a jury will inevitably speculate as to why the trial has been adjourned for a period of several days or weeks. It has been speculated that one reason for this power is that the ruling may be in relation to only certain counts on the indictment and, therefore, the trial could take place on counts not related to the appeal (Taylor et al (2004) 88). This would only partially solve the problem as there would no doubt be speculation, but judges are used to telling juries that a count has been withdrawn from them. The difficulty is, however, that this would ordinarily lead to a formal acquittal and thus a knowledgeable jury would be able to identify why a count has been withdrawn rather than the defendant being formally acquitted of it. It would seem more straightforward to discharge the jury pending any appeal and this would be the more likely scenario.

The Court of Appeal has three options open to it when determining an appeal (s 61):

- **Uphold the ruling.** This will lead to the acquittal of the defendant on those counts that are affected by the ruling.

- **Reverse the ruling.** If the court does this then it may order that the trial is resumed or started afresh with a new jury.

- **Vary the ruling.** It may be that the prosecution are only partially successful. When this happens the Court of Appeal has the right to decide whether to acquit the defendant or to order the trial to continue/begin again.

Unlike in respect of appeals by defendants, the Court of Appeal has a much more limited discretion in deciding whether to overturn a ruling; it may only do so when it is wrong in law, involved an error of law, or was irrational (s 67) and this draws an immediate comparison to judicial review (Dennis (2004) 624) and this will certainly restrict the use of the power as irrational (meaning *Wednesbury unreasonableness*; see 5.1.2.2 above) is a relatively high threshold; mere disagreement will not suffice.

The Court of Appeal was only permitted to order the resumption of a trial or order a fresh trial when it considered that it was in the interests of justice to do so (s 61(5), CJA 2003). The *Criminal Justice and Immigration Act 2008* (CJIA 2008) has amended this provision and states that the Court of Appeal should only acquit the defendant when it is satisfied that an offender could not receive a fair trial if the matter was resumed or a new trial resumed. However, the Court of Appeal, albeit *in dicta*, has suggested that the interests of justice remain valid. In *R v A* [2008] EWCA Crim 2186 the court ruled that whilst Parliament has altered s 61(5), it is notable that the Court of Appeal must grant leave (permission) before an appeal may be brought. The court suggested that the wider interests of justice must be considered when deciding whether to permit leave to be granted (at [9]). Their Lordships suggest that if it would never be in the interests of justice for a new trial to take place then leave will simply not be granted. On a semantic level the decision is correct in that leave is required and this is frequently granted or denied after a full hearing, but it would also seem that this is an attempt by the Court of Appeal to circumvent the intentions of Parliament. Such an approach could not be taken if, as with most defence cases, the issue of leave was dealt with separately to the determination of the appeal.

Perhaps surprisingly no statistics are published on the use of the power under s 58 and so it is not possible to state how many applications for leave are made and how many applications are successful. It would obviously be of interest to those within the justice system if such statistics were published and there would seem no reason why the CPS or the *Court and Judicial Statistics* could not make this available.

13.4.2.2 Evidentiary rulings

The second type of appeal is that which relates to evidentiary rules. This owes its background more to Auld as the Law Commission had rejected the idea of an appeal against anything other than a terminatory ruling (Dennis (2004) 624–625). However, s 62 permits evidentiary rulings to be appealed in certain circumstances. There are a number of differences between s 58 and s 62 appeals. The first is that the range of offences is more limited. Section 58 appeals can be brought in any case tried on indictment whereas s 62 appeals can only be brought in those cases that have been prescribed (Sch 4). The second is that the appeal can only be brought in respect of a ruling that takes place before the opening of the defence case (s 62(2)) and this, in effect, limits the matter to rulings on prosecution applications although the vast majority are likely to be dealt with at the Plea and Directions Hearing stage (see 12.2.1 above). The third, and perhaps most significant, is that there is no requirement that the evidential ruling would be a terminal ruling: indeed if the result of the evidentiary ruling was to cause the acquittal of the person then it is more likely that s 62 would be the more appropriate appeal. That said, an appeal is only possible where it significantly weakens the prosecution case (s 63(2)) although quite what this means in practice is open to interpretation (Dennis (2005) 622).

The final difference between the sections is that an unsuccessful appeal will not automatically lead to the acquittal of the defendant. The Court of Appeal has the right to uphold, vary, or reverse the ruling made by the trial judge, and can decide whether to allow the trial to continue or start again (s 66). It may only acquit the defendant where the prosecution state that they do not wish the prosecution to continue (s 66(2)(c)), presumably in circumstances where the Court of Appeal either upholds or varies the ruling.

Areas of similarity between ss 58 and 62 are that appeals may be expedited (s 64) and the grounds upon which the Court of Appeal can determine the appeal remain the same (s 67).

It has been suggested that the case for the prosecution rights of appeal is strong (Dennis (2005) 626) and, since they are restricted solely to decisions of the law by the judge, this is probably true. Trial judges are not immune from mistakes and if, as has been suggested, the purpose of the criminal justice system is to enforce the criminal law (Dennis (2000) 945) then the public have the right to expect that mistakes that occur before the final determination of an appeal can be put right. The prosecution are sometimes thwarted by perverse or incorrect rulings and until now had no avenue available to them: the defendant would be acquitted. It was difficult to identify how that necessarily served the best interests of the criminal justice system.

13.4.3 Double jeopardy

It was noted in Chapter 12 that at the time of plea, a person can enter two special pleas known as *autrefois convict* and *autrefois acquit*, that being the person has previously been tried and either convicted or acquitted. Traditionally this was a barrier to any subsequent proceedings but the CJA 2003 has altered this position and it is now possible for a person who has previously been acquitted to be retried for the offence. This differs from a prosecution appeal in two ways. The first is that it is not an immediate remedy in the way that an appeal is. Where the prosecution believe that a judge has erred in law and that this resulted in the termination of proceedings prior to the jury retiring, then the more appropriate response will be to use the powers under Part 9 of the CJA 2003 (see 13.4.2 above). The second is that a person can be retried even if it was the decision of a jury to acquit the defendant whereas an appeal is only possible from decisions by the judge.

It has to be recognized that the proposals to modify double jeopardy were, and are, extremely controversial as it was considered to be a long-standing freedom (see, for example, Liberty (2003) 15–16 and Dennis (2004) 619) although, interestingly, it is not an absolute right in terms of either the ECHR or the EU *Charter of Fundamental Rights* (Dennis (2004) 636–637). The pressure for reform of the rule appears to stem from the *Macpherson Report* into the death of Stephen Lawrence (Taylor et al (2004) 96–97). Stephen Lawrence was a black teenager who was murdered in an unprovoked racist killing. The subsequent investigation by the police was flawed and led to the acquittal of those who were accused of his murder. The Macpherson Inquiry examined all issues surrounding the case, including allegations that the police themselves were racist in the handling of the investigation, and also the conduct of the prosecution. Recommendation 38 of the *Macpherson Report* suggested that the protection of double jeopardy should be removed. This was followed by a Law Commission report which held that there was an arguable case for the restriction of the right of double jeopardy but only to murder. This, in turn, was examined by Auld in his review of the criminal justice system and he ultimately questioned why the power should be restricted to murder and argued for a wider restriction (Auld (2001) 631–634). Ultimately this led to the introduction of the power contained in Part 10 of the CJA 2003.

It is important to note that the double jeopardy rule is not totally abrogated as it applies only to specified offences (although the number of offences is extremely wide and can be added to without the need for primary legislation (Taylor et al (2004) 100–102)). Also, it is not just for the prosecuting authorities to decide to bring a new prosecution; they must first seek permission to do so and for the acquittal to be, in effect, quashed (s 76 CJA 2003). The application must be brought with the personal consent of the DPP (Dennis (2004) 626) and is heard by the Court of Appeal (Criminal Division).

The language of the statute appears to suggest that the Court of Appeal has little say in whether the acquittal should be quashed, with s 77(1)(a) stating that if the conditions are met, then the court 'must make the order applied for'. However, it is not necessarily so straightforward since the second of the two conditions is that it is in the interests of justice for the acquittal to be quashed (s 78). This quite clearly provides the court with discretion as they can take almost any matter into consideration when deciding what is in the interests of justice. In tandem with this is the first condition which is that an acquittal can be quashed only where there is 'new and compelling' evidence to suggest that the acquittal should be set aside (s 78).

It has been suggested that the need for compelling new evidence is directly linked to the justification for permitting an exception to the double jeopardy rule in that new evidence may cast doubt on the efficiency of the criminal justice system (Dennis (2000) 945 and Dennis (2004) 631). In other words, new evidence (for example, DNA evidence which was perhaps unavailable at the time of the trial (Taylor et al (2004) 105)) may demonstrate that the criminal justice system has failed a victim and society, and that if the purpose of the criminal justice system is to enforce the criminal law then perhaps such a tainted acquittal should be quashed in the same way that a tainted conviction is (Dennis (2000) 945). Setting aside the objections to any interference with double jeopardy this point is well made. Whilst there are many reasons why the quashing of a conviction will be preferable to the quashing of an acquittal, it cannot be doubted that there have been some acquittals that, for any number of reasons, are extremely dubious and where the criminal justice system appears to be as faulty as it was in the heights of the miscarriages of justice era. The more salient question, however, is whether this justification can permit a draconian change to a fundamental right to the finality of a trial.

It is clear from the wording of the statute that the procedure is considered to be exceptional, and the fact that there are so many stages to any retrial perhaps demonstrates this. In terms of new evidence, it has been noted that although this takes the form of evidence that was not *used* at trial, the suggestion is that the mere oversight or negligence of a prosecutor in not using the evidence at the trial would not be sufficient to justify quashing an appeal (Dennis (2004) 633). The Act does not, however, require the court to consider whether this would have an impact on the acquittal (p 634) and to this extent it may be contrasted with, for example, appeals against conviction by a convicted person where the court must consider the safety of the conviction. However, it is submitted that the court will undoubtedly consider this issue when considering the 'interests of justice' as the potential impact of the evidence must, it is submitted, be a factor.

A criticism of the proposal to relax the rule of double jeopardy was that it could undermine the finality of decisions, leaving those acquitted with the constant nagging worry that they would never be left in peace by the authorities (Liberty (2003) 16) but the Act includes two quite significant safeguards (independent of those discussed above) against repeated investigations. The first is that the timing of any application to quash an acquittal is crucial since, by statute, the prosecution may only make an application against an acquittal once (s 76(5)). It is important to note that the statute expressly states only one *application* and not one order quashing the conviction. Accordingly if the application is rejected then that is the end of the matter even if, in future years, further compelling evidence is adduced. Similarly if the retrial ends in a further acquittal (other than in circumstances whereby a prosecution appeal under Part 9 of the Act can be brought) then no further applications can be brought. The second is that investigations into the acquitted persons are constrained by the Act (s 85). The Act restricts the power of arrest, search, and seizure in connection with an acquitted person, permitting it only with the written application of the DPP. Further, the application can only be made by someone of chief-officer rank (s 85(4)) which ensures that only the most significant cases are likely ever to be the subject of any application.

Case box *William Dunlop*

The first application under Part 10 of the CJA 2003 was made in November 2005 when the DPP gave personal consent to apply to the Court of Appeal for an order quashing the acquittal of William Dunlop for the murder of Julie Hogg (see CPS (2005)). The murder of Julie Hogg had been a cause célèbre in the North-East of England and, to an extent, the wider United Kingdom for many years. Dunlop had been accused of the murder and had stood trial twice, testifying each time (denying the allegation), but the juries could not reach a conclusion and he was formally acquitted.

In 2000 he was charged, and convicted, of perjury following a confession he made to a prisoner that he did, in fact, kill Hogg. In 2005 the DPP applied to the Court of Appeal presumably, in part, on the basis that the 'confession' was new and compelling evidence (it has been suggested that admissions by defendants are likely to be fruitful forms of new evidence (Dennis (2004) 633)).

The application was granted and in 2006 Dunlop pleaded guilty to murder and became the first person to be convicted of an offence having previously been acquitted. In October 2006 he was sentenced to life imprisonment.

One issue that will need to be raised in any subsequent trial will be what will the jury be told? In simple (immediate) retrials it is not uncommon for the jury not to be told anything about the original trial. Where there has been a significant gap (eg the Court of Appeal has quashed a conviction and ordered a retrial) then it is often the case that juries are directed as to the fact that there was an original trial but not to take this into account. What will the position be here? Berlins argues that a difficulty here is that if the jury are aware of the test for quashing an acquittal (new and compelling evidence) then they may question how they could ignore this evidence and not consider it so compelling as to convict (Berlins (2005) 15) but does that not turn the jury into a rubber-stamp (ibid)? It could be argued that the jury will not know that this is the test but given that juries may now include members of the criminal justice system in their ranks this cannot be guaranteed so how should a jury be directed? As yet there is no guidance on this point. In reality, however, it may well be that it is academic because the quashing of an acquittal will lead to a guilty plea on the basis that the defence will realize that it has no answer to the 'compelling' evidence.

Retrospectivity

It has been noted that the first case to be referred to the Court of Appeal seeking the quashing of an acquittal is that which relates to a murder committed in 1989 and this demonstrates an important aspect of the provisions, that being that they are retrospective. To an extent it is easy to see why this is the case: the very nature of the pressure leading to the interference with double jeopardy would imply retrospectivity but this is a significant departure from the usual rule that criminal laws cannot be retrospective.

It has been noted that the argument against retrospectivity is, in effect, the same as the arguments against the provision itself (Taylor et al (2004) 105) and that the approach is likely to be compliant with the ECHR because the issue is whether the person knew *at the time of the conduct* that it was illegal (p 106) which they would. Part 10 of the CJA 2003 does not render conduct that was lawful in the past unlawful under new laws but rather applies only when a person was acquitted of committing a crime then. On that basis it can be argued not to be an interference with Article 7. Any conviction will be based upon the substantive law then (although evidential changes since the trial will be implemented) and any punishment will be based on the maximum sentence at the time the offence was committed and not based on any changes that have been brought about since the acquittal.

The powers under Part 10 of the CJA 2003 have been rarely exercised. There have, at the time of writing, been only five applications and only two have been successful (the case of *Dunlop* discussed above and *R v A* [2009] 1 WLR 1947). This reinforces the fact that the courts—and indeed the CPS—are reluctant to step beyond double jeopardy and that an acquittal will ordinarily be the end of the matter save where there are strong public interest considerations that the acquittal amounts in itself to a miscarriage of justice.

13.5 Appeal against sentence

It is not just a conviction that will give rise to an appeal: the sentence imposed by a court can also be the subject of review. Sentencing is perhaps one of the most crucial aspects of a criminal trial as it is gives rise to emotions surrounding the proper disposition of a convicted person. Sentencing has usually marked one of the principal battlegrounds between politicians and the judiciary and is certainly an area where the legislature has increasingly become involved. This was perhaps best demonstrated in mid-2006 when a furore erupted over the sentencing of sex offenders (see, for example, the case of 'Sweeney' (Gillespie (2005b)) and *Attorney-General's Reference (Nos 14 and 15 of 2006)* [2006] EWCA Crim 1335). Over the past decade there has been an increase in 'mandatory' sentences where Parliament has sought to limit the discretion of judges, although these have been robustly contested by the courts who have normally found reasons justifying an exception where they believe the interests of justice so require (see, for example, *R v Blackall* [2005] EWCA Crim 1128). Against this background it is not surprising that sentences give rise to appeals and it is also notable that since 1988 the prosecution has a limited right to appeal against sentences, this being perhaps indicative of the political reality of sentencing.

13.5.1 Appeal by convicted person

The more usual appeal is that which is brought by the defendant. The defendant, when considering an appeal, is perfectly entitled to bring an appeal against both conviction *and* sentence even though this is the equivalent of saying, 'I did not do it, but if I did do it, I was sentenced too harshly!' Leave is required to appeal against sentence in the same way as with an appeal against conviction. In 2009 5,443 applications for leave to appeal against sentence were received of which 1,204 (22 per cent) were granted by the single judge and a further 670 were brought before the full court. Seventy-three per cent of sentence appeals were successful, a considerably higher percentage than those relating to conviction.

Whereas appeals against conviction will normally be dealt with by a panel of three judges, the same is not true of appeals against sentence and indeed it is more common for an appeal to be heard by two judges. This increases the number of potential panels of the Court of Appeal (Criminal Division) that can sit on these matters.

In the same way that an appeal against conviction is not an exercise in the appellate court deciding whether they would have reached a different conclusion, an appeal against sentence is examining whether a sentence was imposed correctly. Sentencing is perhaps more difficult in that in connection to a conviction it is possible to decide factors that may undermine the safety of a conviction whereas a sentence must reflect the individual characteristics of an offender. Sentencing is often said to be more of an art and not a science (see, for example, *Attorney-General's Reference (No 77 of 1999)* [2000] 2 Cr App R(S) 250 at 252 per Rose LJ) meaning that it is not possible to produce a mathematical formula to decide what an appropriate sentence must be. Accordingly, unless the sentence is illegal or procedurally flawed then the court must decide whether the judge could properly have reached his decision.

The two particular areas that the court concentrates on are the factual basis upon which a sentence was imposed and whether it is manifestly excessive.

13.5.1.1 Factual basis

A particular problem with convictions in the Crown Court is that it is not always clear what the factual basis is upon which a person is convicted. The reason for this is that sometimes a person will, as a matter of law, have committed an offence but the manner in which a person has committed the offence will make a significant difference to the sentence.

👁 **Example** Grievous bodily harm

Causing grievous bodily harm is an offence contrary to ss 18 or 20 of the *Offences Against the Person Act 1861* (depending on the *mens rea*) and is committed by the infliction of grievous (meaning 'really serious') bodily harm.

Let us take an example. Derek is accused of causing grievous bodily harm to Paul after they had been fighting. The prosecution case is that Derek attacked Paul in an unprovoked manner and stamped on Paul's head. Derek denies this and says that he attacked Paul after he had called him names, and that he had hit and kicked him.

Derek cannot deny that he is guilty of grievous bodily harm but, since stamping is an aggravating factor (see *Attorney-General's Reference (No 59 of 1996)* [1997] 2 Cr App R (S) 250) and provocation may be a mitigating factor, if he were to be sentenced on the basis of the prosecution case he could expect a more severe penalty than if he were sentenced on the basis of the facts put forward by the defence.

How should a court resolve the matter? It was seen in an earlier chapter that where the matter is by plea then the court has a number of options open to it. The most appropriate is that a written basis of plea is tendered (if the prosecution disagree with this basis then they could seek to try the defendant) and this, therefore, sets the factual background upon which a judge should sentence (*R v Kesler* [2001] 2 Cr App R(S) 126). The other alternative is that where a jury returns a verdict of guilty the judge can, after hearing all the evidence, decide what the likely facts accepted by the jury are (*R v Solomon and Triumph* (1984) 6 Cr App R(S) 120). This is the more complicated scenario, however, and the judge must make clear that not only is his assessment consistent with the jury's verdict, but also that he expressly states what factual basis he is basing the sentence on (see, for example, *R v Ibrahima* [2005] EWCA Crim 1436).

In these situations the Court of Appeal will simply examine whether the judge was entitled to assume the factual basis upon which he acted and whether the sentence was accurate in light of those facts.

13.5.1.2 Manifestly excessive

The most usual ground cited by appellants is that the sentence imposed by the judge is 'manifestly excessive' and should be reduced on appeal. 'Manifestly excessive' is not contained within statute but has been the traditional approach by the Court of Appeal to reviewing sentences on appeal and continues, in part, because of the doctrine of precedent. It is also a useful mechanism by which to ensure that too many appeals are not sent to the court and reinforces the point that sentencing is an art not a science.

The general basis upon which the court will act is to decide upon a range of sentences for which a person convicted of a crime is subject to and normally to interfere only when the matter is outside of this range. A classic example of this can be provided by the *dicta* of Ackner LJ (as he then was) in *R v Waddingham* (1983) 5 Cr App R(S) 66 when he differentiates between an excessive sentence and a severe sentence (p 69), the point being that a tough sentence within the range of discretion by the sentencing judge cannot be interfered with. In *R v Bibi* (1980) 2 Cr App R(S) 177 the Court of Appeal argued that it tried to achieve a consistency of approach rather than of precise mathematical comparisons and that accordingly the starting point is to identify the range and then to examine the aggravating and mitigating features.

Mitigation is the usual way in which the Court of Appeal will alter a sentence, usually arguing that a judge has not given sufficient credit for a particular factor. However, the Court of Appeal is entitled to take account of information that the sentencing judge did not have available to him, and it is not unusual for it to refer to how the person has behaved in prison pending his appeal (although this was strongly disapproved of in *Waddingham* (p 69)).

13.5.2 Unduly lenient sentence

Prior to the system of prosecution appeals the only substantive appeal the prosecution had was in connection with unduly lenient sentences. The right of the senior appellate courts to increase sentences upon appeal was removed in 1966 with the establishment of the Court of Appeal (Criminal Division) (now incorporated in s 11(3) CAA 1968) but this was soon regretted and in 1972 Dr David Thomas, perhaps the leading authority in the field of sentencing, called for a power to review lenient sentences (Thomas (1972)). During the 1980s there was increased concern over the consistency of sentencing (see Shute (1994) 746). In fact the issue of sentencing has perhaps been the most controversial topic, in part because it demonstrates the tension that will invariably exist between the elected politicians and the judiciary, especially when media attention focuses on individual cases. Eventually the pressure led to the government introducing a scheme whereby the prosecution could refer certain offences to the Court of Appeal for re-sentencing where it was thought that the sentence was 'unduly lenient'.

The statutory power for this provision is contained within ss 35 and 36 of the *Criminal Justice Act 1988* and it provides a power for the Attorney-General to refer an unduly lenient sentence to the Court of Appeal but only if it is a qualifying sentence, meaning an offence that is triable only on indictment or is prescribed by statutory instrument for this purpose (s 35(3)). The latter has proved quite controversial in part because the list of prescribed offences has not kept pace with statutory reform; for example few of the either-way offences contained in the *Sexual Offences Act 2003* has been prescribed (see Gillespie (2005b)) yet sentencing for sex offences was one of the reasons why the power was introduced.

The power has grown in use with the number of cases rising from ten in the first year of its use (Shute (1994) 747) to 108 in 2009 (A-G Office website). The Attorney-General or his deputy, the Solicitor-General, must examine each complaint personally,[7] even though members of their legal secretariat (qualified lawyers) will have reviewed the cases and provided a summary. It must be seriously doubted whether this is actually necessary. Given that the DPP has been given the authority to seek the leave of the Court of Appeal to appeal against an acquittal (see 13.4.3 above) it seems an absurd waste of time to demand the law officers to give personal consent and the jurisdiction could easily be exercised by the Crown Prosecution Service.

⮑ THE LAW OFFICERS

The Attorney-General (A-G) and his deputy, the Solicitor-General (S-G), are known as the 'Law Officers'. The S-G is by virtue of s 1 *Law Officers Act 1997* the formal deputy of the A-G and can perform any of his functions.

The A-G and S-G are political appointments and are members of one of the Houses of Parliament. The current A-G and S-G are members of the House of Commons (Rt.Hon. Dominic Grieve QC and Edward Garnier QC respectively) but prior to this, Lord Goldsmith was A-G sitting in the House of Lords.

Traditionally if the A-G or S-G are not already Queen's Counsel upon appointment this distinction will be given to them. Although the term Solicitor-General implies otherwise, the first solicitor to hold the post of S-G was the Rt Hon Harriet Harman QC who was appointed in 2001. Prior to that time all holders of the post were barristers.

As political appointees the Law Officers must resign when asked by the prime minister to do so and/or when the government falls. Neither is of cabinet rank although the A-G will attend cabinet when required. Although political, the A-G and S-G's primary role is to be the principal legal advisors of the government and they act apolitically when performing their legal functions.

It is important to note that even if the matter is a qualifying offence it is not certain that an offence will be altered; the sentence must be 'unduly lenient'. Theoretically leave is required from the Court of Appeal to bring such an appeal but in *Attorney-General's Reference (No 24 of 1991)* (1992) 13 Cr App R(S) 724 the Court of Appeal indicated that it was administratively preferable for the substance of the matter and the leave to

---

7. *Hansard*, HL Deb, vol 653, col 882 (14 October 2003) per Lord Goldsmith.

be heard at the same time (pp 725–726). This, however, confuses the substantive and leave steps and undoubtedly causes delay and wasted court time (Gillespie (2005b) 8).

An illustration of the meaning of 'unduly lenient' can be found in *Attorney-General's Reference (No 4 of 1989) (1990) 90 Cr App R 366* where the Court of Appeal stated that it would not interfere with a sentence when it thought it was different to that which it would have imposed but gave the following definition:

> A sentence is unduly lenient...where it falls outside the range of sentences which the judge, applying his mind to all the relevant factors, could reasonably consider appropriate. (p 371 per Lord Lane CJ)

The requirement to have regard to the range of sentences undoubtedly sets the threshold reasonably high: the sentence must be outside the normal range of sentences. This can be contrasted with the appeal against sentence by the defendant where the court is prepared to interfere at a much lower range. Even if the court does decide that a sentence is unduly lenient any alteration of the sentence is discretionary (Gillespie (2005b) 9). Accordingly, the Court of Appeal could decide that it is not going to interfere with a sentence irrespective of the fact that it is unduly lenient (see, for example, *Attorney-General's Reference (No 1 of 2003) [2003] EWCA Crim 1051*).

Rather controversially, the Court of Appeal argued that there was an element of 'double jeopardy' involved in a prosecutorial appeal in that a prisoner faces the trauma of being re-sentenced. This invariably leads to a discount being awarded and the courts have said that this is especially relevant where a person is to be imprisoned after initially being handed a non-custodial sentence. It is possible to see the justification for a discount under these circumstances but it is less easy to justify the discretion when an offender is already incarcerated, where all that is being discussed is the length of incarceration and not the possibility of being deprived of liberty once again (see Gillespie (2005b) 9). Persons subject to an unduly lenient sentence have been convicted of a specified offence and the sentence imposed was one that was outside the usual range of sentences, ie almost certainly less than that which the person had expected to receive. Is any trauma caused in such circumstances?

The government believed that giving a discount for 'double jeopardy' was wrong, especially in the most serious offences. The CJIA 2008 has amended the law so as to preclude a discount for 'double jeopardy' being given where the sentence imposed is a discretionary life sentence (mandatory life sentences were already exempt from this principle by the CJA 2003) or certain other sentences, most notably imprisonment for public protection. Where a determinate sentence is being reviewed, however, the principle still exists and the court continues to give a discount (see, for example, *Attorney-General's Reference (No 42 of 2008) [2008] EWCA Crim 2660*.

13.6 Appeals to the Supreme Court

It is possible to appeal against a decision from the Court of Appeal to the Supreme Court (s 33 *Criminal Appeal Act 1968*). Either party can appeal the matter irrespective of who brought the matter to the Court of Appeal (ie if the defendant appealed against conviction to the Court of Appeal the prosecution can appeal to the Supreme Court). For the matter to be heard by the Supreme Court it is necessary for the Court of Appeal to certify a point of general public importance is raised in the case (s 33(2)) and leave must be sought either from the Court of Appeal or the Supreme Court directly. An interesting issue arose in *R v Dunn* [2010] EWCA Crim 1823 where the Court of Appeal refused to certify a point of public importance. The appellant sought to argue that this was a breach of Article 6 ECHR because the Court of Appeal was, in essence, sitting in judgment on its own decision and was biased. The appellant sought to argue that since the Court of Appeal would not wish to be reversed by the Supreme Court it could, by declining to certify a point, prevent a case from reaching the Supreme Court. Perhaps unsurprisingly the Court of Appeal ruled against the submission noting that the certification point was separate from the merits and that an impartial observer would not consider it to be biased when making the decision. The requirement for points of law to be certified exists in both the civil and criminal jurisdiction and is seen by the courts as a method of ensuring that only the most important cases appear before the Supreme Court. As was seen from Chapter 6 the Supreme Court has the capacity to only hear a limited number of cases and the certification process is a part of the filter mechanism.

13.7 Miscarriages of justice: the Criminal Cases Review Commission

It has been noted already that there was, during the 1970s and 1980s a series of miscarriages of justice that began to undermine public confidence in the criminal justice system. Part of the difficulty with the miscarriages were that they centred on terrorism trials and the person with responsibility for deciding whether to refer a matter back to the Court of Appeal, following an unsuccessful appeal after trial, was the Home Secretary and there was at the very least the appearance of bias in terms of whether to refer a matter to the court. The office of Home Secretary became increasingly political recently with Michael Howard, David Blunkett, and Charles Clarke adopting an extremely combative attitude towards the criminal justice system and, in particular, the imprisonment of offenders. Whilst a politician was responsible for decisions to refer matters to the Court of Appeal, ie considering whether the criminal justice system had made a terrible mistake, there was concern that politics might interfere.

The *Criminal Appeal Act 1995* (CAA 1995) removed the political aspect of the decision from the Home Secretary through the establishment of the *Criminal Cases Review Commission* (CCRC) which from 1997 replaced the Home Secretary as the referring body for fresh appeals (s 9 CAA 1995). There are two principal methods by which the Commission can become involved. The first (and more usual) is that a convicted person will make an application to the Commission for a matter to be referred. There were early fears that the Commission would be overwhelmed by applications (Zander (2007) 728) and although there has been a significant backlog at times, it would appear that the Commission has managed to clear the backlog whilst concentrating on key cases (for details of the backlog see CCRC (2005) 25 and for a wider discussion see Kerrigan (2006) 126–127). The second way that the Commission may become involved is that the Court of Appeal can direct that the Commission investigate a matter and report to it (s 15 CAA 1995). This power is rarely exercised (CCRC (2005) 32) but it is a useful power where the Court of Appeal suspects that an issue may arise in a case before it. A direction under s 15 allows the case to be investigated whereas the Court of Appeal does not, of course, have any such power and merely adjudicates upon appeals.

Although the Commission is undoubtedly independent, it is interesting to note that not everyone necessarily believes that this is preferable. Some suggest that a difficulty with the Commission is that it is not directly accountable to Parliament in the way that the Home Office, through the Home Secretary, was (Nobles and Schiff (2000) 224). That is not to say, however, that there is no accountability and the Commission must issue an annual report to the Justice Secretary (Sch 1 CAA 1995) and they can be, and indeed have in the past been, called before Parliamentary Select Committees to discuss their work. Aside from accountability others argue that there is less freedom to refer matters since political pressure could sometimes have persuaded the Home Secretary to refer cases where there was little prospect of success whereas the Commission can only refer where there is a 'real possibility' of success (Nobles and Schiff (2000) 224–225). Whether this is an appropriate criticism, however, must be seriously questioned since the Court of Appeal is overburdened with work and so referring hopeless cases to the court for political reasons does not seem a particularly appropriate way to proceed.

The issue of 'real possibility', however, can cause problems with some suggestions that this means that the 'lurking doubt' cases will never be referred since the Commission needs to identify some tangible ground (Nobles and Schiff (2000) 221). It has been suggested that as an abstract term it is relatively meaningless (Kerrigan (2006) 133) and that this means that the Commission must take notice of the working practice of the Court of Appeal (Ashworth and Redmayne (2010) 391) and that, in essence, this means that something 'new' (not necessarily evidence) is required before a matter could be referred. Where the 'new' matter is evidence there would appear to be an additional hurdle because not only should the Commission ask itself whether this would affect the safety of the conviction, it must also consider whether the evidence would, in fact, be admissible within the Court of Appeal (ibid). Where the matter is one of due process it is perhaps easier to deal with since the court has identified that human rights requirements will usually mean that the safety of such convictions will be questioned, and accordingly the discovery of due process arguments may assist the Commission but only where they were not known at the time of the trial.

The CJIA 2008 has also resolved one question about 'old' appeals. The CCRC had begun to send cases to the Court of Appeal where the sole ground of appeal was that statutory law had overridden the previous common-law rules under which the person had been convicted, ie the law had changed. The Court of Appeal itself would ordinarily refuse to allow leave to appeal to defendants in such cases but this was not possible when the matter was referred by the CCRC since leave is not required. The CJIA 2008 amendment allows for the Court of Appeal to dismiss the appeal where the only ground for the appeal is that there has been a new development in the law and where, had the appellant himself petitioned the court, leave would not have been granted (s 43 CJIA 2008).

Ashworth and Redmayne argue that the Commission does, when deciding which cases to refer, get its balance correct and this would seem to be borne out by the statistics. By 2009/10 the CCRC reported that 70.1 per cent of cases referred to it by the Court of Appeal succeeded (CCRC (2010) p 22), suggesting that the CCRC is largely referring the correct cases to the Court. Perhaps the more difficult issue to examine is that of whether sufficient cases are being referred. By the year 2009/10 it was reported that since its creation, only 454 cases had been referred to the Court of Appeal out of 11,871 cases completed (ie not just applications received but those that had been reviewed) (CCRC (2010) p 21) meaning that the referral rate is 3.8 per cent. It is always going to be difficult to identify whether sufficient cases are being referred (Ashworth and Redmayne (2010) 392) in part because the CCRC suffers from the same difficulty the Court of Appeal has in that some convicted persons will have nothing to lose by applying (the Commission, in contrast to the court, does not have the power to order the loss of time served). Many convicted persons will simply be applying because they disagree with the decision rather than because they can identify any particular fault in the process.

The resources of the Commission must, however, have an impact on the work of the body and successive annual reports of the chair of the Commission complain that the CCRC is under-resourced, and the 2009/10 report indicated that staffing within the Commission had reduced from 40.9 full-time equivalent casework staff to 35.4 (CCRC (2010) p 19) which is a significant drop. The chair of the CCRC also noted that the CCRC had been subject to four-years of real-time reductions in its budget (CCRC (2010) p 6). This perhaps returns us to the issue of accountability since it is ultimately a matter for the executive, through the Justice Secretary, to decide the budget of the Commission and this means the executive is still able, to an extent, to influence the appellate system, albeit at a policy level rather than at an individual level.

 ## Summary

This article has examined how an appeal from a decision of a first instance criminal court is dealt with. In particular, it has shown that:

- The paths of appeals differ depending on the mode of trial of the original criminal hearing.
- There are two potential criminal appeal avenues from a summary trial: either to the Divisional Court (by way of case stated or (exceptionally) judicial review) or to the Crown Court.
- Appeal from the Crown Court is to the Court of Appeal (Criminal Division).
- An appeal ordinarily requires leave (permission) but appealing to the Crown Court from the magistrates' court does not require leave.

 ## End-of-chapter questions

1. In *R v Hanratty* [2002] 3 All ER 534 the Lord Chief Justice said: 'We do however emphasise that there have to be exceptional circumstances to justify incurring the expenditure of resources…including those of this Court, on a case of this age.' This was in connection with a murder case that took place in 1962 and for which the offender was executed later that year. The judgment in this case alone consisted of 215 paragraphs spread over eighteen pages in the law reports. In *R v Nicholson* [2004] EWCA Crim 2840 the Court of Appeal quashed a conviction for theft that dated back to 1957. The Court stated that it

did not condone the referral of historic cases but accepted that an error had been made in this case. Should the Commission refer historic cases or do you think that its time and money would be better spent in referring cases where the applicant is still in, or has been recently released from, prison?

2. Kerrigan (2006) argues that the Commission is not using its powers correctly in referring miscarriages of justice that occur in summary trials. Should the CCRC deal with summary matters or is it designed to protect public confidence through examining only serious cases that are heard in the Crown Court?

3. Read pp 397–401 of Ashworth and Redmayne (2010). Was it right to abolish the rule of double jeopardy? Can the powers be abused by the police or are there sufficient safeguards built into the legislation?

 ## Further reading

Kerrigan K (2006) 'Miscarriages of justice in the magistrates' court: The forgotten power of the Criminal Cases Review Commission' *Criminal Law Review* 124–129.

This is a fascinating article that considers the power of the CCRC to appeal decisions within a summary trial. It raises important issues about the status of convictions (ie whether a summary conviction is as important as a conviction by the Crown Court).

Leigh LH (2006) 'Lurking doubt and the safety of convictions' *Criminal Law Review* 809–816.

This is an interesting article which examines how appeals are determined by the Court of Appeal, including where there is no flaw in the trial process.

Roberts S and Malleson K (2002) 'Streamlining and clarifying the appellate process' *Criminal Law Review* 272–282.

This is an interesting critique of the Auld proposals in respect of criminal appeals, particularly the prosecution right of appeal.

Spencer JR (2006) 'Does our present criminal appeal system make sense?' *Criminal Law Review* 677–694.

This is a comprehensive article which examines the history of criminal appeals and discusses, in particular, the absurdity of two appeal mechanisms from a summary trial.

 For multiple choice questions, updates to this chapter and links to useful websites, please visit the Online Resource Centre at

www.oxfordtextbooks.co.uk/orc/gillespie_els3e/

PART IV

Civil Disputes

14

Civil Litigation

By the end of this chapter you will be able to:

- Understand the basic elements of civil litigation.
- Identify the three 'tracks' through which cases are heard.
- Identify the broad approaches the courts take to the issue of costs.
- Understand how a small claims matter proceeds through the court.
- Understand how a judicial review proceeds through the court.

Introduction

It is now time to turn our attention away from the criminal justice system to civil procedure. Although the criminal justice system is probably responsible for the majority of the headlines and stories within the media, the civil justice system is more frequently used. The civil system straddles numerous different type of cases from public child-law cases (where the courts have to decide whether a child should be removed from its parents) through divorces to high-value litigation (eg the Wembley dispute where the parties sued for a combined total of £66,000,000) and then through to public remedies such as judicial review.

This chapter will take a slightly different approach to the issue of litigation. It is divided into three distinct sections. The first discusses some of the general issues relating to civil litigation and then sections two and three will detail some hypothetical case studies. Each part will examine one aspect of the civil justice system and detail how a case will proceed through the process. The aspects that will be examined are the small claims court and judicial review.

14.1 Civil litigation

The civil justice system partners the criminal justice system in providing a forum through which disputes of law can be resolved. The disputes, however, can be quite varied. It is often said that the English Legal System does not operate a separate court system for 'public law' in that there are no separate courts that deal with matters relating to the resolution of disputes between the state and the citizen. However, this is not strictly true since, as you will see from related modules, there is now a distinct body of law known either as *Administrative Law* or *Public Law* which details how citizens can hold the government to account for their actions. Indeed arguably there is now a de facto separate court in that that there is now a court known as the Administrative Court where such matters are heard. However, technically this is just part of the High Court of Justice and so the convention may still hold. Setting aside public-law matters the civil justice system predominantly concerns disputes between citizens. Chapter 15 details alternative bodies that have been created to resolve certain specialist disputes, known as tribunals, and Chapter 16 details methods of resolving disputes without recourse to litigation.

14.1.1 The Woolf reforms

In the 150 years between 1850 and 2000 there were sixty reports that examined the state of litigation (Andrews (2000) 20) but perhaps the more important of these are the recent ones, especially those reports into civil litigation conducted by Lord Woolf. The Woolf reports, which led to the establishment of the Civil Procedure Rules (CPR) regime, provided a framework for the wholesale reform of the civil justice system. Woolf had found that the civil system remained crippled by high costs, excessive delays, and complexities of trials. Lightman J, speaking extrajudicially, argued that this was endemic within the system and suggested that litigation was analogous to a game of cricket:

> In summary, each side prepares its team for the contest. One side in turn goes into bat...and faces the bowling of the other side...then the other side takes its turn at the wicket...Throughout, an independent third party umpire...watches, listens, and enforces the rules, and at the end of the game gives his decision as to the winner. (Lightman (2003) 236)

Lightman J also argued that this analogy was complete because 'both are slow and boring' (ibid). It could probably be taken further by suggesting that although the average person may understand the broad principles of both cricket and the law, they probably do not know the specific rules and tactics of the game without assistance. He argues that the principal difficulty with civil litigation is, therefore, the fact that it is adversarial.

Lightman J is not alone in this belief and it has been suggested that the adversarial nature of proceedings is an impediment to justice. Indeed it has been said:

> There is...a fundamental error in the way in which, on the whole, attempts at reform of civil justice have so far been approached. It is that they have...accepted that [trials] should remain, primarily, a system for resolution of disputes by trial and judgment...(Davies (2006) 33)

The objection of some is that an adversarial approach to dispute resolution is, in essence, merely a 'gladiatorial' contest between two parties with each seeking to 'trick' the other and make the position more complicated and certainly more time-consuming (Lightman (2003) 239). Woolf argued that these criticisms could be met without the need to abandon the principles of adversarial litigation if there were two principal changes. The first is that there would be an encouragement to participate in alternative dispute resolution, and the second was that rather than being a passive umpire the judge should assume control of the proceedings. An important aspect of this change is that the court may make procedural orders on its own motion rather than wait for either party to apply for directions (Andrews (2000) 26). It has been suggested that the result of these changes is that the parties can no longer either individually or collectively set the evidential or procedural agenda but it has also been noted that such powers could, if misused, threaten 'a serious loss of impartiality and the risk of prejudgment by the court' (Andrews (2000) 33). The remedy for the latter would be an appeal but this would be contrary to the overall objective which is to reduce delays and costs.

What of the push towards alternative dispute resolution (ADR)? ADR is discussed elsewhere in this book (Chapter 16) but does the CPR encourage ADR in preference to litigation? Lightman argues that it should since his (judicial) experience is that properly managed mediation can settle amicably most disputes with lower costs (Lightman (2003) 241) but he notes that the courts cannot force someone to engage in ADR. Thus the CPR provides incentives to engage in ADR, for example permitting it to be taken into account at the costs stage, but does not require it. Davies is critical of this and suggests that unless ADR is brought within the court system—ie by stating that disputes must proceed through ADR before litigation may begin—then there is no incentive for lawyers to advise their clients to proceed through ADR (Davies (2006) 41).

Nevertheless the Woolf reforms are generally considered to be a step forward. How they are put in practice will be examined in the rest of this chapter.

14.1.2 Civil Procedure Rules

The procedural rules governing civil disputes are now, in effect, codified—ie all the rules are set out in a document and it means that all parties are aware of their responsibilities and how a court will treat their cases. The Civil Procedure Rules (CPR) are currently on draft 53.[1]

⮕ REFERRING TO CPR

In order to refer to the CPR and accompanying practice direction in an understandable way, I will be referring to them in the following manner.

- **Rules.** The CPR consists of 79 parts, each with individual rules. The convention CPR Part. Rule will be adopted: CPR 31.2 means rule number 2 in Part 31 of the CPR.
- **Sub-rules.** These will follow the usual convention of brackets, eg 31.2(1).
- **Practice Directions**. Whilst it is technically one practice direction, in essence each Part has its own practice direction relating to it. The convention PD Part.Paragraph will be adopted: PD 31.7.6 means the Practice Direction relating to Part 31, paragraph 7.6.

All CPR and Practice Directions are available publicly on the Internet and the Online Resource Centre accompanying this book provides a link to them.

14.1.2.1 Underlying principles

It is notable that the CPR contain a definition of purpose (Rule 1.1),[2] known as the 'overriding objective' which states:

(1) These rules are a new procedural code with the overriding objective of enabling the court to deal with cases justly.

(2) Dealing with a case justly includes, so far as is practicable–

    (a) ensuring that the parties are on an equal footing;

    (b) saving expense;

    (c) dealing with the case in ways which are proportionate–

        (i) to the amount of money involved;

        (ii) to the importance of the case;

        (iii) to the complexity of the issues; and

        (iv) to the financial position of each party;

    (d) ensuring that it is dealt with expeditiously and fairly; and

    (e) allotting it an appropriate share of the court's resources, while taking into account the need to allot resources to other cases.

---

1. At the time of writing: Autumn 2010.
2. Note that the rules are numbered n.n and do not follow the convention followed in legislation.

In essence the CPR overriding objective is to attempt to set out a definition of the purpose of litigation. Lightman has suggested that the purpose is that:

> [t]he law and the legal system should be a protection, a safeguard, a source of peace of mind, to which recourse should be available by all at an affordable cost (Lightman (2003) 236).

He suggests that this is what the CPR should assist in encouraging through the Woolf reforms. However, he remained somewhat sceptical as to whether this has happened yet. His major suggestion, perhaps mirroring that of Davies (above), is that the system should move to a more inquisitorial approach (p 246). It can be seen immediately, however, that the CPR's overriding objective appears to enshrine the adversarial system by encouraging the court to ensure, so far as is practicable, that the parties are on an equal footing (CPR 1.1(2)(a)), which suggests that the spectre of two gladiators fighting for the eventual win remains in place.

The consequences of this adversarial approach are that specific rules of disclosure ensure that both sides have advance sight of the evidence. In this way the court can be presented with detailed information without the need to adjourn, but it does nothing to encourage agreements as to the evidential basis of the case. Disclosure is an important part of civil litigation and the court has specific powers to deal with non-disclosure, including rendering the documents inadmissible without the leave of the court (CPR 31.21), although it would be unlikely to do so where the parties acted in good faith.

⊃ COOPERATION

It has been held that the overriding objective of the CPR, including the duty to cooperate, means that it is not possible to take advantage of a technical breach of the rules (see, for example, *Hertsmere Primary Care Trust v Estate of Rabindra-Anandh* [2005] EWHC 20. This is different from the 'old' approach to litigation where opposing sides would not infrequently take advantage of technical breaches or mistakes by opposing sides.

The notion of proportionality contained within the primary objective is also important. In the past there have been cases where people have fought over relatively small sums of money with the costs easily eclipsing the sum awarded in compensation. There is little point in such a battle and the courts are not there to settle spurious claims. The CPR ensures that matters are kept in proportion (to the extent that this is possible) and this includes assessing how the case should proceed.

It was noted above that Woolf had identified that the courts had not taken a particularly proactive stance in case management prior to the introduction of CPR with the parties having the main responsibility. The rules are designed to reverse this onus and ensure that the court has the primary responsibility for case management (CPR 1.4(1)). The court should maintain active case management through, for example:

(a) encouraging the parties to cooperate with each other in the conduct of the proceedings;

(b) identifying the issues at an early stage;

(c) deciding promptly which issues need full investigation and trial and accordingly dispose summarily of the others;

(d) deciding the order in which issues are to be resolved;

(e) encouraging the parties to use an alternative dispute resolution;

(f) helping the parties to settle the whole or part of the case;

(g) fixing timetables or otherwise controlling the progress of the case;

(h) considering whether the likely benefits of taking a particular step justify the cost of taking it;

(i) dealing with as many aspects of the case as it can on the same occasion;

(j) dealing with the issue without the parties needing to attend at court;

(k) making use of technology; and

(l) giving directions to ensure that the trial of a case proceeds quickly and efficiently.

(CPR 1.4(2))

This reinforces the perception that civil proceedings post-Woolf will be more tightly controlled and it is notable that many of these 'case management' steps are designed to facilitate the avoidance of court. In some sectors of the law it was a popular maxim that a party had lost if it reached court, and to an extent this remains true with counsel spending considerable time in attempting to settle a case amicably rather than use the courts. The early steps within rule 1.4 are also important as it demonstrates that the judge is not just an umpire in this dispute; the rule permits him to decide what the issues of relevance are, and this can limit the full extent of the case, requiring perhaps reduced disclosure. Without this rule every issue raised by the claimants would be dealt with even if it were speculative.

An important issue in respect of the CPR is that law should be accessible. Woolf noted that one of the barriers to traditional civil litigation was that it was simply not understandable by many of the users of the service, requiring the expense of lawyers. Whilst many still prefer to engage lawyers, and indeed with moderate-to-high value claims it would be desirable to do so, the CPR introduced a simpler way of dealing with matters. One of the most important principles was the abolition of 'legalese', ie the language that was unique to the law and normally based on Latin. Many familiar aspects of the language, eg 'writ' (now a 'claim form') and 'affidavit' (now 'witness statement') have been swept aside. The courts have stated that the ordinary meaning of words should ordinarily be used (*Vinos v Marks & Spencer plc* [2001] 3 All ER 784) and this has the intention of ensuring that the law remains accessible to those who wish to litigate in person. This is reinforced by the overriding objective where the court should ensure that parties cooperate: this could mean that where one side is not familiar with the technical aspects of a case the implications of the opposing side's actions should be explained to them by their lawyers.

14.1.2.2 Enforcement

The CPR aims to ensure that decisions are dealt with justly and empowers courts to take control of the proceedings in order to ensure an effective case management process; but how do the courts enforce this? There are a number of possibilities, the most extreme being the ability to dismiss an application/claim if the person bringing the claim fails to adhere to an order of the court (CPR 3.4). It is also possible to award summary judgment (ie permit the application/claim to succeed without the need for a hearing) if the respondent fails to adhere to ruling as to a defence.

Striking out or awarding judgment are extreme sanctions and would normally be exceptional courses of action. One alternative to the absolute action is to limit the sanction by striking out (or awarding summary judgment) in respect of part of the claim/defence. This may be appropriate where, for example, either party has provided information in respect of all but one aspect of the claim or defence. Any decision as to these powers is subject to the overriding purpose of CPR and, therefore, this will only apply where it is 'just' to do so.

The more usual sanctions are an 'unless' order or a costs order.

'Unless' orders

An 'unless' order is, in effect, a warning; it is where a court will reiterate the requirement and provide for an automatic sanction if it is breached (CPR 3.5). Theoretically there is no need for breach to have occurred prior to an 'unless' order; a court could impose it prior to breach where the other side adduces sufficient evidence to demonstrate that it is unlikely that the party will comply. However, it appears more usual for them to apply after the non-compliance with a procedure.

Sime argues that the preference is for the date and sanction to be imposed on the face of the order.

 Example Time limit

The claimant has failed to respond to a direction requiring further details of their claim. The respondent applied to the court for it to enforce the directions, the hearing taking place on 1 June 2010. The judge decides that the claimant should have six working days to comply or the judge will waive interest for a full month. The order would be phrased as:

Unless the claimant serves further details of his claim as identified by the respondent by 4 pm on day and/or date the claimant shall, if the claim succeeds, lose interest on the claim amounting to one calendar month.

The alternative is to place a 'countdown' onto the order by stating that the sanction will arise *n* days after the delivery of the order. This would be used where the party in default did not attend the hearing (Sime (2005) 280).

Costs

Perhaps the most flexible resource available to a judge is costs (Sime (2005) 459). It has already been noted that the costs involved in litigation can be significant, and whilst the CPR was supposed to reduce these to an extent, they remain an important part of the litigation process. The general rule is that the loser is responsible not only for the costs of either bringing or defending the action, but also for the costs of the other side (CPR 44.3(2)). There are, of course, exceptions to this and one of the more important exceptions is where the judge decides to use costs as a sanction against non-compliance with the rules (see, for example, *Re Elgindata Ltd (No 2)* [1992] 1 WLR 1207 and now CPR 44.3).

Where, therefore, further delay is introduced because a party does not comply with a direction it is likely that the party causing the delay will be liable for all the costs incurred through that delay regardless of whether they ultimately succeed. Where a hearing is required to seek compliance then it is quite likely that the costs could be quite significant. Sime notes that non-compliance has now been taken to include not coming within the ethos of the CPR reforms, most notably through a breach of the overriding objective (Sime (2005) 456), eg by failing to cooperate or concentrating on issues that are not strictly relevant.

The flexibility a judge has over costs includes the possibility of deciding that an interim costs order should be made; ie instead of waiting till the end of the proceedings and settling the costs in the usual manner, the judge could order the defaulting party to pay costs immediately, or even decide that interest can be added to the costs. In effect this means that although the costs will be for a particular fee that sum will grow according to the statutory interest rate from the date incurred or a date fixed by the judge (CPR 44.3(6)).

Wasted costs order

Perhaps the most draconian costs order that can be made is that known as the wasted costs order. This is an order of the court which requires the lawyer to be personally responsible for some, or all, of the costs in respect of an action (s 51(6) *Supreme Court Act 1981* (SCA 1981)). Normally, of course, it will be the litigants rather than the lawyer who will be responsible for any costs but this order is designed to mark the court's disapproval of inappropriate, unethical, or negligent conduct by a lawyer.

A party (including the party the lawyer represented) may apply for a wasted courts order or the court may do so on its own motion where it believes that it is just to do so. The lawyer has the right to make representations to the court as to *why* an order should not be made against him but ultimately it is for the judge to decide.

Where the order is made at the end of proceedings and upon the application of a party it is possible that the wasted costs order will be a deferral, ie the order is removed from the total costs bill owed to the lawyer.

Answering enforcement

It is quite possible that a party will admit that they have not complied with a direction for whatever reason and the rules provide for them to be able to apply for an extension of time during which the ruling or direction will be adhered to. Sime makes the point that this differs from an application to extend time prior to the deadline passing (Sime (2005) 281) and at the very least this would almost certainly involve the party paying additional costs. Granting an extension is discretionary but there will be circumstances when granting the extension will be justified and, indeed, it can be argued that it will often be 'just' to grant the extension and allow the litigation to proceed as planned. This will not necessarily mean that a sanction will not be imposed but it may mitigate it slightly. At the very least it is likely that the party failing to comply will be responsible for extra costs but they may not be punitive.

14.1.3 Identifying the court

It was noted in Chapter 3 that there are a number of civil courts but the two primary ones for our purposes are the *county court* and the *High Court* which is, of course, divided into three divisions. Woolf argued that there was too great a distinction between the county and High Courts and the CPR has established a single set of rules that govern all cases regardless of where they begin. This replaced the previous situation where the county and High Courts had their own rules (known respectively as the

County Court Rules and Rules of the Supreme Court).[3] It is often said that a litigant has the right to choose the court in which the action will begin but this is not strictly true. There is a residual right to start proceedings in any court but only where the rules or customs do not require the action to start in a particular court.

Table 14.1 Identifying the court

County court	Small claims actions
	Consumer Credit Agreements under £25,000
	Most domestic tenancy issues
	Personal injury cases under £50,000
	General actions under £25,000
	Most divorce cases
High Court: QBD	Judicial review (will be heard in the Administrative Court)
	Personal injury cases over £50,000
	Admiralty decisions (normally heard in the Admiralty Court)
	Commercial matters (heard in the Commercial Court)
	Defamation
	General proceedings of a significant nature requiring common-law remedies
High Court: Ch D	Sale, exchange, or partition of land
	Mortgages
	Trusts and the execution of estates
	Most company law matters
High Court: Fam D	Complex divorce cases
	Complex child and family cases
	Cases requiring the inherent jurisdiction of the court (mainly public child-care or medical cases)

That said, there will always be exceptions particularly where, for example, important issues relating to the *Human Rights Act 1998* are involved. There is also the opportunity for cases to be transferred between divisions if the case raises particularly complicated situations that the judiciary within the 'home' division would not be familiar with.

14.1.3.1 The wrong court

What happens if a litigant chooses the wrong court? Theoretically where the claim has been lodged for an inappropriate reason the matter could be struck out as an abuse of process (see *Restick v Crickmore* [1994] 2 All ER 112). The more likely sanction, however, is that the matter will be moved to the correct court and the claimant will bear the costs related to such transfer. Indeed s 51(8) SCA 1981 states that if the claim succeeds a penalty of up to 25 per cent of the overall costs may also be deducted as a result of the

---

3. The Rules of Supreme Court still exist (although they are now known as the Rules of the Senior Courts) as they provide for issues in respect of the particular jurisdictions of the Senior Courts (ie Crown Court, High Court, Court of Appeal). The CPR, however, provides for the rules of civil litigation.

inappropriate action. Where it is a bona fide mistake it is more likely that the transfer and actual costs of transfer would be imposed.

14.1.3.2 Transfer

Regardless of whether the claimant believes that the matter has begun in the correct court, it can be transferred to another court (usually county court to High Court or vice versa) upon an application by a party (most likely a respondent) or the court itself. A party may choose a transfer for any number of reasons, not least the fact that High Court proceedings will generally be more costly than county court matters. There is also the issue of venue: the vast majority of High Court matters are heard in London although both Queen's Bench and Family Division judges will travel on circuit and certain court centres (eg Cardiff, Leeds, Manchester, and Newcastle) will ordinarily have at least one High Court judge in attendance during each term. The judges can also be supplemented by 'deputy judges' (see Chapter 7) who may be circuit judges acting as a judge of the High Court or a recorder; but, even with these judges supplementing the permanent judiciary most matters will be heard in London.

There is also the difficulty that because of the small number of High Court judges available (not least because judges of the Queen's Bench Division will also sit in the Crown Court and the Court of Appeal) there will ordinarily be longer delays in the High Court than the county court and this may be a reason why either a party or the court itself will transfer the matter.

The shortage of High Court judges has long been a matter of concern for the judiciary and Woolf had noted this problem and suggested that care should be taken to ensure that matters were brought before a High Court judge only when necessary and not where desired. This decision will be based not just on monetary value but also complexity and the issues raised by the case. The notion of complexity is quite controversial since why should it automatically follow that High Court judges (or indeed members of the profession 'acting' as High Court judges) will necessarily be more competent than their circuit judge colleagues? It was seen in Chapter 7 that the qualifications for appointment differ slightly between circuit and puisne judges but in practice they are drawn from the same calibre of persons.

14.1.4 Allocating tracks

Whilst there is now a single set of procedural rules that govern litigation, it is still possible to differentiate between the forms of litigation. It will be remembered that Woolf had suggested that litigation should wherever possible be simplified. A system of 'tracks' was set up to deal with most litigation save where specific rules set out specialist procedures (eg judicial review, divorce proceedings, etc). There are three principal tracks:

- Small claims track
- Fast track
- Multi-track.

It is a judicial decision as to which track a case will be assigned to, but where there is consensus between the parties then this will normally be adhered to.

14.1.4.1 Small claims track

This is the simplest track and will be discussed below. As a basic rule any general dispute under £5,000 will be assigned to this track (CPR 26.6) although this is subject to some exceptions, most notably:

- personal injury where the compensation claim for pain and suffering is over £1,000
- claims by tenants requiring landlords to undertake more than £1,000 of work
- claims by tenants relating to harassment by landlords or unlawful eviction
- claims involving disputed allegations of dishonesty.

Even where the claim falls within these bands if it raises issues of complexity then it may be removed from the small claims track (CPR 26.7). The parties can consent to a higher-value claim being heard in the small claims track but the judge has to approve this. Where the claim is only nominally higher, however, then this may be an attractive proposition not least because of the costs involved.

14.1.4.2 Fast track

The second track is the fast track and it is generally used for the next band of litigation. Where a claim broadly falls between £5,000 and £15,000 it will be allocated to the fast track. Where the exceptions to the small claims court apply they will normally fit within the fast track. The financial band is only one aspect however and a matter will only be placed within the fast track where there is an expectation that the trial will ordinarily last no longer than one day and involve no more than two experts (CPR 26.6). Where the expected length of the trial is more than one day then this will not automatically lead to the case being assigned to the multi-track but it becomes more likely.

The matter will be heard only in the county courts by either a district or circuit judge, including a deputy judge. An advantage of the fast track procedures is that they become easier to timetable since they will ordinarily last one day. This trial length is often achieved as a result of standard procedures setting down how the trial will proceed (CPR 28.2, 28.3). If these procedures are adopted then after the initial paperwork (see below) the trial should ordinarily take place within thirty weeks of the directions hearing (CPR 28.2). The rules provide that as much of the directions as possible should take place by agreement and this is in compliance with the overriding objective of the CPR.

To further expedite the trial an indexed bundle of documents contained in a ring binder must be lodged within the court not less than three but not more than seven days before the trial. There is an expectation that the judge will read all the documents contained within the bundle (PD 28, 8.2) and this does raise again the question as to whether litigation is now adversarial or inquisitorial. The judge is likely to waive opening speeches (Sime (2005) 265) and will only welcome submissions on the contentious arguments. That said, however, judicial activism can only go so far without it inviting a submission that it interferes with the party's rights under Article 6 of the *European Convention on Human Rights* (ECHR) (the right to a fair trial).

Costs in the fast track are not as simple as those within the small claims track but neither are they as complicated as in multi-track cases. Part 46 of the CPR deals with the costs regime in the fast track and their purpose is to place strict limits on costs, thus attempting to make the fast track accessible to ordinary litigants.

According to CPR 46.2(1) the costs awarded are currently limited as in Table 14.2.

Table 14.2 Table of costs

Value of claim	Fixed costs
Up to £3,000	£485
£3,001–£10,000	£690
£10,001–£15,000	£1,035
£15,000–	£1,650

These costs can be varied under two principal circumstances. The first is when the court decides not to adopt the fast-track costs scheme (but that would be rare and effectively only used to demonstrate disapproval of a party's conduct) and the second would be when additional legal representation was required. The general rule is that a fast-track case should normally only require an advocate (when in the county court this can be either a barrister or solicitor). If, however, it was necessary to have an additional legal representative (most likely a solicitor accompanying a barrister) then if the court agrees this is necessary then additional costs of £345 can be awarded (CPR 46.3).

14.1.4.3 Multi-track

The third, and most complicated, track is that of the multi-track. This is, in essence, the 'default' track and is used where a case falls into neither the small claims nor fast track. This is perhaps the most complicated track in that it deals with all cases that do not fit into either the small claims or fast tracks. The procedures, therefore, have to be sufficiently robust to apply equally to a claim of £20,000 or £20 million. One way to differentiate between the different classes of case is to use standard directions in respect of smaller claims (Sime (2005) 266). The principal steps can be summarized as shown in Diagram 14.1.

14.1.5 Payment into court

The main steps of the small claims track are presented in the later sections of this chapter, but in both the fast track and multi-track there can be a significant tactical ploy known as payment into court. It has already been noted that an objective of the civil litigation system is to encourage parties, so far as it is possible to do so, to reach a settlement. The rules surrounding payment into court is a classic example of this.

The rules are now set out in Part 36 of the CPR and amount to two distinct forms, known as 'Part 36 offers' and 'Part 36 payments'. The principal tactical advantage in their use is that they can limit the costs payable by the losing party. Accordingly where a party believes there is a risk that they may lose in whole or part but contest the quantum (the amount the claim is for) they may decide to make an offer to settle the claim.

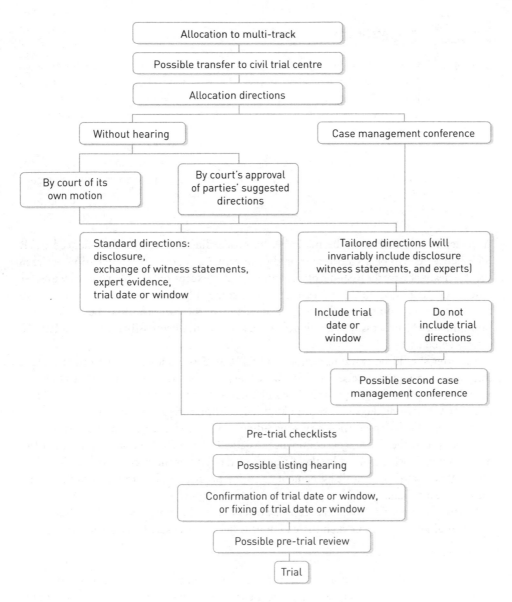

Diagram 14.1 Multi-track procedure

From Stuart Sime, *A Practical Approach to Civil Procedure* (9th edn)(2006) by permission of Oxford University Press.

14.1.5.1 Part 36 offers

The Part 36 offer is the modern version of a mechanism known as the *Calderbank offer* (see *Calderbank v Calderbank* [1976] Fam 93). The essence is that prior to the trial the parties can discuss the claim and make offers to settle. The status of the offers are 'without prejudice' meaning that, apart from when deciding costs, they do not form part of the evidence of the case if, at trial, the defendant decides to contest liability.

> ### 👁 **Example** Part 36 offer
>
> Shopwivus Ltd own a series of supermarkets and Miss Moneybags attended the Anytown branch where she claims she slipped on a grape that was on the floor. She has launched a claim for £25,000 in respect of pain, suffering, and loss of employment. Shopwivus Ltd believe that Miss Moneybags was injured, in part, through her own fault and that they do not believe that her injuries were as bad as she suggests.
>
> They write to Miss Moneybags making a Part 36 offer to settle the claim for £10,000.
>
> If Miss Moneybags rejects the offer then she cannot adduce the letter in court to prove that Shopwivus Ltd are admitting partial liability; the letter cannot be mentioned until the judge is called upon to rule as to costs.

An offer should ordinarily be made before proceedings have been commenced (CPR 36.3) since, as will be seen, there should ordinarily have been communication between the parties prior to the issuing of proceedings. An exception to this rule, however, is where the claim does not involve money but some other form of relief (eg access to land, the prohibition of a nuisance) is being claimed, then an offer may be made at any point during the process. In part this is because it will not be possible to make a Part 36 offer (see below).

An offer should be made in writing and CPR 36.5 provides a series of formal steps that demonstrate the precise terms on which the offer is made, eg whether it relates to the whole claim or some part of it. It should make clear that the offer is open to acceptance for twenty-one days and should be titled 'without prejudice save as to costs'.

If the offer is accepted then any proceedings will automatically lead to proceedings being stayed if they had been commenced (CPR 36.15). The person making the offer must pay any costs incurred by the claimant to the date of the acceptance (CPR 36.13) although where there is a disagreement as to the precise total of these costs the courts may make a ruling.

Where a claimant declines to accept the offer but the judgment is less than that which was contained in the offer then the claimant is liable for costs as discussed below.

14.1.5.2 Part 36 payment

The more usual Part 36 action is that of the payment, in part because this will ordinarily happen once the action has begun. Frequently an offer will not be made because the would-be respondent wishes to see whether the claimant will actually issue proceedings (with the possible costs implications) and to identify the precise nature of the claim.

A Part 36 payment, as its name suggests, involves money actually being transferred whereas an offer is simply that: an offer to settle the matter. The payment is not made directly to the claimant, however, but is instead lodged with the courts. A specific form, known as a Part 36 notice, must be served upon the claimant which makes clear what the precise nature of the payment is. It is important to be clear as to whether the sum is inclusive of interest (CPR 36.22) although it is usual for it to be inclusive (Sime (2005) 449) not least because the general principle in litigation is that monetary claims will incur interest.

As with an offer, the claimant has twenty-one days in which to decide to accept a payment. If the payment is accepted and it was in respect of the whole claim then the proceedings are automatically stayed and a decision on costs is made. The offeror will be responsible for all the costs in proceedings up until the date of acceptance, subject to the precise nature of the costs being reviewed by the court upon disagreement.

Late acceptance

Although there is a twenty-one-day deadline on the acceptance of a payment the money may remain in court if the respondent so wishes and it is possible to accept the payment at a late stage. The usual rule is that unless there is consent by all parties, acceptance will require the permission of the court (and this will ordinarily only be given if the person making the payment accepts). Where the payment is accepted after the twenty-one-day deadline then the issues of costs becomes slightly more complicated. The offeror is responsible for costs until the twenty-one-day deadline. The claimant is then responsible for all costs from the twenty-first day until the date of acceptance unless the court orders that it is in the interests of justice not to do so. It has been suggested that one reason why a court may waive the usual rule is if the claimant accepted after the time limit because of a failure of the offeror to disclose all relevant documents (Sime (2005) 452).

14.1.5.3 Failure to meet Part 36

The reason why careful consideration of a payment (or offer) is necessary is because of the consequences of not accepting an offer and failing to meet the Part 36 payment. A failure occurs when judgment is given for the claimant but the damages awarded by the judge is the same or less than that which was paid into court. In these circumstances the claimant will be responsible for all costs incurred from the time after the elapsing of the payment (ie normally twenty-one days after the payment was made). This can be not insignificant and indeed it is conceivable, in multi-track cases, that the costs could actually exceed the compensation granted, meaning that the claimant will win in principle but lose in reality, having to pay more in costs than that which he receives in compensation.

The rule is normally strict and a safeguard in the system is that ordinarily the judge will not be aware of any Part 36 offer or payment (CPR 36.19). Accordingly, the judge will not be tempted to set relief at a different level and he should not alter it when he becomes aware of the existence of the Part 36 matter (see, for example, *Crouch v King's Healthcare NHS Trust* [2004] EWCA 1332). However, if the judge does become aware of the existence of the payment then it will not automatically lead to the judge withdrawing from the case but, rather, the judge must decide whether it is possible 'in the interests of justice' to carry on (*Garratt v Saxby* [2004] 1 WLR 2152). However, it must be questioned whether this is compliant with Article 6 ECHR, the right to a fair trial. Whichever party loses there will be a suspicion that the damages were set with the payment into court in mind.

14.1.6 Interest

Where a fixed sum of money is being claimed then it is also possible to claim interest on money owed and if interest is to be claimed then this must be factored into the claim together with specified wording. The interest will be divided into two parts:

* interest up until the date of the claim (eg filing the form)
* interest after the date.

Obviously the former will be known but the latter will not. After the sum claimed has been placed on the form, the following wording is used:

> The claimant claims interest under section 69 of the County Courts Act 1984 at the rate of 8 per cent a year, from [date money owed] to [date of claim form] of £[amount] and also interest at the same rate up to the date of judgment or earlier payment at a daily rate of [amount].

It is necessary to calculate the rate of interest. The rate is set by the government and is currently 8 per cent (s 35A SCA 1981) and *simple interest* is calculated (ie it is a fixed daily rate of interest). In order to calculate the daily rate the money owed must be multiplied by 8 per cent and then divided by 365. That figure will be quoted at the end of the statement. In order to calculate the interest owed already the daily rate must be multiplied by the number of days the debt has been owed for. The amount is always quoted in pounds (eg if 50 pence is owed it is expressed as £0.50) and calculated in days.

If, for example, there is a fixed claim for a sum of £500 and the claim had lasted for 25 days then it would be possible to calculate the interest. The amount claimed is £500 so the daily rate of interest will be £0.10 so the total for the 25 days is £2.50. Of course when the sums are so small interest will be minimal but consider the interest in the *Wembley* stadium litigation where tens of millions of pounds were being disputed!

14.2 Small claims court

This section marks the beginning of the second part of this chapter where the procedure in civil litigation will be set out according to two example case studies. The first is in respect of the small claims court, more properly known as the small claims track under the CPR.

It is important to note at the outset that the small claims procedure differs quite radically from all other types of litigation in that it is designed to be as informal as possible. Indeed of all the tracks this is perhaps the one that can be contrasted the most from the adversarial system. The hearings rarely take place in a courtroom but more usually in an informal room within a county court and usually before a district judge. The small claims track is designed to be fully accessible to members of the public and so far as possible the use of lawyers is to be avoided in this track. The system is designed to allow anyone to access this track.

Example   Faulty television set

In order to discuss the small claims track we will use a case example.

Amy Daventry is a resident of Northampton. She buys a television costing £250 from Screens 'R' Us Ltd, a national company with a branch in Northampton (their Head Office is in Carlisle). After one month Amy's television blows up. She contacts Screens 'R' Us who say that 'it is nothing to do with us, that is what they do'. They offer to put her in contact with a repair service who will fix it for £150. She declines the offer.

If you refer to your *Contract Law* book you will see that the scenario above is a very simple contract matter. Since this is a private transaction between a shop and a consumer, the *Sale of Goods Act 1979* applies, and this includes the provision that items should be 'fit for purpose', which clearly it is not. The law makes clear that she can expect a refund under these circumstances and that as the seller it is the responsibility of Screens 'R' Us. How would Amy receive a refund?

14.2.1 Initial action

Before issuing proceedings it will be first necessary for Amy to contact Screens 'R' Us to formally inform them that she believes she has a claim. It was noted that the overriding objective of the CPR is that court action should arise only when necessary and this applies equally to small claims. Therefore by writing to the store it is possible that they will realize their obligation and provide a refund.

Amy is under no obligation to send the letter recorded delivery although it is advisable to do so as this provides evidence that communication was possible. The letter can be sent to either the store or the Head Office (see below).

The main issues that must be contained within the letter are the details of the claim. Accordingly, Amy should set out when the television was purchased (preferably adducing evidence to that effect although not the original), the problem with the goods, a short statement of why she believes it is the responsibility of the retailer (ie state the law), and her request, ie that she should receive a full refund.

If there is no answer or the retailer writes back to say that it is not their responsibility then Amy may feel that she now has no option but to bring an action. In order to ensure that the procedure is as simple as possible, the Court Service produces a series of leaflets explaining the process and also allow the forms to be downloaded from the Internet. The Online Resource Centre that accompanies this book provides a link to these forms and leaflets allowing you to access them.

14.2.1.1 Issuing the claim

The first action is to fill in the claim form (known as form N1) and this is relatively simple. For small claims like this it is unlikely that additional details will be required and the two sides of the form will suffice. There are five areas of the form that most concern us.

Claimant and defendant details

It may seem obvious but the most important aspects of the form are at the very beginning where the claimant must enter his (or in our case, her) name and address. The details of the person who will become the defendant in this case must also be set out. Where it is a company that is being sued then there are two principal addresses that can be used. The first is the registered company address of the company. All companies either limited by guarantee or listed publicly on the stock market must have a registered address and this will be listed with *Companies House*, an official body which organizes the administrative requirements of companies. However, where a company trades at a number of locations it is possible to list one of the addresses at which the company trades (rule 6.5(6)).

Brief details of claim

This is perhaps the one section of the form that is not titled particularly clearly. This section is not an invitation to list all of the precise details of the claim as this comes later, but rather it is a summary of the *nature* of the claim and what remedy is being sought. It is important within this section to make clear what the relationship between claimant and defendant is and thus why it is within the court's jurisdiction.

Value

Assuming that the claim is for money (as in our example) then in this section of the form the *amount* of money being sought would be claimed. Where a fixed sum of money is being claimed then this amount would be included. Where it is not possible to know exactly how much is to be recovered then, in order to ensure that the correct track will be identified from the beginning, one of four possible forms of words should be used:

- 'not more than £5,000'
- 'more than £5,000 but less than £15,000'
- 'more than £15,000'
- 'I cannot say how much I expect to recover'.

The latter should not ordinarily be used but the remaining three will ordinarily map onto the tracks discussed above.

The cost of issuing proceedings will ordinarily be entered into the 'value' field as a separate entry. As this is the small claims court this will only be the actual court fee and not any preparatory expenses, eg legal costs.

Particulars of claim

The particulars of claim can be given at two points; either with the claim or served separately within fourteen days. In small claims proceedings there is little point in waiting and it is highly exceptional for the particulars to be served separately. The space on the form will be used to set out *specifically* what the case for the claimant is. It is essential that the particulars set out why the claimant believes that the money is owed by the defendant and for what legal reasons. It is not necessary in small claims proceedings to use 'legalese' but it should allow both the defendant and court to understand what the argument of the claimant is.

In our case study the matter is a simple contract matter governed by the *Sale of Goods Act 1979* (as amended) and the particulars will be quite brief.

Statement of truth

Although the small claims court is a relatively informal experience it is still the formal resolution of a dispute by the courts. It is a serious offence deliberately to mislead a court and thus most documents will require a 'statement of truth' to be signed. Where a lawyer has prepared all the documents then this will ordinarily be completed by them and they will testify that they *believe* the facts to be true. It has already been noted that for small claims procedures it would be unusual for a lawyer to be involved and it is more likely, therefore, that the claimant him/herself would sign the form.

When the claim form has been completed then the claimant must photocopy it and the 'notes for defendant on replying to the claim form'. The claimant must have a copy for themselves, each defendant will need a copy, and the court itself will require one. All copies are either sent by post or personally delivered to the court who will place the appropriate official stamp on them and send them on.

A fee must be paid to the court at the time of delivering the claim form (either by post or in person). The fees differ according to the value of the claim and for small claims are currently as set out in Table 14.3.

Table 14.3 Small claims fees

Value of claim	Fee (£)
Up to £300	30
£300.01 to £500	45
£500.01 to £1,000	65
£1,000.01 to £1,500	75
£1,500.01 to £3,000	85
£3,000.01 to £5,000	108

14.2.1.2 The defendant's response

The defendant will, as noted above, be sent a copy of the claim form and the appropriate notes for completion. A 'response pack' will also be sent. A copy of the forms and response pack is included online—it is not replicated here as it can be a lengthy form. However, in essence, the defendant has four options open to him:

- admit the whole of the claim
- admit *some* of the claim but deny the rest
- deny the whole of the claim
- counterclaim.

In fact the options are slightly increased since a counterclaim can be combined with an admission and partial admission of the claim. A counterclaim is where the defendant argues that the claimant owes money. It is not necessary to discuss in detail the process of counterclaiming but in essence the defendant becomes the 'claimant' for that part of the claim and the claimant becomes the 'defendant'. To avoid doubt and ensure consistency, however, the claimant and defendant continue to be so labelled for the duration of the proceedings. We will not cover counterclaims in this section as to do so could only confuse matters and this 'walkthrough' is simply an illustration of how civil litigation can occur and is not designed to be a comprehensive analysis of all aspects of the civil litigation system.

Admission of the claim

The most straightforward situation is that the defendant admits the claim and decides to settle the claim. No money is paid to the court but instead the defendant tells the court he admits the claim and will pay the money to the claimant. When the claimant receives the money he will notify the court that the matter is settled. An advantage of the small claims court is that this can occur relatively quickly, especially where a major business is the defendant. The consequences for a business of losing a judgment can be significant as it will be entered onto a register to which credit agencies have access. Whilst a prompt settlement will lead to the entry being withdrawn the initial damage occurs.

Also, where there is an arguable case many businesses will simply pay the money owed in a small claims case as it would cost more for them to fight it (as no legal costs can be paid the 'costs' of their in-house or contracted legal department who would inevitably deal with such matters would probably be more than the amount claimed).

It is for this reason that the small claims track is particularly useful for consumers. As there is no liability for costs, the 'threat' of a court summons (which, as seen from the costs above, will not cost much money to issue) can often settle customer-relations disputes. Whether this is a satisfactory use of court administration and time is perhaps more questionable and arguably consumer disputes, eg disputes governed by the *Sale of Goods Act 1979* or the *Supply of Goods and Services Act 1982* could perhaps be better dealt with through alternative dispute resolution or an Ombudsman-type body.

Admission of part of the claim

One possibility is that the defendant admits part of the claim but not all of it. In these circumstances the defendant explains to the court what part of the claim he admits and what part he is contesting and why. The defendant would normally pay the amount admitted although this need not be done at once. The claimant will then be asked whether he accepts the partial admission as full settlement or whether he wishes to pursue the matter for the remainder.

 Example Smoke in the kitchen

Susan purchases a new saucepan but when it is first used it burns badly causing intense smoke damage to the wall by the cooker. Susan believes that the whole kitchen should be repainted because painting only one wall would not look right. The sellers of the saucepan believe it is possible to paint one wall.

Here, the seller may well admit liability but contest the damages that are being asked for. In this case, a partial admission will be made whereby the seller accepts to refund the cost of the saucepan and for the work involved in painting one wall. They deny that it is necessary to pay for full redecoration.

Susan would have to decide whether to accept this partial admission or seek a hearing to decide whether her full claim would succeed.

Denial of the claim

Where the defendant contests the entire claim then he must tender a defence which is a formal statement saying *why* he contests the claim. This is also part of the response form. In the small claims court it is usual for the defence to be supplied at the time of acknowledging the service of the claim but this need not occur and it is possible to acknowledge receipt of the claim within fourteen days and serve a defence within twenty-eight days (CPR 15.4).

14.2.1.3 Defendant does not respond

It is possible that the defendant will simply fail to respond. Although the claim form is a formal document issued by the county court it is amazing that many people, firms, and companies will simply ignore the form hoping that 'it will go away'. In fact it rarely does and refusing to respond to a claim can cause significant complications, allowing the claimant to seek 'judgment by default' (Part 12 of the CPR).

A judgment by default is when the court rules without any consideration of the merits of the case. If a claimant can demonstrate to the court that a valid claim has been filed and served (which is ordinarily easy in small claims situations since the court will serve the claim on the defendant) and that no defence has been served within the appropriate time then the claimant can ask for judgment to be entered on his behalf.

Where the claim is for a fixed sum, eg in our example with Amy, then this will proceed without any requirement for a hearing and can be completed on papers. The claimant completes the necessary form and this is then laid before a judge who will make the appropriate order. Where the claim is not for a fixed sum then it is likely that a short hearing will be necessary as the judge will require sufficient information to allow him to make a decision on the amount of money that should be paid. In either case no fee is payable for the judgment to be made in default.

Setting aside a judgment by default

Whilst a judgment by default is a judgment of the county court and can be enforced like any other judgment, there exist special measures by which a defendant can ask for the judgment to be set aside. This is not an appeal as it is heard by the same level of court but is simply a request to the court that he should have the opportunity to contest the matter and that it should proceed to trial.

An application to set aside a judgment by default is discretionary: the judge does not *have* to set aside the judgment (save where the judgment was wrongly made before the expiry of the time a defendant has to respond (CPR 13.2)) and ordinarily will not do so unless there is good reason to do so. The defendant must make an application to the court on the appropriate form. A fee is payable for this (currently £75) and the claimant will be entitled to make representations as to whether the judgment will be set aside.

Apart from when a judgment was made in error, there are two grounds (CPR 13.1) upon which to ask a court to set aside a judgment:

(a) the defendant has a real prospect of successfully defending the claim; or

(b) it appears to the court that there is some other good reason why–

    (i) the judgment should be set aside or varied; or

    (ii) the defendant should be allowed to defend the claim.

Ground (a) exists because it is in compliance with the general principles of the CPR that justice should be done. If a person is not liable then they should not ordinarily be required to pay damages. The court will, however, wish to question why the defendant failed to respond.

One of the most common forms of applications to set aside judgments arises because the defendant has moved property and thus the forms were served on an incorrect address. In those circumstances the courts will ordinarily grant the application as it cannot be said that the defence had a true opportunity of defending the matter (see, for example, *Akram v Adam* [2004] EWCA Civ 1601).

In reality where there is a 'good reason' for the delay or where the application is made just after the relevant defence time elapsing the court will ordinarily grant the applications. In part this is because it does not prejudice the claimant's case; they have not necessarily incurred any extra expenses (since no fee is payable for judgment in default) nor does setting aside a judgment in default mean the pre-judging of the case; it simply states that the matter should proceed to the hearing.

14.2.1.4 Allocation of track

Where a claim is for more than £1,500 the matter must be allocated a track. Disputes under £1,500 will be allocated to the small claims track automatically and no fee is charged for this. Where, however, the claim is for over £1,500 even if it is under the £5,000 (under which a matter is ordinarily assigned to the small claims track) then an application for allocation must be made. This requires the payment of a fee of £35 (which is recoverable from the defendant if the claim succeeds) and, for small claims matters, it will ordinarily be undertaken on papers without the need for a hearing.

14.2.2 The hearing

Eventually the matter will proceed to a hearing. Whilst, theoretically, the defendant has only fourteen to twenty-eight days to file his defence and to admit the claim in reality the defendant can choose to settle the matter at any point up to the hearing and the court would simply acknowledge that the dispute is settled and make the appropriate orders.

Assuming that for our example Screens 'R' Us have decided to contest the matter (we will assume they have filed a defence saying it is not their responsibility as they do not manufacture the televisions) then the matter must proceed to a hearing. Theoretically the parties can agree to dispense with the hearing and invite the judge to make a ruling purely on the papers (CPR 27.10) but it is unlikely that this would ever happen as most parties will wish to comment on the evidence they are adducing. A final fee has to be paid before the hearing takes place and this depends on the amount of money that is claimed:

Less than £300	£25
Less than £500	£50
Less than £1,000	£75
Less than £1,500	£100
Less than £3,000	£150
Less than £5,000	£300

Whilst this fee is recoverable if the claimant wins it must be noted that this, together with the other fees, means that even the small claims court can be relatively expensive.

A significant advantage of the small claims track is that of informality; indeed informality is enshrined in the rules (CPR 27.8(2)). It has been noted that lawyers will ordinarily not be involved and appearing at the hearing with a lawyer is not necessarily advantageous; in fact some would argue it could be an impediment as the judge expects small claims matters to be settled informally. The hearing will take place in the county court but it is exceptionally rare for the matter to be heard in an actual courtroom. Small claims track matters are ordinarily heard in the judge's room, known as 'in chambers'. That said, however, they remain public hearings and members of the public could request to sit in on the proceedings. Ordinarily, however, they will not do so and will want to watch something slightly more exciting!

The court will notify both parties of the date of the hearing and changing the date requires an application to the court. In small claims tracks they prefer not to alter the date of a hearing except for good cause, even when there is agreement between the parties. If either party does not turn up then the matter may proceed by summary judgment where the judge either dismisses the claim (where the claimant does not turn up) or gives judgment in default (where the defendant fails to attend).

Assuming that both parties do attend then the matter will be heard. The judge will ordinarily be a district judge and so will be referred to as 'Sir' or 'Madam'. Although it is a formal hearing, the strict rules of evidence do not apply to the small claims track and the judge is able to proceed in which ever way he feels appropriate to meet the overriding objective of the CPR (CPR 27.8). In essence, therefore, the hearing has the feeling more of an arbitration process than a traditional court hearing. Witnesses may still be called and whilst they do give sworn testimony the formal rules of examination are not followed, in part because it would be unreasonable to expect a lay person to be familiar with the rules of evidence. The judge will normally control the testimony and can ask questions himself.

Judgment will normally be given immediately after the case has been presented and orders and costs drawn up at that point in time. Written decisions would not normally be granted.

14.2.3 **Post-trial**

After the hearing there are two issues of relevance that need to be considered briefly: enforcing the judgment and appeals.

14.2.3.1 Enforcement

Hopefully when judgment is entered the opposing party will settle the matter promptly but what of the situation where the person refuses to pay? In this situation enforcement proceedings must begin. The most usual way of enforcing a (money) judgment is to seek execution against goods through a warrant of execution. The person to whom money is owed applies to the court (and pays the relevant fee—which will be added to the debt) and if the court agrees (as it inevitably will) then an order is made and the matter is passed to the court-appointed bailiffs. The bailiffs are then empowered to seize goods to the value of the claim (this being the value they will realize, ie not how much they cost but how much they can be sold for). An often misunderstood point, however, is that bailiffs have no automatic right to enter property: they must gain lawful entry.

Under s 89(1) *County Courts Act 1984* (as amended) it is not possible to seize:

(a) such tools, books, vehicles and other items of equipment as are necessary to [the debtor] for use personally by him in his employment, business or vocation;

(b) such clothing, bedding, furniture, household equipment and provisions as are necessary for satisfying the basic domestic needs of the debtor and his family.

What precisely amounts to 'as are necessary' will always be open to debate but luxury items (for example televisions, hi-fi equipment) are unlikely to be considered necessary. The debtor normally has at least one more opportunity to settle the debt prior to the goods being sold but if he does not do so then the items are sold and the money (less the bailiff's fees) is forwarded to the creditor.

Where a debtor has other assets (eg bank accounts, investments, etc) or where they receive a regular salary then there are other possible ways of securing the judgment through, for example, asking the court to impose a 'third-party debt order' on the assets or requiring an employer to deduct a proportion of the debtor's salary until the debt is settled (Sime (2005) 480–484).

14.2.3.2 Appeal

Like most proceedings it is possible to appeal against the decision of the district judge but it is restricted to questions of law. Part 52 of the CPR deals with appeals and either side can appeal.

 Example More about the television set

Let us assume that the district judge, for whatever reason, upheld in part Amy's claim. Instead of awarding her the £250 the television cost, he awarded the £150 it would cost to get it fixed.

Amy may wish to appeal against this decision even though she 'won' because she believes the judge erred in not giving the full amount.

The first stage is to serve notice on the court and parties that an appeal is to be lodged and this is done by completing form N164 and paying the requisite fee. Permission to appeal is required (CPR 52.3) and unless the district judge granted permission to appeal then form N164 will also serve as a request for permission. The permission will only be granted if the relevant judge believes that there is a 'real prospect of success' or where there is 'some compelling reason' to do so (CPR 52.3(6)). Unlike in criminal cases where an appeal is heard in a superior court, an appeal from a decision of a district judge in the small claims track will ordinarily be made to a circuit judge sitting in the county court, ie it will stay in the same court but the level of judge will rise.

It is notable that the form continues with the 'user-friendly' access and it is designed so that anybody can complete it. An appeal must ordinarily be lodged within fourteen days but this can be extended by permission of the court. The appeal hearing will not be a rehearing but rather a hearing deciding whether the judge erred in law. Whilst only decisions of law can be raised on appeal, if the appeal succeeds the appellate court (ie the circuit judge) will ordinarily dispose of the case rather than remitting it for a rehearing (Practice Direction, Pt 27, 8.3). This is a welcome development as there would appear to be little reason for a rehearing when most small claims track cases will be very simple and it is difficult to see how the court would do anything other than follow the District Judge.

 Example The outcome of the appeal

Amy has persuaded the circuit judge that the district judge erred in not treating the contract as fundamentally breached. The circuit judge orders that Screens 'R' Us pay the £250 rather than remit it back to a district judge with a direction to do the same.

Prior to the forty-second update to the CPR (which came into force in October 2006) the position as regards costs for small claims was not favourable to litigants. Although costs were strictly limited during the initial trial this was not the case during an appeal and indeed it was not uncommon for lawyers to be engaged to present an appeal, seriously escalating costs. There was concern that the threat of an appeal could undermine the small claims process.

The forty-second update, however, introduced a system whereby the costs on appeal are limited to the court fees and travelling expenses, ie the same as that which could be awarded during the original trial. This was a major shift but must be considered a welcome step. An advantage of changing this fee regime is that it suggests that lawyers will no longer be engaged for an appeal and the dispute will remain between the parties. Whilst it is unlikely that the appeal will change from being a consideration of alleged mistakes of law rather than a rehearing, it will have to become more informal and presumably the circuit judge presiding will adopt a similar approach to that adopted by the district judge during the first trial. Presumably the rules of evidence etc will also be relaxed and ensure that the small claims procedure in its entirety is an accessible method of resolving disputes in respect of relatively small amounts of money.

QUESTION FOR REFLECTION

Is extending this costs regime helpful? Is there not a danger that by restricting costs each party will have nothing to lose by bringing an appeal and, accordingly, incurring delays and unnecessary litigation in the county courts? Do you think there are any solutions to this? How should the leave provision apply to small claims track appeals?

LISTEN TO THE PODCAST

For guidance on how to answer this question and a discussion of the main issues, listen to the author's podcast on the Online Resource Centre:
www.oxfordtextbooks.co.uk/orc/gillespie_els3e/

14.3 Judicial review

In this section the concept of judicial review will be examined. The introduction of the CPR, and its changes to traditional terminology, has had a particular impact upon the way that judicial review cases are termed.

JUDICIAL REVIEW: CASE CITATIONS

The traditional manner of citing judicial review cases is *R v* [body to be reviewed], *ex p* [person or body seeking the review], eg:

R v Criminal Injuries Compensation Board, ex p A [1999] 2 AC 330

In this case, Mr(s) A sought to judicially review a decision of the Criminal Injuries Compensation Board. The Crown (*R or Regina*) is represented but in name alone—the Crown has no automatic place in proceedings.

The modern way of citing judicial review cases is *R* (*on behalf of* [person or body seeking the review]) *v* [body to be reviewed], eg:

R (on behalf of Greenfield) *v Secretary of State for the Home Department* [2005] UKHL 14

The change is largely cosmetic but it does perhaps more accurately reflect the 'players' in that it is X *v* Y and not an ex parte matter which was always somewhat confusing. The fact that the Crown is still, in theory, bringing the matter is indicative of the fact that it is the judiciary that is reviewing the matter. The judiciary act on behalf of the Queen in this matter in ensuring that a public body has acted properly. Given that most public bodies act on behalf of the Queen (most notably the government who act in her name) this does lead to the rather novel situation where the Crown is holding itself to account!

When the 'new' system is being used it should also be noted that sometimes the 'on behalf of' words are omitted from case reports (eg *R (Greenfield) v Secretary of State for the Home Department* [2005] UKHL 14) although they should always be present on official documents relating to the case.

The second 'walkthrough' that will be undertaken to assist in understanding how civil procedure works is that of a judicial review. There has, in recent years, been a significant growth in the number of judicial reviews (LCD (2005) 23), in part because courts are more ready to challenge decisions of the executive or public bodies. This part of the chapter will *not* examine the substantive law relating to judicial review as this will be covered in other subjects but rather the purpose is to allow you to understand how a review proceeds. This will hopefully be of assistance when you learn about judicial reviews as you can understand how a case proceeds.

As before, an example will be used to assist us in understanding how a case proceeds.

 Example A mother's march

Matilda wishes to campaign against the decision of the (fictional) Rutland County Council to close a nursery in Smallville. She has organized a number of parents and they wish to march two miles down the centre of Smallville to the offices of Rutland County Council where they will make speeches and wave placards. The protest is planned to take place the day a Home Office minister is due to visit Smallville and so the Chief Constable of the (fictional) Rutland Police has decided to ban the march because he doesn't want the town to look unruly. Matilda wishes to challenge this decision. She visits the Chief Constable but he refuses to back down and thus she wishes to take action in court.

14.3.1 Pre-hearing matters

Part 54 of the CPR governs applications for judicial review and this contains detailed rules that must be undertaken in order to make a judicial review. Whilst it is possible that a review could be undertaken by a litigant in person, and some are, it is more usual for lawyers to be engaged in the process because of the complexity of the issues. In any event the public body that is going to be reviewed will certainly use lawyers and there can be liability for costs if the review is lost.

14.3.1.1 Public bodies

The first issue to note is who is subject to judicial review. The precise details of this will be discussed in depth during other modules and have controversially developed through time (see Barnett (2011) 727–729). The CPR states (54.1(2)) that judicial review can be invoked:

to review the lawfulness of—

    (i)   an enactment; or

    (ii)   a decision, action or failure to act in relation to the exercise of a public function.

The controversy of course exists over what amounts to a 'public function' although many are obvious, eg inferior courts or tribunals, members of the executive (including ministers, the police, prison staff, Inland Revenue Commissioners, etc) and public bodies (eg healthcare trusts, universities, etc). Also certain regulatory bodies can be subject to judicial review (eg British Medical Association) but not bodies that regulate private activities (see, for example, *R v Football Association Ltd, ex p Football League Ltd* [1993] 2 All ER 833).

For the purposes of our example there is little difficulty for Matilda as the police are members of the executive and subject to review.

14.3.1.2 Standing

Once a body is capable of being judicially reviewed it is then necessary to decide whether a person has any right to claim the review. Not everyone will have the right to review a decision because they may not be affected by it. Traditionally the test for whether a person can make an application was known as *locus standi* but it is now known as 'standing' and the test is set out in s 31(3) SCA 1981:

[the claimant]…has a sufficient interest in the matter to which the application relates.

The statute does not helpfully set out what 'sufficient interest' means but it has been suggested that the 'essential idea is to exclude busybodies' (Sime (2005) 492). In essence it is necessary to show some link between the claimant and the issue being reviewed and in many cases this will not be difficult (Southey and Fulford (2004) 6).

👁 Example   More about the march

If we refer back to our example, it would be extremely difficult for anyone to argue that Matilda does not have any standing in this matter since she is the one who wants to organize the protest. If however Hazel, who lives 200 miles away, wants to challenge the decision because she 'feels strongly about the right to march' it is unlikely that she would have standing because there is no link.

That said, it has been pointed out that some abuses of power may be so widespread that any citizen will ordinarily have the power to intervene (Southey (2004) 8, and *R v Somerset County Council and ARC Southern Ltd, ex p Dixon* [1997] COD 323).

It has been suggested that the issue of standing can be decided at one of two stages: either at the permission stage or when the full hearing takes place (Elliott (2005) 513). It may appear most logical that standing is decided at the preparatory stage but in *R v Inland Revenue Commissioners, ex p National Federation of Self-Employed and Small Businesses Ltd* [1982] AC 617 the House of Lords argued that this need not be the case and actually it will sometimes be decided at the actual hearing so that the court has the opportunity of looking at the totality of the case in deciding whether someone has sufficient interest.

Human rights

Before leaving the issue of standing, it will be first necessary to examine the position in respect of applications under the *Human Rights Act 1998*. Section 7(7) of the HRA 1998 expressly states that when deciding whether to permit someone to bring an action under s 7 of the Act (which permits someone to bring proceedings claiming a breach, or future breach, of their rights) the court must make reference to Article 34 of the ECHR. Article 34 defines a 'victim' and it has been suggested that the definition of victim under the ECHR is more restrictive than the test ordinarily adopted by the courts when making decisions under Part 54. However it is not necessarily easy to identify any practical issue because many issues raised as human rights issues would also be relevant under the grounds of judicial review (Elliot (2005) 542).

 Example Human rights issues

If we refer back to our example Matilda's application may, or may not, raise human rights issues. On the one hand she could use s 7 HRA 1998 because the right to protest is contained within Articles 10 (freedom of expression) and 11 (right of assembly) of the ECHR. However she could also complain about the decision using only domestic law.

In fact, in this scenario it would make no substantive difference since Matilda would be considered a victim under Article 34 as well as having ordinary standing under s 31.

14.3.1.3 Timing

Judicial-review actions are supposed to be timely: they are designed to review either decisions recently made or decisions that are about to be made. The rules state (CPR 54.5):

The claim form must be filed–

    (a) promptly; and

    (b) in any event not later than 3 months after the grounds to make the claim arose.

Note that this rule is not saying that the time limit is three months; it is saying that the *maximum* time limit is three months. If a court believes that undue delay has been taken before lodging the claim then it may refuse leave or a remedy (s 31(6) SCA 1981) notwithstanding the fact that it may still be within 'time' for the purposes of the CPR (s 31(7) SCA 1981) although some question whether this is compatible with Article 6 of the ECHR (Southey (2004) 94).

That said, it is important to note that the court does have a discretion to extend time limits (CPR 3.1) but it would be exceptional for the court to do so in judicial review cases. Where it may do so, however, is if the issues raised are so important it would be inappropriate to reject an application and leave the question unanswered (p 99).

 Example Time limit

We return to the example of Matilda. Let us assume that the protest was organized two months in advance of the date of the march. If Matilda left the judicial review proceedings to the week before the date of the march then it is quite possible that the court would refuse to entertain the judicial review on the basis that she had not acted promptly.

14.3.1.4 Making the application

Assuming that the Chief Constable has refused to reconsider his decision, then Matilda may wish to proceed in making an application. Any application must be made on the appropriate form (N461; the Online Resource Centre accompanying this book reproduces a copy of this form) and applications can only be addressed to the High Court (s 31 SCA 1981). Cases will be heard in the Administrative Court which was set up in 2000 (see *Practice Direction (Administrative Court: Establishment)* [2000] 1 WLR 1654) and replaced the previous Crown Office List. This was in response to a review of judicial-review procedures (Elliott (2005) 442) that had called for the establishment of a dedicated 'court'. Although referred to as a court and one that has its own 'lead' judge (currently Mr Justice Collins) and office (the Administrative Court office) it is part of the Queen's Bench Division of the High Court.

The form itself must be completed and served on the appropriate persons. This will always mean the body which will become the respondent (ie the body which is to be judicially reviewed) but where that body is an inferior court or tribunal, all parties to the case must also be served (Practice Direction 54, 5.1).

The claim form is relatively straightforward and requires the claimant to record their details and those of the respondent(s). It then asks for details of the decision that is to be reviewed, so in our example this would be the decision to ban the protest. A separate box exists on the form (p 2) to allow a respondent to list the Articles of the ECHR they believe to have been breached. However, the discussion on 'standing' must be borne in mind when deciding whether human rights issues are raised.

The form then asks for a series of details:

- the statement of grounds (these can be sent separately)
- the remedy claimed (a prerogative order and possibly damages but more likely simply the prerogative order)
- any other applications (for example, extension of the time limit)
- statement of facts (these can be sent separately).

Full details (and copies) of the documents that the claimant wishes the court to consider should also be enclosed with the claim form (CPR 54.6 and Practice Direction 54, 5.9). The bundle is particularly important and it should be paginated. The statement of grounds and statement of facts should be cross-referenced with the bundle of documents. A judicial review differs from most applications in that facts are a secondary issue. The purpose of a review is to decide whether the reviewing body should have reached the decision it did and thus the resolution of factual disputes is not central to a judicial review (Elliott (2005) 443). It is for this reason that cross-examination of witnesses is not normally available (see below).

Grounds

Perhaps the most obvious issue that jumps out from the form is the statement of grounds. Again, it is not possible in this chapter to detail precisely the grounds for judicial review as this will be the subject of several lectures in other modules, but it is necessary at least to raise them. Perhaps the most famous detailed examination of the grounds of judicial review was set out by Lord Diplock in *Council of Civil Service Unions v Minister for the Civil Service* [1985] AC 374 where his Lordship identified (at p 410) three principal grounds:

- illegality—the body has no lawful right to make that decision or has exceeded its powers in making the decision
- Irrationality—he referred to this as 'Wednesbury unreasonableness' (see *Associated Provincial Picture Houses Ltd v Wednesbury Corporation* [1948] 1 KB 223 and

Wade and Forsyth (2009) 312–313)) which, in effect, means that a decision is so perverse that no properly directed body could reach such a decision

- procedural impropriety—the body failed to adhere to the rules which govern its decision-making or it has flouted the rights of natural justice.

In essence these grounds continue to exist but they have been supplemented by additional grounds such as the duty to give reasons and legitimate expectation (Southey (2004) 31).

 NATURAL JUSTICE

Natural justice is the term given to the basic rules governing the adjudication of disputes. The two principal rules are the right to have a dispute raised in court (ie access to court) and that no person shall be a judge in their own cause (ie rule against bias).

Remedy

The form also requires the claimant to indicate what remedy they seek. The most usual remedies are the prerogative orders:

- quashing order (ie an order that quashes the decision that is being reviewed, returning the position to that which it was before the decision was made)
- mandatory order (ie requiring the body to take a particular action or decision)
- prohibiting order (ie prohibiting the body from taking a particular action or decision).

The prerogative orders can be combined, eg both a quashing and mandatory order could be made. This would have the effect of quashing the previous decision and then telling the body how they must rule when the matter is returned to them (cases are often returned to the lower court because the court has no jurisdiction to rule on the substantive issue).

Example Judicial review of criminal proceedings

In Chapter 13 it was noted that one option available to both defendants and the prosecution is to judicially review the decision of the magistrates' court in criminal matters. The Administrative Court will hear this matter but it is a civil court. The jurisdiction on trying summary criminal matters is with the magistrates' court and so the matter must be returned to it. As an inferior body, however, the High Court can tell the court how to rule.

An example, therefore, is that Dominic has been convicted of common assault but complains that the chairman of the bench commented 'I have known police officers all my life, and they never lie' and prevented the defendant from adducing evidence to show that the arresting officer had fabricated evidence. This could amount to an irrational decision (it could also amount to other breaches but for this example we will use irrationality) and thus if the defendant succeeds it is possible that the court will make a quashing order (quashing the decision to convict) and a mandatory order (requiring the bench to acquit). The matter proceeds to the magistrates' court, which must follow the mandatory order and no retrial will take place. If only a quashing order was made then a retrial would need to take place.

Other remedies available include the ability to make an injunction (although more often this could be achieved by a prohibiting order), the award of damages, or even a simple declaration. Damages are exceptional in judicial review cases and will normally only be permitted where there is a recognized head of liability (Southey (2004) 186).

 QUESTION FOR REFLECTION

What remedy or remedies would Matilda seek in our example?

LISTEN TO THE PODCAST

For guidance on how to answer this question and a discussion of the main issues, listen to the author's podcast on the Online Resource Centre:
www.oxfordtextbooks.co.uk/orc/gillespie_els3e/

14.3.1.5 Replying to the claim

Once the form has been served on each person (and note that it is the responsibility of the claimant to serve the papers and not for the court to send them out) then the respondent party and any interested parties must decide whether they wish to be heard on the matter. This is known as 'acknowledgement of service' and must be made on a separate form (N462) which allows the respondent to choose whether they intend to contest some or all of the claim or accept it. The form can also be used by interested parties to signal an intention to make a submission to the court.

The form also permits the served parties the opportunity to name other interested parties who may wish to join the action. Those persons will then be served with the claim form. The acknowledgement must be filed within twenty-one days of being served (CPR 54.8) and include a summary of the argument that they will make at trial. A failure to make an acknowledgement of service need not prevent the person from participating in the hearing (CPR 54.9) but it would normally prevent them being involved at the permission stage.

14.3.2 Permission stage

The need for permission has already been discussed but how is this decided? There are two possibilities: a decision on papers and a decision by hearing.

14.3.2.1 Papers

It will be remembered that the claimant must file the papers that they wish the court to consider when the claim form is submitted. The Practice Direction makes clear that the usual event will be for permission to be decided on papers alone (Practice Direction 54, 8.4). This is a marked change from the traditional way that leave (the original name for 'permission') was handled but the review on judicial review considered that it was administratively and judicially burdensome for routine matters (Elliott (2005) 473).

The judge will now consider the matter by looking at the papers filed by both the claimant and defendant, again something that has recently changed since traditionally leave was an *ex parte* matter, ie it was based solely on the case advanced by the claimant. There are strong reasons for preferring the *inter partes* system where all parties are able to make, at least brief, written statements as it assists the judge in understanding whether there is an arguable case.

Elliott notes that there is no single test for permission to be given (Elliott (2005) 474). As judicial review is a discretionary action a court does not *have* to give permission even if there is a justiciable decision and thus where a person could have brought the complaint through another branch of the legal process this may be a ground for refusing permission. However, the overall decision is simply an arguable case (*R v Inland Revenue Commissioners, ex p National Federation of Self-Employed and Small Businesses Ltd* [1982] AC 617). This is because any higher threshold would transform the permission stage into the final determination, something that the recent reforms were designed to move away from.

In essence the permission stage is simply designed to weed out weak or improper cases but at least one commentator argues that the new reforms are a retrograde step:

> The claimant has from the outset to go to the trouble and expense of assembling all the relevant materials and must disclose its case in full to the defendant. The defendant need no more than give its defence in outline. In the normal course of things, the claimant will have no opportunity to rebut the allegations made by the defendant because permission will be decided on the papers...(Cornford (2000))

This is an interesting criticism and hints at the fact that there may not be parity between the parties. If this is so then potentially it raises an 'equality of arms' argument under Article 6 of the ECHR. However the counter-argument is that it is a sensible approach and that full disclosure by the defence is not required as it is simply a matter of deciding whether the matter should be heard—and where the defence statement highlights a disagreement that cannot be proved it may perhaps signal that the matter requires resolution and permission should be given.

14.3.2.2 Hearing

Although the Practice Direction states that a matter should normally be undertaken by papers, the rule is prefixed by the word 'generally' (Practice Direction 54, 8.4) and thus the court retains the discretion to require a hearing.

The usual reason for a hearing to occur is where a decision is made at the papers stage not to grant permission. In these circumstances the claimant can ask (as of right) for a hearing to take place (CPR 54.12). This is expressly *not* an appeal but reconsideration (CPR 54.12(3)). The difference between reconsideration and an appeal is that an appeal would ordinarily take place before a higher judge or in a higher court but reconsideration takes place in the same court although not normally by the same judge. Also, an appeal would normally be restricted to correcting errors of law whereas reconsideration is simply listening to expanded arguments. That said, if after reconsideration the decision is still not to give permission then an appeal may be sought to the Court of Appeal (Civil Division). Leave is required from the Court of Appeal for such an appeal (CPR 52.15(1)) but the court when determining leave may, in effect, decide the determination of the appeal by deciding to grant permission instead of leave to appeal (CPR 52.15(3)). The consequence of such permission is that the matter would 'return' to the High Court for trial, albeit almost certainly by another judge.

A permissions hearing will ordinarily take thirty minutes (Southey (2004) 147) and this is perhaps indicative of the fact that permission is a matter of 'weeding out' rather than substantive resolution but it also sends a signal that the judge is very much in control of the proceedings rather than advocates attempting to present their case according to their own demands. Neither the defendant nor any interested party needs to attend a hearing unless the court directs otherwise (Practice Direction 54, 8.5) and indeed if they do attend the general rule is that the claimant will not be responsible for the costs of their attendance irrespective of the outcome (Practice Direction 54, 8.6). The latter is an important exception from the usual rule of civil litigation costs and is perhaps indicative of the fact that it remains a preliminary issue and one that (theoretically) is identifying whether the claimant has demonstrated an arguable case. That said, many defendants will appear at the permission hearing since if they can persuade the judge to deny permission then they will save the time and costs involved in defending a judicial review. Where the review is anticipatory (ie it seeks to challenge something that relates to the future—in our example the march occurs in the future) this has the advantage in ensuring that alternative arrangements do not have to be made pending a hearing (as the decision would ordinarily be 'stayed' pending review; however, it is possible to bring expedited judicial reviews and indeed there are 'duty' judges available all day and night to provide for emergency matters).

14.3.3 The hearing

Assuming that permission is given (in 2009 only 24 per cent of applications were given permission: *Judicial and Court Statistics 2009*, p 158) then the next stage is to consider the hearing. However, getting to that stage still requires one of two further procedural matters. All documents must now be filed with the court at the time of the claim form but before any hearing can take place a further fee (currently £180) has to be paid to the court within seven days of permission being given.

If the defendant has not already done so (and ordinarily they will not have done so) then a detailed defence must be served on the court and claimant following permission being given (Practice Direction 54, 10.1). The same is true of those interested parties who wish to be heard on the matter.

14.3.3.1 Skeleton arguments

Prior to attending the hearing, a skeleton argument must be filed by all parties. The claimant must serve his skeleton argument (on the defence and on the court) not less than twenty-one days before the hearing (Practice Direction 54, 15.1) and the defence and other interested parties not more than fourteen days (Practice Direction 54, 15.2). The difference in dates reflects the fact that the defence will ordinarily have time to consider the arguments of the claimant.

A skeleton argument (Practice Direction 54, 15.3) will ordinarily contain:

(a) a time estimate for the hearing including judgment

(b) a list of the issues

(c) a list of the legal points to be taken (authorities must be provided and properly referenced in the bundle—see *Practice Direction (Citation of Authorities)* [2001] 1 WLR 1001)

(d) a chronology of events

(e) a list of essential documents to be read by the judge(s) prior to the hearing

(f) a list of persons referred to.

14.3.3.2 In court

A judicial review will ordinarily be in public within a courtroom, ordinarily in the Royal Courts of Justice in London. For civil matters a judicial review will typically involve a single puisne judge sitting (and so he or she will be referred to as My Lord/My Lady); in criminal matters, however, the hearing will normally be before a Divisional Court. Traditionally this would involve a Lord Justice of Appeal and a puisne judge sitting but recently it is becoming more common for two puisne judges to sit.

Hearings are often extremely quick, in part because it would be very rare for witness testimony to be heard. Since a judicial review is about the propriety of a decision rather than factual disputes there would not normally be any reason for witnesses to be adduced. That said, however, in *R (on the application of PG) v London Borough of Ealing and another* [2002] EWHC Admin 250 the Administrative Court held that it retained the right to hear oral evidence if exceptionally it was needed and indeed for witnesses to be tendered for cross-examination. The learned judge presiding, Munby J, argued that any prohibition on this would arguably be incompatible with Article 6 (at [20]) but it is important to note that it will be extremely rare for witnesses to be heard.

The order of the speeches follows the usual convention with the claimant speaking first followed by the defendant and then any interested parties. Not everyone need be represented at the hearing and it is possible for written submissions to be submitted instead.

14.3.3.3 Remedy

The remedies available to the court have already been set out but it is important to note that judicial review is a discretionary procedure and thus even where a claimant satisfies the court that an error has been made the court can still decide not to act. However, it is more likely than not that a court will make an order, especially in situations like our example of Matilda where a ruling will have a significant impact on future conduct. The main reason for denying a remedy would be where the mistake was a technical one and the deficiency would not have made any real difference to the substantive matter (Southey (2004) 178). This would be most likely in situations where procedural impropriety was being alleged.

👁 **Example** Use of a leisure centre

Let us assume that in order for the Peabody District Council to restrict the leisure centre's opening hours it is necessary to seek permission from (a) the Council Leader, (b) the Mayor, (c) the Leader and Mayor of the neighbouring District Council, and (d) the (fictional) Department for Administrative Affairs.

For some reason although all bodies were contacted the Department for Administrative Affairs' reply was not received. A judicial review is brought by Jim Naseum, who uses the leisure centre after work. The court finds that the Department's permission was not granted (and to that extent the procedure was flawed) but that it was simply because the letter was lost in the post. The letter had given permission.

Here the court may well deny relief on the basis that it would be academic to do so as the Council would then simply obtain the necessary permissions immediately after the hearing.

Where a court does intend to grant relief, it will make an order that will be served on all parties stating clearly what the order(s) say and mean, and provide for any timescales.

 QUESTION FOR REFLECTION

Think back to our example featuring Matilda. What relief do you think Matilda would be granted?

LISTEN TO THE PODCAST

For guidance on how to answer this question and a discussion of the main issues, listen to the author's podcast on the Online Resource Centre:

www.oxfordtextbooks.co.uk/orc/gillespie_els3e/

14.3.4 **Post-hearing matters**

A number of factors need to be briefly considered in connection with post-hearing matters. The three of most relevance are: enforcement, costs, and appeals.

14.3.4.1 Enforcement

Any relief (other than a declaration which is simply a statement of findings) is an order of the High Court and must be followed. Unlike money judgments where a procedure has to be followed to secure compliance (see, for example, 14.2.3.1 above) any of the prerogative orders must be followed as of right. If a quashing order has been made alone then the decision that was the subject of review is quashed and the position of the parties is as though the decision were never made. Accordingly, it is open to the body to seek to make the decision again although this time in a proper manner. The CPR make clear, however, that the court does not *have* to remit the matter back to the authority to make another decision and could, if it believes there 'is no purpose to be served in remitting the matter' make the decision itself (CPR 54.19). If this occurs the decision is treated as though it were taken by the proper body and all consequential steps from that decision will occur naturally.

Where a prohibiting order has been made then the defending body is legally required *not* to take the action listed in the order. Where a mandatory order has been made the converse is true: the body *must* take whatever action is listed in the order. Breaches of such orders are punishable as contempt of court which is punishable by either imprisonment or a financial penalty or both. In a landmark ruling, *M v Home Office* [1994] AC 377 the House of Lords ruled that ministers of the Crown can be in contempt of court for breaching a prerogative order although it was suggested that any finding may be somewhat unenforceable. At least one academic has suggested that this is nonsensical and that it could devalue judicial review since non-enforceability potentially handicaps any adjudication (Harlow (1994) 623). Nevertheless judicial review decisions are routinely complied with by the government, in part because it would be politically inexpedient not to.

 QUESTION FOR REFLECTION

Would it ever be possible for an order under judicial review to be enforced against the government? The Secretary of State for the respective government department is ultimately responsible for the actions of the department and it is inconceivable that a court would ever imprison a Secretary of State for failing to adhere to an order. Does that mean that orders are unenforceable?

14.3.4.2 Costs

Costs remain an important aspect of any procedure and judicial review is no exception. No special rules exist in respect of judicial review costs and so the general rules set out in Part 54 of the CPR apply. These have been discussed already but the main issue that will often arise in judicial review cases is as to who wins? It will be quite common for the claimant to succeed on one of his grounds but not on others. Does this mean that he has won the review? The answer appears to lie in the broad discretion the court has as to costs, allowing them to apportion costs in such a way to reflect those grounds where a claim succeeded and those grounds where it did not (Southey (2004) 206). In other words, a claimant may not receive all of their costs but only a proportion of them.

The other difficulty in respect of judicial review proceedings is the discretionary nature of the proceedings. Does a claimant still 'win' if the claim succeeds but the court declines to offer a relief? The answer, it would appear, is 'yes' because the courts will separate out the decision from the relief (Southey (2004) 207) but where the court believes that the claim was academic and did not resolve issues of importance then it is possible that costs will be varied.

The final issue to note here is where it was a judicial body that was being reviewed, eg the magistrates' court or a tribunal. In those circumstances costs will not ordinarily be ordered against the defendant (especially since justices have personal liability) unless they acted 'in flagrant disregard of elementary principles' (Southey (2004) 211) in which case costs may be used to demonstrate the court's disapproval of the conduct. The other exception is where the court or tribunal wastes costs. The classic example of this is that the general rule is that justices or a tribunal will not appear before the court at a hearing. This is because the court is, in essence, supposed to adopt a neutral stance (Southey (2004) 140). That is not to say that the matter will not be contested; it will but ordinarily it will be the interested party that will undertake the opposing position.

14.3.4.3 Appeal

A judicial review can be the subject of further appeal in certain circumstances although the rules differ depending on the type of case.

Criminal cases

Where the judicial review is in respect of a decision of the magistrates' court then the only appeal that lies against the decision of the High Court is to the Supreme Court (s 1 *Administration of Justice Act 1960*). This is, in part, because it is not a decision of 'first instance' but rather a type of appeal; the matter being heard originally by the magistrates' and/or Crown Court. Leave for appeal is required to take a matter to the Supreme Court and whilst theoretically the Administrative Court can grant such permission, it would be extremely rare that it would do so and leave will normally be sought from the Supreme Court itself. Like all appeals to the Supreme Court, leave will only be granted if the matter raises a 'point of public importance' and it has to be accepted that they are comparatively rare.

Any appeal must be made within fourteen days of the decision of the Administrative Court (s 2) and notice of an application for leave must be served on the defendant and all interested parties.

Civil cases

As a general rule civil matters are the subject of an appeal to the Court of Appeal (Civil Division). Leave to appeal is required (CPR 52.3). This can be granted by the High Court itself or by the Court of Appeal. The latter would be used where the High Court has refused permission to appeal (Practice Direction 52, 4.7). Seeking permission from the Court of Appeal is not an appeal of the decision *not* to grant leave in the High Court but is a substantive matter in its own right. The decision would ordinarily be taken by a single judge of the Court of Appeal.

An appeal can only be made on the grounds that the judge has made an error of law but the proper exercise of discretion is, theoretically, a matter of law and so where the judge has declined to award a remedy this could be the subject of an appeal. The complication, however, is that the appellate courts will ordinarily not interfere with the discretion of a judge unless it is obviously wrong. Accordingly, there is a higher burden for the would-be appellant to discharge.

 # Summary

This chapter has provided an overview of the civil justice system and, in particular, looked at how a case proceeds through the small claims track or a judicial review. It has also:

- Noted that the courts are strongly supporting alternatives to litigation, particularly alternative dispute resolution (ADR) initiatives.

- Identified that a series of rules (known as the Civil Procedure Rules) govern the conduct of litigation and the overarching principle is that the judge must ensure that a case proceeds justly.

- Noted that these rules apply to all litigation regardless of which court the matter is to be heard in.

- Identified that there are three 'tracks' through which litigation proceeds—two of these tracks (fast track and multi-track) span both the county court and High Court, with the value of the claim deciding in which court the matter will be heard.

- Discussed the fact that judges have the ability to use costs orders in a flexible manner so as to 'control' proceedings and penalize parties that do not conduct themselves in the most appropriate manner—the ultimate sanction is a 'wasted costs order' which makes the lawyer for the party personally responsible for some or all of the costs.

- Noted that costs can also be used as a 'negotiating tool' where the defendant can make an offer to the claimant, or pay money into the court, to encourage a settlement—if, at trial, the judge does not award more money than that which was paid into court, the claimant is responsible for a significant proportion of the costs.

End-of-chapter questions

1. Read Lightman G (2003) 'The civil justice system and legal profession' 22 *Civil Justice Quarterly* 235–247.

   Lightman J in this article discusses civil litigation and he suggests that even recent reforms have not altered the general position that delays and costs remain problematic. The learned judge also places the blame for much of this on lawyers. To what extent do you believe that the judge is right? What are the incentives for lawyers to act quickly if they are paid daily?

2. Read the following articles: Andrews N (2000) 'A new civil procedural code for England' 19 *Civil Justice Quarterly* 19–38; and Davies GL (2006) 'Civil justice reform: Why we need to question some basic assumptions' 25 *Civil Justice Quarterly* 32–51.

   Andrews' article was written just after the introduction of the CPR and Davies' after five years of implementation. Davies believes that little has changed over the years and suggests that the problems of litigation will not be solved until we move away from the adversarial system. Would it be possible to move to an inquisitorial approach? What would the advantages and disadvantages of such an approach be?

 # Further reading

Lewis P (2006) 'The consumer's court? Revisiting the theory of the small claims procedure' 25 *Civil Justice Quarterly* 52–69.

This is an interesting article which considers the small claims track and how it has changed. It was initially set up as a way of ensuring ordinary citizens could litigate to enforce their rights but Lewis questions whether it is now being used by companies to enforce small debts against individuals.

Peysner J (2003) 'Finding predictable costs' 22 *Civil Justice Quarterly* 349–370.

This article considers the operation of fixed costs and assesses how the scheme operates in practice whilst drawing a comparison with other costs regimes.

Zuckerman AAS (2005) 'CPR Part 36 Offers' 24 *Civil Justice Quarterly* 167–184.

This is a comprehensive article which examines the approach the judiciary takes to Part 36 offers and its impact on the fees regime.

 For multiple choice questions, updates to this chapter and links to useful websites, please visit the Online Resource Centre at

www.oxfordtextbooks.co.uk/orc/gillespie_els3e/

15

Tribunals

By the end of this chapter you will be able to:

- Identify the type of disputes that are heard by tribunals.
- Understand how tribunals are constituted.
- Discuss the accountability of tribunals.
- Understand how a matter is heard by the Employment Tribunal.
- Understand how a matter is heard by the Investigatory Powers Tribunal.

Introduction

Not every dispute will necessarily be dealt with before a court. In this chapter it will be demonstrated that some disputes will be settled before they reach court, but other cases will never proceed before a court but will instead be heard by a different body. A system of tribunals has been created to deal with specific statutory issues. They are administrative rather than purely legal bodies and the rules will often vary between tribunals.

This chapter will take the same format as the previous chapter. The first part of the chapter will examine many of the key common aspects of the jurisdiction of tribunals. The second part of the chapter will examine the procedure followed by two very different tribunals through the use of case studies.

15.1 The tribunal system

The Senior President of Tribunals, Carnwath LJ, has commented:

> There is no doubt…that tribunals represent one of the most important pillars of the system of justice in this country…It is fair to say that more people bring a case before a tribunal than go to any other part of the justice system. (cited in Buck (2006) 459)

This is a worthy point and demonstrates the importance of a 'parallel' system of justice that exists alongside the courts. Tribunals are administrative bodies that are created by statute to resolve certain disputes. There are currently over seventy tribunals although there is a core of just over twenty tribunals that exercise judicial authority regularly. The use of tribunals became quite widespread in the latter half of the twentieth century where it was considered that their use would be preferable to allowing courts to settle administrative disputes. In part, this response was also to minimize pressure on the judicial process by diverting these disputes from the courts.

Whilst tribunals are not strictly courts, they must adhere to the general principles of due process and a key finding of the *Franks Report*, the report of a committee that was set up to examine how tribunals worked, was:

> In the field of tribunals openness appears to us to require the publicity of proceedings and knowledge of the essential reasoning underlying the decisions; fairness to require the adoption of a clear procedure which enables parties to know their rights, to present their case fully and to know the case which they have to meet…(Franks (1957) 10)

This is probably the distillation of the minimum requirements of due process but is not directly comparable to the judicial system. Since the *Franks Report* the number of tribunals has increased and their importance within the English Legal System has grown. After the *Woolf Report* into civil litigation it was thought that a review of tribunal justice would also be needed, in part to identify whether a separate system of dispute resolution was required alongside a reformed court system. Assuming that such a system was necessary (and the abolition of tribunals was never seriously on the agenda) then their status and effectiveness needed to be discussed in a way similar to the *Woolf* reforms. Together with the *Auld Report* into the criminal justice system this meant that there were, in effect, three reports that covered the entire justice system.

The task of examining the tribunals was given to Sir Andrew Leggatt, a former Lord Justice of Appeal, and he reported in 2001. Leggatt argued that tribunal justice carries with it two advantages: the first is that it consists of a mixture of legal and expert assistance, and the second is that their preparation and hearings should be simpler and more informal than courts (Leggatt (2001) para 1.2). However, he also found that the development of tribunals was ad hoc rather than systematic and that this had created a situation where there was no consistent application of justice within the tribunal system (Leggatt (2001) para 1.3).

15.1.1 Independence

One difficulty that was perceived by Leggatt was the independence of the tribunals. They were paid for by the departments which they oversaw and their staff were appointed by the respective Secretaries of State (Leggatt (2001) para 1.19). Given the increasingly judicial nature of the work that they undertake this would invite questions about the independence of the tribunals, including inviting arguments about the compatibility of the system with Article 6 of the European Convention on Human Rights (ECHR) (Leggatt (2001) paras 2.11–2.17). Certainly if reference is made to the earlier discussion on judicial independence (see 7.5 above) then it is clear that the appointment of the judiciary is a key concept defining independence and has led to incompatibility with Article 6 on previous occasions (*McGonnell v United Kingdom* (2000) 30 EHRR 289 and *Davidson v Scottish Ministers (No 2)* [2004] UKHL 34).

Leggatt concluded that tribunals should have the same independence as courts and they should be brought under a single department, preferably through a single executive agency. The government intended to legislate to do this (and has now done so as detailed below) but as an interim stage in 2006 the Tribunal Service was created as an executive agency of the (then) Department for Constitutional Affairs (DCA) (later Ministry of Justice) which assumed responsibility for most tribunals. The DCA purported to transfer jurisdiction administratively, stating that since the tribunals were the responsibility of its Secretaries of State they could choose administratively to transfer responsibility to the Secretary of State for the DCA, the Lord Chancellor.[1] Whilst primary legislation would have been tidier, the administrative consolidation worked at least in terms of consolidating procedures.

Eventually the government legislated and the *Tribunals, Courts and Enforcement Act 2007* (TCEA) has transformed the structure of the tribunals. Most notably, s 1 of the Act amends the *Constitutional Reform Act 2005* to ensure that the guarantee of judicial independence contained therein (see 7.5.2.1 above) also applies to the tribunal judiciary.

---

1. *Tribunal Service: Framework Document*, p 4.

15.1.2 Senior President

A Senior President of Tribunals is created by s 2 TCEA 2007. Originally the Senior President was to be appointed by the Lord Chief Justice but the statute now requires that appointment is made by the Queen on advice of the Lord Chancellor (s 2(1)). The Senior President will ordinarily be appointed by consultation with the Lord Chief Justice (and his equivalents in Scotland and Northern Ireland) but if this is not possible then the matter is referred to the Judicial Appointments Commission (Sch 1 TCEA 2007).

The first Senior President is Lord Justice Carnwath who has been the Senior President (designate) for several years whilst the legislation was being drafted. His responsibilities include coordinating the work of tribunals and, in particular, representing the views of the tribunal judiciary (Sch 1, Part 4, TCEA 2007). In order to discharge this duty the Senior President has the statutory power to lay written representations before Parliament (Sch 1, Part 4, TCEA 2007) and he does not need the permission of, for example, the Lord Chief Justice to do so. It has been noted that this gives the Senior President proper power as President in his own right and not as a delegate of the Lord Chief Justice (Carnwath (2007) 3).

It is no accident that the Senior President is a Lord Justice of Appeal given that the head of the Employment Appeals Tribunal and Asylum and Immigration Tribunal are both puisne judges. Whilst the Presidents continue to have leadership within their own tribunals the post of Senior President is obviously central to their coordination. The day-to-day (administrative) work of the Tribunal Service is the responsibility of the chief executive who liaises closely with the chief executives of all the tribunals brought under the auspices of the agency.

However there remains one tribunal that stands separate from the others, and this was with the approval of Leggatt (Leggatt (2001) para 3.11). This tribunal is the Investigatory Powers Tribunal (see below) and it has a unique jurisdiction. The tribunal, as will be seen, is more regulatory than others and also has a key investigatory process that others do not have. The tribunal is staffed by those who hold high judicial office or are eligible for a senior judicial appointment (see para 1, Sch 3, *Regulation of Investigatory Powers Act 2000* (RIPA 2000)). A president and vice-president must be appointed, both of which must be senior members of the judiciary (para 2, Sch 3). Currently these positions are filled by Mummery LJ (President) and Burton J (Vice-President). Having a Lord Justice of Appeal and puisne judge as its senior judges demonstrates a commitment to judicial independence and this is further strengthened by the fact that all members of the tribunal are appointed by letters patent (s 65 RIPA 2000) which means they can only be dismissed in the same way as members of the senior judiciary, ie only by an address of both Houses of Parliament (para 1(5), Sch 3).

15.1.3 Oversight

The TCEA 2007 created a new statutory body known as the *Administrative Justice and Tribunals Council* (s 44 TCEA 2007). The Council includes the Parliamentary Commissioner for Administration and between ten and fifteen appointed members (Sch 7, TCEA 2007). To reflect the fact that tribunals have a UK-wide remit, the appointees include appointments made in concurrence with Scottish and Welsh ministers (meaning devolved ministers rather than Westminster ministers). One of the appointed members will be made chair and the rest sit on the main Council. Committees of the

Council are created for the devolved bodies but as these are not part of the English Legal System they will not be considered here.

Along with having general duties on the administration of justice, the Council has specific duties in respect of tribunals, namely:

- to keep under review, and report on, the constitution and working of tribunals
- consider and report on any other matter that relates to tribunals or that the Council deems to be of special importance
- consider and report on any matter referred to the Council that relates to tribunals.

The Council may also scrutinize and comment on legislation that relates to tribunals. Presumably this includes draft legislation since otherwise scrutiny and comments are of little use since, of course, legislation is supreme and cannot be easily challenged in court (see Chapter 2).

In addition, a Tribunal Procedure Committee is created (Sch 5 TCEA 2007) which will include nominees of the Senior President, Lord Chancellor, Lord Chief Justice (and his equivalents in Scotland and Northern Ireland). The Committee is to produce Tribunal Procedure Rules which are, in essence, the equivalent of the *Civil Procedure Rules* and *Criminal Procedure Rules* used in the court system.

15.1.4 Composition of tribunal panels

One of the distinctive features of the administration of tribunals is that they involve a mixture of both judicial and lay members (Wikeley (2000) 484). More than this, it is not only each tribunal that will have a mix of judicial and lay members but also each constituted tribunal panel (ie the panel hearing each case) will involve such a mixture. Normally the judge will be the President of the bench and the lay members will sit alongside the judge. A comparison can arguably be drawn with appeals from magistrates' courts in the Crown Court (see 13.2.1 above) in that the lay members must take the law from the President but so far as decisions of fact are concerned, they hold an equal vote.

The background of lay members differs between the tribunals. For example, those who sit as lay members of the Employment Tribunals represent employers and employees, and one from each should normally sit (reg 8 *The Employment Tribunals (Constitution and Rules of Procedure) Regulations 2004*). The Social Security Tribunals differ with only lawyers, accountants, and members of the medical profession sitting together with those who worked (in a voluntary or salaried) position in connection with disabled persons (Wikeley (2000) 486). This demonstrates that the purpose of lay members is not strictly comparable to lay magistrates; they are not representing society as a whole, but rather they are designed to have some relevant experience that can assist the legal President. Certain appeal tribunals (ie tribunals that hear appeals from other tribunals) do not contain lay members but instead consist of a judge sitting alone. This is ordinarily because the appeal consists solely of issues of law (see below) but is relatively controversial in that most appellate courts, as has been seen, will consist of more than one person. That said, not all appeal tribunals sit in single panels and the Employment Appeals Tribunal (EAT), for example, continues to sit with lay members.

The appointment of judicial members has changed recently, in part to reflect the wider constitutional changes and also because of the *Human Rights Act 1998* (HRA

1998). Members are now selected by the *Judicial Appointments Commission* (JAC) (s 85 *Constitutional Reform Act 2005* when read in conjunction with Sch 14 and see Part 2 TCEA 2007) and appointed formally by the Lord Chancellor although the Lord Chancellor has strictly limited powers over vetoing any appointment by the JAC. The Commission and the powers of the Lord Chancellor in respect of them were considered in an earlier chapter of this book (see 7.3 above). The principal advantage of this change is that it introduces independence from the government. Previously, members tended to be appointed by the Secretary of State relevant to the tribunal. This did lead to concerns about their independence and impartiality, something that has been commented on (Leggatt (2001) para 2.20 and see 15.1.1 above). It was noted when discussing the judiciary that a series of claims were made under the HRA 1998 regarding the compatibility of part-time members of the judiciary with the ECHR. Similar concerns were raised with tribunals, this culminating in the Employment Appeals Tribunal, which it will be remembered, is a superior court of record, ruling that the previous system of making short-term appointments without clear guidelines on reappointment was incompatible (*Scanfuture Ltd v Secretary of State for Trade and Industry* [2001] ICR 1096). The government conceded that change was needed and as an interim measure the Lord Chancellor altered the appointment of tribunal members in a way similar to the action he took in respect of recorders.[2]

Another benefit of the introduction of the JAC is that it may also assist with the background of members. As with the court judiciary, women and members of the ethnic minorities are under-represented (Bailey et al (2007) 235 although some argue this has now changed (Falconer (2007)) and an independent body may assist in altering this. The socio-economic background of lay members is more complex, especially since many of the lay members are not 'lay' in the strictest sense but are members of relevant professions.

15.2 Structure of tribunals

It has already been noted that the TCEA 2007 has altered the structure of tribunals, but what is the current system? The Act creates two tribunals, known as the 'First-Tier Tribunal' and the 'Upper Tribunal'. The First-Tier Tribunal consists of six chambers, known as:

- Social Entitlement Chamber
- Health, Education and Social Care Chamber
- Taxation Chamber
- General Regulatory Chamber
- Immigration and Asylum Chamber
- War Pensions and Armed Forces Compensation Chamber.

These chambers will deal with the work of some of the pre-existing tribunals. For example, the *Criminal Injuries Compensation Appeal Panel* forms part of the *Social Entitlement Chamber* whilst the *Mental Health Review Tribunal* and the *Care Standards Tribunal* are subsumed within the *Health, Education and Social Care Chamber*. The

2. LCD Press Notice 284/00.

First-Tier Tribunal is, in essence, the equivalent of a first-instance jurisdiction even though this jurisdiction may include an appeal from an administrative judgment (eg Criminal Injuries Compensation).

The Upper Tribunal consist of four chambers: the *Administrative Appeals Chamber*; *Tax and Chancery Chamber*; *Lands Chamber*; and *Immigration and Asylum Chamber*. The Upper Tribunal largely deals with appeals from the First-Tier Tribunal although some complicated first-instance matters on, for example, tax and land can also form part of their work.

The First-Tier Tribunal and Upper Tribunal are not the only tribunals in existence, even in the medium term. It has already been noted that the *Investigatory Powers Tribunal* sits outside the structure but this is perhaps because of its specialist work (see 15.4.2 below). However other tribunals—that are more in line with the First-Tier and Upper Tribunals—also exist outside the system, most notably the *Employment Tribunals* and *Employment Appeals Tribunal*. These tribunals are within the *Tribunal Service* but do not feature in the revised structure although the government is likely eventually to include the *Asylum and Immigration Tribunal* within the new structure (Buck (2008)). The Employment (and Appeal) Tribunals are more difficult to locate within the structure easily, not least because the *Employment Appeals Tribunal* is considered to be a superior court of record.

15.2.1 Appeals

As noted above, appeals from the First-Tier Tribunals will ordinarily now proceed to the Upper Tribunal (s 11 TCEA 2007). Appeals from the Upper Tribunal will proceed to the Court of Appeal (Civil Division) (s 13 TCEA 2007). A further appeal is only permitted on matters of law and only with leave to appeal from either the Upper Tribunal or the Court of Appeal (Civil Division) (s 13(3)).

The TCEA 2007 left unanswered an interesting question over the judicial review of tribunals. It will be noted (see 15.3 below) that most tribunals were ordinarily considered to be inferior bodies and thus subject to the judicial review of the High Court. Would the same be true of the revised tribunal structure? The First-Tier Tribunal remains an inferior body but the TCEA 2007 purports to transfer the judicial review jurisdiction over this tribunal from the High Court to the Upper Tribunal (s 15 TCEA 2007) and thus the High Court should decline jurisdiction and instead leave this to the Upper Tribunal (in part based on the rule that judicial review by the High Court should only be permitted where no alternative remedy exists). The precise delineation between the judicial review jurisdiction of the Upper Tribunal and the High Court is still unclear (for a discussion see Buck (2008)).

What of the Upper Tribunal? It is clear that the Upper Tribunal is a superior court of record (s 3(5) TCEA 2007) but this is not conclusive by itself since, of course, the Crown Court is also a superior court and it is reviewable for matters other than trials on indictment. The answer to the question is to be found in the decision of the Court of Appeal (Civil Division) in *R (on the application of C) v Upper Tribunal* [2010] EWCA Civ 859. The Court of Appeal held that the Upper Tribunal is subject to judicial review because it does not have the same status as the High Court, not least because its jurisdiction is based on statute rather than the inherent jurisdiction to resolve matters. The Court of Appeal also noted that the belief that a superior court of record could not be reviewed has never been clarified by the English courts and is not recognized by the

Scottish courts (which may be relevant as the First-Tier and Upper Tribunals are UK bodies, not simply bodies of England and Wales). The court preferred to reason that as Parliament is aware of the High Court's power to judicially review, it would have used express words to divest the Upper Tribunal from this power had it so intended, and in the absence of such language, the Tribunal is theoretically at least reviewable.

However, the court noted that the fact that it can be reviewed as a matter of law does not mean that it will be in practice or identify what it may be reviewed for. The court noted that judicial review related to various grounds, some of which were controlled by discretion, but that it would be a dereliction of the High Court's duty to let a court or tribunal act in excess of its authority or where it had denied a party a fair hearing (at [26]). However, in terms of other matters of judicial review (eg procedural impropriety etc) the court noted that Parliament had created the tribunal system to be an independent and self-sufficient system that should correct its own errors of adjudication.

Accordingly, the Court of Appeal held that the Upper Tribunal is amendable to judicial review by the High Court where it purports to exercise jurisdiction it has not been given by Parliament or where it denies the right to a fair trial through, for example, allowing someone to sit as judge who should not. At one level this decision could be considered to be a reasonable compromise in that such challenges will be rarely brought: and the Court of Appeal is stating that where the judicial review is in respect of their adjudication then a review will not be heard and the ordinary appellate rules should apply. On another level, however, this can be said to be a fudge. A right of appeal exists from the Upper Tribunal to the Court of Appeal (Civil Division) on matters of law (s 13 TCEA 2007). The jurisdiction of the Tribunal and the right to a fair trial are both matters of law and so it must be questioned whether it is truly necessary for the High Court to claim the right to judicially review the Tribunal rather than, for example, allowing the Court of Appeal to correct such an error. It may have perhaps been simpler to do this but the courts are slow to limit their own jurisdiction.

15.3 Court or tribunal?

The key question in this area that needs to be answered is what, if anything, is the difference between a court and a tribunal. The answer is not easy, not least because certain tribunals are actually considered to be superior courts of record (see, in particular, the Employment Appeals Tribunal: s 20(2) *Employment Tribunal Act 1996*), that is to say the equivalent of the High Court.

Some argue that the difference is as regards their jurisdiction. There are two parts to this argument. The first is that a court will ordinarily have general rather than specific jurisdiction, ie its work will not be limited to one small aspect of the law, whereas tribunals are created by statute to examine certain specific areas (eg the Employment Tribunal which examines employment issues, the *Special Educational Needs and Disability Tribunal* (now within the *Health, Education & Social Care Chamber* of the *First-Tier Tribunal*) which allows parents and children to ensure that their educational needs are appropriately resourced by the appropriate authorities). As a rule of thumb this can be quite a useful test but it is often said that it is flawed because specialist courts do exist, most notably the Bankruptcy Court (which deals with bankruptcies), the Commercial Court (which deals with high-value commercial transactions between companies, often relating to trade marks), and the Admiralty Court (which deals with disputes relating to shipping). However, it could be argued that this does not contradict the point which is made because technically these 'courts' are not individual courts but rather groupings within the Queen's Bench Division of the High Court of Justice (see 6.2.4 above). Accordingly the overarching body—the High Court—does still have general jurisdiction.

The second aspect to the argument about jurisdiction concerns not just the area of law but also the type of decision reached. It is sometimes said that tribunals are there to ensure that administrative actions have been taken correctly. Whilst this is undoubtedly true for some tribunals (eg the *Land Tribunal* (subsumed within the Upper Tribunal) which examines questions about compensation arising from the compulsory acquisition of land by government) it becomes less clear for other tribunals (eg the Employment Tribunals). Also, it cannot be determinative since the High Court has a reviewing jurisdiction through the doctrine of judicial review and one of the three grounds for invoking this procedure is procedural impropriety, ie not following the correct administration (see *Council of Civil Service Unions v Minister for the Civil Service* [1985] AC 374).

It can be seen therefore that it is not simple to identify what the difference between a court and tribunal is. At one point it was thought that perceptions may be the difference: ie the executive views tribunals as administrative bodies although the judiciary views them as judicial or quasi-judicial bodies (Franks (1957) 9). Leggatt suggested that there were three tests to decide whether a matter should be heard by a tribunal or court ((2001) paras 1.11–1.13):

1. Participation. Tribunals are considered to be inclusive and are designed, so far as possible, to be dealt with without the need for a lawyer.

2. Special expertise. Where a matter is outside the knowledge of the tribunal of fact a court will ordinarily permit the parties to adduce expert evidence by calling witnesses. Tribunals, however, will ordinarily consist of a legally qualified chair with experts sitting alongside them.

3. Specialist administrative expertise. Tribunals specialize in dealing with the combination of law and administration that relates to administrative or regulatory bodies. The absence of this would ordinarily leave judicial review as the only option.

However, it is not clear that this necessarily helps because many of these factors can be applied to both. For example, the absence of representation (which is discussed below) is also a feature of the small claims court although this is perhaps not as significant since the small claims court is perhaps not representative of a 'court' and indeed the scheme is often considered closer to arbitration than litigation (see 15.2.1 above). However, Leggatt was not necessarily suggesting that these factors will only be found in a court but that it makes it more likely that a matter will be heard in a tribunal.

To an extent it can be argued that the distinction between tribunals and courts is not particularly relevant. Modern tribunals are bound by the HRA 1998 in the same way as are courts (s 6(3)(a) states a 'public authority' includes a 'court or tribunal') and the disputes heard by tribunals will almost certainly be considered a 'right or obligation' within the meaning of Article 6(1) of the ECHR. On that basis it could be legitimately questioned whether there is any significant disadvantage that arises from a matter being heard by a tribunal rather than a court. The two issues that tend to give concern are issues of precedent and representation.

15.3.1 Precedent

The importance of precedent to the English Legal System has been noted already (see, most notably, Chapter 3 above) but what is the position with tribunals setting precedent? It has been suggested that this can be a way in which they differ from the courts:

> [A] tribunal is...in a radically different position from a court of law. Its duty is to reach the right decision in the circumstances of the moment, any discretion must be genuinely exercised, and there must be no blind following of its previous decisions. (Wade and Forsyth (2004) 931)

Before examining what this means it is necessary to pause to consider whether this is 'radically different' from courts of law. Decisions of the county court do not set precedent nor, it will be remembered, do decisions of the High Court when it is sitting as a court of first instance (see 3.2 above). However, it is clear that the courts need to follow the precedent of higher courts and also will normally be slow to depart from its own decisions even when technically not bound by them.

However, the point made by Wade and Forsyth is that a tribunal is (supposedly) concentrating on the individual facts of the case at hand rather than adopting a consistent approach to principles. However, is this necessarily either correct or appropriate? It has been suggested that whilst this was true historically the modern role of tribunals requires them to interpret legislation in a similar way to the courts (Buck (2006) 465). Accordingly, it can be questioned whether it would not be more appropriate for their interpretations to be consistent? It will be remembered from Chapter 3 that the principle of *stare decisis* is considered to be a fundamental principle of English justice and so the abandonment of this policy at tribunal level could be construed as a lowering of fairness.

In fact it would be naive to suggest that there is no precedent within the tribunal system. Certain tribunals publish their decisions and allow them to be cited (the most obvious examples being the Employment Appeals Tribunal and the (then) Care Standards Tribunal). Also, most tribunals are inferior bodies (the principal exceptions being the Employment Appeals Tribunal, Investigatory Powers Tribunal, and the Immigration Tribunal) and may (unless prohibited by statute) be the subject of judicial review. If they are subject to judicial review then they are required to follow the rulings of the High Court (now Upper Tribunal in some cases—see 15.2.1 above) and thus a rudimentary form of *stare decisis* is created.

Even where a tribunal is not subject to judicial review it is possible that rudimentary precedent will be created. It had been customary to differentiate between first- and second-tier tribunals and it has been suggested that precedent replicates the appellate structure and the relationship between the tribunals (Buck (2006) 466), and this has now been formalized by the TCEA 2007 reforms (see 15.2 above).

⊙ FIRST- AND SECOND-TIER TRIBUNALS

It is customary to refer to 'first-tier' and 'second-tier' tribunals. In essence first-tier tribunals were those tribunals that exercise original jurisdiction, ie they make findings of fact and provide an appropriate relief or declaration. Examples of this would include the Employment Tribunal and now the First-Tier Tribunal itself.

Second-tier tribunals are appellate tribunals and are more concerned with ensuring that a person who believes a decision made by a first-tier tribunal has been wrongly made has a means of redress. Perhaps the classic example of this is the Employment Appeals Tribunal. Leggatt proposed a single second-tier tribunal be created to hear appeals from most first-tier tribunals (Leggatt (2001) para 6.10) but he did accept that a small number of tribunals would be excepted from this regime and appeals would proceed direct to the courts (Leggatt (2001) para 6.14) and that as a consequence alternative appeals, including judicial review, should no longer be permitted (Leggatt (2001) para 6.30). As noted above, this is the position that has now largely been created (see 15.2 above) although certain first- and second-tier tribunals exist outside of this structure.

Leggatt considered how precedent should work following his reforms. He suggested that first-tier tribunals should not set precedent (Leggatt (2001) para 6.19), ie a first-tier tribunal would not be bound by the previous decision of a first-tier tribunal. This would appear somewhat logical and comparable to first instance decisions of courts. However, Leggatt also ruled out decisions of second-tier tribunals automatically creating precedent (Leggatt (2001) para 6.24) because he believed that it would be a barrier to access since users of tribunals would be required to be familiar with decisions of the second-tier tribunal. However, others suggest that precedent in tribunals could actually assist tribunal users, not least by efficiently clarifying and developing the law (Buck (2006) 465) and ensuring that someone seeking advice is able properly to predict the law. The compromise suggested by Leggatt is that some decisions will set precedent but others will not (Leggatt (2001) para 6.26). The tribunal itself would select which decisions would become precedent and these would be published.

This suggestion can be immediately contrasted with the position in the courts where it has been held that it is *not* for a judge passing judgment to decide what does, or does not, create precedent (see 3.3.2 above). Also, it is not immediately clear how this system will assist users of tribunals as they must become familiar with certain precedents. Presumably, however, since there will be a small number of binding precedents these could be accompanied by summaries prepared and publicized on, for example, tribunal websites.

It is too early to say how precedent is working following the reforms of the TCEA 2007 but this is something that will need to be watched closely. As the Upper Tribunal beds in it is quite possible that precedent will become established. This, together with the other reforms of the TCEA 2007, are arguably bringing tribunals closer to full-court status and the challenge will no doubt be ensuring that their accessibility to the public remains intact.

❓ QUESTION FOR REFLECTION

If tribunals adjudicate on questions of law (including the application of a statutory provision) rather than just examine whether an administrative process has been followed, should the system of *stare decisis* not apply in the same way as it does in the court system? One of the reasons why it does not appear to be followed literally is the informal nature of tribunals (Leggatt (2001) para 6.24) but is this a valid excuse? Should a person seeking justice before a tribunal not expect a consistent approach to be taken as to the law?

LISTEN TO THE PODCAST

For guidance on how to answer this question and a discussion of the main issues, listen to the author's podcast on the Online Resource Centre:
www.oxfordtextbooks.co.uk/orc/gillespie_els3e/

15.3.2 Representation

It has been seen that in both the civil and criminal justice system it is not strictly necessary to employ a lawyer to represent oneself in court. However, with the exception of certain proceedings in the magistrates' court (eg guilty pleas to driving offences) or small claims court it is probably more desirable if lawyers are engaged, but what is the position with tribunals?

A principal advantage of the tribunal system is said to be that they are informal and user-friendly (Wade and Forsyth (2009) 771). All of the tribunals try to make themselves accessible to those that need to access them. This includes the provision of step-by-step instructions on how to access the service.[3]

An example of accessibility is the fact that there are extremely wide rights of audience in most tribunals. Not only can the applicant act as a litigant in person during a tribunal but he has the choice to engage a lawyer (unless specifically prohibited by statute) or take any other person as representative (see, for example, s 6 *Employment Tribunal Act 1996*). A difficulty with engaging a lawyer is the fact that legal aid (or equivalent) is not generally available for tribunals, and where a tribunal does not specifically permit a lawyer to be engaged it is unlikely that the rules of the tribunal will permit the fees to be reclaimed by the successful party. Where legal aid has failed many bodies have stepped in. Those who belong to a trade union will normally be given representation, with most unions employing workers who specialize in tribunal litigation. The Citizens Advice Bureau (CAB), an independent charity, has also begun to adopt a representation service for those areas of work within its expertise (usually employment, rent, and social welfare). Even universities have entered this sector with some undergraduate law programmes including a 'law clinic' whereby undergraduates, under the supervision of staff (who frequently hold professional practice certificates), undertake legal work in the community including providing representation before clinics.

If representation is permitted by others then this does raise the question whether tribunals are litigant-friendly. It is one thing suggesting that a lawyer does not need to be engaged, but if a representative (eg a union official or CAB worker) is useful then does this not mean that legal representation would be useful? There is evidence to suggest that representation was beneficial to those using tribunals (Leggatt (2001) para 4.21) and yet despite this there is strong resistance to the use of representation in tribunals. Some argue that engaging a lawyer would simply add to costs, delay, and complexity (Bailey et al (2002) 1077 and see Leggatt (2001) para 4.21). Why is it that the lack of legal representation is considered to be an advantage? Is it truly an advantage or is this a justification that is used to disguise the fact that it would be expensive for lawyers to be used in all tribunals?

It is difficult to argue against the suggestion that representation is helpful because the representative is almost certainly familiar with the tribunal process and will

---

3. The Online Resource Centre that accompanies this book provides links to the principal tribunal websites which will allow you to access the materials available and understand how to initiate proceedings.

therefore be able to structure the submissions in an effective way that demonstrates the claim made. A litigant in person is unlikely to have legal training and yet is being asked to put forward an argument based, in part at least, on law, something they are unlikely to know anything about. It has been noted that the right to representation, including legal representation, has not traditionally been considered a principle of natural justice (Wade and Forsyth (2009) 789) but the decision of the European Court of Human Rights in *Steel and Morris v United Kingdom* (2005) 41 EHRR 22, which suggested that Article 6 could require legal assistance to be provided where lack of it would lead to an inequality of arms, does take a further step towards identifying a right to legal representation. Whilst it may be thought that an inequality of arms may not exist within a tribunal system of justice it is conceivable to identify circumstances. A spin on the facts of *Steel and Morris* is possible whereby a private individual is seeking to refer a large multinational corporation to an employment tribunal. Other examples may include situations where it is a private individual against the state where one party (the state) can afford to engage leading counsel whereas the individual litigant may not. However, the counter-argument is that the decision in *Steel and Morris* was based, in part, on the fact that High Court proceedings are inherently formal and technical. Since tribunal proceedings are not then it could be argued that the same level of representation is not required.

In this era of restricted public legal funding (discussed in Chapter 9) it is perhaps unrealistic to expect an absolute right to legal representation. The current system relies on specialized lay persons stepping into the breach but is this appropriate? In a now rather dated report, Bell noted that there was a perception that tribunal justice did not consider that lawyers needed to be engaged but thought that tribunals should be more inclusive (Bell (1975) 19). To some degree this has been taken on board by the tribunals through the provision of guidance to bringing a case, but can a litigant in person ever be considered comparable to a professional representative? It has been suggested that a fundamental principle of tribunal justice is that tribunals are adversarial (Wade and Forsyth (2009) 783) but it is not clear why this is the case. It is suggested that deviating from the adversarial process means that favouritism could be shown but this does not automatically follow. An inquisitor can remain independent and it has been noted elsewhere that there is a tendency in the civil litigation system to move away from strict adversarial approaches.

Is the solution therefore not to adopt a more inquisitorial system? In that way the emphasis is placed on the tribunals and not the litigants but this may not necessarily be welcome as it could lead to more focus on the constitution of the tribunal, including a consideration as to whether all members (including lay members) should be better rewarded as they will need to alter their approach to a case. The conundrum as to rights of audience looks as though it will continue for some time yet.

QUESTION FOR REFLECTION

Tribunals are, potentially, dealing with extremely important issues, including the integrity of litigants (in, for example, employment disputes or disputes before the *Care Standards Tribunal* (now *Health, Education and Social Care* Chamber of the First-Tier Tribunal) which decides, inter alia, upon the suitability of teachers to work with vulnerable members of society) and certain disputes will concern significant sums of money. Is it right, therefore, that the engagement of a lawyer should be exceptional in such cases?

What advantages and disadvantages is there to the routine appointment of lawyers (including state-funded lawyers where appropriate)?

🎧 LISTEN TO THE PODCAST

For guidance on how to answer this question and a discussion of the main issues, listen to the author's podcast on the Online Resource Centre:
www.oxfordtextbooks.co.uk/orc/gillespie_els3e/

15.4 The tribunals

So far we have identified some of the core themes that exist in relation to the use of tribunals as a form of administering justice. In this section of the chapter this will be placed into context by providing an illustration of how certain tribunals operate.

15.4.1 Ordinary (open) tribunals

For many tribunals their work is open and may be watched by members of the public in the same way that court hearings are. The hearings usually take place in designated rooms that have the appearance of modern civil courtrooms although usually everyone is all on the same level and usually there is no coat of arms.

Will a user of a tribunal notice any difference between a court and a tribunal? Some of the controversies surrounding any distinction between court and tribunal have been noted above but in practice what would a person see? For this purpose the Employment Tribunal will be examined.

👁 **Example** Employment Tribunal

The Employment Tribunal is one of the more well-known tribunals. During the year 2009/10, over 236,000 cases were accepted by the Employment Tribunal (Annual Report)—a significant increase from 2008/9 when approximately 150,000 cases were accepted. To cope with this significant workload the Tribunal sits on multiple occasions at numerous locations. Its jurisdiction is set out, inter alia, in the *Employment Tribunals Act 1996* and covers over seventy different types of employment dispute. The tribunals used to be known as Industrial Tribunals but were renamed Employment Tribunals by s 1 *Employment Rights (Dispute Resolutions) Act* 1988.

In the same way that both civil and criminal courts have rules governing their procedure, so does the Employment Tribunal, these being contained within Sch 1 *The Employment Tribunals (Constitution and Rules of Procedure) Regulations 2004*, SI 2004/1861 (as amended by *The Employment Tribunals (Constitution and Rules of Procedure) (Amendment) Regulations 2008*, SI 2008/3240. Reference must be made to these rules in order to progress a case although the tribunal does produce a series of guides to progressing a case.

Rule 14(2) states:

> the tribunal shall seek to avoid formality in...its proceedings and shall not be bound
> by any enactment or rule of law relating to the admissibility of evidence in proceedings
> before the courts of law.

There are two important aspects to this rule. The first is that proceedings should be informal and the second is that ordinary rules of evidence should not apply.

It is often said that an advantage of tribunals is their informality (Wade and Forsyth (2009) 784; Leggatt (2001) para 1.24) but is this true? The suggestion of informality is supposedly in contrast with the formality of court proceedings. However, it is less clear that this occurs. For example, in order to apply to the tribunal it is necessary to complete an application form which is then served on the respondent. This is directly analogous to the position before a court although it is accepted that this is because the courts have, in recent years, made their forms more user-friendly. However, the analogies do not stop there and there is a tightly controlled pre-hearing regime that must be undertaken. Within the Employment Tribunal this includes a case management hearing (rule 17) which discusses how the hearing will be undertaken. Issues such as the number of witnesses and witness statements to be heard will be discussed together with the admissibility of other evidence. The likely length of the final hearing should also be discussed at this hearing. In other words, it can be seen that the tribunal is also keen to avoid delays and will structure matters so far as possible. By requiring witnesses to be disclosed and statements to be exchanged etc the process is becoming more formalized since there will be sanctions for failing to undertake such action.

Before the hearing takes place there will also be a pre-hearing review (rule 18) which will ordinarily decide whether there is a prima facie case. This will involve a person demonstrating that they have, for example, suffered unfair treatment or discrimination. Types of evidence that could be adduced at this stage include witnesses, witness statements, and documentary evidence. This will be a hearing that takes place in public. Can this be easily described as informal?

The hearing itself takes place in public too. It has already been noted that rule 14(2) states that the tribunal is not bound by rules of evidence. This theoretically means that any evidence that is relevant can be heard. This can be contrasted with the traditional position in the courts where the probity of evidence was considered to be a relevant factor. Traditionally, hearsay (which for our purposes can be summarized as second-hand evidence) was not permitted by the courts although in recent years this has changed (see *Civil Evidence Act 1995* and *Criminal Justice Act 2003*).

It has been noted already that tribunal proceedings tend to remain adversarial even though rule 14(3) states:

> the tribunal...shall make such enquiries of persons appearing before it and witnesses as
> it considers appropriate and shall otherwise conduct the hearing in such a manner as it
> considers most appropriate for the clarification of the issues before it generally to the just
> handling of the proceedings...

This could be construed as permitting an inquisitorial approach (see, in particular, the right to 'make enquiries' and the 'clarification of issues'). Adopting a more inquisitorial approach could potentially make proceedings more informal and would certainly allow a contrast to be made with the courts.

However there is little evidence to suggest that tribunals are using this power and the adversarial model remains supreme.

Not only is the adversarial system used but all of its formalities are. Rule 27(2) states that witnesses may be called and whilst it is to be hoped that witnesses will give evidence voluntarily, the tribunal does have the right to issue a witness summons (s 7(3)(d) *Employment Tribunals Act 1996*) and this is backed by the creation of a criminal offence of failing to attend (s 7(4)). Where witnesses do attend then they will ordinarily give their evidence on oath (rule 27(3)) which means that false testimony constitutes perjury. It is difficult to see how this can be considered an informal approach. Whilst rule 27(2) relaxing the rules of evidence will mean that the technicalities of examination-in-chief and cross-examination need not be followed to the letter (see 12.3.2 for a discussion of this), the examination of witnesses remains a key skill and one that the average lay person does not possess. If we return to the issue about representation discussed above it can be seen that this is where a lay person could be disadvantaged. If the litigant is not a member of a union then it may be difficult for them to obtain a representative without privately financing it (and for which they are unlikely to be recompensed). Yet is a litigant in person likely to know how to conduct a cross-examination without assistance?

Further difficulties with proceedings have been noted by Leggatt:

> At the hearings, users can experience some quite old-fashioned processes. Examples include a legal representative reading out in full a paper submission which is already in front of all the parties; witnesses being asked to read out their written statements; or witnesses being taken slowly through detailed, uncontroversial, factual material where simple confirmation that the position is as set out in the documents would suffice. (Leggatt (2001) para 1.23)

In these circumstances it is difficult to see how it can be properly claimed that a tribunal is more informal than a court hearing. Indeed the only issues that appear to differ are the absence of lawyers and the fact that the tribunal will ordinarily consist of both a legally qualified member and two lay members. Given that all members are paid and most civil matters within a court are heard by a single judge it must be questioned whether this is an advantage of the tribunal system. The same can be said of other tribunals, eg the *Care Standards Tribunal* (now *Health, Education & Social Care Chamber* of the *First-Tier Tribunal*) which, inter alia, is called upon to adjudicate upon the suitability of a person working with children or vulnerable adults. Again a legally qualified chair will sit with two lay members but do the lay members (who will frequently have a background in social services or education) add anything to the adjudication? Within the criminal justice system the decision as to the suitability of a person to work with children is something that a judge himself is entrusted with (see, for example, s 29A *Criminal Justice and Court Services Act 2000*).

15.4.2 Closed tribunals

Not every tribunal is open to the public and certain tribunals will sit in private. Some of these tribunals will be dealing with relatively mundane matters (eg appeals relating to the determination of tax) but others can be dealing with extremely sensitive work. Perhaps the most restrictive tribunal is the *Investigatory Powers Tribunal* (IPT) which was created by Part IV of RIPA 2000, a statute which (as its name suggests) regulates the use of covert investigation powers by the state. The tribunal has been described as:

> being different from all others in that its concern is with security. For this reason it must remain separate from the rest and ought not to have any relationship with other tribunals. (Leggatt (2001) para 3.11)

Although Leggatt is correct to argue that its work relates to security it is less clear as to what this means exactly. There are currently over forty bodies that are authorized to use some or all of the powers within RIPA 2000 (see, for example, the *Regulation of Investigatory Powers (Directed Surveillance and Covert Human Intelligence Sources) Order 2003*, SI 2010/521) and whilst some undoubtedly deal with security matters (eg GCHQ, the Security Services (MI5), and the Secret Intelligence Service (MI6)) others may appear less important (eg the Food Standards Agency or the Gaming Board for Great Britain).

The powers that are available to these bodies are extremely sensitive and are outside the scope of this book and their use of the powers can be very controversial. The detailed use of the powers will frequently be kept secret, even during a criminal trial, through a process known as *public interest immunity* (PII) (Ashworth and Redmayne (2010)). Whilst the Act provides for the regulation of these powers through a body known as the *Office of the Surveillance Commissioners*, this body does not examine individual complaints but focuses on whether the powers are, in general, being used appropriately. The use of covert surveillance against a person is a prima facie breach of Article 8 of the ECHR in that it is an interference with a person's private life (see, for example, *Malone v United Kingdom* (1985) 7 EHRR 14). If used appropriately this will not matter as it is justified under Article 8(2) but how can this be tested?

It has been noted already that courts, both civil and criminal, are prima facie public bodies and should sit in public and provide for a public pronouncement of the decision. The powers available under RIPA 2000 are so sensitive that the government would not wish them to be discussed in public because it could assist those that they could be used against (ie criminals could use the knowledge to develop anti-surveillance techniques). The HRA 1998 requires (s 7) that someone who believes the powers are being used against them inappropriately should have the right to take action against authorities and the IPT is this action. Section 65(2) RIPA 2000 states that an action can *only* be brought in the IPT. In *R (on the application of A) v B* [2009] UKSC 12 the Supreme Court upheld this provision of RIPA 2000 and rejected an argument that the *Human Rights Act 1998* required that there should be access to the ordinary courts. The Supreme Court held that the IPT had been given exclusive jurisdiction by Parliament and that the courts had no jurisdiction to hear matters within s 65 of RIPA even where they did not relate to the regulation of investigatory powers.

The rules of the tribunal are loosely set out in secondary legislation (*Investigatory Powers Tribunal Rules 2000*, SI 2000/2665) but RIPA 2000 itself states (s 68(1)) that the tribunal shall decide its own procedure in respect of complaints. It is taken to mean that the tribunal can, therefore, issue its own rules but also that it may alter them depending on the circumstances. This rule is subject to the rules set out in the statutory instrument but the tribunal, as the sole arbitrator of claims under the HRA 1998, has used its authority to strike down at least one section of the rules (that which requires it to sit in secrecy; see below). Accordingly the position appears to be that where the rules are incompatible with the ECHR the tribunal reserves the right to be the ultimate arbitrator of its own procedure, in part because of the fact that decisions of the tribunal are not ordinarily the subject of an appeal.

Unlike a traditional matter, the adjudication of a matter raised in the IPT could lead to an investigation of the matter. Members of the tribunal are empowered to require the Intelligence or Security Services Commissioners to assist them (rule 5(1)(b)) or to require any public authority to disclose to it such documents and information as it requires (rule 5(1)(c)). It can be seen, therefore, that the adjudication appears to take the form of an inquisitorial hearing rather than a simple adjudication. This is taken further by the fact that there is no disclosure of documents; indeed the statutory rules make it clear that the general rule is that the claimant will *not* be given any details of information provided by the state bodies (s 69(6) RIPA 2000 and rule 6).

The IPT does not, unlike most other tribunals, have to hold a hearing, the rules making clear that any hearings are purely discretionary (rule 9(2)) although there may be concerns as to whether this is necessarily compatible with the ECHR since Article 6 is generally taken to mean that there is a right to access a court (or tribunal) where a civil right or obligation is in dispute. As has been noted, covert surveillance is a prima facie breach of Article 8 and thus it is a matter of civil rights or obligation. Accordingly, a person should ordinarily have a right to judicial adjudication although it is less clear whether this right requires an actual hearing or whether it is merely a judicial determination of the issues which could, for example, mean the matter being disposed of by an examination of the relevant papers.

Even if hearings do take place, however, they are unlikely to take the format of the traditional adversarial approach with both sides being in the same room hearing and challenging all the evidence. Rule 9(4) states that it is possible to hold separate hearings for the different sides and at least one commentator has suggested that this will be the normal position (Fenwick (2001)). Again this must raise questions over its compatibility with Article 6 of the ECHR since this places significant restrictions on the ability of a person to conduct their case.

Assuming that hearings are held, the statutory rules are quite clear about their nature:

> The Tribunal's proceedings, including any oral hearings, shall be conducted in private. (rule 9(6))

In other words all matters relating to the tribunal are held in secret with members of the public and press excluded. Again this raises questions about compliance with basic freedoms under both domestic and ECHR jurisprudence where the traditional rule is that hearings are in public. There has always been the opportunity for courts to sit in camera (meaning in secret) where it is necessary to protect information in the interests of security or other public interest matters but this has always been the exception to the rule. The rules purport to state that tribunal activities can *never* be in public and the tribunal has decided that this is incompatible with basic rights and overturned this rule (Langdon-Down (2003) 22). Some have suggested that this may lead to more transparency, and certainly it is interesting that the website for the tribunal is examining the possibility of listing its rulings in public (although, of course, the rulings will be sanitized in terms of party names and operational details) and this is to be welcomed.

It can be seen, therefore, that the IPT operates in a significantly different way from both ordinary tribunals and the courts. Certainly it makes a clear contrast from courts where there are more rigid and formalistic approaches to the adjudication of matters and where the adversarial model of justice remains important. This distinction continues when it relates to evidence. Like the Employment Tribunal the IPT has wide powers over evidence but its rule is formulated slightly differently:

> The Tribunal may receive evidence in any form, and may receive evidence that would not be admissible in a court of law. (rule 11(1))

Arguably this is very similar to the form of words adopted for the Employment Tribunals but it is expressed in a stronger way, making clear that there is no doubt that the IPT can receive inadmissible evidence. This can be contrasted immediately with both civil and criminal courts where certain evidence, particularly in respect of covert surveillance, would ordinarily not be admissible in evidence. This would appear to support the earlier argument that the IPT adopts an inquisitorial rather than adversarial system when deciding whether a person's rights have been infringed.

Example Inadmissible evidence—telephone taps

The use of 'telephone taps' (more properly known as an interception of communication) has always been controversial within the English Legal System. Section 17 of RIPA 2000 makes clear that the product of an intercept (ie the actual conversation) is not admissible in evidence. Let us take an example.

The police suspect Mandy is involved in the importation of a large quantity of illegal drugs. In order to find out where the drugs originate, they place an intercept onto Mandy's telephone. They hear Mandy talking to Alan and she is heard agreeing to buy 20 kilos of heroin to be imported into Whitby docks.

For whatever reason the drugs do not appear in Whitby. Technically speaking the conversation between Mandy and Alan amounts to a criminal offence (a conspiracy) but since s 17 RIPA 2000 applies, the police cannot adduce the transcript of the telephone conversation and so it is unlikely that any conspiracy could be proven.

Since the IPT can receive any evidence, however, including inadmissible evidence, they could ask for transcripts. Let us assume that Mandy has complained to the IPT that she believes her telephone has been tapped and that the police have been listening to conversations with her lawyer, thus breaching legal professional privilege. Not only can the IPT ask the police whether they have intercepted any conversations but it could demand the transcripts which would allow it to decide whether legal professional privilege has been breached.

Looked at in this way it would appear that removing any barrier to admissibility would seem to be a safeguard but it can also work against a private citizen. The IPT will frequently have to decide whether it was appropriate for the state to use covert investigation powers and this will include examining the type of person the defendant is. Although it is often said that the criminal law is not concerned over the probity of evidence (see *R v Sang* [1980] AC 402), the criminal law does have strict rules concerning some aspects of admissibility. Perhaps the most notable is in respect of the admissibility of confessions (see s 76 *Police and Criminal Evidence Act 1984* (PACE 1984); note that confession means a statement wholly or partially adverse to the person making it (s 82) and not just the 'classic' example of a confession seen in television shows) and also rules on misconduct by state officials (see, for example, s 78 PACE 1984) and on abuses of process through, for example, entrapment (see *Attorney-General's Reference (No 3 of*

2000); R v Looseley [2001] UKHL 53). However, since the IPT can receive any evidence then it does not matter how the state agencies gathered the evidence (illegally or inappropriately) it will still be perfectly admissible.

The secrecy of the IPT invariably leads to questions being raised as to whether it is a fair system, especially since it rejects many of the adversarial principles that are so coveted in other aspects of the judicial system. The fact that a person is not necessarily able to be involved with the full case nor able to see the evidence on which the state relies must certainly raise questions as to fairness even if these are unproven. These questions are perhaps given more weight by the fact that according to the Intelligence Services Commissioner's report (the Commissioner reports to Parliament (via the prime minister) on activities relating to surveillance) there were 157 applications made to the IPT in 2009 (the last year for which figures were produced). Of these, fifty-eight were resolved by the end of that year, with sixty-seven of the seventy-five cases held over from the previous year also being resolved (ISC (2010) 12). Of these 125 cases only a single case led to a complaint being upheld (and the Commissioner notes that this means that this is only the fourth occasion when the tribunal has upheld a complaint). The details of the complaint have not been published but it is said that it did not relate to any of the agencies over which the Intelligence Services Commissioner had jurisdiction (ibid). This is an extraordinary statistic and either means that RIPA 2000 is working extremely well with all agencies closely adhering to the law, or alternatively raises concerns as to the independence and work of the IPT.

15.4.3 A single system?

The previous two sections have demonstrated that tribunal justice is disparate and some forms of tribunal work (most notably those tribunals that are interpreting and applying the law rather than considering the validity of administrative functions) are almost directly analogous to court work. During the review undertaken by Leggatt some suggested that the Employment Tribunals should be moved to within the judicial system rather than the administration system and that a new court could be created (Leggatt (2001) para 3.21). This was rejected by Leggatt (para 3.24) in part because he believed that the multi-panel system would be difficult to achieve in the judicial system. Certainly it would be unique. Although courts do frequently sit with more than one member (most notably the Divisional Courts of the High Court, the Court of Appeal, and the House of Lords) they are multiple members of the judiciary rather than a mixed bench. The only example of a mixed bench is when the Crown Court sits as an appellate court but even then it is not truly mixed since the justices belong to the magistracy and are, theoretically at least, members of the judicial system.

However it was noted above that it must be questioned whether a mixed panel necessarily adds anything. Even if it does, however, it would be possible to create a separate court for the employment tribunal and the parent statute would state the composition of the panels. In the criminal arena there has been consideration given to a similar composition for fraud trials (see, for example, Auld (2001) 200–204; this proposal was rejected but s 43 *Criminal Justice Act 2003* allows for a judge to sit alone without a jury on serious fraud cases) and so it would not be unprecedented. Certainly it is difficult to see how these tribunals can be considered anything other than de facto courts and, of course, the Employment Appeals Tribunal (the second-tier tribunal of the Employment

Tribunal) is, as a matter of statute, a superior *court* of record (s 20(3) *Employment Tribunals Act 1996*) and so there is already a blurring between courts and tribunals.

At the other end of the spectrum there exist tribunals that are kept outside of the court system for the sake of convenience. Perhaps the classic example of this is the IPT, the work of which was discussed above. It has been noted above that the IPT is neither analogous to an (administrative) tribunal nor a court. Unlike the EAT the IPT is not a superior court of tribunal although its members are appointed by letters patent (s 65(1) RIPA 2000) which means they have security of tenure. The courts have suggested that the IPT has many of the characteristics of a court (*Ewing v Security Service* [2003] EWHC 2051) but it is *not* a court. To an extent, establishing it as a court would cause significant problems since it operates in such a different way from the rest of the judicial system. It would also cause difficulties in that there is no appeal from the tribunal (s 67(8) RIPA 2000 permits an appeal to be brought only in circumstances identified by the Home Secretary through delegated legislation; no statutory instrument has ever defined these circumstances) and it would, therefore, become the only court from which there is no appeal. In any event it is suggested that the absence of a right of appeal is somewhat extraordinary and potentially a breach of Article 6 of ECHR. Certainly the fact that every petition laid before the IPT has been rejected does suggest that consideration must be given urgently to an appeal system allowing for the review of its decisions.

Leggatt recommended that all tribunals other than the IPT were brought within a single system (Leggatt (2001) paras 3.8 and 3.11) but even though the TCEA 2007 has come close to doing this, it has been noted that not all tribunals are within the system. If the work of tribunals is so disparate would it not be better either properly to categorize work into either courts or tribunals or recognize that there needs to be different tribunals to undertake this work? Leggatt feared that if some tribunals were moved to the court system then some of the advantages (most notably the informality and speed of decision-making) might be lost. However, as has been seen, these perceived advantages may not necessarily be true in practice and careful thought should be given as to whether it is possible to talk about 'the tribunals' as a collective body distinct from the court structure.

 ## Summary

This chapter has examined the jurisdiction of tribunals and noted their increasing role within the justice system. In particular it has:

- Noted that tribunals have existed for many years but traditionally operated as an oversight system for administrative issues.

- Identified the fact that in recent years the number of tribunals has increased and their work has included questions of law and not just administrative propriety.

- Discussed the independence of tribunals and noted that in 2006 the government sought to bring about a degree of independence through the creation of the Tribunal Service.

- Discussed whether tribunals are separate from the judicial system or whether there is an argument that they should be recognized as courts.

- Identified that tribunals see themselves as being more informal adjudicating bodies where traditional rules of evidence do not necessarily apply.

- Considered whether litigants in a tribunal should be represented.

End-of-chapter questions

1. Read Chapter 4 of the Leggatt Report (available online). Do you think tribunals are truly accessible to ordinary members of the public or do you still require the services of someone who knows the law and procedure? Is there any way of making them truly accessible and would this be desirable?

2. Read *Ewing v Security Service* [2003] EWHC 2051 where the High Court decided that the IPT bore many of the characteristics of a court. Also read Fenwick (2001). Is the IPT really a tribunal or is it a court? What, if any, are the differences and do you believe that the tribunal can properly be said to safeguard a citizen's human rights?

Further reading

Bradley AW (2002) 'The tribunals maze' *Public Law* 200–202.

This short article considers the proposals in the *Leggatt Report* to consolidate the tribunals into one service with a smaller number of tribunals.

Buck T (2006) 'Precedent in tribunals and the development of principles' 25 *Civil Justice Quarterly* 458–484.

This is an interesting piece that considers whether precedent exists within tribunals, whether precedent should exist in tribunals, and, if so, how it would operate.

Burton M (2005) 'The Employment Appeal Tribunal: October 2002–July 2005' 34 *Industrial Law Journal* 273–283.

This article is written by Burton J, the then President of the Employment Appeal Tribunal, and considers the significant changes that have occurred to the tribunal over a three-year period.

For multiple choice questions, updates to this chapter and links to useful websites, please visit the Online Resource Centre at

www.oxfordtextbooks.co.uk/orc/gillespie_els3e/

16

Alternative Dispute Resolution

By the end of this chapter you will be able to:

- Understand why the pressure for ADR arose.
- Define ADR and explain the three principal forms of ADR.
- Identify how the courts are able to persuade litigants to use ADR.
- Appreciate some of the advantages and disadvantages of ADR.

Introduction

It has been seen in the previous chapters that there are several different ways in which disputes can be resolved formally through the invocation of the judicial system. However, court proceedings are not the only ways in which disputes can be resolved and in recent times there has been an increase in alternative dispute resolution (ADR). This has been used as either a preliminary option prior to litigation or sometimes as a complete alternative to litigation.

This chapter will examine how ADR has grown and consider its application and some difficulties that may arise through its use.

16.1 Shift from adversariality?

It has been noted numerous times in this book that the English Legal System is based on the adversarial system of litigation. In essence this means that both sides separately prepare their respective submissions and then they arrive in court and participate in a quasi-gladiatorial contest until the tribunal of fact (in civil trials this usually being a judge) pronounces the winner. The manner in which this contest occurs was seen in Chapter 12 and even in tribunals, a system of justice that is usually considered to be more informal, the adversarial system remains intact with both sides still competing against each other.

Yet in recent times there has been an increasing debate as to whether the adversarial system is the appropriate way of resolving all disputes. To an extent this was realized in specialist proceedings, perhaps most notably in proceedings relating to the welfare of a child. The *Children Act 1989* makes clear that the best interests of the child must be the court's paramount consideration (s 1) and this has led to the conclusion that in certain proceedings, most notably child-protection proceedings, the full adversarial system is unhelpful and that making the proceedings more inquisitorial can be of assistance (see, for example, the comments in *L (A Minor)(Police Investigation: Privilege)* [1997] AC 16).

Even within ordinary litigation it is now becoming increasingly accepted that the adversarial system is not always of assistance and that it inherently involves both extensive cost and delay (Davies (2006) 32). It has also been suggested that it involves two further disadvantages; an imbalance of power (which could be likened to the 'equality of arms' principle contained within Article 6 of the *European Convention on Human Rights* (ECHR) (see 5.2.3.4 above)) and the restriction of civil legal aid (see Chapter 9) means that the adversarial system allows the rich to exploit the law (Davies (2006) 32). It is difficult to argue against these and although Article 6 will try to level the 'battleground' so far as possible, eg through exchange of documents (although this is not an automatic right: see for example *Secretary of State for the Home Department v MB* [2006] EWCA Civ 1140) or the provision of legal assistance (see, for example, *Steel and Morris v United Kingdom* (2005) 41 EHRR 22) it is simply a fundamental part of the legal system.

Wider concerns exist over the adversarial system, not least being whether it encourages the resolution of disputes and the discovery of the facts or merely seeks to identify who has the better advocate. The advocate in adversarial systems, whilst being under a professional duty not to mislead the court, owes a duty to his client and will act in a partisan way before the neutral umpire (Boon and Levin (2008) 12), seeking to exploit the weaknesses of the opposing side whilst at the same time trying to hide their own weaknesses. Not only are the lawyers inherently partisan but most witnesses almost certainly will be, not least by the labelling of witnesses as being 'for' or 'against' a side (Davies (2006) 32). A witness will not be called unless it is thought that they would assist the argument being put forward by the party, not whether or not the person has anything to contribute to the finding of fact.

The adversarial system ensures that lawyers are central to the process. Since the analysis and presentation of evidence is key to the adversarial approach, one requires a lawyer who is able to assimilate the facts quickly and apply them with an appropriate knowledge of law. This by itself is not sufficient however since a lawyer must also advocate the points, ie use persuasion to encourage the tribunal of fact to make the appropriate rulings. In a market society such as England and Wales, this means that the best lawyers will always be in demand and can therefore charge significant fees. This not only makes litigation expensive but also creates a power imbalance between those who can afford these fees and those who cannot (Davies (2006) 37). This position is arguably aggravated by the fact that civil legal aid in many disputes is severely restricted (see Chapter 9). If there is a quest for a fair resolution should wealth be a factor?

For all of these reasons there has now been an acceptance that alternatives to the adversarial system of justice may be appropriate. Arguably one of the easiest to implement is to encourage disputes to be resolved other than by recourse to litigation. This has led to the establishment of alternative dispute resolution (ADR).

16.2 What is alternative dispute resolution?

The first point to discuss is perhaps to try to identify what ADR is. The Department for Constitutional Affairs defines it as:

> The collective term for the ways that parties can settle civil disputes, with the help of an independent third party and without the need for a formal court hearing (cited in Shipman (2006b) 182).

Perhaps one of the most important aspects of this definition is the recognition that there is more than one type of ADR although some commentators have suggested that it is difficult to identify precisely what constitutes ADR (Boon and Levin (2008) 409). Other commentators argue that ADR can be divided into two classes, those being adjudicative and consensual (Shipman (2006b) 182). The former is customarily called arbitration and, as will be seen, is not dissimilar to court proceedings and this has led to some criticisms as to whether there is anything 'alternative' about ADR (Boon and Levin (1999) 373). If both litigation and arbitration involve an independent third party adjudicating upon the decision then what are the advantages of using ADR? One possibility is the fact that arbitration is ordinarily more informal in character than court proceedings, is held in non-ceremonial surroundings, and, perhaps more importantly, treats each case on its individual facts without being bound by precedent (Shipman (2006b) 182).

Consensual forms of ADR are less reliant on adjudicating the decisions and are designed more to persuade the parties to reach an agreement between themselves (Shipman (2006b) 183). The most common forms are negotiation, mediation, and conciliation although the former is probably not a form of ADR but is instead a standard part of the litigation system. Other commentators agree with this division in ADR and at least one commentator has suggested that we should stop using the term ADR and think about it as either 'agreement' (consensual ADR) and 'determination' (adjudication) (Evans (2003) esp 230–232).

16.2.1 Arbitration

Arbitration is the most formal of the ADR forms and does involve an independent person adjudicating upon the dispute, ie making a decision rather than merely facilitating an agreement between the parties. Usually the arbitrator will be an expert in the field of the dispute (Bevan (1992) 7) and although formal the proceedings will be quicker and more informal than litigation. The informality arises from the fact that there are no strict rules of evidence and it is unusual for parties to interrupt each other.

Arbitration will ordinarily occur under one of two circumstances. The first is in commercial disputes where a contract includes a clause within it stating that disputes will ordinarily be the subject of arbitration. The second possibility is when the parties voluntarily agree to invoke an arbitrator once a dispute arises. Again this is relatively common in high-value commercial cases where the costs of litigation would be high.

The decision of an arbitrator is normally binding and the courts will rarely interfere with the decisions (see Phillips (2004) 158) and indeed legislation exists to limit the courts' ability to judicially review decisions of certain arbitrators (see *Arbitration Act 1996*).

⤵ ACAS EMPLOYMENT ARBITRATION SCHEME

The *Employment Rights (Dispute Resolution) Act 1998* (ER(DR)A 1998) legislated for something known as the Advisory, Conciliation and Arbitration Service (ACAS)[1] Employment Arbitration Scheme. This is considered to be an alternative to the use of Employment Tribunals and deals with allegations of unfair dismissal or flexible working legislation.

The scheme only applies where both parties agree to it and the decision of the arbitrator is binding. The ER(DR)A 1998 provides that decisions of the arbitrator are enforceable in the county court as though they were decisions of a court.

The arbitrator will be neutral and does not need to be legally qualified but all are given training and are familiar with the employment relations field of work. ACAS state it provides a 'speedy, informal, private and generally less legalistic alternative to an Employment Tribunal hearing'.

16.2.2 Mediation

Mediation is one of the forms of consensual ADR and although it still involves an independent third party the responsibility of the mediator is to assist the parties in reaching a settlement rather than adjudicating on disputes.

---

1. The Online Resource Centre accompanying this book provides a link to the ACAS website.

Mediation is therefore assisted negotiation. Whereas negotiation will normally involve both parties simply trying to put forward their own positions, mediation will involve the independent third party structuring the process of negotiation and attempting to find solutions to obstacles that may impede a settlement. It has been suggested that the skill of a mediator (and presumably a conciliator) is similar to that of a diplomat (Evans (2003) 230) in that they must try to persuade both parties that reaching an acceptable compromise would be better for both parties than the matter resorting to litigation.

Unlike arbitration, mediation is not binding nor will it necessarily reach a settlement. It is quite possible, therefore, that the parties will not agree and need to resort to litigation in any event. However, it is favoured because it is informal and normally an inexpensive way of attempting to resolve issues before positions become entrenched by litigation.

⮑ FAMILY PROCEEDINGS

The *Family Law Act 1996* (which has now been repealed) tried to make mediation compulsory in divorce cases. It was widely ridiculed at the time of its inception and it was considered to be virtually unworkable (see Roberts (2001)).

However that is not to say that mediation does not occur in family proceedings, and arguably it is one of the areas where it is most suited. Contested divorce cases can become extremely expensive and acrimonious and yet the issues may not be so very divisive. Many solicitor firms specializing in family law now offer mediation to divorcing couples and indeed many of these schemes are either free or heavily subsidized by the *Legal Services Commission*.

16.2.3 Conciliation

Differentiating between mediation and conciliation is not always easy and indeed one commentator argues that they are interchangeable terms (Bevan (1992) 15). Certainly both are consensual forms of ADR but where a difference may arise is in how the meetings take place. With mediation it is usual for both parties to be physically present in the room with the mediator and discussing the strengths and weaknesses of their case. Conciliation differs in that it is more usual for the conciliator (the independent third party) to meet with the parties separately and, in effect, 'shuttle' backwards and forwards between the parties with offers and counter-offers.

Conciliation is not infrequently used where the positions adopted by parties are particularly entrenched or where there is misunderstanding between the parties. Since the two sides do not meet there is a reduced danger of them 'play-acting' by trying to destabilize the other party or try to place blame for the dispute occurring in the first place. It is possible that after the early rounds of negotiation the parties may be brought together in which the case the difference between mediation and conciliation becomes uncertain at best.

Like mediation, conciliation is voluntary and will not necessarily succeed. Where conciliation efforts do break down it is more likely that the matter will proceed to either arbitration or litigation. It is worth noting that conciliation (and mediation) is a relatively informal process and thus even where contracts stipulate arbitration as the means of resolving disputes it is not unusual for the parties to try conciliation first, especially where it is hoped that the relationship between the parties will continue beyond the dispute.

⊙ CONCILIATION

Conciliation is often used in industrial disputes. A good example would be where trade unions and employers disagree over work conditions, health and safety, etc. It is often used to try to settle disputes before strike action takes place. The alternative is either lengthy industrial disputes or litigation being brought where an employer seeks to interfere with strike action or where the trade union seeks declarations regarding health and safety legislation. By using conciliation, however, both sides can understand what the other's position is and try to reach a compromise that is suitable to both sides. A key to the success of conciliation is that the conciliator must be completely impartial. ACAS is often used in this role because of the reputation it has accrued over the years.

16.3 Encouraging ADR

ADR potentially offers an opportunity to avoid litigation with all of the disadvantages that this can potentially bring (see Chapter 14). The civil justice system has identified ADR as an important part of the civil system and the *Civil Procedure Rules* (CPR) encourage the use of ADR prior to litigating; indeed, the judge is able to 'encourage' the use of ADR where he believes it may be of assistance (CPR 1.4(2)(e)). Yet at least one commentator has questioned whether this is, in effect, merely lip-service. It has been suggested that the whole ethos of the civil justice system continues to be that a trial is inevitable (Davies (2006) 34). By this the commentator is suggesting that all the rules of court etc require people to correspond as though proceedings are going to be initiated or progressed (eg requiring the service of a claim form within a set period of time, requiring claim details and defences to be exchanged). The CPR continues this because unless action is contemplated the CPR will not be engaged and realistically CPR 1.4(2) applies by the time a directions hearing arises since a judge will have been assigned to the case. By the stage that the judge 'encourages' ADR it may well be that the opportunity for less formal resolution has passed with both sides now believing (upon the advice of their lawyers) that they have an arguable case in court.

Not every court adopts this approach, however, and indeed in essence the small claims court (Chapter 14.2) is actually arbitration albeit with a district judge as arbitrator (see *Scarth v United Kingdom* (1998) 26 EHRR CD154 for an illustration of the consequences this may have). This explains the absence of formal rules of evidence, the absence of legal representation, and the informal procedure. Certain admiralty and commercial decisions are also subject to standard ADR notices which require the parties to consider ADR at any early stage, but again both of these require the claim to have already been made. Perhaps one solution is to reconsider the concept of the limitation period, and allow for the period to be 'stayed' whilst legitimate attempts at ADR are made.

⊙ LIMITATION PERIOD

It is not possible to bring an action for historical wrongs except under highly exceptional circumstances. The *Limitation Act 1980* sets out the maximum period in which proceedings must be launched. Good examples are that personal injury matters must begin within three years (s 11) and ordinary torts within six years (s 2). Not every limitation is contained within the Act. For example, libel proceedings must be brought within one year (s 5 *Defamation Act 1996*).

An advantage of such a proposal would be that it would ensure that not every dispute would automatically proceed to the courts, but it could also be questioned whether this is anything different to staying proceedings once the claim and defence have been served, something that is already possible under the CPR (CPR 26.4).

Assuming that a claim has been made then CPR 1.4(2)(e) may be triggered but precisely how judges are to encourage ADR is not spelt out expressly in the CPR. The courts have used their discretion in respect of costs (see 14.1.2.2 above) to provide an incentive, with the courts refusing an order to pay the successful party's full costs where an opportunity for ADR was unreasonably rejected (see, for example, *Dunnett v Railtrack plc* [2002] EWCA Civ 303 but cf *Halsey v Milton Keynes General NHS Trust* [2004] EWCA Civ 576 and see Stilitz and Sheldon (2003) 301–306). Certainly where the judge has suggested ADR and either party refuses to take this up, it is highly likely that the courts will exercise their discretion to make an order governing the recovery of costs (Shipman (2006b) 206–207).

⮕ JUDICIAL PERSUASION

Prior to the establishment of the CPR it appears there was considerable frustration by members of the judiciary who would have liked to suggest ADR. Bevan cites Philips J as he then was who stated that he 'often wanted to bang the parties' heads together in cases where he couldn't see why they continued to fight' (Bevan (1992) 8).

CPR 1.4 would now appear to give judges the power to (metaphorically) bang the litigants' heads together by adjourning proceedings whilst ADR is attempted.

That said, the key to this must be the appropriateness of using ADR. At least one commentator has suggested that sometimes ADR is used inappropriately and that in some cases it would be preferable to seek a quick judicial ruling rather than attempt to settle the matter through protracted negotiations (Evans (2003) 232). Indeed Evans argues that where the respective lawyers have made a serious attempt at settling the matter it may be that there was little point in proceeding through ADR. There is also the question as to which types of cases will be suited to ADR. Lord Irvine, the then Lord Chancellor, had argued that ADR was unlikely to have any role in public law disputes, ie to displace judicial review proceedings (Stilitz and Sheldon (2006) 306) but the courts have taken a different line and suggested that some public-law disputes could be suitable for ADR (see, for example, *R (on the application of Cowl) v Plymouth City Council (Practice Note)* [2001] EWCA Civ 1935 and Stilitz and Sheldon (2006) 307–310).

Where ADR will not be of assistance is where the matter relates to a matter of law rather than fact since decisions of law should be made by judicial authorities (Stilitz and Sheldon (2006) 311) but many disputes do not raise questions of law but rather the construction of an agreement or the application of the law. In either situation it is quite possible that ADR could assist the parties in obtaining a compromise acceptable to both parties. The courts have recognized, however, that sometimes the positions of both parties will be such that attempting ADR would not be advisable, and perhaps the classic example of this is where one party is alleging inappropriate conduct (eg discriminatory or dishonest conduct) where neither mediation nor conciliation would be likely to succeed (Shipman (2006b) 196). Similarly, arbitration is unlikely to add anything to such disputes with the consequences going beyond financial compensation and thus they become arguably more appropriate for litigation.

❓ QUESTION FOR REFLECTION

It was noted above that Davies believes that the civil justice system works on the presumption that proceedings will occur and although ADR can be encouraged, this will only occur once a claim has been initiated. Should there be a requirement to undertake ADR *before* initiating a claim for certain actions (eg libel, personal injury, etc)? Is the danger of using costs as the 'weapon' that this is not a particularly potent weapon for wealthy litigants?

🎧 LISTEN TO THE PODCAST

For guidance on how to answer this question and a discussion of the main issues, listen to the author's podcast on the Online Resource Centre:
www.oxfordtextbooks.co.uk/orc/gillespie_els3e/

16.4 Reaction of lawyers

How have lawyers reacted to the concept of ADR? There are two issues to consider here: where lawyers are advising clients and where lawyers are acting as the independent third party within an ADR process.

16.4.1 Advising ADR

It has been noted that one aspect of the adversarial process is that the principle of orality assumes a position of almost supreme importance (Phillips (2004) 154). This means that the legal process becomes wedded to the idea that only oral evidence and argument can resolve disputes, which can be a barrier to negotiation and alternative sources of resolution. Certainly there is a disincentive for disputes to proceed to ADR since at the heart of most ADR processes is informality and that it can be undertaken without the use of a lawyer. Given that it can be undertaken by the parties without lawyers is there any incentive for legal advisors to recommend ADR?

It has been noted by commentators that the professional codes of practice do not expressly refer to whether a matter should proceed to ADR (Boon and Levin (2008) 418) although, that said, it must come within the overall duty to act in the best interests of the client, including setting aside considerations as to which would be the most profitable form of resolution for themselves.

16.4.2 Lawyers as arbitrators or mediators

Some have argued that notwithstanding the concerns above, lawyers have welcomed ADR on the basis that it opens up new avenues of work for lawyers as they are able to put themselves forward as independent arbitrators or mediators (see, for example,

Boon and Levin (2008) 417). Certainly one of the principal purposes of the *Arbitration Act 1996* was to ensure that the United Kingdom became one of the leading centres in the world for arbitrating on disputes (Boon and Levin (1999) 378).

Certainly in England and Wales there are a large number of lawyers who will now offer their services during ADR. However there is some dispute as to the ethical standards expected of lawyers working within ADR. Where the lawyer is acting as a mediator or arbitrator, can he be said to be acting in a legal capacity for the purposes of the rules of the professional bodies? Most rules relate to client care or the conduct of litigation, neither of which is strictly relevant here. The traditional approach has been to state that they are separate (Bevan (1992) 27) and to an extent this still holds with the Bar Code of Conduct making clear that a person who acts as an arbitrator or mediator is not 'supplying legal services' (para 1001 of version 8). Yet there is certainly a need for guidance since it has been said 'ethics are at least as central to the mediator's role as they are to the advocate's role' (Boon and Levin (2008) 426).

Professional associations for arbitrators and mediators do exist and these will impose their own codes of conduct. However, there is no requirement for a person who wishes to act as an arbitrator or mediator to be a member of any association meaning that it is possible to conduct ADR in an unregulated manner.

❓ QUESTION FOR REFLECTION

Is it realistic to divorce arbitration and mediation from the role of a solicitor or barrister? Is it not more likely that the arbitrator or mediator has been sought because he is a lawyer? Assuming that this is correct, then would it not be more appropriate to state that where a lawyer acts as an arbitrator or mediator he should be bound by the Code of Conduct of either the Law Society or Bar Council?

🎧 LISTEN TO THE PODCAST

For guidance on how to answer this question and a discussion of the main issues, listen to the author's podcast on the Online Resource Centre:

www.oxfordtextbooks.co.uk/orc/gillespie_els3e/

Indeed some commentators have questioned whether lawyers are necessarily appropriate for sitting as an arbitrator or mediator (Boon and Levin (1999) 384–393). Certainly they are not the only professionals who act in this capacity and it is not uncommon for architects, surveyors, and other professionals to be used, especially in arbitration where it is preferable for an expert to be involved so that they can make an appropriate adjudication. What can a lawyer bring to ADR? It has been suggested that they bring independence but this is arguably no different from other professions. Do they have the requisite skills? Lawyers are used to the adversarial process and thus concentrate more on the process than the issues (Bevan (1992) 37). This is the opposite of what ADR is supposed to do, especially the consensual models where the independent third party is supposed to be facilitating an agreement. Are lawyers appropriately trained to do this? Whilst they now tend to be trained in the art of negotiation, this tends to continue to follow an 'adversarial' model whereby each party adopts the approach of marshalling the arguments and identifying what their best strategy is. This is something that differs dramatically from mediators and questions must be raised as to whether lawyers are fully able to engage with this process. Of course, the solution is to undertake staff development training to learn how to be an arbitrator or mediator but this returns us to the argument as to professional codes of conduct and whether there should be an *obligation* to do so.

16.5 The future of ADR

So far we have identified many advantages of ADR and noted that the legal system is beginning to treat ADR seriously. The increase in the number of lawyers training to be arbitrators and/or mediators demonstrates a real recognition that ADR can be a valid alternative to litigation. However, what is perhaps more open to debate is whether additional changes need to be made to ensure that ADR becomes more central in the resolution of disputes.

In the state of Queensland, Australia, the law was changed to provide the court with the power to order a matter to proceed to mediation even if either party objected (Davies (2006) 41). There was also a greater push for the use of voluntary ADR and the cumulative effect of this was dramatically to reduce delays in the justice system (from two years to three months) as a result of fewer cases proceeding to trial (Davies (2006) 43). Delay continues to be a problem within the English Legal System and accordingly it may be that the courts in England and Wales need to adopt this approach and make ADR compulsory. Arguably this is a simple extension of the current position adopted by the courts who are currently using costs as a way of encouraging ADR but it would be a more formalized and open system. An advantage of moving to this position is that it would be transparent. A party would know exactly what will happen if they reject the idea of ADR and can make a balanced judgement accordingly. The current position does not bring this clarity since the judge has a discretion over costs and so the decision to award costs and the amount of these costs will vary depending on the individual judges.

However, it is vital that ADR is used only where it is realistic to do so. It has been noted that it is somewhat ironic that ADR has as one of its purposes the desire to reduce costs and yet it can, in certain circumstances, actually increase costs (Davies (2006) 48). This is because where ADR is likely to fail all that will be achieved in undertaking the process is further delays to the case being disposed of by court, and the costs of the independent third party accruing.

This perhaps demonstrates a potential dilemma for ADR. Mediation and conciliation are not binding and thus at any point the parties could decide to withdraw from the process and begin litigation. It is unlikely that this would be altered. Arbitration on the other hand is binding and the courts will seek to uphold the arbitrator's decision. In essence, therefore, arbitration becomes the formal resolution and is only subject to judicial review under exceptional circumstances. However, arbitrators do not set precedent and thus cases could be disposed of differently which may be unfair as it means any relief depends on the arbitrator and not necessarily on the merits of the case. Questions are beginning to be asked whether arbitration is fair and even whether it is compatible with the ECHR.

In order to understand this it is necessary to return to the ACAS employment scheme as this best demonstrates the potential way in which arbitration is being used as an alternative to the courts. It will be remembered that this scheme runs parallel to the system of Employment Tribunals but that a claimant must choose which scheme to use (see 16.2.1 above) and the scheme will only apply where there is an agreement between the parties. This seems fine in principle but does the claimant necessarily understand the consequences of their decision?

Using arbitration could be extremely advantageous from the point of view of an employer. There will be no legal representation so that legal expenses will be reduced. Indeed because the arbitration scheme is considerably less formal than even a tribunal there will be less preparatory work which further reduces legal costs. Another key advantage for employers is the privacy (Busby and Middlemiss (1999) 153). Tribunal proceedings are public proceedings and may be reported as such, including the finding and details of any award. Arbitration on the other hand is private and the parties are normally required to undertake, as part of the contract of arbitration, that they will *not* discuss the proceedings or award.

A tribunal is, as has been seen, a quasi-judicial body and it is required to interpret and apply the law. Each Employment Tribunal is presided over by a legally qualified member (see 15.1.3 above). Yet this is not the same for the arbitration scheme; indeed it is highly unlikely that the arbitrator will be legally qualified, with it being more likely that it is a member of the human-resources profession. A tribunal is required to follow precedent, an arbitrator is not. A consequence of this is that the law may not be considered as important as the factual basis of the claim, potentially undermining the claimant's position. These consequences become more serious when one remembers that a claimant will, if he chooses the arbitration option, lose all the right to petition a tribunal or launch an appeal. This is supposed to ensure that one of the key elements of arbitration, its binding nature, is upheld (Busby and Middlemiss (1999) 158), but it does create a situation in which a claimant loses a significant right. If a tribunal errs on the law or makes an award that is incompatible with precedents set, the claimant may petition the Employment Appeals Tribunal. This option is not open to someone who accepts the arbitration scheme.

A key question that needs to be asked is whether a claimant necessarily understands this when they choose which track to use. There is no requirement for a person to seek independent legal advice before choosing the arbitration scheme yet the choice has a significant impact on that person's legal rights. The imbalance of power between employer and employee may heavily influence this decision. An employer who suggests arbitration may influence an employee who thinks that arbitration places them on a 'level playing-field' and without the need to engage expensive lawyers. A person who is not a union member may find that they approach ACAS for advice on what to do, not least because ACAS provides general guidance on employment rights. Is it likely that ACAS will encourage claimants to use their scheme?

It is commonly accepted that Article 6 of the ECHR provides a right of access to the courts and not just a fair trial once accessed. However, access merely means the ability to have a dispute resolved and accordingly the ACAS scheme could be considered to be compatible to this extent. If there is no proper understanding by the claimant that accepting the scheme leads to their legal rights being de facto extinguished, or where there is an inequality of arms over the choice to turn away from the law, it is possible Article 6 could be engaged. Where Article 6 may also be relevant is in relation to appeals. If an error of law is made by an arbitrator there is no avenue of appeal. A person has the right to a fair trial and this includes the right to expect adjudicators to follow the law. Denying an appeal in the circumstances set out above would seem to be a denial of justice and potentially a breach of Article 6.

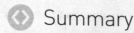 Summary

This chapter has examined the use of ADR within the civil justice system. In particular it has:

- identified that there has been a shift away from the 'pure' form of an adversarial trial, although not to a full inquisitorial system
- noted that ADR is often cheaper and more informal than civil litigation, meaning disputes can sometimes be resolved more quickly and more amicably than through litigation
- discussed the three principal forms of ADR: arbitration, mediation, and conciliation
- noted that some contracts will now include an arbitration clause within them, meaning that disputes must proceed through arbitration first
- discussed the merits of the ACAS employment arbitration scheme, including noting that it potentially reduces the legal avenues open to someone claiming a breach in employment rights
- noted the finality of arbitration where courts are reluctant to interfere with the decision of an arbitrator.

End-of-chapter questions

1. Read Davies (2006). Is there a case for moving away from the adversarial system of justice? What would the difficulties be with such an approach?

2. Read Roberts (2001). Why were the mediation proposals in the 1996 Act dropped? With many divorces is there not a danger that clients are arguing over relatively small assets, leading to acrimony and high legal bills? Would mediation not ensure a smoother transition through divorce?

3. Why do you think there is no right of appeal against the decision of an arbitrator? Is there a danger that by allowing an appeal to exist it would detract from the whole point of arbitration? It could allow an unhappy side simply to engage in expensive litigation after deciding that they did not like the decision of the arbitrator. Could an appeal be restricted to errors of law? One difficulty with this presumably must be the fact that arbitrators are not legally qualified so would they understand the legal principles they would then have to uphold? If only legally qualified arbitrators were used, how would this differ from a tribunal?

Further reading

Busby N and Middlemiss S (1999) 'Arbitration: A suitable mechanism for adjudication of unfair dismissal claims' 18 *Civil Justice Quarterly* 149–161.

   This article was written soon after the introduction of the *Employment Rights (Dispute Resolution) Act 1998* and considers the use of the scheme in the employment arena.

Genn H (2002) 'Court-based ADR initiatives for non-family civil disputes', http://www. hmcourts-service.gov.uk/docs/adr_initiatives.pdf.

   This web page presents the report of Professor Genn who was examining the use of ADR in non-family civil disputes. It makes some interesting points about the perceptions of counsel and the judiciary over the use of ADR in complex commercial cases.

Roberts S (2001) 'Family mediation after the Act' 13 *Child and Family Law Quarterly* 265–273.
This article considers the reasons for the introduction of the *Family Law Act 1996* and its eventual abandonment. The article also discusses ways in which mediation continues to be used by family practitioners.

For multiple choice questions, updates to this chapter and links to useful websites, please visit the Online Resource Centre at

www.oxfordtextbooks.co.uk/orc/gillespie_els3e/

17

The Future

Introduction

The English legal system is always evolving; this is in part a result of the common-law nature of the system and also reflects the political realities of the day, with governments deciding how they wish to shape the legal system. In this concluding chapter a number of predictions will be made as to what are the principal changes that are likely to be made in the coming years.

There are four aspects that will be examined:

- 'English' legal system
- funding legal services
- LSA 2007 firms
- Alternative Dispute Resolution (ADR).

17.1 'English' legal system

In Chapter 1 it was noted that when we talk about the English Legal System we actually mean the legal system of England and Wales because the law does not differentiate between England and Wales (see 1.1.1.1 above). Devolution has begun to bring some changes, with the right, for example, to use the Welsh language in pleadings and indeed in court. However, devolution in Wales has always been more limited than in Scotland and Northern Ireland, almost certainly reflecting the fact that the latter countries have always had a separate legal system and body of laws.

In essence, the Welsh Assembly was undertaking executive acts by performing the duties that the Secretary of State of Wales had traditionally undertaken. It could not, therefore, pass legislation in its own right although it did have limited power to amend legislation that had already been passed. The *Government of Wales Act 2006* (GoWA 2006) is designed to increase the powers of the devolved Welsh Assembly. In political terms it creates an executive (government) separate from the Assembly and this government would undertake the executive work delegated to it by Westminster (Part 2 GoWA 2006). Westminster would also allow the Assembly to act in its stead for certain delegated legislation (ie statutory instruments) where it was within the devolved matters (Part 3 GoWA 2006).

👁 Example Transport

The Welsh Assembly has delegated authority over highways and transport. It could, theoretically, therefore pass legislation governing the signage on roads or providing for bus lanes in each town etc.

More controversially, the GoWA 2006 also provides for the possibility of the Welsh Assembly assuming powers relating to *primary legislation* (Part 4 GoWA 2006). This would allow the Assembly to pass statutes in the same way that the Scottish Parliament may do so. This could, in essence, mean that separate laws could exist in England and Wales for the first time in nearly five centuries. However there are two limits to this power. The first is that the Assembly will have limited competences with Westminster retaining control over many aspects of the law.

👁 Example Welsh language

The use of the Welsh language would be a matter that the Assembly would have competence on (para 20, Sch 7 GoWA 2006). Accordingly it could pass a Welsh Language Act stating that all written forms must be available in both Welsh and English. However this power does not extend to the use of the Welsh language in courts (ibid) and accordingly the Welsh Assembly could not order all court forms to be available in both languages or for court hearings to take place only in Welsh.

The second, and perhaps more significant, restriction is that the Welsh Assembly will only gain these powers following a referendum in Wales (s 103 GoWA 2006). This referendum could only occur with the consent of both Houses of Parliament (s 103(4)) and the Welsh Assembly. Two-thirds of Assembly members must vote for the measure in the Assembly (s 103(5)). The referendum is to be held on 3 March 2011 (an Order in Council being made in December 2010) following the agreement of the Welsh Assembly and Westminster Parliament, and at the time of writing its result is not known.

Accordingly in the future it is likely that the laws applicable in England and in Wales will differ. Will this mean that the English and Welsh legal systems become distinct? Probably not. The legal system, in terms of the mechanism of the application of the law, the court structure, and the rules of court, are not delegated powers and thus the Assembly, even after a referendum, would have no authority to alter this. Accordingly it is likely that this book will be discussing the legal system of England *and* Wales for a considerable period of time.

17.2 Funding legal services

In each of the two previous editions of this book I predicted that the funding of legal services would be an issue that would continue to be topical and this continues to be the case. The global 'credit crunch' at the end of the last decade has meant that public spending has had to be curtailed: the new coalition government was elected on a mandate to cut spending and legal aid is an easy target for any government as it is easy to sell such cuts to the public as an attack on 'fat cat' lawyers. The reality is very much different but it is likely that funding will remain controversial. The tension over funding exists over both civil and criminal matters although they perhaps raise slightly different issues.

17.2.1 Civil litigation

The Labour government began a process whereby the civil courts should, in essence, become 'self-funding', ie that, broadly speaking, civil litigation should be cost-neutral to the state save where it features as part of an action. The coalition government has not (at the time of writing) suggested that it disagrees with this approach. The logic of such an approach is that the losing party should be able to pay for the costs of litigation and that the arbitration of civil disputes is not a matter that the state should have to pay for. Many would question this, especially in circumstances where the state is the defendant to an action (eg actions against the police, NHS, etc). Allied to this suggestion is that contingency fee arrangements can shift the risk from the state (through legal aid) to the lawyers. Of course whilst this is true, it does potentially mean that a number of people are denied access to justice because a lawyer will only take on a strong case under a contingency fee.

Allied to the issue of funding are the changes to the legal profession under the *Legal Services Act 2007* (LSA 2007), especially the growth in so-called 'Tesco Law' (see 17.3 below). A large organization can perhaps offer certain legal services but with lower overheads because of their existing structures. This may include, for example, car insurance companies that decide to employ in-house lawyers to do all the work instead of contracting it out to individual solicitor firms and counsel. The pre-existing 'brands' that are currently offering legal services (albeit through subcontracting rather than by directly employing lawyers) demonstrate possible ways in which alternative funding sources may become reality. A number of these 'brands' are operating subscription or insurance-type policies whereby free legal advice is given in return for a fixed payment. To an extent this is nothing new since most car insurance policies provide the same but it does demonstrate an 'easy' way to fund litigation: is it possible that with the advent of 'Tesco Law' such practices may become more popular, with those who have 'legal insurance' able to undertake litigation. However, as with private medical insurance, it can be legitimately questioned whether this benefits all those in need or whether it is simply a service of use to the middle classes.

It is increasingly difficult to see how a person who is injured or suffers a contractual wrong, but who is from a low to middle-income family, will be able to afford litigation. The 'fast track' might offer fixed fees but it can quickly become reasonably expensive. Even the small claims track has become relatively expensive, as demonstrated in Chapter 14. A person who wishes to claim £4,000 in respect of, for example, a breach of contract case would have to find upwards of £400 in court fees. Whilst these may be recoverable if a claim is successful, that is still quite a lot of money to find in advance, especially where there is a chance that the claim may fail. The small claims track was supposed to be an informal and cost-effective way of resolving disputes, something it has arguably failed to become.

What of those situations where there is arguably no winner or loser? The government's determination that civil courts are self-funding has even reached towards the family courts. Whilst it could be argued that a couple divorcing should not unreasonably have to pay fees that are commensurate with real costs (although there remain arguments that the state, which prescribes the rules under which a person may separate, should provide a service to resolve disputes) it is less easy to reconcile this concept with public child-care proceedings.

Public child-care proceedings are where the state seeks either to take a child away from its parents or place it under the supervision of a local authority (ie the state albeit at local level). Surely this is a classic example of where a fee regime should take into account the fact that the overriding objective is to safeguard children at risk of harm rather than making courts cost-neutral? Yet the previous government altered the fee arrangements within the family courts so that there was a significant increase in the court fee required to initiate, for example, public child-care cases. It is difficult to see how this approach can be justified: the care and welfare of a child should not be a matter of finance.

The then government argued that child safety was not disadvantaged because there was an increase in funding to local authorities but this misses the point. It is never possible to be sure how many children are at risk in a given year. If the government gives local authorities a finite budget for child-care proceedings what happens when that budget is used up? With increased fees it will be increasingly difficult for an authority to find new money to initiate proceedings.

A major difficulty with this approach is that any funding is not ring-fenced. Accordingly the new (and future) money could be diverted elsewhere. Access to justice in such matters should not be a question of finance. It is not just the issue of local authorities having to find the money. There has been concern over the past twelve months that some local authorities perhaps initiate child-protection proceedings too quickly (although on other occasions they have been criticized for acting too slowly). A parent has to be able to challenge such proceedings and this means being able to have access to a lawyer. In many instances this will be contingent on legal aid and it is imperative that funding arrangements do mean that parents are able to put the state to test when it decides to interfere with its family life.

17.2.2 Criminal litigation

The government has not attempted to suggest that the criminal courts need to be self-funding since they are obviously a different status. However the Labour government was committed to means-testing in the criminal courts and the coalition government has shown no desire to backtrack from this.

The argument in favour of means-testing is that those who can afford to pay for their defence costs should do so. However, does this not neglect a more significant issue, at least for those who are acquitted? The state is suggesting that they have committed a criminal offence and, by constitutional convention, they are innocent until proven guilty. Finding the money to pay barristers and solicitors is not easy: private defence work can be expensive. Why should an innocent individual need to pay money (which he may not have: the means-testing will include many middle-income families who are unlikely to have much disposable income after the mortgage, bills, and other loans are taken into account) to defend himself from the state's accusations? Whilst those who are acquitted may be able to recoup the money from central funds this is discretionary and may not be the full amount that has been spent on the defence.

❓ QUESTION FOR REFLECTION

Should someone accused of a crime have to pay? Think about the costs involved in, for example, a murder or rape trial? It is likely that a QC, a junior barrister, and a solicitor will have to be engaged to defend such a matter. The costs of this are likely quickly to escalate into a five-figure sum. Is it realistic to suggest that most people could afford such sums or are they likely to be forced to go for a cheaper team who may be less qualified? Is that truly justice given that the person may be innocent?

Very High Costs Cases (VHCC) remain controversial. It was seen in Chapter 9 that the LSC had to back track on its draconian proposals to funding such cases, but it is likely that this will continue to be a flashpoint. A difficulty with this form of trial is that it is used only for the most serious and complex cases and thus all parties will wish the very best barristers to appear. The best barristers can, not unreasonably, charge large money and whilst it can be questioned why the state should pay for such representation, it is a fundamental principle of justice that a person is not placed at the risk of a loss of liberty simply because the state will not pay for a barrister capable of such complex work. The panel of counsel who could be funded for VHCC ended in 2010 and it has been decided not to replace this but to have individual contracts with counsel whilst a new scheme is created. Quite what this new scheme will be is not known but it is likely that the LSC will be looking to trim costs once again. Kenneth Clarke QC, the current Lord Chancellor and Secretary of State for Justice, in a speech on criminal justice reform said, 'I cannot believe that it is right that one per cent of criminal cases, the so-called "very high costs cases" consumes 50 per cent of the Crown Court legal aid budget'. Of course, many will quibble about the one per cent/50 per cent statistic but it marks a clear statement that criminal legal aid budgets are to be squeezed. This is undoubtedly something that will be returned to in the coming months and years.

17.3 Legal Services Act 2007: new firms

It was noted in Chapter 8 that when the LSA 2007 is fully implemented it could transform the legal landscape in terms of what we traditionally understand a legal firm to be. Whilst a small number of firms have been created to allow, for example, non-lawyers to take on management positions or to allow barristers or legal executives to become partners in a legal firm, the take-up has perhaps not been what one might have thought. In part, this is because LDPs are the interim stage and remain quite restrictive in that only 25 per cent of any management within a practice can be non-lawyers. The fact that an LDP is only an interim stage may well put people off creating them as it is quite possible that when Alternative Business Structures (ABSs) are created the LDPs will be forced to change into an ABS, creating additional expense. Assuming that LDPs do not need to restructure themselves then it is quite possible that their number will grow. It may be particularly attractive for solicitors and barristers seeking to join together to produce a firm that is able to undertake all types of work.

A barrister engaged in an LDP will continue to be regulated by the Bar Standards Board (BSB) although the LDP itself will be regulated by the Solicitors Regulatory Authority (SRA). It will thus be incumbent on the SRA and BSB to cooperate closely although it is unlikely that the LDP regulation would cause any conflict with the personal responsibilities of individual counsel.

The consequences for the independent Bar are potentially significant and it is likely that in the medium term the form of independent practice will change. The advent of

LDPs will mean that chambers may shift from being a collection of individual barristers into a true partnership or company. To an extent such a step would be logical since much of the modern arrangement of chambers has the hallmarks of a partnership in all but name. Barristers share administrative support, employ support staff, have management committees to run chambers, and are normally led by a 'head of chambers' who is a senior partner in all but name. A barrister who breaches the rules of chambers can be asked to leave. Of course this does raise an interesting issue if an LDP was to be created. Currently a barrister in chambers is an independent practitioner and thus if asked to leave has little legal recourse. However, if he is within an LDP he potentially has employment rights (although this would depend on the governance structure of an LDP, ie whether it is a partnership or company).

A formal partnership could bring other uncertainties. There will be difficulties entailed with barristers joining or leaving the partnership and it will raise an interesting question in respect of pupillage. Will the ruling in *Edmonds v Lawson* [2000] QB 501 (see 8.2.2.3 above) have to be changed if chambers becomes a formal partnership? Where it is a collective of individual self-employed barristers the Court of Appeal found it difficult to argue that a pupil was employed. However, a partnership is a legal entity and accordingly it may then be possible to argue that there is employment. This is something the BSB will have to consider carefully when deciding whether to relax the rules.

The most radical change will be when ABSs are permitted, and it is this which will be most closely watched. ABSs are the ultimate aim of the LSA 2007 as it will allow for ordinary businesses to employ lawyers and yet offer legal services to the public. Somewhat light-heartedly this has become known as 'Tesco Law' but this friendly description perhaps accurately predicts the future. Major supermarkets and other service providers are interested in offering legal services as they believe that it would fit into their existing suite of products. Certainly there is some logic to this and it is likely that we will see big corporations adopting ABSs to allow for legal insurance or in-house services to be offered. It is quite possible that a wide number of organizations, including charities, could employ lawyers to, for example, write wills although given the administration involved in creating an ABS it may be better simply to contract this work to a particular legal firm.

This will be radically different from existing structures and does raise issues about the ethics of practice. If a lawyer is managed by a commercial enterprise will there be pressure to squeeze on costs? To cut corners? Each lawyer will be accountable to their individual regulator but how will this fit into a commercial structure? If a lawyer disagrees with a corporate instruction because he believes it is contrary to the ethics of practice will this act as a defence in disciplinary proceedings? The Legal Services Board will have to think carefully how it is going to regulate such bodies, ensuring that a lawyer's 'higher duty' to the courts and the law is not watered down.

Apart from these large corporate bodies it is less easy to predict who else may try to use ABSs. Presumably this will depend on the extent of regulation, something that will not be known for some time. It is conceivable that certain professions may wish to create an ABS to allow themselves to offer a 'one stop shop', for example, accountants and lawyers or architects and lawyers. There could be some advantages in this but it will all depend on how complicated the regulatory framework is (bearing in mind that accountants and surveyors are subject to their own professional regulation). If it is too extensive then many will decide that it may be too problematic, yet if it is too light then it raises issues about whether legal responsibilities and ethics arc being minimized. It should make for an interesting few years.

17.4 ADR

A squeeze on legal aid and increasing costs of civil litigation is likely to mean that there will be increased emphasis on ADR. Chapter 16 noted that ADR has a long history in the English Legal System but it perhaps still does not play the role that it could. Many family disputes should be dealt with by the process of ADR and the new President of the Family Division, Sir Nicholas Wall P, controversially stated that the more educated a parent the more likely it was that they would engage in 'battle' over custody etc in court. Whilst many will question the perceived link to education, if it were replaced by the term 'wealth' then it may make more sense. Certainly, if you speak to many family lawyers they will provide stories of a bitter divorce where the child becomes a 'prize' and where contact issues form part of the overall battle. This cannot be in the best interests of the child or indeed the families and simply means that costs rise. The difficulty is, of course, how this position can be remedied. Is it for the courts to impose ADR on reluctant parties? This was contemplated by the *Family Law Act 1996* but was thought to be too difficult to implement properly. Access to the courts is seen as a fundamental principle and challenging this viewpoint is not easy.

ADR is already popular in respect of commercial contracts where it is not unusual for contracts now to include a provision that disputes should be settled by ADR initially. This is to be welcomed and certainly the *Civil Procedure Rules* should encourage this in other branches of the law. Of course, a difficulty with ADR is that some forms, most notably arbitration and mediation (its two principal forms), are reliant on the parties cooperating and where cooperation is not forthcoming it becomes difficult for ADR to operate. The recent review of costs undertaken by Lord Justice Jackson has noted the importance of ADR and perhaps the costs regime needs to be altered to give greater encouragement, including altering the costs regime where a party proposes, or refuses, ADR.

17.5 Conclusion

It has been shown in this book that the English Legal System is a complex system that seeks to uphold justice, both civil and criminal. There are undoubtedly tensions within the system and unfairness exists in both the civil and criminal systems. It is unlikely that the perfect system of justice will ever be created because people are involved at every stage and people are fallible. The legal system is constantly updated and reforms are likely to continue because the law touches everyone of us every day—every time you purchase something (contract law) or every time you go outside (criminal law: we seek to be protected from attacks or burglaries)—and thus it will always be a political issue. The good news for those of you studying law, of course, is that means there will always be a need for lawyers...

Bibliography

Abel R (2003) *English Lawyers between Market and State* (Oxford: OUP).

Adams JN and Brownsword R (2006) *Understanding Law*, 4th edn (London: Sweet & Maxwell).

Allen R and Hill H (2002) *Study Guide: Human Rights Act 1998*, 2nd edn (London: Lord Chancellor's Department).

Andrews N (2000) 'A new civil procedural code for England' 19 *Civil Justice Quarterly* 19–38.

Ashworth A (1980) 'The binding effect of Crown Court decisions' *Criminal Law Review* 402–403.

Ashworth A (1993) 'Plea, venue and discontinuance' *Criminal Law Review* 830–840.

Ashworth A (2004) 'Delay in criminal proceedings: Unreasonable delay (AG Ref (No 2 of 2001)' *Criminal Law Review* 574–576.

Ashworth A and Redmayne M (2010) *The Criminal Process*, 4th edn (Oxford: OUP).

Ashworth A and Strange M (2004) 'Criminal law and human rights' 2 *European Human Rights Law Review* 121–140.

Atrill S (2003) 'Keeping the executive in the picture: A reply to Professor Leigh' *Public Law* 41–51.

Auld Rt Hon Lord Justice (2001) *A Review of the Criminal Courts of England and Wales* (London: HMSO).

Bagaric M and McConvill J (2005) 'The High Court and the utility of multiple judgments' 1 *High Court Quarterly Review* 13–43.

Bailey SH, Ching JPL, Taylor NW, Smith PF, Gunn MJ (2007) *Smith, Bailey and Gunn on the modern English Legal System*, 5th edn (London: Sweet & Maxwell).

Baksi C (2005) 'World at their feet' 102 *Law Society Gazette* 26–28.

Barendt E M (1998) *An Introduction to Constitutional Law* (Oxford: OUP).

Barnett H (2011) *Constitutional and Administrative Law* 8th edn (London: Cavendish Publishing).

Beernaert M (2004) 'Protocol 14 and new Strasbourg procedures: Towards greater efficiency? And at what price?' 5 *European Human Rights Law Review* 544–557.

Bennion FAR (1990) *Bennion on Statute Law*, 3rd edn (Harlow: Longman).

Berlins M (2005) 'Clarify jury's role under double jeopardy law', 14 November 2005.

Bevan AH (1992) *Alternative Dispute Resolution: A lawyer's guide to mediation and other forms of dispute resolution* (London: Sweet & Maxwell).

Beyleveld D and Pattinson D (2002) 'Horizontal applicability and horizontal effect' 118 *Law Quarterly Review* 623–646.

Bingham T (1995) 'Judicial ethics' in R Cranston (ed) *Legal Ethics and Professional Responsibility* (Oxford: Clarendon Press).

Bingham T (2000) *The Business of Judging: Selected essays and speeches* (Oxford: OUP).

Bix B (2003) Jurisprudence: *Theory and Context*, 3rd edn (London: Sweet & Maxwell).

Blake M and Ashworth A (1998) 'Some ethical issues in prosecuting and defending criminal cases' *Criminal Law Review* 16–34.

Boon A and Levin J (2008) *The Ethics and Conduct of Lawyers in England and Wales* 2nd edn (Oxford: Hart Publishing).

Boyron S (2002) 'In the name of European Law: The metric martyrs case' 27 *European Law Review* 771–779.

Bradley A (2003) 'Judicial independence under attack' *Public Law* 397–407.

Brownlee ID (2004) 'The statutory charging scheme in England and Wales: Towards a unified prosecution system' *Criminal Law Review* 896–907.

Buck T (2006) 'Precedent in tribunals and the development of principles' 25 *Civil Justice Quarterly* 458–484.

Buck, T (2008) *Transforming Tribunals: Going Live* 158 *New Law Journal* 1599–1600.

Busby N and Middlemiss S (1999) 'Arbitration: A suitable mechanism for adjudication of unfair dismissal claims' 18 *Civil Justice Quarterly* 149–161.

Calvert-Smith D and O'Doherty S (2003) 'Legislative technique and human rights: A response' *Criminal Law Review* 384–390.

Cammiss S (2006) 'I will in a moment give you the full history' *Criminal Law Review* 38–51.

Cape E (2004) 'The Rise (and fall?) of a criminal defence profession' *Criminal Law Review* 401–416.

Carnwath, Sir Robert (2007) *Administrative Justice and Tribunals Council: Getting there at last!* Available online at: http://www.judiciary.gov.uk/docs/speeches/tribunals_ajtc_speech_201107.pdf.

Carter, The Lord (2006) *Legal Aid: A market-based approach to reform* (London: Department for Constitutional Affairs).

CCRC (2005) *Annual Report 2004–05* (London: Criminal Cases Review Commission).

CCRC (2008) *Annual Report 2007–08* (London: Criminal Cases Review Commission).

Chalmers D, Hadjiemmanuil C, Monti G and Tomkins A (2006) *European Union Law* (Cambridge: CUP).

Choongh S (1998) 'Defendant's right to elect jury trial under threat—again' *Justice of the Peace* 936–938.

CJA (2003) *Annual Report 2003* (London: Commission for Judicial Appointments).

CJA (2004) *Annual Report 2004* (London: Commission for Judicial Appointments).

Clementi D (2004) Review *of the Regulatory Framework for Legal Services in England and Wales* (London: HMSO).

Cobley C (1995) *Child Abuse and the Law* (London: Cavendish Publishing).

Cooke R (2006) 'A constitutional retreat' 122 *Law Quarterly Review* 224–231.

Cooper J (1998) 'Parliamentary debates on the Human Rights Bill' *European Human Rights Law Review* 1–4.

Coppel J and Supperstone M (1999) 'Judicial review after the Human Rights Act 1998' 3 *European Human Rights Law Review* 301–329.

Corker D (2002) 'Trying fraud cases without juries' *Criminal Law* Review 283–294.

Cornford T (2000) 'The new rules of procedure for judicial review' 5 *Web Journal of Current Legal Issues*, http://webjcli.ncl.ac.uk/2000/issue5/cornford5.html.

Cownie F, Bradney A and Burton M (2010) *English Legal System in Context*, 5th edn (Oxford: OUP).

CPS (2004) *Code for Crown Prosecutors* (London: Crown Prosecution Service).

CPS (2005) DPP *Refers William Dunlop Case to Court of Appeal as First under Double Jeopardy Law*, CPS Press Release, 10 November 2005.

CPS (2006) *Annual Report and Resource Accounts 2005–06* (London: Crown Prosecution Service).

Craig, P (2008) *The Treaty of Lisbon, process, architecture and substance* 33 *European Law Review* 137–166.

Curzon LB (2002) *Dictionary of Law*, 6th edn (Harlow: Longman).

Cuthbert M (2003) *Law Student 2000*, http://www.ukcle.ac.uk/directions/previous/issue7/cuthbert.html.

Darbyshire P (1984) *The Magistrates' Clerk* (Chichester: Barry Rose).

Darbyshire P (1997) 'An essay on the importance and neglect of the magistracy' *Criminal Law Review* 627–643.

Darbyshire P (2000) 'Raising concerns about justices' clerks' in S Doran and J Jackson (eds) *The Judicial Role in Criminal Proceedings* (Oxford: Hart Publishing).

Darbyshire P (2008) *Eddey and Darbyshire on the English Legal System*, 9th edn (London: Sweet & Maxwell).

Darbyshire P (2002) 'Magistrates' in M McConville and G Wilson (eds) *The Handbook of the Criminal Justice Process* (Oxford: OUP).

Davies GL (2006) 'Civil justice reform: Why we need to question some basic assumptions' 25 *Civil Justice Quarterly* 32–51.

DCA (2005) *Judicial Appointments in England and Wales: Policies and procedures* (London: Department for Constitutional Affairs).

DCA (2006) *Useful Information for Magistrates* (London: Department for Constitutional Affairs).

Denning, Baron (1995) *The Road to Justice* (London: Stevens & Sons).

Dennis I (2000) 'Rethinking double jeopardy: Justice and finality in criminal process' *Criminal Law Review* 933–951.

Dennis I (2004) 'Prosecution appeals and retrial for serious offences' *Criminal Law Review* 619–638.

de Thane (2003) 'Positive obligations under the European Convention on Human Rights: Towards the human rights of victims and vulnerable witnesses' 67 *Journal of Criminal Law* 165–182.

Devlin P (1956) *Trial by Jury* (London: Stevens & Sons).

Dingwall G and Harding C (1998) *Diversion in the Criminal Process* (London: Sweet & Maxwell).

Doran S (2000) 'The necessarily expanding role of the criminal trial judge' in S Doran and JD Jackson (eds) *The Judicial Role in Criminal Proceedings* (Oxford: Hart Publishing).

Doran S (2002) 'Trial by Jury' in M McConville and G Wilson (eds) *The Handbook of the Criminal Justice Process* (Oxford: OUP).

Dunn R (1993) *Sword and Wig: Memoirs of a Lord Justice* (London: Quiller Press).

Dwyer DM (2005) 'Rights brought home' 121 *Law Quarterly Review* 359–364.

Dyer C (2005) 'Judges speak out against erosion of independence by government', *Guardian*, 26 April, p 6.

Eekalaar J (1997) 'The death of parliamentary sovereignty: A comment' 113 *Law Quarterly Review* 185–187.

Elliott M (2005) *Beatson, Matthews and Elliott's Administrative Law: Text and materials*, 3rd edn (Oxford: OUP).

Elwyn-Jones, The Lord (1983) *In My Times: An autobiography* (London: Weidenfeld & Nicolson).

ETS (2008) *Annual Report and Accounts 2008* (London: Employment Tribunal Service).

Evans A (2003) 'Forget ADR—Think A or D' 22 *Civil Justice Quarterly* 230–234.

Evans R and Puech K (2001) 'Reprimands and warnings: Populist punitiveness or restorative justice?' *Criminal Law Review* 794–805.

Fairgrieve D (2001) 'The Human Rights Act 1998, damages and tort law' *Public Law* 695–716.

Fairhurst J (2010) *Law of the European Union*, 8th edn (London: Pearson Education).

Falconer of Thoroton, Lord (2007) 'Judicial diversity', a speech at Wragge and Co, available online at: http://www.dca.gov.uk/speeches/2007/sp070201.htm.

Feldman D (1998) 'Remedies for violations of convention rights under the Human Rights Act' *European Human Rights Law Review* 691–711.

Feldman D (2002) *Civil Liberties and Human Rights in England and Wales*, 2nd edn (Oxford: OUP).

Fenwick H (1997) 'Procedural "rights" of victims of crime: Public or Private ordering of the criminal justice process?' 60 *Modern Law Review* 317–333.

Fenwick H (2001) 'Covert surveillance under the Regulation of Investigatory Powers Act 2000, Part II' 65 *Journal of Criminal Law* 521–536.

Fenwick H (2007) *Civil Liberties and Human Rights* 4th edn (London: Cavendish).

Fitzmaurice M (2003) 'The practical working of the law of treaties' in MD Evans (ed) *International Law* (Oxford: OUP).

Flood J and Whyte A (2006) 'What's wrong with Legal Aid? Lessons from outside the UK' 25 *Civil Justice Quarterly* 80–98.

Fortin J (2009) *Children's Rights and the Developing Law*, 3rd edn (Oxford: OUP).

Foster NG (2010) *Foster on EU Law* 2nd edn (Oxford: OUP).

Franks O (1957) *Report of the Committee on Administrative Tribunals and Enquiries* Cmnd 218 (London: HMSO).

Freedman L (2005) *The Official History of the Falklands Campaign: Volume 2* (London: Routledge).

Fredman S (1998) 'Bringing rights home' 114 *Law Quarterly Review* 538–543.

Fredman S (2006) 'From deference to democracy: The role of equality under the Human Rights Act 1998' 122 *Law Quarterly Review* 53–81.

Genn, H (2009) *The attractiveness of senior judicial appointments to highly qualified practitioners* (London: UCL).

Gibb F (2010a) 'Top family law post vacant after challenge to government critic', *The Times*, 4 March.

Gibb F (2010b) 'Supreme ambition, jealousy and outrage', *The Times*, 4 February.

Gillespie AA (1998) 'Child abuse prosecutions and the Human Rights Act 1998' 150 *New Law Journal* 620–621.

Gillespie AA (2001) 'Curfew and bail' 151 *New Law Journal* 465–466.

Gillespie AA (2005a) 'Reprimanding juveniles and the right to due process' 68 *Modern* Law *Review* 1006–1015.

Gillespie AA (2005b) 'Reviewing unduly lenient sentences' 10 *Archbold News* 5–9.

Gillespie AA (2006a) 'Sentencing: The spider's web' 156 *New Law Journal* 1153–1154.

Gillespie AA (2006b) 'Caution ahead: Teachers, vetting and the law' 18 *Education and the Law* 19–30.

Glidewell I (1998) *The Review of the Crown Prosecution Service* (London: HMSO).

Goodhart A (1931) *Essays in Jurisprudence and the Common Law* (Cambridge: CUP).

Gower J and Hammond A (2000) *Review of Prosecutions Conducted by the Solicitor's Office of HM Customs and Excise* (London: HMCE).

Gray C (2003) 'The use of force and international legal order' in MD Evans (ed) *International Law* (Oxford: OUP).

Greenwood C (2003) 'The law of war' in MD Evans (ed) *International Law* (Oxford: OUP).

Griffith, A (2008) *CLACs: Are they worth it?* (London: Advice Services Alliance)

Griffith JAG (1997) *Politics of the Judiciary*, 5th edn (London: Fontana).

Grove T (2002) *A Magistrate's Tale* (London: Bloomsbury).

Hailsham, The Lord (1990) *A Sparrow's Flight* (London: Collins).

Hale B (2001) 'Equality and the judiciary: Why should we want more women judges?' *Public Law* 489–504.

Hale of Richmond, Baroness (2005) 'The House of Lords and women's rights or am I really a Law Lord' 25 *Legal Studies* 72–84.

Harlow C (1994) 'Accidental loss of an asylum seeker' 57 *Modern Law Review* 620–626.

Harris BV (2002) 'Final appellate courts overruling their own "wrong" precedents: The ongoing search for principle' 118 *Law Quarterly Review* 408–427.

Harris DJ, O'Boyle M and Warbrick C (1995) *Law of the European Convention on Human Rights* (London: Butterworths).

Harris, DJ, O'Boyle M, Bates, E and Buckley C (2009) *Law of the European Convention on Human Rights* 2nd edn (Oxford: OUP).

Harris JW (1991) *Precedent in English Law*, 4th edn (Oxford: Clarendon Press).

Harris JW (1997) *Legal Philosophies*, 2nd edn (London: Butterworths).

Heslett, R (2010) 'Under new management' *Law Society Gazette*, 3 June 8.

Higgins, Her Excellency Judge (2003) 'Reflections from the International Court' in MD Evans (ed) *International Law* (Oxford: OUP).

HM Crown Prosecution Service Inspectorate (2004) *Violence at Home: A joint inspection of the investigation and prosecution of cases involving domestic violence* (London: HMCPSI).

Home Office (2006) *Quashing Convictions—Report of a review by the Home Secretary, Lord Chancellor and Attorney-General: A consultation paper* (London: Home Office).

Hoult P (2005) 'Press round-up: "Crony" controversy as Potter becomes Family President' 102 *Law Society Gazette* 10.

Hoyano A (1997) 'A study of the impact of the Revised Code for Crown Prosecutors' *Criminal Law Review* 556–564.

Hucklesby A (2001) 'Police bail and the use of conditions' 1 *Criminology and Criminal Justice* 441–463.

Hucklesby A (2002) 'Bail in criminal cases' in M McConville and G Wilson (eds) *The Handbook of the Criminal Justice Process* (Oxford: OUP).

Irvine of Lairg, Lord (2003) 'The impact of the Human Rights Act: Parliament, the courts and the executive' *Public Law* 308–325.

ISC (2010) *Report of the Intelligence Services Commissioner for 2009* (London: HMSO).

Jackson, Rt Hon Lord Justice (2010) *Review of Civil Litigation Costs: Final Report* (London: HMSO).

Jones TH (1999) 'Judicial bias and disqualification in the Pinochet case' *Public Law* 391–399.

JSB (2005) *Annual Report 2004/05* (London: Judicial Studies Board).

JSB (2010) *Annual Report 2009/10* (London: Judicial Studies Board).

Kavanagh A (2005a) 'Unlocking the Human Rights Act: The "radical" approach to section 3(1) revisited' 3 *European Human Rights Law Review* 259–275.

Kavanagh A (2005b) '*Pepper v Hart* and matters of constitutional principle' 121 *Law Quarterly Review* 98–122.

Keogh A (2006) 'Carter: The crunch' 156 *New Law Journal* 1149.

Kerrigan K (2006) 'Miscarriages of justice in the magistrates' court: The forgotten power of the Criminal Cases Review Commission' *Criminal Law Review* 124–129.

King M and May C (1985) *Black Magistrates* (London: Cobden Trust).

Klug F (1999) 'The Human Rights Act 1998, *Pepper v Hart* and all that' *Public Law* 246–273.

Klug F and Starmer K (2005) 'Standing back from the Human Rights Act: How effective is it five years on?' *Public Law* 716–728.

Lammy D (2004) *Speech to the Black Solicitors' Network* (London: Department for Constitutional Affairs).

Langdon-Down G (2003) 'A fair hearing' 100 *Law Society Gazette* 21–24.

Langdon-Down G (2005) 'The future of family law: Family fortunes' 102 *Law Society Gazette* 20.

Law Commission (2001) *Law Commission Report No 267: Double jeopardy and prosecution appeals* (London: HMSO).

Law Lords (2003) *Law Lords' Response to the Government Consultation on a Supreme Court* (London: House of Lords).

LCD (2005) *Annual Report 2004–05* (London: Lord Chancellor's Department).

Leach P (1999) 'Automatic denial of bail and the European Convention' *Criminal Law Review* 300–305.

Legg T (2004) 'Brave new world: The new Supreme Court and judicial appointments' 24 *Legal Studies* 45–54.

Leggatt A (2001) *Tribunals for Users: One system, one service* (London: HMSO).

Leigh I (2002) 'Taking rights proportionately: Judicial review, the Human Rights Act and Strasbourg' *Public Law* 265–287.

Leigh LH (2006) 'Lurking doubt and the safety of convictions' *Criminal Law Review* 809–816.

Leng R (2002) 'The exchange of information and disclosure' in M McConville and G Wilson (eds) *The Handbook of the Criminal Justice Process* (Oxford: OUP).

Lewis G (1997) *Lord Hailsham: A life* (London: Pimlico).

Liberty (2002) *Magistrates' Courts and Public Confidence* (London: The Civil Liberties Trust).

Liberty (2003) *Liberty's Briefing on the Criminal Justice Bill for the House of Lords,* http://www.liberty-human-rights.org.uk/pdfs/policy03/crim-jus-lords-june-2003.pdf.

Lightman G (2003) 'The civil justice system and legal profession' 22 *Civil Justice Quarterly* 235–247.

Littlewood M (2004) 'The Privy Council, the source of income and *stare decisis*' *British Tax Review* 121–145.

Love, G (2010) *Oh brave new world! Lisbon enters into force* EU Focus 1–14.

Loveland I (2009) *Constitutional Law, Administrative Law and Human Rights: A critical introduction,* 5th edn (Oxford: OUP).

Lyon A (2005) 'Two swords and two standards' *Criminal Law Review* 850–863.

Madhloom L (2010) 'Videos and supremacy of EU law: does a failure to notify nullify domestic law' 74 *Journal of Criminal Law* 496–500.

Majid A (2004) 'Jury still out on deaf jurors' 154 *New Law Journal* 278.

Malanczuk P (1997) *Akehurst's Modern Introduction to International Law,* 7th edn (London: Routledge).

Malleson K (2004) 'Creating a Judicial Appointments Commission: Which model works best' *Public Law* 102–121.

Malleson K (2006) 'Rethinking the merit principle in judicial selection' 33 *Journal of Law and Society* 126–140.

Manchester C, Salter D and Moodie P (2000) *Exploring the Law: The dynamics of precedent and statutory interpretation,* 2nd edn (London: Sweet & Maxwell).

Marshall G (2003) 'The lynchpin of parliamentary intention: Lost, stolen or strained' *Public Law* 236–248.

Mason D (2004) 'A ticking time bomb?' 154 *New Law Journal* 1601.

Masterman R (2004) 'Section 2(1) of the Human Rights Act 1998: Binding domestic courts to Strasbourg' *Public Law* 725–737.

Masterman R (2005) 'Determinative in the abstract? Article 6(1) and the separation of powers' 6 *European Human Rights Law Review* 628–648.

Mathijsen PSRF (2004) *A Guide to European Union Law,* 8th edn (London: Thomson Sweet & Maxwell).

Mayson, S. (2007) 'Something for everyone?' 157 *New Law Journal* 1073–1074.

McConville M (2000) 'Plea bargaining: Ethics and politics' in S Doran and JD Jackson (eds) *The Judicial Role in Criminal Proceedings* (Oxford: Hart Publishing).

McConville M (2002) 'Plea bargaining' in M McConville and G Wilson (eds) *The Handbook of the Criminal Justice Process* (Oxford: OUP).

McConville M and Mirksy CL (2005) *Jury Trials and Plea Bargaining: A true history* (Oxford: Hart Publishing).

McConville M, Hodgson J, Bridges L and Pavlovic A (1994) *Standing Accused: The organisation and practices of criminal defence lawyers in Britain* (Oxford: Clarendon Press).

McCoubrey H and White ND (1999) *Textbook on Jurisprudence,* 3rd edn (London: Blackstone Press).

McEwan J (2000) 'Co-operative justice and the adversarial criminal trial: Lessons from the Woolf Report' in S Doran and JD Jackson (eds) *The Judicial Role in Criminal Proceedings* (Oxford: Hart Publishing).

McEwan J (2002) 'Special measures for witnesses and victims' in M McConville and G Wilson (eds) *The Handbook of the Criminal Justice Process* (Oxford: OUP).

McGlynn C (1999a) 'Women, representation and the legal academy' 19 *Legal Studies* 68–92.

McGlynn C (1999b) 'Judging women differently: Gender, the judiciary and reform' in S Millns and N Whitty (eds) *Feminist Perspectives on Public Law* (London: Cavendish Publishing).

McKay W (2004) *Erskine May's Treaties on the Law, Privilege, Procedures and Usage of Parliament,* 23rd edn (London: LexisNexis).

McVea, H (2004) *Legal Disciplinary Practices: Who needs them?* 563–573.

Merrils J (2003) 'The meaning of dispute settlement' in MD Evans (ed) *International Law* (Oxford: OUP).

Millett, The Lord (2003) 'The Pinochet case: Some personal reflections' in MD Evans (ed) *International Law* (Oxford: OUP).

Morgan J (2004) 'Privacy in the House of Lords, again' 120 *Law Quarterly Review* 563–566.

Morgan P (2010) 'Don't let politicians dangle baubles in front of judges', *The Times*, 24 June.

Morgan R and Russell N (2000) *The Judiciary in the Magistrates' Courts* (London: Home Office).

Munday R (2005) 'Bad character rules and riddles: "Explanatory Notes" and true meanings of s 103(1) of the Criminal Justice Act 2003' *Criminal Law Review* 337–354.

Myers A and Flannery L (2004) 'Wannabe barristers?' 154 *New Law Journal* 1698–1699.

Narey M (1997) *Review of Delay in the Criminal Justice System* (London: Home Office).

Neff SC (2003) 'A short history of international law' in MD Evans (ed) *International Law* (Oxford: OUP).

Ni Aolain F (2002) 'Truth telling, accountability and the right to life in Northern Ireland' 5 *European Human Rights Law Review* 572–590.

Nicol D and Marriott J (1998) 'The Human Rights Act, representative standing and the victim culture' *European Human Rights Law Review* 730–741.

Nicolson D (2005) 'Demography, discrimination and diversity: A new dawn for the British legal profession?' 12 *International Journal of the Legal Profession* 201–228.

Nicolson D and Webb J (1999) *Professional Legal Ethics* (Oxford: OUP).

Nobles R and Schiff D (2000) *Understanding Miscarriages of Justice* (Oxford: OUP).

Nyikos SA (2003) 'The preliminary reference process: Changing opportunity structures and litigant desistment' 4 *European Union Politics* 397–420.

Olowofoyeku AA (2000) 'The *nemo judex* rule: The case against automatic disqualification' *Public Law* 456–475.

OJC (2010) *Annual Report 2009–10* (London: Office for Judicial Complaints).

OSC (2005) *The Annual Report for 2004–05* (London: Office of the Surveillance Commissioners).

Otton P (2002) 'The role of the judge in criminal cases' in M McConville and G Wilson (eds) *The Handbook of the Criminal Justice Process* (Oxford: OUP).

Oulton D (1994) 'Independence of the judiciary: A review' 21 *Journal of Law and Society* 567–570.

Pace M (2005) 'Litigation and money laundering after *Bowman v Fels*' 4 *Journal of Personal Injury Law* 345–350.

Pannick D (1987) *Judges* (Oxford: OUP).

Pannick D (1992) *Advocates* (Oxford: OUP).

Pannick D (2005) 'Judges must be able to take up any position once they're off the bench' *The Times* 12 July.

Pannick D (2008) 'Should judges respond to criticism?', *The Times*, 27 November.

Phillips F (2004) *Ethics of the Legal Profession* (London: Cavendish Publishing).

Pickles J (1992) *Judge for Yourself* (London: Coronet).

Pinder J (1998) *The Building of the European Union*, 3rd edn (Oxford: OUP).

Plattern H (2004) 'LDPs: Fusion or confusion?' 154 *New Law Journal* 846.

Ponting C (1987) '*R v Ponting*' 14 *Journal of Law and Society* 366–372.

Prime T and Scanlan G (2004) '*Stare decisis* and the Court of Appeal: Judicial confusion and judicial reform' 23 *Civil Justice Quarterly* 212–227.

Rackley E (2002) 'Representations of the (woman) judge: Hercules, the little mermaid and the vain and naked emperor' 22 *Legal Studies* 602–624.

Roberts S (2001) 'Family mediation after the Act' 13 *Child and Family Law Quarterly* 265–273.

Roberts S and Malleson K (2002) 'Streamlining and clarifying the appellate process' *Criminal Law Review* 272–282.

Robins J (2009) 'Legal Disciplinary Practices: Race for the Title?' *Law Society Gazette*, 9 April 12.

Robins R (2005) 'Inn a time warp?' 102 *Law Society Gazette* 19–20.

Rogers J (2003) 'Applying the doctrine of positive obligations in the European Convention on Human Rights to domestic substantive criminal law in domestic proceedings' *Criminal Law Review* 690–708.

Rogers J (2005) 'Shoot, identify and repent?' 155 *New Law Journal* 1273–1274.

Rose D (2003) 'The great divide' 14 *Law Society Gazette* 22.

Rothwell R (2005) 'The Inn crowd' 102 *Law Society Gazette* 22–23.

Rowbottom J (2005) 'Obscenity laws and the Internet: Targeting supply and demand' *Criminal Law Review* 97–109.

Rutherford A (2001) 'Race and criminal justice' 151 *New Law Journal* 117.

Sanders A (2002) 'Prosecution systems' in M McConville and G Wilson (eds) *The Handbook of the Criminal Justice System* (Oxford: OUP).

Sanders A and Young R (2010) *Criminal Justice*, 4th edn (London: Butterworths).

Sentencing Guidelines Council (2004) *Reduction in Sentence for Guilty Plea* (London: SGC).

SGC (2006) *Draft Guideline on Allocation* (London: Sentencing Guidelines Council).

Shelton D (2003) 'International law and "relative normativity"' in M D Evans (ed) *International Law* (Oxford: OUP).

Shipman S (2006a) '*Steel and Morris v United Kingdom*: Legal aid in the European Court of Human Rights' 25 *Civil Justice Quarterly* 5–19.

Shipman S (2006b) 'Court approaches to ADR in the civil justice system' 25 *Civil Justice Quarterly* 181–218.

Shute S (1994) 'Prosecution appeals against sentence: The first five years' 54 *Modern Law Review* 745–772.

Shute S (2004) 'Punishing murderers, release procedures and the "tariff", 1953–2004' *Criminal Law Review* 160–182.

Shute S, Hood R and Seemungal F (2005) *A Fair Hearing? Ethnic minorities in the criminal courts* (Cullompton: Willan Publishing).

Sime S (2005) *A Practical Approach to Civil Procedure*, 8th edn (Oxford: OUP).

Smith JC (1999) 'Commentary on *R v F Criminal Law Review* 306–307.

Smith RKM (2004) '"Hands-off parenting?" Towards a reform of the defence of reasonable chastisement in the UK' 16 *Child and Family Law Quarterly* 261–272.

Solley S (2002) 'The role of the advocate' in M McConville and G Wilson (eds) *The Handbook of the Criminal Justice Process* (Oxford: OUP).

Soothill K (1997) 'A cautionary tale: The Sex Offenders Act 1997, the police and cautions' *Criminal Law Review* 482–490.

Southey H and Fulford A (2004) *Judicial Review: A practical guide* (Bristol: Jordan Publishing).

Spencer JR (2006) 'Does our present criminal appeal system make sense?' *Criminal Law Review* 677–694.

Sprack J (2004) *A Practical Approach to Criminal Procedure* (Oxford: OUP).

Stevens R (2002) *The English Judges: Their Role in the Changing Constitution* (Oxford: Hart Publishing).

Stevens R (2003) *The Independence of the Judiciary: View from the Lord Chancellor's Office* (Oxford: Clarendon Press).

Stevens R (2004) 'Reform in haste and repent at leisure: Iolanthe, the Lord High Executioner and Brave New World' 24 *Legal Studies* 1–35.

Stilitz D and Sheldon C (2006) 'ADR and public law' *Public Law* 299–319.

Stone R (2010) *Textbook on Civil Liberties and Human Rights* 8th edn (Oxford: OUP).

Supperstone M, Stilitz D and Sheldon C (2006) 'ADR and public law' *Public Law* 299–319.

Tata C and Stephen F (2006) '"Swings and roundabouts": Do changes to the structure of legal aid remuneration make a real difference to criminal case management and case outcomes?' *Criminal Law Review* 722–741.

Tata C, Goriely T, McCrone P, Duff P, Knapp M, Henry A, Lancaster B and Sherr A (2004) 'Does mode of delivery make a difference to criminal case outcomes and client satisfaction? The Public Defence Solicitor experiment' *Criminal Law Review* 120–135.

Taylor, The Lord (1992) *The Judiciary in the Nineties* (Richard Dimbleby Lecture).

Taylor R, Wasik M and Leng R (2004) *Blackstone's Guide to the Criminal Justice Act 2003* (Oxford: OUP).

Thomas DA (1972) 'Increasing sentences on appeal: A re-examination' *Criminal Law Review* 288–307.

Thomas PA (1992) 'From McKenzie's friend to Leicester assistant: the impact of the poll tax' *Public Law* 208–220.

Thornton P (2004) 'Trial by jury: 50 years of change' *Criminal Law Review* 683–701.

Travis, A and Hirsch A (2010) 'Alarm bells ring after Tories revive pledge to repeal Human Rights Act', *Guardian*, 20 May..

Tridimas T (2003) 'Knocking on heaven's door: Fragmentation, efficiency and defiance in the preliminary reference procedure' 40 *Common Market Law Review* 9–50.

Tur RHS (2003) 'Legislative technique and human rights: The sad case of assisted suicide' *Criminal Law Review* 3–12.

Turner A (2004a) 'The Human Rights Act: Was it worth it?' 168 *Justice of the Peace* 685.

Turner A (2004b) 'New practice direction on failing to answer bail and proceeding in a defendant's absence' 168 *Justice of the Peace* 81.

Vezzoso S (2006) 'The incentives balance test in the EU Microsoft case: A pro-innovation "economics-based" approach' 27 *European Competition Law Review* 382–390.

Vos G (2006) 'Objective opportunities' 156 *New Law Journal* 433.

Wade HWR (1996) 'Sovereignty: Revolution or evolution' 112 *Law Quarterly Review* 568–575.

Wade HWR and Forsyth CF (2004) *Administrative Law*, 9th edn (Oxford: OUP).

Wade HWR and Forsyth CF (2010) *Administrative Law*, 10th edn (Oxford: OUP).

Wade W (1998) 'Human rights and the judiciary' 5 *European Human Rights Law Review* 520–533.

Wadham J (2004) 'Investigations into deaths in police custody and the Independent Police Complaints Commission' 4 *European Human Rights Law Review* 353–361.

Weatherill S (2010) *Cases and Materials on EU Law*, 9th edn (Oxford: OUP).

Webb J (2005) 'Legal disciplinary practices: An ethical problem in the making?' 8 *Legal Ethics* 185–194.

White RCA (1997) 'Rights brought home' 22 *European Law Review* 517–518.

White RM (2006) 'Investigators and prosecutors or, desperately seeking Scotland: Re-formulation of the "Philips Principle"' 69 *Modern Law Review* 143–182.

Wickremasinghe C (2003) 'Immunities employed by officials of states and international organizations' in MD Evans (ed) *International Law* (Oxford: OUP).

Wikeley N (2000) 'Burying Bell: Managing the judicialization of social security tribunals' 63 *Modern Law Review* 475–501.

Williams G (1955) *The Proof of Guilt* (London: Stevens).

Wilson H (1994) 'The County Court judge in limbo' 144 *New Law Journal* 1453.

Windlesham, Lord (2005) 'The Constitutional Reform Act 2005: Ministers, judges and constitutional change: Part 1' *Public Law* 806–823.

Windlesham Lord (2006) 'The Constitutional Reform Act 2005: The politics of constitutional reform: Part 2' *Public Law* 35–57.

Woolf, The Lord (2001) *The Needs of a 21st Century Judge* (London: Judicial Studies Board).

Woolf, The Lord (2005) *Review of the Working Methods of the European Court of Human Rights* (Strasbourg: Council of Europe).

Zander M (2007) *Cases and Materials on the English Legal System* 10th edn (Oxford: OUP).

Index